VOICES
OF FILM
EXPERIENCE
1894 to the present

VOICES OF FILM EXPERIENCE

1894 to the present

EDITED BY

Jay Leyda

RESEARCH BY

DOUG TOMLINSON

AND

JOHN HAGAN

Macmillan Publishing Co., Inc.
NEW YORK
Collier Macmillan Publishers
LONDON

Macmillan Publishing Co., Inc.

866 Third Avenue, New York, N.Y. 10022

Collier Macmillan Canada, Ltd.

Library of Congress Cataloging in Publication Data

Main entry under title: Voices of film experience.

Bibliography: p.
1. Moving-pictures—Biography. / I. Leyda, Jay, 1910–
PN1998.A2V66 / 791.43'028'0922 [B] / 77-2569
ISBN 0-02-571600-X

First Printing 1977

Printed in the United States of America

This anthology is
dedicated to
the memories of
Sidney Meyers and James Agee

———————————————

Preface

On Interviewing as a Craft

"As an art form?" Not quite. "As a business?" It is often more than that. "As communication?" Spoken words have to be examined with as much suspicion as print on a page—where the spoken interview usually finds itself anyway.

Our aim was to chase and then to examine words spoken or written by people who work in films. Anywhere. Any time. Any job. Do these people tell us something about their problems, their solutions, their failures, their relationships with the film people they work with? Or are they merely enjoying the game of talking to the press? Or are they rehearsing the anecdotes they plan to dine out on? We've tried to be severe enough to eliminate whatever doesn't illuminate the tangle of motives and authority that brings any film into being. But I will not be surprised if exaggeration—or worse—has sneaked in here and there, with varying degrees of falsification. We cannot say we weren't warned; here is one interviewer (James Conaway) shocked by the revelations of a former interviewer (Jean-Luc Godard):

> And, in the end, he asked me to make up this article. He claimed to have invented whole interviews with Jean Renoir and Roberto Rossellini, and "they contained no more lies than truth."*

In this book there will be more truths than lies. Even while you are being intoxicated by the sound of your own voice, you are revealing more of reality, often, than you are aware. A sensitive, knowing interviewer can sometimes penetrate defensiveness, exhaustion or a bad mood: he may find that such obstacles can turn into the means of getting beneath the artist's surface. But no formula always works; each person interviewed presents a new set of problems to the interviewer. Even so prepared a conversationalist as Lindsay Anderson concluded that "[John] Ford is pretty well interview-proof."

Another, more subtle warning came from Antonioni:

> I don't feel, in any case, that the things a director has to say about his own work really go very far towards illuminating it . . . and in my own case, I know enough about myself to know that anything I said would just define

* *A section of Sources for all quotations follows this preface.*

a particular moment or state of mind, or throw a certain light on the imaginative process.

Yet that, for us, seems the most substantial contribution to art history that we can demand of the speakers here.

One reason for this book's form and material: the people who make our films have gradually become the weakest voices in describing their motives and ideals and methods. Their voices are almost drowned in a deluge of criticism and analysis—often as misinformed as it is sometimes arrogant and unhelpful. Eisenstein and Bergman are among the few who have addressed their audiences outside their films. Possibly unconsciously, many film people use a channel eagerly offered to them—journalism, and especially the interview. Mixed with a great quantity of dross, the very things we want to know about studio problems and conflicts are often revealed in newspaper interviews; in combing through a richly unselective clipping file, such as that of the British Film Institute (where this book was born), one can sense an occasional sigh of relief by the interviewee that the interviewer has assumed the initiative that makes it possible for the film person to touch the subject that concerns him most—his work. One intelligently sympathetic question is often enough to make the artist trust the questioner.

Of course, even the most seriously intentioned interviewer encounters resistances of all sorts. The commonest one, "If I say what I really think, it may do me harm," is hard to cope with, particularly since it usually remains unstated. An experienced interviewer has described this and other damaging factors:

> A person rarely tells everything he knows or expresses his innermost opinions because he is afraid of offending someone or some group and thus jeopardizing his position, job, or career, or of exposing himself to libel. Also, ulterior motives can affect an interview so that it becomes a tool for expounding special points of view or for furthering self-esteem and self-promotion.

Staged interviews, often guarded by a trembling or bullying public relations employee, are practically doomed from the start. The blocking protest of Mizoguchi that "A film maker has nothing worth saying to say," is hard to take seriously, given his well-known dislike of interviews. Dustin Hoffman's first encounter with an interviewer left a permanent scar:

> They've already decided what you are . . . I had just Beacon-waxed my floor and she came in, smelled, and says, "You been smoking pot in here?" And I said, "That's Beacon wax." And she says, "Come on . . . I know what you people do."

These and related obstacles account for many of the voices missing here. Yet we decided to depend on scraps of reality, no matter how incomplete, to convey the many sides of the film-making process. We have aimed, in uncovering these scattered and unexpected revelations, to demonstrate the benefits of a link between film people and their audience, a way for film people to open a continuing discussion of film problems and hopes.

We have found, happily, interviewers on both sides of the Atlantic who have learned the different facets of their craft so thoroughly that they can pull from each film-interviewee exactly what he or she has yearned to say, which is also what we want most to hear, especially if it concerns an actual experience on a particular film. From abroad we have Kevin Brownlow's campaign to catch America's film past before it vanishes, without our seeing it go. Lotte Eisner, David Robinson and Louis Marcorelles are unusually reliable European interviewers, as are Luda and Jean Schnitzer, who are now helping to complete Georges Sadoul's task of bringing voices from those countries of Eastern Europe and Asia where interviewing is not taken seriously and any right-minded generalities serve. The three interviewers who made *Bergman on Bergman* possible deserve special mention for concrete usefulness. The interviewing energies of the staffs of *Films & Filming* (Gordon Gow in particular), *Sight & Sound* and *Screen* have produced remarkable results. Some of the responsible English questioners—Penelope Gilliat, Charles Higham and Gavin Lambert— are now working this side of the Atlantic. Here, we can also be grateful for the scrupulous and searching interview methods of Lillian and Helen Ross, and of Peter Bogdanovich, in an earlier phase of his career. Working valuably away from home are Gideon Bachmann, Donald Richie and G. Roy Levin. We should add that among the many memoirs now available to collectors of "voices," it was encouraging to find the honesty of Mary Astor's *A Life on Film,* Karl Brown's *Adventures with D. W. Griffith* (with more promised), and Mae West's *Goodness Had Nothing to Do With It.* Rudy Behlmer, editor of *Memo from: David O. Selznick,* should have special credit for his care and success in choice and arrangement. In its oral history project the American Film Institute is collecting a rich store of testimony.

We apologize to those readers (and users) who would have preferred this miscellany to have been arranged in orderly categories by profession; we decided to allow the alphabet to govern the arrangement, so that a member of one profession could talk about other jobs as well as his own in making a film. We've tried to make an index that would catch these essential cross-references. The nature of the best materials ruled out a chronological arrangement.

In limiting the speakers to their film experience we have had to sacrifice many valuable words and acts: Mr. and Mrs. Robert Redford's persistent conservation campaign, Gloria Swanson's advice on diet, Vanessa Redgrave's and Joanne Woodward's political sincerities, the many backgrounds and careers on stage and television; all belong in their lives as artists, but someone else will have to gather those threads. In fact, there is plenty of room and material for those who are unsatisfied with this anthology of film experience to compile ones of their own.

Isn't it strange to open a film book where critics only ask the questions?

Jay Leyda

Sources

in *Preface*

Godard-Conaway, in *The New York Times Magazine,* 24 Dec 72
Antonioni, interviewed by Michèle Manceaux for *L'Express;* trans. in *Sight &
        Sound,* Winter 60/61
Anderson, in *Sequence,* New Year 52
Steen, in *Hollywood Speaks!* (NY 1974)
Hoffman, interviewed by Leonard Probst for *Off Camera* (NY 1975)

A

Agee, notes to *Man's Fate* in *Films,* Nov 39
Aldrich, interviewed by Charles Higham and Joel Greenberg for *The Celluloid
        Muse* (Chicago 1969)
Alexeieff & Parker, in *Film Culture,* Spring 64
W Allen, interviewed for *The New Yorker,* 4 Feb 74
Allgeier, in *Die Filmwoche,* No 52, 1932
Altman, interviewed by Robert Ebert for *The Chicago Sun-Times;* repr. *The
        Calgary Herald,* 13 Apr 74
    interviewed by Larry Gross for *Millimeter,* Feb 75
Alvarez, interviewed by Rodi Broullon, Gary Crowdus and Allan Francovich
        for *Cinéaste,* Vol. 6; No. 4 (1975)
Anderson, interviewed by Joseph Gelmis for *The Film Director as Superstar*
        (NY 1970)
    in Notes for a Preface, *If . . .* (London 1969)
Anger, interviewed for *Spider,* 15 Apr 65; repr. *Film Culture,* Spring 66
Anhalt, interviewed by William Froug for *The Screenwriter Looks at the
        Screenwriter* (NY 1972)
Anstey, contribution to *The Technique of Documentary Film Production,* by
        W. Hugh Baddeley (London 1963); revised ed. Focal Press, 1975
Antoine to André Lang (1924), in Sadoul-Morris, *Dictionary of Films* (Berke-
        ley 1972), p. 8
Antonioni, quoted in Sadoul-Morris, *Dictionary of Films* (Berkeley 1972), pp.
        10, 140
    interviewed for *Bianco e nero,* June 58
    interviewed for *The Times,* 29 Nov 60

interviewed by Pierre Billard for *Cinéma 65*, Nov 65
interviewed by students of the Centro Sperimentale, 16 Mar 61; trans. for
    Film Culture, Spring 62
interviewed by J.-L. Godard for *Cahiers du cinéma*, Nov 64; trans. by
    Rose Kaplin for *Cahiers du Cinéma in English*, Jan 66; repr. in *Inter-
    views with Film Directors* (NY 1967)
Arcand, interviewed by Judy Wright and Debbie Magidson for *This Magazine*,
    Nov–Dec 74
Arvidson, in *When the Movies Were Young* (NY 1925)
Arzner, interviewed by Guy Flatley for *The New York Times*, 20 Aug 76
Asquith, in *Films & Filming*, Feb 59
Astaire, interviewed by Morton Eustis for *Theatre Arts Monthly*, May 37
    interviewed by Carol Saltus for *Interview*, June 73
Astor, in *A Life on Film* (NY 1971)
Astruc, in *L'Écran français 144*, 30 Mar 48
    interviewed by J.-L. Godard for *Arts*, 20 Aug 58; trans. in *Godard on
    Godard* (London 1972)
Attenborough, interviewed by Gordon Gow for *Films & Filming*, June 69
Audran, interviewed by Francis Wyndham for *The Sunday Times Magazine*,
    9 Sep 73
Autant-Lara, in *La Revue du cinéma*, Nov 1930
Avery, interviewed by Joe Adamson for *Take One*, Jan–Feb 70
Axelrod, interviewed by John Hanhardt for *Film Comment*, Winter 70–71
Ayres, interviewed by Arthur Lewis for his *It Was Fun While It Lasted* (NY
    1973)

B

Babochkin, in *Face of the Soviet Film Actor* (Moscow 1935); trans. for *Kino*
Baker, interviewed by Clive James at the National Film Theatre, 2 Nov 72
    interviewed by Margaret Tarratt & Kevin Gough-Yates for *Films & Film-
    ing*, Aug 70
Ball, interviewed (18 Jan 74) by the American Film Institute for *Dialogue on
    Film*
Barrault, interviewed by Luce & Arthur Klein for *Theatre Arts Monthly*, Oct 47
Barrymore, quoted by Spencer M. Berger in *Image* (Rochester), Jan 57
Barsacq, in *Ciné-Club*, Oct 47
Bass, interviewed by Philip Oakes for *The Sunday Times*, 9 Dec 73
Bassori, interviewed by Paul-Louis Thirard for *Positif*, Oct 69; trans. *Atlas*,
    Feb 70
Beaton, in *Cecil Beaton's My Fair Lady* (NY 1964)
Becker, quoted in Sadoul-Morris, *Dictionary of Films* (Berkeley 1972), p. 55
Bellocchio, interviewed by W. Starr, G. Crowdus & M. T. Ravage for *Film So-
    ciety Review*, Jan 72
Belmondo, interviewed by Bernard Frizell for *Horizon*, Nov 61
Benedek, in *Sight & Sound*, Oct–Dec 52
Benton & Newman, interviewed by James Childs for *Film Comment*, Mar–
    Apr 73

Ingmar Bergman, interviewed by Cynthia Grenier for *Playboy,* June 64
   interviewed by Lars Olof Lothwall for *Films & Filming,* Feb 69
   in Henderson's *The Image Maker* (Richmond 1971)
   interviewed by Stig Björkman, Torsten Manns & Jonas Sima for *Bergman
      on Bergman* (Stockholm 1970); trans. by Paul Britten Austin (London 1973)
   translated by Alan Blair for *The New Yorker,* 21 Oct 1972
Ingrid Bergman, interviewed by Lillian & Helen Ross for *The Player* (NY 1962)
Berkeley, interviewed by Mike Steen for *Hollywood Speaks!* (NY 1974)
Bernhardt, interviewed by Charles Higham & Joel Greenberg for *The Celluloid
   Muse* (Chicago 1969)
Bertolucci, interviewed for *Newsweek,* 12 Feb 73
   interviewed by Joseph Gelmis for *The Film Director as Superstar* (NY 1970)
Bitzer, in *Billy Bitzer, His Story* (NY 1973)
   interviewed by Beaumont Newhall for *D. W. Griffith,* by Iris Barry (NY 1940)
Blackton, in lecture at University of Southern California, 20 Feb 1929; repr.
   Koszarski's *Hollywood Directors*
Blitzstein, answering questionnaire in *Films,* Winter 40
Blondell, interviewed by Charles Higham for *The New York Times,* 20 Aug 72
Boetticher, interviewed by Bertrand Tavernier for *Budd Boetticher: The West-
   ern* (London 1969)
Bogarde, interviewed by Gordon Gow for *Films & Filming,* May 71
   interviewed by Mark Shivas for *The Guardian,* 4 Apr 70
Bogdanovich, interviewed by Gordon Gow for *Films & Filming,* June 72
Boleslawski, interviewed by Otis Wiles for *Filmgoers Famous Films Supple-
   ment,* 1934(?)
Bolt, interviewed by Ivan Butler for *The Making of Feature Films* (London 1971)
   interviewed by Barry Pree for *Transatlantic Review,* 64
Boorman, interviewed by Gordon Gow for *Films & Filming,* Feb 72
Booth, interviewed by Kevin Brownlow for *The Parade's Gone By* (NY 1968)
Borgnine, interviewed by Clyde Gilmour for *The Toronto Star,* 2 Dec 72
   interviewed by Barry Norman for *The Times,* 10 Feb 73
Borowczyk, interviewed by Peter Graham for *Films & Filming,* Apr 65
Box, in *The Making of Feature Films* (London 1971)
Brackett, in *The Quarterly of Film, Radio & Television,* Fall 52
Brakhage, comments in *Take One,* Sept–Oct 70
Brando, interviewed by Chris Hodenfield for *Rolling Stone,* 20 May 76
Brault, interviewed by P. M. Evanchuck for *Motion,* Jan–Mar 75
Bresson, interviewed by Peter Graham for *The Montreal Star,* 16 July 66
   quoted in Sadoul-Morris, *Dictionary of Films* (Berkeley 1972), pp. 228, 294
Britten, answering questionnaire in *Films,* Winter 40
Brook, interviewed by Penelope Houston & Tom Milne for *Sight & Sound,*
   Summer 63; repr. in *Interviews with Film Directors* (NY 1967)
L Brooks, in *Film Culture,* Spring 72
   in *Image* (Rochester), Sep 56

R Brooks, interviewed for *Directors at Work* (NY 1970)
    interviewed by Paul Mayersberg for *Hollywood: The Haunted House* (London 1967)
    interviewed by Ian Cameron, Mark Shivas & Paul Mayersberg for *Movie*, Spring 65
C Brown, interviewed by Kevin Brownlow for *The Parade's Gone By* (NY 1968)
K Brown, in *Adventures with D.W. Griffith* (NY 1973)
Brownlow, in *Monthly Film Bulletin*, Apr 76
Brunius, in *Photographie et photographie du cinéma* (Paris 1938)
Buñuel, interviewed by François Truffaut for *Arts*, 21 July 55
    interviewed by Jacques Doniol-Valcroze for *Cahiers du cinéma*, July 54
    interviewed for *Cahiers du cinéma*, July 54; trans. in Aranda's *Luis Buñuel* (London 1975)
    interviewed by Francisco Aranda for his *Luis Buñuel* (London 1975)
    interviewed by Michel de Castillo for *Cinéma 65*, Mar 65
    interviewed by George L. George for *Action*, Nov–Dec 74
Burstyn, interviewed by Ann Guerin for *Show*, Dec 72
Burton, interviewed by Clive James at the National Film Theatre, 11 Sep 72

C

Cacoyannis, interviewed by Stephen Chesley for *Impact*, Spring 72
Cagney, interviewed by Philip Oakes for *Sight & Sound*, Winter 1958–59
    interviewed by Charles Champlin for *The Toronto Star*, 7 March 73
Caine, interviewed for *London Daily Mail*, 8 Aug 66
    interviewed by Sydney Edwards for *The Evening Standard*, 15 Dec 72
Canutt, in *Action*, Sept–Oct 71
Capra, in *The Name Above the Title* (NY 1971)
    interviewed for *The American Film Heritage* (Washington 1972)
    quoted by Robert Bookman in *Yale Alumni Magazine*, June 72
Cardiff, interviewed by Ivan Butler for *The Making of Feature Films* (London 1971)
    in *The People* (London), 24 Aug 58
Carle, interviewed for *Cinema Canada*, Apr–May 73
Casares, in *World Theatre 8*, 1959
Cassavetes, interviewed by David Austen for *Films & Filming*, Sep 68
    interviewed for *Films & Filming*, Feb 61
    interviewed by Joseph Gelmis for *The Film Director as Superstar* (NY 1970)
    interviewed Jan 71 for *Dialogue on Film*, No. 4
    interviewed by Judith McNally for *Filmmakers Newsletter*, Jan 75
Cassel, interviewed by Ronald Hayman for *The Times*, 12 Feb 72
Cavalcanti, interviewed by Elizabeth Sussex for *Sight & Sound*, Autumn 75
    interviewed by Kevin Glover, Jim Hillier, Alan Lovell and Sam Rohdie for *Screen*, Summer 72
Chabrol, interviewed by Noah James for *Take One*, Sept–Oct 70
    interviewed by Ronald Hayman for *The Times*, 13 May 72

Chang, in *China Reconstructs,* Jan–Feb 54

C Chaplin, in *My Autobiography* (London 1964)
>in *American Magazine,* Nov 1918
>interviewed by Francis Wyndham for Chaplin's *My Life in Pictures* (London 1974)

G Chaplin, interviewed by Jim Trombetta for *Crawdaddy,* July 76

Chase, interviewed by Jim Kitses for *Film Comment,* Winter 70–71

Chayefsky, in *Saturday Review,* 21 Dec 57

Cherkasov, in *Notes of a Soviet Actor,* trans. G. Ivanov-Mumjiev and S. Rosenberg (Moscow 1957)

Chevalier, interviewed by Roderick Mann for *The Sunday Express,* 3 Sep 64

Chin, in *Dazhong Dianying,* No. 21, 1958; trans. for *Dianying*

Christie, interviewed by Nina Hibbin for *The Morning Star,* 4 Feb 67

Chukhrai, interviewed by Hermann Herlinghaus; trans. *Film Culture,* Fall 62
>interviewed for *Soviet News,* 31 July 62

Clair, interviewed by John Baxter and John Gillett for *Focus on Film,* Winter 72
>to Charensol, quoted in Sadoul-Morris, *Dictionary of Films* (Berkeley 1972), p. 13
>in *American Cinematographer,* Feb 41
>interviewed by Theodore Strauss for *The New York Times,* 11 May 41
>interviewed for *The New Yorker,* 29 Nov 58

Clarke, in *Sight & Sound,* Spring 61
>interviewed for *The Sunday Times,* 17 June 61
>interviewed by Susan Rice for *Take One,* Nov–Dec 70
>interviewed for *Films & Filming,* Dec 63

Clift, interviewed by Roderick Mann for *The Sunday Express,* 16 Aug 59
>interviewed for *The Sunday Telegraph,* 28 Aug 66

Clothier, interviewed by Tim Hunter for *On Film,* 1970

Clouzot, interviewed by Sidney Smith for *The Daily Express,* 9 Dec 55

Cobb, publicity for *Lawman* (1970)

Cocteau, conversations with André Fraigneau for *Cocteau on the Film;* trans. by Vera Traill (London 1954)
>in *Diary of a Film;* trans. by Ronald Duncan (London 1950)

Colman, interviewed by Sheilah Graham for North American Newspaper Alliance, 1937
>interviewed by John Barber for *Leader Magazine,* 3 Apr 48

Conklin, interviewed for *The Evening Standard,* 14 May 64
>in interview by Kevin Brownlow with Minta Durfee for *The Parade's Gone By* (NY 1968)

Connery, interviewed for *The Sunday Express,* 14 Feb 65

Copland, interviewed by Bill Moyers for PBS, WNET, Mar 76

Coppola, interviewed by John Cutts for *Films & Filming,* May 69
>interviewed for *Time,* 13 Mar 72

Corman, interviewed by Bill Davidson for *The New York Times Magazine,* 28 Dec 75
>interviewed by Joe Medjuck & Allan Collins for *Take One,* Jul–Aug 70
>interviewed by Joseph Gelmis for *The Film Director as Superstar* (NY 1970)

Cortez, interviewed by Charles Higham for *Hollywood Cameramen* (London 1970)
Costa-Gavras, interviewed by Dan Georgakas & Gary Crowdus for *Take One*, July–Aug 69
> interviewed by David Austen for *Films & Filming*, June 70
> interviewed by Martin Knelman for *The Globe & Mail*, Toronto, 29 Sep 73

Cotten, interviewed for *Action*, May–June 69
Courant, in *Film Culture*, Vol. 2, No. 3, 1956
> interviewed by Ernest Dyer for *Cinema Quarterly*, Autumn 34

Coutard, in *Sight & Sound*, Winter 66
> interviewed by Peter Lennon for *Show*, 17 Sep 70

Crawford, interviewed by Lillian and Helen Ross for *The Player* (NY 1962)
> in Crawford and Jane Kesner Ardmore, *A Portrait of Joan* (NY 1962)

Crisp, interviewed for *Films & Filming*, Dec 60
Cukor, interviewed by Robert Hughes for *Cukor & Co* (NY 1971)
> interviewed by Gavin Lambert for *On Cukor* (NY 1972)
> interviewed by Richard Overstreet for *Film Culture*, Fall 64; repr. in *Interviews with Film Directors* (NY 1967)

Czinner, interviewed for *News Chronicle*, 8 Jan 60

D

B Daniels, interviewed by Kevin Brownlow for *The Parade's Gone By* (NY 1968)
> interviewed by Patricia Keighran, 1933(?)

W Daniels, interviewed by Charles Higham for *Hollywood Cameramen* (London 1970)
> in *Picturegoer's Famous Films Supplement*, 1935

Darrieux, interviewed by Ronald Hayman for *The Times*, 16 Oct 71
Dassin, interviewed by Gordon Gow for *Films & Filming*, Mar 70
Daves, interviewed by Paul Mayersberg for *Hollywood: The Haunted House* (London 1967)
Davis, in *The Lonely Life* (NY 1962)
De Antonio, interviewed by Michel Ciment & Bernard Cohn for *Positif*, Feb 70; trans. by Thomas Waugh for *Jump Cut*, No. 10/11
De Broca, interviewed by Paul Gardner for *Transatlantic Review* (1969)
Decae, interviewed for *Les Lettres françaises*, 22 July 70
C De Mille, interviewed for the New York *Dramatic Mirror*, quoted by Charles Higham in *Cecil B. DeMille* (NY 1973)
W De Mille, quoted in Peter Milne's *Motion Picture Directing* (NY 1922)
Demy, interviewed by Mark Shivas for *The Sunday Times Magazine*, 17 Jan 65
De Seta, interviewed by Gérard Langlois for *Les Lettres françaises*, 15 Oct 69
De Sica, interviewed by Pier Luigi Lanza
> interviewed by Thomas Wiseman for *The Evening Standard*, 25 May 57
> introduction to the published script of *Miracle in Milan* (NY 1968)
> interviewed by Derek Malcolm for *The Guardian*, 1 July 72
> interviewed by Ronald Hayman for *The Times*, 15 July 72
> interviewed by Martin Knelman for *The Globe & Mail*, Toronto, 25 Dec 71

Deutsch, in *Hollywood Quarterly*, Jan 46

Diamond, interviewed by William Froug for *The Screenwriter Looks at the Screenwriter* (NY 1972)
Dietrich, interviewed by Sydney Edwards for *The Evening Standard,* 2 June 72
    interviewed by Peter Bogdanovich for *Esquire,* Jan 73; repr. in *Pieces of Time* (NY 1973)
Disney, interviewed by Fletcher Markle for "Telescope Program," CBC-TV
Donen, interviewed for publicity, 1965
Donner, interviewed by Ian Cameron & Mark Shivas for *Movie,* Fall 65; repr. in *Interviews with Film Directors* (NY 1967)
    interviewed by Gordon Gow for *Films & Filming,* July 69
Donskoy, discussion in *Film-Direction* (Moscow 1939); trans. for *Kino*
K Douglas, interviewed by Roger Ebert for *Esquire,* Feb 70
    interviewed by Gordon Gow for *Films & Filming,* Sep 72
M Douglas, interviewed by Lillian and Helen Ross for *The Player* (NY 1962)
Dovzhenko, in autobiographical sketch of 1935
    interviewed by Georges Sadoul for *Les Lettres françaises,* 6–12 Dec 56
Dreyer, interviewed by Peter Lennon for *The Guardian,* 21 Dec 64
    interviewed by Michel Delahaye for *Cahiers du cinéma,* Sep 65; trans. in *Cahiers du Cinéma in English,* No. 4, 66; repr. in *Interviews with Film Directors* (NY 1967)
    in *Pageant,* Dec 62
    answering questionnaire in *Film: Book I* (NY 1959)
    interviewed for *The Guardian,* 21 Dec 64
    in radio interview of 1954; printed in *Om Filmen* (Copenhagen 1959)
    interviewed by Borge Trolle for *Film Culture,* 41, Summer 66
Dupont, in *The New York Times,* 11 July 1926; repr. in *Spellbound in Darkness,* ed. by George C. Pratt (Greenwich 1973)
Duras, interviewed by Lee Langley for *The Guardian,* 7 Sep 68
Duse, letter to the Ambrosio Company; trans. *Sight & Sound,* Summer 60
Dwan, interviewed by Kevin Brownlow for *The Parade's Gone By* (NY 1968)
    interviewed by Peter Bogdanovich for his *Allan Dwan* (NY 1971)

E

Eason, interviewed by Ezra Goodman for *The Fifty-Year Decline and Fall of Hollywood* (NY 1961)
Eastwood, interviewed by Tony Toon for *Photoplay,* May 69
    interviewed by Graham Peters for *The Daily Mirror,* 31 Jan 70
Edwards, interviewed by Stuart Byron for *The Village Voice,* 5 Aug 71
Eisenstein, "The Birth of a Film"; trans. *Hudson Review,* Summer 51
    letter to Léon Moussinac, 16 Dec 1928, published in Moussinac's *Sergei Eisenstein* (Paris 1964); trans. D. Sandy Petrey
    letter to Salka Viertel, 27 Jan 32, published in *Sight & Sound,* Autumn 58; repr. in Salka Viertel's *The Kindness of Strangers* (NY 1969)
    in *The Film Sense* (NY 1942)
Eisler, in *World Film News,* May 36
    answering questionnaire in *Films,* Winter 40
Evans, interviewed by Derek Prouse for *The Sunday Times,* 28 May 61

F

Farrar, in her *Such Sweet Compulsion* (NY 1938)

Farrell, interviewed by Guy Flatley for *The New York Times,* 2 Feb 69

Fassbinder, interviewed by John Hughes & Brooks Riley for *Film Comment,* Nov–Dec 75

Fegté, quoted in *Hollywood Director* by David Chierichetti (NY 1973)

Fellini, interviewed for *Les Cahiers de la R.T.B.,* Brussells 62
>   interviewed by Leonardo Fioravanti for *Bianco e nero,* Feb 60
>   interviewed for *Life,* 20 Dec 63

V Fields, interviewed for *Dialogue on Film,* in *American Film,* June 76

W Fields, in *The Evening Journal,* New York City, 9 May 36

Finch, interviewed for *Films & Filming,* June 64
>   interviewed by Philip Jenkinson for *Radio Times,* 7 Oct 71

Finney, interviewed by Ronald Bryden for BBC-2; published in *The Listener,* 24 Aug 67
>   interviewed by Hunter Davies for *The Sunday Times,* 26 Nov 67
>   with Mary Ure, interviewed by Louis Marcorelles for *Sight & Sound,* Spring 61

Fisher, in *Films & Filming,* July 64

Flaherty, interviewed by Roger Manvell for *Cinema 1950;* repr. in Calder-Marshall, *The Innocent Eye* (London 1963)
>   quoted in Richard Griffith, *The World of Robert Flaherty* (NY 1953)

Fleischer, interviewed for *Films & Filming,* Oct 62
>   interviewed by Gordon Gow for *Films & Filming,* Dec 70

H Fonda, interviewed by Lillian and Helen Ross for *The Player* (NY 1962)
>   interviewed by Jack Stewart for *Henry, Jane and Peter: The Fabulous Fondas* (NY 1976)
>   in *Films & Filming,* Feb 63
>   interviewed by Roderick Mann for *The Sunday Express,* 13 Sep 59
>   interviewed by Peter McDonald for *Radio Times,* 2 Nov 72

J Fonda, interviewed by Jack Stewart for *Henry, Jane and Peter: The Fabulous Fondas* (NY 1976)

P Fonda, interviewed for *The Image Maker* (Richmond 1971)

Forbes, interviewed by David Haworth for *The Guardian,* 7 Oct 65
>   interviewed by Dick Adler for *Town,* Dec 65

Ford, interviewed by Lindsay Anderson for *Sequence,* New Year 52
>   interviewed by Peter Bogdanovich for his *John Ford* (NY 1967)
>   interviewed by Jean Mitry for *Cahiers du cinéma,* Mar 55; trans. by Andrew Sarris in *Films in Review,* Aug–Sep 55
>   interviewed by Burt Kennedy for *Films & Filming,* Oct 69

Foreman, interviewed for Edinburgh *Evening News,* 1 Sep 58
>   interviewed by Mary Blume for *International Herald Tribune,* 5 Apr 68
>   in *Film Comment,* Winter 70–71
>   interviewed by Penelope Houston and Kenneth Cavander for *Sight & Sound,* Summer 58

Forman, interviewed by *Czechoslovak Life,* July 67
>   interviewed by Ian Wright for *The Guardian,* 1 Oct 65

quoted by Joseph Skvorecky in *All the Bright Young Men and Women* (Toronto 1971)

interviewed by Joseph Gelmis for *The Film Director as Superstar* (NY 1970)

interviewed by Lee Langley for *The Guardian,* 18 Aug 71

interviewed by Ann Guerin for *Show,* Feb 70

interviewed by Harriet Bolt for *Film Comment,* Fall 70

interviewed by Tom Burke for *The New York Times,* 28 Mar 76

Fox, interviewed for *Upton Sinclair Presents William Fox* (NY 1933)

Franju, interviewed by Ronald Hayman for *The Times,* 28 Nov 70

interviewed by G. Roy Levin for *Documentary Explorations* (Garden City 1971)

Frankenheimer, interviewed by Gerald Pratley for *The Cinema of John Frankenheimer* (NY 1969)

interviewed by Ronald Hayman for *The Times,* 1 May 71

Franklin, interviewed by Kevin Brownlow for *Sight & Sound,* Summer 69

Frederick, interviewed by Adela Rogers St. Johns for *Photoplay,* Sep 1926

Freund, interviewed by Jay Leyda for *A Tribute to Carl Mayer* (London 1947)

interviewed by Oswell Blakeston for *Close-Up,* Jan 1929

Friedkin, in *Take One,* July–Aug 71

interviewed by Rex Reed for *The Toronto Star,* 17 Nov 73

interviewed by Marci McDonald for *The Toronto Star,* 19 Jan 74

Fuller, interviewed by John Walker for *The Guardian,* 9 Sep 69

interviewed by Stig Björkman for *Movie,* Winter 69–70

G

Gance, interviewed by Kevin Brownlow for *The Parade's Gone By* (NY 1968)

Garbo, interviewed by Mordaunt Hall for *The New York Times,* 24 March 29; repr. in *Spellbound in Darkness*

Gardner, in *Film Library Quarterly,* Fall 69; repr. in *The Documentary Tradition,* ed. by Lewis Jacobs (NY 1971)

Garfein, interviewed by Albert Johnston for *Film Quarterly,* Fall 62

Gargan, in *Why Me?* (Garden City 1969)

Garmes, interviewed by Charles Higham for *Hollywood Cameramen* (London 1970)

Gaudio, in *The Journal of the Society of Motion Picture Engineers,* Aug 37

Gauntier, in manuscript of *Blazing the Trail* (completed in 1928); and *Woman's Home Companion,* Oct 1928

Gentleman, interviewed in *Take One,* Sep 68

Gerasimov, interviewed (1964) by Luda and Jean Schnitzer for *Cinema in Revolution;* trans. by David Robinson (London 1973)

Germi, interviewed by Robert Coughlan for *Life,* 20 Dec 63

Giannini, quoted in *Time,* 16 Feb 76

interviewed by Joan Sutton for *The Toronto Sun,* 18 Mar 76

Gielgud, in discussion with Derek Hart on BBC-2, Mar 66

interviewed by Michael Billington for *The Times,* 17 Apr 67 interviewed by Michael Elliott for The Third Programme, BBC; published in *The Listener*, 2 Oct 69

Gilliatt, interviewed by Betty Lee for *The Globe & Mail*, Toronto, 4 Sep 73

interviewed by James Childs for *The Hollywood Screenwriters* (NY 1972)

Gish, quoted in *Take One*, Sep–Oct 73

interviewed by Sheridan Morley for BBC-2 Late Night Line Up; repr. in *Films & Filming*, Jan 70

Glennon, in *American Cinematographer*, Feb 30

Glenville, interviewed for *Films & Filming*, Apr 64

Godard, interviewed for *Cahiers du cinéma*, Feb 62; trans. in *Godard on Godard* (London 1972)

interviewed for *Le Nouvel Observateur*, No. 100; trans. in *Take One*

interviewed by Tom Milne for *Sight & Sound*, Winter 62–63

interviewed for *Cinéma 65*, Mar 65

interviewed by Kenneth Tynan for *The Observer*, 5 Sep 65

Goddard, interviewed by Meriel McCooey for *The Sunday Times Supplement*, 4 June 72

Goldman, letter to Paul Rotha, quoted in Calder-Marshall, *The Innocent Eye* (London 1963)

Goldwyn, interviewed by Lindsay Anderson, for *Sequence*, New Year 51

Golovnya, in *Iskusstvo Kino*, Aug 53; trans. for *Kino*

interviewed by Luda and Jean Schnitzer for *Cinema in Revolution*; trans. by David Robinson (London 1973)

Grant, interviewed by Frank Rasky for *The Toronto Star*, 4 June 76

Grayson, in *Bryn Mawr Alumnae Bulletin*, Apr 46

Greene, in preface to *The Third Man and The Fallen Idol* (London 1950)

Grierson, transcript of BBC-TV program, "The Projection of Britain," 23 Nov 54; repr. in *Documentary Diary* by Paul Rotha

in *Cinema Quarterly*, Spring 33; repr. in Forsyth Hardy, ed., *Grierson on Documentary*

Griffith, interviewed by Henry Stephen Gordon for *Photoplay*, Oct 1916

quoted by Stroheim

Guinness, interviewed by Gerald Bowman for *The Evening News*, 25 Jun 55

interviewed by Cecil Wilson for *The Daily Mail*, 1 Dec 61

interviewed by Roderick Mann for *The Sunday Express*, 19 Dec 65

interviewed by Ronald Hayman for *The Times*, 7 Aug 71

Gwenn, interviewed for *The Film Weekly*, 17 Oct 1931

interviewed by Philip Slessor for *Film Pictorial*, 2 Dec 33

H

C Hall, interviewed by the American Film Institute for *Dialogue on Film*, Oct 73

interviewed by Win Sharples, Jr. for *Filmmakers Newsletter*, Nov 73

P Hall, interviewed by Gordon Gow for *Films & Filming*, Sept 69

Hani, interviewed by Joan Mellen for *Voices from the Japanese Cinema* (NY 1975)

Hardwicke, interviewed by Lillian and Helen Ross for *The Player* (NY 1962)

Hardy, interviewed by John McCabe for *Mr. Laurel & Mr. Hardy* (NY 1961)

Harris, from a BBC recording, in *Films & Filming*, Apr 65
Harrison, in his *Rex, An Autobiography* (NY 1975)
Harryhausen, in *The Making of Feature Films* (London 1971)
Hart, in *My Life East and West* (NY 1929)
Harvey & Clark, interviewed by Roger Hudson for *Sight & Sound*, Spring 66
Hawks, letter to Kevin Brownlow (1967) for *The Parade's Gone By* (NY
      1968)
    interviewed for *Take One*, Nov–Dec 71
    interviewed by Jacques Becker, Jacques Rivette & François Truffaut for
      Cahiers du cinéma, Feb 56; trans. by Andrew Sarris
    interviewed by David Austen for *Films & Filming*, Oct 68
Hayakawa, in *Films & Filming*, Feb 62
Hayden, in *Wanderer* (NY 1963)
    interviewed by Paul D. Zimmerman for *Newsweek*, 3 Jan 72
Head, interviewed by Donald Zec for *The Daily Mirror*, 2 Nov 70
    interviewed by Margaret Hogan for *The Globe & Mail*, Toronto, 14
      Sep 74
Hecht, quoted by Stephen Fuller in *Film Comment*, Winter 70–71
Henry, interviewed by William Froug for *The Screenwriter Looks at the
      Screenwriter* (NY 1972)
A Hepburn, interviewed by Peter Evans for *The Daily Express*, 1 Oct 65
K Hepburn, interviewed by David Robinson for *The Times Saturday Review*,
      24 Nov 73
    interviewed by Paul King for *The Toronto Star*, 5 Oct 74
Herlth, to Lotte Eisner for *Murnau* (Berkeley 1973)
Herrmann, in *The New York Times*, 25 May 41; repr. in *Focus on Citizen Kane*
      (Englewood Cliffs 1971)
    interviewed by Ted Gilling for *Sight & Sound*, Winter 71–72
    interviewed by Christopher Palmer for *Crescendo*, Apr & May 73
Heston, from his *Ben-Hur* diary, extracted in *American Film*, Apr 76
    interviewed by James Delson, for *Take One*, July–Aug 71
    interviewed by Gordon Gow for *Films & Filming*, May 72
Hitchcock, interviewed by François Truffaut for *Hitchcock* (NY 1967)
    interviewed by Peter Bogdanovich for *The Cinema of Alfred Hitchcock*
      (NY 1963)
    in an Academy discussion of *Rear Window*; published in *Take One*,
      Nov–Dec 68
    interviewed by Arthur Knight for *Oui*, Feb 73
Hoellering, interviewed by Ben Brewster & Colin MacCabe for *Screen*,
      Winter 74–75
Hoffman, interviewed by Leonard Probst for *Off Camera* (NY 1975)
Hoffmann, interviewed for *Die Filmwoche*, 1928, No. 13; 1932, No. 10
Hoge, in *Action*, May–June 69
Holden, interviewed by Lillian & Helen Ross for *The Player* (NY 1962)
    interviewed by Stuart Byron for *The Village Voice*, 5 Aug 71
Hopper, interviewed for *Jack Nicholson, Face to Face* (NY 1975)
Hornbeck, interviewed by Kevin Brownlow for *The Parade's Gone By* (NY
      1968)
Horner, interviewed for *Hollywood Quarterly*, Fall 50

Horton, interviewed by Bernard Rosenberg and Harry Silverstein for *The Real Tinsel* (NY 1970)

Houseman, in *Run-Through* (NY 1972)
    interviewed for *Sight & Sound*, July–Sep 53
    interviewed by Chris Chace for *The New York Times*, 21 Apr 74

Howard, interviewed by Thomas Baird for *World Film News*, Feb 38

Howe, interviewed by Charles Higham for *Hollywood Cameramen* (London 1970)
    in *American Cinematographer*, Oct 37

Hubley, in *Sight & Sound*, Winter 61–62

Hugo, in *Ciné-Miroir*, 11 Nov 27; trans. in Sadoul-Morris, *Dictionary of Films* (Berkeley 1972), pp. 275–6

Huston, interviewed by David Robinson for *Sight & Sound*, Winter 72–73
    interviewed by Gene D. Phillips for *Film Comment*, May–June 73
    interviewed by Art Buchwald for *The Washington Post*, 7 Apr 57
    interviewed by Gideon Bachmann for *Film Quarterly*, Fall 58
    interviewed by Clive James at the National Film Theatre, 14 Sep 72
    interviewed by Dan Ford for *Action*, Sept–Oct 72

I

Ichikawa, interviewed by Donald Richie for *Sight & Sound*, Spring 66

Imai, interviewed by Joan Mellen for *Voices from the Japanese Cinema* (NY 1975)

Inge, interviewed by Digby Diehl for *Transatlantic Review*, 1967

Ingram, contribution to Peter Milne's *Motion Picture Directing* (NY 1922)

Ioseliani, interviewed by Valeri Fomin for *Once There Was a Singing Blackbird* (Moscow 1974)

Ivens, in *The Camera and I* (Berlin–New York 1969)

J

Jackson, interviewed by Peter Mezan for *Esquire*, May 72
    interviewed by Rex Reed for *The Toronto Star*, 23 Jan 71
    interviewed by Martin Knelman for *The Globe & Mail*, Toronto, 30 Oct 71

Jancso, interviewed by Gyula Maar for *Filmvilag*; trans in *The New Hungarian Quarterly*, Autumn 67
    interviewed for *The New Hungarian Quarterly*, Winter 68
    interviewed by Tibor Hirsch for *The Image Maker* (Richmond 1971)
    interviewed by Ronald Hayman for *The Times*, 16 May 70

Jaubert, in *World Film News*

Jaworsky, interviewed by John Hanhardt and Gordon Hitchens for *Film Culture*, Spring 73

Jewison, interviewed by Gordon Gow for *Films & Filming*, Jan 71
    interviewed for *Directors at Work* (NY 1970)

Jones, interviewed by Fred Baker for *Movie People* (NY 1973)

Jutra, interviewed by Kirwan Cox for *Cinema Canada*, Apr–May 73

K

Kanin, interviewed by Penelope Houston & John Gillett for *Sight & Sound*,
Summer 72
in *Tracy & Hepburn* (NY 1971)
B Kaufman, quoted in Sadoul-Morris, *Dictionary of Films* (Berkeley 1972),
p. 17
interviewed by Edouard de Laurot & Jonas Mekas for *Film Culture*,
Summer 55
M Kaufman, in *Proletarskoye Kino*, No. 4, 1931; trans. by Alexander Brailov-
sky for *Experimental Cinema*, No. 4, 1932
Kazan, interviewed for *Directors at Work* (NY 1970)
interviewed by Michel Ciment for *Kazan on Kazan* (London 1974)
interviewed by Rex Reed for *The Toronto Star*, 12 Feb 72
Keach, interviewed by Sydney Edwards for *The Evening Standard*, 17 Mar 73
interviewed by Richard Fisher for *Filmmakers Newsletter*, June 73
Keaton, interviewed by Kevin Brownlow for *The Parade's Gone By* (NY 1968)
interviewed by Christopher Bishop for *Film Quarterly*, Fall 58; repr. in
Interviews with Film Directors (NY 1967)
Kelly, interviewed by Clive Hirschhorn for *The Sunday Express*, 1 Nov 70
interviewed by Peter McDonald for *Radio Times*, 19 Oct 72
interviewed by Charles Hamblett for *The Guardian*, 12 Nov 73
in *Action*, Mar–Apr 69
Kendall, interviewed by Peter Evans for *The Daily Express*, 16 Jan 59
Kende, interviewed for the press release on *Red Psalm*
Kerr, in *The Star*, London, Jan 1–4, 51
interviewed by Ronald Hayman for *The Times*, 2 Sep 72
Kobayashi, quoted in Sadoul-Morris, *Dictionary of Films* (Berkeley 1972), p.
246
interviewed for the *Asahi Weekly*, 12 Oct 62
interviewed by Leo Bonneville for *Séquences*, Apr 68
Koch, in *Casablanca: Script & Legend* (NY 1973)
in *Film Comment*, Winter 70–71
Korda, interviewed by Stephen Watts for *Cinema Quarterly*, Autumn 33
Kotcheff, interviewed by A. Ibranyi Kiss, George Koller & Harris Kirshenbaum
for *Cinema Canada*, June–July 74
interviewed by John Katz for *Cinema Canada*, July-Aug 75
Kozintsev, posthumously published notes for *The Tempest* in *Iskusstvo Kino*,
Aug 75
Kräly, interviewed for *The Motion Picture Classic*, undated
S Kramer, interviewed by Roderick Mann for *The Sunday Express*, 15 Feb 63
interviewed by Betty Lee for *The Globe & Mail*, Toronto, 25 Sep 71
Kubrick, in *Films & Filming*, June 63
interviewed for *American Cinematographer*, June 68
interviewed by Penelope Houston for *The Saturday Review*, 25 Dec 71
interviewed for *Sight & Sound*, Spring 72
Kuleshov, interviewed (1965) by Luda and Jean Schnitzer for *Cinema in
Revolution;* trans. by David Robinson (London 1973)
in *Iskusstvo Kino*, Mar 40; trans. for *Kino*

Kurosawa, interviewed for and quoted in Donald Richie, *The Films of Akira Kurosawa* (Berkeley 1965)

L

Lamarr, in unidentified English newspaper, 27 May 56
Lambart, notes on *Begone Dull Care*, 1949(?)
Lancaster, interviewed by Derek Malcolm for *The Guardian*, 4 Aug 72
Lang, interviewed by Peter Bogdanovich for *Fritz Lang in America* (London 1967)
    interviewed by Gretchen Berg for *Take One*, Nov–Dec 68
    interviewed for *Film Pictorial*, 5 Jun 37
    interviewed for *Films & Filming*, June 62
Lansbury, interviewed by Gordon Gow for *Films & Filming*, Dec 71
    interviewed by Ronald Hayman for *The Times*, 29 Jan 72
La Roque, interviewed by Bernard Rosenberg and Harry Silverstein for *The Real Tinsel* (NY 1970)
Lassally, interviewed by Roger Hudson for *Sight & Sound*, Summer 65
Lathrop, in *American Cinematographer*, Nov 65
Laughton, interviewed by Patrick Murphy for *The Sunday Express*, 3–10 Dec 33
Laurel, interviewed by John McCabe for *Mr. Laurel & Mr. Hardy* (NY 1961)
Law, interviewed by Gordon Gow for *Films & Filming*, Apr 72
Lawson, in *Film: The Creative Process* (NY 1964)
Leacock, in a letter of 23 Feb 67
    interviewed by G. Roy Levin for *Documentary Explorations* (Garden City 1971)
Lean, interviewed for *Films & Filming*, Jan 63
Lee, interviewed by Peter Bess for *Variety*, 4 July 73
Leger, quoted in Sadoul-Morris, *Dictionary of Films* (Berkeley 1972), p. 22
Leigh, interviewed by Ronald Bryden for *The Observer*, 7 Jan 68
    interviewed by David Lewin for *The Daily Express*, 16 Aug 60
Leighton, interviewed for *The Evening Standard*, 27 Aug 71
Leisen, quoted in *Hollywood Director* (NY 1973) by David Chierichetti
Leiterman, interviewed by Alan Rosenthal for *The New Documentary in Action* (Berkeley 1971)
    interviewed by George Koller for *Cinema Canada*, March 72
Lelouch, interviewed by Ronald Gold for *Variety*, 13 July 66
Lemmon, interviewed for *Films & Filming*, Nov 60
    interviewed by Steven Greenberg for *Film Comment*, May–June 73
LeRoy, interviewed by John Gillett for *The Scotsman*, 27 Oct 70
    interviewed by Jack Stewart for *Henry, Jane and Peter: The Fabulous Fondas* (NY 1976)
Lester, interviewed by Ivan Butler for *The Making of Feature Films* (London 1971)
    interviewed in *Directors at Work* (NY 1970)
Levine, interviewed by Robert Muller for *The Daily Mail*, 31 July 61
Lewin, interviewed by Bernard Rosenberg and Harry Silverstein for *The Real Tinsel* (NY 1970)

J Lewis, in *The Total Film-Maker* (NY 1971)

R Lewis, in *Theatre Arts Monthly*, June 47

Lewton, interviewed for *The Los Angeles Times;* quoted in Joel Siegel's *Val Lewton* (NY 1973)

Lloyd, interviewed (1963–64) by Kevin Brownlow for *The Parade's Gone By* (NY 1968)

    interviewed by William Cahn for *Harold Lloyd's World of Comedy* (NY 1964)

Loden, interviewed by Derek Malcolm for *The Guardian*, 9 Dec 70

Logan, interviewed by Ann Guerin for *Show*, Sep 72

    interviewed by Gordon Gow for *Films & Filming*, Dec 69

Lollobrigida, interviewed for *The Times;* repr. in *The Globe & Mail*, Toronto, 3 June 67

Loos, in letter (1964) to Kevin Brownlow for *The Parade's Gone By* (NY 1968)

    interviewed by Alanna Nash for *Take One,* Sep–Oct 73

    interviewed by Leonard Maltin for *Film Fan Monthly*, Mar 67

Loren, interviewed by Lillian & Helen Ross for *The Player* (NY 1962)

Lorre, interviewed by Elwood Glover for "Assignment," CBC, 29–31 May 62

Losey, interviewed by Tom Milne for *Losey on Losey* (London 1967)

    interviewed by Peter von Bagh for *The Cinema of Joseph Losey* (London 1967)

    quoted in Sadoul-Morris, *Dictionary of Films* (Berkeley 1972), p. 38

    interviewed for *Films & Filming*, Oct 63

    interviewed by Francis Wyndham for *The Sunday Times*, 29 Nov 64

    interviewed by Alexander Walker for *The Evening Standard*, 17 June 69

    interviewed by Michael Billington for *The Times*, 5 Sep 70

Love, in unidentified English newspaper, 1956

Loy, interviewed by John Barber for *Leader Magazine*, 4 Dec 48

    interviewed by Rex Reed for *The New York Times*, 13 Apr 69

Lubitsch, in letter (1947) to Herman Weinberg for *The Lubitsch Touch* (NY 1968)

    interviewed for *The New York Times*, 16 Dec 23; repr. in *Spellbound in Darkness*

    interviewed by William Stull for *American Cinematographer*, Nov 29

Lucas, interviewed by Clyde Gilmour for *The Toronto Star*, 25 Aug 73

Lugosi, in press-book for *The Raven*, 1935

Lumet, interviewed by Dale Luciano for *Film Quarterly*, Fall 71

    interviewed for *Films & Filming*, Oct 64

    interviewed (1968) by Fred Baker for *Movie People* (NY 1973)

Lumière, interviewed by Georges Sadoul for *Sight & Sound*, Summer 48; repr. in *Film Makers on Film Making* (Bloomington 1969)

Lye, in *World Film News*, Dec 36

M

MacLaine, interviewed by Robin Bean for *Films & Filming*, Feb 62

Maddow, interviewed in Apr 74

Magnani, interviewed by Cecil Wilson for *The Daily Mail*, 28 Apr 61

Mailer, interviewed by Joseph Gelmis for *The Film Director as Superstar* (NY 1970)

Makavejev, interviewed by Elena Pinto Simon for the *University Film Study Center Newsletter*, Dec 75

Malle, interviewed by G. Braucort for *Écran*, 25 May 74; trans. by Barbara Leaming for *Thousand Eyes*, June 76

Mamoulian, interviewed by Andrew Sarris for *Interviews with Film Directors* (NY 1967)

    interviewed by David Robinson for *Sight & Sound*, Summer 61

    interviewed by Jack Jamison for *The New Movie Magazine*, Sep 35

Mancini, interviewed by Catherine Stott for *The Guardian*, 29 Dec 71

F Mankiewicz, interviewed by George Csaba Koller and A. Ibranyi-Kiss for *Cinema Canada*, Apr–May 73

H Mankiewicz, interviewed by Morton Eustis for *Theatre Arts Monthly*, June 37

J Mankiewicz, interviewed by Gordon Gow for *Films & Filming*, Nov 70

A Mann, interviewed by Barry Pattison and Christopher Wicking for *Screen*, July–Oct 69

March, interviewed by Lillian and Helen Ross for *The Player* (NY 1962)

Marsh, interviewed by Bernard Rosenberg and Harry Silverstein for *The Real Tinsel* (NY 1970)

Marvin, interviewed by Grover Lewis for *Rolling Stone*, 21 Dec 72

G Marx, interviewed by Robert Altman, Jon Carroll and Michael Goodwin for *Take One*, Sept–Oct 70

S Marx, a footnote in his *Mayer and Thalberg* (NY 1975)

Mason, interviewed by Ivan Butler for *The Making of Feature Films* (London 1971)

Mastroianni, interviewed by Leonardo Fioravanti for *Bianco e nero*, Feb 60; trans. by Rosalie Siegel in *Fellini* (NY 1969)

Mayer, in testimony (1947) before the House Committee on Un-American Activities

    interviewed by David Lewin for *The Daily Express*, 14 July 55

Maynard, interviewed by Helen Ludlam for *Screenland*, July 1929

McBride, interviewed by Joseph Gelmis for *The Film Director as Superstar* (NY 1970)

McCarey interviewed by Serge Daney and Jean-Louis Noames for *Cahiers du cinéma*, Feb 65; trans. by Rose Kaplin for *Cahiers du Cinéma in English*, Jan 67

McDowell, interviewed by Sydney Edwards for *The Evening Standard*, 31 Dec 71

    interviewed by Andrew Bailey for *Rolling Stone*, 2 Aug 73

McLaren, in *Canadian Film News*, Oct 53

    interviewed by Alan Rosenthal for *The New Documentary in Action* (Berkeley 1971)

    interviewed by Susan Carson for *Weekend Magazine* (Montreal), 30 Mar 74

Medvedkin, contribution to *A Life in Film* (Moscow 1971)

Medwin, press release for *O Lucky Man,* 1973
    press release for *If . . . ,* 1969
Mekas, in *The Village Voice,* 24 June 65; reprinted in his *Movie Journal*
    (NY 1972)
Méliès, in his memoirs, published in Bessy, *Georges Méliès, Mage* (Paris
    1945 & 1961)
Melville, interviewed by David Austen for *Films & Filming,* June 70
Menjou, in *It Took Nine Tailors,* by Menjou and M. M. Musselman (NY 1948)
Metzner, in *Close-Up,* June 33, Mar 32, Sep 32
Meyerhold, in a lecture of 1918; trans. by Edward Braun in *Meyerhold on*
    Theatre (London 1969)
    interviewed for *Teatralnaya Gazeta,* 7 Aug 1916; trans. for *Kino*
Milestone, interviewed by Hal Hall for *American Cinematographer,* Jan 1931
Miller, in *One Reel a Week,* by Fred J. Balshofer and Arthur Miller (Berkeley
    1967)
    interviewed by Charles Higham for *Hollywood Cameramen* (London
    1970)
    in *American Cinematographer,* Mar 37
Milner, in *American Cinematographer,* Jan 35, Mar 38
L Minnelli, interviewed by George Anthony for *Impact,* March 72
V Minnelli, in *I Remember It Well,* by Minnelli and Hector Arce (NY 1975)
Minsky, interviewed by Tom Hutchinson for *The Guardian,* 9 Feb 71
Mitchum, interviewed by Clive James at the National Film Theatre, London,
    7 Sep 72
Mitra, interviewed by Kavery Dutta for *Filmmakers Newsletter,* Jan 75
Mix, in *Pictures,* 19 Mar 1921
Mizoguchi, quoted in Sadoul-Morris, *Dictionary of Films* (Berkeley 1972),
    pp. 377, 322
Mocky, interviewed for *Films & Filming,* Oct 61
Mohr, interviewed by Bernard Rosenberg and Harry Silverstein for *The*
    Real Tinsel (NY 1970)
Montagu, interviewed by Peter Wollen, Alan Lovell and Sam Rohdie for
    Screen, Autumn 72
Montague, statement repr. in *World Film News,* Feb 38
Moorehead, in *Action,* May–June 69
Moreau, interviewed by Michel Delahaye for *Cahiers du cinéma,* Jan 65
    interviewed for *The Times,* 7 Jan 67
    interviewed by Richard Eder for *The New York Times,* 30 June 76
Morris, interviewed by Allen Eyles for *Focus on Film,* No. 8, 71
    interviewed by John Russell Taylor for *The Times,* 22 July 67
Mozhukhin, memoirs in *Pour vous,* 1 Feb 39; trans. for *Kino*
Muni, interviewed by Lewis Funke and John E. Booth for *Actors Talk About*
    Acting (NY 1961)
    press sheet on *The Life of Emile Zola* from Warner House, London 37
Munk, interviewed by Stefania Beylin for *Polish Film,* Sep 61
Murnau, quoted (1922) in *Murnau* (Berkeley 1973) by Lotte Eisner
    in *McCall's Magazine,* Sep 1928

N

Nagel, interviewed by Bernard Rosenberg and Harry Silverstein for *The Real Tinsel* (NY 1970)

Neame, interviewed by George Hughes for *Amateur Photographer*, 28 March 73

Negulesco, interviewed by Charles Higham and Joel Greenberg for *The Celluloid Muse* (Chicago 1969)

Nelson, in *Action*, Nov–Dec 68

Newman, interviewed by Grover Lewis for *Rolling Stone*, 5 July 73
    interviewed by Lillian and Helen Ross for *The Player* (NY 1962)
    interviewed by Michael Billington for *The Times*, 8 Feb 69

Niblo, in *American Cinematographer*, July 1930

D Nichols, interviewed for *National Board of Review Magazine*, March 36
    in *Great Film Plays*, ed. by John Gassner and Dudley Nichols (NY 1959)

M Nichols, interviewed by Joseph Gelmis for *The Film Director as Superstar* (NY 1970)
    interviewed by Ronald Hayman for *The Times*, 15 Sep 71

Nicholson, interviewed by Bill Davidson for *The New York Times Magazine*, 28 Dec 75
    interviewed by Robert David Crane and Christopher Fryer for *Jack Nicholson, Face to Face* (NY 1975)
    interviewed by John Russell Taylor for *Sight & Sound*, Summer 74

Nureyev, interviewed for *The Globe & Mail*, Toronto, 9 Feb 74

Nykvist, interviewed by David Denby for *The New York Times*, 25 Apr 76
    interviewed by Robert Avrech and Larry Gross for *Millimeter*, July–Aug 76

O

Odets, interviewed by Roderick Mann for *The Sunday Express*, 11 Oct 64

Olivier, interviewed by Kenneth Harris for *The Observer Review*, 9 Feb 69

Olmi, interviewed by John Francis Lane for *Sight & Sound*, Summer 70

Marcel Ophüls, in press release
    interviewed by C. Peary and M. Turim for *The Velvet Light Trap*, Summer 73
    interviewed for *Critic*, Nov–Dec 72

Max Ophüls, interviewed by Francis Koval (1950); repr. in *Masterworks of the French Cinema* (London 1974)
    letter to Howard Koch, 5 Sep 56

Ornitz, interviewed by Win Sharples, Jr. for *The Filmmakers Newsletter*, Feb 74

O'Toole, interviewed by Lewis Archibald for *Show*, Jan 73
    quoted in *Time*, 17 Feb 67

Ouspenskaya, interviewed by Grace Wilcox for *Screen & Radio Weekly*, 1939

Owen, interviewed by Natalie Edwards for *Cinema Canada*, June–July 73
    in *Canadian Cinematography*, Jan–Feb 67

Ozu, quoted in Donald Richie's *Ozu* (Berkeley 1974)
    quoted in *Cinema*, Winter 72–73

P

Pabst, interviewed by Winifred Bryher for *Close-Up*, Dec 1927
 interviewed for *The Times*, 1932
Pacino, interviewed by Leonard Probst for *Off Camera* (NY 1975)
Page, interviewed by John Whitely for *The Sunday Times*, 4 Aug 68
Pagnol, interviewed by Peter Lennon for *The Guardian*, 16 Apr 69
Palance, interviewed by Timeri Murari for *The Guardian*, 22 July 71
Palmer, in *Change Lobsters—and Dance* (NY 1975)
Parrish, letter to *Sequence*, Autumn 49
Pasolini, interviewed by Leslie Childe for *Scene*, 19 Feb 63
 quoted by Kevin Gough-Yates in *Studio International*, Mar 69
 interviewed by Gideon Bachmann for *The Guardian*, 13 Aug 73
Passer, interviewed by Peter Lennon for *The Guardian*, 4 Mar 67
Peck, interviewed by Michael Billington for *The Times*, 9 Nov 68
 interviewed by Clive Denton for *Marquee*, June–July 76
Peckinpah, interviewed by John Cutts for *Films & Filming*, Oct 69
 interviewed by Stephen Farber for *Film Quarterly*, Fall 69
 interviewed by Derek Malcolm for *The Guardian*, 27 Oct 69
 interviewed for *Time*, 20 Dec 71
Penn, interviewed by Joe Medjuck for *Take One*, Sep–Oct 68
 interviewed by Joseph Gelmis for *The Film Director as Superstar* (NY 1970)
 interviewed by Michael Billington for *The Times*, 10 Apr 71
 interviewed by Gordon Gow for *Films & Filming*, July 71
Perelman, interviewed by John Hall for *The Guardian*, 30 Nov 70
 interviewed by Mary Blume for *Herald-Tribune* (Paris), 31 May 67
Peries, in *Sight & Sound*, Autumn 57
Perkins, interviewed for *Cinema*, Mar–Apr 65
 interviewed by Roderick Mann for *The Sunday Express*, 11 Sep 70
 interviewed by Robin Bean for *Films & Filming*, July 65
Perry, interviewed by Kay Loveland and Estelle Changas for *Film Comment*, Spring 71
 interviewed by Judy Klemesrud for *International Herald Tribune*, 2 Aug 73
Philipe, in *L'Écran français*; trans. in *Sequence*, Spring 49
Picker, interviewed (1968) by Fred Baker for *Movie People* (NY 1973)
Pickford, interviewed (1965) by Kevin Brownlow for *The Parade's Gone By* (NY 1968)
 in her *Sunshine and Shadow* (Garden City, N.Y. 1955)
Pierson, interviewed by Robin Bean for *Films & Filming*, Sep 69
Pinter and Donner, interviewed by Kenneth Cavander for *The Transatlantic Review*, 1963
Pleasence, in *Films & Filming*, Aug 62
 interviewed by Arthur Taylor at the National Film Theatre, 18 May 72
Poe, interviewed by Michael Dempsey for *Film Comment*, Winter 70–71
Poitier, interviewed by Lillian and Helen Ross for *The Player* (NY 1962)
 interviewed for *Dialogue on Film*, in *American Film*, Sep 76

Polanski, interviewed for *The Times*, 8 Apr 64
> interviewed by Arthur Taylor at the National Film Theatre, 10 Feb 72
> interviewed by Lee Langley for *The Guardian*, 10 May 65
> interviewed by Joseph Gelmis for *The Film Director as Superstar* (NY 1970)

Pollack, foreword to published screenplay of *They Shoot Horses, Don't They?*, with the novel by Horace McCoy (NY 1969)

Polo, letter to *Cheerio!* published 13 Sep 1919

Polonsky, interviewed by Jim Hillier and Kingsly Canham for *Screen*, Summer 70
> interviewed by Nina Hibbin for the *Morning Star*, 24 Jan 70

Pontecorvo, interviewed by PierNico Solinas for published screenplay of *The Battle of Algiers* (NY 1973)

Porter, in *The Moving Picture World*, 11 July 1914; repr. in Koszarski's *Hollywood Directors*

Préjean, in *The Sky and the Stars* (London 1956)

Preminger, interviewed by Paul Mayersberg for *Movie*, Nov 62

Preston, interviewed by Lillian and Helen Ross for *The Player* (NY 1962)
> interviewed for *Screenland*, Oct 39

Prévert, interviewed by Peter Lennon for *The Guardian*, 7 Mar 61

Previn, in *Music Face to Face* (London 1971)
> interviewed by Edward Greenfield for *The Guardian*, 10 July 71

Price, interviewed for *Films & Filming*, March 65
> interviewed by David Austen for *Films & Filming*, Aug 69

Pudovkin, in *Film Technique* (London 1933); trans. by Ivor Montagu in *Film Acting* (London 1935); trans. by Ivor Montagu
> interviewed by Mikhail Mikhailov for Moscow Radio, 18 Apr 44; printed in *Documentary Newsletter*, No. 3, 44

R

Rackin, interviewed by Robert B. Fredrick for *Variety*, 26 Aug 72

Raft, in *The People*, 17 Nov 57

Raimu, in press release for *La Femme du Boulanger*, 38

Raizman, in *Cinema Chronicle*, July 45

Raphaelson, interviewed by Herman Weinberg for *The Lubitsch Touch* (NY 1968)

N Ray, in *Movie*, May 63

S Ray, interviewed by Ved Mehta for *The New Yorker*, 21 Mar 70
> in *Sight & Sound*, Spring 57; repr. in *Film Makers on Film Making* (Bloomington 1967)
> interviewed by Ann Leslie for *The Times*, 22 Jan 73

Redford, interviewed by Martha Weinman for *The New York Times Magazine*, 7 July 74
> interviewed by Laurence Luckinbill for *Esquire*, Oct 70

L Redgrave, interviewed by Roderick Mann for *The Sunday Express*, 13 July 69

M Redgrave, interviewed by Gerald Bowman for *The Evening News*, 30 July 55 interviewed by Lillian and Helen Ross for *The Player* (NY 1962)

V Redgrave, interviewed for *Radio Times,* 30 Sep 71

Reed, quoted in Sadoul-Morris, *Dictionary of Films* (Berkeley 1972), p. 373
    in the *Oliver!* souvenir book, 1968

Reiniger, interviewed by Paul Gelder for *The Guardian,* 13 Feb 73
    in *Radio Times,* 15 Jan 60

Reisz, interviewed for *The Times,* 19 May 60

Remick, interviewed by Lillian and Helen Ross for *The Player* (NY 1962)
    interviewed by Arthur Taylor at the National Film Theatre, 15 June 72

Renoir, in his *My Life and My Films;* trans. by Norman Denny (NY 1974)
    interviewed for O.R.F.T., 1961; trans. in published screenplay of *The*
        Rules of the Game (NY 1969)
    interviewed by Louis Marcorelles for *Sight & Sound,* Spring 62; repr.
        in *Interviews with Film Directors* (NY 1967)
    interviewed by Satyajit Ray for *Sequence,* New Year 1950

Resnais, interviewed by Peter Lennon for *The Guardian,* 14 Mar 63
    interviewed for *Cahiers du cinéma,* Sep 61; trans. by Raymond Durgnat
        for *Films & Filming,* Feb 62; repr. in *Film Makers on Film Making*
        (Bloomington 1967)
    and Robbe-Grillet, in *Films & Filming,* Mar 62; repr. in *Film Makers*
        on Film Making (Bloomington 1969)
    interviewed by Richard Roud for *Sight & Sound,* Summer 69
    interviewed by Adrian Maben for *Films & Filming,* Oct 66

J Richardson, interviewed for *The Times,* 7 Dec 71

T Richardson, interviewed by Norman Berry for *The Daily Mail,* 13 Sep 61

Ritt, interviewed by Bob Ellison for *The Toronto Star,* 11 Dec 65
    interviewed by Michael Billington for *The Times,* 18 March 69

Roach, interviewed for *The Times,* 17 Aug 61
    interviewed by Bernard Rosenberg and Harry Silverstein for *The Real*
        Tinsel (NY 1970)
    in *Films & Filming,* Oct 64
    interviewed by Kevin Thomas for *Screen* (India), 7 June 68

Robbe-Grillet, interviewed by Barbara Bray for *The Observer,* 18 Nov 62

Robertson, interviewed for *Photoplay,* July 69
    interviewed by William Hall for *The Evening News,* 15 Apr 68

Robinson, in *All My Yesterdays* (with Leonard Spigelgass) (NY 1973)

Robson, interviewed by Dennis Peary for *The Velvet Light Trap,* Fall 73
    interviewed by Joel Siegel for his *Val Lewton* (NY 1973)

Rocha, interviewed by Antonio de Figueredo for *The Guardian,* 1969

Rock, interviewed by Bernard Rosenberg and Harry Silverstein for *The Real*
    Tinsel (NY 1970)
    interviewed by John McCabe for *The Comedy World of Stan Laurel*
        (Garden City, N.Y. 1974)

Roeg, interviewed by Timothy Wilson for *The Guardian,* 3 Apr 71

Rogers, in *The Autobiography of Will Rogers* (Boston 1949)
    interviewed by Rob Wagner for *Screenland,* Oct 1929

Rohmer, interviewed by Fred Barron for *Take One,* Sep–Oct 72

Roizman, interviewed by Mike Benderoth for *Millimeter,* Feb 75

Romm, trans. in *Screen* (India), 29 Apr 60
    interviewed by Oleg Belyavsky for *Soviet Film*, 4 , 1966
Rooks, interviewed by Don Druker, 22 Sep 73
Rosay, for *The Evening Standard Saturday Magazine*, 2 Jan 60
Rosher, interviewed by Kevin Brownlow for *The Parade's Gone By* (NY 1968)
    interviewed by Lotte Eisner for *Murnau* (Berkeley 1973)
Rossellini, quoted in Sadoul-Morris, *Dictionary of Films* (Berkeley 1972),
        pp. 317, 272
    interviewed by Elizabeth Frank for *The Northern Chronicle*, 15 March
        60
    interviewed by Victoria Schultz for *Film Culture*, Spring 71
    interviewed by Philip Strick for *Sight & Sound*, Spring 76
Rossen, interviewed by Daniel Stein for *Arts in Society*, Winter 66/67
Rotha, in his *Documentary Diary* (London 1973)
Rouch, in *Cahiers du cinéma*, Jan 65
    interviewed by G. Roy Levin for *Documentary Explorations* (NY 1971)
Rozsa, interviewed by Christopher Palmer for *Music & Musicians*, Dec 72
    interviewed by Benny Green for *Record & Show Mirror*, 14 Nov 59
Ruddy, interviewed by Barry Norman for *The Times*, 19 Aug 72
K Russell, interviewed by John Baxter for his *An Appalling Talent* (London
        1973)
    interviewed by Rex Reed for *The Toronto Star*, 4 Dec 71
    interviewed by John Baxter for his *An Appalling Talent* (London 1973);
        extracted in *Observer Review*, 26 Aug 73
    interviewed by Lee Langley for *The Guardian*, 26 Oct 67
R Russell, interviewed by Mike Steen for *Hollywood Speaks!* (NY 1974)
Ruttmann, quoted in Sadoul-Morris, *Dictionary of Films* (Berkeley 1972),
        p. 31
Ryu, in *Sight & Sound*, Spring 64

S

Sagan, interviewed by Forsyth Hardy for *Cinema Quarterly*, Winter 32
Sanda, interviewed for *Unifrance*, July 71
Schell, interviewed by Lillian and Helen Ross for *The Player* (NY 1962)
Schlesinger, interviewed for *Films & Filming*, May 63
    interviewed by Gordon Gow for *Films & Filming*, Nov 69
    interviewed by Michael Billington for *The Times*, 30 June 71
    interviewed by David Spiers for *Screen*, Summer 70
    interviewed by Gene Phillips for *Film Comment*, May–June 75
Schneider, interviewed for *Newsweek*, 12 Feb 73
    interviewed for *Time*, 22 Jan 73
Schüfftan, publicity for *Mademoiselle Docteur*, 1937
Schulberg, in *The Saturday Review*, 3 Sep 55
Scofield, interviewed by Tom Hutchinson for *The Guardian*, 4 Aug 71
    interviewed by Alex Harvey for *The People*, 12 Feb 67
Scorsese, interviewed by Steve Howard for *Filmmakers Newsletter*, March 75
    interviewed by Guy Flatley for *The New York Times Magazine*, 8 Feb 76
Scott, interviewed for *Dialogue on Film*, Jan 75

Sellers, interviewed by Clive James at the National Film Theatre, 19 Oct 72
Selznick, in *Memo from: David O. Selznick* (ed. Rudy Behlmer, NY 1972)
Sembène, interviewed by Guy Hennebelle for *L'Afrique litteraire et artistique;* trans. by Robert Mortimer in *African Arts*, Spring 72
Sennett, quoted in Chaplin, *My Autobiography* (London 1964)
    in Sennett, *King of Comedy* (as told to Cameron Shipp, Garden City, N.Y. 1954); repr. in *Film Makers on Film Making* (1967)
Shamroy, in *American Cinematographer*, Aug 59
Sharif, quoted by Oscar Barnes for *The New York Herald-Tribune*, 9 Aug 64
    interviewed by Roderick Mann for *The Sunday Express*, 12 Feb 67
Shub, in *Sovietskoye Kino*, Nov–Dec 34; trans. in *Kino*
    in her *In Close-Up* (Moscow 1959)
Shukshin, discussion trans. by Margaret Wettlin, *Soviet Literature*, Sep 75
    posthumously in *Sovietsky Ekran*, May 75
Siegel, interviewed by Barry Norman for *The Times*, 15 Sep 73
    interviewed by Stuart Kaminsky for *Take One*, March–Apr 71
    interviewed by Peter Stamelman for *Millimeter*, July–Aug 76
Signoret, in *Films & Filming*, June 62
    interviewed by Mary Blume for *The Daily Mirror*, 24 Nov 73
    interviewed by Lillian and Helen Ross for *The Player* (NY 1962)
Siodmak, interviewed by John Russell Taylor for *Sight & Sound*, Summer–Autumn 59
    interviewed by Charles Higham for his *Ava* (NY 1974)
Sirk, interviewed by Jon Halliday for *Sirk on Sirk* (London 1971)
Skolimowski, interviewed by Michael Billington for *The Times*, 3 Apr 71
Slocombe, interviewed by Roger Hudson for *Sight & Sound*, Summer 65
    interviewed by Ivan Butler for *The Making of Feature Films* (London 1971)
    quoted by P.H.S. in *The Times*, 16 Jan 69
F Smith, interviewed by Mike Steen for *Hollywood Speaks!* (NY 1974)
L Smith, in *American Cinematographer*, Vol. 2, No. 22
Snow, interviewed by Charlotte Townsend for *Artscanada*, Feb–Mar 71
Sorenson, in *Motion Picture Magazine*, July 1927; repr. in *Spellbound in Darkness*
Sorkin, interviewed by Gideon Bachmann for *Cinemages 3*, 1955
Starewicz, interviewed by Louis Saurel for *Cinémonde;* trans. in *American Cinematographer*, Feb 1930
Steiger, interviewed by Ronald Hayman for *The Times*, 31 Oct 70
    interviewed by Roderick Mann for *The Sunday Express*, 31 Oct 65
    interviewed by Fred Baker for *Movie People* (NY 1973)
Steiner, interviewed by Bernard Rosenberg and Harry Silverstein for *The Real Tinsel* (NY 1970)
Sternberg, interviewed by Kevin Brownlow for *The Parade's Gone By* (NY 1968)
    quoted in Sadoul-Morris, *Dictionary of Films* (Berkeley 1972), p. 9
    in *Film Culture*, Winter 55; repr. in *Film Makers on Film Making* (1967)
Stevens, interviewed at the American Film Institute for *Dialogue on Film*, May–June 75
Stewart, interviewed for *Films & Filming*, Apr 66

Stoney, interviewed by Alan Rosenthal for *The New Documentary in Action* (Berkeley 1971)

Stradling, Sr., quoted in *American Cinematographer,* Oct 51

Streisand, interviewed by George Perry for *The Sunday Times Magazine,* 12 Nov 69

Stroheim, quoted in Peter Noble, *Hollywood Scapegoat* (London 1950)
    quoted in Lewis Jacobs' *The Rise of the American Film* (NY 1939)

Struss, interviewed by Charles Higham for *Hollywood Cameramen* (London 1970)
    interviewed by John and Susan Harvith for *Karl Struss* (Ann Arbor 1976)

Sturges, interviewed by Paul Mayersberg for *Hollywood: The Haunted House* (London 1967)

Surtees, in *American Cinematographer,* Oct, Nov 51; revised for repr. in *Films in Review,* Apr 52
    interviewed by Peter Greenberg for *Action,* Jan–Feb 76

Sutherland, interviewed by Kevin Brownlow for *The Parade's Gone By* (NY 1968)

Swanson, interviewed for *The Times,* 16 Oct 61

Sweet, interviewed by Anthony Slide for *The Griffith Actresses* (London 1973)
    interviewed by Bernard Rosenberg and Harry Silverstein for *The Real Tinsel* (NY 1970)

von Sydow, interviewed by Alexander Walker for *The Evening Standard,* 2 Sep 66

T

Tao, interviewed for *Dazhong Dianying,* No. 6, 1957; trans. for *Dianying*

Tashlin, interviewed by Peter Bogdanovich for *Pieces of Time* (NY 1973)

Tati, interviewed by Penelope Gilliat for *The New Yorker,* 27 Jan 73
    interviewed by Peter Waymark for *The Times,* 15 Nov 71
    in press-book for *Playtime,* 1967
    interviewed by Harold C. Woodside for *Take One,* July–Aug 69

Taylor, interviewed by Roderick Mann for *The Sunday Express,* 12 Aug 62

Thalberg, in a public statement on 20 Mar 29
    quoted in *Thalberg, Life and Legend* (NY 1970)

Thompson, interviewed by Ken Ferguson for *Photoplay,* Sep 69

Thomson, answering questionnaire in *Films,* Winter 40

Thulin, interviewed by David Haworth for *The Guardian,* 1 Apr 65
    interviewed by Mary Blume for *The International Herald Tribune,* 8–9 Feb 69

Tiomkin, interviewed by Christopher Palmer for *Crescendo,* Aug 72

Tisse, in *Sovietsky Ekran,* 11 Dec 26; trans. for *Kino*

Toland, in *Theatre Arts Monthly,* Sep 41
    interviewed by Lester Koenig for *The Screen Writer,* 1949
    in *Popular Photography Magazine,* June 41; repr. in *Focus on Citizen Kane* (Englewood Cliffs, 1971)
    in *American Cinematographer,* Feb 41

Topol, interviewed by Rex Reed for *The Toronto Star,* 13 Nov 71

Totheroh, interviewed (in 1964 and 1967) for *Film Culture*, Spring 72
Tourneur, interviewed for *Films & Filming*, Nov 65
    interviewed by Charles Higham and Joel Greenberg for *The Celluloid Muse* (Chicago 1969)
Towne, interviewed by American Film Institute for *American Film*, Dec 75
Tracy, quoted in Garson Kanin, *Tracy and Hepburn* (NY 1971)
Trintignant, interviewed by Peter Lennon for *The Guardian*, 10 Feb 66
Truffaut, introduction to *The Adventures of Antoine Doinel* (NY 1971)
    interviewed by Gordon Gow for *Films & Filming*, July 72
    interviewed for *Cahiers du cinéma*, Dec 62; trans. in *Film Quarterly*, Fall 63
    interviewed by Louis Marcorelles for *Sight & Sound*, Winter 61–62
    in *Films & Filming*, July 62
    interviewed by Suni Mallow for *Filmmakers Newsletter*, Dec 73
Trumbo, interviewed for *Film Society Review*, Oct 71
Turner, quoted in Anthony Slide, *Early American Cinema* (NY 1970)

U

Ullman, interviewed for *Time*, 4 Dec 72
    interviewed by Barry Norman for *The Times*, 7 Mar 73
Ustinov, interviewed by Michael Scott at the National Film Theatre, 21 June 66

V

Valentine, in *American Cinematographer*, Oct 42
Van Dongen, quoted in A. Calder-Marshall, *The Innocent Eye* (London 1963)
Van Dyke, interviewed by Harrison Engle for *Film Comment*, Spring 65
Varda, interviewed by Mark Shivas for *The Sunday Times Magazine*, 17 Jan 65
    interviewed by Jacqueline Levitin for *Women & Film*, June 74
Vertov, in *Sovietskoye Kino*, Nov–Dec 34; trans. for *Kino*
Vidor, letter (1962) to Kevin Brownlow for *The Parade's Gone By* (NY 1968)
    in *A Tree Is a Tree* (NY 1954)
    interviewed by Charles Higham and Joel Greenberg for *The Celluloid Muse* (Chicago 1969)
    in *King Vidor on Film-Making* (NY 1972)
    in *Films & Filming*, May 55
Visconti, interviewed by Penelope Gilliatt for *The Observer*, 10 Sep 61
    interviewed by Mark Shivas for *The Guardian*, 4 June 70
Vitti, interviewed by John Marble for *The New York Times International Edition*, 24 Mar 67
    interviewed by Barry Norman for *The Daily Mail*, 17 May 67
Voight, interviewed at the American Film Institute (11 Apr 73) for *Dialogue on Film*, June 73

W

Wajda, interviewed by Ronald Hayman for *The Times*, 27 May 72
Walker, interviewed by John and Susan Harvith for *Karl Struss* (Ann Arbor 1976)

Wallach, in *Films & Filming*, May 64
Walsh, interviewed by James Childs for *Sight & Sound*, Winter 72–73
    quoted by Robert Bookman in *Yale Alumni Magazine*, June 72
Walters, interviewed by John Cutts for *Films & Filming*, Aug 70
Walthall, interviewed by Dorothy Donnell for *Motion Picture Classic*, Nov 1925
Wanger, interviewed by Bernard Rosenberg and Harry Silverstein for *The Real Tinsel* (NY 1970)
D Warner, interviewed by Philip Jenkinson for *Radio Times*, 30 Sep 71
H Warner, interviewed by Logan Carlisle for *Screenland*, Aug 1929
J Warner, interviewed by Paul King for *The Canadian* (*Toronto Star*), 28 July 73
Watkins, interviewed for *Film Society Review*, Mar–May 72
    interviewed by Alan Rosenthal for *The New Documentary in Action* (Berkeley 1971)
Watson, quoted in *Photoplay*, May 1928; repr. in *Spellbound in Darkness*
Watt, in his *Don't Look at the Camera* (London 1974)
    in *Documentary Newsletter*, Feb 43
Wayne, interviewed by Guy Flatley for *The New York Times*, 30 Dec 73
Webb, interviewed by Christopher Palmer for *Crescendo*, Mar 73
Wegener, in *Sein Leben und seine Rollen* (Hamburg 1954)
Welles, interviewed by Huw Weldon for Monitor, BBC-TV; shown 13 Mar 60
    interviewed by Juan Cobos, Miguel Rubio and Jose Antonio Pruneda for *Cahiers du cinéma*, Apr 65; trans. by Rose Kaplin in *Cahiers du Cinéma in English*, Nov 66; repr. in *Interviews with Film Directors* (NY 1967)
Wellman, interviewed by Kevin Brownlow for *The Parade's Gone By* (NY 1968)
    interviewed by Clyde Gilmour for *The Toronto Star*, 1975
    in *A Short Time for Insanity* (NY 1974)
Wertmüller, interviewed by E. Servi Burgess for *Women & Film*, June 74
West, interviewed by Scott Eyman for *Take One*, Sept–Oct 72
Westmore, interviewed by Mike Steen for *Hollywood Speaks!* (NY 1974)
    in *American Cinematographer*, Jan 38
Wexler, interviewed by Michael Shedlin for *Take One*, July–Aug 71
White, interviewed by Kathlyn Hayden for *Picture Show*, 4 May 29
Wicki, interviewed for *Films & Filming*, Apr 62
Widmark, interviewed by Lillian and Helen Ross for *The Player* (NY 1962)
    interviewed by Roderick Mann for *The Sunday Express*, 28 May 61
Wilder, interviewed by Michael Billington for *The Times*, 19 Aug 69
    interviewed for *The Times*, 8 Feb 62
    interviewed by Roderick Mann for *The Sunday Express*, 31 July 60
    interviewed by Martin Levine for *The Toronto Star*, 2 Jan 73
    interviewed by Charles Higham and Joel Greenberg for *The Celluloid Muse* (Chicago 1969)
    and Diamond, interviewed for *Dialogue on Film*, in *American Film*, July–Aug 76
Williams, interviewed by John Carpenter for *The Evening News*, 19 Mar 59
Winner, interviewed by Mark Carducci for *Millimeter*, Feb 75

Winters, interviewed by Philip Oakes for *The Sunday Times*, 2 May 71
 interviewed by Roderick Mann for *The Sunday Express*, 11 July 65
 interviewed by Lewis Funke and John E. Booth for *Actors Talk About Acting* (NY 1961)
Wise, interviewed by Ralph Appelbaum for *Filmmakers Newsletter*, Apr 76
 interviewed for *Directors at Work* (NY 1970)
 interviewed for *American Film*, Nov 75
Wiseman, interviewed by Donald E. McWilliams for *Film Quarterly*, Fall 70
Wood, interviewed by Philip Oakes for *The Sunday Times*, 28 Dec 69
Woodward, interviewed by Scott MacDonough for *Show*, Feb 73
Wyler, interviewed by Ken Doeckel for *Films in Review*, Oct 71
 interviewed for *American Film*, Apr 76
 in *The Screen Writer*, Feb 47
 interviewed by George Perry for *The Sunday Times Magazine*, 12 Jan 69
 in *Documentary Film News*, Vol. 7, No. 6
 letter to *Sequence 8*, Summer 49
Wyman, interviewed by Rex Reed for *The New York Times*, 6 Oct 68

Y

M York, interviewed by Barry Norman for *The Times*, 8 Apr 72
S York, interviewed by William Hall for *The Evening Standard*, 24 Aug 63
 interviewed by Elizabeth Prosser for *The Sun*, London, 10 June 69
Young, interviewed by Ivan Butler for *The Making of Feature Films* (London 1971)

Z

Zanuck, in *Films & Filming*, Nov 62
Zanussi, interviewed by Boleslaw Michalek at the Pesaro Film Festival, 1970
Zeffirelli, interviewed by Barry Norman for *The Daily Mail*, 7 Feb 66
 interviewed by Sheila Huftel for *The Guardian*, 2 March 68
Zinnemann, interviewed by Richard Schickel for *Show*, Aug 64
 reported by Albert Johnson for *Sight & Sound*, Autumn 55
 interviewed by Gene Phillips for *Focus on Film*, Spring 73
 interviewed by Peter Lennon for *The Guardian*, 24 Aug 63
Zouzou, interviewed by Ann Guerin for *Show*, Feb 73
Zsigmond, interviewed at the American Film Institute for *Dialogue on Film*, Oct 74
Zukor, interviewed by Aljean Harmetz for *The New York Times*, 4 Feb 73

Acknowledgments and thanks to the many kind individuals and publishers and libraries that helped us make this anthology of film practice. The first encouragement (and patience) came from the staff of the British Film Institute; the first blanket permissions were given by Kevin Brownlow and Jonas Mekas. Michael Ostroff and Eric Bauman assisted the research in Canada. Granada Television broadcast the interviews from the National Film Theatre in London. The Gottesman Foundation and the National Endowment for the Humanities are warmly thanked for their assistance in completing this book. More details will be found in the SOURCES, beginning on page xi.

The surest reference books at our elbows were *The Film Index* (1941) and *The New Film Index* (1975), Georges Sadoul and Peter Morris's *Dictionary of Films* (1965–1972), Leslie Halliwell's *The Filmgoer's Companion* (Fourth Edition, 1974), *The World Encyclopedia of the Film* (1972) and *The Oxford Companion to Film* (1976). John D. Smith was the hero of the final typing.

J. L.
D. T.
J. H.

VOICES
OF FILM
EXPERIENCE

1894 to the present

A

James A G E E [1910–1955]
Born in Knoxville, Tennessee. His film scripts prepared him for the film direction that tragically was never realized. One project was an adaptation of Malraux's Man's Fate:

Important, on the fog, and on the timbre of film all the way through, to make this clear: that smooth and lyric fog (as in *Zoo in Budapest* [1933] or *The Informer* [1935]) is not meant and is to be avoided. By taking its resonance from that of the bell I mean that that should be the rhythm of the grain in the film, as if produced of the sound. All the film should be grainy, hard black and white, flat focus, the stock and tone of film in war newsreels, etc., prior to the invention of panchromatic. No smoothness and never luminous. It should not seem to be fiction. . . .

The use of the disembodied voice and choric voices is of course exceedingly dangerous: they could with much difficulty avoid the mistakes made in the voicing of poetic radio plays. The problem would be to find the right voice —entirely untrained, un'cultivated' and above all unhistrionic; capable of coloring and intensifying a monotone without departing it. The chorus voices, too: same desperate avoidance of the mass-chant type of tone: not in unison, very dry: voices not of poetic performers but of literal persons. When they sing the few notes its massiveness should come of many crowded and untrained voices, of which many sharpen and flat the pitch.
——Agee, notes to scenario of *Man's Fate*, in *Films*, Nov 39

Robert A L D R I C H
Born 1918 in a wealthy Rhode Island family. First film jobs at RKO in 1943, first TV direction in 1952, and first film direction, The Big Leaguer, *1953. Before this first film Aldrich had the advantage of assisting several American directors of value.*

Apache [1954] was an inexpensive Red Indian epic that could have been better. A great deal of what I wanted to say about the Red Indians in it was lost. The original script ended with the hero, Massai (played by Burt Lancaster), going back up to a shack to be shot needlessly in the back by Federal troops.

That was the script I'd been given, that was the script I'd approved, and that was the script I'd shot.

Two or three days before the shooting on the picture was due to finish, United Artists prevailed upon [the producer] Hecht to shoot two endings. I don't know how it is in other countries but in this country when you have somebody suggest two endings you know they're going to use the other one. So I refused to shoot the alternate ending, and for about two days Burt agreed that the original ending was what this picture was all about. Then, for reasons best known to himself, he changed his mind. Now once Burt had changed his mind it made little difference if I refused to direct the other ending, because the next day they could get someone who would. The point was lost because a $500-a-week director had no hope of prevailing against Hecht-Lancaster and United Artists.

[The picture] was seriously compromised. You make a picture about one thing, the inevitability of Massai's death. His courage is measured against the inevitable. The whole preceding two hours become redundant if at the end he can just walk away.

. . . You learn from good directors and bad directors: When we were making *M* [1950], Losey was doing a sensational job.

We came to the final scene where David Wayne as the child-killer is cornered, as in the Fritz Lang original [1931]. Luther Adler had to deliver his defensive eulogy of Wayne. Adler did it in rehearsal and it was just brilliant. There wasn't a dry eye on the sound stage. Everybody applauded. But he never, never got it again; didn't come close to it; didn't come halfway towards getting it. One would have thought that anybody with half a goddamned brain would have remembered that always. I should have been smarter.

We came to the scene in *Attack* [1956] where Eddie Albert has to break down and grab the slippers. I made the same mistake as Losey: [Albert] left the performance in the rehearsal hall. It never got on film. What's there is quite good—we cut and edited it to make it look as good as possible. But he was brilliant in rehearsal. The actor has a right to expect the director to know his limitations sufficiently well to know what he's capable of and to be sure that his best work is captured on film, because he might not have the particular kind of talent that can do it over and over and over again.

———Aldrich, interviewed for *The Celluloid Muse* (Chicago, 1969)

Alexandre A L E X E I E F F & Claire P A R K E R
Born 1899 in Kazan, Alexeieff began work in Paris at the age of 20 as theater-designer and book illustrator. His first film work, A Night on Bare Mountain *(1933–34): for this and later films he and his wife, Claire Parker, invented and perfected several new and ingenious means of artificial film animation, described by him here:*

. . . I was afraid of the Eldorado atmosphere which held the motion picture studios prisoner; the theater had already taught me the role played by chance in collective creations, distorting the intentions of the individuals who participate in them. I considered the animated cartoon good for comics, not for the poetic atmosphere which was the life-substance of my engravings. I would have to invent a motion picture technique such that I might, entirely alone, make pictures with half tones, grays, and indistinct forms. I made this invention and built the first pin-screen in association with an American, Miss Claire Parker of Boston, who later became my wife. We illustrated together *Night on Bare Mountain* by Mussorgsky.... We had a success in the press unequaled for an 8-minute film; the newspapers and reviews predicted the most brilliant future for us, but not a single motion picture distribution circuit beyond the motion picture theater Panthéon in Paris and the Academy Cinema in London asked for our film.

Since 1951 we have been developing the technique of a new kind of animation: instead of recording frame-by-frame a stationary object, we often record frame-by-frame moving objects which are connected with compound pendulums. We have built in Paris a robot, driven by a compound pendulum, which draws on one frame of the film while the camera makes one long exposure. After having thus made one frame, we rewind the robot which executes the following frame in a like way, etc. The results thus obtained are new, and very useful in certain particular cases, notably in the case of abstract pictures....

But what I care for above all in animation is the power to master the tempo of thought and emotions in the audience. It pleases me to construct over a period of four months a synthesis whose presence on the screen will last only one minute, during which the audience cannot withdraw its attention for even a fraction of a second.

———Alexeieff (1956), in *Film Culture*, Spring 64

Woody A L L E N [Allen Stewart Konigsberg]
Born 1935, in Flatbush, Brooklyn. Background of radio and TV writing and soliloquies, plus a clarinet that he has never put aside. First film script: What's New, Pussycat? (1966).

If people only knew how little control you have over films. You're constantly dealing with catastrophes. I like them. Of course, the mishaps of editing add to them. Editing *Play It Again, Sam* [1972], I would suddenly get hysterical with laughter, and the other people in the place wouldn't know why. It would often be when I'd put half of a scene at the end and half at the beginning. That can sometimes work wonderfully. It's one of the good accidents in life. Most accidents are negative. But in entertainment and—er—*art* there's something about a serrated edge....

Once I've done a script of my own I try not to read it again, because it becomes a little bit less funny. I don't rehearse a film. I never know where I'm going to put the camera. Funniness is organic, like sitting around with a lot of people when something loopy happens. What you write is not what you shoot at all. I've shot the middle of a movie again and again and eventually put it somewhere else. I love annihilating film when we're cutting it. Getting it down from 124 minutes to 89 minutes may be the perfect length for something funny, don't you?

———Allen, interviewed for *The New Yorker*, 4 Feb 74

Sepp ALLGEIER [1895–1968]
German cameraman of skill and alertness who began his professional career before 1914; he made his specialty the "mountain films" that were particularly popular in the Germany of the 1920s and 1930s. His most important studio film was Das Tagebuch einer Verlorenen (1929). *He also contributed work to propaganda and newsreel films of the Nazi period* (Olympia, Feldzug in Polen, *etc.*).

The first ski film was realized in 1913; Dr. Tauern, Dr. Rohde and Fanck formed the team which planned the film. I became the fourth of the group. It concerned an ascension of the Monte Rosa on skis, an exploit that had been realized before only two or three times. The film was completed in three days. On this occasion I got acquainted with the dirty tricks of the oil mechanism: the oil in the camera froze in the severe cold. Later on, we mountain camera-men found the solution to use petroleum instead of oil. The Monte Rosa film was quite a success, contrary to what we had expected.

——Allgeier, in *Die Filmwoche*, No. 52 (1932)

Robert ALTMAN
Born 1925 in Kansas City, Missouri, and graduated in engineering from the University of Missouri. In air force during war, and a free-lance writer after-ward, for magazines, radio and films.

For *The Long Goodbye* [1973], we did an interesting thing. The camera never stopped moving in that film. We'd lay our camera tracks along one side of the room we were shooting in, and I'd have the grip push the camera platform very slowly from one side to the other, then back again.

At the same time, the camera would be moving, very slowly, up and down. And, very slowly, zooming in and out. All the time. The idea was to make the audience feel like eavesdroppers, always craning their necks to see what was happening.

——Altman, interviewed for *The Chicago Sun-Times*, repr. in *The Calgary Herald*, 13 Apr 74

Sound is supposed to be heard, but words are not necessarily supposed to be heard. I am trying to divorce the audience somewhat from literature and from theater, which is based on literature. In those areas it's the words that the character uses that is important. I think in film it's what the character does not say, what you don't hear. Now again, in this film [*Nashville*, 1975] we're using the 8-track sound system and in the theaters we're adding 16 tracks. But we're really going after the simplicity of having audiences hear what they would hear. There's no way to do that with one microphone, or with one guy mixing it there on the set, so we're getting it separated so we can get the quality we got on *California Split* [1974]. We hope this picture will be much better because that was the first time we'd tried this system.

——Altman, interviewed for *Millimeter*, Feb 75

Santiago A L V A R E Z
*Born 1919 in Havana. After two visits to the United States, active in founding
a left cine-club in Havana whose members produced the first films of the Institute Cubano del Arte e Industria Cinematográficos (ICAIC) three months after
the revolution of 1959. Alvarez himself has become one of the most inventive
makers of documentary and newsreel films.*

. . . In 1939, I lived in the United States, working as a dishwasher and working
in the coal mines in Pennsylvania. It was here in the United States that I
started to become politically conscious and when I went back to Cuba I became a communist. American imperialism is the greatest promoter of commu-
nism in the world. In fact, it was my experiences here that form the roots of
Now [1965], my film against racial discrimination in the U.S. . . .

I really started learning about the cinema in 1959 . . . the first newsreels
that we made [at ICAIC] were influenced by traditional newsreels. They were
not revolutionary in a formal sense, but the content was revolutionary. After
we had completed about 20 of them, we started to look for new, expressive
cinematic forms for the newsreel.
———Alvarez, interviewed for *Cinéaste*, Vol. VI, No. 4 (1975)

Lindsay A N D E R S O N
Born 1923 in Bangalore, India, in a military family.

My films are subjective, both the features and the shorts. Subjective to me. In
a certain way, an artist's films are all about himself. And my films are really
about myself. So when I make a film about Covent Garden market [*Every
Day Except Christmas*, 1957] and those workers and it is idealized, this is actually a part of myself and the way I look at life, the way that I look at my
fellow human beings. I'm trying to make other people share that way of looking at life. It doesn't mean that I'm not capable of being cynical or satirical
about them, which I can also be in a different context. . . .

Moral influence can't be measured. The artist does contribute to the moral
climate of his time. . . . Did a film like *The Grapes of Wrath* [1940] play any
part in arousing a social conscience in America? Or was it the *result* of the
social awareness arising out of New Deal politics? Which is cause and which
is effect? We are a part of history and we also make history.

. . . For instance, I am rather struck by *If* . . . [1969] in this context.
If . . . was not created in any way with a conscious knowledge or analysis of
student movements in France, Berlin, Tokyo, London, and Columbia University. None were heard of in that way when the script was being written. The
fact that when we were shooting the scenes of student revolt and massacre
for *If* . . . , the events of May [1968] in Paris and Berlin and New York actually
were happening is a very extraordinary coincidence. . . .

Ambiguity is extremely important. Much of *If* . . . is ambiguous, in the
sense that people can take bits of it in very different ways. You find certain
people in an audience responding very differently to certain things that happen. I don't quarrel with that. I don't want to tell them exactly what they are
to think at each moment.
———Anderson, interviewed for *The Film Director as Superstar* (NY, 1970)

We specially saw *Zéro de conduite* [1933] again before writing [on *If . . .*] started, to give us courage. And we constantly thought of Brecht, and his definition of the "epic" style. David [Sherwin] referred to Kleist from time to time. John Ford ("old father, old artificer") and Humphrey Jennings (romantic-ironic conservative) were in the bloodstream.

——Anderson in Notes for a preface, *If . . .* (London 1969)

Kenneth A N G E R
Born in Santa Monica, California, in 1932. A child actor in films who carried his film interests into directing at the age of 7. The Spider *interviewer asked him about the film he was working on in 1965:*

Well, right now it's hung up because I've run out of money. When I got the Ford Foundation grant, I was completely breadless, and I conscientiously paid off lab bills and things like that. So by the time I'd taken care of my debts there was a piece missing of the $10,000, and then I got a used station wagon, and some extra equipment I needed. And so a friend and I set off across the country from here to New York to film. The material I'm filming is teenagers in relationship to machines. And one of the machines that across the country they're hung up on in a popular sense, I mean like aside from the transistor, is the car. And so my film is ostensibly about teenagers and drag racing and kustom cars.

——Anger, interviewed for *Spider*, 15 Apr 65

Edward A N H A L T
Born in New York City, 1914.

In the case of *The Boston Strangler* [1968], for example, in Gerald Frank's book, which was real, DeSalvo was a guy who got his kicks by killing women. He killed 14 women, and he was very open about his kicks. I've heard his tape, illegally, and he keeps saying in his confession that it was the only way that he could come. Well, I did that in the screenplay, but I found it dull. I found that if you strangle one woman, you strangle two. After you strangle enough women, then it just doesn't move anymore—which is one of the things that's wrong with escalating violence, dramatically. So I had to invent something that was more interesting to me and, therefore, presumably would be to the audience. I believe that people write for themselves. I really pay no attention to anything else. But to me, I had to make him more interesting, so I made him a dual personality. The good DeSalvo didn't know what the bad DeSalvo was doing, which is certainly one of the oldest devices in the world. But it worked on the screen, and not only that, the people who read the book never realized they weren't seeing reality.

——Anhalt, interviewed for *The Screenwriter Looks at the Screenwriter* (NY 1972)

Edgar A N S T E Y
Born 1907 in Watford, Hertfordshire. A founder-member of Grierson's docu-
mentary group and production head of the Shell Film Unit during the war.
Before his retirement, he established British Transport Films (1949), where
he assigned a young director to make his first noticed film, Terminus *(1960):*

It was obvious that we must be strictly honest. If we were not, the audience
(which knows about stations) would not believe any of it. This meant showing
some unattractive aspects of the life of a station. . . .

We shot the film largely by a newsreel technique, with a hand-held
camera operated by a television cameraman who had real genius for capping
the sudden drama of the moment. People today are so used to being photographed with 16 mm. and 8 mm. cameras that they were rarely bothered—
this was 35 mm. But that was all the same to them. Those who were aware
of anything unusual were put at their ease by John Schlesinger's enthusiastic
explanations and carried on quite naturally. . . .

Among all these people we planted our actors. They each had a part to
play, among the ordinary passengers. . . .

These controlled episodes did of course provide an opportunity for more
complete shot-by-shot continuity, but in general there was no shooting script
for *Terminus.* . . . A film like this should go on growing beyond the written
word. You look at the "rushes" and new ideas come to you.
———Anstey, in *The Technique of Documentary Film Production*
(London 1963)

André A N T O I N E [1858–1943]
Founder of one of the most influential theaters (and methods) in modern
theater history, the Théâtre Libre. After his retirement from the direction of
the Odéon in 1916, translated his artistic aims into films, most of which have
been lost to modern viewers.

I had an idea for a film [*L'Alouette et la mésange*, 1922]: the life of boatmen
on the canals in Flanders. I send Grillet ahead to look for a location. I arrive
with the artists. We leave Antwerp on one barge and we go up the Escaut.
Since everything was shot on the voyage this enhanced the photography. Very
striking! It ended with a man being sucked into the mud one night and the
next day the barge floated anew tranquilly in the light and the silence.
———Antoine to André Lang (1924), in Sadoul-Morris,
Dictionary of Films, p 8

Michelangelo A N T O N I O N I
Born in Ferrara, 1912. This most articulate and logical of Italian directors en-
tered the film world through journalism and film criticism. Then he worked as
scenarist and assistant director with Rossellini, Carné, Visconti, and De Santis.
His first independent work was a series of documentary films that he looks back
on as an essential part of his education. After his debut in fictional films with

Cronaca di un amore (1950), *he made four other sensitive films that won for him a discriminating but small public, until his first great surprise,* L'Avventura, *shown to a jeering, booing audience at the 1960 Cannes film festival.*

... I have been told that Pavese and I are somewhat similar. His intellectual experiences coincided tragically with his personal experiences [he committed suicide in 1955]. Could the same be said of me? Doesn't the fact I'm here in the process of making films suggest optimism? For me, I want to have my characters part of their surroundings and not to separate them from their everyday environment. Also you won't find one single *champ-contre-champ* [field-reverse field] in *Le Amiche* [1955]. The technique is instinctive and derives from a desire to follow the characters in order to unveil their innermost hidden thoughts.

Il Grido [1957] has a theme that is very important to me and is the first in which I handled emotional problems in a different way. Previously, my characters were often passive about their emotional crises. In this film we have a man who reacts, who tries to do something about his unhappiness. I treated the character with more compassion. I wanted to use the landscape to express his psychology. It is the landscape I remember from my childhood, but seen through the eyes of a man who returns after an intense cultural and emotional experience.

———Antonioni, quoted in Sadoul-Morris, *Dictionary of Films*, pp 10, 140

Naturally I cannot work out camera movements at my desk, I have to think about them at the studio.... I follow the characters with the movements I have already worked out, and I correct them later if need be. I compose my scenes from behind the camera. Certain directors—for instance, René Clair—work in a different way ... but I cannot understand how they manage to shoot from little designs and plans they have drawn on paper ahead of time.

———Antonioni, interviewed for *Bianco e nero*, June 58

I see my film as narratives, *romans par images*. . . . In a way I suppose I do actually write with the camera. Of course I am always credited with a script, and there has to be something actually written down on paper to satisfy the producers and so on. But I don't work from a written script. My work begins when I look through the viewfinder of the camera—that is for me the moment of creation. Sometimes it is only then that I understand what shape the action will take. It is often the plastic elements—the actors, the decors even—which determine the direction of a scene.

———Antonioni, interviewed for *The Times*, 29 Nov 60

Q: Do you prefer to record the sound on the set or to dub it afterwards?
A: When I can, I prefer recording on the set. The sounds, the noises, and the natural voices as picked up by microphones have a power of suggestion that can't be obtained with dubbing. Moreover, most professional microphones are much more sensitive than the human ear, and a great many unexpected noises and sounds often enrich a sound track that's been made on the set.

Unfortunately, we are still not advanced enough technically to be able to use this system all the time. Shooting outdoors, it's hard to get good sound. And dubbing also has its advantages. Sometimes I find that the transformation of a noise or of a sound becomes indispensable for certain special effects. Thus in certain cases it is necessary to change the human voice. . . .

Q: Do you shoot any sequences from several angles so as to have greater freedom when you edit?

A: Until *Red Desert* [1964], I always filmed with a single camera, and thus from a single angle. But from *Red Desert* on, I began using several cameras with different lenses, but always from the same angle. I did so because the story demanded shots of a reality that had become abstract, of a subject that had become color, and those shots had to be obtained with a long-focus lens. . . .

Q: How much do you have to do with the cutting of your films?

A: I have always had an editor at my side on all my films. Except for *Cronaca di un amore* this editor has been Eraldo da Roma. He is an extremely able technician with vast experience, and a man who loves his work. We cut the films together. I tell him what I want as clearly and precisely as possible, and he does the cutting. He knows me, he understands immediately, we have the same sense of proportion, the same sensibility concerning the duration of a shot.

——Antonioni, interviewed for *Cinéma 65*, Nov 65

I prefer to get results by a hidden method; that is, to stimulate in the actor certain of his innate qualities of whose existence he is himself unaware—to excite not his intelligence but his instinct—to give not justifications but illuminations. One can almost trick an actor by demanding one thing and obtaining another. The director must know how to demand, and how to distinguish what is good and bad, useful and superfluous, in everything the actor offers.

——Antonioni, interviewed (16 Mar 61) by students of the Centro Sperimentale, Rome; trans. for *Film Culture*, Spring 62

[On *The Red Desert*] I used the telescopic lens a great deal in order not to have deep-focus, which is for good reason an indispensable element of realism. What interests me now is to place the character in contact with things, for it is things, objects and materials that have weight today. I do not consider *Red Desert* a result: it is research. I want to tell different stories with different means. . . . With color, you don't use the same lenses. Also, I perceived that certain camera movements didn't always jell with it: a rapid panoramic sweep is efficacious on brilliant red, but it does nothing for a sour green, unless you're looking for a new contrast. I believe there is a relationship between camera movement and color. A single film is not sufficient for studying the problem in depth, but it's a problem that must be examined. I made, for this reason, some 16mm tests. They were very interesting, but I was unable to achieve, in the film itself, certain effects I had found by this means.

——Antonioni, interviewed for *Cahiers du Cinéma in English*, Jan 66; trans. Rose Kaplin

Denys A R C A N D
Born in a Quebec village, 1941. Educated in Montreal, where he enjoyed theater work. Joined the National Film Board in 1962, and then moved back in 1967 to his native village of Deschambault.

I went back to the NFB as a freelance and presented *On est au coton* [1970] as a project. They were fool enough to accept it. . . . The original project was about technocracy. People at the time were always talking about computers and the skills of managers. I wanted to take a crew of 7 of the most technically brilliant minds that I could find—an engineer from IT&T, a specialist in mathematics—and confront them with a problem that I thought would be without solution . . . I chose the textile workers problem. After one month of shooting, these people said . . . it was impossible. They said, "It is a problem of the whole society . . . it is not a scientific matter. It is a political matter, you would have to have a revolution, and we can't plan a revolution on our computers. Sorry, we are managers."
Q. What was the problem exactly?
The textile workers' lives. How could you better the lives of these people.
. . . It was the first film that was really censored by the NFB. I had no prior indication. I worked on the assumption that everything would go well. . . . People in the textile mills asked us: "Why are you always shooting films about poor people? We know poor people. We know our story. We don't have to see it on the screen. Why don't you show us rich people? We never see rich people and that would be interesting for us." We said, "Okay, who would you like to see?" They replied: "The president of Dominion Textiles, we would love to see him." So we decided to include a sequence of the president [King] in *On est au coton*. . . .
    When I finished *On est au coton*, the Film Board decided to invite Mr. King to see the film because he had a very important part. He came and . . . just sort of had a heart attack during the film. . . . Then the Film Board told me that if I removed the portion on Mr. King, the film would be released. Now I am very sorry that I agreed. I thought at the time they were sincere. I removed the part. Then we had another screening and the NFB said it was OK. They cut the negative and printed a copy. That is the copy that now circulates underground.
                    ——Arcand, interviewed for *This Magazine*, Nov–Dec 74

Linda A R V I D S O N [Mrs. D. W. Griffith 1884–1949]
Born in San Francisco, where she began her career as a child actress. She married David Griffith, a fellow actor, in 1906, a long and unhappy marriage.

[*After Many Years* (1908)] was the first movie without a chase. That was something, for those days, a movie without a chase was not a movie. How could a movie be made without a chase? How could there be suspense? How action? *After Many Years* was also the first picture to have a *dramatic* close-up—the first picture to have a cut-back. When Mr. Griffith suggested a scene showing Annie Lee waiting for her husband's return to be followed by a scene of Enoch cast away on a desert island, it was altogether too distracting.

"How can you tell a story jumping about like that? The people won't know what it's about."

"Well," said Mr. Griffith, "doesn't Dickens write that way?"

"Yes, but that's Dickens; that's novel writing; that's different."

"Oh, not so much, these are picture stories: not so different."

[Mack Sennett] played policemen mostly—and . . . a French dude. But he was very serious about his policeman and his French dude. From persistent study of Max Linder—the popular Pathé comic of this day—and adoption of his style of boulevardier dressing, spats, boutonniere, and cane, Mr. Sennett evolved a French type that for an Irishman wasn't so bad. . . . In *Father Gets in the Game* [1908] . . . Sennett is seen as the gay Parisian papa, the Linder influence plainly in evidence.

——Arvidson, in *When the Movies Were Young* (NY, 1925)

Dorothy ARZNER
Born 1900. A successful film editor at the Paramount Studio who was given the opportunity to direct.

Paramount was the best of all the studios because they gave me my start as a director in 1927 with *Fashions for Women*. I also liked working for Sam Goldwyn. Oh, he would blow his top and the writers would be carted off to the hospital with ulcers, but I'd just wait for him to settle down and then I'd explain why things couldn't be the way he wanted them. You have to learn how to handle producers. Goldwyn gave me everything I wanted in the way of sets, lighting, cameramen and costumes, but he also gave me the job of making Anna Sten look like a great actress. He had spent a year grooming her, telling everyone that she would be greater than Dietrich, greater than Garbo, and then when she opened her mouth, out came these monosyllables. The only thing I could do was not let her talk so much.

. . . Joan [Crawford] had been a hey-hey girl and the public didn't seem to want that anymore. But I thought I was going to direct Luise Rainer in *The Girl from Trieste*, Molnar's intimate case history of a young girl who is forced to take to the streets. I was out scouting locations when I got the news that Miss Rainer had been suspended for marrying a Communist and that Joan would replace her in the movie, which was now being called *The Bride Wore Red* [1937]. Right away, I knew that would be synthetic, but Mayer knelt down, with those phony tears in his eyes, and said, "We'll be eternally grateful to the woman who brings Crawford back." I never liked that man; he wasn't honest and he didn't keep his promises. He used to duck out the back door of his office when he saw me coming.

A director must realize what is inside a person, bring it out, and eliminate the flaws. I took Freddie March out of a road company of *The Royal Family* and put him into *The Wild Party* [1929], and he said to me, "I always know when I'm doing a scene right by looking out at your face. Your face is my barometer." The director is the only one who knows what it's all going to look like in the end. It's *pictures*, after all—the actors' faces, the composition, the movement, how the whole thing is orchestrated. And he'd better have a fairly good story to start with, too. I never had a great story, but I used to tell myself, "I'm the only woman director [in Hollywood], so I'd better not complain."

———Arzner, interviewed for *The New York Times*, 20 Aug 76

Anthony A S Q U I T H   [1902–1968]
Born in London. Youngest son of First Earl of Oxford and Asquith by his marriage to Margot Tennant. First British director to join newly formed Association of Cinematograph and Allied Technicians.

I believe as strongly as anyone that visual movement is a vital element in the cinema; but I believe that in a sound film it must not be imposed on the aural flow, or even be a casual fellow-traveler. It must be the partner of an indissoluble marriage. And this is never more true than when you have long dialogue scenes involving several characters.

   This is a problem which is constantly arising in filming the plays of Bernard Shaw, of which I have done two—*Pygmalion*, in 1937, and *The Doctor's Dilemma* this year [1959]. The heart of a Shaw scene is nearly always a verbal one. The dialogue is closely knit, but elaborate. It is almost impossible to break up such scenes into small sections without destroying the general rhythm and also making it far harder for the actors.

   I prefer, therefore, to do such scenes in one continuous take. At the same time I try to achieve the different emphasis of long-shot, medium-shot and close-up by devising movements for the actors and the camera which will give me the gradations at the right moment, without having to interrupt the scene with a cut. It is what I might call a legato technique.

   Sometimes into these scenes I interject a staccato chord, as it were, by a sudden cut in to a big close-up. . . .

———Asquith, in *Films & Filming*, Feb 59

Fred A S T A I R E [Frederick E. Austerlitz]
Born in Omaha, 1899. A vaudeville and musical comedy team with his sister Adele. Considered unsuitable for film work.

In the old days, they used to cut up all the dances on the screen. In the middle of a sequence, they would show you a close-up of the actor's face, or of his feet, insert trick angles taken from the floor, the ceiling, through latticework or a maze of fancy shadows. The result was that the dance had no continuity. The audience was far more conscious of the camera than of the dance. And no matter how effective the trick angles and cockeyed shots might have been in themselves, they destroyed the flow of the dance—a factor which is just as important on the screen as on the stage. . . .

   On the stage you are bound by the limits of a 40-foot proscenium arch, whereas in the pictures you have a little more scope, though not much more, as the dance should not wander all over the lot. What the first approach is, is almost impossible to tell. Often the story, the character, or a piece of music will be the inspiration for a dance routine. Sometimes the conception will come right out of the blue. You get an idea that it would be swell to do a dance on roller skates, or to your own shadow. When this happens, you have to fit your idea into the book, or, perhaps, even build the book around the idea. For instance, I had the idea for the *Top Hat* [1935] dance long before that film.

—Astaire, interviewed for *Theatre Arts Monthly*, May 37

Q. Was it in *Carefree* [1938] that one dance needed 28 takes?

A. [In that one] the dress kept hitting me in the face . . . and the very first take was the one we used . . . and the exhaustion—it was all one take, I remember the whole thing, we didn't cut into anything at all. It was on a stage, and we were trying to make it look like a stage. But you go to a movie, you don't want to see a stage show, you want to see a *movie*. And you get angles and things that are very attractive. The numbers I like the best that we did are those that were not stuck on just one thing. . . .

Q. Weren't most of the dances in the early films all done that way, though?

A. You just cannot photograph everything that way . . . I don't know how I ever did it, or how anybody ever does it—you just sweat yourself out, I used to lose 10 pounds or something—and you could have done it much easier by cutting in to pieces, and getting an angle and moving in, and using the medium. . . . Well, I used it—all my best numbers were done the other way.

Q. You mean by cutting?

A. Oh, absolutely. . . . "Top Hat"—you think that was all one take? It *looks* like one take, because we were very careful to see that it did.

—Astaire, interviewed for *Interview*, June 73

Mary ASTOR [Lucile Langhanke]
Born 1906 in Quincy, Illinois, one of the few movie beauty contest winners who made a film career for herself, chiefly through her own beauty and talent, plus some help from an imaginative photographer, Charles Albin, and lessons from John Barrymore.

[*Beau Brummel* (1924)] was filmed at an easy pace, no production schedule, no pressure from the front office [Warner Brothers]. If we had been working hard on a difficult scene, we'd be given a rest.

The routine of making a silent was similar to that of today as far as the actors and directors were concerned. A scene was blocked out, rehearsed and shot. . . . Except for a special scene that could not be taken again—a battle scene, a car falling over a cliff—there was only one camera, and that was mounted on a tripod and hand-run with a crank. If you said the words, "a thousand and one," neither fast nor slowly, you had the rhythm of one turn of the crank for normal speed. . . .

Perc and Ern Westmore were handling makeup and hairdressing on *Don Q* [1925]: as I remember, it was the first time these departments had been created. Greasepaint came in a stick—somewhat like a big lipstick. Stein's Pink #2, I remember, was what I used. And it was pink, whitish pink. It was applied in streaks all over the face, and then smoothed until it filled every pore. With a towel wrapped turbanlike around the head, you leaned over and using a powder puff loaded with a pinkish powder slapped it all over until the grease had absorbed it. Really very similar to the methods clowns use. Eyebrows disappeared, eyelashes were coated, lips covered. Then it was brushed off nice and smooth. Lipstick was a dark red. Reds went black on film, but if the tone was too light, one's mouth would look white. . . .

One day in the makeup room Perc Westmore and I played around with mixing the Stein's Pink with just a touch of the brown eye shadow. We melted it together and stirred it up and put it on, and there was an ivory cast to the color. . . . It was the beginning of panchromatic makeup. I wish I had held a patent on it! . . .

In [*Holiday* (1930)] it was impossible to "overlap," which is natural in conversation. In fact one couldn't pick up a cue very quickly; there had to be time for the sound man to switch off one mike and switch on another, and that required a beat more than is natural. And the sound man was king. If he couldn't hear it, we couldn't shoot it. . . . You couldn't talk and pace up and down. For example, if the action started with you standing beside a table and then included a move to a chair by the fireplace, you could speak into a mike at the table, but you couldn't talk on the way over; you'd have to wait until you sat down—where there was another mike in the fireplace! . . .

Stage 18—or was it 16?—where the interiors [of *Red Dust* (1932)] were filmed; hot, no air conditioning then, just big fans; damp from the constant use of rain machines. Vic [Fleming] being tough about our complaints, "So what! Everybody sweats in the tropics. Let it show, that's the way it is."

The Mason jar of moths released each scene to flutter and bat their way around kerosene lamps for realism. (Of course they preferred the brighter, hotter lights offstage, and Props had to try and shoo them back into the scene.) . . .

We had completed several days on the back lot on the rubber plantation set. Shots of Clark [Gable] carrying me through the mud, gasping from the force of the monsoon.

We had just finished the continuation on the stage inside where he carries me up the veranda steps into my bedroom, soaking wet, breathless.

Fleming said, "Okay, let's move in on a tight two." . . .

Now Clark was a husky guy and a good sport, but it was not practical for him to be a hero and hold me up for the hour or so the shot would take to line up and shoot. So first of all, a stool had to be found which was the correct height to support most of my weight. Out of sight, of course; they were cutting about elbow high . . . the carpenter was taking a tape measurement from the bottom of my fanny to the floor, and getting the legs sawed off the stool. Lighting was being blocked in, and in those days there were lots of lights. We were hedged in by them, in fact. It was getting very, very hot.

Harold Rosson, the head cameraman, said, "You can step out for a minute, Clark and Mary. Give me the stand-ins."

We cooled off and had a smoke at the big open doorway. I had my usual bad-tempered argument with the makeup man about too much makeup. . . .

"Okay, but *no* lipstick, Harry—you know what Mr. Fleming said. All that rain, I'd never have any makeup left."

"Looks so naked."

"That's what he wants." . . .

The weird part of it all is that it never occurred to anyone, including Clark and me, that all this might have had a bad effect on the mood, or on our ability to play a love scene convincingly. But that's the way it was. The way it always is. The way it is today, on any movie set. . . .

Personally I thought Muni was a very attractive man, and as an actor he was very scholarly and as dedicated and hardworking as the character he was playing [in *The World Changes* (1933)] . . . I didn't approve of his method of working: his total attention to externals, makeup, hair, clothing, manner of walking, gesturing. Every word of the script memorized and actually recorded and rerecorded before he ever went on the set. And the theory that if your eyes twinkled you conveyed humor, if you shook your fist and shouted and allowed spittle to form on your lips, presto! you were an angry man. Okay. So I didn't agree with him. . . .

We had a more than adequate schedule for the picture [*The Maltese Falcon* (1941)]. Because John's script was well prepared, and because he took time in rehearsal, the shooting went very quickly. Often there is much time lost in lack of preparation. There was and is too much of "Let's rehearse with film" in the hopes that something might happen that would be spontaneous and fresh, and wouldn't happen again. . . . Of course, if you have actors who come unstuck, . . . because they lack any kind of professional firmness, or ability to get with it, to concentrate, then it all takes time. . . . The *Falcon* was a jigsaw puzzle, and each scene related to what had happened before and what was to happen—precisely. In emotional levels, in tempos, in cadence of speech and movement. . . .

I have heard people say [Bogart] wasn't *really* a good actor. I don't go along with that. It is true his personality dominated the character he was playing—but the character gained by it. His technical skill was quite brilliant. His precision timing was no accident. He kept other actors on their toes because he *listened* to them, he watched, he *looked* at them. . . .

I worked out the way this poor alley cat [in *Act of Violence* (1948)] should look, and insisted firmly (with [Zinnemann's] help) that the one dress in the picture would *not* be made at the MGM wardrobe, but be found on a rack at the cheapest department store. We made the hem uneven, put a few cigarette burns and some stains on the front. I wore bracelets that rattled and jangled and stiletto-heeled slippers. I had the heels sanded off at the edges to make walking uncomfortable. I wore a fall, a long unbecoming hairpiece that came to my shoulder. And I put on very dark nail polish and chipped it. I used no foundation makeup, just too much lipstick and too much mascara—both "bled," that is, smeared, just a little. Zinney said, "You look just right!" And camera helped with "bad" lighting.

——Astor, in *A Life on Film* (NY, 1971)

Alexandre A S T R U C
*Born in Paris, 1923. Studied law, wrote a novel and film criticism, founded
cine-clubs and announced a theory that he tried on an amateur basis before
getting the chance to work professionally. His theory (at age 25, see below)
has been a key statement for young French filmmakers since 1948, though
the films directed by Astruc himself have not been the proudest examples of its
validity.*

After having been in turn a circus sideshow, an entertainment like the old-
fashioned music hall and a method of making a record of the sights of a given
period, the cinema is becoming, little by little, a language. A language in the
sense that it is a medium in which and by which an artist can communicate
his thoughts, no matter how abstract, or set down his obsessions exactly as he
can today in an essay or a novel. That is why I call the new age of the cinema
that of the *Camera-stylo.* The term has a very exact meaning. It means that
the camera will tear itself progressively away from the tyranny of the visual,
the picture for picture's sake, the immediate story, the concrete, to become
more and more a means of writing as supple and subtle as written language
. . . the scenario-writer should direct his own film. Better, that there should be
no scenario-writer, for in such a form of cinema the distinction between
scenario-writer and director has no meaning.
·—Astruc in *Écran français,* 144, 30 March 48

. . . *Une Vie* [1958] is the story of a couple, but above all the story of the
solitude in which a woman is compelled to confine herself by the negative
drive of a man who is her only link with the world . . . I tried to describe a
woman as one normally portrays men, and vice versa. My heroine needs
cerebral contructions. This is why I am delighted to have been able to work
with Maria Schell, whose acting, her way of building a character, is based
on a masculine principle. Christian Marquand, on the contrary, has a much
more feminine style. . . .
    Claude Renoir and I have tried to use color as a dramatic element rather
than purely for its decorative value. . . . What *is* difficult is the transitions.
In autumn, because of the sun and the leaves, the façade of a house becomes
yellow. Then one goes indoors with a character into a violet salon. It's very
tricky. It is the same when you are cutting from a long shot to a close-up and
don't want a shock effect. A film in color must be ten times more carefully
planned than one in black and white.
——Astruc, interviewed for *Arts,* 20 Aug 68;
trans. in *Godard on Godard,* 1972

Richard A T T E N B O R O U G H
*Born in Cambridge, 1923. Trained at Royal Academy of Dramatic Art and
entered films in Coward's* In Which We Serve *[1942]. His first direction is
described below.*

. . . Before [*Oh What a Lovely War* (1969)] started shooting, I talked to
the whole crew. And by the whole crew I mean 160 people, I don't just mean

the key people. I talked about the problems involved in the subject matter, the problems involved in pure logistics, and the whole total concept that I hoped to achieve on the screen. So the whole unit knew what I was aiming at. They knew about the change of style that had to take place. They knew about the fragmentation and the lack of story line. And when we came down to each sequence, I explained the same problems to the actors involved in that sequence.

I spent a whole day with the actors who were playing members of the family that we call Smith, I told them that they would, within an abnormally short space of time, have to convey the quintessence of an emotion, of a state of mind, which in a normal film might occupy a scene lasting two minutes. For instance, take the scene where Mary Wimbush as the mother is watching her son Harry going up onto the stage to enlist, in a response to the song "I'll Make a Man of You" which is sung by Maggie Smith. Now I had to tell Mary that in two shots, one lasting four seconds and one lasting five seconds (as a matter of fact, I didn't know the exact timing at that stage, but I did know they would be very short), she had to say everything to an audience about a mother's feelings as she sees her son going to join up: the terror, and yet that ridiculous but inevitable sense of pride; all that, in that moment. And this required an incredible preparation in the mind, to know exactly, to be absolutely clear in the mind as to what she was conveying at a particular moment. . . .

———Attenborough, interviewed for *Films & Filming*, June 69

Stéphane AUDRAN
*Born in Versailles, 1933. She has worked in films and theater, and has ap-
peared in many of the films directed by her husband, Claude Chabrol,
beginning with* Les Cousins [1958].

My favorite designer is Karl Lagerfeld, and he has taught me a lot about what to wear in films. The clothes must be fashionable, but not too fashionable, or they will date before the film comes out. In the Buñuel [*The Discreet Charm of the Bourgeoisie* (1972)] it was important to wear no loud colors, nothing too noticeable. And for the night scenes one had to wear something light, but Buñuel insisted that it should not be too light. It was complicated! That was one thing Buñuel told me: the other was "Don't think about anything at all." And he forbade the actresses to make up; we rehearsed, then shot the scene without a pause. But Delphine Seyrig, Bulle Ogier and I were meant to be bourgeoises—that was the whole point—and I suppose we are bourgeoises, so we were always secretly fixing our makeups and hairdos. Buñuel had a strange contraption like a periscope with which he used to spy on us and catch us out.

———Audran, interviewed for *The Sunday Times Magazine*, 9 Sept 73

Claude AUTANT-LARA
*Born in Luzarches, France in 1903. Entered films as set designer, assistant to
René Clair, and as a maker of experimental films* (Faits divers, 1923). *Was
the first to experiment with Henri Chretien's anamorphic lens process* (the

Hypergonar system), later (1953) exploited as CinemaScope. This first film,
Construire un feu, begun in 1927 and completed in 1930, was based on a
Jack London story:

We are fully aware of the interest that the Hypergonar people showed in the special production of *Construire un feu*. I hasten to add that this realization was, in no way, intended to illustrate all the possibilities of the Hypergonar system about which I learnt fully only when the cutting and the realization of our sketches had long been completed.

For *Construire un feu* the application was very simple: The main top screen relating the objective action of the film was filmed with an ordinary camera, without Hypergonar. Similarly for the bottom screen, the subjective one: the two films were juxtaposed on the same image by extending the focal length, and during projection the synchronization of the two screens is perfect . . . Moreover, here is how . . . the Hypergonar was used for the final scenes of the film:

At the claim, under the tent, a man is awaited by his companion: in the night, while the latter thinks that his friend is arriving and prepares the soup, the gold searcher weakens and falls a few miles from there. His friend tries to while away the waiting by distracting himself; the other slowly agonizes imagining himself far from any help.

These scenes, that a current production would present in succession, are here represented simultaneously and are juxtaposed with the help of the Hypergonar.

————Autant-Lara, in *Le Revue du cinéma,* Nov 1930

Tex A V E R Y
Born in Dallas, 1907. First animation experience with Charles Mintz and
Walter Lantz. Collaborated with Chuck Jones at Warner Brothers where they
invented Bugs Bunny and other characters.

. . . We found out early that if you did something with a character, either animal or human, that couldn't possibly be rigged up in live action, why then you've got a guaranteed laugh. If a human can do it, a lot of times it isn't funny in animation; or even if it is funny a human could do it funnier. . . . Actually, we used any kind of distortion that couldn't possibly happen, like a character getting himself stuck in a milk bottle. You couldn't get Chaplin in a milk bottle. . . .

I've always felt that what you did with a character was more important than the character itself. Bugs Bunny could have been a bird. Donald Duck could have been any character that blew its top every 10 feet. It isn't what you see on the screen, it's what they say and do that builds up their personality. As a character Bugs Bunny has an awful lot in common with Max Hare from *The Tortoise and the Hare* [1934], one of Walt Disney's old *Silly Symphonies.* . . . But if you look back, why, my goodness, there's a rabbit that looked a heck of a lot like Bugs Bunny, a far as the drawing goes. But he wasn't Bugs Bunny without the gags that we gave him.

————Avery, interviewed for *Take One,* Jan–Feb 70

George AXELROD
Born in New York City in 1922. Before becoming a successful playwright and scenarist, worked as a radio and television scriptwriter.

What happened [in *The Manchurian Candidate* (1962)] was, I knew what I wanted and Frankenheimer figured out how to do it, 360 degree pan. Then, as a matter of fact, I cut the sequence. How this happened was that one of the crafty ways one worked with Sinatra is to put all his scenes first. You get him in and out of the picture as fast as you can because his attention span is, one could say, somewhat limited. We got him in and out in 23 days. As he was leaving town, he wanted to see a rough cut of all his scenes, and the one thing we hadn't touched was this complicated dream sequence, on which we must have shot about 6,000 feet. So I said, "Look, I know what it should be, let me make a rough cut. I'll just cut from the script." So the cutter and I went away and did it in about half an hour. And we never changed it.

——Axelrod, in *Film Comment*, Winter 70–71

Lew AYRES [Ayer]
Born in Minneapolis, 1908. Played banjo in touring jazz band before achieving a screen test at Pathé.

. . . The role of Paul in *All Quiet [on the Western Front* (1930)] was originally to be played by Douglas Fairbanks, Jr. I'm not sure what happened, whether he turned it down or wasn't chosen. . . .

I'd just done a picture with Garbo, the last of her silents [*The Kiss* (1929)]; Pathé dropped my option, and there was nothing ahead for me. Actually, it was a critical period for the industry as well. It took a lot of courage for Hollywood to make a film where, in the end, the boy and the girl don't walk out into the sunset hand in hand. . . .

What a thing to do in those days, to show Americans that there was another world outside . . . Carl Laemmle [Jr.] was the producer but the credit really belongs to Millie [Lewis Milestone]. . . . Even though Carl had the final say, in any dispute he generally yielded to Millie, who had far more experience than either of us. Actually, Laemmle and I were nearly the same age, pretty young. . . .

——Ayres, interviewed for Lewis, *It Was Fun While It Lasted* (NY, 1973)

B

Boris BABOCHKIN [1904–1975]
Worked in itinerant theaters. Began acting in films in 1927. One role, in
Chapayev (1934), *established his place in film history:*

The two Vasilievs read it in turns. Georgi Vasiliev sang the songs. In its first
version the scenario was so long that we sat from 10 P.M. to 3 A.M. The
material was so fascinating, intimate and exciting, that it already contained
the seed of the film's future success. This very night, walking home, I showed
how Chapayev would wear his cap, and I suggested the "Black Raven" song
to the Vasilievs. Frankly, the image of Chapayev was clear to me, but Petka,
whom I was to play, was not so easily imagined. Nevertheless, I agreed to
play Petka, for the interests of the film were now mine. It did not occur to me
that I might be asked to play Chapayev. I only urged the Vasilievs to
make no mistake in casting this role. I was eager for them to persuade
Khmelyov to play it. In describing the inadequacies of several candidates,
and with no ulterior motive, I showed them how this or that actor would
handle the role. They asked me to try the makeup, so I put on the cap and
moustaches of the commander. A few days later I signed the contract to play
the role of Chapayev.
——Babochkin, in *Face of the Soviet Film Actor* (Moscow, 1935)

Stanley BAKER [1928–1976]
*Born in South Wales: Noticed in school play and soon appeared on London
and Birmingham stages.*

Q. Can you tell us something of your relationship with [Joseph] Losey because you've done several pictures with him since *Blind Date* [1960]?
    A. Well, I don't know what to say about my relationship with Losey
except that I think that it was Losey who really made me first properly aware
about being an actor—probably how involved an actor should be in what he
is doing—up until that stage everything was full of excitement. . . .
    Q. All sorts of terrible things have happened to *Eve* [1962] since it was
made—it's a very hard picture to see and people fought for control over it—
did you realize it was in this kind of trouble when you were making it?
    A. . . . It was a difficult picture for Losey to make because he was at

odds with the producer of the film. They didn't feel they were making the same film—it's sort of hard when you are working on the same film and then when it came out the producers took Losey's film and they put their own version together and they showed it, to his disapproval, naturally—I mean he didn't agree with the cut that they showed and finally after a lot of hard work he got his own cut and he showed it in Paris I believe—and I believe there was one print in this country that was shown—Losey's version. That's very sad when you're making a film if the producer has one idea and the director has another idea and it clashes in the middle and then the public really don't know where they're at because they don't know which film they're watching really and Losey believes quite clearly that his version is far better than the producer's—and the producer believes that his version is far better than Losey's. I've seen both versions—I believe Losey's version is far better than the producer's. But I mean that's personal taste.

———Baker, interviewed at the National Film Theatre, 2 Nov 72

Q. What sort of role did Harold Pinter play on *Accident* [1967]?

A. As with most of Losey's pictures we had a period of preproduction when we sat down together—Harold Pinter as well—and thrashed out what everybody was about which is quite normal when you're dealing with some-one like Losey. But at that stage, most scriptwriters drop out entirely and I think that's probably a good thing because it must be an anxious time for them, but Pinter was quite different. He was there most days and because he had been involved with the previous discussions with the actors he knew what we were all trying to achieve, and if, as an actor, you needed reaffirm-ing about any particular point you could always get an intelligent and objec-tive reply from him. It was marvelous that he was there but I wouldn't use it as a method for most writers. It could be dangerous; it depends on the attitude of the writer.

Q. How did you achieve the superb pace and throwaway dialogue at the dinner table and round the tennis court? You know, the "All of a heap" and Uriah Heep stuff?

A. A lot of that came out of the actors themselves and the playing of the scene. It wasn't written down specifically in black and white. We were only able to use that sort of Pinterish dialogue because we were working with him before and were involved in the situation.

———Baker, interviewed for *Films & Filming*, Aug 70

Lucille B A L L
Born in Jamestown, New York in 1911. Moved from chorus line to studio contracts.

. . . I was in pictures and I didn't dig it too much because I wasn't typecast. I like to be typed. I made my mind up to that a long time ago, and when television came along I said, "Gee, this is my chance to be typed," which is quite the opposite of what most people want to do. To me I thought that was marvelous because I'd been 15 years in pictures and I'd always be playing someone else even though I was maybe the same type of career girl, maybe the same type of model, or same type of prostitute or whatever the hell it was. But still there was a similarity to everything, but it wasn't a type—a real recognizable type so if you'd see me you could recognize me from pictures past. . . . So I said, I want to be—what do I want to be? I had to stop and think. And I thought, well, of the 30 pictures I've made or 32 or whatever it was, what did I like best? I could only find but 3 or 4 scenes in those pictures that I cared anything about and I put them all together and I found out they were domestic scenes, where I was housewife—I don't know, maybe normal, natural, somewhat silly—but I loved the domestic scene. So I started from that. . . .

Buster [Keaton] was a personal friend. I never got a chance to work with Buster until 2 months before he died. . . . Fabulous, fabulous man with props . . . he taught me about props and the value of taking care of them and checking them yourself, and even how to make some of them, but how to make them work especially.

————Ball, interviewed for *Dialogue on Film*, 18 Jan 74

Jean-Louis B A R R A U L T
Born in Vesinet, France, 1910. Since 1946 has headed the Renaud-Barrault Company.

You have to *feel* the camera. Jean Gabin has the sense of it. Sometimes you give too much, sometimes not enough, and the result is very often unexpected. In *La Symphonie fantastique* [1942] I had a hysterical fit that was awful. I had to control the measure of sensitivity and then it was better. Another time I thought I was too intense and there was nothing at all on the screen.

————Barrault, interviewed for *Theatre Arts Monthly*, Oct 47

John B A R R Y M O R E [Blythe] [1882–1942]
Born in Philadelphia. Before the peak of his stage career, he entered films (1913) as a comedian:

I found that I overacted many of the scenes, that missing the stimulus of the audience I became indiscreet. . . . I had been prewarned, but I had a feeling that if I worked hard enough I could make the electricians and the camera-men laugh and they would take the place of a theater audience. The result was woeful and unreal.

————Barrymore, quoted in *Image* (Rochester), Jan 57

Léon B A R S A C Q [1906–1969]
Born in the Crimea. Studied at l'Ecole des Arts Decoratifs in Paris and worked as assistant to Jean Renoir before the first film he designed, La Marseillaise, *1938.*

All collaborators on a film have their besetting sin: you have to demonstrate to them, whenever they collaborate, that the contribution of their field is a major one for the realization of the film in question. This holds true for the scriptwriter, as well as for the cutter, the director, the cameraman, the designer, the composer and even the producer, not forgetting the "star."

For a René Clair film such competitions never take place. For the whole team, as well as for the public, it's simply a René Clair film.

This miracle derives from a strong personality, from an extraordinarily lucid mind. One often quotes his statement (the irony of which his admirers fail to discern): "A film is made on paper, the job in the studio is a mere pleasure party." . . .

In describing my work in *Le Silence est d'or* [1947] I describe the work of a designer placed in ideal conditions. It is beneficial to me as this represents a very rare happening.

I would like to characterize first in some words the studies for the settings, the period of the preparation. Having read the first script, a conversation with René Clair allows me to establish the list of settings with indications of the needs of the production: The main angles of the shots, entrances, exits, transitions between various settings, particularly important details, necessitating special research, etc. . . .

The equipment of our studio included also about 12 settings painted as trompe-l'oeil. These background canvases had to serve for different scenes showing different views of 1906. For this matter, too, we appealed to a film veteran, Amédée Prévot, Zecca's appointed designer in 1906, precisely.

It was the exterior setting of the big boulevards which presented most complications. It was out of the question to film on the real boulevards or in any real street. The modern shop windows, the street lamps, the signs represented all too evident anachronisms; on the other hand, the necessity to have the advertising procession of Mi-Careme pass through numerous extras dressed in the style of the period, and night views, very difficult to light, made this enterprise more costly than the construction of a special setting for the shots.

————Barsacq, in *Ciné-Club*, Oct 47

Saul B A S S
Born 1920 in New York City. A graphic artist who made a career of designing film titles and, later, as a scene planner.

I had a fantastic crash course in direction from Hitchcock and I'll always be grateful for that. But when [*Psycho* (1960)] came out everyone went wild about the shower-bath murder which I'd done, almost literally shot by shot, from my story board. And then Hitchcock had second thoughts. In the book with Truffaut he says that I directed the sequence because he was ill on that day. But after he saw it he hated it and directed it himself all over again. I hate to say this, but that story's not true. The man's a genius. But why should a genius get away with being so greedy?

————Bass, interviewed for *The Sunday Times*, 9 Dec 73

Timité BASSORI
With La Femme au couteau (1969) *Bassori initiated a film industry in the*
Ivory Coast. The interviewer asked how such a beginning is made:

It's not easy, believe me! The aid I get from Ivory Coast Television is a
provisional kind—one that, in a sense, condemns me to making what they
think will be obvious financial successes. . . . And then the production costs
are unbelievable. . . .

There's another thing that's even more irritating—all the money we had
to spend *outside* the Ivory Coast just in order to get the film completed. The
final processing of the negative, the cutting, the addition of a sound track, the
making of prints—all these had to be done somewhere else. We just don't
have enough technicians or facilities. Along with the high cost of film stock
itself, in the end the total amount spent outside our own country amounted
to more than half the budget! . . . I had to bring in my own personal funds; I
had to go around borrowing money. It was a real adventure, I can tell you
that.

———Bassori, interviewed for *Positif*, Oct 69; trans. in *Atlas*, Feb 70

Cecil BEATON [Walter Hardy]
Born in London, 1904. Fashionable photographer and designer; his greatest
film successes were in the costumes for Gigi (1958) *and* My Fair Lady (1964):

Monday, 25 February [1963]. The morning went by with diversions and
interruptions. The only positive work, which lasted half an hour, consisted
of making preliminary ground-plans for Higgins's house. Gene [Allen, art
director] is practical and encouraging. We have used the 3 floors of Dr.
Gottfried's house in Wimpole Street which, with adaptations, suit Shaw's
elaborate comings and goings. We chortled because we had really started.
George Cukor cracked that he expected to see the job finished by the
evening. . . .

I am a parasite in George Cukor's room until the furnishings for my
office arrive. We work in close harmony, and every aspect of the picture is
discussed, from the style of lighting to be suggested in different scenes to the
types of people who would be invited to the ball. George is in tearing spirits,
and our bungalow rings with his laughter. Sometimes I am impatient and
nervous to get some of my ideas on paper. But George is content to talk.

George likes to talk his ideas. He needs an audience. That's the way he
works. He says he can't imagine my enjoying being by myself for hours upon
end, closeted only with my drawings. With people around him, his ideas
come twirling out of his brain like caramel on a revolving machine. . . .

Friday, 15 March. With Gene, I went through all the details of the
various architectural elements to be incorporated in the Higgins's households:
picking cornices, details of panelings, moldings, balustrades and typical pieces
of English *art nouveau* 1910.

It has taken us a month to collect our thoughts in trying to find a
style to present Shaw as a film-musical, for this style must be consistent.

We must romanticize the exteriors. The buildings will be imperceptibly elongated and painted in exaggerated light-contrasts to create a slightly heightened effect to the ordinary.

Wimpole Street presents the greatest difficulties. When have you seen a studio street scene that is successful?

Thursday, 11 April . . . This is, from a costume point of view, a play about three women—Eliza, Mrs. Higgins, and Mrs. Eynsford-Hill. They are surrounded by people who are all dressed as important characters. In this production there are virtually no "extras" and, with the exception of the tails at the Ball, and the gray frock-coats at Ascot, there are no "repeats." Even the men in the cockney scenes are being created as individual characters, whose prototypes are to be found in Phil May, Belcher, or photographs of the period. Among the 400 women at the Ball and at Ascot, there is not one costume that has not been specially designed, or re-created from museum sources, with the care and attention given to a principal's clothes.

Wednesday, 3 July . . . Geoff Allan, a burly, somewhat top-heavy-looking youth from the outskirts of London, has become an expert at "aging" clothes. Today he was breaking down Eliza's little jacket in which she first visits Higgins's house. Everyone who had seen the coat in a test agreed that the black velveteen appeared too elegant and rich-looking. In an effort to save the garment, Geoff decided to take drastic measures. He asked me, "Suppose it doesn't survive?" "Go ahead. At worst, we'll have to get a new one." Geoff put the coat in a boiling vat. After a few hours the black velvet had become a cream colour. Geoff now started to make the coat darker, many shades darker. Putting a spoon in dye, he smeared its surface, leaving the light patches where the sun might have faded the collars and shoulders. He purposely left paler the material at the edges and in the creases. The coat was then dried out in a furnace. To me, it now looked like something found in an ancient Egyptian tomb: it was as hard and brittle and brown as poppadum. With blazing eyes, Geoff then brought out a wire brush and gave the garment a few deft strokes, saying, "This bit of pile will soon disappear." It did. Later Geoff said, with avid enthusiasm, "I'll take the thing home tonight and sew frogs on it again—coarsely, with black thread, and I'll sew them with my left hand. Then, with my right hand, I'll rip them off. Then I'll knife the seams open here as if it's split. Afterwards, with coarse thread, I'll patch it. Of course, the collar will have to be stained a bit as if Eliza had spilled coffee on it (no, she would drink tea . . . it will have to be tea stains), and there must be greasy marks on the haunches where she wipes her dirty hands. Naturally the skirt will have to be made muddy around the hem, because, you see, she sits when she sells her violets, and the skirt, and petticoats also, would seep up the wet."

———Beaton, in *Cecil Beaton's My Fair Lady* (NY, 1964)

Jacques B E C K E R [1906–1960]
Born in Paris; parents were friends of the Cézanne and Renoir families. Jean Renoir's assistant from 1931 to 1939. Completed his first film, Dernier atout, *after his return from captivity in Germany in 1942. The following remarks describe the making of his greatest success,* Casque d'or (1952):

I don't like criminals. A "perfect crime" thriller is dependent on psychiatry. I'm not interested in recounting clinical cases, but in human beings. I found the visuals during the writing of the script. As I wrote it, visualizing the scenes, I gave only the minimum essential dialogue to the characters. . . . Companeez was only involved in the last fifth of the script.
———Becker, quoted in Sadoul-Morris, *Dictionary of Films*, p 55

Marco BELLOCCHIO
Born in Piacenza, Italy, in 1939. Studied acting and direction at the Centro Sperimentale in Rome; directed three short films before I Pugni in tasca (Fists in the Pocket, *1966).*

G. How do you characterize *Nel nome del padre* [1971]? Exactly what is the film all about?
A. Clearly it was our intention and ambition to go beyond a simple boarding-school situation and to illustrate the society; not abstractly but by indicating a certain condition of youth, a debasement, a kind of education that is not limited only to the Catholic boarding schools but which has existed—and still exists—in all kinds of schools, education that makes cowards and hypocrites of us all.
There is a scene that I think turned out rather well and which synthesizes this attitude of the educators, the Establishment people—the scene when the boys run up the stairs and spit on the marble bust of the founder of the school. The teachers see this but condone it; by allowing the young people this kind of outlet in the present, they can screw them better in the future in the things that matter. It is a pecular kind of freedom in Italy that permits a future domination, a kind of "controlled" freedom that is typical of the Church.
———Bellocchio, interviewed for *Film Society Review,* Jan 72

Jean-Paul BELMONDO
Born 1933 in Neuilly (Seine).

As soon as I was dressed for the role [in *A bout de souffle,* 1959] with that hat on my head and the cigarette in the corner of my mouth, I felt at ease in the character. All I needed was a tic. Jean-Luc Godard, the director, has a habit of pinching his lower lip, and I thought I ought to do that. But I wasn't comfortable with it. Then I remembered Humphrey Bogart's gesture of rubbing a finger across his lip. I was ready to go.
———Belmondo, interviewed for *Horizon,* Nov 61

Laslo BENEDEK
Born in Budapest, 1907. Worked in German, French and English films, and moved to Hollywood in 1937, assisting Joseph Pasternak at MGM. First direction, The Kissing Bandit (1948).

When faced with long dialogue scenes [in *Death of a Salesman,* 1951], I do not hold with the school that believes in moving around the actors incessantly and in panning or dollying around frantically for the sake of "giving it movement." Unless the movement of the actors and that of the camera is dictated by the inner dynamics of the scene, I find it distracting and irritating. The scenes of this play fall into two categories: reality and imagination. The realistic scenes I tried to handle as simply and naturally as possible, both in staging and in camera treatment. (In the scene, for instance, of Linda's great speech in the kitchen: "Attention must be paid . . ."—I deliberately strove for an almost static quality and for a complete simplicity of background in order to avoid any distraction). In these scenes I depended primarily on the dialogue and the power of the performances.

It was the other aspect of the play that offered interesting cinematic possibilities, logically dictated by its very nature. Relating the last 24 hours of Willy Loman's life, the play blended and integrated the real happenings of this one day with his memories and fantasies, stretching back over many years and distant places. In presenting this story, the play borrowed freely from motion picture technique. The reason for this, I believe, is obvious. The very process of remembering, of the fantasy, of the daydream or even of imagination is essentially similar to the motion picture. They have in common the vivid movement, the quick transitions, the "dissolve," sometimes the vagueness of out-of-focus images, sometimes the precision of a close-up.
————Benedek, in *Sight & Sound,* Oct–Dec 52

Robert B E N T O N & David N E W M A N
While working at Esquire *they collaborated on writing* Bonnie and Clyde (*1967*).

Newman: Of all the things we've done *What's Up, Doc?* [1972] is the project we felt least personally involved with. One night the phone rang, and it was Peter [Bogdanovich]. He said, "I've got a deal with Streisand and Ryan O'Neal, and no script. I want to do a remake of *Bringing Up Baby* [1938], and we can do it like [snap!] that." We said, "Look, Peter, we can't get involved in a thing like that. We have preproduction starting on *Bad Company* [1972] in five weeks."

Benton: Peter said, "Hawks did it with [Dudley] Nichols and [Hagar] Wilde in six weeks and eleven days. We can do it in seven." When Peter decides he wants something, he has this incredible tenacity.

Newman: Anyway, he called back and they held out a lot of money, which we needed. Peter said, "Ah, that'll be fine. We'll do it in a snap." We met with him and hashed out this story, doing the first draft in a week and a half, which was a remarkable feat for us—although it looked like it had been done in a week and a half. Then we went out there and did a second version, and then left for preproduction on *Bad Company*. The script [of *What's Up, Doc?*] wasn't ready yet and that was obvious. It was staying-up-all-night kind of writing. Buck Henry came in and did the third version. But it was fun working with Peter because we'd spent all our lives watching the same movies, and all our reference points were the same.
————Benton & Newman, interviewed for *Film Comment,* Mar–Apr 73

Ingmar BERGMAN
Born in Uppsala in 1918, son of a pastor to the Swedish royal court. Trained in theater, assisting at opera; entered films in 1940, as scenarist. First film direction, Crisis (*1945*).

Do you know what moviemaking is? Eight hours of hard work each day to get 3 minutes of film. And during those 8 hours there are maybe only 10 or 12 minutes, if you're lucky, of real creation. And maybe they don't come. Then you have to gear yourself for another 8 hours and pray you're going to get your good 10 minutes this time. Everything and everyone on a movie set must be attuned to finding those minutes of real creativity. You've got to keep the actors and yourself in a kind of enchanted circle. . . .

————Bergman, interviewed for *Playboy*, June 64

Q. You shot quite lengthy sequences in *The Shame* [1968] which you didn't at first think were suitable?
   A. I've always done so, that has been my practice for the last 10 to 15 years. You see, one has to begin somewhere in a film; when you do, you're likely to be far out from the center of eventual interest, you find yourself disoriented. No matter how well you prepare, you don't really know how a film's going to look when you've finished it. Above all, you're not sure of the tone, and that's tremendously important . . . for which reason I always have a margin of at least a week for retakes, usually at the tail end of the production. . . .
   Q. When you've written your manuscript and it's ready for you to start shooting, it's pretty well set up as a visual continuity. Do you work in such a way with your imagination that you can then "close your eyes" and see the film as a sequence of pictures?
   A. No. Well, bits and pieces of it, yes. But it would be intolerable, for me and for those working with me, if, at every moment, I were to try and shape the film by force, if I insisted on a sequence of detailed, preconceived pictures to illustrate the conception I had as I envisioned or wrote the script. . . .
   While that original conception must always be in the background, I must not let it become too dictatorial, since, for one thing, I must be prepared to modify it when I switch from writing to directing. For another, my actors, too, have a right—to say nothing of an obligation—to draw straws, to choose among alternatives. The whole process is essentially creative. You write down a melodic line and after that, with the orchestra, you work out the instrumentation.
   If *Smiles of a Summer Night* [1955] hadn't been an international success, I would have been virtually finished. I had just had *The Seventh Seal* refused, in manuscript. When *Smiles of a Summer Night* became a success, after its showing at Cannes, I drove to Cannes to see Carl-Anders Dymling and laid that script on the table and told him: "Now or never." Then he accepted it.

————Bergman, interviewed for *Films & Filming*, Feb 69

. . . *Persona* [1966] was a very strange thing because I wrote the script without thinking of anything. I just wrote it and it was very complicated for me to understand what I had written. I had to reshoot some scenes two or three times before when I was on location. We made it once again and that time I thought it was all right. That was very complicated. But it was charming and nice because there were just two actors and it did not cost too much. I did not feel too guilty. You always feel it's not your money—not my money. I don't spend my money. I spend the money of the company. When I was young they always told me that I spent company money and now I think there's still a little guilt.

—Bergman in Henderson's *The Image Maker* (Richmond, 1971)

When I was making *Crisis* [1945], Victor Sjöstrom was the only living person who could even talk to me or I had the least respect for. All through that dreadfully unhappy period he was kind to me. After he'd seen the day's rushes he'd come in and have a chat. If the entire production wasn't canceled—Sjöstrom was artistic director out here at Rasunda in those days—it was almost entirely his doing. At that moment Ingmar Bergman's to-be-or-not-to-be as a film director really hung by a thread! But Sjöstrom chatted with me in the mornings and was decent to me. . . . He gave me the benefit of his own immense experience. I felt safe with him.

But then along came Lorens Marmstedt and looked at my rushes in a sort of cold fury and called me an incompetent bloody amateur—swore we'd have to scrub the whole production—that he'd have to call in Hasse Ekman to make the film instead. . . . "Bloody soul-shakers," he called us, acting out our private lives in public, a bunch of traitors; no, worse, charlatans, who were throwing away his money. . . . But one thing he did teach me . . . and taught me thoroughly, and I'm eternally grateful to him for it. He taught me to look coldly and objectively at my own rushes.

[*The Seventh Seal*, 1956] got shot in 35 days. You know that scene where they dance along the horizon? We'd packed up for the evening and were just about to go off home. It was raining. Suddenly I saw a cloud; and [Gunnar] Fischer swung his camera up. Several of the actors had already gone home, so at a moment's notice some of the grips had to stand in, get some costumes on and dance along up there. The whole take was improvised in about 10 minutes flat.

The script [of *A Passion*, 1969] had been written straight off the cuff; it was more a catalog of moods than a film script. Usually I solve most of the technical problems at the script stage; but here—both for lack of time and as a challenge to myself—I chose to cross my bridges as I came to them. This meant I had a lot to do all the time. I shot scenes, saw they were wrong, and had to remake them.

And then, too, it was almost the first time we'd worked in color. The first time we'd used color we'd made it entirely by the book [*Now About These Women*, 1964]. But with *A Passion* we'd got it into our heads we were going to make a *noch nie da gewesenes* color film. And for the first time in many many years Sven [Nykvist] and I clashed. I began to suffer from twinges of stomach ulcer, and Sven's giddiness came back. Two lunatics staggering about, looking at our takes, and hating. . . . Because we couldn't get it the way we wanted, we reshot a great deal. The more sensitive sort of color film wasn't available at that time, the sort which has double-x sensitivity. It was all terribly tough going.

Q. How was the supper scene in *A Passion* done? How much of the conversation is yours and how have the actors improvised? Is this scene [dubbed], too?

A. No, it isn't. The whole thing was perfectly simple. The script told them more or less what they were to talk about—the devil knows whether they did, though! The evening before, we met and went through what each of them should talk about. I explained the scene plan and the situation. They were to sit around a table, such or such food was to be served, such or such a red wine. Each actor had a clear idea of where he or she stood in the film. Then the camera was turned, first on one, then on the second, then on the third, then on the fourth, and the conversation was allowed to take whatever course it liked.

Q. Was that scene shot at a late stage in the filming?

A. Yes, it was one of the last. Otherwise we couldn't have it. Liv [Ullmann] has a remarkable bit, too, where she suddenly begins defending her marriage and her voice becomes somehow wild and shrill and strange. Really good actors—who know their parts inside out and have a pretty good idea of what it's all about—can make up their own words. It works fine. And it doesn't have to be nonsense, either.

———Bergman, interviewed for *Bergman on Bergman* (Stockholm, 1970);
trans. by Paul Britten Austin (London, 1973)

As I turn this project [*Cries and Whispers*, 1972] over in my mind, it never stands out as a completed whole. What it most resembles is a dark, flowing stream—faces, movements, voices, gestures, exclamations, light and shade, moods, dreams. Nothing fixed, nothing really tangible other than for the moment, and then only an illusory moment. A dream, a longing, or perhaps an expectation. A fear in which that to be feared is never put into words. I could go on indefinitely describing key and color, and we shouldn't be any the wiser. We had better get started.

———Bergman, in *The New Yorker*, 21 Oct 72

Ingrid BERGMAN
Born 1917 in Stockholm. Attended Royal Dramatic Theater School.

... I always try to figure out why a person behaves the way she does. I have to make my own foundation, my own little staircase. It's possible that the audience will never get it, but I always have to try my own way. When I played the part of Anastasia [in 1956], I believed she was the Czar's daughter, so I played it that way. The director told me I played it so sincerely that everybody would believe she was the Czar's daughter. But my own idea was that she *was;* otherwise I couldn't have played it. How could I play it and lie? When I do a part, I always invent characteristics to bear out what I understand the part to be. If it is clear in your head, you can convey it. It's the little things that the audience sees. This we learn from films. I always want an explanation for everything in a part. What does this mean? *Why* open a window? I have to have it terribly clear in my mind. Then I try to behave as though I were another person. But I use my own ways. If you play 20 parts, you are certainly bound to repeat things, but I try within my limits to make each character a different person. There is a kind of acting in the United States, especially in the movies, where the personality remains the same in every part. I like changing as much as possible. The Swedish idea of acting is that you do change; you play another person each time. To me, doing that is natural.

——Bergman, interviewed for *The Player* (New York, 1962)

Busby B E R K E L E Y [William Berkeley Enos] (1895–1976)
Born in Los Angeles. Worked in New York theater.

Q. What brought you to Hollywood back in 1929?
   A. Eddie Cantor was going to do a picture called *Whoopee* [1930] for Sam Goldwyn, and they wanted me to direct all the musical numbers. It was my first time to work with Cantor. I did three more pictures with him at Goldwyn: *The Kid from Spain, Palmy Days,* and *Roman Scandals.* I started showing sequences of close-ups of pretty girls with *Whoopee.* It had never been done before.
   Q. From the Goldwyn Studio you went over to Warner Brothers?
   A. Yes. I was under contract at Warner's for 8 or 9 years. The first film I did there in 1933 was a milestone in musicals called *42nd Street.* Darryl Zanuck produced it. It started a new popularity for musicals. It starred Dick Powell, Ruby Keeler, and Warner Baxter. Ginger Rogers had a featured part. Most of the same cast was in *Gold Diggers of 1933.* There was an earthquake in Los Angeles when we were shooting that. At the time it hit I had 50 beautiful girls up 35 feet high on platforms. I shrieked and hollered to them not to jump. They would have killed themselves. I yelled, "Sit down! Sit down!" No one was hurt, but the walls of the stage were shaking.
   Q. Why did you use only one camera to film what is known as your spectacular ensemble numbers?
   A. Because I knew exactly what I wanted to shoot. I did my cutting with the camera. That is, the cutter had to put it together the way I shot it. I set every shot in every film I ever made. I got behind the camera and showed the operator exactly what I wanted.

——Berkeley, interviewed for *Hollywood Speaks!* (NY, 1974)

Curtis [Kurt] B E R N H A R D T
Born in Worms, Germany, 1899. First film work in Berlin, moved to France in 1934, to Britain in 1935.

. . . At the end of 1939 or the beginning of 1940, I came to the United States and immediately signed with Warner Brothers.
   The first thing that hit me here, and hit me hard, was that I no longer had

the authority that I had had before. In Germany, France and Italy before World War II, the director was in charge of the whole artistic side of the film including the script and the choice of the story.

In America, I found that the producer was the number-one man and that the director was supposed to take a script, make a few changes if he felt like it, and then shoot it. My earliest memory of Warner Brothers in 1940 is of somebody handing me a script and saying: "You start shooting Monday." And I was used to having three, four, or five months preparation!

It's not true that Bette [Davis] had anything to do with the lighting of her close-ups. I saw to it that she didn't assume any authority that didn't belong to her, which was often quite a struggle. I would never have an actor tell me where to put my camera or anything like that. Once a director lets an actor interfere, he is lost. That's why I could never work with Sinatra or Marlon Brando. It would be out of the question because these guys assume rights and attitudes which properly belong to the director. Let them direct themselves, if they know how.

[Payment on Demand, 1951] had some very fascinating flashback effects using negatives and transparent sets, incorporating a technical innovation of my own invention. Frankly, I cannot understand why it hasn't been used since. It was all a play with light. In part of it, Bette Davis had to play a thirteen-year-old girl, and I had her sort of impressionistically in the middle ground of the set. When we reverted to the past—the cameraman was the late Leo Tover—the foreground became dark, the background lit up and the walls disappeared, because the walls were actually transparent. But you couldn't discern that when they were illuminated for foreground action; they were like screens. As soon as you took the light off them and moved into the background, the walls vanished.

———Bernhardt, interviewed for *The Celluloid Muse* (Chicago 1969)

Bernardo B E R T O L U C C I
Born in Parma, 1941, the son of a well-known poet and film critic. His own poetry was awarded an important Italian prize at the time his interest in film was expressed in working as assistant to Pasolini.

When I was 10, I would spend Saturdays and holidays at the movies, seeing one at 2 o'clock, another at 4 and maybe a third at 6. . . .

From the day I began work with Pasolini [on Pasolini's first film, *Accatone*, 1961], I stopped writing poetry. Poetry was only a means of expressing myself until I could find the real way—making movies. . . . For Pasolini each shot, each zoom, was the first in the history of the cinema. . . .

Three months before the shooting [of *Last Tango in Paris*, 1972] was to begin, [Brando] insisted I come to Hollywood and spend 2 weeks talking about Paul. I didn't want to talk about Paul, so I went to Brando's house that first day and told him everything I knew about the character in 30 minutes. Then I said, "Let's talk about ourselves, about our lives, our loves, about sex. That's what the film is going to be about."

. . . We were about to shoot a scene in which Brando was supposed to cry, when he came to me and said, "I don't know how to do it." Earlier, he had told me about a terrible nightmare he'd had about his children, and so I said, "Think of the nightmare." He looked at me and for a second I thought he wanted to kill me. I knew I had asked him to violate his intimate self, and I was about to change the scene when he said, "Okay, I'll do it."

———Bertolucci, interviewed for *Newsweek*, 12 Feb 73

I swear to you that I absolutely don't even know how this split screen [*Partner*, 1968, in which one actor plays dual roles] was done technically. I have this technique in my imagination. I don't know how to use the camera. But I know what I want. I want each take to be a film in itself. I am against editing. I would like to make a film of one long take. I feel that editing renders films all alike, gives them a brushing of conventionality. I want to do as many long takes within a single film as possible. I prefer to do an interior editing inside my head.

This forces me to find solutions that are not the usual solutions of editing —of, you know, making the establishing shot and then the close-up and so forth. It forces me to find unconventional solutions. For each shot I must have a new idea. For example, in *Partner*, in the shot of Pierre Clementi and the double in front of the mirror, this for me in my mind was a little thing. Because in the interior of my mind I had 3 dissolves of light fading on first one and then the other character. I am forced to invent continuously because I don't want to use cutting and editing and the usual conventions.

. . . I create my film in the shot, not in the editing room. What comes later is arranging the scenes. I am not re-creating a reduced original vision. I am just creating order out of the chaos of my selections. And I must be objective enough to eliminate scenes that don't work, as I did with several very long takes in *Partner*.

———Bertolucci, interviewed for *The Film Director as Superstar* (NY 1970)

Billy B I T Z E R [Johann Gottlob Wilhelm Bitzer, 1874–1944]
Born in Boston. Mechanic and electrician before working (1896) as news cameraman for the Biograph Company of New York City.

On the studio roof [of the Biograph Company, 1899] we were making pictures that ran on an average of 75 feet apiece. There was no story. The set consisted of two large Japanese screens spread to make a background, a table, and a few chairs. If it was a domestic scene, I put paper roses in a vase on the center of the table. If it was a home of wealth, the table was removed and a large potted palm was placed by the Japanese screen. Two potted palms indicated even greater wealth. Having no actors, we would just take anyone handy. According to the number of people we could gather together, the plot was born.

The Interrupted Message [1900] was my first staged attempt at a movie (I had taken only newsreels and railroad "scenics"). For the new venture, director, cameraman, props and writer were all rolled up in one Billy Bitzer. We used a couple of women from the building for the feminine lure and a man from the lobby bar for the comedy bit. . . . The man was relating an experience, with many gestures, when there was a knock on the door. . . . He opens the door, accepts the letter, puts it on the table, but continues his rapid talking as he seats himself. He reaches to the floor to retrieve his handkerchief, but instead picks up the end of the tablecloth, which he sticks in his pocket. (On the end of the tablecloth we had a hook.) At last he reads the message. On it I had written "You're a lousy actor." He hadn't expected this, looked around helplessly in astonishment, then jumped to his feet, dashing from the room. As he dashed out, the hook in his pocket pulled off the tablecloth, thereby upsetting one of the women. This was the effect we wanted, as petticoats were amazingly attractive in an era when ladies dressed to suggest rather than reveal.

There was a lot of speculation among cameramen about the Méliès camera, built in France before 1904. All we could do was guess how he worked out all his film fantasies himself. His magic tricks intrigued cameramen like me who were not permitted to waste company film experimenting. At the end of a film roll, there is always some left over, and this I used for experimental purposes, though I never discovered the secrets of the Méliès magic.

It has been asked many times whether Griffith or Bitzer should be credited with the fadeout. It probably should be neither one. . . . I had been so preoccupied with the mechanics of the camera that I did not pay that much attention to what was later lauded as a marvelous achievement. To me it was just another day's work. If Mr. Griffith asked for some effect, whether a fadeout or whatever, I tried one way or another to produce what he wanted. When it worked successfully, we were hailed as inventors.

——Bitzer, in *Billy Bitzer, His Story* (New York, 1973)

[The single camera with which he photographed the *Birth of a Nation,* 1915] was a $300 Pathé machine, with a 3.5 2-inch lens interchangeable with a wide-angle lens—that is, you had to screw one out and screw the other in its place. . . . It was a light camera, and it was easy to pick it up and come forward for a close-up, back for a long shot, around for a side angle. But there were times when I wished that Mr. Griffith wouldn't depend on me so much, especially in the battle scenes. . . . The fireworks man shooting smoke bombs over the camera—most of them exploding outside the camera range and D. W. shouting "Lower, lower, can't you shoot those damn bombs lower?"

——Bitzer, interviewed for Iris Barry, *D. W. Griffith* (New York, 1940)

In filming Sherman's march to the sea, we needed cannons and had arranged to get some. . . . The crew bringing them out to Universal Field was held up, and while we were waiting, Griffith noticed a family group on the hill nearby. At his direction, I inched the camera unobtrusively up to them, all the while pretending we were after shots of the valley below. Later, the combined scenes, edited by Jimmy and Rose Smith, would vary the long panorama shot with this little intimate picture of a mother and her child caught in the grip of war.

The reason we had to have the camera dolly [for the big shot in Belshazzar's court] was that the balloon, which we tried first, did not work. I had to get the entire set in full view—a real bird's-eye view—from the air, then zoom downward gradually to the dancing virgins of the Sacred Fires on the steps, then zoom into the big banquet hall, for many yards, and finally pinpoint a little toy chariot . . . as it moved across the floor. . . . Now remember that the whole set was about three-eighths of a mile long and that I had to start suspended in the air 150 feet high. When we tried it first in the balloon, the trouble was that the basket rocked. . . . But Huck Wortman [the set designer] worked it all out fine with his next construction. The dolly was 150 feet high, about 6 feet square at the top and 60 feet wide at the bottom. It was mounted on 6 sets of four-wheeled railroad-car trucks and had an elevator in the center. . . .

This great dolly was moved backward and forward by manpower; 25 workers pushed it smoothly along the rails. Another staff operated the elevator, which had to descend at a regular rhythm as the railroad car moved forward. The whole scene had to be filmed in one continuous shot, in focus at every level.

————Bitzer, in *Billy Bitzer, His Story* (NY, 1973)

James Stuart B L A C K T O N [1875–1941]
Born in Sheffield, England, and came to the United States at the age of 10. Worked as a newspaper journalist and illustrator. In 1896 made a short animated film for the Edison Company. Formed the Vitagraph Company with Albert Smith in 1897.

. . . The Spanish American War broke out. It gave a very big impetus to the motion picture interests. The first war picture made by the firm of Blackton and Smith was *Tearing Down the Spanish Flag*. That was the first picture we made with our improved machine. It was made the day after the declaration of war with Spain. It was taken in our 10′ × 12′ studio room. Our background was the building next door. We had a flag pole and two 18″ flags, one of them an American one and the other a Spanish flag. Smith operated the machine and I, with this very hand, grabbed the Spanish flag and tore it down from the pole and pulled the Stars and Stripes to the top of the flag pole. That was our very first dramatic picture and it is surprising how much dramatic effect it created. The people went wild. Of course, it was war time and their emotions ran high and then while the flags were but 18″ in size the picture showed a big 36′ flag. That was the beginning of making the miniature look like the real large thing.

. . . Pop Rock . . . had a lot of these Mutoscopes he had hired from the Mutoscope Company and when he joined us we pooled our pictures together, what he had and what we had, and started out to do a large exhibition business, and also to make some films. Mr. Rock brought in one day a list of the takings of the various pictures for that day. They were as follows:

United States Battleship at Sea	1 day	$ .25
Joseph Jefferson (*Rip Van Winkle*)	1 day	.43
Ballet Dancer	1 day	1.05
Girl Climbing a Tree	1 day	3.65

We had been trying to decide just what kind of pictures to make and from this list we finally came to the conclusion that the people wanted to see more of the *Girl Climbing a Tree* type.

———Blackton, in lecture given at the University of Southern California, 20 Feb 1929; repr. in Koszarski's *Hollywood Directors*

Marc B L I T Z S T E I N   (1905–1964)
Born in Philadelphia.

Q. Does your musical imagination have to fit itself to particular details, dramatic or visual, of the film sequence; or is it free to produce its own musical terms for the essence or quality of the sequence as you see it?

A. There is no choice here. The music must satisfy both the film's needs and musical needs. I sense here an expression of an attitude that greatly hampers progress in this medium. No one has yet used music in films in *all* its potentialities. The usual serious use has been as psychological underlining. Music rarely stands erect alongside of other dramatic means. A song sometimes actively promotes the dramatic action, but once the characters stop their song and begin to use speech the music beats a hurried retreat to the background and hides there, hoping no one will notice it. This half-disappearance of the music is suicide for it, aesthetically and as a medium. Better use no music. The word "integration" is thrown around a lot in an optimistic way, but there are few attempts at complete integration and collaboration of dialogue and score. In my last two film scores, for *Valley Town* [1940] and *Native Land* [1940–41], I have tried to exploit this terra incognita. In the introductory reel of *Valley Town*, writer and composer worked so closely together that full phrases of music and of commentary (the documentary film's "dialogue") dovetailed in an alternating planned continuity. The sound of, and, more importantly, the significance of the words gained musical meaning and the music really collaborated without receding to accompaniment. This could be called a foreground relation. Another example—in *Native Land*, where the music cries aloud *with* the cries of the farmer's wife and, in rising panic, screams *against* her screams. . . .

Besides the music's reflection of the forms of the film and its separate sequences, it must have a form of its own. A film-composer who follows shot by shot abjectly is a poor film-composer. An example of the dramatic advantages of a well-shaped piece of music is Honegger's work for the sequence of speech-devices in *Pygmalion* [1938], which produced a thrilling *musical* sequence. In the first "historical" sequence of *Native Land*, the score answers unifying musical necessity as well as the dramatic action. I have tried to assist the spiritual depth of the sharecropper sequence in this film by giving the most simple and direct form to the music's structure—a song, sung by chorus and Robeson. Also to be mentioned is the dramatic value of silence, which only in the film really can be achieved.

———Blitzstein, answering questionnaire in *Films*, Winter, 40

Joan BLONDELL
Born in New York City, 1909, in a theatrical family. Stage role with James Cagney in Penny Arcade *in 1929 led to both being brought to Hollywood for the film version,* Sinners' Holiday *(1930).*

We worked twice as hard in those days. We started work at 5 in the morning, which meant getting up at 4. Makeup, all that junk, then *whammo on the nose!* Straight over to the set at 8, knowing all your lines. We'd work clean through the day until after sundown, then on Saturday and always right through Saturday night. They'd bring in sandwiches like straw for the horses and we'd finally make it into bed on Sunday morning as the sun hit the pillows. Damn good thing we were young!

——Blondell, interviewed for The New York Times, 20 Aug 72

Budd BOETTICHER
Born in Chicago, 1916.

I directed some films under the name of Boetticher Jr. . . .

The Bullfighter and the Lady [1951] was my first film under the name of Budd Boetticher. . . .

John Ford supervised the editing, in quite peculiar circumstances.

We were working in the same studio [Republic]. I was waiting for Herbert J. Yates to come back, who had gone off to Europe with Vera Ralston. My film was stuck. So one day I picked up the telephone and called Ford:

"Mr. Ford? I'm Budd Boetticher. . . ."

"Oh yes. Good, I want to see your film." . . .

That was the beginning of a long association with John Ford, although we never actually worked together. He took charge of almost all the editing of *The Bullfighter and the Lady*. I had one or two disappointments, because he cut passages I liked, especially bits with the horses, but Ford had a right to say "I want it like that," and for once I had to do what somebody said. I wasn't satisfied with the editing, but just the fact of having been helped by John Ford did me a lot of good. I was put under contract by Universal.

——Boetticher, interviewed for Budd Boetticher:
The Western (London, 1969)

Dirk BOGARDE
Born in London in 1920. Began as actor with Amersham repertory company in 1939. Served in World War II in army intelligence.

One is never allowed to see any rushes on a Visconti film, and he himself never sees any for the first 2 months—then he sees them in a block. [In working on *The Damned,* 1969] I found a lot of changes had to be made from what I was used to—I had to do without a stand-in, for example. And I'd always gone with a director to rushes—but doing without that is not important if you trust the director—after all, I'm an old experienced man.

——Bogarde, interviewed for Films & Filming, May 71

... And then one day [in Rome] I was being fitted for a suit and I learned from the tailor that I was supposed to be filming in Austria the next day. From a tailor! I confirmed that it was true and drove all through the night and arrived green the next morning. There was nobody around when I got there. I asked where is Signor Visconti and was told that they'd been shooting all last night and wouldn't be working that day.

Actually the picture [*The Damned*] had all kinds of money problems and delays through bad organization, and because it was so far behind schedule, I had to go to Tunisia and Hollywood for *Justine* [1969] before it was finished. So there was a two-month gap on *The Damned* and I flew back over the Pole to do a couple of scenes in Terni to help complete the picture. It was madness.

It wasn't Visconti's insistence on perfection that delayed things, though he is a stickler for detail. For instance, the set for the vast family dining room had a carpet on the floor, which was quite wrong, and he insisted that it be taken up and replaced by an oak floor. So shooting stopped for 5 days while that was laid. He was right, of course. If my hat ever became too rakish in angle, Visconti would always notice and straighten it again. And like all great directors, he has no compunction about what he does to get what he wants. He brought the whole of Dusseldorf's traffic to a halt for a funeral scene, and a complete village in Austria was taken over during its only month of tourism and flooded with Nazi flags and hundreds of men in uniform.

——Bogarde, interviewed for *The Guardian*, 4 Apr 70

Peter BOGDANOVICH
Born 1939 in Kingston, New York. While working as critic, biographer and interviewer, joined Roger Corman's crew in 1966.

I used [black-and-white photography in *The Last Picture Show* (1971)] because I didn't want the film to look pretty. I didn't want it to be a nostalgia piece. ... Color always had a tendency to prettify, and I didn't want that. Orson Welles encouraged me. In fact, he suggested I do it in black and white, at one time when we were talking about how to achieve depth of field and sharpness of image in a certain way, he said, "You can't do it in color—you'll have to do it in black and white." Well, several months before that, the writer Larry McMurtry had also suggested that we shoot it in black and white. And I said, "Of course it should be in black and white, but I don't think that anybody's going to let me do it"—and I just sort of let it go. I realized, being a fellow with a memory about movies, that if I were making this film even 15 years ago, this is the kind of film that would have been shot in black and white. And since those days were better in terms of filmmaking, and nobody was put under the restriction of being told they had to shoot in color because of television, the great directors who used both color and black and white made the right choices. Ford would shoot *Wagonmaster* [1950] in black and white and then he'd shoot *The Quiet Man* [1952] in color, then go back and shoot in black and white for *The Sun Shines Bright* [1953] and shoot *Mogambo* [1953] in color. You alternated, you know, depending on the story and not on any kind of economic consideration. However, I didn't think I'd be allowed to make that kind of choice for *The Last Picture Show*. But then when Orson suggested it—rather forcefully—I said I thought he was right and that I'd ask the producer, Bert Schneider. He knew Bert himself, because I'd introduced them, and he said, "I think Bert will go along with it." So I went and talked to Bert, and indeed Orson was right, Bert was rather sanguine about it.

———Bogdanovich, interviewed for *Films & Filming*, June 72

Richard B O L E S L A W S K I (1889–1937)
Born in Warsaw. Educated at University of Odessa. From 1906 to 1915, actor at Moscow Art Theater.

The moment a player reaches the stage, he also becomes a guesser. But with Miss Garbo, I discovered that when she comes to her day's work, there is no guessing on her part. . . .

[In *The Painted Veil*, 1934] we had a scene with Miss Garbo. She was to cross a room, pick up a lamp, light it with a match, hook the lamp to a wire concealed in her dress, lift the lamp to an exact height where the electric bulb would not shine in the lens, then walk to the door, listen, and enter another room. In addition, this pause at the door was the most difficult moment in her entire part in the picture.

Yet Miss Garbo accomplished it with only one rehearsal and after only 20 seconds of concentration before we turned the camera over. Her craftsmanship is all in the day's work to her. Still, like the real actor who knows he works with emotions, she never hesitates to laugh, to joke or to play when the opportunity arises.

———Boleslawski, for *Filmgoers Famous Films Supplement*, 1934

Robert B O L T
Born in Sale, Cheshire in 1924.

If you took the novel *Dr. Zhivago* as it stands and treated it as a shooting script incident by incident the resulting film would run at least 60 hours. Therefore, in the film you can have only a twentieth of the book—therefore, you have to turn it into something not merely shorter, but quite different. . . .

If you are going to reduce a book to a twentieth of its length, you can't go snipping out pieces here and there, up to nineteen-twentieths. You have to take in and digest the whole work to your own satisfaction and then say, "Well, the significant things, the mountain peaks which emerge from this vast panorama are such-and-such incidents, moral points, political points, emotional points, and those are all I can deal with in dramatic form—all I *should* deal with." Then you lock the book in a cupboard and retell the story—its significance rather than a full sequence of events. . . . Once the peaks have emerged, the problem is how to link them. You are under the necessity of inventing incidents which do not occur in the book—threads which will draw together *rapidly* a number of themes, where Pasternak might have taken 10 chapters. Another point is that you cannot take your dialogue from the novel to any extent. The characters have to become your characters—you make them your own, make them speak as you would have them speak. You do all this, relying on the fact that you have *understood* the book, that your feeling about it is an adequate and accurate one. . . .

In *A Man for All Seasons* [1967] I quite deliberately made the king several years younger than he in fact was at the time, because what I felt to be essential about his relationship with More was something which was more obvious when the king was in his earlier years. I felt it justifiable to play about with the time scale, partly because it was kept vague (no ages were mentioned) and partly because it represented the truth, as I felt it, about their relationship.

——Bolt, in *The Making of Feature Films* (London 1971)

Working on *Lawrence of Arabia* [1962] was hectic. All rather like a rugby scramble really. Both David Lean and Sam Spiegel are terribly experienced and professional men. I didn't know what I was doing, but I was kept under constant pressure and enjoyed it all. I came to learn that the problems of film writing were very like those of writing plays: classical problems——such as telling the story, economy of language, feeding the audience here, starving them there, etc.

——Bolt, interviewed for *Transatlantic Review* (1964)

John BOORMAN
Born in London in 1933 and established himself in the American film industry.

The fragmentation [of *Point Blank* (1968)] was necessary to give the character and the situations ambiguity, to suggest another meaning beyond the immediate plot. And this process of fragmentation began during the preparation of the script, but it also continued and merged into the process of making the film. I like to work on my own scripts, but not alone. I like to talk them out—and act them out. In the scripting phase, the screenplay writer and I are locked in a room, working every day. There was one problem in *Point Blank* that was never solved in the scripting period—the confrontation between [Lee] Marvin as Walker and Carroll O'Connor as one of the top men in the gang's organization. I wanted to suggest in this scene that Walker was never going to get what he wanted—that the money he was seeking was merely a symbol of revenge. And we never determined precisely how to do the scene until I got Marvin and O'Connor together in my house one weekend, and we rehearsed the confrontation in different ways. They improvised, and gradually the tension increased until it grew so great that suddenly O'Connor burst out laughing. And that was so wrong, it was right. And he did it again, and this time he said, "Don't ask me for money. I never carry any with me. I always use checks. I've got only eleven dollars on me." That's what we used in the completed film.

——Boorman, interviewed for *Films & Filming*, Feb 72

Margaret BOOTH
Born in Los Angeles. Her brother, Elmer Booth, acted in the Griffith Company.

I had just come out of school, and I started as a patcher with the D. W. Griffith Company. While I was there, I learned to cut negative; in the old days we had to cut negative by eye. We matched the [work] print to the negative without any edge numbers. We had to match the action. . . . But it was very tedious work. Close-ups of Lillian Gish in *Orphans of the Storm* [1921] would go on for miles, and they'd be very similar. . . .

This lasted a few months, then I went to work in the laboratory at Paramount, assembling the tinted sections for release prints. That lasted two or three weeks. Finally, I went to work for Mr. [Louis B.] Mayer at the old Mission Road studios. . . . At Mission Road was a remarkable director, John M. Stahl. I became his assistant. I used to stand by him while he cut, and he asked me to come in with him to see his dailies in the projection room. This way he taught me the dramatic values of cutting, he taught me about tempo— in fact he taught me how to edit. . . .

Learning how to cut was hard going because Stahl was a very hard taskmaster. He was a perfectionist; he kept doing things over and over again. He shot every sequence so it could be cut in many different ways.

Irving Thalberg was that way, too. In *Romeo and Juliet* [1936] I had five versions of the balcony scene. One with tears, one without tears, one played with close-ups only, another played with long shots only, and then one with long shots and close-ups cut in.

———Booth, interviewed (1965) for *The Parade's Gone By* (NY, 1968)

Ernest B O R G N I N E   [Ermes Effron Borgnine]
Born in Hamden, Connecticut, 1917. After serving in navy, studied acting and obtained roles in television and theater, before beginning his film career in 1951.

[The fight in *Bad Day at Black Rock* (1954)] was shot in a single take and Tracy watched from the sidelines while his double and I went through the motions of the fight. By his own wishes, Spence hadn't thrown a punch in front of a camera since he hit Clark Gable in the mouth in *Boom Town*, in 1940. . . .

[Delbert] Mann knew me from live television plays he had directed in New York, and he thought I could play Marty. But Chayefsky was skeptical— and the role certainly was a far cry from the bad-guy parts I had just been doing in Hollywood.

I had to get the western twang out of my voice and start talking like a Bronx butcher before Chayefsky would listen. Then I auditioned by reading practically the whole script aloud, with Paddy himself reading all the other parts.

After a while we got to the point where my old Italian mother in the story is encouraging Marty to overcome his shyness and get out and meet some girls. She tells him, "Go on, put on your blue suit and go down there. You'll meet a lot of tomatoes." And Marty looks at her with his whole soul in his eyes and says, "All right, I'll put on my blue suit, but you know what I'll get from it? A broken heart. Maw, I'm just an ugly, ugly man!" Right at that point the role got under my skin so much that I turned around and started to bawl. And when I turned back and looked at Chayefsky a moment later, he was crying. And so was Delbert Mann. And at that instant I said to myself, "You've got it!"

———Borgnine, interviewed for *The Toronto Star*, 2 Dec 72

I couldn't think how to play this part [in *The Revengers* (1972)]. Just couldn't. What could I do? Then I received a great hurt in my life and suddenly the answer came to me: I'd play the part as a woman. I made this woman my character and played her as a man and he came out in that movie as the most no-good, back-stabbing rascal you ever saw, one minute all sentimental tears and the next minute totally vicious. It was a beautiful character to play and I pulled out all the stops. . . . I had a beautiful feeling of revenge, too.

———Borgnine, interviewed for *The Times*, 10 Feb 73

Walerian B O R O W C Z Y K
Born in Kwilicz, Poland in 1923. His most successful animation after leaving Poland was The Concert of Mr. and Mrs. Kabal (1962).

Q. How exactly did you conceive that diabolic couple?
A. I don't really know. They just came to me. I had not made any comic films up till then, and I wanted a change. I planned to make a series of separate episodes, concerning a circus, a cabbage, a voyage to the moon, etc., and *The Concert* was one of these. But I subsequently decided to make instead a single full length film, simply called *The Theater of Mr. and Mrs. Kabal,* which I have been working on for the last nine months or so. What I've tried to do with *Kabal* is keep the drawing fairly naturalistic—I mean I don't deform the human figure any more than the average newspaper cartoon. The trouble with so many animated films nowadays (I am thinking especially of the Yugoslavian school and those influenced by it) is that they crib from Picasso and suppose that that is enough to make their style modern. They reduce the human figure to a circle and a few dots and squiggles; and if you're not Picasso this won't do. They also overlook the fact that the cinema is *movement,* and that the draftsmanship must be dynamically tuned to this movement. If the drawing is already greatly deformed, a deformed or grotesque movement loses impact. If the drawing remains basically naturalistic, then it can, by contrast, interact with any distortion of movement. When you then incorporate the sound track—grossly neglected in the majority of films—the possibilities for interaction between draftsmanship, movement, and sound become enormous.

———Borowczyk, interviewed for *Films & Filming*, Apr 65

John B O X
Born 1920.

There must be nothing arbitrary about the background. *That* must be the place where *this* person is at *this* time—and the audience must be convinced of its inevitability. The designer must not be self-indulgent, his background must never distract from the character in the foreground. . . .

In *A Man for All Seasons* [1967] nothing was put in a set unless it was functional. Not a chair was placed in a room unless it was sat on. I was not principally interested in the architecture, but in the atmosphere and the habits of the people of the period. Take that early scene where Wolsey is confronted by Thomas More. Fred Zinnemann's intention was to present Wolsey as power and authority. That, to me, meant a feeling of claustrophobia which would accentuate the character and power of Wolsey, and would involve the audience with Thomas More as he was confronted by the great man of the time. So we put Wolsey in a small room to emphasize his largeness. He wears red robes, so we don't want any other colors to lead your eye away from the central figure, so the walls become a darker shade of the same red. There are no corners in the room. The table at which he sits is smaller than it would have been in reality, to accentuate Wolsey's size. We had to have a window because he looks out of it, a table because he is sitting at it, a candle because he needs light. Nothing else was necessary, emphasizing just claustrophobia and the power of the political cleric. . . .

Then take Fagin in *Oliver!* [1968]. Until I knew the color of his coat, and until his makeup and whiskers were correctly worked out, I was uncertain about what should go behind him. Period architecture and period clothing can conflict on the eye and become disturbing. Which comes first? The clothing. Get the character right in his clothes before you move into the background. They should look like clothes, not costumes.

——Box, in *The Making of Feature Films* (London, 1971)

Charles BRACKETT (1892–1969)
Born in Saratoga Springs, worked as screenwriter, then in teamwork with Billy Wilder. Sunset Boulevard (1950) *was perhaps their most striking collaboration:*

[Norma Desmond] was also tragic. Perhaps we should have told about her with a more audible lump in our throats. We thought it effective to suppress the pitying sounds and let the audience find the pity for themselves.

——Brackett, in *The Quarterly of Film, Radio & Television*, Fall 52

Stan BRAKHAGE
Born in Kansas City, 1933, attended Dartmouth College, and established an independent filmmaking center in Colorado.

Another thing is that I had given up editing in the conventional sense of the word. My drive throughout here [*Scenes From Under Childhood* (1970)] was to take whole sections of shooting and lay them in in relation to, and fortified by, superimposition of other material—either supportive in color or texture, or other whole series of shots that went with them rather than to take the shooting as the material, and start breaking it up and all that extreme mentality or intellectuality of editing. Which, for a film like this, I tend to get more and more suspicious of.

Getting suspicious of memory processes led me to a great suspicion of taking too much for granted—how can I put this in a balanced way?—that (as Eisenstein gave us) the art of film is in the editing. I think he certainly made one there, and there's a great power there, but I have been too dependent on just that kind of creativity which tends to be very intellectual, like the term implies: editor. An editor is very censorial, a censor who moves in there and tries to tidy things up.

———Brakhage, comments published in *Take One,* Sep–Oct 70

Marlon BRANDO
Born in Omaha, Nebraska, 1924.

A lot of directors want to know everything. Some directors don't want to know anything. Some directors wait for you to bring everything to them. . . .

[John Huston] gives you about 25 feet. He's out in the background. He listens. Some guys listen, some guys are auditory; some guys are visual. Some guys are both. He's an auditory guy and he can tell by the tone of your voice whether you're cracking or not. But he leaves you alone pretty good. . . .

Chaplin is a man whose talent is such that you have to gamble. First off, comedy is his backyard. He's a genius, a cinematic genius. A comedic talent without peer. You don't know that he's senile. Personally, he's a dreadful person. I didn't care much for him. Nasty and sadistic and mean. . . .

———Brando, interviewed for *Rolling Stone,* 20 May 76

Michel BRAULT
Born in Montreal, 1928. While in university began his film work as cameraman with Claude Jutra.

When I returned to Canada from Europe after working with Jean Rouch on *Chronique d'un été* [1961], I met Pierre Perrault who suggested that we do this film [*Pour la suite du monde* (1963)] with the people of Le Coudre. Up to that time all the cinéma vérité was a confessional type of filmmaking. They were not complete films with a beginning and an end. This film for me was a challenge—to try to tell a story without having a script.

The story involves us asking local people to return to the traditional method of trapping whales by placing poles in the form of a trap that then relied on the rise and fall of the tides to catch the whales. . . . At the end of 6 months we were very desperate because we still hadn't caught a whale. It was not at all like the good old times when they used to trap 30 to 40 whales each rise and fall of the tide. Eventually one did get caught, a beautiful white whale, which saved us from being humiliated.

None of that film is staged. We suggested several things to the people, but it was up to them to act or not to act on that suggestion.

You will notice in *Pour la suite du monde* that only the old people talk: We had contact with the young people, but never would they naturally carry on with their activities in front of the camera. They were quite shy; the older people were not shy at all.

———Brault, interviewed for *Motion,* Jan–Mar 75

Robert BRESSON
Born 1907, in Bromont-la-Mothe. Studied philosophy and classics. He was a painter before making his first film, a satire, Les Affaires publiques, *in 1934:*

I never use professional actors nowadays. After my first films *Les Anges du Péche* [1943] and *Les Dames du Bois de Boulogne* [1945], I realised that my type of cinema required total amateurs. In those two films, I literally had to stop the actors acting. For in my opinion the moment actors interpret a part and their faces assume certain expressions, the result cannot be true cinema, only filmed theater. People say I'm influenced by Carl Dreyer; but Dreyer and the rest of them all produce filmed theater—I have been influenced by no one. I am a painter as well as a director, which perhaps explains why I feel the meaning must reside in the image alone. People who have never acted before are more easily harnessed to my visual style than professionals who are set in their ways.

——Bresson, interviewed for *The Montreal Star*, 16 July 66

I wanted to make a film that would re-create the visual and aural integrity of the "trial and death of Joan of Arc" [1962]. . . . The problem was that of a film entirely in questions and answers. But I was content to use the monotony like a unified background against which the nuances would be more clearly seen. . . . Joan's replies to the questions put to her serve not so much to give information about present or past events as to provoke significant reactions on Joan's face, the movements of her soul . . . I see her with the eyes of a believer. I believe in the marvelous world whose doors she opens and closes. . . . One might say she was a more perfect being than we are, more sensitive. She combines her five senses in a new way. She sees her voices. She convinces us of a world at the farthest reach of our faculties. She enters this supernatural world but closes the door behind her.

——Bresson, quoted in Sadoul-Morris, *Dictionary of Films*, p 294

Benjamin BRITTEN (1913–1976)
Studied with Frank Bridge and John Ireland.

Q. Is there anything in composing music for the film sequence that necessitates a change in your usual method of composition?
    A. Usually greater speed, so that one is not so free to reject as when composing in one's own time. In moments of greatest emergency, one has to write straight into the orchestral parts, which is not my usual method! Personally, even in times of ease, I always write film music straight into score—which is not such a feat as it sounds since I use as small an orchestra as possible.

——Britten, answering questionnaire in *Films*, Winter 40

Peter BROOK
Born in London, 1925. At Oxford University, made film adaptations of Laurence Sterne's A Sentimental Journey. *A theater director since 1945:*

During the period I was working with Sam Spiegel on *Lord of the Flies* [1962], for instance, there were altogether about 7 screenplays. In the end we had one which wasn't to my mind the picture I was going to make; but it also seemed to me we'd reached a point where the only thing I could do was to accept it, and then trust to the fact that we were going to be far away on an awkward island and might cheat another script on the spot. I emerged from this period with a 140-page document into which I'd put meaningless but fantastically impressive camera directions. . . . "The camera tracks slowly back, and as it begins to rise it discloses over the top of a palm, left of screen. . . ." This document was hardly touched or seen again, and of course it bears no relation to the finished film. It did come in very useful, though, as something to show people when we were raising money privately to make the picture; and because of the way we were doing *Lord of the Flies*, entirely independent of any production setup, I was then able to go ahead and make the film actually without a script. . . .

From a standpoint of strict story-telling [in *Lord of the Flies*], and in order to get a certain result in a certain space of time, I'm mad if I don't use some technical aids, including having a timetable, getting what I'm going to shoot that day down on paper, and using a man with a couple of lights when the sun goes in. . . . I've had an extraordinary case of this on *Lord of the Flies*, where we used two cameramen as a consistent technique right through the picture. If this particular story were to be caught on celluloid in the time and conditions available, I realized that I must put every penny we had into an unlimited supply of film stock. This meant that I could stop the gaps of time and money and children and everything else running out by keeping on shooting, speaking through shots, going back without cutting the camera.

———Brook, interviewed for *Sight & Sound*, Summer 63

Louise BROOKS
Born in Cherryvale, Kansas, 1906. A student of Ruth St. Denis and a Ziegfeld Girl before her film debut in The Street of Forgotten Men *(1925).*

[William Wellman] directed this opening sequence of *Beggars of Life* [1928] with a sure, dramatic swiftness lacking in the rest of the film. Its pace did not accord with [Benjamin] Glazer's artistic conception of the tragedy and thereafter the action grew slower without increasing the film's content. Only Wallace Beery's entrance into the film saved it from Glazer's cultured supervision. Neither God nor the devil could have influenced Beery's least gesture before the camera. Having been briefly a tramp as a boy, he developed his character with authority and variety. His Oklahoma Red is a little masterpiece. . . .

So intrigued was I by the quiet sadism practiced by Billy behind the camera, especially in his direction of women, that I began to investigate his past life. From him I learnt nothing because he was extremely shy in conversation with women. A slim handsome young man, more than a director he resembled an actor who was uncertain in his part.

———Brooks, in *Film Culture*, Spring 72

To other people surrounding [Pabst] he would talk endlessly in that watchful way of his, smiling, intense; speaking quietly with his wonderfully hissing precision. . . . But to me he might speak never a word all morning, and then at lunch time turn suddenly and say, "Loueess, tomorrow morning you must be ready to do a big fight scene with Kortner.". . .

That was how he directed me [in *The Box of Pandora* (1928)]. With an intelligent actor he would sit in exhaustive explanation; with an old ham he would speak the language of the theater. But in my case, by some magic he would saturate me with one clear emotion and turn me loose.

——Brooks, in *Image*, Sept 56

Richard B R O O K S
Born 1912 in Philadelphia. A novelist brought to Hollywood to write, but he was soon directing his own scenarios.

It doesn't make any difference how much simulated blood is spilled, so long as it has style and action and movement. Excitement. And you do not have to take a position on the issues. Then you can enjoy it. A picture like *The Professionals* [1966], which is a western done in pretty good style, could be very successful, but *In Cold Blood* [1967], where you are forced to believe in something happening, and they know that something like it happened, becomes rather frightening, and you withdraw from it. Many people don't want to see it because they think, "Well, maybe it's too gory or something." And even when they hear it's not, they say, "Well, then it's depressing," which it is. But it also asks the audience to identify. That's why the picture was made in black and white, and in that style, so that people wouldn't think that they're watching a movie, but rather that they are watching an event that's taking place. That's why it was cast with hardly known people, and the studio didn't want to do that. And I knew they wouldn't want to do that. After all, it's not a mystery story. It's not a matter of "who did it." It's not a matter of rooting for them to "get away with it" or rooting for them to "get caught." You know all the facts beforehand. You know who did it, how it was done, to whom it was done, what happened to those who did it.

In the actual murder in *In Cold Blood*, I removed all the sound—there was no sound effect—except that each of the flashbacks had one specific sound that could be identified with the scene. The very first time, for example, was when he was in the washroom in the bus station, and he imagined himself being a famous nightclub artist or something. All you hear is applause, which wasn't there. So he did hear the applause that was important to him. The next time was when he thinks about himself as a child with his mother and father. His mother—where she's riding a horse—and she and he are at the rodeo or something or preparing for the rodeo. She ropes a calf and then takes him for a ride on the horse, and there is no sound at all except the horse's hoofs, when he's finally on the horse. There's another flashback when he's a child in the room with himself as a grown-up, and his mother is with another man, and no sound effects until the father hits her with his belt, and that's all there was, and during the actual murder the only sound is that of the shotgun and footsteps. That's all. There's not a gurgle. Not a scream. Just not a thing.

——Brooks, interviewed for *Directors at Work* (NY, 1970)

What we started to do with color [in *The Brothers Karamazov* (1958)] was to open up the field because both John Alton and myself felt that color could sometimes give us what we did not have by going to Russia to make the film in the first place. Russia wanted us to make the picture in the Soviet Union, but New York said that that would make it a Communist movie. So I said— Dostoevsky was a long time before this. How can I create Russia in a backlot? I'll have to make everything at night or in interiors. It's impossible—you'll make it, and stay away from those people. We felt color could create for us a mood, and Dostoevsky very often wrote in this sense. When all his words were added together in a particular chapter they created a mood; all the Karamazovs really existed in a conditioned atmosphere, and we tried to create that conditioned atmosphere with color, because, after all, most of the film was made in the interior.

We used the colors specifically in what we thought those colors represented to us. And we even made some tests beforehand to see if when we saw the color on the screen, whether those colors would still give us what we felt was the effect.

——Brooks, interviewed for *Hollywood: The Haunted House* (London 1967)

. . . I found a piece of music about 3 years before I did *Blackboard Jungle*. Driving home late at night from a poker game I heard this piece of music on one of those small stations and the rhythm interested me very much. I didn't remember its name. When I was planning to write *Blackboard Jungle* I asked the music store if they could get it for me. They finally came up with the record: "Rock Around the Clock." So 6 to 8 hours a day while I wrote the script I played this record in the office. I felt that this record was indicative of young people's attitudes. When we began to shoot this film I played this record quite often on the stage through the dialogue so that the body movements would have this feeling, then dubbed some of the dialogue later.

——Brooks, interviewed for *Movie*, Spring 65

Clarence B R O W N
Born 1890 in Clinton, Massachusetts, he was educated as an engineer and trained as an automobile mechanic. In 1915 he joined Maurice Tourneur as an assistant and editor. While filming The Last of the Mohicans (*1920*) *Tourneur had a bad accident, and Brown completed the film.*

. . . The only 2 people who knew anything about [a film being made] were the director and cameraman, so they had to edit it between them. I used to watch this process with interest. I once saw Tourneur with 20 pieces of film in his mouth. I got it into my head that I could do it. Within a month I was editing his pictures and writing his titles, relieving him of that end of the business entirely. I took to cutting like a duck to water; timing meant a great deal to me, having been an engineer and having dealt with inches, feet, rods, acres, and so forth. I think you'll find in all my pictures that I take trouble over tempo. . . .

I would finish cutting a picture in 2 weeks. It took about 4 weeks to shoot a picture; and because Tourneur hated exteriors, I worked the rest of the time doing [his] exteriors with my own cameraman. While he was shooting in the studio, we would exchange casts and work as 2 units.

. . . We made [*The Last of the Mohicans*] at Big Bear Lake and Yosemite Valley. I had learned by this time never to shoot an exterior between 10 A.M. and 3 P.M. The lousiest photography you can get is around high noon when the sun's directly overhead. . . .

We were up at 4 A.M. and we stopped at 10. We wouldn't go out again till 3 P.M.—but we shot till 6 and so we had a full day's shooting. I never shot an exterior in flat light in my life—until color came out. In color, it doesn't make too much difference. . . . As you go to infinity, the color gets weaker and weaker until you get depth, even with flat light. . . .

In *The Last of the Mohicans* we made much use of lighting effects and weather atmosphere. We used smokepots to create the suggestion of sunrays striking through woodland mist. The rainstorm in the forest was simply a fire engine and a hose. We got clouds because we waited for them, and used filters. Clouds normally did not register on the old ortho film.

When the girls are escaping from the Indian ambush, I put the camera on a perambulator. We built it from a Ford axle, with Ford wheels, a platform, and a handle to pull it down the road. We follow the girls running away; suddenly, [an Indian, Wallace Beery, blocks] their path. The camera stops—the perambulator stops—and this accentuates the girls' surprise. . . .

[Garbo] was a shy person; her lack of English gave her a slight inferiority complex. I used to direct her very quietly. I never gave her a direction above a whisper. Nobody on the set ever knew what I said to her; she liked that. She hated to rehearse. . . .

She took her work seriously, though. Her attitude was this: she came on the set at 9, made up and ready for work. She worked hard. At 5:30 or 6, when she was done, she was through. That was it. There was always a signal on the set—her maid would come in and hand her a glass of water. She would then say good night and go home.

. . . Whenever I had to direct a New York stage actor, I did an imitation of him. "This is how you're playing it," I would say. "Is this how a human being behaves? You're talking to me when you make a scene. It's intimate. The camera is there, and I'm here, right beside it. But you're projecting yourself way out to an audience."

I would never impose a performance on an actor, however. That was one of the troubles with Lubitsch's pictures. He was one of the greatest directors, but every player that ever worked for him played Ernst Lubitsch. He used to show them how to do everything, right down to the minutest detail. He would take a cape and show the star how to put it on. He supplied all the little movements. He was magnificent, because he knew his art better than anybody. But his actors followed his performance. They had no chance to give one of their own. . . .

I want everything an actor knows. If it's a woman, she'll know more about playing a woman than I know. I want to get her angle on the picture. So I always rehearse without giving a word of direction. I follow them around, and watch, and listen, and I get their interpretation first. If their interpretation doesn't agree with the one I have in mind, then we begin to talk. . . . If we couldn't get it right, we kept at it. I fought schedules all the time. I shot till I got it right.

———Brown, interviewed (1965, 1966) for *The Parade's Gone By* (NY 1968)

Karl B R O W N
Born 1896 in Versailles, Pennsylvania.

[Griffith] could compress [the four gospels for *Intolerance*, 1916], and that is just what he did. It was a matter of picking key episodes of this best known of all biographies and playing them for all they were worth. We did the marriage at Cana with painstaking attention to detail.

I say "painstaking" because that was forced upon us by the confusions and contradictions of the four different versions by the four different writers. They were long on character but short on description. They told us all about who was who but nothing about what was what. How were we to know what Jerusalem, or the temple, or Golgotha, or the house at Cana actually looked like? Huck Wortman had to be given some idea so he'd know how to lay out the sets. Herbert Sutch had to know exactly how everybody dressed so he could plan costumes for Goldstein to make. What was the furniture like? Or, for that matter, what was the actual physical appearance of Christ during his life as a man on earth? . . .

Griffith cut the knot of bewilderment with a single decisive stroke. People believe only what they already know. They knew all about how people lived, dressed, and had their being in biblical times because they had been brought up on Bible pictures, Bible calendars, biblical magic-lantern shows, Christmas cards, Easter cards, pictures of every incident with which we were concerned. Never mind whether these pictures were accurate or not. Follow them in every detail because that's what the people believe to be true, and what the people believe to be true *is* true—for them—and there's no budging them.

Out of all this vast and varied series of preparations the first of the great Babylon sets took form and finish and became ready to use. This was the exterior of the Babylon wall, and around this a battle was to swirl.

Well, now, we had the set; we had the equipment; Siegmann had lined up the men—a couple of thousand of them—you'd be surprised how a really big set can eat up people; the costumes were ready; the dressing tents, the size of circus tents, were ready; and even the latrines had been dug, not silly little privies such as we used in Delta but big, majestic twenty-holers as befit the majesty and dignity of our production. The cameras were ready. We had film, carefully ordered from Eastman so as to have but one emulsion number to shoot on. This film had been tested for sensitivity, gradation, and how it would work in our now makeshift developing solutions. We were as ready as we would ever be.

All that remained to be done was to do it. . . .

Griffith used dozens of assistants, each in charge of this unit or that. There was [Woody] Van Dyke. Then there was Monte Blue, who stuck close to Griffith through all the battle, because Monte gave the signals to the various unit directors scattered through the crowds. Crowds, plural, because we had one attacking crowd on the ground to storm the walls and another on the walls to defend them. Monte presented a very warlike appearance because he wore 2 heavy .45 revolvers, one on each hip, with a number of different-colored flags under one arm. The revolvers were loaded with blanks, and they were for signaling purposes only. A yellow flag meant one thing, a red one another, a green something else. Monte was a very busy man. And of course, down in the crowd or up on the walls, we had our tried-and-true actor-assistants, all in costume, leading their various groups in whatever maneuvers the shots or flags called for. Elmer Clifton, George Siegmann, Joe Henabery, and even Spec Hall had been pressed into service.

So the battle was on, with everybody yelling, throwing things, and being as obnoxious to one another as possible. The towers, pushed by elephants, advanced toward the walls.

———Brown, in his *Adventures with D. W. Griffith* (NY, 1973)

Kevin B R O W N L O W
Born 1938 in Crowborough, Sussex. Worked in cutting rooms while beginning It Happened Here, *shot between 1956 and 1963.*

Andrew [Mollo] and I first tackled the matter of schedule [for *Winstanley,* 1975]. Should the picture be shot in 8 weeks flat, or should we aim at week-end shooting, spreading the 8 weeks over a year to capture the seasons? As it happened, the seasons didn't have much to do with it. We were ruled more by the availability of the cast. We tried first to cast the film with professionals, and either agents turned us down because we could only pay the Equity minimum, or the actor we selected (i.e., Eric Porter for Parson Platt) rejected the script. With some relief, therefore, we decided to cast nonprofessionals (with the exception of the role of Lord General Fairfax, for whom we wanted Jerome Willis). Miles Halliwell was already cast as Winstanley, and he was extremely helpful in suggesting people for other parts. It seemed as though he waited until we were absolutely desperate— then introduced us to a friend, such as David Bramley (Parson Platt), who looked absolutely right. We cast entirely from appearance; and so few people looked right that we were forced to take acting ability on trust. Using non-professionals obliged us to settle for a sporadic schedule and weekend shoot-ing, which meant that we had to hold a sizeable cast together for a daunting length of time. But we could capture the changing seasons—very important in so visual a film—and, to Andrew's and my delight, we could grow our own crops!

———Brownlow, in *Monthly Film Bulletin*, Apr 76

Jacques B. B R U N I U S [pseud.] (1906–1967)
A critic and cinéaste long associated with Renoir.

In the summer of 1936, while working with Renoir on his film *Une Partie du campagne*, we decided that some scenes should take place between characters who would be more than 10 meters away from each other. But it was only with great difficulty that we managed to find very old lenses [that would give this depth of focus]: a few made by Zeiss, and one Bausch & Lomb that opened to 3.5. . . .

——Brunius, in *Photographie et photographie du cinéma* (Paris, 1938)

Luis BUÑUEL
Born 1900 in Calanda, Aragon. Studied at Jesuit College in Saragossa and Madrid University. First professional theater work: Manuel de Falla's puppet opera, Maestro Pedro. In Paris assisted Jean Epstein and Mario Nalpas.

Technique is no problem for me. I have a horror of posed shots, and I detest unusual angles. Sometimes I work out with my cameraman what we think is a superbly clever perspective; everything is arranged down to the very least detail, and then when the time comes for shooting, we burst out laughing, throw the whole plan out, and simply shoot with no special camera effects.

——Buñuel, interviewed for *Arts*, 21 July 55

For me *Los Olvidados* [1950] is effectively a film of social argument. To be honest with myself I had to make a film of a social type. I know that this is the way I see things. Apart from this, though, I did not want in any respect to make a thesis film. I had seen things which had distressed me very much, and I wanted to put them on the screen, but always with the sort of love I have for the instinctive and irrational that you can find everywhere. I've always been attracted by the strange and unknown, which fascinated me without my being able to say why.

Q. You had Figueroa as cameraman, but you used him in a completely different way from his usual style. Did you prevent him from making beautiful images?

A. Naturally, inasmuch as the film did not lend itself to them.

Q. He must have felt very miserable.

A. Very miserable . . . It's true. I have to say that I didn't behave with him like a director conceding favors in terms of "Come then, my friend, since you are so eager to do it. . . ." But the essentials are true. After 11 days shooting, Figueroa asked Dancigers why they had chosen him to do a film which any newsreel cameraman could have done. He was told: "Because you're a very quick and very commercial cameraman." It's true. Figueroa is fantastically quick and very good. It's a guarantee. At the start he was terrified of working with me. We could never agree. But I think he developed a lot, and we became very good friends.

——Buñuel, interviewed for *Cahiers du cinéma*, July 54; trans. in
Aranda's *Luis Buñuel* (London, 1975)

[*Wuthering Heights, Abismos de Pasion*, (1954)] is a film I wanted to make at the time of *L'Age d'or* [1930]. It's a key work for Surrealists. I think it was Georges Sadoul who translated it. They liked the side of the book that elevates *"l'amour fou"* above everything—and naturally as I was in the group I had the same ideas about love and found it a great novel. But I never found a backer, the idea languished among my papers and the novel was filmed in Hollywood 8 or 9 years later. I hadn't thought about it any more until Dancigers, who had two stars under contract, Mistral and Irasema Dilian, both very known in Spain, asked me to make a film from a script I didn't like. Then he reminded me that I'd once mentioned my adaptation of *Wuthering Heights,* and I showed it to him. He accepted it. Really, I was no longer interested in making this film, and I didn't try any innovations. It remains the film I conceived in 1930, a 24-year-old film, but I think it's faithful to the spirit of Emily Brontë. It's a very harsh film, without concessions, and it respects the novel's attitude to love. . . .

[The *Tristan* music] was my own fault. My negligence. I went to Europe, to Cannes, and left the composer to add the musical accompaniment; and he put the music throughout the film. A real disaster. I intended to use Wagner just at the end, in order to give the film a romantic aura, precisely the characteristic sick imagination of Wagner. Still, I think that my first version reflects the spirit of the novel much better than the one made in Hollywood.

———Buñuel, interviewed by Aranda for his *Luis Buñuel* (London, 1975)

Q. How do you establish your script?

A. At first, I work only on an idea according to the sources of inspiration about which I have been speaking to you a moment ago. When I have finished a film I usually don't know what to film next, but once an idea appears or is caught, the film shapes itself. When I know what I want, the collaboration with the script writers starts (I have been working several times with Luis Alcoriza; for a long time my usual scriptwriter is Julio Alejandro; recently, I have been working with Jean-Claude Carrière for *Le Journal* [*de femme de chambre,* 1964]). They stimulate me, they push me to advance faster in editing and most of all, they write, whereas I am very lazy in that respect; however, we always follow the idea established by myself at the beginning. A written script undergoes considerable modifications during the work on the sound stage. For *Viridiana* [1961], for instance, the script sequences were ready when I left Mexico for Spain. The renewal of contact with my native country conveyed new ideas to me, not only during the reconsideration of the script effected in Spain, but also during the shooting.

Q. Do you fix all details of the script from the beginning, before shooting?

A. As a rule, yes; but all characters change, undergo an evolution during the shooting. . . .

Q. Do you improvise a lot when you produce?

A. A lot, and in accordance with the means available at that moment. I work very quickly and this compels me often to use only one setup for several scenes and even to eliminate some scenes.

Q. How did you prepare for *Los Olvidados* [1950]?

A. At first I wanted to understand and *see.* I love to *see* things. I disguised myself in blue overalls and went to live in a shantytown. Believe me, it is very difficult to understand poverty, to enter it. It is a world of its own, closed.

Q. And what contribution does surrealism make to this kind of work?

A. An enormous contribution. A camera is a collective eye. If I had been satisfied to look at and photograph, I would have arrived at a perfectly impersonal documentary, without any precise significance. My goal was to show all of it and without taking stands, to make us understand what the poverty of these kids really is.

———Buñuel, interviewed for *Cinéma 65*, Mar 65

Shooting is really a bore. What is important is the writing of the script and the editing of the footage. It is during the writing stage that I get all my ideas, all my inspiration. Images come to me spontaneously, sometimes completely unrelated to the story line, and I incorporate them into the script. Then I follow my screenplay practically without deviating from it.

———Buñuel, interviewed for *Action*, Nov–Dec 74

Ellen B U R S T Y N [Edna Rae Gillooly]
Born in Detroit. Left high school at 17, worked as model and dancer. In 1957 —wins lead in Broadway production of Fair Game.

... [*The King of Marvin Gardens* (1972)] is not an ordinary film in any way. It's very ambiguous. Bob [Rafelson] loves ambiguity. ...
   Bob is terribly secretive about his work. He wouldn't let us talk about the script, I'm surprised he let us read it.
   ... Mr. Minnelli's way of directing [on *Goodbye, Charlie* (1964)] is to do the scene for you and then you imitate him—not one of the more stimulating ways of working.
   ... I've never seen anybody like [Billy Friedkin, directing *The Exorcist* (1973)]. He runs everything. Every single detail. He knows everything that's happening everywhere—on the set, the production, the script—and does it well, perfectly, easily and demands perfection from everybody else, nicely. There is no such thing as anybody saying, "We couldn't get what you wanted, it doesn't exist," you can't say that. He'd just say, "Well, what does that mean? Get it! I want it yesterday!"

———Burstyn, interviewed for *Show*, Dec 72

Richard B U R T O N [Jenkins]
Born in Wales, 1925. First film in England, The Last Days of Dolwyn (*1948*). *His success began in Hollywood in 1952.*

[*The Robe* (1953)] was a very funny film to make because we were asked if you please by the Head Office not to smoke on the set or drink because it was a holy picture and the stars were myself and Vic Mature and it's very difficult to stop Mature and the immature Burton from having the occasional drink so it was a pretty hectic set—sort of nun spies around them—monks watching us every second of the time. It was rather interesting, too, because one of the supporting actors got a young girl into trouble at the time and there was a tremendous hubbub and brouhaha trying to conceal the evidence from the press because it was a holy picture.
   [*Cleopatra* (1963)] seemed to be beset with difficulties from the very

beginning because it first started with Elizabeth of course playing Cleopatra and Peter Finch playing Caesar and a very good actor [Stephen Boyd] playing the part that I played. . . .

. . . And they built the whole set—whatever it was—the Forum or something on the backlot of Pinewood and started shooting in November which is not looking forward enough is it to the English climate—as a result of which Elizabeth had triple pneumonia or something and nearly died—that held the film up for a year because she really was very very ill indeed . . . so then Peter Finch and Stephen Boyd had to go elsewhere, they had to work—they couldn't wait around for Elizabeth to recover so then they recast it, replaced the director and recast it with Rex and myself playing Caesar and Mark Antony but there was no script and yet they had to do it for—I don't know—for some reason they had to do it then—and so Joe Mankiewicz—an able man who directed and wrote it—was writing the scenes tonight to be acted tomorrow. So that didn't help very much either. What they should have done of course was to close the whole thing down and let Joe alone for 6 months to write the script and we all come back and do it but they insisted that it had to be done in that way. So Joe might write a scene for which there was no set—that kind of thing—and typical of the confusion of the film was I was in New York in *Camelot*—it was a huge hit—and Joe Mankiewicz called me and asked me if I'd like to play Mark Antony with Elizabeth and Rex and I said I'd be delighted when do you start and he said September 16th or something like that and I said well I can't do it because I'm in *Camelot* and I'm contracted to go to December 3, shall we say, and he said don't worry we'll buy you out. Which they did. They paid $50,000 to Lerner & Loewe and Moss Hart and bought me out of the show.

———Burton, interviewed at the National Film Theatre, 26 Oct 72

C

Michael C A C O Y A N N I S
Born in Cyprus in 1922. Came to study in England from where he broadcast to Greece for BBC during World War II.

I've known this particular property [*The Trojan Women* (1971)] so long. I prefer to feel things rather than analyze them. I'm really an emotional and physical director and I think that my mind works and keeps in step. I don't try to philosophize too much about what I do. I try not to reproduce academically or historically, because you fall into inevitable traps of ignorance. All you can do is use your own evocative powers in terms of today of looking into the past. If one were going to make a film about ancient Greece and one were to restore the Parthenon the way it was, it would be a shocking and an untrue image; I would use it as it is today because it is much more evocative of the truth than from the contemporary viewpoint. . . .

I direct every actor differently according to their experiences, their personality, their art, and sometimes I even show them what I would do. I say don't imitate that, but maybe you recognize some kind of truth in what I am doing that will remind you of something and sometimes that works, too.
——Cacoyannis, interviewed for *Impact,* 1972

James C A G N E Y
Born in New York City, 1889. A vaudeville dancer brought to Hollywood in the sound boom.

I went into show business strictly from hunger. Starvation helps to turn you into a good actor, I guess. I was a dancer at first and for five years I played vaude-ville. Then I had a bit part in a Maxwell Anderson play, *Outside Looking In.* My first film was something called *Sinners' Holiday* [1930] with Joan Blondell. . . .

I've just finished a picture called *Never Steal Anything Small* [1960]. The closest thing to it, I'd say, was *The Threepenny Opera.* It's all about a bunch of crooks who try to operate on big-business lines. It's witty, and it has some good radical lyrics. Films must have some comment to make. They've got to keep moving. The old-style gangster film is as dead as mutton. We've said all there is to say, and we've said it in so many ways. I suppose at the time they fulfilled some kind of public need. But now that need has gone.

I directed my first film last year, a remake of *This Gun for Hire* [1942], called *Shortcut to Hell* [1957]. A director who is also an actor has special problems. If you have youngsters in the cast, they tend to imitate you. I kept telling them, "For God's sake don't do anything like me. Be yourself. Mannerisms only get in the way. . . ."

——Cagney, interviewed for *Sight & Sound,* Winter 58–59

What not many people know is that right up until 2 days before shooting [of *Public Enemy* (1931)] started, I was going to play the good guy, the pal (Edward Woods played it in the end).

——Cagney, interviewed for *The Toronto Daily Star,* 7 March 73

Michael C A I N E   [Maurice Micklewhite]
Born 1933 with a Cockney accent that he has well exploited in the more naturalistic trend of British films.

What I do is to show the sadness of the man—whether he is Alfie, or Warren in this film [*Hurry Sundown* (1967)]. The sadness of a man who destroys others and destroys himself.

——Caine, interviewed (in Baton Rouge, Louisiana) for
London *Daily Mail,* 8 Aug 66

[Joseph] Mankiewicz is bloody marvelous. He knows what you should want and he also knows when you've got it. He's one of those directors who says nothing if he likes it but if he starts going on and starts questions you know you haven't got it.

——Caine, interviewed for *The Evening Standard,* 15 Dec 72

Yakima C A N U T T
Born 1895 in Colfax, Washington; stunt man, director of westerns and second units.

One of the things I started to discuss with Ford [on *Stagecoach* (1939)] was a sequence in which the stagecoach came to a stream and saw the stage station burned by Indians on the other side. The script called for the coach to be lashed with logs and floated down the stream to escape the danger.

"I don't know about that, Mr. Ford," I answered. "It seems to me you can do almost anything if you have enough time and money."

With Ford's approval, I went to work on devising a way to float that stagecoach. Some fellows over at Paramount helped me devise some hollowed-out logs which could be attached to the coach, two on each side. They had to be planned just right—big enough to float the coach, but high enough for the wheels to reach the ground.

Then I devised an underwater cable which could be fastened to the front lead tongue and pulled by an offstage truck on the other side of the river. It was attached with a pelican hook which could be tripped when the coach reached the shore. I had the 6 horses in regular harness, but hooked together so they could be towed along if they quit swimming.

Ford okayed my plans and sent me up to Kernville with a crew to test the rig. I got it all set up and telephoned Ford in Hollywood.

"Put eight people in it tomorrow and see if it works," he told me.

I did it and telephoned him that everything went fine. "Okay, we'll be up tomorrow to shoot it," he said.

When the company arrived, everything was ready to shoot. I put on pads to double for Andy Devine as the driver. Ford shot the crossing in one take.

Afterward he asked me: "Do you think Andy could drive it across?"

"Don't see why not," I said. "The way it's rigged, all he has to do is hold onto the reins."

"Okay, I want to do it again at closer range so I can see all the principals." It worked fine the second time, too.

—Canutt, in *Action,* Sep–Oct 71

Frank C A P R A
Born in Palermo, Sicily, 1897; trained as engineer at Cal Tech, later worked for independent comedy companies before getting a job at Columbia Studio in 1921.

... [Barbara] Stanwyck gave her all the *first time she tried* a scene, whether in rehearsal, or in long shots which served only to geographically orient the audience. All subsequent repetitions, in rehearsals or retakes, were but pale *copies* of her original performance. . . .

And the crews had problems. I had to take the "heart" of the scene—the vital close-ups of Barbara—first, and with multiple cameras so she would have to do the scene only once. Multiple cameras aggravate the difficulties of lighting and recording in geometrical progression, i.e., 4 times as complex with 2 cameras, 8 times with 3 cameras.

On the set I would never let Stanwyck utter one word of the scene until the cameras were rolling. Before that I talked to her in her dressing room, told her the meaning of the scene, the points of emphasis, the pauses. Her hairdresser Helen had become her confidante. I let Helen give her the cues from the other actors. I talked softly, not wishing to fan the smoldering fires that lurked beneath that somber silence. She remembered every word I said—and she never blew a line. My parting admonition was usually this: "Remember, Barbara. No matter what the other actors do, whether they stop or blow their lines—you continue your scene right to the end."

—Capra, *The Name Above the Title* (NY 1971)

In *American Madness* [1932], for the first time, I purposely speeded up the shooting of every scene by about 40 percent above normal. Not with the camera but actually with the actors ... I just upped the pace ... I did that in practically all of the pictures I made, except for mood scenes where pace was not a factor. But in normal scenes, I shot them about 40 percent faster than normal and then they seemed to be normal on the screen. . . . There was an urgency to the scenes that seemed to work.

—Capra, in discussion (1971) at the American Film Institute (*The American Film Heritage,* Washington 72)

Nobody wanted to play in *It Happened One Night* [1934]. Actors don't like comedies much. They're not dynamic like melodramas—nobody gets hurt, nobody gets killed, nobody gets raped. So we couldn't get a girl to play this thing. We offered the part to Miriam Hopkins, Myrna Loy, Connie Bennett, and Margaret Sullavan, and all of them turned it down, and finally we got hold of Claudette Colbert. She was on a four-week vacation and she liked money, being French. We offered her twice as much as she was getting at Paramount if she would do the picture in the 4 weeks' vacation, and she finally agreed.

Now we needed a leading man. We wanted Robert Montgomery from M-G-M. Louis B. Mayer, head of M-G-M, owed Columbia a star for some past deal they had made. But Robert Montgomery didn't want to play the part. You must understand that I worked for Columbia Pictures, which was Poverty Row. It was Siberia to the M-G-M stars. So we were about to abandon the picture because nobody wanted to play it. I said maybe it wasn't any good anyhow, the hell with it, let's give it up, when Louis Mayer called Harry Cohn, head of Columbia, and said, "Herschel, I have a bad boy down here I'd like to punish. I want you to use Clark Gable—I want to punish him." So Mr. Cohn told me, "We've got to make the picture now," and he said, "We've got to make it—Louis Mayer wants to punish Clark Gable."

But it was this picture that made him a very big star. Too bad he didn't continue with this lighter kind of he-man character rather than the unfunny he-man character.

———Capra, quoted in *Yale Alumni Magazine*, June 72

Jack CARDIFF
Born in Yarmouth, 1914. A child actor in films until 1927, when he became camera assistant to Ray Rennahan.

The hallmark of simple lighting is Rembrandt—light/dark/light/dark. I thank God the school is nearly extinct which taught people to use light all over the place. Spot-rails round the set are the cause of this unnatural spread from all sides—it totally destroys realism. Everything is, of course, much easier nowadays. When I was photographing *Black Narcissus* [1946] . . . the key light on an actor's face had to equal over 1,000 candlepower, now we need only 80.

Even in the black-and-white days I "improved on nature," mainly by the use of filters, to make the sky darker and sharpen contrasts. I used dark red or infrared filters for night shots. In addition we had graduated filters, of varying densities from top to bottom. . . . These will enable a scene which is too bright in the upper or lower part of the view (a glaringly hot desert, for instance) to be modified at will by moving or reversing the filter. . . .

Here are two examples of improving on nature. Some years ago I was on top of Mount Vesuvius, filming an actual eruption of the volcano. . . . The lava . . . wasn't behaving at all dramatically in the camera. We decided to make it come out more quickly, so we shot it at about 6 instead of the usual 24 frames per second. Its color didn't come out very well, either, so we didn't equalize the change in exposure by shutting down the lens diaphragm. This meant that the lava was very overexposed. The joint result was an explosion on the screen of fast-moving, bright red, menacing lava, instead of the sluggish, dull-colored stuff it naturally was. In *Western Approaches* [1944] during the war, I needed a close-up to fit in with a previous scene which had been shot in the sunshine. This looked impossible, as we were at sea, with a dark, dirty gray sky. So I used an incandescent orange-yellow light, without the usual blue filter to correct it, overexposed it deliberately to bring out the sky a pure white, and gave instructions for it to be printed with 10 points of blue. The final picture looked exactly like the sunrise at the start of a perfect blue-skied summer day.

————Cardiff, interviewed for *The Making of Feature Films* (London 1971)

Marilyn [Monroe] was so keen to make a hit in *The Sleeping Prince* [*The Prince and the Showgirl,* 1957] that she brought her personal Method dramatic coach [Paula Strasberg] over from New York with her. No one in the studio had bargained for that.

When Olivier gave directions for Marilyn to act in a scene she listened then went into consultation with her Method coach. So, in a way, she was being directed by two people.

I do not know what the coach used to whisper in Marilyn's ear. But there was a story floating round the studio that someone heard the coach say to her before a big scene:

"Relax. Think of soothing things. Think of Coca-Cola and Frank Sinatra!" It was a situation that would have driven a lesser man than Olivier mad. But not once did that magnificent man give by the flicker of an eyelid, the slightest sign of strain or irritation.

————Cardiff, in *The People* (London), 24 Aug 58

Gilles C A R L E
Born in Maniwaki, Canada, 1929.

. . . We shot only with available light [in *La Mort d'un bucheron* (1973)], and mainly hand-held camera. We had to wait for the light to be proper. It takes a lot of time but the result is much better. It's truer.

. . . I chose my locations with windows everywhere, and lots of light coming through. So I could have my people coming into the sun . . . Their shadows . . . It's just beautiful. Beautiful scenes. I didn't have any Elemacks, any dollies, nothing! I just shot hand-held most of the time. Sometimes, the feeling of *La Mort* . . . is like 8mm. What I really worked on was the actors. The actors and the truth of the situation. [*The True Nature of*] *Bernadette* [1972] is so organized, planned and all that, that I began to feel as if I were caught. I had to shoot what I had to shoot. . . . If this section was shot, the link to the other one had to be shot. You're not free anymore. In *La Mort* . . . I felt much freer. . . .

I don't improvise with actors. I wrote my dialogue for this film completely, to the last word, and didn't change a bit of it. But the writing of the dialogue is much different. It's not the same as *Bernadette* at all. It's dialogue taken from life. (Which is much harder to write.) *Bernadette's* dialogue was more organized. It's part of the structure, and it's a little "bright" in a very intelligent way. You can be bright sometimes and be unintelligent. So you have to forget this. I'm not bright. I'm just real.

——Carle, interviewed for *Cinema Canada*, Apr–May 73

Maria C A S A R È S
Born in La Corunna, Spain, 1922. A hospital nurse during Spanish Civil War; took refuge in France at end of war, and studied acting at the Conservatoire. First film: Les Enfants du paradis (*1944*).

On the set [of *Les Dames du Bois de Boulogne* (1945), Robert Bresson] was a tyrant who wanted to take the place of everything, exacting to within a millimeter, to within an inflection. A tear must drop just so and not otherwise —a look be raised in a precise and not always convenient way! The phrase must be scanned as he desired it, and I have seen him walking up and down in front of me, beside himself, repeating for 20 minutes a little phrase I was supposed to say spontaneously, *"Ah! Jean, vous m'avez fait peur!"* In order to find the intonation he considered adequate and impose it on me before shooting.

What then becomes of the actor? A robot? A tool? A marionette? I should never stop if I were to detail the history of that film, from the beginning when Lucienne Bogaert and I drank brandy after brandy by the desire and order of Robert Bresson (he was making us drunk, he said, to quell our nerves— and our personalities, too, I thought) to the end when, discouraged, exhausted, vanquished, nearly all the actors would abandon on reaching the studio anything resembling a life or will of their own, to drag before our gentle tyrant (for he was gentle besides everything else!) what he wanted: a body, a voice he had chosen as you choose an ornament you think will look well on the chimneypiece.

——Casarès, in *World Theatre 8*, 1959

John C A S S A V E T E S
Born in New York City, 1929, into a Greek immigrant family. Experienced in varied theater forms before entering films as actor and as director.

Shadows [1960] was an experiment. It predominantly came out of a workshop. We were improvising on a story, one that was in my mind. It was my secret. Every scene in *Shadows* was very simple; they were predicated on people having problems that were overcome with other problems; at the end of the scene another problem would come in and overlap. This carried it forward and built up a simple structure. Once I had the structure it was a matter of writing a character breakdown and then working on that with the individual. There was a struggle because firstly I had never done a film before, and secondly the actors had to find the confidence to have quiet at times, and not just constantly talk. This took about the first 3 weeks of the schedule. Eventually all this material was thrown away, and then everyone became cool and easy and relaxed and they had their own things to say, which was the point.

——Cassavetes, interviewed for *Films & Filming*, Sep 68

I learned [in working as a film actor], for instance, that in a motion picture you have marks to hit, and the lighting cameraman always lights for you at a certain mark. The actor is expected to go through a dramatic scene, staying within a certain region where the lights are. If he gets out of light just half an inch, then they'll cut the take and do it over again. So then the actor begins to think about the light rather than about the person he is supposed to be making love to, or arguing with. So with *Shadows* we tried something completely different in that we not only improvised in terms of the words, but we improvised in terms of motions. So the cameraman also improvised, he had to follow the artists and light generally, so that the actor could move when and wherever he pleased. A strange and interesting thing happened, in that the camera, in following the people, followed them smoothly and beautifully, simply because people have a natural rhythm. Whereas when they rehearse something according to a technical mark, they begin to be jerky and unnatural, and no matter how talented they are, the camera has a difficult time in following them.

——Cassavetes, interviewed for *Films & Filming*, Feb 61

In *Faces* [1968] Al Ruban did the lighting and I had a great operator who worked the camera. They had individual pride in their work. But they also realized that they were a part of an overall thing. It wasn't decisively important how beautiful their photography was, except to them personally. The question was: "What are we working for?" And the obvious answer was that we were working for these people [the actors]—we're not dealing with objects and walls—to look better. Now it doesn't really make any difference whether the wall behind them is white, dark, black. I don't think it means anything to anybody. It's what these people are thinking, what they're feeling. And that's the drama of the piece.

So when we did the film, the operating was handled by following the people. It's as simple as that. It was absolutely hand-held. No harness. And I think we used only about 3 set shots in the picture. But the idea was, "How do we get to these people the fastest, quickest, most expedient way before that little feeling that they have disappears?" That's the important thing. So sometimes we'd shoot when the lights weren't ready. We'd shoot whenever the actors were ready. We were slaves to them. All we were there to do was record what they were doing. . . .

The emotion was improvisation. The lines were written. The attitudes were improvised, as they always are, but I think a little more deeply in this case. The reactions to leading performers were not modulated. In other words, if somebody had a smaller part, he didn't have to bend to the film's superstar role and didn't have to listen to the hero's sad story. He could do what his character would really do, without fear of offending the main actor—who keeps a tight rein, in commercial filmmaking, on everything happening in his scenes.

In that sense, it was improvised. I really didn't care if they stuck to their lines. But they did stick close to the dialogue, anyway. I didn't know this while we were shooting, because I don't look at a script during the actual filming. I'm not really listening to dialogue. I'm watching to see if they're communicating something and expressing something. I don't know if they're stumbling or carrying on or overlapping or anything. I'm just watching a conversation. You're not aware of exactly what people are saying. You're aware of what they're intending and what kind of feeling is going on in that scene.

————Cassavetes, interviewed for *The Film Director as Superstar* (NY 1970)

So I found that by writing scenes for [*Husbands* (1970)] that we might never use, and writing them again and again and again, that everything that we had written and improvised was, therefore, in our minds, used and usable. We had investigated, then studied it. We knew what we were capable of saying to each other and doing with each other, so we got to the point where we could just give any kind of improvisation. We had a scene written, but it wasn't very good. It wasn't very clear. It just seemed that these people were there, the extras that had been hired to cover the set. I didn't like the scene that we were doing, so I just said, "Let's improvise this scene here. Put beer on the table and whiskey on the table." I didn't know what we would do. We started and I knew that Peter [Falk] and Ben [Gazzara] would catch on, and that the rest of the people would pick it up, because they weren't going to break the reality.

Q. Did you like working as a director who didn't say anything?

A. I hated it. It's terrible. It's painful, and terrible, and too disciplined for me. What happened was that, in a sense, it was really an emotional improvisation. I felt that I couldn't gain anything by using direction to make the scene better, telling Peter to all of a sudden behave in a certain way, creating a situation as you usually do in a film. You create a situation. The lack of action was what the picture was about, you see, so if I stimulated action by directing, it would be bad, wrong. Sometimes the guys would just sit there. I mean, somebody dies; I don't know anybody that knows anything to do. I couldn't tell you now what I would do in a situation like that.

Directors don't really get along with a crew, because usually a crew isn't involved, unless it's the way you work where you're working with people. I walk in as a director and meet my cameraman. He's got his crew and that is his army. The guy in the sound department has his army, and the painter has to check with the cameraman to see whether to put shiny walls over there. At what point can I have some kind of a rapport with the operator? The guy is so conditioned that he has to look to his boss to find out if what he is doing is okay, or he has to look to the studio to find out if it is okay. I think this holds true in terms of union jobs.

————Cassavetes, interviewed Jan 71 for *Dialogue on Film*, No. 4

We're distributing *A Woman Under the Influence* [1974] ourselves because the studios have had no interest in it. And if they did come to us, we wouldn't sell it cheaply because we've taken our risks and expect to be paid well for it. After all, who the hell are they? Unless they finance the production, they're a bunch of agents who go out and book theaters; that's what it really boils down to. Sure, being a distributor is a craft in itself, and if they had done a better job we'd all be in better condition.

————Cassavetes, interviewed for *Filmmakers Newsletter*, Jan 75

Jean-Pierre C A S S E L   [Crochon]
Born in Paris, 1932.

[Renoir] arrives on the set [of *The Vanishing Corporal*, 1962]. We have the impression that he does not know anything about the story, about the film, nothing. "Bonjour. You slept all right? What do we do today? Sit down and read the script." "We've learned the lines." "No, no, sit down and read it like a telephone directory." We sit down and read it, flatly, without acting. "My friends, please, it's fantastic. Marvelous. We shoot immediately. Put the camera here." We shoot only 3 or 4 hours afterward, but no one knows why.

We change everything and you have the impression that you change it, but it's him. "Maybe it's better if you're here. You don't think so? No, no, stay there." Afterwards you go here but it's exactly a game, and when we shoot, he puts his hat off. He never says "Action." He says, *"Messieurs les comédiens, s'il vous plait."* And you act, and at the end he never says "Cut." The first time we did the first scene of the film and we finished the scene and nothing. And with Claude Brasseur we continued, and suddenly it's "What a pity we have to stop." And we look at him and he's crying. "Thank you, thank you. Just once more for pleasure. For my pleasure." And we played it. And we were in love with this man all the time.

[On *Les Fêtes galantes*, 1965] You cannot move in the direction of René Clair. Because it's comedy, and he knows comedy is one, two, laugh, one, two, three, laugh, one, two, three, four, laugh. If you do one, laugh, one, two, three, four, laugh, it's different. It's frustrating. When I worked for him my pleasure was to ride a horse, to fight, to run. But with René Clair it was impossible. You had to ride horse just exactly like that. It's like puppet theater, and always far from the actors. Never the lens is close-up. Not once in the film, and he shoots always with something between the audience and the actors—a glass of water or a door or a wall.

Chabrol never gives an explanation, never a speech. But he gives many tiny things about the attitude of the character. For example, he told me that when I run after her in the street to offer her my sweets, I should stammer a little and he did not tell me why. And I did it and I understood. Because the man is so upset. And it's brilliant to give me something just before we shoot the scene. And he gives many tiny things so you do exactly the right movement at precisely the moment.

——Cassel, interviewed for *The Times*, 12 Feb 72

Alberto C A V A L C A N T I
Born in Rio de Janeiro, 1897. His first European film work was as a designer.

Rien que les heures [1926] was an accident, because my first film [*Le Train sans yeux*] was shot in the studios in Germany and the producers didn't pay the bills and the film was held up by the studios, who wouldn't release the negative for copies. . . . So I got a few friends together, and we said, "We must do a film at all costs, because we are going to miss this winter. . . ." We made a script, and it was the cheapest film you could imagine. It cost at the time 35,000 old francs, which is nothing at all. We had no studio. We shot everything [?] in the streets, and of course we cut it very quickly. . . . It is a clumsy social document, but it is a social document about the lack of work, about the lives in miserable places. It had a lot of trouble with the censors, you know.

—Cavalcanti, interviewed by Elizabeth Sussex for
Sight & Sound, Autumn 75

Q. What exactly was the nature of your collaboration with [Benjamin] Britten and [W. H.] Auden on *Coal Face* [1936] and *Night Mail* [1936]?

A. We all worked together very well. Britten is a very comprehending composer. He wasn't obsessed by musical rules, and he understood fully what was necessary in a sound track. Auden was able to work very fast. For *Night Mail* we scratched marks on a loop of negative film to correspond with the "beats" of the engine sound. This was projected while the poem was spoken by Stuart Legg. He timed his reading to the scratches, which appeared as flashes on the screen.

Q. Did Harry Watt actually direct *Night Mail* alone?

A. I'm almost sure that Harry Watt did all the shooting. Basil Wright gave lots of ideas at every stage.

Q. How closely scripted were the documentaries of this period?

A. *Night Mail* was not very closely scripted before shooting. *North Sea* [1938] is the only film which I remember was very closely scripted. That was, though, based on the existing log of a sea incident which had actually happened, and there was also another reason for its being closely scripted. I had brought Carl Dreyer to visit the unit and had introduced him to Grierson who immediately, in almost Mussolini-like fashion, decreed that Dreyer should direct *North Sea.* Dreyer was given the log of the real incident, took it away and wrote a script. I read the script and refused to have anything more to do with it. Whatever Dreyer's other virtues as a filmmaker, he had no documentary sense. For example, when these tough Scottish fishermen see the rescuing trawler, he had them bursting into tears! Can you imagine that! I had a big quarrel with Grierson over this, but fortunately Dreyer had by this time found other employment and so the matter went no further.

—Cavalcanti, interviewed for *Screen,* Summer 72

Claude CHABROL
Born in Paris, 1930. Gave up a career in pharmacy to join the group of critics on Cahiers du cinéma, *and made his first film,* Le Beau Serge, *in 1958.*

As far as I'm concerned I find myself much less influenced by Hitchcock than I used to be. Now, as far as the conceiving and shooting of a film, I find myself much closer not to Hitchcock, but to Fritz Lang. . . .

Where Hitchcock uses 10 shots in a film, I try to use 3. Hitchcock's shooting is dynamic and his shots are frightening for their movement. When Lang wants to show fear he succeeds in doing it exclusively by the direct relationship between the actors and the decor. This interests me more at this particular moment.

Hitchcock's effect on the spectator is purely a physical one. In Hitchcock you see the person who is fearful; in Lang you see not only the person who is fearful but also you feel fear yourself. . . .

. . . The plot is just for the audience. I don't like the plot too much, you see—what I like is what people are at the beginning of a scene and what they are at the end of a scene. I'm primarily interested in their relationships, and the plot is just a means to get at the behavior of the characters.

Q. Is this why, for instance, you reveal the identity of the murderer so early in *Le Boucher* [1969]?

A. Of course, I am not interested in solving puzzles. I am interested in studying the behavior of people involved in murder. If you don't know who the murderer is, that would seem to indicate that he is not interesting enough to be known and studied.

Q. I was very conscious of the color yellow in *Le Boucher*.

A. Each time I make a film, I try to choose a color for each person. Not necessarily the color they wear, but a color that corresponds with them. Color has a very different effect on people according to the person involved.

——Chabrol, interviewed in *Take One*, Sep–Oct 70

In *Que la bête meure* [1969] it can be admitted that Charles does kill Paul, though most of the spectators think it's his son who does it. It's a simplification, of course, but with the Charleses and the Pauls it's the old trick of the lamb and the wolf. Not that I'm against wolves. I'm very sensitive to circumstances, and in certain circumstances the need to survive becomes the only law. And to survive it's sometimes necessary to act like a wolf. In war, for instance, if you act like a lamb, you won't last long, though it's awful to have to make yourself into a wolf. Of course there are men—and women too—with no goodness at all in them. I believe though that man is naturally good, but that it's quite easy for him to become evil. He always has the wolf potential, and if he hasn't got the strength to become a wolf, he can always become a fox, like the Jean-Pierre Cassel character in *La Rupture*. I prefer the character Jean Yanne played in *Que la bête meure*. The wolves have a certain grandeur, the foxes never, and they aren't even intelligent. . . .

I can tell you very precisely what I wanted to do in this film. My intention was that the audience shouldn't howl with disgust on seeing a woman kiss the mouth of a dying man who's been butchering women all through the film. I wanted to arrive at a point where that would seem quite normal, and the film's viewpoint is really more that of the butcher than the schoolmistress, who isn't entirely blameless either. . . .

——Chabrol, interviewed for *The Times*, 13 May 72

CHANG Chun-hsiang
Born 1911, in Kiangsu Province, China.

Directors, like scenario writers and actors, now have a new conception of their work. One of their chief responsibilities is to see that people depicted on the screen are not only true to life but show real development in response to the problems they face. . . .

We have also found that sharp images emerge only when writer, actor, and director have strong likes and dislikes for the characters they create.

——Chang, in *China Reconstructs,* Jan–Feb 54

Charles C H A P L I N
Born in Kennington, London in 1889. Appeared in music hall as early as 1894. In 1914, he went to work for Mack Sennett at Keystone and soon was directing and writing his own shorts.

Under Sennett's direction I felt comfortable, because everything was spontaneously worked out on the set. As no one was positive or sure of himself (not even the director), I concluded that I knew as much as the other fellow. This gave me confidence; I began to offer suggestions which Sennett readily accepted. Thus grew a belief in myself that I was creative and could write my own stories. . . .

I made about 5 pictures and in some of them I had managed to put over one or two bits of comedy business of my own, in spite of the butchers in the cutting room. Familiar with their method of cutting films, I would contrive business and gags just for entering and exiting from a scene, knowing that they would have difficulty in cutting them out. I took every opportunity I could to learn the business. I was in and out of the developing plant and cutting room, watching the cutter piece the films together.

Now I was anxious to write and direct my own comedies, so I talked to Sennett about it. But he would not hear of it; instead he assigned me to Mabel Normand, who had just started directing her own pictures. This nettled me, for, charming as Mabel was, I doubted her competence as a director; so the first day there came the inevitable blowup. We were on location in the suburbs of Los Angeles, and in one scene Mabel wanted me to stand with a hose and water down the road so that the villain's car would skid over it. I suggested standing on the hose so that the water can't come out, and when I look down the nozzle I unconsciously step off the hose and the water squirts in my face. But she shut me up quickly: "We have no time! We have no time! Do what you're told."

That was enough, I could not take it—and from such a pretty girl. "I'm sorry, Miss Normand, I will not do what I'm told. I don't think you are competent to tell me what to do."

The scene was in the center of the road, and I left it and sat down on the curb. Sweet Mabel—at that time she was only 20, pretty and charming, everybody's favorite; everybody loved her. Now she sat by the camera bewildered; nobody had ever spoken to her so directly before.

. . . With more experience I found that the placing of a camera was not only psychological but articulated a scene; in fact, it was the basis of cinematic style. If the camera is a little too near, or too far, it can enhance or spoil an effect. Because economy of movement is important you don't want an actor to walk any unnecessary distance unless there is a special reason, for walking is not dramatic. Therefore placement of camera should effect composition and a graceful entrance for the actor. Placement of camera is cinematic inflection. There is no set rule that a close-up gives more emphasis than a long shot. A close-up is a question of feeling; in some instances a long shot can effect greater emphasis.

An example of this is in one of my early comedies, [*The Rink* (1916)]. The tramp enters the rink and skates with one foot up, gliding and twirling, tripping and bumping into people and getting into all sorts of mischief, eventually leaving everyone piled up on their backs in the foreground of the camera, while he skates to the rear of the rink, becoming a very small figure in the background, and sits among the spectators innocently reviewing the havoc he has just created. Yet the small figure of the tramp in the distance was funnier than he would have been in a close-up.

They say babies and dogs are the best actors in movies. Put a twelve-month-old baby in a bathtub with a bar of soap, and when he tries to pick it up he will create a riot of laughter. All children in some form or another have genius; the trick is to bring it out in them. With Jackie [Coogan] it was easy. There were a few basic rules to learn in pantomime and Jackie very soon mastered them. He could apply emotion to the action and action to the emotion, and could repeat it time and time again without losing the effect of spontaneity.

There is a scene in *The Kid* [1921] where the boy is about to throw a stone at a window. . . .

Having worked out the mechanics of the scene, I told Jackie to watch me, emphasizing the points: "You have a stone; then you look at the window; then you prepare to throw the stone; you bring your hand back, but you feel the policeman's coat; you feel his buttons, then you look up and discover it's a policeman; you throw the stone playfully in the air, then throw it away, and casually walk off, suddenly bursting into a sprint."

He rehearsed the scene 3 or 4 times. Eventually he was so sure of the mechanics that his emotion came with them. In other words, the mechanics induced the emotion. The scene was one of Jackie's best, and was one of the high spots in the picture.

——Chaplin in *My Autobiography* (London 1964)

I always aim for economy of means. By that I mean that when one incident can get two big, separate laughs, it is much better than two individual incidents. In *The Adventurer* [1917], I accomplished this by placing myself on a balcony, eating ice cream with a girl. On the floor directly underneath the balcony I put a stout, dignified, well-dressed woman at a table. Then, while eating the ice cream, I let a piece drop off my spoon, slip through my baggy trousers, and drop from the balcony onto this woman's neck.

The first laugh came at my embarrassment over my own predicament. The second, and the much greater one, came when the ice cream landed on the woman's neck and she shrieked and started to dance around. Only one incident had been used, but it had got two people in trouble, and had also got two big laughs. . . .

One of the things I have to be most careful about is not to overdo a thing, or to stress too much any particular point. I could kill laughs more quickly by overdoing something than by any other method. If I made too much of my peculiar walk, if I were too rough in turning people upside-down, if I went to excess in anything at all, it would be bad for the picture. Restraint is a great word, not only for actors but for everybody to remember.

———Chaplin, in *American Magazine*, Nov 1918

Any time that I was really stuck for an idea, I would retire to my dressing-room and tell the others: "I have to go into the Gethsemane!" Sometimes I'd be there for days with my chin on my chest, staring at nothing, saying over and over to myself: "There *must* be an answer to this!" The *real* hard work is in thinking, just thinking. For several days I would be in agony—then the word would go round the studio: "Fine! Charlie's got it!" It would probably be a very small idea—but something that could be elaborated while we were doing it until it turned into a good, inventive gag. It doesn't matter how serious the story is—it all amounts to a bit of business or a gag. In the end, everything is a gag.

———Chaplin, interviewed for *My Life in Pictures* (London, 1974)

Geraldine C H A P L I N
Born 1944, to Charles and Oona Chaplin.

[Robert Altman] is magic. Before shooting, there's usually a week or 10 days when he's around a lot; he makes you feel very excited about your part. When you start shooting he's not around so much as *behind*, but in such control.

I adore being manipulated. An example is the whole character in *Nashville* [1975]. I really thought I wrote all those monologues in the car cemetery, and I *did* write them, but he knew what I was going to write because he gave me like 6 or 7 things, key words or something—all that was already implanted. People say that Bob allows you the most enormous freedom and that they're creating their own part, which is an enormous lie. Everyone's lining up in the exact direction he wants them to go. He gives you the *impression* you're creating, and that marvelous ego trip, but you're the same marionette you are with other directors.

———Chaplin, interviewed for *Crawdaddy*, July 76

Borden C H A S E [Frank Fowler] (1900–1971)
Born New York City. Unusual variety of jobs before he began writing for pulps and films.

I came back out in '44 for Metro, on a deal for Al Rubin. That didn't work out and then I did *This Man's Navy* [1945]; Sam Marx was the producer. He put me on it and I came up with the idea. Then the next thing that I heard, Allen Rivkin came to me and he said that he'd been assigned to it and I would write one piece and he would write another piece and so forth. I said, "Go ahead, write." Then I sat down and wrote the whole damn thing. When I did that, I turned it in pretty quick and he said, "Hell, you're not collaborating, you're competing." I said, "You're goddamned right I am. I'm trying to write you off this thing—aren't you trying to write me off it? If you're not, you're stupid." So we didn't become very good friends, but Sam decided my script would go. Billy Wellman directed it, and I had a good time on that with Billy. . . .

——Chase, interviewed for *Film Comment,* Winter 70–71

Paddy CHAYEFSKY
Born in New York, 1923. Reputation established as a writer of television plays.

So you can forget box-office stars. The art film must be made, quite frankly, in the hurried, slipshod way that any other low-budget Grade B film is made. The production of an art film is a shoestring business, demeaned by haggling and skimpiness. The lower the budget, the more chance of profit, so the whole idea is to keep your expenses down. This means slicing days off your shooting schedule, cutting out scenes that would enhance the picture but are not dramatically vital, telescoping three sets into one. In *Marty* [1955] we gave up several delightful photographic touches because we simply could not afford the 50 extras or the fact that the scene would have to be shot on Sunday, which is triple-time. You are forced to yield those elegant little colors and gentle shadings that make the difference between the good and the beautiful. In *The Goddess* [1957] we skimped nothing once we started actual production, but there were several long conferences before the first day of rehearsal whose only purpose was to cut costs. John Cromwell, the director, Milton Perlman, the producer, George Justin, the production manager, and I sat scripts in hand, the tenor of the conference being something like this: "Do we absolutely need that big Hollywood party scene, because it will cost a fortune to construct such an elaborate set, to rent such expensive costumes, to hire 200 extras, and to spend one whole shooting day on this one scene." And the answer was: "No, we don't absolutely need it," and the scene was cut from the script despite the fact it would have given charm and delight to a clumsy transition. Or the assistant director, Charlie McGuire, who laid out the shooting schedule, would be instructed to "keep our Maryland location shooting down to one week, no matter what that means." It means, frankly, racing through difficult and sensitive scenes, settling for half of what you really want, eating your heart out in a frustrated fury of unfulfillment. John Cromwell and I let a lot go by in *The Goddess* because we couldn't afford to spend any more time arguing with Kim Stanley for a more profound insight in her acting or for the cameraman to give us a more exquisitely shadowed mood in the lighting.

We took what we could get as well as we could get it. Fortunately, or rather calculatedly, we had fine talents to work with, and the pressure of time doesn't mean Miss Stanley isn't superb in her performance or that Arthur Ornitz, the cameraman, hasn't lit some lovely scenes. The point is, an art film is never half as good as it should be. An art film must be low-budget, and low-budget means you sacrifice some art.

——Chayefsky, in *Saturday Review,* 21 Dec 57

Nikolai CHERKASOV (1903–1966)
Born in St. Petersburg. An actor since 1918.

Sooner or later every actor comes across a role that opens up new vistas before him, that perfectly suits his abilities. I was sure that Polezhayev [in *Baltic Deputy* (1937)] was just that kind of role. It was the chance I had been longing for.

The studio tested several well-known actors for the role. I decided to do my best to get the part. I do not recall any other instance when I tried so hard or worried so much. . . . I virtually forced myself on the directors, giving them scores of reasons why I was sure I would succeed. I was told, and quite rightly, too, that Professor Polezhayev was 75 while I was only 32, but I countered this by saying that he was so young in spirit that only a young actor could play him. . . .

My first test was not successful. But the second proved much better. The directors favored me and I got the role, despite the fact that the top officials of Lenfilm and certain other film workers had no confidence in me. . . .

Carried away by his enthusiasm for pictorial composition [in *Ivan Grozny*], Eisenstein molded expressive, monumental *mises-en-scène*, but it was often difficult to justify the content of the form he was striving to achieve. In some of his *mises-en-scène*, extremely graphic in idea and composition, an actor's strained muscles often belied his inner feelings. In such cases, the actor found it difficult indeed to mold the image demanded of him. Eisenstein insisted that his ideas be carried out. This insistence infected us. . . .

My confidence in the film waned and my worries grew with each passing day. After watching scenes of the second part run through I criticized some episodes, but Eisenstein brushed my criticism aside, and in the end stopped showing me edited bits altogether. In films, it is the director who has the last word.

——Cherkasov, *Notes of a Soviet Actor* (Moscow 1957)

Maurice CHEVALIER (1888–1972)
Born in Paris; made his debut as singer and entertainer in 1900. Between 1911 and 1914 first appeared in short film comedies.

René Clair came to me with a picture [*Le Silence est d'or* (1947)] about an old man who adopts a daughter and then falls in love with her.

Now the girl, you see, eventually ran away with a young fellow and the old man was desperate.

I liked the story, but I said I would not do it if they insisted on my being desperate. I did not want to be desperate.

"Let me push her to the younger fellow," I said, "and then meet an older woman and fall for her. That is how it should be." And René let me do it this way, and it was a great success.

——Chevalier, interviewed for *The Sunday Express*, 3 Sep 64

CHIN Shan
Born 1911 in Hunan Province, China. Actor, playwright, director.

... The Peking Film Studio discussed with me their wish to make a color film of this play [*Ballad of the Thirteen Hills Reservoir*], using the same shock tactics with which we had prepared the play, to finish the film by October First [National Day], and distribute it to all the villages of the country to propagandize the urgency of building irrigation schemes throughout China. We studied how such a film could be made, writing the script, doing set construction, location work, editing, sound, and all, knowing that we could not exceed 45 days altogether. We knew it would be difficult but we knew that such a vital task must be accomplished. The party organization asked me to have the script ready in 3 or 4 days. It was, and I then showed this to all responsible comrades, including the play's author, T'ien Han. Between August 4 and 12 I listened to their opinions and made alterations. I changed some scenes entirely, and then showed it again to T'ien Han and the responsible comrades. The script took its final form on August 20 [1958], and we started shooting.

———Chin Shan, in *Dazhong Dianying*, No. 21, 1958

Julie CHRISTIE
Born in Assam in 1941 and educated in England and France.

This [*Far from the Madding Crowd* (1967)] is the third film I've worked on with John Schlesinger, I understand him and know how his mind works.
　　As far as Schlesinger is concerned, you work *with* him. I tell him what I think and he tells me what he thinks and it is a two-way process. But he's always a step ahead of me, which pulls me along.
　　When it comes to David Lean, you work *for* him. He tells you exactly what he wants and what he says goes. But he's a super person for bringing you further along than you ever dared to believe you could go.
　　Truffaut? He's a marvelous director. But he doesn't give you any preconceived idea of the character. He leaves you rather in the air. You have to keep your ears open, picking up what you can. Still, he performs the miracle just the same.

———Christie, interviewed for *The Morning Star*, 4 Feb 67

Grigori CHUKHRAI
Born in Melitopol, Ukraine, in 1921. Served in parachute corps during World War II, wounded five times. After war resumed studies at State Film School, where he trained with Yutkevich and Romm.

After graduating from VGIK, I went to the Kiev Studios. Since I am Ukrainian, I wanted to work in the Ukraine. For two and a half years I worked as an assistant to directors Levchuk, Ivchenko, and Braun. I dreamed about my own films, and particularly, about filming *The Forty-first*. But the directors of the

Kiev studios rejected my proposal. Instead, they offered me a project of theirs which I rejected. . . . I went to Moscow. There I proposed my plan to the Art Committee of the Mosfilm Studios. At that time, Ivan Pyriev was the director of the Mosfilm Studios. He patiently listened to me for two hours, while I explained to him what I wanted to do and how. After that, he called in my two teachers, Sergei Yutkevich and Mikhail Romm. He also called in the chief dramaturge of the school, and said to them: "This young man wants to film Lavrenyev's story, *The Forty-First*. What do you have to say about this, you, his teachers?" Yutkevich said: "I have nothing against it. He should try it." Romm supported me even more strongly, and so did the chief dramaturge.
———Chukhrai, interviewed for *Film Culture*, Fall 62

The exposure of the cult of the individual proved to be a turning point not only in the political life of our country, but also for the destiny of Soviet art as a whole.
    In cinematography, the cult of the individual showed itself not only in the form of unrestrained praise of Stalin, but chiefly as a whole system of dogmatic standards and demands having nothing to do with art or real life.
———Chukhrai, interviewed for *Soviet News*, 31 July 62

René C L A I R [Chomette]
Born in Paris, 1898; began his career after the war as a journalist and film actor (for Feuillade and Protazanov). Helped to rediscover and popularize the French fantasists and comedians of the beginning of the century, and drew upon this source for his first films.

. . . In *Le Million* [1931], I discovered this farcical play—it was a farcical play in the beginning, you know, from which I took only the little part, it was what we call in France a vaudeville, a farce. It was very much based on languages, you see, and I hated that because I was still a silent picture director. I wanted an atmosphere of foolishness, and we decided it should not be realistic. And then we started to adopt the principle of putting some gauze between the actors and the sets, which created an illusion of unreality in spite of the fact that you could see real objects behind. I think it is one of the most interesting experiments that has been made in sets—by my colleague [Lazare Meerson] and me—It was a terrific problem for the director of photography; having the gauze over the sets, you could not use the counter light (i.e. backlight).
———Clair, interviewed for *Focus on Film*, Winter 72

[In preparing *A nous la liberté* in 1930] I was closest to the extreme left. I wanted to attack the Machine, which led men into starvation instead of adding to their happiness. I was wrong to use the operetta formula, but I thought it would enhance the satirical nature of the film more than would a realistic style.
———Clair to Charensol, in Sadoul-Morris, *Dictionary of Films*, p 13

To my mind, sets and their dressing should be held as simple as possible. There should be only such furniture as must be actually used in the scenes.

For instance, when we started *Flame of New Orleans* [1941], art director Jack Otterson gave me some lovely sets. When I saw the designs, and later the finished sets, I was delighted. But later, when they brought the set-dressings and furniture in, I felt something was wrong. The dark furniture and patterned upholstery looked wrong against the classic simplicity of Otterson's well-designed monochromatic sets.

So I had them remove all the furniture except those pieces actually to figure in the action of the picture. One large set, for example, contains only a mirror, a chair, a table, and a grandfather's clock, all of them specially refinished in the same colors as the set-walls, but a slight darker tonal value. I even had them take out the carpeting and replace it with a hardwood-finish flooring.

In reality, that set looks bare. But on the screen, it won't. Between the action of the players, Otterson's artistic set-design, and the skill of my old friend Rudy Maté, A.S.C., who is directing the photography, I'm confident that no one in any audience will notice the scarcity of furniture. On the contrary, the set will seem normal—an attractive room. . . . And by eliminating surplus furnishings, we'll keep that background from stealing the scene from the players.

———Clair, in *American Cinematographer*, Feb 41

But to adapt oneself to another country is difficult nevertheless. There is a new language to learn, and that for me is very important because always I have written my own scripts or at least collaborated very intensively on the preparation. To me it has always seemed foolish the producers should pay a man, say $50,000 to write a script, and then pay a director twice as much to stage it. With me, the preparation of the script is all important, it is written in great detail and very slowly. When it is finished an assistant director should be able to shoot it. But such a procedure is now difficult for me because I know little of the English language.

Another problem for me in Hollywood is that one must work with the stars and it is hard to find today the actors for my kind of comedy. The Buster Keatons and those like him are not available, and though I should like very much to do a film with someone like W. C. Fields that is impossible because Fields is practically a director-producer himself. When one works with a star the picture usually must be for him or her rather than for itself.

———Clair, interviewed for *The New York Times*, 11 May 41

When I went to Hollywood, some years ago, I was hired as a director, but presently, since I am a writer, I collaborated on a script [*The Flame of New Orleans*(?)]. When my agent suggested that I ought to be paid for this endeavor, the producer said okay, he'd give me one-tenth of my salary as director as a fee for writing. I had to tell him it should be the other way around. I believe in the script. And yet, even with a meritorious script, you never know what will appeal to the public. I put two lines in *A nous la liberté* about a belt line coming to a halt because one individual refused to be mechanized, and they turned into the funniest scene in the picture.

———Clair, interviewed for *The New Yorker*, 29 Nov 58

Shirley C L A R K E
Born in New York, 1925. Her first career was as a dancer, before she discovered film.

... I started in films the same way as many filmmakers, by doing everything myself. I was writer, director, cameraman, editor, sound engineer, and lab messenger. I enjoyed it and learned a great deal about the craft. Yet having real pros helping me was an amazingly happy experience and better still made it possible for me to concentrate on making the film. I don't go with the view of some independent directors that technical proficiency results in mere slickness. It's up to each filmmaker how much control and knowledge he needs in order to be spontaneous. For me, spontaneity is an effect, not a method. I feel that the actors and the director are freer to improvise—that is, to create intuitively—when they are surrounded by order and not in the midst of chaos.
———Clarke, in *Sight & Sound*, Spring 61

I don't think anything worth while is really improvised. If I set out to walk to the corner, I suppose I improvise my steps along the way, but at least I know where I'm going. The final version of *Shadows* [1959] was not improvised at all in the sense that it was just made up as they went along; by that time they all knew exactly where they were going and shot it in about 8 weeks, though admittedly it all developed from improvisation. I think it may well be useful as preparation, and I am certainly all for leaving actors as much latitude as possible to contribute creatively, changing dialogue and suggesting business; but then it is the director's job to pick his actors right in the first place so that they can understand the character they are playing and what they suggest is to the point and then to be ready always to decide at a moment's notice exactly what is right and what is not in their suggestions. Keeping things fresh and spontaneous in this way is one thing, full scale improvisation quite another. In fact I used to have a little notice up on the set reading "Spontaneity is an effect, not a method."
———Clarke, interviewed for *The Sunday Times*, 17 June 61

Most of my films are messages to other filmmakers about things they are doing that I question. Things I would like them to take a look at. A very good example and the clearest one is *Portrait of Jason* [1967] which was made to show Ricky [Leacock] and Penny [Donn Alan Pennebaker] the flaws in thinking about cinéma vérité. If you take 12 days of shooting and edit only the climax points, you get crap. My theory was that you don't take out the "boring parts" —the way someone reaches those climaxes or an idea or whatever. *Jason* is 2 hours of real time, not film time. The film took 4 hours to make because we had to stop every 10 minutes to reload the camera. All we shot is there. I would leave a scene in even if there were things in it I didn't dig. I don't believe there is any such thing as "documentary reality." Right away there's an opinion given when you ask a question. All of this evokes very conscious playing at not-acting. There is no difference between a traditional fiction film and a documentary. I've never made a documentary. There is no such trip.
———Clarke, interviewed in *Take One*, Nov–Dec 70

The Cool World [1963] was based on a novel by Warren Miller. But we wanted to get into the reality of what is happening now. The novel was written in 1958–59 and when we started shooting the film it was '62: and there was quite a different set of circumstances. Carl Lee went throughout Harlem gathering together talented children from actual street gangs. We then interviewed many other children at which a whole series of questions were asked: Did they have a gun? Would they want a gun? Would they hold up an old man? and so on. From those answers and from Carl's own experiences in Harlem we developed the second stage, which was a shooting script.

Then we went out to shoot. A great many scenes are improvised. The kids are given a lead-in to what they are to accomplish in general in the scene. At all times they were asked if this was something they would do, or wouldn't do; if they believed it, or if they didn't believe it. If they said no, we didn't do it.

——Clarke, interviewed for *Films & Filming*, Dec 63

Montgomery C L I F T   (1920–1966)
Born in Omaha, Nebraska. Worked in Broadway plays before his first films in 1948, The Search *and* Red River.

I'd lost 12 pounds to play the part [in *The Young Lions* (1958)] you see, and had my ears glued forward. I wanted to look like a rodent, that's why. Lean and slim like a rodent. Or let's say a rat passing for a mouse. But they didn't see that. Oh, no. All they saw was that my face looked different and they shrieked.

——Clift, interviewed for *The Sunday Express*, 16 Aug 59

I could never play a part like *The Search* [1948] again. Too much innocence. One grows cynical. . . . I am not a good judge of my own work. Some things I have done I like. *The Young Lions* maybe, and *Nuremberg* [1960]. . . .

But there is so little good screen acting. Ah! To be jealous of an actor. This is the highest compliment—jealousy! To loathe an actor for his performance, to say "I wish I had done that." How often do I feel like that? . . . Laurette Taylor. And now Simone Signoret, and Larry Olivier, of course. And Marlon, in his early roles.

——Clift, interviewed for *The Sunday Telegraph*, 28 Aug 66

William H. C L O T H I E R
Born in Decatur, Illinois, 1903. To California in 1923. Filmed in Mexico and Spain. First job for John Ford as second cameraman on Fort Apache, *1948.*

Q. How did you and William Wellman approach *Track of the Cat* [1954]—particularly in terms of its unusual color?

A. Bill Wellman had the idea; he came to me and explained what he had in mind. He wanted to make a color picture with very little color—in black and white, in a sense. And that's exactly what we did. . . .

The result was that for the first time, I think, you really saw color in people's faces. You were immediately conscious of the color of a person's eyes, because there was no surrounding color. It became a very interesting challenge, and a great pleasure. I am only sorry that I couldn't have made a picture like that again.

Wellman is a wonderful man, and he had a great concept of making a film. He used to come to work in the morning with a small slip of paper, the size of the palm of my hand. And on that slip of paper, he would have every shot written down that he was going to make that day. He knew when he walked on the set in the morning exactly what he was going to do; there was never any doubt in his mind.

Q. Did Ford work fast when he was shooting?

A. Yes, indeed. Ford would always do his day's work. He would come to work at 9:00 in the morning and go home early in the afternoon, but he made all the setups he wanted to make.

He had a wonderful expression. Sometimes I'd ask, "Do you want to get a closer shot in this scene?" He would say, "If I do, they'll use it, and we don't need it." And we wouldn't shoot it. Ford was one of the old school: everything he shot was put in the picture. So, we didn't shoot a lot of setups, but we shot a lot of picture.

Q. What kind of rig do you like to work with? What cameras do you like?

A. Well, I like to work with a camera that's set up on a platform. I don't go for this hand-held stuff very much. . . . Personally, I like to work with Mitchell BNCs. The last two pictures I made with Mark Armstead's converted BNC—a magnificent camera. It's a reflex, in that you just look through the lens when you're shooting; in the past, we would look through the finder. I am using it on this picture for Mr. Hawks, too [*Rio Lobo*, 1970].

I work with the same crew whenever I can. Unfortunately, there are times when I can't. A cameraman in my classification makes a lot more money than an assistant cameraman. I may make only one picture a year. I can't expect my crew to wait for me to go to work; they have to earn a living. But if I make 2 or 3 a year, I can keep my boys with me all the time. In 20 years, I have had only 2 gaffers—20 years, 2 gaffers! And I keep operators, too, when I can.

The big stars in our industry, over the years, have been men, and I make a point of photographing John Wayne or Jimmy Stewart in a way that's complimentary, the way they should look. You know, some cameramen forget that these people are concerned about how they look; after all, they're not juveniles anymore. The cameraman should take little pains with lighting them, making them look good. Because they're the ones who are footing the bill; they're the ones who are keeping us in business.

Q. You evidently like doing Westerns. . . .

A. I've made so many Westerns. I wouldn't want to do anything else. If I had an offer to make a musical, I'd turn it down; I just don't like to make that kind of a picture. I like to make outdoor pictures. And I've been very fortunate in being able to do just that.

——Clothier, interviewed for *On Film,* 1970

Henri-Georges C L O U Z O T   (1907–1977)
Born in Niort, France. Abandoned naval school and diplomatic career to work as journalist on the Paris-Midi. *Worked as assistant director to Litvak and Dupont; in 1932–33, in Berlin to direct and to write French versions of German films.*

[*Les Diaboliques* (1955)] is just a thriller. There is no special moral to it— it is not even what I'd call a serious piece. I just produced it as I would a game.

I took an ordinary detective novel, transposed it into a different setting, even with different circumstances, rewrote it 4 times in a year, and then filmed it in 11 weeks.

Making a horror film is a game. You don't have to be morbid or sadistic or brutal. You have to be what I like best—efficient.

———Clouzot, interviewed for *The Daily Express,* 9 Dec 55

Lee J. C O B B   [Leo Jacob]   (1911–1976)
Born in New York City; in theater before making his first films in 1937.

Q. Could you tell me the best piece of advice you could give?

A. The best piece of advice I could give might be for the young actor or actress! When we're young, we have such a keen sense of injustice, and for that reason we hesitate to compromise. We know what you're asking is not quite right, and so no, we won't. My advice, after this long and tortuous life of mine is, don't die pure. Live to fight another day. If I didn't do a series, which no one believes is the loftiest goal for the artist—if I didn't do that series, I wouldn't have been able to do *Lear,* for instance. I lived to fight another day. In a comparative sense, for an American actor, I've had a relatively rich professional life. I say, for an American actor. I think in another culture, in another atmosphere. I might have had a richer life. I envy some of my colleagues in England. They have a heritage. It's not our fault—we're young, brash, we don't miss what we've never known. That is as a nation. So we don't have the alternatives, the places to work, to study, to experiment, to fail.

———Cobb, in publicity for *Lawman,* 1970

Jean C O C T E A U   (1889–1963)
Born in the Paris suburb of Maisons-Laffitte.

. . . As I was nearly at the end of *Le Sang d'un poète* [1930], the sweepers were told to clear up the studio just as we had started on our last shots. But as I was about to protest, my cameraman [Périnal] asked me to do nothing of the kind: he had just realized what beautiful images he would be able to take through the dust raised by the sweepers in the light of the arc lamps. . . .

I'm quite as interested in the use of sound as in the use of images. When we were making *Le Sang d'un poète,* as the sound film had just appeared, we kept experimenting till we were quite exhausted. We kept building up walls and then demolishing them, trying in vain to obtain the sound of a crash. At last in desperation I hit upon the discovery that the only way to get that sound was by crumpling up two newspapers simultaneously. It happened to be the *Temps* and *L'Intransigeant* (one of which is printed on stiffer paper than the other). In the same film, with the exception of Rachel Berendt's voice, who dubbed for Miss Lee Miller, all the voices are my own, disguised. The chatter in the theater box consists of various phrases said by me and made to overlap in the mixing.

———*Cocteau on the Film* (London 1954); trans. Vera Traill

During the production of La Belle et la bête (1945) *Cocteau kept a record published as* Diary of a Film; *the following extracts are from the English edition* (1950), *trans. by Ronald Duncan:*

[August, on location]

A good day. Emile Darbon [production manager] complains that I don't get on with the schedule quick enough but keep stopping to take extra shots, which the company haven't allowed for. But it's these extras, the inspiration of the moment, which enliven and enrich a film. I am delighted with those I've taken and am sure they will help. I took one today of an open cart-shed full of ladders, ploughshares, forks, baskets, ropes, and bundles of faggots....

[September]

Packed up this afternoon ready to go to Senlis. Smoke machines, red powder, magnesium torches, and a thousand mechanical bits and pieces, none of which I dare forget. Everybody who works on a film knows the awful and implacable responsibility which settles on a director and forces him to hide his own doubts and overcome his own weaknesses. The slightest sign of indecision on his part demoralizes his unit. I suppose that's why, in the long run, film directors, knowing that they must appear sure of themselves, become so overbearing....

[14th October]

It seems I was right to fight against diffuse lighting and the use of gauzes. For yesterday's pictures were a thousand times more robust and had got that clean, sculptured line in the lighting which I admire so much in Périnal. It isn't kind to women, but it does bring out their character. Alékan is gradually finding his balance and a style or whatever it is that corresponds to the way I tell a story, gesticulate or write. He's most helpful and I'm very grateful to him. He's never difficult or tries to prove I'm wrong. Our unit becomes more and more homogeneous.

[29th October]

Alékan tells me that the stuff I think good is considered by some people at the studio as hopeless, badly lit and a mess. But of course, he doesn't know that I have had years and years [of this], and every time anybody tries anything out of the ordinary, people just sneer. They can't see over their own rut or recognize anything which they haven't known before. It is now accepted that poetic things must be soft, whereas in my opinion poetry is precisely the opposite, something almost mathematical. And I'm pushing Alékan in precisely the opposite direction away from what these fools think is poetic. He is slightly bewildered—he hasn't struggled as long as I have....

[December, at the Joinville studio]

Exhaust ourselves putting finishing touches to the set at the last minute. The dust which the rapid motion (to make it appear slow on the screen) throws up may have its own advantages of atmosphere. As Josette [Day, playing Beauty] goes along the corridor, one of the female figures carved in the top of the stairs turns its head to the right, and its plastered arm lifts the curtain. We made an 80-frame slow-motion shot of this. . . . A runthrough (backwards) of the candles being lit as though by magic. It looks exactly as though it had been taken straight. Reminds me of Méliès, Robert Houdin, or *Le Sang d'un poète*. There's plenty of harshness and strangeness in it, and a touch of violence, too. I like it better than what I really intended.

[15th December]

. . . Marais has had to keep his makeup [as the Beast] on for 15 hours at a stretch, with the result that I daren't ask him to do a single retake. Some night visitors come and have a look at us working in Beauty's set, but they soon get tired. They didn't realize that film work was so hard. They watch for a few minutes and off they go, exhausted. And we remain to endure the martyrdom of the blazing arcs or to freeze when they're turned off.

[April 1946, recording]

. . . This quite fantastic synchronization by which, at my request, Georges Auric has not kept to the rhythm of the film but cut across it, so that when film and music come together it seems as though by the grace of God. . . .

What's so astonishing for me . . . is the accidental synchronization which does occasionally occur. . . . What I must do is to make notes of this and reproduce the accident by design. Sometimes a burst from the chorus envelops a close-up, isolates it, and cancels its effect. At other times it focuses for me; and the orchestra seems to quicken the tempo of a sequence.

In *Le Sang d'un poète* I changed the musical sequence where it became too closely related to the picture. This time I shall respect the sequence but I shall direct its use more precisely. The result will be a counterpoint. That is to say, they will not run together both saying the same thing at the same time, neutralizing each other.

Ronald C O L M A N (1891–1958)
Born in Surrey. After some stage and screen experience in England, came to the United States where he entered films in 1921.

All top actors in Hollywood should free-lance like myself, Freddie March, and John Boles. But most of them lack courage to cut themselves adrift from a long-term contract. They are afraid they won't get work. All I know is I could make 10 pictures a year if I wanted to. So could March. And we can choose our stories and only appear in those we like. I'm now trying to persuade William Powell to free-lance. Bill is in a position to pick and choose his material and he's crazy to continue making 5 films a year. It is just as bad to make 5 pictures a year as it is to make one picture every 5 years, like Chaplin.

———Colman, interview (1937), North American Newspaper Alliance

Any picture you make is hard work. . . .

So you might as well strive for something that gives you the feeling of an accomplishment when it's finished. You don't get that reaction from straight roles. That's why we wanted to change. . . .

It's very difficult to get yourself into a particular mood day after day without retaining a portion of that mood in your private life.
———Colman, interview for *Leader Magazine*, 3 Apr 48

Chester C O N K L I N   (1888–1971)
Born in Iowa.

[Sennett would] be there in front of the camera laughing and you'd break your neck to make him laugh. That was one secret of the Keystone's success.
———Conklin, interviewed for *The Evening Standard*, 14 May 64

I remember one rainy morning, Roscoe Arbuckle, Ford Sterling, and myself were sitting in the dressing room playing pinochle. Charlie [Chaplin] wandered in and went up to the makeup bench. In those days we used crepe hair a lot. Charlie held up various pieces of this crepe hair under his nose, then looked at himself in the mirror. Finally, he found a piece that he liked, and he stuck it on there with spirit gum, went over and got Roscoe Arbuckle's hat and his pants, my coat (a cutaway, we called it in those days . . .), and he took his own cane and went out on the set. This was a hotel set, built for Mabel Normand's picture, *Mabel's Strange Predicament* [1914], and Charlie went into the lobby and started clowning around doing the drunk act he'd done on vaudeville. He'd get his foot stuck in the cuspidor and couldn't get it out—all that kind of thing. Everyone had gathered around and was laughing. Sennett stood back of the crowd and watched. Finally, he went up to Charlie and said, "Listen, do what you've been doing when we shoot this picture with Mabel and Chester." Well, of course, it wound up that he stole the picture from us.
———Conklin, interview with Minta Durfee (1963?) for
The Parade's Gone By (NY, 1968)

Sean C O N N E R Y
Born in 1930, in Edinburgh.

My only grumble about the Bond films is that they don't tax one as an actor. All one really needs is the constitution of a rugby player to get through those 19 weeks of swimming, slugging, and necking.
———Connery, interviewed for *The Sunday Express*, 14 Feb 65

Aaron C O P L A N D
Born 1900 into a Brooklyn commercial family.

I had an interesting experience with the music I wrote for *The Heiress* [1949]. There is a scene in which the heiress girl decides to elope, against the wishes of her parents, with her young man. And they decide at eleven o'clock at night he knows a minister who will come and marry them and he'll go and get him—this is around 1905 on Washington Square in New York. And he'll come and he'll marry them there and then. And so off the young man goes to get the minister. And she's waiting. Now, that's a great scene for music because nobody is saying anything. And yet you can't have it silent. So the composer has a real chance to get his innings in.

She's waiting for the carriage to come by the house. . . . And each time she hears a carriage come she rushes out to the stoop of the house and thinks that's him and it always turns out, you know, it isn't him. It happens 3 or 4 times. And nobody is saying anything.

So I wrote a very romantic sort of music. She's waiting and—you see the final carriage go by, she decides he's not coming, she's been jilted. She goes back very dejected into the house. And we took the picture out, as they do, to one little moviehouse that didn't know it was going to see a tryout of a film. And when that scene was played and she turned away, the audience laughed. Well, that was murder. The director [Wyler] came to me and said, "Copland, this is impossible. If they laugh at her, then we don't have a story. They won't take her seriously. They don't care about her. You've got to do something to save the scene. You've got to stop them from laughing." I said, "Well, how can I stop them from laughing if they want to?" He said, "Do anything you like, but stop them from laughing." Then I went back and I thought, this is a rather interesting problem. Maybe I *can* stop them from laughing. So I threw out the music I had written and wrote a completely different sort of music, very hectic and dissonant, more dissonant than you are used to hearing in a film theater, certainly—sort of modern-music style hectic. And they took it out to another little theater without warning. They showed the same scene. And there wasn't a sound in the house. The audience probably wasn't—didn't know music was going on. But it created a tense and taut kind of feeling around— I felt it myself when I heard the thing—which prevented them from thinking of it as funny.

It was a very good illustration to me, the power of music of the film theater to kind of control the emotions of an audience, even against—when they don't know their emotions are being played with.

——Copland, interviewed for "Bill Moyers' Journal," WNET, Mar 76

Francis Ford C O P P O L A
Born 1939 in Detroit; attended Hofstra College and UCLA. Began in films by writing and directing Dementia 13 *in 1962.*

Q. How did *Dementia 13* [1963] [title in England: *The Haunted and the Hunted*], the film you directed under Roger Corman's banner, come about?

A. Well, we were shooting *The Young Racers* [1962] in Europe, and I knew that whenever Roger takes a crew on location he can't resist the temptation of doing a second picture, having already paid the crew's expenses there. I played on this, managing to convince him that I should direct it. At this time Roger wanted to make a movie molded on the success of *Psycho* [1960], so I told him a zesty horror scene which more or less turned him on. He then agreed to my going ahead with a film of my own, giving me a check for $20,000, providing it was called *Dementia*, providing it had lots of violence, and providing it was shot in Ireland. . . . Then Roger went back to America leaving me on my own. It was then I met a British producer named Raymond

Stross. Well, I started to tell Stross about the film I was planning to make—a picture, incidentally, that had yet to be written—and he became so interested that he wanted to buy in, taking over the British rights for a flat deal of $20,000. So now I had $40,000 to play around with, enough for 9 days' shooting at Ardmore Studios and 2 weeks more out in the countryside.

Q. Did Roger leave you entirely alone?

A. On the shooting, yes. On the editing, no. We had big disagreements. He insisted on dubbing the picture the way he wanted it, adding "voice-overs" to simplify some scenes; worse, he also hired a fellow named Jack Hill to shoot some extra scenes. Roger wanted some more violence added, another ax murder at least—which he got, though not from me.

Q. *Is Paris Burning?* [1966] You were involved in that weren't you?

A. I could write a book about the troubles we had—the silly, petty, dumb things with the French government; it was just an insane mess. Paul Graetz, the French producer, was no help. And René Clément, the director, was even worse. Nobody would speak up. They were all terrified. They just wouldn't admit that there were any Communists in France during the war. Or if there were we were never to use their names. It came down to that. Why? Because the de Gaulle regime didn't acknowledge their existence—then or now. You see, the whole essence of the plot, as I saw it, was the battle between the Communists and the de Gaullist faction for control of the city when the Germans moved out. . . . That was the story. And if we couldn't have that, I couldn't see where there was a movie to be made.

Q. How did *You're a Big Boy Now* [1967] come about?

A. Well, I bought the original novel with my own money while working on *Is Paris Burning?* During the day I used to write *Is Paris Burning?* and at night I used to tinker with *Big Boy*, trying to get the thing down on paper. The reason I laid out my own money for the book was this: I knew that if Seven Arts ever got wind of my writing a screenplay on their time, then they could legally make claim to it; but if I owned the book as well as writing the screenplay, then they would have to bargain with me as owner of that book. Which is exactly what happened.

——Coppola, interviewed for *Films & Filming*, May 69

I saw important ideas in this book [*The Godfather*, 1972] that had to do with dynasty and power. Puzo's screenplay had turned into a slick contemporary gangster picture of no importance. It wasn't Puzo's fault. He just did what they told him to do. It was my intention to make this an authentic piece of film about gangsters who were Italian, how they lived, how they behaved, the way they treated their families, celebrated their rituals.

——Coppola, interviewed for *Time*, 13 March 72

Roger C O R M A N
Born 1926, in Detroit/Los Angeles? Worked at various studio jobs before co-producing Highway Dragnet *from his own script in 1954. Same year made his directorial debut with* Five Guns West.

. . . For 2 years after I came back [from England] to Los Angeles, I was a bum. I knocked around from 1951 to 1953, trying to figure out what I was going to do with my life. I also starved a lot. I worked just long enough to qualify for unemployment [insurance] and then I'd quit and collect from the government. I worked as a stagehand at a local TV station and, finally, as a reader for a literary agent. While I was with the agent, I saw all the crap that was coming in from guys who were writing scripts for B movies. I said to myself that this looked like an easy way to make a buck so I sat down and spent a lot of nights doing a script called *Highway Dragnet*. I showed it to my boss . . . and he sold the script to Allied Artists for $4,000. It all was so easy I could hardly believe it.

———Corman, interviewed for *The New York Times Magazine,* 28 Dec 75

Q. Did you work very closely with Daniel Haller on the art direction of your Poe films?

A. We would discuss the sets and Dan would kind of sketch them out on a napkin at lunch, and that would be it. . . . Dan used to walk out on the set and he'd take a piece of chalk, make a mark, and say, "Start it about here." Then he'd walk out about 15 feet and say, "Well, that looks reasonable, bring it out to here." And I think he was totally correct, because they got themselves so wound up in the studio in such needless detail on sets. You know: "This wall is going to be 35 feet, 14 inches." It means nothing whatsoever in a motion picture. The set will change with every lens you use anyway. We built up a collection of sets on the Poe pictures, and one of the reasons Haller was never that accurate was that we would take standing units, and if a flat was anywhere near what we wanted, we used it. The pictures got more elaborate because we constantly added to the collection of flats with each picture, so that the building got bigger and bigger.

———Corman, interviewed for *Take One,* July–Aug 70

. . . I use a lot of hand-held work. But I use hand-held work primarily when there is movement within the shot itself. I feel that when there's violent movement the hand-held camera leads you into the movement. So if I'm photographing a fight or a chase or something like that, as I did in *The Wild Angels* [1966], possibly a fast group of people dancing, something like that, I'll go among them with the hand-held camera.

. . . I would be more likely to use multiple cameras in something like *The St. Valentine's Day Massacre* [1967], when Hymie Weiss sent his parade of cars down the streets of Cicero and blasted Al Capone's headquarters. I had laid something like a thousand squib [simulated bullet explosions] on the front of the building when the cars came through so it was a one-take shot. I think I had 3 cameras mounted around in different areas, photographing that, because once they shot up the front of the building, that was it. On something like that, I'll use multiple cameras.

Other than that, though, I prefer to use one, on the basis, hopefully, that there's one best way to photograph a scene. . . .

I'm a believer in both instinct and preparation. I think you have to go in prepared and then you have to be able to throw away your preparation, if something better occurs. But if you go in just with the vague hope that something brilliant will happen on the spot you could be in a lot of trouble.

———Corman, interviewed for *The Film Director as Superstar* (NY, 1970)

Stanley CORTEZ [Krantz]
Born 1908 in New York City; educated at New York University. Began his photographic career in the studios of successful portrait photographers. Entered film work in 1926.

While I was working at R-K-O, Welles was preparing [*The Magnificent*] *Ambersons* [1942], rehearsing it; I had access to the stages, a privilege at that time. Welles . . . had 8 sets upstairs and downstairs, and Orson was rehearsing on all these actual sets. And I said to myself, "I'm sorry for the guy who has to photograph this damned thing."

There was a man who was very close to Orson called Jack Moss. He was a great magician, and helped Welles learn magic. Jack mentioned to me that Welles was going to use an R-K-O camera staff. I said, "That's fine, they're all good." But meanwhile Orson had seen some of the stuff I did at Universal: *Danger on the Air* [1938], *The Black Cat* [1941] and so on. And the tests I made for David Selznick. After talking to Jack I went to New York for David to make some tests for George Cukor. While I was there, Jack called me and . . . said, "Orson wants you to do his picture for him!". . . Over the phone we agreed on a contract—Selznick, Welles, and myself. I left New York Sunday, arriving in Hollywood Monday at noon. I met Orson Welles for the first time in my life on the Monday night on the set, and we started shooting Tuesday morning. I had no chance to make a test of anybody.

You remember the opening scene I shot? It came well into the picture, and it showed the family at dinner. Joe Cotten made a speech about automobiles. I shot the scene, feeling tired after the all-night flight . . . when we all assembled to see the first day's work we were all so on edge; me especially . . . to fly from New York and start straight away, my God! Then we saw it and Orson was delighted. . . . Immediately there was a *rapport*. From then on, to work with Orson was a fantastic experience.

He gave me complete freedom, but every one of his suggestions was of enormous importance. We did the sleigh scene in an ice plant . . . and I tried to get the feeling of Currier and Ives prints. We used the ice plant chiefly so that we could show the breath of the people on the air. . . . It was a most difficult thing, because the lights would break . . . we used 5,000 watt, 10,000 watt, and they shattered in the cold. I used a lot of arc light on the snow, throwing it in at an angle to suggest sunbeam glare. There's a certain purity in the light that I wanted.

For one sequence, when the camera explored the Amberson mansion after everyone has left it, I took the shoes off my operator and with a heavy Mitchell camera he walked up the stairs with it and through the rooms. We used a periscopic finder, and a 31-inch lens. He had to move, we had to "choreograph" him like a ballet dancer as he walked so the weight was not unbearably heavy.

In another shot we went through 6 or 7 rooms. When this was being discussed during rehearsal, before I had been hired, I said to the cutter, Bob Wise, "Wouldn't it be wonderful if that could be done in one shot?" Orson must have overheard me because when we came to do the scene, he said, "Can we do this whole scene in one?" I said, "Orson, we can, if you're ready to gamble with me." We did it; every time the camera went through a room, we saw 4 walls and a ceiling! Walls moved on cue, and in went a light on a predetermined line, all while the camera is moving. It was a symphony of movement, noise notwithstanding! . . .

Harry Wild and Russ Metty did some scenes, I remember. Russ photographed the ending in the hospital corridor under the direction of Robert Wise. Harry Wild photographed the scene in the railroad station, done in a kind of forced perspective.

Every day the marvelous team that made [*The Night of the Hunter* (1955)] would meet and discuss the next day's work. It was designed from day to day in fullest detail, so that the details seemed fresh, fresher than if we had done the whole thing in advance. I used to go to Charles's [Laughton's] house every Sunday for 6 weeks before we started and explain my camera equipment to him piece by piece. I wanted to show him through the camera what these lenses would and would not do. But soon the instructor became the student. Not in terms of knowing about the camera but in terms of what he had to say, his ideas for camera. He was very much influenced by Griffith; we ran all the films Griffith made. . . .

Perhaps the most extraordinary thing we did was the shot of a drowned girl in a car underwater, her hair streaming. We used a wax dummy for Shelley Winters. . . . We used the tank at Republic. I hauled in a huge crane from which I suspended a platform, and powerful arcs that would penetrate the water to create that ethereal deathlike something you had in the water. We used two cameras, one actually in the water, the other shooting through glass. We engaged Maurice Siederman, who did *Kane* and *Ambersons*, to do the hair and makeup on the Winters dummy. We had to create a current in the water to make the hair stream out, without your seeing the current at all. We used wind machines. The underwater cameraman was dressed in a scuba diving outfit, and we had an effect in which the camera is on a hook under water and it tips up and follows a thread, up to the boat. Do you know what it means to do a shot like that? We had another cameraman underwater with the first man and he kicked him in the fanny and up he went along the line to the bottom of the boat! I painted the thread white so it would pick up the contrast.

———Cortez, interviewed for *Hollywood Cameramen* (London, 1970)

COSTA-GAVRAS   [Constantine Gavras]
Born in Athens 1933. While studying for a degree in literature at the Sorbonne, his interest in film transferred his education to l'IDHEC and his apprenticeship was spent under Yves Allégret, Clair and Verneuil. His first film was Compartiment Tueurs, *1965, and his third film,* Z (1968), *received worldwide attention.*

. . . From the beginning we had decided to do [Z] as a study of political crime. We did not want sentimental feeling to interfere with that. Had we shown the [Lambrakis] funeral, the film would have been more revolutionary, but also more sentimental. . . . As for newsreel, we had also decided from the beginning that it would be a completely directed film with well-known actors playing the major roles. I do not like the use of documentary material in a film like this because I think it cheapens it. I have been working on a documentary, however, which deals with the funeral of George Papandreou. Most of the footage was shot by Greeks hidden in the crowd, and then the film was brought out of Greece secretly. But that is something altogether different.

———Costa-Gavras, interviewed for *Take One*, July–Aug 69

Q. Do you get long to rehearse before shooting [Z]?

A. Just half a day; we don't have more than that before we actually start shooting. What we do is to have many discussions with each individual actor about the script and their part in it, during the weeks before we begin filming. I go through the script scene by scene with each one, but the first time we can all get together is actually on the stage. If we find we must stop during the shooting to rehearse a scene then we do so . . . the technical side of filming, the camera positions and movement, I find easy for me . . . the most important thing, the difficult thing, are the performances.

Q. Do you ever improvise dialogue?

A. On Z it was difficult as each scene must say certain things . . . we could change the words slightly, only provided that the meaning remained the same.

Q. How much do you preplan your actual shooting?

A. It depends. I think it is essential to keep film costs down so I usually work out camera angles and movement beforehand: On *The Sleeping Car Murders* I had everything worked out in detail. Because it was my first feature film the producer appointed a "technical adviser" and if, after a few days' shooting, my work was not good enough, technically, then this man would step in and "help" me finish the picture. I stayed up every night working it out shot by shot . . . it was exhausting.

Now I plan things in advance but often change them. On Z I used very little of what I had prepared.

. . . You know, I spent a year and a half, nearly two years, with Z because nobody wanted to back it. I even had a list of actors for the film, who had all agreed to do it for no money, but still nobody wanted to touch that script. . . .

Money was the biggest problem behind Z, but there were others with the Algerians . . . you see, I could only use a part-French crew, the others had to be locals, and their inexperience with working on features made for some difficulties when we started shooting.

———Costa-Gavras, interviewed for *Films & Filming*, June 70

State of Siege [1973] is more difficult. This time we had to fight against the conventions of the thriller. That's why we start with a man who is kidnapped. The audience has to know from the start that he is dead. We decided to cut all suspense; there's no possibility he'll live. We want the audience to concentrate on finding out who this man is and why he has been kidnapped. . . . Three years ago I read about an American official executed by the *tupamaros*. Fifteen had been arrested, and all had been freed but this one. I wanted to find out why. I took a two-week trip to Latin America which I spent talking to people about the case.

———Costa-Gavras, interviewed for *The Globe & Mail*, Toronto, 29 Sept 73

Joseph COTTEN
Born in Petersburg, Virginia, 1905. Career in theater and theater criticism. Worked as actor in Welles's Mercury group, in theater and radio, and with them made his film debut in Citizen Kane (1941).

One night I was faced with playing a drunk scene [in *Citizen Kane*] ... I thought about how to play it. The thing you don't do when faced with a drunk scene is to get drunk. But how do you avoid all the stock clichés of a drunk? Orson and I came to the conclusion that fatigue would be akin to the kind of numbness that too much drinking can bring. So we started shooting after dinner, having completed a full day's work that day. I had nothing to drink, but by 3 o'clock in the morning I was drunk. I felt so heavy-footed and tired that I didn't have to act drunk at all.

I was so tired that I did a tongue-trip. I had the line: "I'd like to try my hand at dramatic criticism," but the words came out: "crammatic crimetism." The line remained in the picture.
———Cotten, interviewed for *Action*, May–June 69

Curtis COURANT
Born 1895 in Germany, of Israeli parents. His career as cameraman began in 1917 on Hilde Warren und der Tod.

... Imagination was sometimes carried to extremes. I cannot resist citing the original *Quo Vadis* [1924], starring Emil Jannings, which I photographed in Rome. At that time special process effects so widely used today were nearly unknown. Full-size replicas of the buildings of ancient Rome were constructed in the gardens of the Villa Borghese instead of miniatures. Every one of the 300 extras was costumed authentically. Forty-five lions from a circus were under contract for the duration of the shooting. Facilities for handling assorted personnel, human and animal, became something of a problem in logistics— a problem not always solved successfully, for one of the extras was killed by the lions, in preparation for the big scene with the Christians in the arena. The scene itself was filmed by turning the lions loose on dummies animated by wires outside the danger area, stuffed with overripe horse meat. My camera and crew were protected by a concrete pillbox enclosure which at least pro- vided safety.

The picture took 9 months to shoot, much of the time being consumed in setting up such spectacular effects. Most elaborate of all was the burning of Rome. The huge sets were put to the torch and after the last day's shooting nothing remained of the glories of ancient Rome. When released, the film was shown, up to this sequence on the normal-size screen. Film from this sequence was hand-colored to increase the effect of the flames. A special projector was used for this sequence with an extra-wide-angle lens, while the aperture of the screen was enlarged by opening the curtains. This was the forerunner of the wide screen today.
———Courant in *Film Culture*, Vol. 2, No. 3, 1956

Q. But that scene you have just been shooting [in *The Iron Duke* (1935)] with that broken gun-wheel you arranged so carefully upon the mound, does your script give you the details of that?

A. Oh, no. Such a scene can be arranged upon the floor. Then I paint my sky-cloth with light to help the composition. That big ballroom set you saw us shooting the other day—every column of it has its roundness touched off by some specially placed light, so that the scene had form and depth and pictorial balance as well as the softness appropriate to candle-illumination. The lighting made it a composition. . . .

Q. To what extent are you limited on the floor?

A. Only by time. I have to have my lamps ready by the time the director is ready. Often perhaps I could go on trying still better lighting. But you cannot hold up a studio where hundreds of salaried players may be waiting.

——Courant, interviewed for *Cinema Quarterly*, Autumn 34

Raoul C O U T A R D

Born 1924 in Paris. Began as army photographer, 1951–56, and then as a photojournalist.

A cameraman's worries over color are growing steadily less, as the stocks become more flexible every year. But all the same: it's when he is working with color film that the cameraman is most aware of the fact that no film stock is as sensitive as the human eye. The problem comes from the fact that any number of techniques and working practices were developed for work with early color stock, such as Technicolor, which was not very flexible. And people have got stuck there.

Here I'll only mention the problem of makeup. Makeup is essential in a color film, for a reason which is easy enough to understand. As the film stock is unstable, the laboratories need something to use as a fixed point from which to work in reestablishing the true colors; and what they work from are the actors' faces. (They also base their color justification firstly on a range of greys which one films right after shooting the scene, and then after that on the faces of the actors.) All makeup men, however, have been trained in the American techniques which date back to the early days of Technicolor. They make up the actors very red, a practice which apparently was necessary for Technicolor. When the laboratory wants to correct this red, it will probably add some blue; and with someone like Godard, who has a passion for filming against white walls, everything goes to pieces if the wall turns blue.

This red makeup is a pointless habit. Amateur photographers know that they can get excellent results if they photograph their wives and children in Kodachrome without putting any makeup on them at all. On *Une Femme est une femme* [1961], Godard asked for a neutral makeup, very light and clear. If there were moments when we had to add a bit of color to correct one or two lighting effects, we decided to have a clear gray over it. We tried it out; and it worked. It's the same thing, however, as with the laboratories: makeup men have their habits, their normal working methods, and it is a crusade to get a more naturalistic kind of makeup out of them. Godard needed to say to them as well: "Gentlemen, keep it simple."

——Coutard, in *Sight & Sound*, Winter 66

Q. What did you feel those first few days as a director [on *Hoa Binh* (1970)]?

A. A painful sense of total solitude. It was a severe demonstration of the difficulty of communication. I realized that apart from communicating on a thoroughly practical level, you cannot really convey to others what is so obvious in your own mind. And I was working with people I had worked with for years! I used to get furious at first when the unit did not seem to grasp what I was trying to express. Once I got so mad I grabbed the camera myself. I cooled down soon enough, but I could not get it out of my head that nobody cared a damn. I remember when they said: "Well, it's midday, let's eat!" I thought: "The bastards, they want to stop and eat!" I had noticed that about directors—they are never hungry, never tired, never want to pee . . . I was so disturbed after the first day's shooting I rang Truffaut and Costa-Gavras. They told me they had exactly the same sensation. The unit is really concerned about the film, but they are concerned about their part of it—the director must carry the full burden alone. There was no disloyalty really, it was just my intense sense of isolation.

——Coutard, interviewed for *Show*, 17 Sep 70

Joan C R A W F O R D [Lucille Le Sueur]
Born 1904 in San Antonio, Texas. Dancing lessons in Kansas City; chorus line in road show and Broadway. An MGM test led to a contract.

[In 1929] I admired Eleanor Boardman, and I watched Greta Garbo on her sets every chance I could get. I grew determined to become a dramatic actress. I started nagging Louis B. Mayer and Irving Thalberg to cast me in more and more dramatic roles. I would hang around the studio and get my hands on the new scripts, then take them home with me to read, and decide on the role I wanted. I relied on my instinct in choosing what was right for me, and my instinct rarely let me down. After deciding that I wanted a certain role, I got up and went after it. The written words weren't too important. I knew that if certain words or phrases stuck in my throat, I could call a little conference right on the set and have them changed to suit me better. I would go off in a corner with the director and the leading man, and together we would decide what we wanted the writer to change. I knew that the writer would be grateful to me. His words were dead words. They were brought to life by me.

——Crawford, interviewed for *The Player* (NY, 1962)

. . . I asked Mr. Mayer to buy *A Woman's Face* [1938], the drama of a terribly scarred woman which Ingrid Bergman had made in Swedish. . . .
   What worried George Cukor was my emotionalism. He anticipated that wearing a scar could affect me as wearing a cape has been known to affect some actors. To offset the possibility, he rehearsed the very life out of me. Hours of drilling, with camera and lights lined up for the opening sequence in the courtroom, *then* Mr. Cukor had me recite the multiplication table by twos until all emotion was drained and I was totally exhausted, my voice dwindled to a tired monotone.

——Crawford, in *A Portrait of Joan* (NY, 1962)

Donald C R I S P (1880–1974)
Born at Aberfeldy, Perthshire. Came to New York in 1906, where he acted
and directed in the theater before joining the Biograph Company, where he
assisted and acted for D. W. Griffith.

. . . From the standpoint of actors, the cast in the original [*Mutiny on the*
Bounty, 1935] was perfect. You couldn't have two more perfect people for
the parts of Fletcher Christian and Captain Bligh than Clark Gable and Charles
Laughton. Of course, Charles Laughton, he *was* Captain Bligh. It was the first
picture that he made in America, for Irving Thalberg, and one which I'll never
forget. When I asked him about his uniform he said, "Mr. Crisp, we took that
out of a British Museum glass case." He took it to a Savile Row tailor, where
the original uniform had been made a hundred and some years before, and
they remade the costume exactly, to fit Laughton. So when he strode down
the deck he looked like a little bantam cock, full of dignity. "Mr. Christian,
come here! How dare you, sir, address me in such a manner!" And Gable was
so offended that he hated the man because he had never heard that type of
talk before, and this photographed all through the picture. It was a wonderful
accident, because he just didn't like Laughton. Later though they became great
friends.
    Q. Does this mean that you didn't rehearse before shooting?
    A. Very little. You see, we saw this conflict and Frank Lloyd just turned
the cameras over and had it all taken right then. Of course it was superb.
                          ——Crisp, interviewed for *Films & Filming*, Dec 60

George C U K O R
Born in New York City in 1899. Started as assistant stage manager in Chicago
in 1918 and directed Broadway plays between 1926 and 1929. Worked as
dialogue director for Paramount, and for Universal on All Quiet on the Western Front *(1930), before co-directing with Cyril Gardner* Grumpy *and* The
Royal Family of Broadway *in 1930.*

You remember when Freddie March says [in *The Royal Family of Broadway*],
"Come on upstairs, everyone, while I take a bath"? Well, it occurred to me,
why don't we follow him all the way up that big staircase and take him to
the bath? It was quite a business, because those huge cranes didn't operate
electrically then as they do now—they were manually operated and very un-
wieldy. Still, we brought it off, we started on him downstairs, carried him and
the whole family upstairs, then cut as he entered the bedroom and followed
him to the shower. It was the beginning of a breakthrough for me, making the
camera much more mobile.
    I directed [*One Hour with You* (1932)] for about 2 weeks. . . . We shot
an English and a French version simultaneously. Then B. P. Schulberg, the
head of the studio, saw a lot of rushes and didn't like them. Lubitsch had now
finished shooting *The Man I Killed* [1932], but they didn't officially "remove"
me. What happened was goddamned agony for me. I was under contract and
had to stay on the picture, on the set, while Lubitsch took over. . . . He shot

things in a highly stylized way that is simply not my own. And we had a different approach to language. Lubitsch never really spoke English very well, and it didn't finally matter in his case, but it led him to things I couldn't do. For instance, he'd cast a very Middle Western actor like George Barbier to play the Emperor Franz Joseph. This is something he'd never have permitted in German, where he was sensitive to the nuances of speech. There was a very pretty German actress called Camilla Horn, and they cast her in some classical German part, and Lubitsch was very amused because she spoke what he called drugstore German.

What dictates your approach very often isn't you, but it's the situation— it's the text. It's what the play tells you. I envy directors who have everything written on a piece of paper and then just go up on set and do it. I can't make up dialogue, but I see things. The actors suggest things to me. . . . Some people are in themselves fascinating, you get them in a strong situation, and you do it simply, and it carries you along with it. Well, [John] Barrymore was that kind of person, and the situation in *Bill of Divorcement* [1932] was very strong. You just "ride it." You do it naturally, I suppose. Something—a clock or something goes off in your head and you think, "That's the way to do it." Sometimes you're not right; sometimes you're too slow. But if it's a good strong situation—and you have interesting people who carry it, and you're in the saddle . . .

[Irving Thalberg] was very knowledgeable and stimulating for a director. Very often, you work with so-called producers who are just damned nuisances. But Irving would make the most unconventional and interesting suggestions of all kinds. For instance, when we did the parting scene from *Romeo and Juliet* [1936], I thought it was very movingly done; and he said "No . . . no . . . no . . . they're too glum." "But," I said, "Irving, they're parting in the morning." And he said, "No, it could be done, in a sense, with a smile." He didn't mean a mechanical smile, he meant a tenderness, a chagrin d'amour . . . a noble and romantic way to say good-bye.

———Cukor, interviewed in *Cukor & Co.* (NY, 1971)

At the time we did *Camille* [1937] Robert Taylor was an up-and-coming young star; he wasn't all that inexperienced. . . .

He worked in very harmoniously with Garbo. She saw to that—although, like all silent-picture people, she liked to tell herself stories about the character she was playing in order to preserve the illusion. It's a very curious thing; they involve themselves more deeply in their parts that way, it becomes less artificial. As a result, she was rather distant with him and he, a very nice young man, was rather hurt.

"You know," she told me, "I do that so I can always tell myself stories about the character I'm playing, whereas if I got to know him too well it would only confuse the images I've been making of myself as *La dame aux camélias* and of Armand."

———Cukor, interviewed by Gavin Lambert for *On Cukor* (NY, 1972)

When M-G-M bought the rights to *The Philadelphia Story* [1940], they made a recording of a stage performance of the play. The idea was to find out where the laughs came. After the picture was made, we checked it against the re-cording and the laughs came quite differently. In the theater all the comedy was in Phil Barry's verbal wit, but in the movie a lot of it was visual, reactions, pieces of business, and so on. That's why I believe in letting comedy "happen" on the screen. When people complain about audience laughter drowning out a funny moment in a movie, I tell them, "Well, you can always go and see it again." It's a very pleasing complaint. The alternative is to go for something mechanical, and you can see the dire results of canned laughter on TV. The actors know the value of comedy, but they have to let it out in a fresh, ap-parently improvised way. Kate Hepburn had done *The Philadelphia Story* on the stage, and there were a couple of scenes with serious overtones in which she wept. I suggested for the movie she didn't weep. She was doubtful at first, then she tried—and it came out much fresher.

The first thing in transferring plays to the screen is not to discombobulate the original, you mustn't tear it apart. On the other hand, you can't just film the actors speaking their lines. You have to find a new "movement" for the screen, and that starts in the writing. Donald Ogden Stewart, who was a friend of Phil Barry's, adapted *The Philadelphia Story* with the greatest modesty and unselfishness. He wrote in a couple of original scenes, but very much in the manner of Barry. He served the thing, he didn't try to star himself, and yet people realized what a subtle piece of work he'd done, because he won the Oscar for the best screen adaptation that year.

——Cukor, interviewed for *Cukor & Co.* (NY, 1971)

The first of the films we [with Ruth Gordon and Garson Kanin] did together was *A Double Life* [1947], for his own company. It was a very happy and very equal collaboration, Ruth and Garson worked very closely together—no ques-tion of a writer trying to get his wife a job. Garson was a brilliant playwright and screenwriter and had the enormous advantage of knowing his metier very well—he'd already directed some successful comedies. Many of the lovely directorial touches in our films together were in the script. (I know this won't sit well with those people who believe in the *auteur* theory, but these films just didn't have one *auteur*.) Ruth and Garson lived in New York then, but they would come out here for long stretches of time and write, and we'd have readings here and they'd stay for the rehearsals. An interesting thing, in these days of improvisation, was how we did the ad libs. I wanted them to sound improvised, but I didn't believe in actually improvising them. Sometimes when I was shooting a scene with several characters, a party scene or something, and we needed a few ad libs, the actors would try them and I felt they didn't work. So I called the Kanins on the phone and told them the problem, and they'd say, "All right," and call me back a little later and I'd write them down. Sometimes these ad libs were just general, but sometimes I felt they had to be more specific. For the dinner party scene in *Adam's Rib* [1949], when a lawyer and his wife are entertaining other judges and legal people with their wives, you couldn't have them just saying, "Oh, good evening!" For things like this I'd call Ruth and Garson and tell them where the scene was going. Later, I was very pleased when people said about that scene how much they liked the small talk. I'm a great believer in that.

——Cukor, interviewed for Gavin Lambert's *On Cukor* (NY, 1972)

Q. So you're not like Hitchcock, then, who feels that once the scenario and dialogues are written the film is all wrapped up—that the actual filming is mere mechanics.

A. Well, Hitchcock is an absolute master. An absolute master. And what you say is very much his style. He's a master of well-thought-out effects. But between you and me I'm not quite sure that he is telling the complete truth. He must improvise with performances sometimes. There was a picture of his called *Suspicion* [1941] where Joan Fontaine gave the most extraordinary performance. Now, I can't believe that that was all mechanical—all planned out ahead of time. Very often it is, especially in his case . . . but not always. He is hiding things from you; he doesn't say how he works, how he achieves effects —easier to say it was all planned in the script and all the rest is mechanics.

For example, we started out with Harry Stradling, who is, by the way, a very talented man. I said to him, "Harry, these sets are well painted, the colors are perfect as they are and we don't want any more color of any kind . . . no filter!" He's rather tough and said that he wouldn't put any color in. Well, when I saw the rushes I discovered that he had snuck a little color in—some little nuances way in the back. So I said to him again, "No color, Harry. No color!" He finally got the idea that I meant business. The set was beautiful, and there was no need to jazz it up with any more color.

Q. What picture was this?

A. *My Fair Lady.* But he was very good about this finally. Cameramen get into all kinds of habits and one has to watch them very carefully. It's best to have someone with an open mind who won't put in all sorts of boring shadows and things like that. You have to give these men their head because they're artists—you have to stimulate them, not let them fall back on habits.

Q. One has the impression that you do quite a bit of documenting before starting a picture. You certainly did for *My Fair Lady,* in any case.

A. Yes, the groundwork must be well gone over. You must be familiar with the climate of your subject down to the smallest details. When I am going to do a picture on New York, I go to New York and look all around, all around. I look at locales with different eyes because when you know you are going to do a film you see things altogether differently, with different eyes. I delve into the texture of life and reality.

For instance, when we were preparing *The Actress* [1953] we went to see an old house that served as a model for the one in the film. It was a wonderful house and had a kitchen with 6 doors. We used that kitchen . . . not exactly the same way, but almost. Reality must be observed, then transmuted. If I were going to film this hotel room I would begin to see it with new eyes. I would look all around, see that newspaper over there, those books. Mind you, I couldn't film it just as it is—I would make notes in my mind about the casual bits of reality and then re-create the whole thing.

You can rehearse up to a certain point, but not too far. For example, Rex Harrison . . . I would not let him rehearse. During rehearsals he had a tendency to give too much of himself and there wasn't enough left for the real thing. Rehearsals are just meant for going through the mechanics of the thing. In the actual being before the camera something must be discovered, there must be an electricity there that can only come the first time something is done. Before, you just go through the motions and let yourself go when your time comes. . . . When you are before the camera things should "happen." Good people will vary it every time, for every take . . . make it fresh, give little changes each time. You know how some dumb actresses will say: "I can't do it unless I believe it." Well, there's truth in that. If you have too much rehearsal it becomes mechanical.

I never tell them what they should do. I coax, persuade, push sometimes. But it's important to let them discover reactions and feelings in the character they're playing. Everything is not perfectly laid out ahead of time, and on the set I'm not a dictator.

——Cukor, interviewed for *Film Culture*, Fall 64

Q. I'd like to ask you about the [scene in *A Star Is Born* (1954)] where the agent goes to visit Mason in the sanitarium. It has such a strange and chilling atmosphere.

A. I'll tell you where I got that from. Years ago, when I was going to direct *Camille* [1937], I went to see Jack Barrymore about playing De Varville, the part Henry Daniell finally played. Jack had put himself into some kind of home in Culver City to stop drinking. He was a friend of mine, and I went to take the script to him. It was an old frame house that called itself a rest home. I went into some dreary, depressing room. . . . Then Jack came in, with a sort of aide called Kelly. He took us into a gloomy sitting room and said, "Can we sit in here, Kelly? Nobody's going to come through and disturb us by pretending he's Napoleon." I reported this episode to David Selznick, who was preparing the first *A Star Is Born* [1937] with William Wellman. They liked the scene so much they included it in the picture. Then, years later, I found myself redoing it.

We had a problem at first with Micawber [in *David Copperfield* (1935)]. I wanted Charles Laughton, who wasn't keen to do it, but we persuaded him. He devised a marvelous makeup and *looked* perfect, but it turned out he just didn't have the geniality or the innocence for the part. We got on very well— in spite of his strange habits, such as a terrific prejudice concerning Jews and needing strange offstage noises to get himself in the mood for acting. He was the first actor I encountered who prepared to make a laughing entrance by going around doing *ha-ha!* sounds for hours. But it didn't work out. We shot for about a week, then he withdrew.

Q. And you got W. C. Fields. In spite of being an outsider in the cast, he worked brilliantly.

A. He was really born to play it, even though he'd never played a real character role before—that rare combination of the personality and the part.

Q. Were there any problems in Fields's having been an act rather than an actor?

A. He was charming to work with; his suggestions and ad libs were always in character. There was a scene in which he had to sit at a desk writing, and he asked me if he could have a cup of tea on the desk. When he got agitated, he dipped his pen into the teacup instead of the inkwell. Another time he was sitting on a high stool and asked for a wastepaper basket so he could get his feet stuck in it. Physically he wasn't quite right, wasn't bald, as Dickens describes Micawber—but his spirit was perfect.

——Cukor in Gavin Lambert's *On Cukor* (NY, 1972)

Paul CZINNER (1890–1972)
Born in Budapest; began his film career in Vienna and Berlin, and emigrated to Britain in 1933. His best-known films, beginning with Nju *(1924) starred his wife, Elisabeth Bergner. After successfully filming ballet and opera performances at Covent Garden, he proposed to film performances of Shakespeare at Stratford and the Old Vic:*

My method has several advantages over a specially made film. The actors don't have to take any instruction in film technique.

They just play their roles in the normal way—and leave the rest to me, my 11 cameras and 350 technicians. We can shoot for as long as an hour without interruption.

——Czinner, interviewed for *News Chronicle*, 8 Jan 60

D

Bebe [Virginia] D A N I E L S   (1901–1971)
Partner in Harold Lloyd's short comedies before her "formal" career began with Cecil B. DeMille.

Dorothy [Arzner] used to hold the film up to the light and cut it in the hand. . . . Dorothy used to cut as we went on those comedies, and it was very helpful to see the cut rushes in the morning. We could keep the pace right. We might have slowed down as we went along, but seeing the cut rushes kept us to the right speed.
　　　　——Daniels, interviewed (1963) for *The Parade's Gone By* (NY, 1968)

At that time [of *Rio Rita* (1929)] it was technically impossible to dub sound, so we had to take an entire orchestra when we went on location. In the open patio scenes the air temperature was often over 100 degrees and the heat did peculiar things to the violins and cellos. Almost all the dancers fainted from the heat, but still the film was completed in 24 shooting days.
　　　　——Daniels, interviewed by Patricia Keighran, 1933(?)

William D A N I E L S   (1895–1970)
As a child, his family brought him from Cleveland to Los Angeles, where he attended the University of Southern California. Continuing his boyhood hobby of photography, his first job in 1917 was as an assistant cameraman. His first work as full cameraman was in short comedies, but he returned to the job of second cameraman in order to work with Stroheim on Blind Husbands *(1919). He followed Stroheim to MGM, where he photographed both* Greed *and* The Merry Widow *(1925), before becoming the permanent cameraman for Garbo's films.*

We were on [*Foolish Wives* (1921)] for some 13 months. Von Stroheim was terribly, terribly slow; there would be constant rehearsal; he would select "types," too, for parts, rather than accomplished actors or actresses. It was his job (he was proud of that) to be more or less a Svengali, to turn the "types" into "great performers." That took a terrible lot of time, *endless* time. . . . The actors and actresses just didn't complain; it was hell for them, but they were ambitious, and would do anything to succeed. Some he would bully, some not.

I remember we had a little girl called Malvina Polo; there was a sequence in which von Stroheim went to her bedroom and there was a rape involved, and she becomes hysterical. We worked all night long on that one scene. She wasn't an accomplished actress, and finally he worked her so hard that she actually became hysterical. That was when he got what he wanted. It was his technique, you might say, to get novices and drive them to the point at which they lived a part, since they couldn't "act" it. Extraordinary, but far too costly, and not practical in any sense of the word.

I experimented with some halolike effects round hair in that picture. I used a thin net like a lady's stocking over the lens. The effect was of a sort of vignette. You could burn it out with a cigarette into different shapes. There was one scene in which we had a monk in a cabin by candlelight; the candlelight made a little crosslight, and von Stroheim liked that.

. . . We were seven months on [*Greed* (1923)]. Much of it was very hard going. We were six weeks in Death Valley during the summer—July and August. It was 132 degrees under the shade of an umbrella. Of course, being a realist [Stroheim] really *had* to have it hot! . . .

We used natural interiors in the scenes in San Francisco. It was one of the first times they had been used. The company rented one whole building. We had a big scene they still talk about: the wedding of McTeague and the girl, and during the wedding procession you see a funeral cortege going by, through the window. In other scenes you see the streetcar passing. It was done without process. There was a problem of getting a correct balance of light between interior and exterior so that it looked as though all the scenes were lit by daylight only, and getting enough light on the people to balance the exposure was hell.

Then we got into the sound period, and the cameras in those butchers' iceboxes. And very few people knew anything about editing sound: there is a scene at the beginning of *Anna Christie* [1930] they often refer to in which the camera travels a long, long way across a wharf, and we had mist and water lapping. Well, the reason for long scenes like that was they just weren't sure how to sound edit!

————Daniels, interviewed for *Hollywood Cameramen* (London, 1970)

Miss Garbo naturally dominates any picture she is in, but she never does it deliberately. She neither struts nor poses. She is a woman of extreme simplicity, on or off the screen.

Another thing characteristic of Miss Garbo is that she never demands favor when she is in front of the camera. If a scene belongs to another actor in the cast, he gets everything he deserves and always with her cooperation.

I have even seen her turn her back to the camera and remain obscurely in the background to give the other actor his opportunity on the screen. In photographing her, we always use big close-ups or long shots. We never compromise with intermediate or full-figure shots. She does things not so much by gestures or postures, but by little things in her eyes. That is why she is superb in the close-ups.

She is good in the long shots because she has such a lovely walk. In fact, she almost runs; the most beautiful walk you ever saw—almost like floating through the air. . . .

She takes direction very easily. Whatever the director demands, she responds wholeheartedly. Should the director be indefinite about his plans, she will outline them for him. I have never known anyone to work as rapidly and readily as she does. . . .

Because of her methodical working program we have developed a very efficient system in filming her pictures, and rarely do we have to retake scenes.
———Daniels, in *Picturegoer's Famous Films Supplement,* 1935

Danielle D A R R I E U X
Born 1917 in Bordeaux. Her film career began at the age of 14.

It is rather unusual to find a director who asks a lot of the actor. Because you don't know what you have inside. The director must know. He mustn't leave you to your own experience, because that's nothing. He has to take from you, but what it needs is a gift. You should give something to be able to take. Ophuls never asked directly for things, never said "Be more sad." He suddenly would speak to you about something completely outside the woman and the film. He would tell you a funny story or a sad story, and you thought "Why is he talking like that to me? It's not the moment." And you realize it's just to give you the mood. He was very funny, very intelligent. [Claude Autant-] Lara is more direct; Ophuls was more complicated. He was very curious, wanted to know everything about everybody. He was full of life and he was rather young to die. At 53, I think. But now people say he was a great, great, great director, and if they'd said that when he was alive, maybe he wouldn't be dead.
———Darrieux, interviewed for *The Times,* 16 Oct 71

Jules D A S S I N
Born in Middletown, Connecticut in 1911. Worked in the theater and directed short films at MGM before making his first feature, Nazi Agent (1942).

. . . Making [*Du rififi chez les hommes* (1955)] was very difficult, on account of the language problem. The real trouble was in communicating with the technicians. With the actors, it was all right. With actors you don't need language to communicate. But in talking to the technicians, it really was a difficult job. I sometimes ask myself whether so much of the film was silent because of my own lack of French.

. . . I did plan [*Uptight* (1968)] beforehand, how I would place the groups. But I drove my script clerk to complete madness by an enormous amount of cheating and recomposing, changing the positions of people quite arbitrarily on the floor. I wanted the character of Corbin [Dick Williams], the real leader of the militants, to be always surrounded with African tonalities, and I didn't have those in the set, which was a bowling alley. So I just plucked actors who wore different clothes and grouped them around him all the time. The script clerk would say, "But *he* was *there* in the last shot, he *can't* be *here* in this one." I just didn't pay any attention to that. So there was cheating and improvisation; and then as I went on, that entire sequence was "cut" as it was shot: there was not a single extra angle or added frame. It grew out of the rehearsal. Again, in the trial scene, I knew broadly how I was going to place the people, but out of the rehearsal came the emphasis and the cutting and the close-ups. In other words, I plan the cutting continuity as I shoot.

——Dassin, interviewed for *Films & Filming*, March 70

Delmer DAVES
Born in San Francisco, 1904. Studied law at Stanford University. Entered films in 1927 as assistant prop man for James Cruze.

It was an experimental film [*Dark Passage* (1947)]. I was the first director as far as I know to use the Arriflex camera. The reason was that this was the first one captured from the Nazis and we rented it from the War Department. The camera *was* Bogart for the first 4 or 5 reels of the picture. We had to invent techniques for handling the camera as if it were a human being. We even invented a shoulder holster so that the camera operator could imitate the walk of a man. In the fight scene, for instance, I had to use the left arm of one man and the right arm of another on each side of the camera in order to give the illusion that you were looking at your own arms. Every shot in that film was a question mark.

In every film I do I like to take on a new challenge. On *3:10 to Yuma* [1957] I studied many of the Westerns that people had made and I discovered that there was one aspect that was not true to my own experience. When I lived with the Navajo Indians for 3 months, I got to know and feel the atmosphere of the desert very well. What was principally wrong in the previous films it seemed to me were the shadow effects. In the desert the shadows are so intense that they're not comparable to other areas. So I got together with the cameraman and tried to create a visual impression that would reflect the feeling of drought. We experimented ahead of time, before we started shooting the film, by not filling the shadows with reflected light. Normally when filming in the desert they use reflectors to lighten the shadows. In *3:10 to Yuma* when a man walks into a shadow he's apt to walk into a black silhouette. It worked so well that when I came to do *Cowboy* [1958] I had the same cameraman, Charles Lawton, Jr., and there we again let the blacks stay. Only this time we were working in color. In the campfire scenes you'll notice that the only areas that are lit at all are the areas that would be lit in reality by the fire. The rest was black as it is in the desert. The use of these blacks in color was radical for that time, which was 1957.

——Daves, interviewed for *Hollywood: The Haunted House* (London, 1967)

Bette DAVIS [Ruth Elizabeth Davis]
Born 1908 in Lowell, Massachusetts. After two years of roles in Broadway plays, brought to Hollywood in 1931.

While I spent countless days posing in bathing suits and evening dresses for fan magazines, I spent my evenings at Grauman's or the Pantages watching the movies from a new vantage point. If I couldn't learn on the set I'd learn from the finished pictures themselves. . . . The difference between the media, intellectually understood, now dawned on me fully. I knew the moment I used a microphone that I didn't have to project my voice as much. I knew the moment I was in the limited range of the camera's eye that my movements were more restricted; but my directors at this point simply told me where to stand. The finer points I had to glean for myself. . . .

[In working on *All This and Heaven Too* (1940)] Tola [Litvak] planned every move beforehand and the camera was his God. I thought of Willie Wyler who would get an inspiration and, on being informed that the camera was already in position, shout, "To hell with the camera. It's the slave, not me!" Tola had it all on paper. His method of directing was never to my taste. There was not the spontaneity or flexibility I found in Wyler.

——Davis, in *The Lonely Life* (NY, 1962)

Emile DE ANTONIO
A teacher and artists' manager before entering his film career.

Words are very important in my film [*The Year of the Pig*, 1969] and in all of my work, and that's how I do the editing: I start with the transcription of the sound track and put all of these pages up on the walls of the big editing rooms where I work and begin to assemble the papers before the film: that's how the structure begins; then I take the film, and I go endlessly from the text to the film and from the film to the text, and I change them around, switching the sheets of paper with each other. I have a good visual memory. When you have so much filmed material, you think of a shot you want and the list of shots is no use because no list of shots can describe everything with precision (you know, the list of shots says: buffaloes, peasants, airplanes, medium shot of buffaloes and peasants). Even if it's well drawn up, it's not as exact as your own memory.

——De Antonio, interviewed for *Positif*, Feb 70; trans. by
Thomas Waugh, *Jump Cut*, No. 10/11

Philippe DE BROCA
Born 1933 in Paris. Worked on documentary films and as assistant director before making Les Jeux de l'amour (1959).

When I was 9, an age when little boys want to be doctors or lawyers, I wanted to be a director. My parents thought this was a funny joke. But I couldn't have lived without making films. My family sent me to the École Technique to study photography. During [my army service], I spent 2 years as a newsreel cameraman, then stayed on another year shooting a documentary on the elephant trail. It was Algeria that shifted my interest to comedy. I decided the real world was just too ugly.

I came back to Paris. I knew that *now* I had to break into film production. So I walked up and down the Champs-Élysées knocking on the doors of every film office. Every secretary knew me! I said I would work for nothing. Then the New Wave hit—and it was a lucky moment. France was suddenly filled with bright young directors. I got a job as assistant on François Truffaut's first film, *The 400 Blows* [1959]. Later I worked as assistant director to Claude Chabrol on *The Cousins* [1958], *Le Beau Serge* [1958], and *Leda* [1959]. After that I said to myself, I cannot be an assistant anymore . . . everyone was young and enthusiastic, and the first directors to succeed immediately helped their friends. Chabrol himself produced my first 2 films with his profits from *The Cousins.* . . .

Jean-Pierre Cassel in *The Love Game* [1959] was really playing two sides of myself—first the fantasist who is crushed when he's forced to acknowledge reality, then the farceur who simply refuses to succumb. Cassel is an excellent comedian who did 3 films for me and I remember telling him, "I'll make *all* my movies with you." Of course I did not. But for those first movies, he expressed exactly what I wanted. When I worked with Truffaut on *The 400 Blows* I was impressed by the rapport between Truffaut and the young actor [Léaud] who played the lead. It was as if Truffaut were directing himself. That must have been in the back of my mind when I chose Cassel.

I made *That Man from Rio* [1964] for political reasons. To be free, to have the money to make what I wanted to. To do this, I needed a very big success. Even so, there were problems. No one wanted to produce *Rio*. It took me 6 months to find a producer and then 5 to write the script. That kind of adventure story always seems very easy, but it isn't. . . . I had certain scenes I wanted in . . . Jean-Paul [Belmondo] escaping on a skyscraper and running through the jungle . . . but the problem was *how*. It is a very naïve film. I think that is why it worked. It won awards but I was not in love with it. It was the kind of movie I wanted to see when I was 14.

After *Rio* I had my freedom, which is vital to a director. In France we have formed a society of directors because we want even *more* freedom. When I say I want to make a film, that means write and direct and edit. There can't be another way.

———De Broca, interviewed for *Transatlantic Review* (1969)

Henri D E C A E
Born in Saint Denis in 1915. Military service as cameraman for French Air Force.

If it is wrong to impose a style (the worst criticism being the statement that the film is mediocre, but that its photography is remarkable), the cameraman is nevertheless of great importance. Astuteness is often necessary. For instance in *Quelle joie de vivre* [1961], I had to finish in the middle of the night a scene that had begun under the dazzling sun; or I had to complete a scene started during the day in a real tunnel in a reconstructed tunnel in the studio that night. On the other hand during the shooting of *Château en enfer* [1969] in Yugoslavia, I was forced to film a snow scene (with a sad atmosphere) while, on this 15 January, there was a magnificent sun.

Naturally, a cameraman must follow evolution. For a cameraman now evolution means more spontaneity in the framing, in the actors' behavior. It is actually out of the question to resort to chalk marks on the floor. Personally, I relearn by watching films. A film such as *Macadam Cowboy* represents a treasure of instruction; however, I would rather use a large scale, such as 70 mm, which allows besides its good definition, to emphasize details that other formats blur. On one image of *La Tulipe noire* [1963], for instance, one notices much more clearly a Dresden porcelain vase than the characters. I am also in favour of color—everything that is possible in black and white is also feasible in color, but the opposite is impossible. In color one can for example obtain a metallic photographic quality, such as in *Le Samourai* [1967]. How do you get that? Very simple, little light and "wide opening" in the studio, overcast sky for open air shots which makes the color slightly duller and softens the contrasts.

We should not forget to mention the work in the laboratory. There, too, the light must be calculated. If one can retouch a face by means of vertical light, it means emphasizing the hollow cheeks of an actor. As we have turned to the actors, I would like to make two acknowledgments—First of all the relationship between the cameraman and the actor is a rather loose one, our functions being very different. On the sound stage everything hampers an actor. As a matter-of-fact, the actor comes only for the shooting and then he is in the hands of the director. If I have to tell the actor something, I tell the director who can communicate it to the actor.

———Decae, interviewed for *Les Lettres françaises*, 22 July 70

Cecil Blount D E M I L L E (1881–1959)
As young men, Cecil and his elder brother William acted and wrote professionally, often under Belasco's direction. By 1912 Cecil's friendship with Jesse Lasky and Samuel Goldfish (Goldwyn) led them to consider the idea of making films. With a cameraman, Alfredo Gandolfi, an experienced East Coast director, Oscar Apfel, and a reluctant stage star, Dustin Farnum, they arrived in Los Angeles on December 20. After finding locations, they began their first production, The Squaw Man (1913), *from the play by Edwin Milton Royle.*

Imagine, the horizon is your stage limit and the sky your gridiron. No height limit, no close-fitting exits, no conserving of stage space, just the whole world open to you as a stage; 1,000 people in a scene do not crowd your accommodations. It was a new feeling, a new experience, and I was enamored with the way Mr. Apfel went about focusing his camera, getting his actors and actresses within range of the lens and the way in which our cameraman followed every move, studied the sun, tried to dodge a cloud, edged his camera into a more advantageous position, and then the artists . . . I felt inspired, I felt that I could do things which the confines of a theater would not permit.

———De Mille, interviewed for the New York *Dramatic Mirror*, 1913

William D E M I L L E (1878–1955)
Born in Washington, D.C.

With such pictures as those in which I specialize . . . pictures that depend considerably for their value on the consistent and progressive development of character, rather than mere physical action, producing in continuity is tremendously effective as well as a great help. . . .

The method of starting with scene No. 1 and proceeding numerically to the conclusion of the picture is of benefit to both players and director. The players' characterizations become well sustained; they take a greater interest in their work as they realize it growing consistently with each day's effort. And the director is able to get a better slant on his story as he watches the whole thing grow and take definite shape from day to day.

———De Mille, quoted in Milne, *Motion Picture Directing* (NY, 1922)

Jacques D E M Y
Born in Pont-Château in 1931. First long film was Lola (1960).

[On *Les Parapluies de Cherbourg* (1964)] Michel [Legrand] and I found that the best solution was to meet every day at home where there's a piano, and to work from 2 o'clock in the afternoon through till 8. We'd have dinner together, talking over what we'd done, and then work till 1 in the morning. We did that every day for nearly a year. I had the lines ready, Michel would read over the scene, we'd talk about it in musical terms, trying to fit the music to the feeling of the scene, looking for the right melody. We'd light on the one that seemed the most suitable and then I'd try to adapt the lines to it. After that, I looked for actors and Michel looked for singers whose voices complemented the faces of the actors. The singers recorded the whole film with the actors present. The actors took away records of the sound track and learned their lines in front of mirrors and so on, so that they could synchronize their lips exactly with the singing. The whole film was shot with playback sound.

———Demy, interviewed for *The Sunday Times Magazine,* 17 Jan 65

Vittorio D E S E T A
Born in Palermo in 1923.

I don't feel uprooted [in France]. On the other hand, it would be impossible for me to work in Germany. I have imagined this film [*L'Invitata* (1970)] in French. Besides, I think that in 30 years there will be a European community for artistic matters. . . .

Does one know beforehand when a writer will write his tenth chapter? No. So why do you want a director to remain faithful to what has been written in the script? What strikes me is this fear of change. People are afraid of changing; they are panic-stricken by the slightest change in the working plan. Fortunately, life is unforeseeable. Some people say, "But you have a script." It is just because everything is planned that it has to be changed. Even the interpreters, such as the musicians and actors, have the right to contribute a personal vision of the author they interpret. One can plan the construction of the Concorde, but in artistic matters this planning takes on monstrous proportions. One forgets too easily that a filmmaker does not produce canned foods. I would like to work again the way I did when I produced short films. . . .

———De Seta, interviewed for *Les Lettres françaises,* 15 Oct 69

Vittorio D E S I C A (1902–1974)
Born in Sora, Italy. A successful stage career before acting in films from 1932.
Directed his first film, Rose scarlette, *in 1940.*

What hit Zavattini and me, at the end of the war, was human solitude.

The real sense of my films is the search of the human solidarity, the fight against egoism and indifference; in *Sciuscia'* [1946] the theme was treated in tragedy. . . .

If the end had been foreseen by me, the film would not have had such a hopeless air. Hope should have been the conclusion. It is the last time that I accept the imposition of the producers. But before *Sciuscia'* I had not such a trust in my possibilities. Now I prefer to leave a film rather than mutilating it.

——De Sica, interviewed by Pier Luigi Lanza

I found that nobody wants to finance my films, so I have to finance them myself. I do this by selling my services as an actor. By appearing in 5 films I can make enough money to support myself and my family and to make one film of my own. It is a great luxury for me to make films and like all luxuries you have to pay for it heavily.

——De Sica, interviewed for *The Evening Standard,* 25 May 57

The filming of *Sciuscia'* . . . was very simple. This little fellow, with the name that was sad and picturesque at the same time, was a legacy from the war. For a whole year, I followed 2 genuine shoeshine boys as they went about their eventful everyday life. They were called Scimmietta and Cappellone. I watched them by the hour going along with their humble affairs in the Via Veneto and did actually come upon them taking a ride on the carousel of the Villa Borghese. One day, after the theft of a gas mask, Cappellone ended up in prison. The drama, not invented by me but staged by life itself, was drawing to its fatal conclusion. I had merely to relate what I had seen and felt during that year. Zavattini [the co-writer], too, recognized the melancholy poetry of that generation of children led astray by the war and provided me with the magnificent theme everyone now knows so well. This is how *Shoeshine* was born. . . .

This method, which I call "being faithful to the character," is perhaps simply an exaggeration of the time-honored principle of acting which gives an overwhelming importance to the so-called *physique du rôle*. Only, in my films, the process of the interpretation is reversed: it is not the actor who lends the character a face which, however versatile he may be, is necessarily his own, but the character who reveals himself, sooner or later, in "that" particular face and in no other. It is not surprising if this face belongs, more often than not, to someone who exercises a profession far removed from that of acting. For instance in my *Umberto D.* [1952], as you may know, is a university professor and a well-known expert on Giotto. In *Bicycle Thief* [1948], Bruno's parents were a workman from the Breda district and a lady journalist who had come to interview me. . . .

——De Sica, in *Miracle in Milan* (NY, 1968)

I also have a dream which may only remain a dream because it is difficult for me to find money. It is to film a [novella] by Flaubert called "A Simple Heart."

It is the story of a servant and I believe it is a masterpiece. I think now I have a French producer interested but I am not sure. I have shown the book to many producers, but they are so vulgar. They do not realize that art has to be severe. It cannot be commercial. It cannot be for the producer, or even for the public. It has to be for oneself.

When I was in Hollywood, I had the same trouble. I wanted to make a film with Thornton Wilder called *Miracle in the Rain*. But we had a vulgar producer who wanted to change everything and in the end we had to give up. It is very difficult sometimes to persuade idiots to be sensible, you know.

———De Sica, interviewed for *The Guardian*, 1 July 72

For *Umberto D.* I try everywhere. I go to pensioners' institutions, to old people's homes. Eventually I meet Battisti in the street and I see he has the right physique for the part. He was a university professor at Florence and he was in Rome to take an examination at the University of Rome and to see Signor de Gasperi at the Ministry. I said, "My name is Vittorio De Sica," and it meant nothing to him. "I would like to offer you a part in a film." "You're mad." "It's an art film. A social film. A moral film. A film which is going to demonstrate the absolute absence of human solidarity and especially the solitude of an old person." "Listen, I'm here for an examination." "I'll wait. What time can I see you?" He told me 6. For fear of losing him I arrived at the university at 5 and I sat by his side during the examination. Then I went home with him because he had to wash, to get ready. I waited. We did a screen test, and he accepted the part against the advice of his colleagues at the university. We made a film. He was marvelous. Afterwards he went to Paris to give a lecture at the Sorbonne, but all the questions were about his experience in making the film.

———De Sica, interviewed for *The Times*, 15 July 72

The Garden of the Finzi-Continis [1971] continues in the style of *Umberto D.* (1951), which was my best and most severe picture. There were no compromises and concessions then; there were none on *The Garden of the Finzi-Continis* either. I was given absolute freedom to make the picture in my own style.

I lived through this period. The same feelings I experienced in life I transpose to the picture. That is a duty of the artist.

———De Sica, interviewed for *The Globe & Mail*, Toronto, 25 Dec 71

Adolph DEUTSCH
Born 1897.

Three Strangers [1946] presented many opportunities for the manipulation of recording qualities. Right in the introduction, for instance, where the close-ups of the principals were used, we decided to match the photographic proximity with a corresponding close pickup of the solo instruments. The image on the screen was big and the tone of the instrument was big. Following the title came the London atmosphere, Piccadilly circus at night, traffic and crowd noise. The music I had written attempted to sound British and at the same time to give the feeling of a lot of things going on simultaneously. Dave

[Forrest, sound engineer] and I agreed that we should attempt to get as much clarity of recording as possible, to bring out the counterrhythms and contrapuntal lines in the orchestra. Later on in the picture we had a scene on the bank of the Thames, a night shot, damp and foggy. The orchestration reflected this mood, which we further enhanced by using a very reverberant pickup. The result was a diffused shimmer of sound like the distant murmur of a metropolis, a perfect accompaniment for the occasion.

——Deutsch, in *Hollywood Quarterly*, Jan 46

I. A. L. DIAMOND [Itek Dommnici]
Born in Ungeny, Romania, 1920. Family came to the U.S. in 1929. Attended Columbia University, where he worked on 4 of the Columbia Varsity Shows.

Q. Milos Forman said recently in reference to his film *Taking Off* [1971] that he likes working with 2 writers in addition to himself because, since they rarely agree, there's always a majority of 2 over one on any given point.

A. Well, the way I work with Billy [Wilder] is that if we disagree violently about something, we throw out both approaches and try to look for a third approach. And a good part of the time, we find something better than either of us had considered originally.

Q. Did you and Billy preview your films and recut them according to audience reaction?

A. No, hardly at all. For one thing, Billy shoots very tightly. The film is designed to be cut a certain way. There's very little leftover footage, and very little coverage of scenes. So usually we'd end up taking 4 minutes out of a picture. We never had preview cards. We just did it to get a feel of the audience and how they were reacting to it. I remember the preview of *Some Like It Hot* [1958]. We took it to the Bay Theater in Pacific Palisades and there was a Tennessee Williams picture playing on the same bill. It was a middle-aged audience, and the picture just lay there. Nothing happened. And I remember when we came out, Joe Mankiewicz was there and he put his arm around Billy's shoulder and said, "Well, it happens to all of us." That was on a Wednesday night. Now, without cutting a frame, we took it out again on Friday night to the Village Theater in Westwood, where there was a young UCLA audience, and the house came down. And it was the same picture. Nothing was changed. Not one frame. So go tell about previews.

——Diamond, interviewed for *The Screenwriter Looks at the Screenwriter* (NY, 1972)

Marlene DIETRICH [Maria Magdalena Dietrich von Losch]
Born in Berlin in 1901. Acted in the theater before her first film, Der Kleine Napoleon (1923).

People give me all the credit for *The Blue Angel* [1930], but it was all Von Sternberg's. I didn't want to sing "Falling in Love Again" like that. I wanted to sing it quite differently, sentimental with lots of German soul. But not at all. He showed me how to sing it. At the time I thought the film was awful and vulgar and I was shocked at the whole thing. In those days you did as the director told you and did not complain. Remember, I was a well-brought-up German girl.

——Dietrich, interviewed for *The Evening Standard,* 2 June 72

I didn't know what I was doing—I just tried to do what [Von Sternberg] told me. I remember in *Morocco* [1930], I had a scene with Cooper—and I was supposed to go to the door, turn and say a line like, "Wait for me," and then leave. And Von Sternberg said, "Walk to the door, turn, count to ten, say your line and leave." So I did and he got very angry. "If you're so stupid that you can't count slowly, then count to twenty-five." And we did it again. I think we did it 40 times, until finally I was counting probably to 50. And I didn't know why. I was annoyed. But at the premiere of *Morocco*—at Grauman's Chinese Theater—when this moment came and I paused and then said, "Wait for me," the audience burst into applause. Von Sternberg knew they were waiting for this—and he made them wait and they loved it.

Yes. I was terrific in that [*Touch of Evil,* 1957]. I think I never said a line as well as the last line in that movie—"What does it *matter* what you say about people. . . ?" Wasn't I good there? I don't know why I said it so well. And I *looked* so good in that dark wig. It was Elizabeth Taylor's. My part wasn't in the script, you know, but Orson called and said he wanted me to play a kind of gypsy madam in a border town, so I went over to Paramount and found that wig. It was very funny, you know, because I had been crazy about Orson—in the forties when he was married to Rita and when we toured doing his magic act—I was just crazy about him—we were great friends, you know, but nothing. . . . Because Orson doesn't like blonde women. He only likes dark women. And suddenly when he saw me in this dark wig, he looked at me with new eyes. Was this Marlene?

——Dietrich, interviewed for *Esquire,* Jan 73

Walt DISNEY (1901–1966)
Born in Chicago. After army service returned to Kansas City and set up an animated cartoon studio with Ub Iwerks.

In the days of *Steamboat Willie* [1928] it was picture first then we used to put the sound on afterwards and in those days you couldn't do what we call dubbing today where you could mix a lot of tracks and it wasn't yet science that you could get away with so we used to have to do everything at one time . . . and we used to have to run the cartoons . . . we'd have the fellows with the sound effects, we'd have the people with the voices, we'd have the orchestra going, and everybody had to synchronize . . . keep that thing right on the button . . . and we had a way of doing it though . . . we had a little kind of a little beep that worked up and down and it was so many of those beeps, you know, and they were all musicians working for me so they could follow those beats . . . when it came to a certain number of beats they would go WHAM . . . or they would go BANG . . . or they would do this or they would pop one of these popguns, you know . . . and they would always fit. . . .

——Disney, interviewed for "Telescope Program," CBC-TV

Stanley D O N E N
Born in Columbia, South Carolina, 1924, a Broadway chorus boy in 1940; as
Gene Kelly's choreographic assistant, went to Hollywood in 1942 with a cast
of Best Foot Forward. *For next 5 years worked as dance director or assistant*
on 14 films.

There's a tendency in our business not to upset any well-geared organization.
Under that theory, I would have remained a dance director. But Metro was
willing to take a chance and the studio let [Gene Kelly and me] co-direct
On the Town [1949] instead of merely doing dance routines. And that established me as a director.

————Donen, interviewed for publicity, 1965

Clive D O N N E R
Born 1920 in London. Entered films as a cutter in 1942.

. . . People talk about improvisation as though it were like the Method, something you lay on a scene. As though, if you improvised a scene, and this was
a technique which you used well, it would come out as something that was
evident and good, creatively viable. I don't think improvisation is that. I think
it's just a technique. It depends a lot on the actors concerned, on how flexible
they are, on how uninhibited they are, on the nature of the scene, on how
important the scene is. There may be a scene in which I want to make certain
plot points and character establishment points very carefully. In that case, I
might very well not want to use those sorts of improvisation techniques; they
might lead me into something which would blur the necessary clarity of the
points that I believe ought to be made in the scene.

————Donner, interviewed for *Movie*, Fall 65

. . . Here is a play [*The Caretaker* (1963)] about 3 men who do nothing but
talk the whole time. But it was what was going on that was unsaid, between
the men, that was important. And therefore the way they were to move around
the scene, and their relationship to each other, gave me a style of shooting it
that arose literally from the text. Which is where it all has to come from
basically, whether it be a very set script or whether it's something as loose as
a few pieces of paper; it all comes from the text. And the style arose from the
texture of the piece. To me it was not a piece about claustrophobia, which is
what people went on about, but a piece about people being obsessed with
themselves. They each lived in their own little caissons, as it were. And when
they broke out to make contact with each other, then you had them face to
face; but the rest of the time they were moving around in a very, very limited
space, and stylistically there were very few problems. The danger I had to
avoid was the possibility of becoming overindulgent and pretentious in compositions. You know, with all that junk in that room, it would have been very
easy to have thrown in a great many arty compositions which would have no
significance to the people in the drama. The Pinteresque tensions, and the
primal battle for ascendancy, were manifestations of self-interest. So it was a
question of letting the actors play it naturally within that room. It was in a
derelict house in Hackney, which we took over for the filming. I mean, obvi-

ously, I blocked it out for them, but once that had been done they provided the pictures for me: they gave me the images. Rather than getting stuck into a "basic-two-shot-, over-shoulder-close-ups, single-close-ups" pattern . . . or into a sort of archaic rococo. It just happened . . . in the room there.

Of course, the silences are really the things that *make* that particular work of Pinter's. I remember Harold said to me one day, "You know, it's the shape of the pauses that's important." And once you've got that, then you have a series of fascinating images with three highly contrasting chracters: all of them give you a particular line on how you should photograph them, and where they should be in relation to one another, how close they should be to one another, whether they're facing one another or not.

. . . Aston, for example [Robert Shaw] moves very little, and when he does it's very slow and deliberate and for a very definite purpose. Davis the tramp [Donald Pleasence] is all over the place, never stops moving. Aston's extremely long speech, when he finally gets around to talking about himself, was in about 3 sections, 3 shots, each of which was very long in itself, because I didn't want to break up Robert's concentration: I thought he would give a better performance if he could have a run at a whole chunk of it. And in any case it seemed to me the right way to shoot it: the camera does move, the attitude between the camera and the actor changes, subtly, and from my point of view always with reason. In one part of the sequence the camera dollies right the way round from one profile to the other, fantastically slowly. I don't think it's disturbing: my fear was that it might be disturbing, but it seemed to me natural, as the man went through the trauma of this experience, for the spectator to examine different parts of his face. And because of the way that Nick Roeg lit it, once again ever so subtly, as the camera changed its view on him the planes of his face and the light and shade on his face also changed.

———Donner, interviewed for *Films & Filming*, July 69

Mark DONSKOY
Born 1901 in Odessa. Best known for his trilogy, The Childhood of Gorky (The Childhood of Gorky, *1938;* Among People, *1939;* My Universities, *1940):*

The idea of the whole film, the aim of each scene and image must be explained by the director to the child-actor in full detail, just as to an adult actor.

The director should not show the child how to act, or he will imitate the director, whose basic task it is to summon the *spontaneous* from the child. He need be shown no more than a hint that he can catch and develop for himself. That's how I worked with Alyosha Lyarsky, who plays the role of the boy Gorky. For example, it was very difficult for me to get sufficient emotion for the episodes that demanded the display of a fiery temperament. Lyarsky possessed considerable but concealed inner power and it was up to me in preparing these scenes to summon memories of his own life that related to the situations of his role; this had the effect of developing strong emotional responses.

Rehearsals with children are necessary, sometimes many rehearsals. But one must not film the child that day—or he will act without spontaneity. Generally in working with children it is very dangerous to overrehearse or over-instruct them. This happened with another talented boy, Igor Smirnov, who plays the role of Lenka, the cripple. Igor himself longs "to be an actor," and this caused his mother to interfere by energetically rehearsing with him at home. As a result of this "preparation" the boy would come to the studio so "drilled" that before he faced the camera he was played out. Every spontaneity and freshness was lost. We almost had to "remake" Igor in bringing back his childlike self.

———Donskoy, discussion in *Film Direction* (Moscow 1939)

Kirk D O U G L A S [Issur Danielovich Demsky]
Born 1916 in Amsterdam, New York. Worked in theater before making film debut in The Strange Love of Martha Ivers (1946):

But you got to fight for what you believe in. I remember in *The War Wagon* [1967], I fought with them for the nude scene. Remember where I was walking away from the camera bare-ass? I said that's the only honest way to shoot it. I'm in the sack, see, and John Wayne's knocking at the door, and we've already established that I wear a gun at all times. So we play the whole scene at the door, me with my gun on, and when I walk back to bed you see the gun is the only thing I'm wearing! Great! You put pants on the guy, the scene isn't honest anymore.

I'm not surprised, though, they wanted to destroy the scene. Dealing with Universal is always . . . well, they were the aces who got me where I lived on *Lonely Are the Brave* [1962]. I wanted to put it through a computer and came up with a nothing title. And things like that . . . And *A Lovely Way to Die* [1968] . . . I hated that one. . . . I said, from now on I'm only doing what I want to do. And now, after 50 pictures and the last 3 damn good ones, it's time to take inventory.

Kubrick once had this great idea. We'd make the world's greatest porno-graphic film. Spend millions on it. And then maybe only show it in one country, like Switzerland, and fly people in to see it. Kubrick. A great director. I thank him for so much that is good in *Paths of Glory* [1958] and *Spartacus* [1960]. You know, at one time with *Paths of Glory*, even Kubrick wanted to cop out. He wanted to rewrite the script, make it a sort of B picture, a commercial thing. But I'm glad we stood by our guns. There's a picture that will always be good, years from now. . . . Certain pictures have a universality of theme. *Champion* [1949] did.

———Douglas, interviewed for *Esquire*, Feb 70

. . . A lot of directors don't relate to the actors at all. . . . But Kazan is an actor's director. He feels for the actor. You sensed that he thought the actor was important. And it's because of that quality that he gets such terrific performances out of actors. He's *with* them. Sometimes a director *dares* you to give a good performance. But Kazan is the opposite; he does everything to get the performance out of the actor. The character I played in *The Arrangement* [1969], like Van Gogh as well, called for an inner emotional and intellectual intensity. In both instances I was portraying a tormented man, who is completely twisted. To depict the different shades of that type of a person is exhausting. It's much more demanding than usual. And it needs a director who can pull all that out of you. So *The Arrangement* and *Lust for Life* [1956] were similar experiences for me in that respect, the one with Kazan, and the earlier one with Minnelli.

———Douglas, interviewed for *Films & Filming*, Sept 72

Melvyn D O U G L A S [Hesselberg]
Born 1901 in Macon, Georgia. A considerable Broadway and trouping career before his first film offers:

My second movie, *As You Desire Me* [1932], based on Pirandello's play, was with Greta Garbo. It was the first of 3 movies I made with her. She was a provocative girl. . . . She wasn't a trained actress—and she was aware of that herself—but she had extraordinary intuitions, especially in the realm of erotic experience. I've never seen anything like her sensitive grasp of colors and shadings. . . . I was a little awestruck by Garbo at first, but I found her a very easy person to be with. We talked about everything, including her aware-ness of how she'd never really learned to be an actress. She was much more adept in the love scenes than in any other scenes. This impression was reinforced in my 2 other pictures with her—*Ninotchka* [1939] and *Two-Faced Woman* [1941].

———Douglas, interviewed for *The Player* (NY, 1962)

Alexander D O V Z H E N K O (1894–1956)
Born in the Ukrainian village of Sosnitsa, to a peasant family.

I wrote the scenario in a fortnight, filmed and edited it in 6 months. . . . *Arsenal* [1929] is completely a political film. In making it, I set myself 2 tasks: to unmask reactionary Ukrainian nationalism and chauvinism, and to be the bard of the Ukrainian working class that had accomplished the social revolution. At that time, however, I lacked the necessary theoretical knowledge for an integrated handling of such a grand theme. As far as I was concerned, there were no questions of style or form involved. I worked like a soldier who fights the enemy, without thought of rules or theory. I daresay if I had been asked then what I was thinking about, I should have answered, like Courbet to a lady's question, "Madame, I am not thinking—I am excited."

———Dovzhenko, autobiographical sketch of 1935

In my new film there will be no mountain peaks, no cliffs, no crimes, nothing to excite the spectator. All will be simple, without big effects. . . .

I have written a film trilogy that has for its frame and subject a Ukrainian village, my village. The first part—I have written it as a play—is set in 1930, during collectivization. The second part is an account of the fiery years of the patriotic war, of the battles between the collective farmers and Nazis. The third part comes up to our time. A great dam is built that places the village at the bottom of a new sea; the village dies under 45 feet of waters that vitalize and impregnate the earth.

I begin the production of this trilogy with its last part, *Poem about a Sea.* The title is perhaps too ambitious; I'd prefer *Prose about a Sea.* I have enjoyed planning my future work for the panoramic screen. . . . In 1930, I saw such a giant screen in Paris and it made a profound impression on me. The long horizontal shape suits the elements in my next film: broad and monochrome steppes, stretching waters of a sea, airplanes, the idea of great spaces. . . .

———Dovzhenko, interviewed for *Les Lettres françaises,* Dec 6–12, 56

Carl-Theodor D R E Y E R (1889–1968)
Born in Copenhagen. In 1912, started to write intertitles for Nordisk film company, then adapted novels and wrote scripts for them.

There was a big Danish company [Nordisk] which made 1,800 short, silent films a year. First I was asked to write subtitles and then I edited many of the films. Then I was asked to write a scenario. Five years of school. It was very good for me. . . .

———Dreyer, interviewed in *The Guardian,* 21 Dec 64

Falconetti had to agree to take the part of Joan with her own face (without any makeup), and I believe it was somewhat of a shock to her when she first saw pictures of herself on the screen: "Am I really so ugly?" she whispered. It did not last long, however, before the artist in her took the lead from the Parisienne, and from then on our work was like a dream. . . .

One cannot ask for a larger sacrifice from a woman, when for the sake of art she renounces her womanliness and her beauty. This Falconetti did day after day, as long as we worked on the film. Every morning when she arrived at the studio she had to agree to take off her makeup and remove her lipstick. She had already agreed to cut her hair short and when the scene of the stake approached, she allowed herself to be shorn bald. She cried that day but upon seeing the takes of that day, she realized that she had not made the sacrifice in vain. . . .

———Dreyer, in *Pageant,* Dec 62

Everything must be rehearsed in such a way that everyone feels the movement and perfectly understands what he is doing. For *Gertrud,* we rehearsed a great deal. And I was very happy with the result. All the more so because all the work was done during the shooting so that the editing no longer posed any problem at all. In three days, the editing was completed. Terminated. Definitive. I thus realized a progress, for *Ordet* [1955] was edited in 5 days and *Day of Wrath* [1943] in 12. Before that, I spent a month, or even longer, on the editing of my films.

Yes, I very much believe in long takes. You gain on all levels. And the work with the actors becomes much more interesting, for it creates a sort of ensemble, a unity, for each scene which inspires them and allows them to live the relationships more intensely and more accurately.

Generally, you find the definitive style for a film at the end of a few days. Here [*Vampyr,* 1932], we found it right away. We started to shoot the film—

starting with the beginning—and, at one of our first screenings of rushes, noticed that one of the takes was gray. We asked ourselves why, until we became aware of the fact that it came from a mistaken light that had been shining on the lens.

The producer of the film [and] Rudolf Maté and I thought about the take, in relation to the style we were looking for. Finally, we said that all we had to do was to repeat, on purpose, every day, the little accident that had happened. Henceforth, for each take, we directed a false light on the lens by projecting it through a veil, which sent the light back to the camera.

After that we had to look for an ending: our first idea was to have the old doctor disappear in the earth, swallowed up by quicksand. But we couldn't utilize that idea, as it was too dangerous for the actor. Therefore we had to find something else. One day, on the way back to Paris after a day of shooting, all the while talking about what we might do, we passed a little house that looked as if it were full of white flames. As we were unoccupied, not yet having found anything, we went into the little house and, once inside, understood that it was a little factory where they worked at reclaiming plaster. The whole interior was white, all the objects were bathed in a white dust and the workmen, too, were all white. Everything partook of that extraordinary white atmosphere. This was utilized by us as a point of departure for another stylistic element of the film.

——Dreyer, interviewed for *Cahiers du cinéma*, Sep 65;
trans. Rose Kaplin for *Cahiers du Cinéma in English*, No. 4, 66

During the German occupation of Denmark I went to Sweden to make a film [*Tva Manniskar*, 1945], based on Louis Verneuil's play *Monsieur Lamberthieu*—interesting because it has only 2 characters. The rights, however, were not available, and so we decided on another play, by W. O. Somin, also with 2 characters only. It goes without saying that if you have but 2 people in a film, the actors must be chosen with great care. I found 2 excellent actors. Both of them were rejected: the man because he had an Adam's apple; the woman because she was not sufficiently well-known and not beautiful. Instead of these I was forced to use 2 artists who were clever enough but who were entirely unsuited for the parts, which in the script are described as follows:

HE has to be young, with a pure mind and heart—without guile or deceit.

An idealist, so immersed in his studies that he sees nothing but his work. . . . For this part I was given an actor of an utterly different kind: mysterious, intriguing, cunning, and even demoniacal.

SHE, his wife, should be young, warm-blooded and sensual, with a slightly tarnished past. . . . As a character she is insincere, she has no difficulty in pretending or lying. She is theatrical and a little affected, with a definite inclination to hysteria.

To play her part I got a sweet, natural and uncomplicated actress who turned the woman into a comfortable little housewife. . . . In both cases I got the exact opposite of what I wanted. . . .

Of course the film was a failure.

——Dreyer, answering questionnaire in *Film: Book I*, (NY 1959)

With actors I consider myself like a midwife who helps him give birth to what he has created.

What at first looks like a series of artistic close-ups in *Joan of Arc* are really very thorough psychological descriptions of the people who tried Joan. . . .

In my new film [*Gertrud*, 1964], which is based on a play by a Swedish author, Hjalmar Soderberg, who had the misfortune to have lived in the shadow of Strindberg, I felt that the dialogue was most important. It is the first time I have attached such importance to the dialogue and I have brought it to the foreground, supported of course by the framing, lighting and so on. Usually the dialogue takes second place to the image. In *Gertrud* I use very long shots—8 or 10 or even 12 minutes. I used long shots, too, in *Ordet*, but not so long as in *Gertrud*.

——Dreyer, interviewed for *The Guardian*, 21 Dec 64

In *Ordet* I was so fortunate as to work with actors who manage on their own to come up with the tone and mood that in my opinion are correct, and this is naturally the right thing. The actor's particular creative act must take place in the actor's own mind. Therefore, in my opinion, a film director's task is mainly to unite the several actors' achievements into a compositional whole.

——Dreyer, a radio interview of 1954, in *Om Filmen*

I look upon facial expressions as being very important, both when there is speech and when there is no speech. I think this is an area that in later years has been sadly neglected in movies. What I have tried to do in *Gertrud* is to have the camera follow the actors. I once called it "flying close-ups." But we have also tried to keep it from becoming a stiff ride; it shouldn't be a drive for the drive's sake. Many times we've had very long shots—up to 8 to 10 minutes. But we've tried to shoot it so that the audience didn't notice the ride. The idea has been to have the actors' faces in focus all the time so that the audience can read their thoughts, eventually one character's thought while the other speaks. Why must a dialogue scene be bound to the idea that one either sees the people in profile or sees one actor with his back turned around? That way, the interplay between the actors can easily be washed out. In a dialogue scene, both faces are important.

——Dreyer, interviewed in *Film Culture*, #41, Summer 66

Ewald-André D U P O N T   (1891–1956)
Born in Zeitz, Germany. Worked as film critic and scriptwriter before directing films. His most distinguished German film was Variety (1925), *which brought him to Hollywood with a contract at Universal. He describes this film in the following quotation:*

Karl Freund is a resourceful cameraman. I found in him a ready ally for my purpose. He was always experimenting, trying to discover new angles, new approaches to familiar scenes. Thus, our introduction of Emil Jannings as Boss Huller, manager and ballyhoo man of a Hamburg sideshow, was by not photographing him full-face, but by accenting his occupation, his ringing of

a bell to call the crowd about his booth. In the prison sequence of the prologue, Jannings keeps his back to the audience.

It was my general aim in the picture to show a simple, childish grown-up,
devoted, lovable, and his reaction to betrayal and duplicity. I tried to portray
the primitive emotions that are in all of us. And I tried to show it, not by
subtitles, but by the lens, which, after all, is our true medium. . . .

The trapeze work, and, indeed, all the shots in the Winter Garden were
difficult to make. For one thing we had to bring a great deal more light into
the theater than normally is used. Then we had to construct observation positions for the camera, so as to photograph the entertainment to the best effect.

For one of the scenes we strapped a camera to another trapeze, facing
Jannings, and operated it electrically from the ground. To make the falling
scene we lowered a camera by cable, slow-cranking all the way. We "shot"
from every angle in the theater, using every device known and a great many
that were invented at the moment.

A trapeze act is interesting when one observes the actual trapeze work.
There is a natural lull in interest as the performers take their positions. To
bridge this gap without causing a break in the action, I had to photograph
the artists from unusual angles. Thus, in one sequence, the audience saw
the actors from below, climbing like monkeys up their rope ladders. The
following scene had to be taken from another vantage post.

Later in the picture, when the very same act had to be shown again,
it would obviously have been quite boring to repeat the identical action.
Therefore, Freund had to move his camera to still another position.

The festival scene, in which Warwick Ward and Lya de Putti figure,
has the appearance of having been an elaborate set. As a matter of fact,
by grouping my extras interestingly, dimming my lights, and showing only
the sparkle and glow of fireworks, I convey the impression of a great celebra-
tion. It was merely the adaptation of the newer stage technique—the use
of a pillar to indicate a great edifice.

Jannings used several makeups for the picture, besides appearing in
many of the scenes with virtually no facial aid whatever. Each change reflected a mood.

———Dupont, in *The New York Times*, 11 July 26;
repr. in *Spellbound in Darkness*

Marguerite D U R A S
*Born in Indochina in 1914. Studied in Paris for a law degree and a licence in
political science. Her first novel,* Les Impudents, *was published in 1943:*

. . . For the first time I didn't feel like starting to write something else immediately. So I thought, right, I'll make a film. What interested me was the
physical aspect of it—*le côté manuel,* of the cinema: it really is the antidote
to literature . . . much simpler.

The difference between writing for the screen and writing a book is
enormous, of course. The main difference is that the screenplay is not something in itself, it's a stage between the film and *le vide,* nothingness. It has
no existence in itself. I know I wrote a screenplay for *Hiroshima mon amour*

[1959] which has been published as a book, but that was because Resnais asked me to approach it as literature; that was something special.

———Duras, interviewed for *The Guardian,* 7 Sep 68

Eleonora D U S E   (1858–1924)
Born in North Italy. Her theater career began at the age of 4, as little Cosette in Les Miserables. *Her national and international fame continued until her death in Pittsburgh. In 1916 the Ambrosio-Caesar Company persuaded her to make her exquisite and only film,* Cenere *(*Ashes*). Then it was universally disliked—now it is a treasure. She recognized its flaws but perceived the medium's future:*

If I were 20 or 30 years younger, I would start afresh in this field with the certainty of accomplishing much. But I should have to learn from the bottom up, forgetting the theater entirely and concentrating on the special medium of this new art. My mistake, and that of many others, lay in employing "theatrical" techniques despite every effort to avoid them. Here is something quite, quite fresh, a penetrating form of visual poetry, an untried exponent of the human soul. Alas, I am too old for it!

———Duse, in a letter of resignation to Ambrosio, 1916

Allan D W A N   [Joseph Aloysius Dwan]
Born in Toronto, Canada, in 1885. Studied electrical engineering at Notre-Dame University where he contributed studies to the school magazine. First film work, as lighting engineer and scenarist, at the Essanay Company, from 1909 to 1915; then with Griffith at Triangle, 1915–1917, where most of his direction was of Douglas Fairbanks's films. He has directed more than 400 films, and has written or produced as many more.

I watched everything [Griffith] did, and then I'd do it, in some form or another. I'd try to do it in another way—I'd try to do it better. And I'd try to invent something that *he'd* see. He finally sent for me and said he was sick of competing, and would I join him at Triangle?

What fascinated me about Griffith? Well, I think his lack of long gesture, his simplicity, and his use of facial expression. He developed a strange new pantomime. I like pantomime anyway, but I don't like the extreme pantomime.

Other actors exaggerated to make up for not having words. His players used short little gestures to get over their point—they were much more realistic. And I saw Griffith was expressing vividly a lot of things with very little effort. . . .

Doug's stunts were not actually great athletic feats, they were good stunts done with great grace. That was the whole key. If Doug had to fight a duel and leap to a table top, I would time his leap—and I would cut the table to exactly the right height to accommodate his ability to leap. And the same with the climbs. Every set that we built I measured for handholds. They were always there, and he would automatically feel for them. A longer-armed man would have been awkward on them, or a shorter man, but with

Doug it was perfect. . . . If he jumped, it was just exactly the distance he could gracefully jump. Never a strain.

                    ——Dwan, interviewed for *The Parade's Gone By* (NY, 1968)

We would work, say, Monday, Tuesday, and Wednesday shooting and make 2 pictures. Then on Thursday and Friday I'd develop and cut them and take Saturday and Sunday off. . . .

And we developed our own negatives. I rented a couple of stores. One was for offices, the other was for the development process, the lab. Our cameraman had to be able to develop film in those days. . . .

I cut the negative—never saw a print . . . we didn't have cutters. And we didn't have any instruments or machines—we did it by hand. I would take the reels and run them through in front of a light. I could read the negative. Wherever I wanted to end a scene, I'd just cut it with a pair of scissors and that'd be a scene. Then I'd get the next scene I wanted and we'd glue it together. When I'd have 1,000 feet—one reel—I'd roll it up and send it to Chicago. . . . They'd simply print it that way when it got to Chicago, and that's the way it stayed. . . .

[*David Harum,* 1915] was the first time we moved the camera. And we didn't get very much praise for it either—nothing but abuse. The scene required David Harum to walk down the street talking to people as he went, to show that he was well acquainted with everybody; he was a horse-trader, quite a foxy old man, and very gay. He'd greet one person and stop to chat with another as he moved down the street. Well, I thought, if you set the camera at one end of the street and start him at the other end you wouldn't see anything; you'd see a fly speck approaching and finally when he got away down near the camera you'd say, "Oh, that's David Harum," but all the rest would have been wasted. So all this atmosphere would have to be made as a series of short scenes: let him walk this far, now put the camera down, let him walk this far—and so on. Well, instead of setting the camera backward each time, it occurred to me, wouldn't it be nice if we could just *move* it backward with him. I said to the cameraman [Hal Rosson], "How can we move it back?" And he laughed at me. Because in those days cameras were anchored or chained down on tripods so there'd be no vibration. He said, "You could pick it up and carry it"—you know, that big heavy thing. So I said, "No, but we can put it on wheels. Now what wheels can we put it on?" Well, the only thing we could think of was the Ford car. . . . Well, we got a farm scraper and we scraped the street flat, got all the bumps out. And then we softened the tires so they wouldn't joggle, we locked the springs and fastened the camera on securely with a few two-by-fours, got it well wired down, so it wasn't bobbley, and it worked great. . . .

[On *Robin Hood* (1922)] Not only did we have this ninety-foot wall, but on top of it were parapets and platforms. And we shot it with double-exposures. We'd put the 5,000 people on the ground for the first exposure—which went halfway up on the film—and then move the same 5,000 people up on the walls for the second exposure, which got the top half of the film. We had to be very careful not to let the people on top drop anything, because if they did, of course, it would disappear halfway down. So we tied their napkins or handkerchiefs to their wrists and took everything loose away from them. But it was a terrific effect—when you looked at the sets on the screen, they were bigger than they really were. They were big enough for anybody, but we still put tops on them with glass shots. That was the most fascinating thing we ever did in films—the old glass shot—it's gone now. We'd have a set of a certain height and then right in front of the camera we put a big plate of glass and an artist would paint on it—in exact proportion to our camera's perspective—the top part of the set, the ceiling, the chandeliers, whatever you wanted there. When you photographed the real thing and the painting, they were lit so they'd tie together. And it made very great effects; nearly any picture of any importance had glass shots in it. And you couldn't tell the difference because it was done so artistically and lit very, very carefully. . . .

It was the first time I used the zoomar lens, [*Tide of Empire,* 1929] which had just been invented. We were on this Western set looking off into the distance and up the hills from where a stagecoach is supposed to come toward us into town. So I got real brilliant. I said, "Here's a great chance to use the zoomar lens. We'll bring the stagecoach right into town with it." So we did. But it looked like the camera must have been on the horses' noses because it came right with them; they were always in close-up and the town finally appeared, but actually you didn't see them approach the town. In fact, the town must have approached the horses since it looked like the stagecoach stood still all the time. Or galloping on a treadmill. The effect was all wrong. The lens also wasn't popular because it wasn't available and it was too costly. And it wasn't an attachment to the camera then—but a gigantic affair that hung out in front of the camera—about 2 yards long and bulky. I think it was just experimental, and later it got to be a practical thing that anybody could use. Though even today it doesn't have the effect of movement, but the effect of extension. It just seems to open up instead of move.

[On *What a Widow,* 1930] I suggested something that had never been done, and may never be done again. I got the nucleus of the cast together and went on some standing sets and photographed the entire picture in 2 days—every scene in master shots, with all the dialogue—but, without costumes or makeup or any extras, and none of the action. It didn't cost much under those conditions. We cut it together and that way we could see and hear the flow of the story—and were able to correct the parts that were weak. And when we went out to make the picture, everything went very rapidly and smoothly because we had already been through it. If it weren't for union problems today, it would still be an excellent system—photograph a picture, look at it and then make it.

———Dwan, interviewed for *Allan Dwan, the Last Pioneer* (New York, 1971)

E

B. Reeves E A S O N   (1887–1956)
Born in Mississippi. First film job as property man. A "second-unit" director
responsible for the spectacular action sequences of Ben-Hur (1925), Cimarron
(1931) *and* The Charge of the Light Brigade (1936), *among many others.*

You can have a small army of people charging across the screen and it won't
matter much to the audience. But if you show details of the action, like guns
going off, individual men fighting or a fist hitting someone in the eye, then
you will have more feeling of action than if all the extras in Hollywood are
running about. That is why real catastrophes look tame in newsreels. You
need detail work and close shots in a movie. Only then does it come alive.
——Eason, interviewed for Goodman's The Fifty-Year Decline . . .
(NY 1961)

Clint E A S T W O O D
Born 1931 in San Francisco. Acted in television films before his career was
changed with an invitation from Italy.

Well, I was pretty well established in the TV series [*Rawhide*]. In fact I'd been
doing it for 7 years—when Sergio Leone sent me the script of *A Fistful of
Dollars* [1964]. It had a style about it which I liked, the character was one
I felt I wanted to play and I thought it would be a good opportunity for
me to break into films in a bigger way, although I'd done movies before. So
I duly signed on the line and it was only then, as it happens, that Sergio was
able to interest a producer in his project, or rather, he interested 2, Harry
Colombo and George Papi.
    It was a Western with a difference. It had realism, without the glamour
of so many Hollywood Westerns, but the distinctive feature was my part
as The Man With No Name, the cigar-smoking, poncho-wearing gunslinger. I
became known as El Cigarillo, and youngsters started wearing ponchos
modeled on mine—that is, blankets with a hole for the head.
    To begin with, it was on a shoestring basis. There was a lack of wardrobe
and to some extent of technical knowledge. But the situation improved as
success came. The second and third movies were more "classy." I got on
famously with Sergio Leone. To begin with, I knew no Italian and he knew

no English. But we managed to communicate. And, of course, it was very agreeable filming in Spain. Sergio, by the way, while working always wears a ten-gallon hat, boots, and sideburns. I suppose it puts him in the right frame of mind.

——Eastwood, interviewed for *Photoplay*, May 69

... The Italians were a little bit panicked by my interpretation of the part because they are not used to silence in films. But I felt the less he said, the stronger he became, and the more he became in the imagination of the audience. I insisted that all the long dialogue of the explanatory scenes was cut. You never knew who he was, where he came from or what he was going to do next.

... The unpleasantness of [the thin black cigars] sometimes put me in the mood for the scene. If I had to be in an unpleasant frame of mind I took a couple of draws and boy, I was right there.

——Eastwood, interviewed for *The Daily Mirror*, 31 Jan 70

Blake EDWARDS
Born in Tulsa in 1922. Served in Coast Guard during the Second War. Writer for radio and television before his directorial film debut with Bring Your Smile Along (1955).

I don't believe in "now" pictures or in "youth" pictures, but in *Wild Rovers* [1971] I tried to portray a view of American history that is perhaps different from what we believed when I grew up. The cowhands who become bank robbers—Bill Holden and Ryan O'Neal—are the good guys and the ranch owner, the capitalist, Karl Malden, the bad guy. The way I filmed it Holden and O'Neal leave behind enough money so that their fellow cowhands on the ranch can get paid that week, but this scene was cut out by MGM. I suppose they felt—what? That the robbers should be more normal villains. Then, I had developed the character played by Tom Skerritt—one of the ranch owner's sons who pursues the robbers—more fully as a repressed homosexual, a man unable to accept the easy, guiltless relationship between Holden and O'Neal. I had a scene of Skerritt going berserk at the end when he kills Holden. But [James] Aubrey wanted this out, and I acquiesced. I think they were afraid of it.

——Edwards, interviewed for *The Village Voice*, 5 Aug 71

Sergei EISENSTEIN (1898–1948)
Born in a well-to-do Riga family; formal education ended in Petrograd in 1917 when he enlisted as engineer in the Red Army. Always excited by theater most of his army years spent in an itinerant army theater, as designer, director, playwright and occasional actor. After demobilization in Moscow, continued to work in theater groups and to study with Meyerhold. Success at the Proletcult Theater led to his first film, Strike *(filmed in 1924 and released in 1925), and to the chief film assignment for the anniversary of the 1905 Revolution, out of which came* Battleship Potemkin *(released in early 1926).*

In order to make a film about a battleship one needs—a battleship. And to reconstruct the history of a 1905 battleship, it must be of exactly that type used in 1905. . . .

Our scouts reported that if we could not trace the *Prince Potemkin of Tauride,* a friend and kinsman of the same class still lived: the mighty, courageous battleship, *The Twelve Apostles.* Chained to the rocky shore, attached to the sea-floor with iron flukes, her sometimes heroic carcass stood in one of the most remote of the many winding inlets. . . .

But the "drama on the quarterdeck" had occurred at sea. Neither from the side nor from the prow of the battleship could the cameraman point his camera without having for background the tall vertical blackness of the cliffs.

The keen eye of the director's assistant, Lyosha Kriukov, who had ferreted out the old iron hulk in the windings of the Sevastopol roadstead, found a way to overcome this difficulty. By swinging about her mighty body 90 degrees, the vessel stood away perpendicularly from the shore, so that her front, taken from the prow, appeared exactly opposite a fissure in the surrounding cliffs and showed clear sky around the whole breadth of her sides! . . .

Not a jot of leeway to the right or left. Not one centimeter to the side! Or the illusion of "open sea" would be shattered.

. . . On the deck of the real battleship was raised the superstructure of a plywood battleship—with laths, beams, and plywood; and by using the old plans preserved in the archives of the Admiralty, the exact outer appearance of the battleship *Potemkin* was reconstructed.

One can almost see in this a symbol of the film itself: on a basis of real history, the past was reconstructed by means of art. . . .

One of the very important roles for the story was that of the ship's surgeon. We searched long for someone to play it, hopelessly, and at last settled on a compromise candidate, a certain actor.

This not quite suitable candidate rode with our filming group in the little cutter toward the cruiser *Komintern,* where the episode of the maggotty meat was to be filmed. I sat pouting at the far end of the cutter, as far as possible from the "surgeon." . . .

I looked over the [other passengers in the cutter] day-laborers who had been hired to hold the mirrors and gauzes during the filming. Among them was an especially feeble-looking man. He was the furnace-man at the drafty, chilly Sevastopol hotel where we killed time when we weren't shooting. "Now why should they pick such feeble fellows to work with the heavy mirrors," the thought lazily wandered through my head. "He's sure to drop a mirror overboard. Or worse—break it. And that would be a bad omen. . . ."

At this point my thoughts came to a halt: the feeble furnace-man had unexpectedly leaped on to another plane of value—from the viewpoint of his physical laboring capacities to the viewpoint of expressive capacities: moustache tendrils and sharp little goatee . . . crafty eyes. . . . Mentally I covered them with the glasses of a pince-nez on a chain. Mentally I exchanged his greasy cap for the officer's cap of the ship's surgeon. . . .

There's a legend that I played the role of the priest in the film. That isn't true. The priest was played by an old gardener from one of the orchards outside Sevastopol. He played the role in his own white beard, combed slightly to the side, and a bushy white wig. . . .

A very essential participant also remains anonymous. . . . This was the guard at the Alupka Palace grounds . . . he stubbornly sat on the head of one of the Alupka marble lions, refusing to let us film it without written permission.

In this crisis we were saved by the fact that there are *six* lions on the Alupka steps. As we ran with the camera from lion to lion, we finally so confused this grim and short-witted guardian of order that at last he disposed of the problem with a flourish of his hand, and let us take the close-ups of the three marble lions that we wanted.

These "roused lions" were a "find on the spot"—at Alupka, where we had gone to rest on one of our "lost" days.

——Eisenstein, "The Birth of a Film," trans. *Hudson Review*, Summer 51

I'm very sorry that the little time I stole from cutting my *October* gave me so few chances to talk movies with you during your visit to Moscow. . . .

From the point of view of construction, *October* is by no means flawless. It's just that in this film that is so much of the "people," of the "masses," I allowed myself to experiment. Despite the fact that my experiments are seldom appreciated (Germany understood not a single one!), they were enough to break the composition of the work as a unity. But, on the other hand, they were also enough to allow me to make deductions which are very, very far-reaching.

I think I'm ready to overturn my entire system. Thematically as well as formally. I think that we shall find the key to pure cinematography on the "other side" of the acted film—that is, in the film as newsreel, as well as in the film [material] itself. And, most amusing of all, this cinematography will be genetically ideological, for its substance will be the screening of . . . (the one essential word in all this hodgepodge doesn't come to mind . . . and no dictionary at hand. Okay, take the German word *Begriff* [concept, idea]. . . .)

Such a tendentious organization is the dance of the gods around Kornilov (*October*, Act III); they are present only to demonstrate our idea of deity. The uncrowning of the Deity . . . the future possibilities in techniques and themes opened by this sort of device makes it well worth being considered something of a failure by the gross audience of snobs. The greatest stupidity (found in almost all German papers) would be to compare *October* and *Potemkin*. *October* is the dialectical denial of *Potemkin!* And the main interest of *October* is in the bits and pieces which do not resemble the "Battleship."

. . . The "proclamation" that I'm going to make a movie of Marx's *Das Kapital* is not a publicity stunt. I believe that the films of the future will be found going in this direction. . . . In any case, they will have to do with philosophy. It is true that I won't get to this for another year, or year and a half, since the field is absolutely untouched. *Tabula rasa*. And it will be necessary to do a lot of sketching before trying to treat such an enormous theme without compromising it. . . .

If you have any questions at all, I could write you at once, since the bad weather means I'll always have time to write. (I'm now finishing *Old and New*).

——Eisenstein, letter to Moussinac, 16 Dec 28; trans. D. Sandy Petrey

You probably know that out of the schedule 4 months and $25,000—we succeeded after 13 months and $53,000 (what a sum!!) in transforming a shabby travelogue into a really major film [*Qué Viva Mexico!*]. The expansion was terribly difficult, due to the bad conduct and management of Sinclair's brother-in-law [Hunter Kimbrough]. . . . To Sinclair he pictured me as liar, blackmailer and God knows what else. Correspondence stopped. Our only contact was through Hunter . . . whereupon the work of 13 months was abruptly halted.

The last episode of the film—with all the elements of Act V—was ripped out, and you know what this means. Just as if Ophelia were ripped from *Hamlet,* or King Philip from *Don Carlos.* We saved this episode, the last before a brief epilogue, and the best as material, story and effect, for the last to be filmed. This episode is the story of Soldadera, the women who by their hundreds followed the Revolutionary army, caring for their men, fighting beside them, bearing their children, burying their men—and then caring for their next men. In showing the Mexican Revolution, this cannot be surpassed in pathos.

And this is the climax, for here is the birth of a new nation, rising after the exploitation and oppression of Spanish rule, as Mexico.

Without it the film loses meaning, unity and final impact; it becomes a display of unintegrated episodes. Each of these episodes now points towards this end and this resolution.

To be practical: we have the army free—500 soldiers for 30 days! 10,000 carbines—50 cannon—also free. We have found the most extraordinary landscapes for our settings. We've resolved the dramatic problem successfully, and it is now a question of $7,000 or $8,000, in order to finish this in a month, and to have a magnificent film (and when I say it, I mean it!). With all its mass effects, no studio could attempt this now! Just imagine, Zalka, 500 women in a boundless cactus desert, the wounded, the children, beds and cooking things, the dead, all dragging and dragged through clouds of dust, followed by 500 white-clad soldiers in straw hats, then the march into Mexico City, past Spanish churches and palaces—for all of which we have the cooperation of thousands from sport organizations—to show the meeting of Villa and Zapata before the Cathedral—the victory of the first Revolution.

And to sacrifice all this for $8,000!—and to let a quarrel (in which, by the way, I am right, and I can prove it with documents) justify Sinclair in stopping the production and in throwing at people a mutilated stump. . . .

One doesn't write such letters often. . . . To have this possibility and to be forced to give it all up. . . !

——Eisenstein, letter to Salka Viertel, 27 Jan 32;
repr. in *The Kindness of Strangers*

. . . It makes no difference whether the composer writes music for the "general idea" of a sequence, or for a rough or final cutting of the sequence; or, if procedure has been organized in an opposite direction, with the director building the visual cutting to music that has already been written and recorded on sound track.

I should like to point out that in *Alexander Nevsky* [1938] literally all these possible approaches were employed. There are sequences in which the shots were cut to a previously recorded music track. There are sequences for which the entire piece of music was written to a final cutting of the picture. There are sequences that contain both approaches. There are even sequences that furnish material for the anecdotists. One such example occurs in the battle scene where pipes and drums are played for the victorious Russian soldiers. I couldn't find a way to explain to Prokofiev what precise effect should be "seen" in his music for this joyful moment. Seeing that we were getting nowhere, I ordered some "prop" instruments constructed, shot these being played (without sound) *visually,* and projected the results for Prokofiev—— who almost immediately handed me an exact "musical equivalent" to that visual image of pipers and drummers which I had shown him.

——Eisenstein, in *The Film Sense* (NY, 1942)

Hanns E I S L E R (1898–1962)
Born in Leipzig and studied with Arnold Schönberg in Vienna. Always in-terested in the problems of film music since his first score in 1925 for Rutt-mann's Opus III.

In 1930 I worked with Granovsky on his film, *Song of Life.* The birth of a child was shown, and the picture of the baby was accompanied by a ballad which depicted all the things which were waiting for the child. This tempted Granovsky to show the same things in the film as well. Music and film depicting the horrors of this world resulted in a combination of picture and sound which at that time created much interest. . . .

In the same year I was working together with Victor Trivas on the film [*Niemansland*]. Of the instances in which we succeeded to employ music and picture in an original way, I would like to quote only one: the beginning of the war. A workman says good-bye to wife and child—on the way to the barracks we see depressed men accompanied by their wives. Martial music starts very softly, gradually increasing until it reaches a fortissimo. While this music is played, good-natured and anxious men turn into ferocious warriors.

——Eisler, in *World Film News,* May 36

Do you work on the music from the script or from the finished filmed sequence?

I work mostly from the film sequence after careful study of the script. After reading the script the composer can make sketches; but for scoring you really need to study the finished sequence. The usual trouble is that you see the film late, and then you are rushed to the recording date. This is dangerous for the quality of the music. Another danger is that after the recording, for several possible reasons, the sequence is cut again. This generally means that the music suffers. There are compromises, however, in which the film is cut to the music, and vice versa. (e.g., In *400,000,000* [1939] several sequences were cut to my music—bombardment, dust-storm, the music composed for the children sequence was cut and edited to fit the picture.)

————Eisler, answering questionnaire in *Films*, Winter 40

Edith E V A N S   (1888–1976)
Born in London. After a career in the theater, she made her first film in 1915.

The makeup [for *The Queen of Spades*, 1949] was a tremendous problem. You remember, I played the old Russian countess who sells her soul to the devil in exchange for the secret of the cards. Well, they decided they couldn't give my face a really ancient texture by greasepaint alone, so they painted on some liquid stuff: one man held my skin while another applied the mixture. And when it dried the result was heavy, thick wrinkles. I thought I looked more like an old Maori woman than a Russian aristocrat.

Then at the end of the day they peeled it off like a layer of skin, and to my speechless horror and chagrin . . . the wrinkles were still there! I nearly died of fright—I thought I was marked for life. Actually, they did discover later that the substance was too strong. They were only allowed to film me once every 3 days, and I suppose it was a wonder it didn't put me off films for life.

————Evans, interviewed for *The Sunday Times*, 28 May 61

F

Geraldine F A R R A R   (1882–1967)
Born in Melrose, Massachusetts. Dramatic soprano brought from Metropolitan Opera to films by Cecil B. De Mille.

The first picture for Lasky and De Mille, *Maria Rosa,* 1915, was concluded in a short time, to everyone's satisfaction. Meanwhile, the playwright and brother of C. B. De Mille, William De Mille, had completed our special scenario for *Carmen* [1915], which enjoyed the same cast as *Maria Rosa.* I was most eager to get to work on it. It was then that I asked Mr. De Mille if we might have music during our scenes, as I was so accustomed to orchestral accompaniment for certain tempi and phrasings, I felt I could better pantomime the rhythm of the effects. A little piano was hastily wheeled on the set and the talented Melville Ellis, who knew every kind of music, Broadway jazz as well as the classics, by heart, inspired all my scenes with his impromptu playing. I believe this started the habit for music "offstage" for all later aspirants to emotional appeal. . . .

This *Carmen* has been a popular subject. . . . Our scenario, however, was based more on the Merimée story, and my biggest fighting moment was a vigorous quarrel in the tobacco factory where the amiable Jeannie Macpherson, Mr. De Mille's right hand scenarist and an actress of no mean ability, loaned herself to my assault in a battle that made screen history. Here I garnered material for the first act of the Metropolitan's scene, that is usually indicated by a phlegmatic chorus lineup.

——Farrar, in *Such Sweet Compulsion* (NY, 1938)

Glenda F A R R E L L   (1904–1971)
Born in Enid, Oklahoma.

When I went out there to do *Little Caesar* in 1930, the talkies were still new. Not many actors could talk, so they shoved the ones who came from Broadway into everything. It all went so *fast* I used to ask myself, "What set am I on today? What script am I supposed to be doing—this one or this one?" Up at 5 every morning, start work at a quarter of 6, work till 7 or 8 at night. By the time you got home, it was 9. Then you had to study your lines, have your dinner and bath and go to bed. You worked till midnight on Saturday. All I ever really wanted was a day off. Our contracts gave us 6 weeks' vacation each year, but they got around that by loaning us out to other studios. I could have gone on suspension, but I had responsibilities—my father to support, my son in military school, all that. . . .

No, Warners never made you feel you were just a member of the cast. They might star you in one movie—I *starred* with Paul Muni in *Hi, Nellie* [1933]—and give you a bit part in the next. I can remember thinking, "Oh, God, I hope it's a small part this time, so I can get some rest." So you weren't Kay Francis. You were still well paid, and you didn't get a star complex. We were a very close group—Cagney, Kibbee, Hugh Herbert, Aline MacMahon, Dick Powell and Joan Blondell. Of course, Bette [Davis] was *always* an outsider.

———Farrell, interviewed in *The New York Times*, 2 Feb 69

Rainer Werner FASSBINDER
Born 1946 in Bad Wörishofen, Bavaria.

Q. Why did you use those white fadeouts [in *Effi Briest*, 1973]?
A. It's one element of alienation, like books which have white pages with black print. According to Kracauer, when the screen goes black, the audience begin to fantasize, to dream, and I wanted the opposite effect through the white. I wanted to wake them. It should not function like most films, through the subconscious, but through the conscious. It's the first film that I know of where the audience is supposed to have its own fantasy, like reading a novel— the first *normal* fiction film. This happens also with Straub, but his films are not normal films. . . . When you read a novel, you imagine your own characters. That's just what I wanted to do in this film. I didn't want to have predetermined characters made for the audience; rather, the audience should continue to work, as in reading a novel.
Q. In all your films, you place the camera at a distance creating an effect of observation. One is not *in* it or *part* of it, but *observing* it. Is this your alienation effect?
A. This is my special attitude toward film. The reason is that I don't want to create realism the way it's usually done in films, but rather that a realism should come about in the audience, in the head of the viewer. It's a collision between film and the subconscious that creates a new realism.
———Fassbinder, interviewed for *Film Comment*, Nov–Dec 75

Ernst FEGTÉ
Born 1900. Art director, chiefly at the Paramount Studio.

Nobody was strong enough to tell Mitch [Leisen] he couldn't do what he wanted, so he just ran away with the picture [*Frenchman's Creek*, 1944], going way over schedule and spending more money. David Lewis was the most wishy-washy producer. All he ever did was play cards on the set with the actors. Mitch and I were both very good at cheating. We loved to use tricks so that it would look like we had fantastic production values without spending nearly as much money as the real thing would cost. We made much use of the hanging miniature technique. We built the first floor of the manor on location in the correct scale so that people could come out of the door on the first floor. But every time there was a long shot showing the whole building, the upper floors were a hanging miniature. It was built an inch to the foot and we hung it so that from a certain angle, the miniature and the real construction fused together. The sunlight hit them both the same way and when you saw it on the screen, you were sure it was a real two- or three-story building. Then we realigned it and came in for a closer shot. When we came back to Hollywood, I took the same miniature and added it on top of a building in the courtyard where they stopped to water their horses. We used another hanging miniature in the first scene in the gaming house. The balconies across the room were hanging miniatures. I did all of this as sort of a second unit while Mitch was off directing the actors, but he understood these things and encouraged me to the utmost.

——Fegté, quoted in *Hollywood Director* (NY, 1973)

Federico F E L L I N I
Born in Rimini, 1920. In Rome, worked as a cartoonist, gagman, co-scenarist, assistant director. First independent film, The White Sheik (1952).

I don't consider myself Rossellini's disciple in the sense that my imaginative world, my way of making films, my characters have a close link with his. The way I would mean it, if I said I was his disciple, would probably be something even deeper than that. He was the man whose example, and whose personality first inspired me to realize, when I was working with him on *Rome, Open City* [1945], and *Paisa* [1946] that the means of expression best suited to my nature was the cinema. It is in this sense that I can say Rossellini taught me something fundamental. . . .

——Fellini, interviewed for *Les cahiers de la R.T.B.*, Brussels 62

I don't really believe in the idea of an actor being required at a given moment to incarnate a particular character. I never try to get a virtuoso performance out of an actor in an attempt to make him express something which, on the human level, on the level of his own personality, I know is just not him. . . . I never make the mistake—for I think it is one—of making the actor enter into a character. On the contrary, I always try to do the opposite, namely to let the character take on the color of whatever actor I have available for the part. One of the things I really try to do . . . is to make friends with an actor before starting work. Naturally, this is not a method that I can recommend to everyone, and even for me making friends can be difficult enough.
. . . The definite casting of minor roles, or indeed sometimes even the main ones themselves, is for me one of the most agonizing moments. Because I fall in love with everyone. For example, I see a character as bald, slurring his r's, nerveless, and with hairy hands, and I see him clearly; I saw him vividly when I was conceiving him. And I start looking round to find that physical presence which will embody my character. And then there comes to

see me a man who is thin, with a lot of hair, with long, artist's hands, and a perfect pronunciation. By the very fact that this is someone alive, speaking and looking at me, someone who has a particular accent, who breathes, who lights his cigarette in a certain way, all this makes him so much more alive than my own imagined creature that I say to myself, "Instead of looking for that particular type, maybe I could use this one." And then I see it will work out just as well, better perhaps, and everything is in the melting pot again, making it all more harassing than ever. Then a second man turns up, not very thin, an average chap, and now I find that this one, too, could bring to my character the authenticity of his own life, of his presence. So you see the casting of a character becomes a real drama, because they would all be good— they all communicate something to me. Any real living person moves me, influences me, stimulates my imagination. . . .

———Fellini, *Bianco e nero*, Feb 60

When I write a story, I never start from the beginning. Maybe it is the middle or maybe the end. In 8½ [1963] it was the end, because the root of that picture was that a friend of mine had committed suicide. I asked myself what might have prevented it. And the thought grew that if somehow, just before he pulled the trigger, his family and friends could have come up to him and shown that they wanted to accept him as he was, and asked him to accept them also for what they were, sharing the conditions of human existence without blame and without demands, he would have been reconciled to life; he would not have fired the gun. But these fragments never compose themselves in advance into a real script. Finally, in my own mind, I know what the picture *is*. Various scenes are written, some with collaborators. I have no system.

———Fellini, interviewed for *Life*, 20 Dec 63

Verna FIELDS

The Savage Eye [1960] I dearly love. . . . I got credit as sound, but I was more involved than that. The main credit was "a film by" Ben Maddow, Joseph Strick, and Sidney Meyers. . . . The 3 men had put the film together, and Gary Merrill had done the narration. They had all the narration in a couple of boxes, and their film all cut in another box and all their trims thrown into cartons. They needed a sound cutter, and they came over and talked to me. They left me a couple of reels to look at, and I was knocked out by the film. I told them I would do it. I ended up working on the film for 7 months.

Nobody had ever told them that you should time your narration to match the picture. The form of the picture was there, but we had to recut constantly. That period was my psychiatric session. I would work most of the day laying out the narration, changing pictures around. In the afternoon Ben and Joe would come over and say, "Why did you put those words here? Let's analyze this." We'd work until 10 or 11 at night in a constant analysis of why certain words create certain effects and certain images. I learned an enormous amount.

Q. Do you see any advantage in the use of multiple cameras?

A. I'm so glad you asked me that because I'm on a real rampage about that. George Lucas used them very carefully [for *American Graffiti*, 1973]. It was thought out very well. He had a short schedule on a difficult picture and decided that was the only way he could do it. But using multiple cameras has suddenly become a very popular thing to do, and it's disastrous. Instead of getting one beautifully staged, well-shot take on something, you're getting 2 or 3 camera angles of the same thing—all mediocre—because the staging cannot be as good as it should be since you have to allow for where the other cameras are. If the lighting is good for the A camera, it may be terrible for the B and C cameras. You're spending a fortune on raw stock and lab. You're running through miles of film out of which maybe you get a little something.

I've been watching dailies on a film using multiple cameras, and they're just awful. I've talked to several cutters I know, and they're all complaining about the same thing. Eight, nine, ten reels of dailies a day, four of which are dailies, and the rest of which are junk.

———Fields, interviewed for *Dialogue on Film*, in *American Film*, June 76

W. C. FIELDS [William Claude Dukinfield] (1879–1946)
Born in Philadelphia. Toured the U.S. as a comedy juggler for over 18 years before joining Ziegfeld in 1915, the year of his first short film, Pool Sharks.

Nobody in Hollywood wanted me. I couldn't get a job anywhere. I went to one studio with a proposition. I offered to write, direct, and act in a short subject for nothing. If the picture went over, all I asked was a chance to make some more shorts, on salary. I was turned down.

Finally Mack Sennett gave me a chance, and my comedies made good. That was when I broke my neck.

I was supposed to ride a bicycle into the rear end of a truck that was backing up. I did that all right, but in falling off the bike, I broke my neck. I should have been able to roll between the back wheels without trouble, but I couldn't move. Everybody yelled at the truck driver, but he couldn't hear. So John Sinclair jumped under there and yanked me out. They piled me into the back seat of a touring car, and I held my head in my hands. A man sat on each side of me to brace me, and we raced for a hospital. Fortunately, the injury was not as serious as we thought at first, or I wouldn't be writing this today.

Then Paramount gave me a chance. I had a sequence in *If I Had a Million* [1932]. After that came a part in *Million Dollar Legs* [1932], and another part in *International House* [1933]. Apparently, I got over, because Paramount signed me to a contract, and I've been working ever since.

———Fields, in *The Evening Journal*, New York City, 9 May 36

Peter FINCH [William Mitchell] (1916–1977)
Born in London; taken to Australia at the age of 10.

It was about 10 years ago that I first felt I would like to direct in films; but at that time I felt that I didn't know enough. So since then I have been lurking around other people's cutting rooms as well as around the cameras on set, and learning the general sum total of the technical aspect of filmmaking. Then I thought I was ready when I made my short, *The Day* [1961], which I very much enjoyed working on. But now I am bogged down with the Italian finance over *The Hero* [unrealized] which will be my first feature as a director. Because of the very nature of the story it has to be a co-production with Italy, otherwise the costs would be enormously high if we had to take a full English crew on location.

It is a lot tougher at the moment when trying to set up productions, because the financiers are all trying to back certainties—which is understandable. The main role in *The Hero* will be played by Alan Bates, who I think is one of the best screen actors we have in England. In England you could probably raise money on his name, but in Italy for instance he is unknown and they won't put up any money on his "name." But I am sticking out for him, because he is right for the part. (Probably if the character was changed to an American and we cast it with an American star, we could get the money tomorrow!). So I'm up against this dreaded thing that we all know—that the actor who is right for the role is not the one that raises the money for you.

To have been an actor is a help in directing; it then helps you in guiding the actors because you are more aware of their problems. You know when an actor is not giving you something because he is nervous, or he has got himself tied up in a knot; and you can then untangle it. One thing though that you must do is to divorce yourself from directing actors to play a part as you would.

. . . Jack Clayton, who I recently worked with on *The Pumpkin Eater* [1963], has his own absolutely vivid style as a director, which you could see after only 3 days' work. One was fascinated to know how that style operated, while at the same time he is really allowing your individual ideas a great freedom. But although on the surface Jack is very calm, I think he suffers enormously inside from a nervous tension—but he never lets anybody see this.

After *The Nun's Story* [1958] which I did with Fred Zinnemann (he had sent me the script, I liked it, said yes, and that was that), I did a film with Angie Dickinson [*The Sins of Rachel Cade* (1961)], which I now think was a terrible mistake. It was the same old trouble; they sent me a script which was *nearly* good (it certainly was not bad) but it needed work on it. They said, "Well, we'll get one of the best writers in Hollywood on it". . . but it just didn't get any better. Also I did this film because Henry Blanke, whom I am very fond of, had produced *The Nun's Story* as well. So I was in a way trapped by friendship and trust, this magical grip that doesn't appear unless it can be done in the first place.

With *In the Cool of the Day* [1963], John Houseman had said "Well, Peter, I had objections to the script and thought it was melodramatic". . . and that the characters weren't properly resolved, and he assured me that it would all be taken care of. I suppose with the best will in the world we tried to take care of it, but it just doesn't work out that way very often. The first script had been written by Meade Roberts, who has a very good reputation. But there is a sort of subtle alchemy around the scripts that once they start to go wrong, nothing will ever save them. There is a rotten core somewhere.

It really is no good getting surgeons in, the script has to be right at the beginning, and it has taken me, I'm ashamed to say, some 30 years to find out that you mustn't listen to anybody at lunch anymore.

——Finch, interviewed for *Films & Filming*, June 64

. . . Murray Head was worried that his part [in *Sunday Bloody Sunday,* 1971] was too much of a cipher. So we all had to work that much harder to make him *real.* That isn't to say you can't perform an act of mental sublimation. Sometimes one just has to work for the bread.

. . . The most important thing is the script. You've just got to insist that it really is the finished script. The number of times I've accepted something on the strength of a treatment, then discovered we were literally writing the lines as we went along. Terrible!

———Finch, interviewed for *Radio Times,* 7 Oct 71

Albert F I N N E Y
Born 1936 in Salford, Lancashire. Works in both theater and films.

. . . I felt that [Karel Reisz] was going about [*Saturday Night and Sunday Morning,* 1960] the right way. I was then 23. I'm not being presumptuous about it, but I felt sympathetic to the way he was doing it, the way he was out to do it. I think Karel is very good with actors; he's very interested in the actors creating a character and not just relying on personality; he's good at encouraging actors to explore the characterization, and I think that's the kind of acting I'm interested in.

Q. Can you give me an example of what he does with actors that makes him better to work with than other directors?

A. When I commit myself to an interpretation or to a way of doing things, I like to believe that it's because I think that's absolutely the way to do it. I like to be convinced that that's the way it should be done. And I think Karel is similar. You know, very hesitant at first, but once he feels that's the way it should be done, doing it that way. We have similar temperaments in that respect.

Q. Did you find it easy acting in front of film cameras?

A. The process of acting, inside oneself, is the same. The manifestation of it is very different. What was marvelous for me at that stage, very exciting, was to work in the Raleigh factory, where certain scenes were shot. The reality of working the lathe, as an actor who'd just worked in the theater for 4 years before that, and trained for the theater the 2 years before these 4, I found very exciting. When I was being photographed working at the lathe, then I could absolutely concentrate on what the character was supposed to do. There was no cheating involved, you know. . . .

I sometimes feel I do take myself too seriously, and it was good to do *Tom Jones* [1963] where instead of walking round the pool and considering what I did, I just said: "Right, I'm going to dive in here, now." Do you know, I did things much more spontaneously. And I didn't mind that the public would see a spontaneous reaction, rather than an artistically created—I hope, achieved —reaction. But the kind of actor that I am, I like to feel that they're seeing something I've worked at, that I've considered other possibilities but this is what I think they should see. I think I have a facility for acting, you know. My danger is, sometimes, that I do it easily. I need the neurosis of making my work more complicated and more difficult than it need be sometimes, in order to escape the feeling of "I'm just getting away with it."

———Finney, broadcast interview on BBC-2, published in
The Listener, 24 Aug 67

We had this location [for *Charlie Bubbles,* 1967] which was a slum clearance area in Salford, about 2 miles of it. I got up there about an hour early, at 7:30 in the morning, still in the dark, to see how we could do the sequence. It was an area I used to know as a boy. I was walking round it when this copper stopped me, wondering what I was doing. "Oh, it's you, Albert." He knows I'm filming in the area.

It gets to 8:00 and I'm still looking round. At 8:10 I can hear the trucks coming round the corner, about half a mile away. It's getting lighter. I know they're going to be here in a minute. They roll up with all the technicians and all the gear. All I want to say is go away, go away. I just don't know what I want to do.

They all pile out, "Hello, Guv, lovely day, isn't it, where's the tea?" then the rest of the lads start arriving. At 8:20 the first assistant asks, "What's the first site, then?" I look around, about 60 people, all waiting for me to make up my mind. . . .

There were 4 moments in [*Saturday Night and Sunday Morning*] when it all came out as I'd tried to do it. People thought I was really like Arthur Seaton, which was good, though I'm not. It occupied my mind completely.

But in *Tom Jones* I just felt I was being used. I wasn't involved. I was doing it on false pretenses. I wasn't after anything. I was bored most of the time. In *Two for the Road* [1967] I felt much the same. I wanted to do a movie like that and it seemed the best in that category I was offered. I'm not making a distinction of quality; Stanley Donen is a smashing moviemaker. I just think it's a pity I haven't done more demanding work in the cinema.

———Finney, interviewed for *The Sunday Times,* 26 Nov 67

Ure: It's an enormous help to be in a real location. When we were doing the last scene in *Look Back in Anger* [1959]—the scene at the railway station where I met Jimmy Porter again—we shot it at 4:00 in the morning and we did it in a single take. We couldn't possibly have managed that in a studio, without the help we got from the atmosphere, the smoke and the rain and the way the station felt.

Finney: In *Saturday Night and Sunday Morning* I felt like that about the scenes where I was working at the lathe. I felt almost like a sculptor—working a real lathe, with real metal, and working it myself. It's wonderful for an actor to be able to pour his concentration into an actual object like this, until in a way it becomes part of him. I found that one of the most exciting things about filming.

Ure: Of course it's important to rehearse properly, to know what you're doing in a scene. But in the cinema—and this is one of the reasons why I find such excitement in films—there is always the chance that something in a shot may go slightly wrong; and in that case you need this little bit of freedom just to give something truly creative. Surely this chance thing is terribly important: some of the best things in the cinema have come about by chance.

    Finney: But if something goes wrong and you have to cope, for want of a better word, you can cope in a way which is good for the film or one which is bad for the film. Even if I'd only dropped a cup and saucer, for instance, I'd like to feel that the way I pick it up would be influenced by the fact that I was in the right rhythm of the scene.

    ——Finney and Mary Ure, interviewed for *Sight & Sound*, Spring 61

Terrence FISHER
Born in London, 1904. Worked as a film editor before directing horror films for the Hammer Company.

One ought to plan a film with costume and set designers before shooting; but I've never had the time or the money. There is the danger of overpreparation, of loss of spontaneity; overrehearsal is the most terrible thing you can imagine. We have a very close association between costume and set designer, though. And the cameraman is very important, of course. The cameraman of *Phantom [of the Opera,* 1962] prefers what he calls natural, neutral color, whereas Jack Asher likes to go for strong color effects. And then you really have to stylize and discipline the color; and the closer you move your camera in, the more you have to bunch your color. One blob of red in the wrong place and the audience isn't looking at the hero, they're looking at a patch of curtain (or something similar) and your whole effect is lost.

    ——Fisher, in *Films & Filming*, July 64

Robert FLAHERTY (1884–1951)
"The father of the documentary film" was born in Iron Mountain, Michigan. His work as an explorer led, almost accidentally, to filming near Hudson Bay. A second, more serious try, led to the making and world success of Nanook of the North *(first shown in 1922):*

The difficulties of film development and printing during the winter were many. The convenience of civilization which I most missed was running water. For instance, in the film washing, 3 barrels of water for every 100 feet was required. The waterhole, then 8 feet of ice, had to be kept open all winter long and water clotted with particles of ice had to be taken, a barrel at a time, from the distance of more than a quarter of a mile away. When I mention that over 50,000 feet of film was developed over the winter with no assistance save from my Eskimo and at the slow rate of 800 feet a day, one can understand somewhat the amount of time and labor involved.

    My equipment included 75,000 feet of film, a Haulberg electric light plant and projector, and 2 Akeley cameras and a printing machine so that I could make prints of film as it was exposed and project the pictures on the screen so that thereby the Eskimo would be able to see and understand wherever mistakes were made.

    One of *Nanook's* problems was to construct an igloo large enough for the filming of interior scenes. The average Eskimo igloo, about 12 feet in diameter, was much too small. On the dimensions I laid out for him, a diameter of 25 feet, Nanook and his companions started to build the biggest igloo of their lives ... the dome's half just over the camera had to be cut away, so Nanook and his family went to sleep and awakened with all the cold of out-of-doors pouring in.

——Flaherty, interviewed for Cinema 1950 (London, 1950)

[Louisiana Story, 1948] was a story built around a derrick which moved so silently, so majestically in the wilderness; probed for oil beneath the watery ooze and then moved on again, leaving the land as untouched as before it came.... For our hero, we dreamed up a half-wild Cajun boy of the woods and bayous [and] we developed the character of an oil driller who would become a friend of the boy, eventually overcoming his shyness and reticence. Then came the difficult business of casting. I spend perhaps more time on this aspect of picturemaking than any other, for I believe the secret of success lies in finding the right people.

We worked day after day, shooting reams of stuff. But somehow we never could seem to make that pesky derrick come alive. . . . Then we hit on it. At night! That's when it was alive! At night, with the derrick lights dancing and flickering on the dark surface of the water, the excitement that is the very essence of drilling for oil became visual.

——Flaherty, quoted in Richard Griffith's
World of Robert Flaherty (NY, 1953)

Richard FLEISCHER
Born 1916, in New York City, son of pioneer animator, Max Fleischer. First work in films on newsreels and shorts for RKO.

When Orson Welles is an actor, he stays an actor. He neither makes suggestions nor offers any advice on the filmmaking itself. I have directed him in 2 films, Compulsion [1958] and Crack in the Mirror [1960], and we got along famously. With a man like Welles you expect him to have his own interpretation, but it has to be an interpretation that the director agrees with. I had no real conflict with him on either film. Sometimes when we didn't agree we argued about it and I must say that Orson would bow to the director's point of view. Being a director himself he knows what it means to the overall film to disobey a director.

Orson can see how a scene is going and if the timing is off a little he'll adjust himself so that the camera will reach its position comfortably—he'll time himself to the camera. Actors less aware will say "I have to go from A to B and I'm going to be there on cue," and they let the camera take care of itself.

Orson has one peculiarity that's really amusing. Dean Stockwell and I got a big kick out of it when we were making Compulsion. When an actor has to perform on camera and speak to someone not being photographed with him, the other actor usually stands next to the camera so that they can look at each other, act and get the cues back and forth as they say the dialogue. Orson is violently against this. "Who'd ever expect anyone to do that?" He wants nothing there, nobody. He doesn't want anyone in his sight line and no one can read the lines to him that he has to cue to. He'll go through the whole scene and say his lines, giving exactly the right pause for the other person to speak his lines, and come in again right on cue.

I think an actor behind the camera would disturb Orson's concentration. He would rather imagine it and concentrate on his own performance than be thrown by another actor who is not really acting. When an actor's behind the camera he's never as good as when he's in front, and in my experience the actor behind the camera invariably stumbles on his lines.

——Fleischer, interviewed for *Films & Filming*, Oct 62

But for *The Boston Strangler* [1968], apart from the alienation, I felt that the best way to get the feeling of a city in terror, and of a general dragnet being thrown out, was to show everything happening at once, rather than each individual image by itself. If you can show a lot of images, of many events happening simultaneously, you get a result that's greater than the sum of its parts. The whole thing is happening all over; it's not just a series of localized events. Also, while life could be going on in a very normal way on one side of the screen, there was this mysterious shadowy outline on the other side of the screen when 2 women discovered one of the bodies: they opened the door, moving from one image to the other, from the normal scene outside the door to the discovery inside the room. You see, the element of surprise was taken away from me in that film by the nature of the story. You knew there were going to be a lot of stranglings, and you also knew that Tony Curtis was the Boston Strangler. So the possibility of suspense was to some extent removed. I had to rely, and build heavily, upon anticipation. Therefore I was not reluctant to show what people were going to see before they saw it. The people on one side of the screen, living normally, and the body on the other—there's anticipation in this. I think I put a bit of suspense back in, this way: for instance the strangler walking through hallways while you saw his next victim on the other side of the screen at the same time.

——Fleischer, interviewed for *Films & Filming*, Dec 70

Henry FONDA
Born 1905, in Grand Island, Nebraska; grew up in Omaha.

It was easy to make the transition to movies. I started to act in the film version of *The Farmer Takes a Wife* [1935] the way I always did for a play, and Victor Fleming, the director, told me I was mugging. And that's all it took. I just pulled it down to reality. You don't project anything for movies. You do it as you would in your own home. Because of all the experience back of me in the same part, it didn't bother me to work out of continuity, the way you do in making a movie. Of course, there's very little personal satisfaction in doing those bits and pieces for a movie. You don't really have any recollection of having created a role. But in the beginning the money made it pretty attractive.

——Fonda, interviewed for *The Player* (NY, 1962)

[Fritz Lang] was too preoccupied with what everything was going to look like. Lang took a whole day to shoot a simple scene with Sylvia [Sidney] and me in *You Only Live Once* [1937]. It's the wedding supper, and the camera starts on an insert of the marriage certificate, then dollies back, sees the plates where we have finished our dinner, and finally sees us. The scene is what we say to each other, and Fritz was all day shooting it. He would dolly back and shoot, then he would stop and take the spoon from my dessert, move the ice cream round a little bit and dirty the dish, and then he would do it again, dirtying her dish a little bit, and then do it again. Then he would move the cup this way and do it, then he would tilt the marriage certificate and do it. He would do it 55 times, he would stand and blow smoke into the scene or something. Now, this is not important . . . this is not using an actor who's a human being, who has learned his craft, and who knows what to do. I have said it to Fritz Lang's face, and I will say it to anybody—he is a great director, but he is not for me. You must know that I love to act, that I love to build a character and have it come out of me.

——Fonda, interviewed for *Henry, Jane and Peter:
The Fabulous Fondas* (NY, 1976)

. . . It is not possible to develop a character in a film as much as you can in the theater. The one chance I had in the cinema was with Sidney Lumet making *Twelve Angry Men* [1957] because the nature of the picture was such. We got the artists together, most of them theater actors, and we rehearsed for 2 weeks like a play. We could have opened in a theater after those 2 weeks; but instead of going to a theater we went onto the sound stages, and photographed it, out of continuity as you have to because of the economics of filming. But those actors had already had for 2 weeks the benefit, and the thrill, of building their parts from the beginning to the end like a graph. This you never have in films, although you might have a director who appreciates rehearsal.

——Fonda, in *Films & Filming*, Feb 63

I've had successes, of course. Like *Mr. Roberts* [1955]. But I despised that film. It was ruined by its co-director, John Ford. I had played the title role on Broadway for 4 years, so I knew about it. Ford didn't. So he made a terrible picture.

Then there was *War and Peace* [1956]. When I first agreed to do it the script by Irwin Shaw was fine. But what happened? The director, King Vidor, used to go home at night with his wife and rewrite it. All the genius of Tolstoy went out of the window. Inevitably, it was a disaster.

——Fonda, interviewed for *The Sunday Express*, 13 Sept 59

I sensed something very special about [*The Grapes of Wrath*, 1940] from the outset. I was a Steinbeck fan and the story had moved me tremendously. John Ford directed it. We had just made 2 films together so we already had a love affair and on top of that it was Ford at his very best.

For months I wouldn't even go close to anyone connected with the film [*Young Mr. Lincoln*, 1939]. Then Ford stepped in and the way he dealt with me was typical of him. He sent for me and I wasn't under contract, I was under no obligation at all to do it, but in front of him I was almost like the recruit before the admiral.

I will never forget going to his office. There was Ford, sitting behind his desk. He had his old felt hat on and, I think, a handkerchief in one hand and his pipe in his mouth. He looked up at me from under his eyebrows. "What the _____'s this about you and Lincoln?" he demanded. "What do you think you're going to play, the Goddamn emancipator. Lincoln's a Goddamn jackleg lawyer in Springfield, for Christ's sake!" I left his office ready to do the film, ashamed of myself and that, of course, was exactly what Ford had intended. He shamed me into doing the picture.

If you do have a disagreement with Ford, it becomes an all-out fight. No half measures.

I've had my share of them with him, too. Total disagreements. One I particularly remember was, again, on *The Fugitive* [1947]. It was over the way to do a scene and Ford finally said: "Okay, we'll shoot it both ways. Your way and my way!" I felt almost triumph. So first we shot it his way. With that he walked away from the whole thing and I never did get to do it my way!
——Fonda, interviewed for *Radio Times*, 2 Nov 72

Jane F O N D A
Born 1937 in New York City. Studied at Vassar College and the Actors Studio.

You might play a scene in which you are face to face with someone. Then you do it over again for a close-up and only your face is seen. You have to get the same intensity of emotion, the same sincerity, even though you are acting all by yourself. Cueing Tony [Perkins in *Tall Story*, 1960], I would read my lines and really put feeling into them. But he just read his, and I couldn't work up the proper reactions. When I realized that, I told him that I'd make a deal with him—if he would read my cues properly I'd do his. Otherwise, I would just throw them away.
——Fonda, interviewed for . . . *The Fabulous Fondas* (New York, 1976)

Peter F O N D A
Born 1939 in New York City.

[The business of "flash cutting" in *Easy Rider*, 1969] was Dennis's [Hopper] idea. Dennis and I agree that dissolves and fades are all triggers that let you off the hook as an audience. If you're fading out a scene, the audience knows that the scene is ending and can relax; dissolve has the same effect. Dennis wanted to have some way of dividing the scenes that weren't either a fade or a cut, and thought up these "flash cuts." I was opposed to them because I still prefer direct cuts. I think that both of those times we cut 6 frames one scene, 6 frames the next, then 6 frames back, 6 frames the next scene, and so forth, could have been accomplished on a direct cut each time. But it is an interesting thing, and Dennis wanted to put it in because it was his gig.
——Fonda, interviewed for *The Image Maker* (Richmond, 1971)

Bryan F O R B E S
Born in London in 1926. Acted in and wrote films before directing Whistle
Down the Wind (*1961*).

I'd been acting around for 20 years and then I was suddenly hailed as a brilliant new discovery. That sickened me—so I decided I'd try my hand behind
the cameras. My trouble as an actor was that I hadn't been through the
Sandhurst of the film industry. I could never be cast as stiff-upper-lip officer
material; I was always the little cockney private in jankers, or I was the joker
of the lower deck. It was bloody arrogant, but I felt I was worth more than
that. . . .

I started writing when a film I was in ran out of words for its leading
actor, Alan Ladd. It was full-dress period stuff called *The Black Knight* [1954].
It was the weekend, and I promised to deliver something on Monday morning.
I read "Morte d'Arthur" in a few hours and then belted out a script with a
liberal sprinkling of "forsooths" and "verilys." It was cheeky, but it worked.
The word got round and soon I was rewriting scripts by the dozen. I was given
£75 a script—that was all a writer was thought to be worth.

The scripts had usually been through the mill 2 or 3 times before they
were thrown to me, and the only comfort I got was that as a rule they weren't
given to anyone else after I'd finished with them.

——Forbes, interviewed for *The Guardian,* 7 Oct 65

. . . When I got the chance to be a director. I went to Carol [Reed] and said,
"Any tips? Are there any secret code words which open the door?"

Q. Did he have any?

A. He had one very useful one. Yes, he said, never cut for an actor. And
I know what he means. It is so easy to destroy actors. I mean, you know, a
director, if he really wants to, can tear an actor to tatters.

Q. Yes, but he can make them, too.

A. Yes, he can either destroy them at the time or after the time, in the
cutting room. It is very easy. You are in a position of great power, really.

Q. What did Reed mean?

A. He meant if you have got to cut a scene because the actor isn't good,
or because he didn't learn his lines right, disguise the fact of why you have
cut. Carol said, "I always carry a nail or a coin in my hand, and if I see an
actor is going to go, I drop it on the floor and say, 'Cut! We must have quiet,
you know. Now, since we have stopped, would you mind doing it again!' "

——Forbes, interviewed for *Town,* Dec 65

John F O R D [Sean Aloysius O'Fearna] (1895–1973)
*Born in Cape Elizabeth, Maine. He came directly from high school in Portland,
Maine to Hollywood to get a job where his brother Francis Ford was a contract
writer-director-actor for Universal. Worked at many odd jobs—prop man,
actor, assistant director—until he directed his first film,* Lucille Love—The
Girl of Mystery, *in 1914. He was 22 when he began directing Westerns in
1917:*

We made about one a week. I directed them and Harry Carey acted them. All those early ones were written by Carey and me—or stolen. We didn't really have scripts, just a rough continuity. . . .

——Ford, interviewed for *Sequence*, New Year 52

Did you improvise a lot with Will Rogers on *Dr. Bull* [1933]?

Well, no writer could write for Will Rogers, so I'd say to him, "This is the script but this is not you—the words will be false coming from you. Just learn the sense of it, and say it in your own words." Some of the lines he'd speak from the script, but most of the time he'd make up his own; he'd stop and let people pick up their cues and then go on; he wouldn't write the lines down, but he'd work it out beforehand and then just get in front of the camera and get the sense of the scene in his own inimitable way.

What was it like working with color for the first time [in *Drums Along the Mohawk*, 1939]?

There was no change really. It's much easier than black and white for the cameraman. It's a cinch to work in, if you've got any eye at all for color or composition. But black and white is pretty tough—you've got to know your job and be very careful to lay your shadows properly and get the perspective right. In color—there it is; but it can go awfully wrong and throw a picture off. There are certain pictures, like *The Quiet Man* [1952], that call for color —not a blatant kind—but a soft, misty color. For a good dramatic story, though, I much prefer to work in black and white; you'll probably say I'm old-fashioned, but black and white is real photography.

When possible do you like to play a scene through in one angle, without cutting it up, as you did in the scene between [James] Stewart and [Richard] Widmark [in *Two Rode Together*, 1961]?

Well, it's better if you can do that, if you get close enough so the audiences can see the faces clearly. Certain directors go by fixed rules—they say you must have a close-up of everything. But we've got this big screen: instead of putting a lot of pockmarked faces on it—big horrible head, eye— I just don't like it—if I can play a scene in a two-shot, where you can see both faces very well, I prefer it that way.

——Ford, interviewed for *John Ford* (NY, 1967)

Q. Do you determine what the camera shall see?

A. With the cameraman. It's done in advance. A good cameraman knows how a shot should be framed. . . .

Q. You never improvise?

A. Oh, certainly—but strictly within the predetermined framework. You can change a cue, modify an incident, but the movement of the camera, like its position, is determined in advance. A director who changes his mind is a director who loses time. You should make your decisions before, not during, the shooting.

——Ford, interviewed for *Cahiers du cinéma*, Mar 55; trans. in *Films in Review*, Aug–Sep 55

It pays to get good actors [in small parts]. I remember in *The Searchers* [1956] I had a scene where all an actor had to do was go through the door and take his suspenders off. I did the scene 35 times, and the actor still didn't do it right. I couldn't figure out [what] was wrong. I said, "For Crissake, don't you realize what you're doing? You're going to bed and leaving your wife outside with Duke Wayne." The actor said, "Christ, I didn't know that. Most of us who play small bits never read the script. We just come in, find out what the director wants, do the part and leave." I shot the scene one more time, and the actor got it right in the first take.

Q. Is it true that you "cut in the camera"?

A. Yes, that's right. I don't give 'em a lot of film to play with. In fact, Eastman used to complain that I exposed so little film. I *do* cut in the camera. When I take a scene, I figure that's the only shot there is. Otherwise, if you give them a lot of film "the committee" takes over after you leave the lot. They're all sure they're picturemakers and that they know exactly how to put a picture together, and they start juggling scenes around and taking over this and putting in that. They can't do that with my pictures. I cut in the camera and that's it. There's not a lot of film left on the floor when I've finished.

———Ford, interviewed for *Films & Filming*, Oct 69

Carl FOREMAN

Born in Chicago, 1914. Came from theater work to Hollywood as story analyst and laboratory assistant.

I was certainly once the lowest-paid screenwriter. That was around 1940 when I was working in Hollywood. The first movie script I ever wrote was for a film called *Spooks Run Wild* [1941], which featured Bela Lugosi and the Bowery Boys. For that I was paid the equivalent of £50. . . .

———Foreman, interviewed for Edinburgh *Evening News*, 1 Sep 58

[*High Noon*, 1952, is still] very moving because of its personal connections. It was the first film I wrote and produced. I was under subpoena while writing it, so much of it is comparable to what was happening. The fact is I was not a Communist, but the guilt by association thing. . . . Friends drop you and in my case it led to a break with my close associates. When *High Noon* was finished I'd been blacklisted and I knew it would be my last Hollywood picture for some time. . . .

I started out to do a film about the UN, but I didn't want outright propaganda, so I thought of the Western background. Anyway, I wanted to do a Western because I never had. And the time for time thing interested me —a film that ran an hour and a half and took place over an hour and a half.

When I got the subpoena I switched. It became very interesting. There are scenes from the film that are taken from life. The scene in the church is a distillation of meetings I had with partners, associates, and lawyers. And there's the scene with the man who offers to help and comes back with his gun and says, "Where are the others?" Cooper says there are no others. Some of my associates were afraid for themselves—I don't blame them—and tried to get me off the film, unsuccessfully. They went to Gary Cooper, and he refused. The director, Fred Zinnemann, too, was very staunch and very loyal. Then they went to the backer, a wealthy lettuce grower from Salinas. He said, "I don't care if Foreman's a ringtailed monkey if he's doing a good job."

———Foreman, interviewed for the *International Herald Tribune*, 5 Apr 68

Well, Bolt is an admirable writer and one of the ornaments of our Guild, and Lean is one of the great directors, and their collaboration has been marvelously successful for both of them over the years. It may be noted in passing that Lean insists on having Bolt with him during the making of their films, and on this score, as well as others, Bolt is to be envied. My own experience with Lean, who I believe is, in his own way, a genius, was not quite so fortunate— in the case of *The Bridge on the River Kwai* [1957]. Writing the script, I found myself thinking along the same lines as Peggy Ramsay because David Lean wishes he could write for himself, he is daemonically particular about what he films and when . . . and David may have thought, among other thoughts, that I was trying to direct his film. In the end, and a hair's breadth from what I thought was the final draft, I asked to go, a considerable sacrifice for me since I had owned the film rights originally and had hoped to break through the blacklist with the film.

David agreed to my departure, I think with relief, and at my suggestion Michael Wilson was brought on for the final draft. In the end, I, at least, found certain confusions and awkward interpolations in the released film which, despite its financial success, betrayed the problems inherent in a director attempting to write a film through and by means of 2 disparate writers. And, ironically enough, neither Wilson nor I received screen credit for our work because we were both then still blacklisted, and the screen-writing Oscar the film received graces the home of someone named [Pierre] Boulle. Yes, there are all kinds of frustrations in writing for films.

———Foreman, in *Film Comment*, Winter 70–71

And as a producer, after making [*The Key*, 1958], what do you feel about the division of the producer's and director's functions?

Well, by and large, one person must dominate a film. Who that is depends on who *he* is and what the film is. Sometimes it's the producer, sometimes the director, very rarely the writer. And I would think there must be someone, ideally, who sets out to make a film, *his* film. I suppose that I will probably always be frustrated until the time comes when I direct a film and get *that* out of my system. Because, though I've worked closely and very amicably with directors, there is always a 5 percent area of no-man's land where no two minds meet. The question of who is right or wrong is not the issue—there's bound to be this divergence of opinion. If you have rehearsals, all these things can be ironed out one way or another; if you're doing a scene which hasn't had much rehearsals, it can be difficult. And there is always the pressure of time, and time is money. However, although both Carol [Reed] and I are strong-willed people, our relationship was a very good one throughout the picture. Ideally, Carol might have been happier entirely alone, and I might have been happier if I had been directing; but we made the effort—let's put it this way—because we have great respect for each other.

———Foreman, interviewed for *Sight & Sound*, Summer 58

Milos FORMAN
Born in Caslav, Czechoslovakia, 1932.

[With collaborators Ivan Passer and Jaroslav Papoušek] Our present way of making films is the result of many factors, which perhaps we do not even realize ourselves. Perhaps it is a reaction to our school years, when Czech films were acted in such a way that there was not an atom of truth in them. And perhaps, too, it is because formerly I invented and constructed so doggedly and laboriously that I got sick of the whole process. Of course I have not given up fabrication altogether—after all, even *Talent Competition* [1963], which was intended purely as a documentary on the Semafor Theatre, in the end turned out to be a film with a slight story about the hopes and dreams that many girls cherish.

Before I made *Talent Competition,* I automatically thought of professional actors—but when we came to the actual filming, I used to get scared. I found that I was afraid of them, full of complexes. And the results of my work with nonactors came as a pleasant surprise, even to me. I had discovered in their mode of expression unforeseeable moments which first of all confused me, but later enraptured me. And when I saw that they had the same effect on the audience I found no reason to avoid using nonactors.

——Forman, interviewed for *Czechoslovak Life,* July 67

The more precise the script, the more time and freedom I have for improvising when I come to the actors. Some of them I've known for years. I meet them and talk to them about the problems of the characters in the film and work their own views and dialogue into the script I am writing.

They see their bit the day before rehearsals. I think it's important that an actor doesn't form a view and say "I am a bad character" because he will then try, falsely, to be bad, and the director is finished. The actors are always very surprised when they see the finished film. In *Peter and Pavla* [1964], for instance, the father thought it was a tragedy and the boys thought it was a comedy. . . .

The director has to be a bit of a hypocrite with the cast. He has an overall picture but he mustn't tell them. I never speak theoretically to them and never, never let them get the idea that we are making big art. If they ever thought that, the whole thing would freeze.

——Forman, interviewed for *The Guardian,* 1 Oct 65

There are basically two types of nonactors. Those who are only able to be themselves—for instance, the mother in *Peter and Pavla*—and others who can act, but these have to be at least one degree more intelligent than the characters which they are playing. This is the case with Peter and his father . . . they aren't really playing themselves, they are doing a deadly straight parody. They reach a ceiling, determined by their own intelligence, while actors are able to spiritually live a role above their own ceiling. . . . It is very advantageous to combine a good actor—it must be a really good actor—with a nonactor. It helps both of them. On the one hand, [the actor] gets from the nonactors that undefinable ability to express himself without affectation. He in turn inoculates them with the very important feeling for rhythm and the expression of a point, which the professional actor possesses ... the value of nonactors lies primarily in their inimitable originality. They have one other tremendous advantage: if I write a bad dialogue or a whole scene, that is if I write it naïvely, or even untruthfully, an actor is able to provide it with the illusion of truthfulness, and thus cover up my mistake. The better the actor, the easier it is to conceal my stupidity. In the performance of a non-actor, who remains constantly himself, my naïveté protrudes like wires out of a broken umbrella. The nonactor is a kind of seismograph. Every stupidity which I commit is to him an earthquake, which causes him to lose his footing.

———Forman, quoted in Skvorecky, *All the Bright Young Men and Women* (Toronto, 1971)

I realized in advance that because the film [*The Firemen's Ball*, 1968] would not be based on the story of one person it would not be helped commercially. Because people like to identify with one person. But in this film it was not possible, because the main personality is a committee, a firemen's ball committee. And it brought problems for me. For example, the shortness of the film is a result of this. I underestimated this fact. When you have one leading character and the audience likes him or her, you can waste a certain amount of time watching just this personality. But when you don't have such a central single personality, you must move quickly.

I shot enough material for a 100-minute film. But this was for me a new experience. I tried to make one main person, a girl who is in the firemen's beauty contest, the leading character in the film. But I found this was impossible. I got more and more interested in describing the atmosphere and events surrounding the ball. So finally I eliminated most of the scenes with the girl, who now has a very small part in the film. And I concentrated more on this collective hero, the committee. I didn't realize the problems when I was writing the script, just when I was cutting the film. Then I understood that this collective hero doesn't keep the film together as solidly as one leading person.

———Forman, interviewed for *The Film Director as Superstar* (NY, 1970)

It [the idea for *Taking Off*, 1971] all started when I read an interview in a paper with the father of a girl who was murdered in the East Village. The interview was fascinating because it showed how *everyone* is leading two lives: the girl, apparently studying, really living with a hippie, mixed up in drugs. The parents, who lead one kind of life in front of their daughter, another when they're alone. At the beginning I thought the film would be about the children, but the more I talked to people, the more I was drawn to the parents. To tell you the truth, I find people of my age [39] much more interesting.

———Forman, interviewed for *The Guardian*, 18 Aug 71

I still want to make this film [*Taking Off*] very much because I think it has a very funny script. But I am absolutely fed up with all negotiations. I tell you something that frightens me. So much energy is spent here on things that never appear on the screen at all. The film, the final product of all that energy, is not a proof of your talent but evidence of your ability as a promoter. So much time and work is spent on negotiations, contracts, money, talking with agents, producers, companies, lawyers, and unions that there is no energy left for what WILL appear on the screen.

——Forman, interviewed for *Show*, Feb 70

Q. So when does the actor feel that he should improvise?

A. On the set. I don't give them the script, that's the first thing. They don't have the script at home, they don't memorize. Not because I don't want them to know what the film is about, I tell them exactly what the film is about, what their part is, but I just don't want them to memorize, to fix some image beforehand. So they come on the set knowing nothing. Now I explain them the situation in every take, I know the script by heart, very exactly, so *I* tell them the dialogue on the set, *exactly* how it's written in the script, but they can't remember even if I repeat it twice or three times. Now they must improvise, they must. They must think what they are speaking about, not only remember what they memorized yesterday.

Q. Do you think that works equally well with actors as with amateurs?

A. Not with everybody, because some actors just lose the earth under their feet if they don't memorize the text. But *if* it works with professional actors, then the result is great. I *love* nonprofessional people, but I love *most* professional actors who are able to do this kind of work. But of course actors trained in theatre acting have trouble with this because the theatre asks the opposite way of working. With improvisation, 90 percent is worthless, but 10 percent is great. I try to capture fresh, real moments, so I try not to do too many takes in order to keep it fresh. Sometimes I don't make long takes, because some actors can't do it. The bed scene in *Loves of a Blonde* [1965] is 10 minutes long, but not everyone could do that.

Q. Who are the professionals and who are the nonprofessionals in *Loves*?

A. The boy and one of the soldiers were actors, and the rest were nonprofessionals. All the girls except Andula really worked at the factory, as did the party official.

——Forman, interviewed for *Film Comment*, Fall 70

With me, story comes first, and actors, and when you have as strong a story as [*One Flew Over the Cuckoo's Nest*, 1975] the action should almost frame itself; you don't have to much calculate framing, you should have going an almost automatic simplicity of composition. Now Haskell [Wexler] though brilliant, if you'd let him he'd exchange the actors for puppets, which would less disturb his lighting and camera angles. Give me similar choice and I'd get rid of the camera, because it always intrudes upon actors and story. Bill Butler, who replaced Haskell, understands this: that, sure, there is eternal conflict between director and cameraman, but it must remain fight which is healthy to the picture, constructive.

——Forman, interviewed for *The New York Times*, 28 March 76

William F O X [Friedman] (1879–1952)
Born in Tulcha, Hungary, and was brought to the United States as a child. After working for a tailor he bought a penny-arcade peepshow. Began film production in 1912.

I went to the Warner Theatre one day, to hear a man [Martinelli?] sing the introductory number of *Pagliacci*. Of course, I went expecting to be thrilled. This was the first person from grand opera who consented to sing for talkies. The picture started, and he was making all the gestures he used on the stage, and the sound I heard was a banjo playing, accompanied by a colored man singing "I Wish I Was in Dixie." Of course the operator had put on the wrong record! And later they ran into this difficulty—they had the problem of shipping the reels to the exhibitor, and if one record was broken, no show could be given. When film gets old you must cut out the brittle part; and of course when this was done, the record and the film did not synchronize. . . .

In the winter of 1925 I was in California, and in the spring I returned to New York. The first day I arrived at my office I was greeted by my brother-in-law, Jack Leo, who said he would like to show me something in the projection room . . . the machine went into operation, and there was a little canary bird in a cage and it was singing . . . following that came a Chinaman who had a ukelele and he sang an English song. . . . "What do you think of it?" I said it was marvelous. Leo said, "It is all right if you think it is marvelous, because I have incurred an expense of about $12,000 without your consent while you were away. . . ." I found that the sound had been recorded on film and that it was reproduced by light from the film to the screen.

. . . They said there was only one way to record sound, and that was in soundproof rooms. . . . We let a contract to build our first soundproof stages on 54th Street and Tenth Avenue. . . .

I called for the inventor, Mr. Case, and said, "I am going to give you a million dollars . . . to make this camera photograph on the outside without a soundproof room."
———Fox, interviewed for *Upton Sinclair Presents William Fox* (NY, 1933)

Georges F R A N J U
Born in Fougères, Brittany, 1912. Military service in Algeria; demobilized in 1932. Worked in the theater before he became involved in film societies, film production and film archives.

I tried to give something unreal to the natural landscape, like the barge in *Le Sang des bêtes* [1949], which cut the wasteground in two without your seeing the water. I knew the slaughterhouses and I knew there was a terrific documentary to be made about them, but you need a poetic and lyrical counterpoint. For a year I went for walks by the canals. Then when I was making the film it took me a fortnight to find the right barge. It has to have the effect of magic. It is real and artificial in the sense that I want to make it look as if it were emerging from the wings in a theater. In my feature films I do the opposite, trying to make them as untheatrical as natural as possible.
———Franju, interviewed for *The Times*, 28 Nov 70

Documentary is to the cinema what the poster is to painting. A poster has a clear, precise question to resolve, which is why there are rarely good posters. The narrower the question, the better your chances of going beyond it. In *En passant par la Lorraine* [1950] if I hadn't noticed that the factories and the steelworks of Hagondange were in the middle of wheat fields, I would never have made the film.

Also, there's a question of conditioning, not so much to condition the audience, but to condition oneself. I've noticed that all the documents—and I'm speaking precisely of documentaries—that I've done have a relationship to subjects I'm afraid of. If I made *Le Sang des bêtes*, it's because I never saw that; if I made *Hôtel des invalides* [1951], it's because I'm antimilitary. If I made *Notre-Dame de Paris* [1957] it's because I'm anticlerical and heights make me dizzy, and if I made *La Lorraine*, it's because I'm afraid of fire, and I condition myself and stay in the fire. Since I'm afraid, then that makes others afraid, obviously. It's a way of sensitizing oneself to violence, and in doing violence. And at that moment comes the result—but it doesn't have anything to do with truth, not a thing to do with it. There's *a* truth, your truth, the filmmaker's truth. It's the only possible truth. There aren't any others. For me, the difference between a documentary and a fiction film is the same thing; if I make one or the other, I've conditioned myself, otherwise I wouldn't make the film. . . .

If you want to make an object stand out, there are two methods. The surrealist solution is to displace the object by putting it in a place where it wouldn't normally be found, where it refinds its quality as object by being unclassed. For example, if you put a piano in the middle of the street, it's much more beautiful.

The other way to make an object stand out is to strip it, deprive it of all ornamentation—which is more difficult. It's generally what one does in documentary. It's what I do in documentary. It's the most difficult solution and difficult to use. I did it in 3 or 4 films. When I made *Le Sang des bêtes* there was a man with a Louis Quinze table in front of him; he was surrounded by a group of men. I had everyone leave, and I left my man all alone in front of his Louis Quinze table. That way, it was right; otherwise, it wouldn't have meant anything. With all the other men, you wouldn't have seen anything. That wasn't by displacement, but by stripping, deprivation. There are two systems, and I know them well because I think I was the only one to apply them to the cinema. But they're only systems—and therefore artificial.
——Franju, interviewed for *Documentary Explorations*
(Garden City, NY, 1971)

John FRANKENHEIMER
Born in Malba, New York, 1930. Before his films he directed 125 television plays. It was the change from live television to tape that sent him into films.

The first thing I do is work intensively and for long periods of time with the writer. Then I read all the related material. Take the case of *The Fixer* [1968]. There was another book published about the actual Mendel Beiles trial called *Blood Accusation,* by a man named Samuels. We had to buy that book because we didn't want somebody going ahead and trying to make the Beiles case. We bought it for very little money, but the main thing is, I really studied that book. I went back through all the newspaper accounts of Beiles and did extensive research on what Russia looked like in that period, methods of transportation, costumes, insides of houses, everything. I try and do as much research as possible on every project, to immerse myself in it, in the period and the milieu. In the case of *The Gypsy Moths* [1969], I did as much work on parachute jumping as I possibly could. I did everything short of jumping for the simple reason I knew I'd feel nothing but terror jumping out of a plane, and it certainly wouldn't help me. But I watched the men who did. I talked to them, spent a lot of time with them. For *The Manchurian Candidate* [1962] I spent a great deal of time looking at newsreels of political conventions, going through all the books on brainwashing and the Korean War.

I find it twice as difficult to work in color as black and white because in color it comes out the way it really is. In black and white it only comes out black, white, and gray, so that you have to work much more closely with the set designer and decorator and cameraman and costume designer than you did in black and white. . . . I thought the natural colors of *The Fixer* were splendid. The jail sequence was almost black and white. We overexposed all the film, then instructed the lab to develop it normally so that we had an extremely thin negative giving muted colors. I really wanted to use color like black and white. I was very careful with every prop, every costume, every set.

[In] *The Manchurian Candidate,* the scene in the Senate Hearing Room with the television cameras. If I hadn't directed live television, I could not have directed that sequence. The flashbacks pleased me. Until then, scenes showing television sets faked the picture you saw on the screen. They said you couldn't photograph pictures on a screen. They just didn't know how to do it. We had technicians in from CBS where I used to work, and they showed them how to do it. Just had to pulse their movie camera so that it would pick up the TV images. In *Seven Days in May* [1964] the use of the screens was even more complicated. We used them in the Pentagon, where the guard could see who was coming up and down the corridor; in the general's office where Kirk Douglas could see Burt Lancaster coming down the corridor, in the telephone conversation between Fredric March and Burt Lancaster—each one had a television to see the other—and of course, during the President's speech. That was quite intricate because we had four monitors there, one for each network. We had it all going from the tape truck, right on those monitors. I could do it only because of my live television training.

I've never made a film in which the dialogue did not have to be changed in some scenes because it didn't sound or play right. I like to have the writer there, but if he isn't there I'll change it if it doesn't play and we have the time. The two best films I've done are *The Manchurian Candidate* and *The Fixer,* and the writer was there at all times.

——Frankenheimer, interviewed for *The Cinema of John Frankenheimer*
(NY, 1969)

It was with a great deal of terror that I approached *The Train* [1964], which was the first action film I'd made. I had no idea how to do it but I remembered something David Selznick had told me a long time ago—"When you're going to do something like that, *really* do it" And he cited the great fire in

Gone with the Wind. When he learned that MGM was going to rip down their back lot and rebuild it he went to Louis B. Mayer, his father-in-law, and he said "Louis B., I'll save you the money. I'll burn it down for you." And he did indeed burn it down. And the same kind of thing happened on *The Train*. I'd heard that the French wanted to rip up one of their big railroad yards because they wanted to change the gauge of the rails and I went to the chief of the SNCF and I said "Sir," I said, "you don't have to worry about ripping this place up—I'll blow it up for you." So the French Army then helped me and we put in 5,000 pounds of dynamite. We used 21 cameras and I tell you it really went up. It was a hell of a blast.

But the accidents in *Grand Prix* [1966] were much more difficult to do than the bombing of the railway yard or the train crashes. Because there were people involved. But we never had a narrow scrape once.

———Frankenheimer, interviewed for *The Times*, 1 May 71

Sidney F R A N K L I N   (1893–1972)
Born in San Francisco. Film career begun in 1915 at the Bosworth Company as an assistant cameraman. In 1916 worked as an assistant director to Griffith.

On *Intolerance* [1916] there were 1,000 idiots on top of the walls of Babylon throwing down burning oil and big rocks made of plaster of paris. Well, if one of them hit you, it could kill you. They were dropping so many things that no one could get the extras up to the walls. I was in charge of a group of 500, and Christy Cabanne had another group of 500. And since I was out in front, I made a speech. You know, a big rousing speech—"Come on, boys, don't be afraid to approach the walls—follow me." I charged toward the walls, thinking and hoping they'd all follow me. It took a lot of courage. "Follow me."—and I'd no sooner got the words out of my mouth than a rock came hurtling from 50 feet up and struck my shield. The shield knocked me cold and my 500 extras went the other way. My mother came across to the studio and said, "Is my son in there?" "Yes," they told her. "His brains are all over the lot."

———Franklin, interviewed for *Sight & Sound*, Summer 69

Pauline F R E D E R I C K   [Pauline Beatrice Libby] (1883–1938)
Born in Boston. A successful theater career led to her entrance into films in 1914 (Hall Caine's novel, The Eternal City, *produced by Adolph Zukor). When her films dissatisfied her, she returned to the theater, and her last years alternated work in both media.*

I made a picture [*Roads of Destiny*, 1921] not long ago because I loved the story. It had tremendous dramatic possibilities. It was sound, honest, big. The woman was a fine woman, a big part. I loved her. I understood her. I don't think I ever worked so hard in my life.... I gave my very heart and soul to that picture. I used to come home at night, crawl into bed and sleep like a child. The other night I saw that picture. And I came home and cried for

3 hours, and then I went down the next morning and signed a long-term contract to go back on the stage. . . .

What I'm trying to say is that there are too many angles to the motion picture business for a lone woman to combat. If I'd been a better picker, had a husband who was a big producer or a fine director, or even a good sound businessman, who could look after my stories, my casts, my releases—I should feel safe. When I left Goldwyn some years ago, I ran into bad luck. I was influenced to do the wrong thing. I didn't see what it would lead to, didn't understand. But I found myself with no one to advise me, no one to give me the surrounding support that I needed. I am an actress—I'm not a director, not a story writer, not a salesman. And—well, I just didn't do the right thing. And since I've never found the right stories in the companies where they wanted me to work, and I haven't found any companies that wanted to make the stories I wanted to do.

— Frederick, interviewed for *Photoplay*, Sep 1926

Karl FREUND (1890–1969)

Born in Konigshof, Bohemia. Entered film work in Berlin in 1908 through offering laboratory and photographic services.

The appearance of a Mayer script was that of a dramatic poem—a detailed recording of every shot and rhythm that he had formed in his imagination. And he was not content to sit down at a desk and imagine his scenes on paper; after repeatedly borrowing a "finder" from me, I finally obtained one for his exclusive use, for it was with a camera-finder that Mayer experimented and rehearsed each shot of each sequence *at home*. He was so persistent in learning *more*, always more about the camera's possibilities, that he often came to my apartment in Berlin in the middle of the night, with a new problem that needed technical advice.

He was just as curious about every part of the many-sided job of film-making. With Emil Jannings, who lived on another floor of the same apartment house, Mayer would try out new ideas and sequences long before they were filmed. In the two and a half months of preparation on *The Last Laugh* [1924], Mayer conferred every day with at least one of us—with Murnau, with the designers Herlth and Röhrig, with Pommer, with Jannings, or with me. It was out of this teamwork that all the innovations in *The Last Laugh* evolved.

I remember the first words that set the camera into motion. Mayer asked me, "Karl, is there any way to film a person's head first in a medium shot and then move in to a great close-up of the eyes alone?" This was for the moment when the aunt discovers that Jannings has been demoted to lavatory-attendant—and it was Jannings's reaction to her discovery that Mayer wanted to heighten. "I guess you'd have to mount the whole camera apparatus on a wheeled platform of some sort."

Carl Mayer immediately comprehended the possibilities of such a device, and the entire *Last Laugh* script was revised with camera movement. Actually, when we came to the shot that had started all this movement, wheels were useless, because the aunt looked down on Jannings from the top of a flight of steps. So we worked out this contraption for a descending approach to Jannings' face; taking a fire ladder that was built in sections that were raised or lowered with a crank, we mounted the Debrie on its top, and chose our *smallest* camera assistant to sit by it to adjust the focus. We all began to look forward to new difficulties—as challenges that required completely original solutions. For the well-known trumpet shot, we suspended the camera in a basket from a bridge that ran the length of the courtyard, and when we found that our pulley couldn't manage the upward movement of the camera-basket, we made the shot downwards—and reversed the film in the camera. When the film had to be a drunken Jannings, I strapped the camera to my chest (with batteries on my back for balance), and played drunk! For the opening shot—down the elevator, across the lobby, and through the revolving door, my camera and I sat on a bicycle in the descending elevator, and rode out through the opened elevator door across the lobby, and through the huge revolving doors. Mayer's imagination had convinced us that we could do anything!

————Freund, interviewed for *A Tribute to Carl Mayer* (London, 1947)

Tartuffe [1924], photographically was quite interesting. The beginning and the end I took in the modern style, allowing the artists no makeup, and using "angles"; while the middle section is soft focus, gauzed and artificial. *Berlin* [1927] was photographed without one person seeing the camera. I would go into a public house, 3 or 4 days before I intended to shoot, and bribe the management to install some powerful lights. After a day or two patrons accepted the lights and ceased to comment. My camera, electrically driven, I would hide in another room, while I sat in a chair in the bar itself and pressed an electrical contact. I always contrived that an electrical fan should be placed near the camera to drown any faint sound that might reach idle ears. Using hypersensitive stock, I managed to get everything that I wanted.

————Freund, interviewed for *Close-Up*, Jan 29

William FRIEDKIN
Born 1939 in Chicago, first professional experience at Chicago's WGN–TV.

The narrative as set forth by Robin Moore's [book *The French Connection*] contained all the raw material for an exciting screenplay, except for a chase sequence. It was on this point that [Phil] D'Antoni [the producer] and I were in full agreement: what we needed most of all was a powerful chase. In fact, our thinking frankly followed formula lines: a guy gets killed in the first few minutes; checkerboard the stories of the cop and the smuggler for approximately 20 minutes; bring the 2 antagonists together and tighten the screws for another 10 minutes or so, then come in with a fantastic 10-minute chase. After this, it was a question of keeping the pressure on for another 20 minutes or so, followed by a slam-bang finish with a surprise twist. . . .

The entire chase [in *The French Connection*, 1971] was shot with an Arriflex camera, as was most of the picture. There was a front bumper mount, which usually had a 30- or 50-millimeter lens set close to the ground for point-of-view shots. Within the car, there were 2 mounts. One was for an angle that would include Gene Hackman driving and shoot over his shoulder with focus given to the exterior. The other was for straight-ahead points-of-view out the front window, exclusive of Hackman.

Whenever we made shots of Hackman at the wheel, all 3 mounted cameras were usually filming. When Hackman was not driving, I did not use the over-shoulder camera. For all of the exterior stunts, I had 3 cameras going constantly. Because we were using real pedestrians and traffic at all times, it was impossible to undercrank, so everything was shot at normal speed. In most shots, the car was going at speeds between 70 and 90 miles an hour. This included times when Hackman was driving, and I should point out that Hackman drove considerably more than half of the shots that are used in the final cutting sequence. . . .

To achieve the effect of Hackman's car narrowly missing the woman with the baby, I had the car with the 3 mounted cameras drive toward the woman, who was a stunt girl. As she stepped off the curb, the car swerved away from her several yards before coming really close. But it was traveling approximately 50 miles per hour.

I used these angles, together with a shot that was made separately from a stationary camera on the ground, zooming fast into the girl's face as she sees Doyle's car and screams. This was cut with a close-up of Doyle as he first sees her, and these 2 shots were linked to the exterior shots of the car swerving into the safety island with the trashcans.

The only other "special effect" was the simulated crash of the train. Since we couldn't get permission to actually stage a crash, we achieved the effect by mounting a camera inside the "approaching" train, which we positioned next to the train that was waiting outside the station. We had the "approaching" train *pull away* and shot the scene in reverse, undercranking to 12 frames per second. Just after what seems to be the moment of impact, we included an enormous crashing sound on the sound track, completing the illusion.

———Friedkin, in *Take One*, July–Aug 71

I started the research [for *The Exorcist*, 1973] in November 1971. The first day of actual shooting was Monday, August 14, 1972, at a hospital on Welfare Island. The original shooting schedule was 105 days. It ultimately wound up 200 days. We were plagued by strange and sinister things from the beginning. It is simply the hardest thing I have ever done in my life.

There are strange images and visions that showed up on film that were never planned. There are double exposures in the little girl's face at the end of one reel that are unbelievable. I had to do a tremendous amount of re-shooting.

Then there was the delay on the trip to Baghdad. I was supposed to go there in the cool spring but because I was so behind schedule I ended up going in the blazing hot summer when it was 130 degrees in the shade and out of an 18-man crew I lost 9 men who dropped out from dysentery and sunstroke.

Ellen Burstyn's back was wrenched and she was out for 2 weeks. Max von Sydow, who is this big, strapping 6'5" guy, was out for a week in the middle of his big scenes. Jason Miller's 5-year-old son was struck down on an empty beach by a motorcycle that appeared out of nowhere and his life was hanging in the balance for several weeks. All of the special effects caused any number of injuries to the actors. The whole thing was a nightmare.

———Friedkin, interviewed for *The Toronto Star*, 17 Nov 73

That was Rex Reed's invention and totally false.

Neither I nor anyone else claimed the devil tried to stop the picture. There was a fire on the set, there was an accident with the sprinkler system; sure, these things happen. But I don't think Jack's death had anything to do with his work on *The Exorcist,* and I don't think Mrs. MacGowran does either. There were never any shadowy images on the film—I never said that.

And as for Linda Blair having a nervous breakdown, that's a vicious rumor and totally untrue.

. . . Linda Blair is the most pulled-together person I know—and I say person, not little girl. Linda Blair is a woman, a very mature beautiful woman. All through that picture she never once complained, was never once a problem, and that makeup took 4 hours to put on every day, and we'd have her in it sometimes 8 or 10 hours at a stretch.

Linda wasn't offended by the language or shocked or surprised by it. You have to have led a pretty sheltered life not to have heard it—it's kicking around the schools.

She'd do a scene then laugh and sip a milkshake. At first it was hard for me to see. Then I saw that that was the way she had to do it. She never once seemed to think of it as anything more than a game.

———Friedkin, interviewed for *The Toronto Star*, 19 Jan 74

Samuel F U L L E R
Born in Worcester, Massachusetts, 1911.

I told [the backer] I had this dream to make a film about the greatest assassins of history. But he wasn't interested in Brutus or any of the others down the line until I mentioned Bob Ford, and he said: "Who?" I said: "He was the man who shot Jesse James." And he said: "Jesse James! We'll make it." I told him that I was tired of writing scripts that were not used, so this time I would direct the film as well. That is how we made *I Shot Jesse James* [1949].

[*Pickup on South Street,* 1953] was [Richard] Kiley's first film and he was scared at that scene, he kept asking if it would hurt. And I'd tell him it wouldn't hurt much and, in any case, we have a dentist standing by. Kiley felt the stairs and said they were hard, and he was worried. He couldn't eat his lunch. Unbeknown to him, I had a very fine stunt man standing by to do the scene, and also a dentist because there is no way not to get hurt, and that is why the stunt man gets extra money.

What I wanted was fear and panic on Kiley's face, and I knew if I told him he was not going to get dragged down those stairs, I was dead, there was no sense in shooting the scene. The man had jitters, and he asked [Richard] Widmark whether he would drag him down fast or slow. And

Widmark said: "Well, you know, I lose myself in my part." So I got the panic I wanted out of him as he ran for the stairs. And I never had anybody really hurt except that one stunt man, and it was just a little tooth.

——Fuller, interviewed for *The Guardian*, 9 Sept 69

I work on the set with a designer, with the wardrobe people, everybody. I rehearse, minimum a week, with the actors. And I rehearse in that week at least 2 days with my whole crew. And we shoot every key scene in the picture without film. Let's say it's Friday. They all go home at 6:00. They rest over the weekend. Monday we repeat that scene. And all the actors are acclimatized now. They're well-rehearsed. They know exactly what to do. It gives me a chance to introduce business.

For instance, you have an actor who has to sit down at a table and he wants to pour himself a glass of water. And for one week I will rehearse him pouring that glass of water. And he says a certain line. For instance he will say: I like Stockholm. And he knows that when he says that line, he must pour himself a glass of water. Now Monday without his knowing it I change that glass of water to another part of the set. I move all my props around. Now when he has the scene, he says—I like Stockholm. There's realism in his face, because he's really looking for the water. And he looks around and I catch a look that's new. And that's what I do through the whole picture. And they never know, whenever they are to shoot a scene, when any business is added.

——Fuller, interviewed for *Movie*, Winter 69–70

G

Abel G A N C E
Born 1889 in Paris, a precocious student whose interest in all the arts led him to theater and to cinema (in this country's first decade) rather than to the solicitor's office that his father expected him to occupy.

At that time [1909], when I was poor, I was doing little parts for films as an actor—at the Gaumont studios, or at Lux—and I was equally disillusioned when I discovered what little importance was given to the actors working there. . . .

When I began writing scenarios, I decided to sell them to Gaumont. I wrote a dozen or so small scenarios—4 or 5 pages—and sold them for 50 to 100 francs. That was a bargain, believe me. You could eat for 3 days on 50 francs, that was all. . . .

I wrote all sorts of little stories, but they were very much cinema stories. Some of these scripts were shot by directors like Albert Capellani and Louis Feuillade, and some of them turned out quite well. I regained a little confidence. Then I had an idea for a film which I wanted to make myself [*La Digue*, 1911]. . . .

Nalpas [of Film d'Art & Pathé Frères] objected to my innovations for exactly the same reason that people disapprove of new ideas today. . . . We used to get orders from Pathé. We were told that if the camera cut off the actors below the knee, then the film would be rejected. The whole body had to be in the frame. . . . It was Ferdinand Zecca who supervised the films. . . .

It was I who raised the first dissenting voice, who sowed the seeds of revolt. As one or two of my films succeeded, they began to accept my ideas—and then they began to copy me. Gradually, I realized the inanity of the sort of thing I was making. I pulled myself up short and said, "Why are people making films which are about nothing but events, when they have at their disposal such a marvelous medium for psychological stories? They go on making films about people chasing each other, killing each other, or trying to commit suicide, but why not films which show feelings instead of just action?"

. . . In the end, Nalpas relented. "Look," he said, "I'll let you have a try. Here's 45,000 francs. Go and make a film." I went away, and in a night or two I wrote the script for the first—*Le Droit à la vie* [1917]. . . .

I tried to suppress the inessential details in an important scene by hanging black velvet behind the actors. In the films in which I did that, no one notices the absence of decor—all they see is the actor. This was really a very good idea, although I know the present generation does not support me. The eye is not distracted by a chandelier, or by the corner of a window. . . .

[*The international reputation of Gance was established by* J'accuse, *1919,* La Roue, *1922, and his masterpiece,* Napoléon, *1927, begun on 17 Jan 1925, with the interior scenes of Napoleon's school, the military academy of Brienne.*] I always spoke a lot before shooting. I would tell the actors and extras everything I had been thinking. "Don't think that because you are only an extra you will not be seen. You will be seen, because my camera will search you out. It is therefore imperative that you do exactly as I say. If you do not, you will have to be cut out of the film." And because these people were simple, they were very good at imitating. I would tell them, "Don't exaggerate! Think of what you are supposed to be, of the period you are supposed to be in. You are no longer in nineteen twenty-six, you are in the Fourth Year of the Republic. . . ."

I found myself becoming bored with the stationary camera, and I wanted to be completely free. The cameramen never refused to do what I asked of them, but they were not particularly pleased at the idea of having to hold the camera. At that time there were no lightweight cameras, and hand-holding was very tiring. Eventually, we invented a sort of cuirasse which, strapped to the chest, supported the camera. . . .

Obviously, I took a great many shots which aren't in the film. In those days, I was trying to find the best ways of getting the best results. With so many innovations, there were bound to be a few failures. . . .

I shot to a high ratio. Film wasn't expensive in those days. I never did much in the way of rehearsals. I found that if a rehearsal was good, the shot would be bad. This was particularly so with the difficult scenes. The first time would be the best.
—————Gance, interviewed for *The Parade's Gone By* (NY, 1968)

Greta G A R B O [Gustafsson]
Born 1905 in Stockholm. While working in a department store hired for 2 advertising films. Made a comedy before her international fame in Gösta Berlings Saga *(1924).*

The interviewer asked if there were a role she would like to play:
Joan of Arc. But it probably wouldn't go so well. I would like to do something unusual, something that has not been done. I would like to get away from the usual. I don't see anything in silly lovemaking. I would like to do something all the other people are not doing. If I could get von Stroheim! Isn't he fine?
If they want me to talk I'll talk. I'd love to act in a talking picture when they are better, but the ones I have seen are awful. It's no fun to look at a shadow and somewhere out of the theater a voice is coming.
—————Garbo, interviewed for *The New York Times*, 24 March 29;
repr. in *Spellbound in Darkness*

Robert GARDNER

My plan [for *Dead Birds*] was very simple. I would choose a man and a boy whose experiences of half a year could be pieced together to provide an understanding of Dani reality. I could not film every moment of their existence for 6 months, nor did I wish to. What I could and did do was to follow them closely and film those events which I thought added insight to the problem of living a Dani life. *Dead Birds* is not an exact chronicle of all events in the Dugum Neighborhood from February to September 1961. There are compressions of time which exclude vast portions of actuality.

——Gardner, in *Film Library Quarterly*, Fall 69

Jack GARFEIN
Born in Mukacevo, Czechoslovakia in 1930. ᴄ̣ ᴠivor of Auschwitz. Worked in New York theater and television, and as assistant on Baby Doll (1956) *and* Giant (1956) *before making his first film,* The Young One (1957).

While I was working on *Something Wild* [1961], the Screen Actors Guild closed me down for a day because I went down the street on which we were shooting on the Lower East Side and talked to the actual people on the block into portraying themselves. The excitement of making a film lies in using people in their neighborhoods, and capturing the actuality of drama going on without people being aware of it. The people were very much better than the extras. They didn't give a damn and paid absolutely no attention to the camera. I went down and found that grimy rooming house, rented the room for $6 a week, and the landlord didn't care who I or Carroll [Baker] was, or why she wanted to live up there. The indifference of the big-city dweller is a very real thing. He didn't even seem very impressed by the fact that we were making a movie there; just as long as he got his rent. But by shooting on actual locations in the city, the visual essence of what might happen to Mary Ann on those streets, when walking through those neighborhoods, adds to the tension of the film. In the bridge sequence, our whole approach was even against suicide. We wanted rather to convey Mary Ann's resignation and fatigue. Finally she gets so hot and looking down, there was this wonderfully cool water. There was only actual sound, there was no dubbing; I wanted [Ralph] Meeker to talk above the sounds of the trucks, so that the music is heard only while she is in her semidelirious state, sitting on the pavement of the bridge. When she leaves with Mike, the music stops, the real world comes back, with all the traffic noises on the bridge.

——Garfein, interviewed for *Film Quarterly*, Fall 62

William GARGAN
Born 1905. Left voiceless after throat operation.

Charles Laughton was Tony [in *They Knew What They Wanted*, 1940]. Years later, Mary and I socialized with Laughton and his wife, Elsa Lanchester, in England, and off the set Laughton could be pleasant company.

On the set, he was the most difficult man I've ever worked with. An inveterate scene stealer, not at all subtle, without any of the charm of Barrymore (or his talent), he was a grubby man who fought and clawed for every inch of celluloid. He'd once played Captain Bligh; now he kept playing Bligh. He'd become a tyrant.

On the set, while we were not shooting, he spent his time knocking the United States. Pretty soon we'd all developed a good-sized dislike for Fat Charles.

But the shooting was worse. In an early scene, Tony, the rancher, has me write a letter to the girl. He stands behind me and tells me what to write; I have to rewrite Tony to make it English and to make it romantic. The camera is up fairly close, on both of us, and as I would look down to start to write, or as I would say something, Laughton—behind me—would begin to writhe, his heavy face hanging over my shoulder like a full moon. Every line I'd speak, every time I'd bend to work on the letter, he'd growl, grimace, wipe his nose, lick his blubbery lips; he'd grovel, rub his hands, do everything but have a fit.

Finally, he had his fit as well.

So did Garson Kanin.

Kanin took it for a while, slowly burning while Laughton fiddled. He was a fine director, perhaps the best I ever worked with, showing me how to play a role both sympathetic and unsympathetic, a wife-stealer you could like, and I just placed myself in his hands. But Laughton needed no direction (Charles knew best); Laughton would take no direction (from an American!). The letter-writing scene dragged on, until Kanin's patience finally snapped and he began to let Laughton have it. Naturally Laughton answered back. . . .
——Gargan, in *Why Me?* (Garden City, New York, 1969)

Lee GARMES
Born in Peoria, Illinois, 1898. Entered films in 1916 in a New York studio before working for Thomas Ince.

My agent got me the job on *Morocco* [1930]. . . . Unfortunately I didn't have sufficient time to make tests of Marlene Dietrich; I had seen *The Blue Angel* [1930], and, based on that, I lit her with a sidelight, a half-tone, so that one half of her face was bright and the other half was in shadow. I looked at the first day's work and I thought, "My God, I can't do this, it's exactly what Bill Daniels is doing with Garbo." We couldn't, of course, have two Garbos! So, without saying anything to Jo [Sternberg], I changed to the north-light effect. He had no suggestions for changes, he went ahead and let me do what I wanted. The Dietrich face was my creation.

[Dietrich] still likes to have the north light to this day. She had a great mechanical mind and knew the camera. She would always stop in the exact position that was right for her.

. . . It wasn't his fault that George [Cukor] was fired [from *Gone With the Wind,* 1939]. It was David [Selznick's]. . . . All the preparatory work was based on Sidney Howard's script, but when we started shooting, we were using

Selznick's. His own material just didn't play the same. Cukor was too much of a gentleman to go to David and say, "Look, you silly son-of-a-bitch, your writing isn't as good as Sidney Howard's."

—————Garmes, interviewed for *Hollywood Cameramen* (London, 1970)

Gaetano (Tony) G A U D I O (1885–1951)

Born in Rome. Trained in a Roman art school. Photographed his first film in 1904, Napoleon Crossing the Alps, *working for Ambrosio Films in Torino. He emigrated to the United States in 1906, where he worked for Carl Laemmle's IMP Company (starting with* Madame Nicotine) *and Mary Pickford, before going to the West Coast and Hollywood for the first time in 1911. In 1938, at the Warner Brothers studio, he photographed his 1000th film.*

During the past year [1936–37] . . . I experimented a bit more with each succeeding picture until the [lighting] technique used in *Anthony Adverse* was fully developed.

It might be termed "precision lighting," because it is achieved almost exclusively with precision lighting tools—spotlights. General floodlighting, formerly used to assure a safe exposure level of illumination over all, is no longer needed or used. Instead, every detail of both actors and set is illuminated by light beams projected from spotlights. There is no difference in the amount of light used, but since every beam can be controlled precisely, there is a tremendous improvement in the result on the screen.

. . . No matter what effect we may be seeking, or what method of lighting we use, we light each actor with several beams, of various intensities, spread, and diffusion, and from several different directions. With all these beams we can either wipe the [face] shadows completely out, or turn them to advantage in giving naturally modeled, three-dimensional effects.

Therefore, if any of you should visit a set where I am making a picture; you would find that all my lighting units are spotlights, arranged on the lamp-rails above the set. Only in rare instances is it necessary to use lamps on the floor. . . .

There is another precision lighting tool that plays a big part in my lighting—the dimmer. When the electricians are getting the lamps ready for rigging a set for me, they know that floodlighting equipment will not be needed, but rather four to half a dozen or more small dimmers. I can then rebalance the lighting by bringing this unit up or that one down, as the players or the camera move about the set.

For instance, in *Zola* [1937], there is a scene played in an artist's studio overlooking Paris. The far wall of the set consisted almost entirely of broad windows and skylights. Now in real life, in such a room, all the illumination would come from the windows, so I illuminated my set in that manner. A series of spotlights on the lamp-rail above the set projected beams down through the skylight and the window. From the opposite rail, just enough diffused light was projected to relieve the shadows caused by this strong key-lighting, and to prevent the scene from being an absolute silhouette. These two angles of light were carefully balanced to produce a natural effect.

This lighting balance was not, however, enough to show up an actor's facial expression if that was important, as it was in one part of the scene. Here is where the dimmers played their part. For a good part of the scene, Muni played with his back to the camera, looking out through the windows. . . . But a little later he had to turn and face the camera, to speak an important line to a friend inside the room. The lighting balance was no longer dramatically correct, for while the semi-silhouette effect was precisely what the eye would actually see in such a room, there was not enough front-light to show clearly the facial expressions. If a big dimmer had been used to raise the intensity of all the front-light, the effect would have been unnatural. So I used a smaller dimmer, wired into the circuits of only the lamps focused upon the one player. . . . As Muni started to turn, the dimmer was slowly operated to bring the intensity of the lamps up to the correct level. When he turned away again, the lamps were dimmed again. . . . Sometimes a simple scene may have a dozen dimmer changes.

——Gaudio, a paper read to the Society of Motion Picture Engineers, published in the Society's *Journal*, Aug 37

Gene GAUNTIER
Her memoirs, Blazing the Trail, *describe her earliest film employment, at Biograph, Kalem and Universal.*

It was [Sidney] Olcott's ambition to finish each one-reel picture in a single day so he held a stop watch on the final rehearsal. If during the actual filming he heard the cameraman say quietly, "Speed up, Sid; film's running out," he would dance up and down shouting, "Hurry up, folks; film's going. Grab her, Jim; kiss her; not too long; quick! Don't wait to put her coat on—out of the scene—hurry now! Out Max? Good lord! Why didn't you hurry? You should have cut across the sidelines."

For the first picture technique did not permit of the action's being stopped midway. If the actors were headed for an exit, outside the carefully marked lines they must be at the end of the scene.

——Gauntier, in *Woman's Home Companion*, Oct 1928

It was the cameraman who held down the temperamental director and usually had the final authority on what could or could not be done. . . . Even as late as 1915 at Universal . . . there was a brief interval when the cameramen were given full authority over all phases of production. There were some 25 of them banded together in a tight little union. If they decided the light was good for photography, a flag was run up on a high flagstaff, a triangular white cotton cloth on which was lettered "Shoot." And if that flag did not fly not a camera crank was turned on exteriors scheduled for that day. . . .

——Gauntier, the manuscript of *Blazing the Trail*, quoted by Jacobs in *The Rise of the American Film*

Wally GENTLEMAN
Entered film in Great Britain with degrees in engineering and fine arts. Came to Canada in 1957 to become the Director of Special Effects at the National

Film Board. He worked on the making of Universe *(1959). It was this film that caught Kubrick's attention.*

No one works with Kubrick, one only works *for* him—one simply becomes an extension of what he wants and this is not what I consider to be good. He has the talent for collecting really good people around him and dissipating their talents in futile chases after some ephemeral thing. But he knows where he is going and he knows what he wants, so the film stands or falls on Kubrick himself. . . .

Kubrick called me down to New York for consultations with him when the script [*2001,* 1968] was at the story-board stage. . . . Kubrick was interested in consulting me on just how these conceptions could be achieved without recourse to normal duping effects. He had repeatedly screened a couple of prints of *Universe* on which tramlines were scored by backwards and forwards visual inspection. . . .

The main novelty in *Universe* was the applications Colin Low had made in getting a huge spatial relationship by using a very small area on the animation stand. This was the most striking thing about *Universe.* The other parallels between *Universe* and *2001* are the integration of three-dimensional models with one-dimensional artwork to render more believable this huge spatial relationship. Also, during the filming of *Universe,* I had become very cognizant of the fact that these things which are apparently happening on a cataclysmic scale can be obtained by shooting high speed into very small areas. In *Universe,* the flame shooting off the surface of the sun was shot on a square inch of cardboard, and this particular effect was in actuality reflections from crenellated tinplate in revolution—a phenomenon that Colin Low came upon when he was looking at a cup of tea in his home and noticed the light dancing across the ceiling. This we sort of harnessed and applied and did this terribly miniature shooting for the huge effect. . . .

My main duty . . . was to advise Stanley on the procurement and setting up of apparatus [for the special effects for *2001*]. I was with Kubrick during the preparatory stages and then the early part of the film production shooting, at which time we were joined by 2 very excellent people from Hollywood. There was Doug Trumbull and Can Pederson, both of whom had a large influence on the whole design of the spacecraft themselves. Kubrick has credited himself with the production and design of the special effects of *2001* which I regard as unflattering to the 4 people who were really involved in the actual design. Kubrick's method was to suggest that he wanted a certain scene and then the sketch artist would pull out 8 different conceptions and then Kubrick would say, "Well, I'd like a piece of this one and a piece of this one and a piece of that one. Now go back and do me another sketch." And then you would have 4 more sketches, and he would come back and say: "I'd like a piece of this one and of that one"—which becomes a terribly time-consuming process. And if in this way he means he designed, then that would be true. . . .

Devices which one uses for supporting or turning models are black velvet columns photographed against black velvet backdrops. One lights the model very carefully, seeing that no spill-light falls on to the actual support column. But then you can be terribly cunning in the way that you support it because if you have a globe that is turning, obviously it has to be supported from somewhere and most people begin to look directly underneath for the support. Whereas in actual fact, what you would do is turn the camera completely upside-down so that what is supporting it is actually hanging it—you run the camera backwards and everything comes out right again.

The technique for flying people that was adopted for use in *2001* is very excellent for concealing not only the wire but also for concealing (what is more important) the creases and the folds in the suit. When you strap a wire harness onto someone's body, where the wire comes out of the clothing, there are always stress lines. To avoid this sort of problem you suspend this person from the ceiling and work with the camera directed up at them and you can't see the support wires. In the scene where Keir Dullea is dismantling Hal, the set is turned vertically so the camera is pointing straight up and he is hanging down by a wire from above.

The weightless shot in the moon shuttle was simply the pen supported on a piece of nylon thread and the pen itself was stuck on a revolving panel of glass when the stewardess picked it off. In front of the camera you erect a large sheet of glass, making sure that you have no reflections in it, and then photograph through the glass with the pen on the other side.

——Gentleman, interviewed for *Take One*, Sept 68

Sergei GERASIMOV
Born in 1906. Joined the FEX Group in Leningrad.

The theoretical part of the training fell to Leonid Trauberg. He did his job with a passion and an extraordinary mastery, conveying to us with immense fervor all the artistic and literary discoveries he had accumulated in his 22 years. Grigori Kozintsev taught the principal matter, called "cine-gesture." It was based on the mathematical precision of American comic and detective films. The actor was required not to "feel." The very word "feeling" was only ever pronounced with derisive grimaces accompanied by scornful laughter from the whole troupe. . . .

This sort of dementia lasted until the appearance of Eisenstein's *Strike* [1924]. The director was officially—our true chief. He was all of 24 years old and for us an old man. We always said, "The Old Man says . . ." "The Old Man thinks that . . ." But Kozintsev remained our undisputed master. And I recall how after having seen *Strike*, he came back to the studio rather thoughtful, and said, "All that we've been doing up to now is baby stuff. We have to review our whole fashion of thinking, everything. We have to look for serious links with real life." And from then on the whole group set itself to read, to argue, to study seriously.

We were then infatuated with the American cinema. Detective films, burlesques, melodramas and of course all the films of Griffith were for us revelations and models. More exactly, we were inspired to redo them better, according to our own fashion. So, emerging from the eccentric period, we fell into the detective melodrama style. This stage was quickly passed, and there soon began to appear new elements, more appropriate to the nascent Soviet cinema. We grew up. We became more lucid, more conscientious. The most important moment of FEKS's activity was *The New Babylon* [1929], inspired by Zola and already a part of the patrimony of our cinematography. From this film dates our transition from the eccentric cinema to the political cinema.

———Gerasimov, interviewed for *Cinema in Revolution* (London, 1973)

Pietro GERMI (1914–1974)
Born in Genoa, studied at the Centro Sperimentale in Rome and worked as assistant to Alessandro Blasetti. His first film, Testimone (1945), *was supervised by Blasetti.*

When I arrive in the morning to start shooting, I never know what I am going to do. I know what the scene is supposed to be, of course—I have the script. But every day is new and different—the weather may be different, the light, the actors and their moods, and yourself. These things don't adjust easily to the film—the film should adjust to them. You don't know about them until you arrive, look around, sniff the air and sense them.

———Germi, interviewed for *Life*, 20 Dec 63

Giancarlo GIANNINI
Born in Spezia, Italy, in 1942.

. . . The scripts that result [from Wertmüller's writing] have the heft of a telephone book. And there are two of them. One version contains extensive dialogue scenes, the other no dialogue at all, representing Wertmüller's attempts to battle her early experience as a playwright and rely more on images. She will actually film two versions of all major scenes, one with talk, one without.

———Giannini, quoted in *Time*, 16 Feb 76

I work with Lina differently. I am involved from the beginning. Other films, I get the script, and we do the film in a month. With Lina, it is, at minimum, a year. I am part of the concept. I work on the script. I stay with it even after filming is completed, to make sure the message stays true. The message. That is everything.

———Giannini, interviewed for *The Toronto Sun*, 18 Mar 76

John GIELGUD
Born in London in 1904, into an English theatrical family. Sir John's acting career began early (his first great London success was in 1926), and the theater has always been of more interest to him than the screen. But it is his occasional screen performance (usually in filmed Shakespeare) that posterity will depend on to judge him as an actor. Nevertheless, he always shows astonishment at the filmmaking process—as in this interview:

. . . One knows that the best things in films are nearly always done by the director. Somebody told me the other day that in the film *The Chimes at Midnight* [1966] with Orson Welles, one of the most effective moments in the film is one in which I (Henry IV) look at Falstaff's body, and then look at Prince

Hal, and so on—there are 5 people. We never did the scene at all. On the last day Orson said; "There's a close-up I have to do of you, just look down there; now look up at me." I never even saw him made up as Falstaff, but it appears that because of the clever cutting, this scene of glances between 5 people is enormously effective. And that shows how much you owe to the cutter and the director when it comes to the screen. You can't really control your performance at all.

——Gielgud, an impromptu interview for BBC–2, March 66

Hitchcock came to me and said that he'd got a marvelous Hamlet part for me to do in modern dress. The idea [of *Secret Agent*, 1936] was that the character, like Hamlet, had to undertake a murder. But I don't think Hitchcock had all that much confidence in me. When we came to make it, all the psychological interest was dissipated. It was quite fun to do, but it didn't really work all that well.

——Gielgud, interviewed for *The Times*, 17 April 67

... Absolute control over your emotions, which can be turned on like a tap at 9 in the morning if necessary, is a very useful and important thing for the actor. In [*The Charge of the Light Brigade*, 1968] there was one little scene at the end which was frightfully important, a very tragic scene, and in the middle of a blazing hot afternoon in Turkey, Tony Richardson suddenly said, "Oh, now we'll do that bit down in the quarry, just get down there and say the lines." I wasn't ready, and if I hadn't been in the character, I wouldn't have known how to treat it, but it came out very well actually. You want to be able to command your powers at any time of the day or night, if necessary, because that's really what you've spent all your career learning how to do.

——Gielgud, interviewed for the Third Programme, BBC; published in *The Listener*, 2 Oct 69

Penelope GILLIATT

Well, there's no doubt that making *Sunday, Bloody Sunday* [1971] was enormously satisfying. When John Schlesinger and I began planning that film, we really thought we were the only two people in the world who would ever believe in it. It came off, I think, because of the work we did before we started filming and the amount of time we spent in rehearsal with Peter Finch and Glenda Jackson.

I coached both of them. Peter is a traditional-style actor who wants to know how to deliver lines. Glenda wants to improvise more, so I'd work with her, switching things around until she was comfortable. As a matter of fact, we became so close, we picked up mannerisms from each other. Even now, people say, "My God, you say that like Glenda Jackson." Or "You laugh just like Glenda Jackson."

——Gilliatt, interviewed for *The Globe & Mail* (Toronto), 4 Sep 73

I always carry big leather notebooks with me, and after I'd made a lot of notes and thought hard about it for a long time, I wrote the complete first screenplay in Boston in 10 days in 1967. The ending came very early on when I was writing in Boston, and it's one of the things that remained quite unchanged through many years of working on the script. I did years of reploughing while we were talking and casting. But no ludicrous, dopey rewrites during shooting. One always changes things after casting, talking with the director, and I suppose because of plain writer's boredom with retracking—you obviously do new things to keep yourself alive and interested—but I never wanted to change the ending.

Q. Is the finished film similar, therefore, to your vision of what it would be?

A. If you've worked on something that's your own, helping to cast it and rehearse it day by day, it's yours and carry the can, yes? The reason most writers don't work for film is that their cut-off point is usually at first draft stage. Forced on them. Or maybe a lot of them can't stand the garbage that long. But the truth about a film is that it's not fully written until you've got the stuff in a rough assembly and then you're looking at it, and you start thinking, "Oh, Christ! That simply doesn't work. What are we going to do about it?" There's no point in saying the mistake was because of the casting, or that the acting wasn't good enough, or whatever else, blah, blah, blah. The only thing for the writer is work out what to do.

When we first saw the first assembly [of *Sunday, Bloody Sunday*] there was a structural problem that I solved by wanting to cut 12 minutes from somewhere near the beginning of the film. For a writer to think of slashing a script in this way is much more ruthless than most film writers generally seem to be with their own work, apparently. I probably wouldn't have been as ruthless if I hadn't been so involved with the film as a whole.

——Gilliatt, interviewed for *The Hollywood Screenwriters* (NY, 1972)

Lillian G I S H
Born in Springfield, Ohio, in 1896.

[Griffith] made *Birth* in 9 weeks and shot only one take for everything except Mae Marsh's death scene. He wouldn't have shot that twice except that she forgot to tie the Confederate flag around her waist, and she'd had it on in the previous scene. He made the film with 300 men, not 18,000 as they advertised.

——Gish, quoted in *Take ⏑ne*, Sep–Oct 73

Q. When you came to make *Way Down East* in 1920, it seems to me that you really did take your life in your hands, particularly with that ice floe sequence. Had you any idea of the dangers involved when you started that film?

A. Yes, when I heard the story I knew it was going to be an endurance test, and I started walking and taking cold baths and getting ready for it. We lost several lives, you know—the girl, Clarine Seymour, who was in *True Heart Susie* [1919], played the part next to mine, and the exposure was too much for her.

Q. But now doesn't that suggest to you that Griffith must have been a very hard man in many ways?

A. No, not at all. He had his face frozen, he was out in the cold longer than any of us—whatever he asked us to do, he did something that was more difficult. In those days we felt the film was important, the most important thing of all—we weren't. Anything he asked, anything that we thought was necessary, we did without question.

Q. But what made that particular ice floe sequence so very dangerous?

A. The ice going over the falls. In the first place, it made so much noise, we couldn't hear the signal that Griffith gave—Richard Barthelmess was a little late in getting that, it was a gesture Griffith made, and he didn't get it the first time, so that I almost went over. And of course I might have been killed—at best I would have been injured probably for life.

Q. Did you never use doubles in those days?

A. Never. It wasn't sportsmanlike. And besides, we felt we moved in a certain way and that the audience could catch a double, they would walk differently, move differently and spoil the film. Or make them think something was wrong. And I think to this day they have that feeling when it's not the same person.

——Gish, interviewed for BBC–2 Late-Night Line Up; repr. in *Films & Filming*, Jan 70

Bert GLENNON (1893–1967)
Born in Anaconda, Montana, educated at Stanford University. Entered films at the Keystone Studio in 1912.

Many people are inclined today to blame the present vogue of multiple camera shooting for the imperfections in photography. Nonsense. It is merely the old, old De Mille technique of picture making plus a few microphones. When Alvin Wyckoff was chief cinematographer for Cecil De Mille, he made all his pictures that way. When I was in the same position, so did I. Now Peverell Marley is doing the same thing. And we used just as many cameras in those days as talkie companies do now, perhaps more.

When we were making *The Ten Commandments* [1923] our general setup was about this: my long shot camera in one spot. Beside it the two-shot camera; then 2 or 3 cameras making close-ups, with only an occasional two-shot, other cameras making angle shots. We would rehearse all morning, and then shoot all the rest of the day. By evening we would have 50 or more scenes in the box—good ones, too. No, multiple cameras can't take all the blame for the shortcomings in artistic lighting.

——Glennon, in *American Cinematographer*, Feb 1930

Peter GLENVILLE
Born 1913 in London. Acted in films from 1939 and directed in theater before his first film, The Prisoner (1955).

The idea of Peter O'Toole and Richard Burton for [*Becket*, 1964] was my idea, which I discussed with producer Hal Wallis, who agreed. I don't believe in having a hard and fast rule of how a scene should be played and imposing it upon an actor. In fact, with good actors that would almost be impossible to do. I believe in having, or endeavoring to have, a true sense of what the author intended by the characters, so in the casting and the original casting you are keeping author's intention well in mind, and then in the detail of the day-to-day work using, exploiting, utilizing, encouraging the particular details and niceties of the actor's personality and to use that in achieving whatever you want to achieve. But I don't believe in having a set idea of how a scene should be played regardless of the actor.

Now after having cast Anthony Quinn and Laurence Olivier in the play I felt, rightly or wrongly, that the film, in that the story dealt with two young men, should be cast rather younger and rather more differently. And naturally one got a completely different emphasis and different focus.

——Glenville, interviewed for *Films & Filming*, Apr 64

Jean-Luc GODARD

Born in Paris, in 1930, educated in Nyon, Switzerland and at the Sorbonne. From 1950 wrote film criticism for various journals, and regularly for Cahiers du cinéma *and* Arts, *before making his first feature film,* A bout de souffle (1959) *from a scenario by his colleague, François Truffaut.*

I improvise, certainly, but with material which goes a long way back. Over the years you accumulate things and then suddenly you use them in what you're doing. My first shorts were prepared very carefully and shot very quickly. *A bout de souffle* began this way. I had written the first scene (Jean Seberg on the Champs-Élysées) and for the rest I had a pile of notes for each scene. I said to myself, this is terrible. I stopped everything. Then I thought: in a single day, if one knows how to go about it, one should be able to complete a dozen takes [shots?]. Only instead of planning ahead, I shall invent at the last minute. If you know where you're going it ought to be possible. This isn't improvisation but last-minute focusing. Obviously, you must have an overall plan and stick to it; you can modify up to a point, but when shooting begins it should change as little as possible, otherwise it's catastrophic.

 . . . Belmondo never invented his own dialogue. It was written. But the actors didn't learn it: the film was shot silent, and I cued the lines.

 . . . *A bout de souffle* was the sort of film where anything goes: that was what it was all about. Anything people did could be integrated in the film. As a matter of fact, this was my starting point. I said to myself: we have already had Bresson, we have just had *Hiroshima*, a certain kind of cinema has just drawn to a close, maybe ended, so let's add the finishing touch, let's show that anything goes. What I wanted was to take a conventional story and remake, but differently, everything the cinema had done. I also wanted to give the feeling that the techniques of filmmaking had just been discovered or experienced for the first time. . . .

If we used a hand-held camera, it was simply for speed. I couldn't afford to use the usual equipment, which would have added 3 weeks to the schedule. But this shouldn't be made a rule either: the method of shooting should match the subject. Of all my films, the one in which the shooting method is most justified is *Le Petit Soldat* [1960]. . . .

What caused me a lot of trouble was the end [of *A bout de souffle*].

Should the hero die? To start with, I intended to do the opposite of, say, *The Killing* [1956]: the gangster would win and leave for Italy with his money. But as an anticonvention it was too conventional—like having Nana win out in *Vivre sa vie* [1962] and drive away in the car. Finally, I decided that as my avowed ambition was to make an ordinary gangster film, I had no business deliberately contradicting the genre: he must die. . . .

But improvisation is tiring. I have always told myself: this is the last time, I can't do it again. It is too exhausting going to bed in the evening and wondering, what am I going to do tomorrow? It's like writing an article in a café at 11:40 when the deadline is noon. The curious thing is that you always do manage to write it, but working like that for months on end is killing. . . .

The only thing is, one never does exactly what one intended. . . . After a certain time, for instance, I realized that *A bout de souffle* was not at all what I thought. I thought I had made a realistic film like Richard Quine's *Pushover* [1954], but it wasn't that at all. In the first place I didn't have enough technical skill, so I made mistakes; then I discovered I wasn't made for this kind of film. There were also a lot of things I wanted to do but which I can't bring off. For instance, those shots of cars looming through the night in *La Tête contre les murs* [1958]. I would also like to compose shots that are magnificent in themselves like Fritz Lang, but I can't. So I do other things. Although I felt ashamed of it at one time, I do like *A bout de souffle* very much, but now I see where it belongs—along with *Alice in Wonderland*. I thought it was *Scarface* [1932].

——Godard, interviewed for Cahiers du cinéma, Feb 62;
trans. in Godard on Godard, 1972

Although I accepted [the offer from Georges de Beauregard] I had no ready idea. Then I read a detective story (from La Série noire) which caught my interest. I had recently seen *The Big Sleep* [1946] with Humphrey Bogart once again, and the idea of a "Humphrey Bogart role" played by a woman like Anna Karina dawned on me. I also wanted the film to take place in France and not in the United States, and I linked the theme to a marginal, obscure episode in the Ben Barka affair. . . .

At the beginning, I tried to make a simple film, and, for the first time, to tell a story. But it's not my nature. I don't know how to tell stories. I want to mix everything, to restore everything, to tell all at the same time. If I had to define myself, I'd say that I am a "painter of letters" as one would say that there are "men of letters." So much so in this film that, although for the first time I followed the mainstream of an anecdote, at the same time I couldn't help placing it in a social context. This context is that in this age, at this time, everything—absolutely everything—is influenced by the United States. Thus the title: *Made in U.S.A.* [1966].

——Godard, interviewed for Le Nouvel Observateur
(No. 100); trans. in Take One

Strictly speaking, it's wrong to say that I use improvisation, except in so far as I always work at the last minute. I always use a written text, though it may often be written only 2 or 3 minutes before shooting. My actors never improvised, in the Actors Studio sense, in *A bout de souffle,* though they did a little in *Une Femme est une femme*. Usually the lines are written at the very last minute, which means that the actors have no time to prepare. I prefer this, because I am not a director of actors like Renoir or Cukor, who can rehearse an actor over and over until he manages to coax out a good performance. I like to sneak up on an actor from behind, leaving him to fend for himself, following his groping movements in the past, trying to seize on the sudden, unexpected, good moment which crops up spontaneously; and so gradually I build up an idea of what I am trying to do myself.

———Godard, interviewed for *Sight & Sound,* Winter 62–63

For me to think about the public means to produce something, good or bad, and then it is up to the public to discuss it. I was never vexed when people did not like what I was producing. What I like is that one likes it and another one doesn't, but that they are enabled to discuss it, to draw the inferences from it, good and bad ones for them. They are free to infer what they want. I only attempt to show them this by means of different forms. For instance, *Le Petit Soldat* [1960] has been severely reproached for showing a confused form, but in this period the opinion of the French was just as confused about the Algerian war—80 percent of the population did not know or did not want to know. I found it encouraging that after the projection of the film people were for or against the war, but in any case wanted to discuss it. . . .

If nothing were happening in the world, I could not produce any more films.

The impossibility or the difficulty to communicate is for me not a fundamental obsession. It is often a starting point of my scripts, just as for Feydeau or Labiche the Husband, the Wife and the Lover.

———Godard, interviewed for *Cinéma 65,* March 65

Pierrot le fou has more improvisation than anything else I have made. Most of it came out of my head just before it was shot. I worked without notes, like a painter. Anything I saw might end up in the picture. Perhaps I have carried this method as far as it will go. . . .

I took 8 weeks to finish shooting—twice as long as usual. The editing was done in a fortnight. We put the shots together more or less as they happened: I don't do many retakes . . . I'm not interested in beautiful images. With Antonioni, the color seems to be inside the camera. With me, it's simply what is in front of the camera. . . .

———Godard, interviewed for *The Observer,* 5 Sep 65

Paulette GODDARD [Pauline Levy]
Born 1911 in Whitestone, New York. Worked as a model and in the theater before entering films.

[Chaplin] changed a lot of things. When I turned up to make *Modern Times* [1936] I was wearing the full glamour rig. Charlie took one look at me, shook his head and said, "That's not it. That's definitely not it." He told me to take off my shoes, change my suit, and remove my makeup. Then he threw a bucket of water all over me. The result is the hairstyle I've worn ever since.

———Goddard, interviewed for *The Sunday Times Supplement,* 4 June 72

John GOLDMAN

To make such a film as *Man of Aran* [1934] requires an extreme awareness, an openness to reception which in my experience is very rare among people. This freedom to be aware was Flaherty's great gift. All the time I was on Aran I never saw Flaherty deliberately pose his camera. The camera was set up and he peered through it. Either what he saw through it was right, or absolutely wrong. Either what he saw had its own life and existence, or it was dead and lifeless, meaningless in its own terms.

When seeing rushes, it is easy to see and reject the shots which are failures, which are lifeless. And Flaherty had a very high proportion of such failures. These having been rejected, the second stage of selection came, and here the difficulties began. During these viewings nothing existed for Flaherty except what was on the screen. Gone was the moment when he took the shot. Gone was any preconceived idea of what he wanted for the film. Gone were any notions of good photography or of focus or exposure. In the theater, he would sit for hour after hour, smoking cigarette after cigarette, heaving with his peculiarly labored breathing, concentrating wholly on the screen. . . .

Then one day, months after the start, Flaherty would suddenly realize that he was looking at a sequence. It was a peculiar sensation. One day a mere collection of shots joined up together; the next, a perceptible semblance of a sequence, seemingly self-generated, organic, belonging. And that, so far as that sequence was concerned, was the end of the second stage in making the film.

The third stage began, similar to the second, but more demanding in patience and perception. Again the projectionists would work day and night. They would have endless strips of paper which they would insert in the reel of film on the projector when Flaherty pressed the buzzer in the theater. "Cut that shot in half.". . . "Take out that long shot, it's dead!" From the first germ of life, the sequence would start to grow up. First, the internal life in the individual shot, then the internal life in the sequence. I recall one sequence growing this way into life and then it seemed to wilt and die, stillborn. "We've been preconceiving," Flaherty said. And so every shot had to be broken down and shuffled up and the reel put back again into rushes.

Then individual sequences would be linked. Disaster. Whole sequences built up and grown after long months of loving care and fatigue would have to go. But never for one instant did Flaherty himself intrude on the film. Always he allowed it to grow from within. . . .

He had definite ideas of what he meant by drama. As a dramatic film director, I found his grammar and vocabulary, using those terms in a film sense, curiously limited. His drama was based solely on suspense and since this was the one weapon in his armory, so to speak, he used it increasingly hard and extended it to a degree that could be said to be monotonous. On the other hand, this suspense drama was ideally suited to his needs. Suspense was always based on revelation, and the revelation delayed until the last possible moment. He was very careful about this exact moment of the resolution of the suspense. This had to be cut as short as possible. He was afraid of anticlimax. One of his maxims was "Never reveal anything." In close-ups of people, he hated full-face shots. He preferred three-quarter profiles, heads shot from behind, anything which did not reveal the full face. The full face showed too much. He disliked medium and mid-long shots because they revealed without hiding. In all his films after *Nanook,* he proceeds from close-ups eventually to a long shot as a payoff. "If they want to know more," he would say, "you know you have got them.". . .

—Goldman, letter to Paul Rotha (1959), quoted in
The Innocent Eye (London, 1963)

Samuel G O L D W Y N [Goldfisch]   (1884–1974)
Born in Warsaw. Office boy before running away to relatives in England. Emigrated to USA at 15. In 1913 formed Lasky Feature Plays with brother-in-law Jesse Lasky and Cecil B. De Mille.

I was very interested in this point you raised about my film [*Edge of Doom,* 1950]. You see, we used no sets at all on that picture. We just went out and we looked for the right location and we used it. We photographed it all on the spot. . . .

Q. But you know as well as I, there are many different ways of photographing a real place. You say yourself you wanted this picture to convey the sense of poverty, but this lighting lushes it all up.

A. Just because it's a realistic picture is no reason for bad photography. I always used the best cameraman. That was Gregg Toland. He died, so I got the next best—Harry . . . Harry Stradling. He did a beautiful job on it.

—Goldwyn, interviewed for *Sequence,* New Year 51

Anatoli G O L O V N Y A
Born 1900.

Pudovkin heard and saw each shot of his films before it was filmed. . . . In filming [*Mother,* 1926] the scene of the mother sitting by her husband's bier Pudovkin and [Baranovskaya] sought for the pose that would convey the feeling that the mother had already sat there a long time, erect and immobile. Pudovkin wanted to convey graphically the sense of empty and silent surroundings. Kozlovsky and I removed everything superfluous from the set. Left in the composition were only the black figure of the mother, the white sheet over the corpse, the open coffin, the gray walls.

In filming it we spoke in whispers, walked on tiptoe. The washstand was filmed separately. Pudovkin gave [me] only one direction: "Film it so that the dripping water can be heard."

—Golovnya, in *Iskusstvo Kino,* Aug 53

Generally Pudovkin concentrated principally on work with the actors. No one respected actors like Pudovkin. . . . He understood that the actor is the incarnation of the character on the screen, the sole incarnation for the spectator, and that the mood of the actor is crucial. Pudovkin revealed enormous tact in working with his actors. It was most striking with Alexei Denisovich Dikii, on *Admiral Nakhimov* [1946]. Dikii was an expansive man. . . . And being a di-

rector as well, he had his own ideas on the way things should be done. Pudovkin cried over it sometimes—literally, somewhere in a corner. Yet at the same
time, what efforts! Not just to achieve his own ends, but to give Dikii himself
the *desire* to play the character as Pudovkin saw him. This was Pudovkin's
greatest accomplishment—without ever constricting the actor, to get him to
think in the same way as the director himself. . . .

Now don't forget that Pudovkin was himself an astonishing actor. If you
were in the place of one of the actors and looked at Pudovkin standing beside
the camera, you would have seen everything the actor did as if in a mirror.
Pudovkin was a very expressive mimic. Moreover he was entirely absorbed in
what was happening (which is inevitable, by the way, for any real director).
He completely let himself go, inside; and it was this that allowed him to seek,
with the actor, the emotional truth of the character. But he never restricted an
actor by asking him to copy him, as some directors do. He sought the truth of
the image in the actor, not in himself.

——Golovnya, interviewed (1965) for *Cinema in Revolution*

Cary G R A N T   [Alexander Archibald Leach]
Born in Bristol, England, 1904.

. . . I must confess it's true that I modeled myself after the blasé drawing-room
pose assumed by my stage idol, Noël Coward. Hand casually plunged in the
pocket, you know. It took me years to get my hand unstuck and acquire the
freedom to simply play myself.

We all create ourselves as we grow older and it's a pity in a way that I
felt most like my true self in my next to last picture, *Father Goose* [1964], . . .
I felt free to perform like an unshaven old gray-haired sot in sloppy denims—
the way I dress when I'm at home. The really relaxed Cary Grant.

——Grant, interviewed for *The Toronto Star*, 4 June 76

Helen G R A Y S O N   (1902–1962)
*Born in Philadelphia; educated in France and Bryn Mawr. Most of her film
work was for the Office of War Information, the best known being* The Cummington Story, *1946.*

The camera crew and I received the script [by Frank Beckwith?] and went to
Cummington. We planned every scene in its actual setting. And it may be
said here that, indoors, documentary directors and cameramen solve difficulties
never encountered in Hollywood studios, where sets are constructed with movable walls and no ceilings. The tiny cottage rooms of Cummington had not
been designed for simultaneous occupation by furniture, floodlights, the large
moving-picture camera on its tripod, and people. A lot of people because the
equipment necessary for indoor shooting requires a large crew of technicians.
The camera director [Larry Madison] had 3 assistants; 2 electricians attended
to the lights; an engineer controlled the Diesel-driven generator in its ele-
phantine truck. I had a script girl. . . . And over all ruled the unit manager.

——Grayson, in *Bryn Mawr Alumnae Bulletin*, Apr 46

Graham G R E E N E
Born in Berkhempstead, Hertfordshire in 1904.

On these treatments Carol Reed and I worked closely together, covering so many feet of carpet a day, acting scenes at each other. No third ever joined our conferences; so much value lies in the clear cut-and-thrust between two people. To the novelist, of course, his novel is the best he can do with a particular subject; he cannot help resenting many of the changes necessary for turning it into a film or a play; but *The Third Man* was never intended to be more than the raw material for a picture.

> ——Greene, in preface to *The Third Man and
> The Fallen Idol* (London, 1950)

John G R I E R S O N (1898–1972)
Born in Kilmadock, Stirlingshire. First film practice, Drifters (1929):

It is the hauling of the herring nets in heavy weather off Smith's Knole in the North Sea and it is, of course, very spectacular. We're in a drifter called *The Mirabel* off Lowestoft. The camera is moving around a very slippery deck indeed, noting detail after detail, and part of the time it is poised perilously up on top of the wheelhouse trying to get the swing of the ship. What seemed new to people 25 years ago was this use of the camera, the detail, the piling of one shot on another and this business of filling the screen as full up as a modern painting. The big close-up, it was a sort of demonstration of a reminder of the camera's power of natural observation, taking all the little bits and pieces and binding them together.

> ——Grierson, on BBC-TV, 23 Nov 54; repr. in
> *Documentary Diary* by Paul Rotha

With Flaherty it became an absolute principle that the story must be taken from the location, and it should be (what he considers) the essential story of the location. His drama, therefore, is a drama of days and nights, of the round of the year's seasons, of the fundamental fights which give his people sustenance, or make their community life possible, or build up the dignity of the tribe. . . .

Flaherty illustrates better than anyone the first principles of documentary. (1) It must master its material on the spot, and come in intimacy to ordering it. Flaherty digs himself in for a year, or two maybe. He lives with his people until the story is told "out of himself." (2) It must follow him in his distinction between description and drama. I think that we shall find that there are other forms of drama or, more accurately, other forms of film, than the one he chooses; but it is more important to make the primary distinction between a method which describes only the surface values of a subject, and the method which more explosively reveals the reality of it. You photograph the natural life, but you also, by your juxtaposition of detail, create an interpretation of it.

The final creative intention established, several methods are possible. You may, like Flaherty, go for a story form, passing in the ancient manner from the individual to the environment, to the environment transcended or not transcended, to the consequent honors of heroism. Or you may not be so interested in the individual. You may think that the individual life is no longer capable of cross-sectioning reality. You may believe that its particular bellyaches are of no consequence in a world which complex and impersonal forces command, and conclude that the individual as a self-sufficient dramatic figure is outmoded. When Flaherty tells you that it is a devilish noble thing to fight for food in a wilderness, you may, with some justice, observe that you are more concerned with the problem of people fighting for food in the midst of plenty. . . .

This sense of social responsibility makes our realistic documentary a troubled and difficult art. . . . The job of romantic documentary is easy in comparison; easy in the sense that the noble savage is already a figure of romance and the seasons of the year have already been articulated in poetry. Their essential virtues have been declared and can more easily be declared again, and no one will deny them. But realist documentary, with its streets and cities and slums and markets and exchanges and factories, has given itself the job of making poetry where no poet has gone before it, and where no ends, sufficient for the purposes of art, are easily observed. It requires not only taste but also inspiration, which is to say a very laborious, deep-seeing, deep-sympathizing creative effort indeed.

——Grierson, in *Cinema Quarterly*, Spring 33; repr. in
Forsyth Hardy, ed., *Grierson on Documentary*

David Wark G R I F F I T H   (1875–1948)
Born in Crestwood, Kentucky.

[*The Birth of a Nation*, 1915] grew as we went! I had no scenario, and never looked again at some few notes I made as I read the book [*The Clansman*, by Thomas Dixon] and which I read to my company before we began. Naturally the whole story was firmly in my mind, and possibly the personal exuberance of which I have told you enabled me to amplify and to implant in the scenes something of the deep feeling I experienced in that epoch that had meant everything, and then had left nothing to my nearest, my kin, and those about me. . . .

There were 6 weeks of rehearsals, before we really began. I think it took something like 6 months to make the picture—that is, the actual photography; but in all I put in a year and a half of work.

It was a big venture in numbers at that time; I suppose from first to last we used from 30,000 to 35,000 people.

That seemed immense at that era, but now, in the piece we temporarily call *The Mother and The Law*, we have used since the first of January about 15,000 people a month [This statement was made in the latter part of April 1916], and I cannot see even the beginning of the end as yet.

With *The Clansman* it was not alone the first expense but the incessant fighting we had to do to keep the picture going, that cost.

We spent over $250,000 the first 6 months, combating stupid persecution brought against the picture by ill-minded censors and politicians who were playing for the Negro vote.

——Griffith, interviewed for *The Story of David Wark Griffith*,
in *Photoplay*, Oct 1916

D. W. Griffith to Stroheim: Take the job but don't do it the way they tell you. Do what you want to do. [Apocryphal?]

Alec G U I N N E S S
Born 1914 in London. Film debut in Great Expectations (1946). *Knighted in 1959.*

Another thing that annoys me is the general assumption that you don't have to act for the screen, the idea that you just dress up in what the wardrobe gives you and then do only what the director says. Ridiculous! There's as much scope for decent acting on the screen as ever there was on the stage, although, of course, it's a different technique. And I can tell you that we're going to do 2 clear weeks of rehearsal before a camera turns on *Arms and the Man* [unrealized].
          ———Guinness, interviewed for *The Evening News,* 25 June 55

I meant to spend a couple of weeks in Glasgow working on the accent [for *Tunes of Glory,* 1960], but I couldn't fit it in. So I borrowed a BBC record of some street interviews up there on VJ-night and kept playing it over.
          ———Guinness, interviewed for *The Daily Mail,* 1 Dec 61

I had no particular policy about my career, other than the fact that I saw the red light one day when I was making a not very good film for Rank called *To Paris, With Love* [1954].
          John Davis (Mr. Rank's No. 2) came on the set one day and called out: *"Give us some pratfalls, Alec. Give us some laughs."* I realized then and there that I just wasn't going to fit in. If things were going that way, I had to think in other terms. Oh dear, yes.
          ———Guinness, interviewed for *The Sunday Express,* 19 Dec 65

[In *The Horse's Mouth,* 1959] It wasn't a question of the grittiness of the voice so much as a question of the accent. Because it seemed to me that it had to be an educated accent and yet if you spoke with an educated accent, a lot of the lines and a lot of situations became not quite believable. If you cockneyed it up a bit, it was false to the creation of the book. So it was a compromise. I tried to find a voice in which no one would be able to detect an accent of any sort, a kind of gritty, rough . . . more or less like air passing out of gravel. And I did find a voice where I thought, "I'll have to use that," and it did the trick for me, finding that, because then I felt myself free to just relax on that and say the lines and be it.
          ———Guinness, interviewed for *The Times,* 7 Aug 71

Edmund G W E N N   (1875–1959)
Born in Glamorgan. Theater work in London and New York City; film roles since the 1916 British short, The Real Thing at Last.

We rehearsed part of the film, *How He Lied to Her Husband* [1931] in this flat, and then Bernard Shaw used the stage of the Palace Theatre with Cecil

Lewis and drilled us himself day after day, displaying the most extraordinary mental and physical agility. Not until we were perfect in every word and movement would he allow us to go before the camera at Elstree. Personally I think Mr. Shaw would make a very good film director. He is ready to adapt himself to new methods. In all the years I have known him, I do not remember him being obstinate about a point.

———Gwenn, interviewed for *The Film Weekly,* 17 Oct 31

Well, I can only give you an instance of my way of working. . . .

Let's take the little East End bookie that I played in *Frail Women* [1931] with Mary Newcomb, at Twickenham. For several weeks before the film started, I spent a good deal of time at racecourses. Not big, exclusive meetings of the Ascot sort, but the crowded "people's meetings" where bookmakers, similar to the one I was to portray, have their stands.

I met bookies, and I came home in the train with them, and I watched them, and talked with them and, of course, made bets with them. Cost me quite a lot, that little bit of "research." But it was worth it. I knew, at the end of it, how a bookie looked, and talked, and a little of how he thought.

———Gwenn, interviewed for *Film Pictorial,* 2 Sep 33

H

Conrad H A L L
Born in Tahiti (son of James Norman Hall), in 1926. Studied under Slavko Vorkapich at the University of Southern California. Camera operator for Mc-Cord, Haller, Crosby and Mohr. Photographed Disney nature films on 16 mm.

. . . There was a lot of hassling during shooting [of *Fat City,* 1972] about not having enough light on the actors. We had the front office looking at the dailies every day, and if they felt it was something that wouldn't project properly at the drive-ins, they would send me a letter and they would telephone somebody on the set who would come over and say something like, "There's nothing on the film." The style I was trying to use comes from the material, which takes place in dingy afternoon bars, and you know how it is at a bar on Fifth Street. It's dark, you can hardly see anything, and then when you come outside, you can hardly see anything because it's pure white. So I went for really dark interiors.

I worked right on the edge, using very little light, wide open stop, and let the windows go completely white so that the exterior material, when it appeared white, would have a sense to it. Because when you looked from the inside out, it was white, so that it had a unifying factor. But I'd be lighting and all of a sudden somebody would say, "There's nothing on the film, you can't see the people." So I'd get a little chicken and throw in an extra light but when I'd see the dailies, it would be perfect, just the way I wanted it. I don't know about drive-ins. I mean, I think there's a great myth about whether shows project well or don't project well at drive-ins, and I doubt whether too many people care what they see at a drive-in. I may be wrong about that. . . .

What happened here was I was not involved in the timing of this picture, and there are many timing problems in this print, as there was in the answer print. I'm sorry that I wasn't involved. I would have made the exteriors even hotter and the interiors slightly darker so that they wouldn't go to that greenish quality. My exteriors were printing about 26 or 30, somewhere in there, and my interiors were printing right on light 20. If you go to light 19, everything gets all milky but if you're on light 20, it's nice and black and rich. The show was pushed for the most part to give it a kind of seedy quality that seemed to fit the material. . . .

It was a 33-day schedule. I could never understand why they took a lot of the material into sets but we had an art director named Dick Silver, a very good art director, and he built a lot of sets.

I could never understand why, I mean of all places, of all movies, this is one that could be made right in those actual skid-row rooms and skid-row bars and those small auditoriums and places where these fights took place. Actually, the novel is set in the very area where we filmed it but for some reason or another, a decision that John Huston made, a lot of the sets were built not on a sound stage but in an auditorium on the Stockton Fairgrounds. I think it's always tough to make sets look *really* real. That first hotel room— that's my favorite shot in the whole picture where Stacy Keach is lying down and he gets up to look for the cigarette and matches. That was a real room that looked like a real room. The rest of it didn't always work that way. . . .

Later on, John turned on me and sided with Ray [Stark] about a scene he felt I had made too obscure, the scene where they're taking the busses in the early morning. It was actually very, very dark. We went out about four o'clock one morning, to what they call the shape-up. It takes place in an area where there's no light, no street lights or anything else. You have a few little fires going, and you hear the bus drivers hawking the type of work their buses would take you to—tomato picking or onion topping or weeding or hoeing or all these kinds of things. There was a sense that I got from it, while wandering through and not seeing anything and having the story told to me through an audio sense, and I don't see what's wrong with doing that in films. The story is what has to be served, and seeing everything is not necessarily the most important element. . . .

For instance, the concept of the barroom scene for me. . . . We had a plank with a hole on it and an Arriflex, so that when he walked down the street and went through the screen door into the bar, we would follow him in until he stopped because his eyes had not adjusted to the dimness. I had purposely not lit the bar interior so we would see nothing past his back, lit from the open doorway. What I wanted to have happen was to see beyond him and not see anything, just the shape of his back before cutting around to the reverse. Well, they never did that. He came in, and they cut immediately to the reverse. I think it would have been much more effective to come in, hear some music and voices and not see anything before you cut around to the silhouette shot and sort of lighten the scene a little bit as it progressed. . . .

Yes, they took out the dream sequences. I liked the dream stuff myself; it shows Tully at an earlier time with his wife. That's one of the pieces I think is missing in this film, his life when he was on top. It's the key to making his dilemma felt.

It was a terrific sequence, it was so different—he was in a suit and he looked young and handsome, and he went into the ring the way they introduce big-time boxers, you know, like Joe Louis. Tully gets up there and the crowd goes wild. It was terrific and his wife was just sensational, sitting down there beautiful as pie, before his life went down the drain. That's what's missing, what his life was like. In order to appreciate what happens when life goes down the drain, you have to know the good times. That's the same as in a love story, if you've got a love story and the love goes bad, you don't get the emotional response out of it unless you've seen the love that's been good. . . .

Talking about it is not like seeing it.

——Hall, interviewed by the American Film Institute,
for *Dialogue on Film*, Oct 73

Q. You once told me that you were able to operate in the bicycle scene in *Butch Cassidy* [1969], with Katherine Ross and Paul Newman. . . .

A. Yes. George Hill let me do that scene; it was mine. I had another operator, and I had two cameras on a lot of the stuff, but I operated one camera throughout the whole shooting of that sequence. I think the rule will be changed, eventually. I've seen some beginnings already.

Q. I once asked Burney Guffey what, of all the changes in film equipment, meant the most to him, and he said "faster film stock."

A. That's a very important change, but lenses have gotten faster, too. As far as I'm concerned, lenses are not fast enough yet. I'd like to not have to light at all if possible, and without having to force develop. I'd like film to be as fast as the human eye, to be able to record someday as the human eye does.

——Hall, interviewed for *Filmmakers Newsletter,* Nov 73

Peter H A L L
Born 1930 in Bury St.-Edmunds. Began his theater work while at Cambridge.

. . . In a film [*A Midsummer Night's Dream* (1968)] how do you make fairies look if you're using a natural location? What does a fairy look like in a real wood? They get dirty and muddy. And they are green, like trees. We found out, during tests and rehearsals before we began shooting, that the fewer clothes they had on the better. I wanted the fairies to look as if they were part of the wood . . . dirty, wet, gleaming, glistening, green. If they stood still, you would hardly see them: natural camouflage. We did muck the color about a bit, quite deliberately. For instance, in the moonlight sequences, Oberon was more silvery. Then sometimes the color transitions, as far as the fairies were concerned, were abrupt. I think it was probably a mistake to do that, because some people thought it was merely carelessness or a technical error. . . .

I used a lot of close-ups, certainly: some people thought this was because the film was financed by CBS Television, and television is a "close-up medium." But if I'd been doing it solely for cinema, I'd still have done it mainly in close-ups, because I believe that if you're using the camera to scrutinize a Shakespearean text and make it more alive and human, you have to shoot close. . . .

That's not because I believe that cinema *is* close-ups. I don't. But Shakespeare on the screen, to me, is close-ups. I want to understand the text better than in the theater. Unless you're going to take quite a different premise, which is perfectly tenable, and express the Shakespearean metaphor by cutting most of the text and replacing it with pictures.

——Hall, interviewed for *Films & Filming,* Sep 69

Susumu H A N I
Born in 1928 in Tokyo. Worked as journalist and still photographer before raising enough money to make a film. His early motion pictures were documentaries and, in 1960, he made his first feature, Bad Boys (Furyo Shonen).

I think that the film *Minamata* [1971] by Tsuchimoto, about those who have suffered from minamata, a poisoning caused by the eating of fish polluted by mercury, is the best documentary made in postwar Japan. You should see it. He was my assistant director for *Bad Boys*. I persuaded many of my assistants to be cameramen; generally speaking, my relationships with those technicians went extremely well. But I was not completely satisfied with those technical machines, so I developed the idea of using 8 mm. In my film *Nanami* [1968] I shot high school students with 8 mm in one brief part. In the film a high school boy shows the hero and heroine a short 8 mm film called *First Love*. It was made by real high school students with our cooperation. Since that time I have been interested in using 8 mm to abolish the distinction between the people who play in a film and the people who watch it. In this film, of course, I made several technical experiments when I found out that 8 mm could be useful for theatrical showings.

——Hani, interviewed for Joan Mellen's
Voices from the Japanese Cinema (NY 1975)

Cedric HARDWICKE (1893–1964)
Born in Worcestershire, near Birmingham.

... In a film, when all is said and done, good cutting can make a good actor out of a donkey. I never go to see myself in the movies—thanks to Bernard Shaw, really. I once said to him that it might be a good idea to go and see yourself, as a way of seeing what you do and learning to correct your faults. You're more likely, he told me, to destroy your virtues. If you watch yourself in the movies, you become terribly self-conscious and begin trying to make yourself like other people, when the one thing you have that counts as an actor is whatever you have that makes you different. You don't ever want to destroy that individuality.

——Hardwicke, interviewed for *The Player* (NY, 1962)

Oliver HARDY [Norvell Hardy] (1892–1957)
In 1913 worked in small comic roles before teaming with Stan Laurel in 1926.
Together they made more than 50 two-reelers that are kept alive on television.

I sit in the lobby and I watch people. I like to watch people. Once in a while someone will ask me where Stan and I dreamed up the characters we play in the movies. They seem to think that these two fellows aren't like anybody else. I know they're *dumber* than anyone else, but there are plenty of Laurels and Hardys in the world. Whenever I travel, I still am in the habit of sitting in the lobby and watching the people walk by—and I tell you I see many Laurels and Hardys.

——Hardy, interviewed for *Mr. Laurel and Mr. Hardy* (NY, 1961)

Richard HARRIS
Born in 1933, Limerick, Ireland. Worked in the British theater before his film
debut in 1958.

With Antonioni I believed at the beginning of *The Red Desert* [1964] that he would give me this participation, because he is a great artist. I assumed he had great respect for my talent because he picked me for it out of *This Sporting Life* [1963], he wrote me many long letters afterwards asking me to do it. When I got to Italy I felt quite the opposite. I felt that Antonioni, after about 5 weeks, I think probably through his own insecurity, found a new formula for making the picture. I think Antonioni's pictures have got his own particular formula and style and he is edging towards something different. But he sort of panicked, and I was then playing a part that I didn't particularly like, I had no sympathy with it at all, and lack of cooperation set in between the two of us.

———Harris from a BBC recording and in *Films & Filming*, Apr 65

Rex HARRISON
Born in Huyton, Lancashire, 1908. Began stage career in Liverpool.

Storm in a Teacup [1937] was directed by Victor Saville, who was a lot of fun, and the director who started to relax me. In *Men Are Not Gods* [1936] I had been directed by a very intense German [Walter Reisch]; Victor was untense, and his very presence helped me to relax. He was an exceptionally easy, large, jolly man, and he made you uncare, so that you started to unwind, to speak the lines casually and naturally, and to think for the camera.

The second film I made with Vivien Leigh was also with Charles Laughton, who, together with the German Erich Pommer, had his own producing company. It was called *St. Martin's Lane* [1938], and was written by Clemence Dane.
... While [Laughton] was making *St. Martin's Lane* he lived in a tree—a tree house, out in the woods. He used to come to work with bunches of wild flowers that he had picked on his "doorstep"; his huge hands carrying those delicate little flowers I shall always remember. It could be very awkward acting with him, because he was so large physically that it was quite difficult to get yourself anywhere near the camera. His bulk seemed to fill the screen.... He could do things in front of the camera totally without shame, without any sense of embarrassment. ...

[Carol Reed asked me] to play in *Night Train to Munich* [1940], co-starring with Margaret Lockwood. ...
Carol Reed is another of those brilliant directors with a gift for relaxing actors.... He's careful, he's technical, he's a perfectionist, and he's marvelous with actors. In *Night Train* we had one scene with a lot of elderly actors. They were all German admirals, and I was a spy, dressed up as a German officer. Charlie France ... kept on forgetting his lines—he must have been about 70. I had very little to do, and only a few lines, and the old man was getting rather flustered, so Carol drew me to one side and said, "Rex, *you* forget *your* lines is this take. Before Charlie has his, you forget yours."

[For *Blithe Spirit*, 1947, David Lean] was only just coming over from film editing to directing. He was given much encouragement by Noël Coward, who saw his potential; even though Noël was disappointed with *Blithe Spirit,* he went on to give Lean *Brief Encounter.* . . . David Lean was ill at ease with comedy and his tension communicated itself to me. I remember one occasion when I had struggled through a scene in rehearsal, and Lean turned to Ronald Neame, his cameraman, and said, "I don't think that's very funny, do you?" Neame echoed, "I don't think it's very funny, no." . . . In those days, I suspect, Lean seemed to feel that actors were an irksome necessity who had to be tolerated until such time as he could get his hands on the celluloid and indulge his real passion, which was for editing.

We rehearsed [*My Fair Lady,* 1964] for 6 weeks before we turned a foot of film, and it was quite a painful business. Though I was trying to adapt the material from stage terms to film terms, I did at least know it, whereas Audrey [Hepburn] was feeling her way through a show she didn't know. . . .

We shot for about 4 months, which is quite a short schedule for this type of film, and I developed my own technique for doing the musical numbers. . . . As I knew the numbers so very well it was perfectly feasible for me to do them live on the set, as long as the director used the two-camera technique to provide for both long shots and close-ups.

In order to go right through the numbers without stopping I had to use a neck mike, a shortwave radio microphone slung around my neck under my clothes. They are used quite a lot in cabarets now, but then was the first time they had been used in a film studio.

———Harrison, in his *Rex* (NY, 1975)

Ray HARRYHAUSEN
Born in Los Angeles in 1920.

"Dynamation" is a very intimate combination of live and model work. My prehistoric animals are always seen with real people. I never merely cut away from one to the other. This is half the value of a fantasy film, and you get much more realism of action—in the fights between men and beasts in *One Million Years B.C.* [1940], for example. . . . In order to create credibility, a model may, indeed, be much more rewarding to work with than a living organism.

. . . All this can take a very long time. . . . Nine months was spent on the model work in *One Million Years B.C.* In *Jason and the Argonauts* [1963] there is a scene where the hero battles with 7 skeletons. All 7 had to be synchronized separately with the live hero. He was photographed first, acting as if he were a sevenfold shadow boxer. Everyone on the set had to *imagine* what was happening. Then the separate pieces were assembled together. This short sequence, lasting only a very few minutes, took nearly 5 months to complete. . . .

Comparatively little Dynamation processing takes place in the laboratory. After the live film is shot, most of the putting together is done photographically in the camera. Even such scenes as that in *One Million Years B.C.,* where the prehistoric bird grabs the girl and flies off with her, was done directly in the camera.

———Harryhausen, in *The Making of Feature Films* (London, 1971)

William S. H A R T (1870–1946)
Born in Newburg, New York. Made New York stage debut at 19 and worked there and on the road for 20 years. Entered films through his friendship with fellow actor Thomas Ince.

What an exquisite pleasure it was to work in *The Bargain* [1914]. I rode 5 horses in the picture, but the principal one was Midnight, a superb coal-black animal that weighed about 1200 pounds. He was nervous, and had broken a director's arm and an actor's leg. But he and I got along finely together. We did skyline rides along the tops of ridges so fast that the camera man could not hold us, no matter how he placed his setup. . . .

I was much pleased with the scenes Barker was getting. We worked well together. When *The Bargain* was finished, it seemed to be in the air that it was a success.

Tom came to me and said, "Bill, I've got a fine part for you in another story Sullivan has just written. I want you to look it over."

I did so. I wrote out some suggestions, starting where I thought it could be strengthened, and both Tom and Sullivan liked them, and Sullivan put them in the story.

On the Midnight Stage [1915] is still playing. It has also been called *The Bandit and the Preacher*. I rode Midnight again in this picture.

I liked my work in *The Bargain* and *On the Midnight Stage*, and I told Tom I would like to stay if he would give me a year's contract. He said that he couldn't; that the company was taking big chances on these 2 pictures; that he would not make any more.

"Bill," he said, "why don't you take up directing? That is where the money is. I will give you a year's contract as a director at $125 a week."

I replied, "No, Tom. I have devoted too many years to acting to quit now. If I am to fail, I'll fail as an actor! Besides, I have no ambition to become a director."

"Well, Bill," he said, "I'm sorry, but that is the best offer I can make and the best advice I can give you."

I said, "All right, Tom. I'm sorry. You know if I don't get back to New York now I'm likely to lose a season's work. I hope the company don't lose any money on these 2 pictures, because I know I talked you into making them. If they blame you, just tell 'em it's all my fault! . . ."

Sullivan wrote a story for me which I considered great. It was *The Aryan* [1916]. The star role was one of those hard-as-flint characters that Sullivan could write so well, but this man had no motive for his hardness. I wrote a beginning for the story and talked it over with Tom and Sullivan. Sullivan gave me a great battle; his argument was that he wanted to create a character that was bad without reason. I finally convinced him that it would be stronger my way and better for the picture, and he allowed me to do it. It proved to be a gripping story. I regard it as the best story Sullivan ever wrote and one of the best Westerns ever made.

As there were 3 large studios under the Triangle banner, I got in the habit of borrowing actors. There was a part in *The Aryan* that I wanted Mae Marsh for. She was tied up in a picture, but Mr. Griffith told me he had a young girl he thought very well of and was just waiting for an opportunity to cast her. When I saw her I grabbed her—she didn't have a chance of escaping. . . . Bessie Love made her first hit in *The Aryan*.

Dear Bessie was a child—she was afraid of me. While the camera was grinding, her little mouth would quiver as she struggled not to cry and gamely fought for the rights of her people. It was just what the part required. It was one of the very finest performances I have ever seen on the screen.

———Hart, in *My Life East and West* (NY, 1929)

Anthony H A R V E Y & James C L A R K
Harvey was born in 1931; turned from editing to direction in 1966 (Dutchman). James Clark's first film work was showing rented films to children (until a screening of Potemkin *produced nightmares) and founding a school film society at Oundle. First cutting-room job at age of 21. Also hopes to move into direction.*

Harvey: If an actor is giving something terribly exciting in terms of performance, I think it is important to stay on his face, even though the conventional thing is to cut every so often to the person he is talking to. I think the audience can imagine the other character's reactions for themselves, and they know he is there so that one doesn't need to keep reminding them. There was a scene in *Lolita* [1962] where Sue Lyon is talking to James Mason and they are all alone in the room: she was so extraordinary that we remained on her for the entire scene without cutting to him at all. This isn't a rule of course: every scene in every film calls for a different treatment. . . .

If I do have a rule at all, it is to look at the actor's eyes. They give you a good guide to the emotion that is going into the performance and sometimes a guide as to where to cut. You could easily be in danger of losing something tremendous if you cut away from an actor too sharply at the end of a speech. You may want to hold on to that misty look in the eyes for another 10 feet or so. But again there is no rule. If two characters are yelling at one another, for instance, it's usually more dramatically exciting to cut sharply.

I don't think there are any basic rules, though there may be conventions which arise from time to time and influences which people accept consciously or unconsciously. Just recently it has become fashionable to dispense with dissolves in getting from one scene to another because audiences have become accustomed to rapid changes of scene. In the old days, you wouldn't dream of going from one sequence to another without some sort of optical mix. Things are much more abrupt now, as they are in life. That's change of style; but there are no rules. You are dictated to entirely by the material. . . . There was another old rule. They used to say, "Don't cut to a scene when the camera is in motion; cut just before the camera starts to move." It was supposed to be ugly on the eye if you cut to a traveling shot from a static shot. But one does it all the time now. One has only to go to a Dick Lester film to see that there are no rules and, if there are, break them.

Q. How did you learn?

Clark: By experience. One can't learn to cut by example, or by analyzing other people's work, or by watching over other people's shoulders. It's not until the stuff is running through your fingers that you can learn to put the magic in it.

Harvey: By looking back on earlier films I've edited. There is a tendency, when you first start editing, to cut too quickly, to be afraid of holding shots. . . . When I first started cutting, I found it was one hell of a strain. I used to wake up at about 3 in the morning having dreamt of the film for what seemed like the last 3 hours. Then I'd write down notes of what I'd been dreaming about, editing notes. . . . In fact, I still do. When one has been on a film for about 9 months, it goes through one's mind like a gramophone record that's stuck and you can't switch it off. . . .

Clark: I find I tend to see life through a moviola, and even in daily life I split things up into cuts as a matter of course. All my dreams are fully edited . . . and well edited, too! I wish I could say the same for all my films.

Harvey: *The Spy Who Came in from the Cold* [1965] is a film where the material dictated something basic in the cutting. It is a story about a failure of a man, essentially a quiet story. There were plenty of opportunities for exciting cutting, as in any spy story. But we found it would have been wrong for this particular spy story. We realized during the editing period that, instead of using hard and dramatic cuts, it would be more fitting to use long, slow dissolves to match the bleak and austere mood of the story. . . .

I had a terrifying experience on *The Angry Silence* [1959]. It was the scene where Dickie Attenborough goes into the works canteen for lunch, a complicated sequence covered by a great number of setups. There is a sea of faces with the camera moving over them, and suddenly we cut to an enormous mouth saying "SHUT UP!" We edited the sequence and thought it tremendous. Some weeks later I took another look at it. I had some new ideas which I thought might improve it. . . . I started again, took it apart, and recut in many versions. . . . None of them was really as exciting. I started to put it back as I had first thought of it—and I couldn't. It was impossible to find the exact timings and rhythms. I finally cut it as closely as I could to the original, but it had lost much of its impact and spontaneity. Since that day, whenever I have had a complicated sequence to put together, I have always had a dupe print made as a record to refer back to. It has proved invaluable, because one's first instincts are almost always right.

Clark: The way I work is to let an editor go away and do what I call a "free assembly," without reference to me but trying to follow the sequence of my shots. Most good editors can follow the way a director has shot a film. Then he'll show me this free assembly for each scene and we'll whittle away at it. The editor may hit it first time. I remember something Tony Harvey did on *The L-Shaped Room* [1962] which was so right that I said, "It's perfect." But he started to work on it again, like a painter who continually paints over, until finally I made him go back and, frame by frame, put it back to the very first way he had assembled it. It's the scene of Leslie Caron walking in a street, a series of overlapping close shots which is supposed in theory to be terribly ugly, just to keep superimposing, without taking her out of frame to keep putting another frame on top. It was perfect, as far as I was concerned.

Harvey: The scene was planned in the script as a series of dissolves. Bryan [Forbes] had shot it in exciting long-shots, medium shots and close-ups, walking past shop windows. I tried an experiment with it by cutting erratically instead of dissolving, so that, watching, you kept going in and out, closer and away again, to show that she was getting dizzy. By losing the dissolves one had injected a nervous feeling that was dead right for the mood of the scene. . . .

On *Dr. Strangelove* [1963] we made our own first cut following the original construction of the script quite closely, so that one flashed backwards and forwards a great number of times between the Airplane, the War Room and the Air Base. It was the most stunning script I have ever read; the way it was constructed was perfect; but it just didn't work in edited film. It was too confusing—you just didn't know where you were half the time. And there was no variation of pace or buildup of tension. We found by experiment that, if we stayed clear for much longer on each setting, everything became clearer and interest was held much more strongly.

Q. What chance does the editor have of getting to know the director's intentions for the film? How much is discussed beforehand, or during filming?

Clark: We don't usually discuss much beforehand: there isn't enough time. Some directors like to have a talk about a scene before they shoot it. John Schlesinger would do that. And I think a discussion of that kind is useful as it helps to clarify the director's own attitude to a scene. He often needs to convince himself of his own decisions.

Harvey: Marty Ritt is extremely concerned that you understand what he's trying to do. He likes to discuss every psychological aspect, the relationships of the characters, the whole mood in fact, and to talk over each scene many times. He really uses people as a kind of sounding board, as John Le Carré once said. Kubrick works very much the same way. He has the most fantastic energy of any man I know. I don't believe that he sleeps more than 4 hours a night. The great beauty of his films is that it's as though he were looking at people through a microscope. He lives for filmmaking. I was 18 months on *Lolita* and a year on *Strangelove*: looking back, I feel I learnt more about films then than at any other time of my life.

——Harvey & Clark, interviewed for *Sight & Sound*, Spring 66

Howard HAWKS
Born in Goshen, Indiana 1896, an engineering student at Cornell, a pilot in the First World War. First film job at Paramount, as prop man in De Mille's unit; an editor in 1922, a scriptwriter in 1924, and directed his first film (The Road to Glory) *in 1926.*

I had great admiration for [De Mille], but I never saw anything that I thought was good. . . . I learned an awful lot from him by doing exactly the opposite. He was a great egotist and he could charm people into doing what he wanted. I once asked Gary Cooper how on earth he could read those goddamn lines. "Well," he said, "when De Mille finishes talking to you, they don't seem so bad. But when you see the picture, then you kind of hang your head."

On the set, he was a Nero. Off the set, he was charming, and he was terribly appreciative. He asked me to help him one time. He'd made a picture that was quite bad. I wrote the titles for the picture, and changed the whole tenor of the story so that it no longer took itself seriously. It became semi-humorous. He previewed it and was very pleased with the laughs he got. The picture was *The Road to Yesterday* [1925]. I was called in very often to help him after that.

———Hawks, in letter to Kevin Brownlow, for *The Parade's Gone By* (NY, 1968)

We had a very simple idea in making *Scarface* [1932]. I asked Ben Hecht whether he'd like to do a gangster picture, and he said, "My Lord, you don't want to do one of those!" I said, "Well, I've got an idea that the Borgia family is alive in Chicago today, and Caesar Borgia is Al Capone." He said, "We'll start tomorrow morning."

We wrote the script in about 11 days, and wrote it for sheer entertainment. We had darn good sources of information about how things happened. Gangsters would come in and say, "Do you want to know how such a killing was done?" I'd say, "I'd love to know, thanks," and we'd do it that way. There wasn't any idea of having any social significance at all. . . .

Q. Were you influenced at all by Ford's *Air Mail* [1932] when you made *Only Angels Have Wings* [1939]?

I never saw it. I was influenced by knowing the characters that were in my story. All of that is true. For instance, I knew the fellow who jumped out of a plane and left someone behind, and nobody would talk to him. And the thing where Grant has to tell his friend about his broken neck—I saw it happen. The only thing we added was that Grant went and stood out in the rain while his friend died.

I did a lot of flying myself. I had dinner one night with some bush pilots down in Mexico, and they told me about this little place where the Grace Line boat stopped, and they had to fly over a hump and they had a man sitting up there. So I wrote it down on a piece of paper, and then one day I went over to talk to Frank Capra about something.

Harry Cohn always knew everyone who came into Columbia, and instead of giving me permission to go and talk to Capra, he asked me to come up and talk to *him*. He said, "Look, I'm stuck, I've got to have a story for Cary Grant and Jean Arthur." I said, "Here's a story I was writing on this morning." I left him, saw Capra, and when I came back [to Cohn's office] he said, "When can you start?" I said, "What do you mean, I haven't got a script written." He said, "You've got to start ten days from now." I said, "Okay, but it's gonna cost you a lot more money."

Q. There are a number of incredible sequences in there. . . .

All those things are perfectly real. . . . Even the condor that came through the cockpit was real. And that location was absolutely real.

Q. Where did you shoot?

Hollywood. . . . A mountain's a mountain wherever you go. . . . You fly a little ways up north and you get all the snow you want.

———Hawks, interviewed for *Take One*, Nov–Dec 71

The tempo in *Scarface* was faster than usual in that period. I generally work with a faster tempo than that of most of my colleagues. It seems more natural to me, less forced. I personally speak slowly, but people generally talk, talk, talk without even waiting for other people to finish. Also, if a scene is a bit weak, the more rapidly you shoot it, the better it will be on the screen. Moreover, if the tempo is fast you can emphasize a point by slowing the rhythm. Similarly, when you have a scene with two characters, don't always use a close-up. When you use close-ups sparingly, the public realizes that they are important. I hate movies which, without any reason, are composed completely of close-ups.

——Hawks, interviewed for *Cahiers du cinéma*, Feb 56; trans. by Andrew Sarris

There is [a lot of ad libbing] in every picture that's any good. You write a story up in a room. With a good actor, the thing comes alive when you get to a set. The actor contributes things, and you think of things for the actor to do—some of the best lines come then, or after you finish the picture. Some of Bacall's best lines in *To Have and Have Not* [1944] don't match her lips at all, because I thought of them after the picture was all over.

——Hawks, interviewed for *Take One*, Nov–Dec 71

Rio Bravo [1958] was made because I saw a picture called *High Noon* [1952], which everybody seemed to think was pretty good, but I didn't like too much. . . . I got into an argument with somebody about how a sheriff would react in a tight situation and that's why I went out and made *Rio Bravo*.

Then after it was finished we found out that we could have told it a lot better, that there were a lot of things we hadn't told, but since the basic framework was still good we went ahead and filmed *El Dorado* [1966]. . . .

Q. Just how much "direction" do you give to players as experienced as John Wayne and Robert Mitchum?

I'd talk over a scene with them while the set was being lit, "We'll be going in there in a minute and I shall start with you. You'll be sitting down over there . . . we want a kind of quiet feeling . . . then out of that comes a burst of anger and you start talking." When they do go in front of a camera they don't realize that they've been set up for it and they work much better for thinking that they're doing it on their own.

You have to run the thing. You have to tell them what to do . . . I don't care who they are. Then they do it, but they do it their own way and in doing so lead you into many, many things.

——Hawks interviewed for *Films & Filming*, Oct 68

Sessue HAYAKAWA (1889–1973)
Film career begun by Thomas Ince in The Typhoon (1914).

At home, when I skimmed through the script of *The Bridge on the River Kwai* [1957] for the first time—quickly, looking for the high points and the scope of the role I had been asked to play, I immediately noted the absence of love interest, and that the entire story unfolded in the jungle. It did not excite me. I saw very little in it, in fact, and when Mr. Spiegel telephoned a day or so later to ask my reaction, I told him I didn't think I would be interested.

I was not alone in my feeling. Halfway around the world from Tokyo, in England, Alec Guinness, whose performance was to win him an Academy

Award, reacted the same way as I. The role of the Englishman, which he was asked to play, did not excite him. He said the role was one of "a dreary, unsympathetic man," and refused not once but 3 times. Even after reconsidering and finally accepting, he arrived in Ceylon with misgivings, brooded—according to news magazine reports, and after a few days on location in the jungle, tried to quit.

My relationship with David Lean was particularly good. Of necessity he is something of a solitary traveler in his profession. He has a keen mind. His insight is deeply penetrating. In his role of director he sees not only the fragments which, woven together, make the whole composition of a film, but the entirety as well.

Mr. Lean and I enjoyed an excellent rapport when we worked together. We never found ourselves in opposition. But he was less than slightly beloved by some of his associates being broiled by the hot sun and infernal humidity of Ceylon during the stifling months we were isolated there. For one member of the technical crew was later quoted as having said, "Lean! The bloody perfectionist! He shot 30 seconds of film a day and then sat on a rock and stared at his goddamn bridge!"

Perhaps he did appear to drag his heels. But he achieved all he desired to achieve. He explored the subject of his responsibility carefully, and was most solicitous when it came to dealing with us, the actors. I never witnessed an instance of his abusing any actor, although it was later revealed that he all but alienated Alec Guinness; for when Mr. Guinness reported to Ceylon from London, Mr. Lean offhandedly informed him that he had really wanted Charles Laughton for the role of Colonel Nicholson. It was some days before Mr. Guinness's unhappiness over this abated. Until it did, the coolness with which each man regarded the other was almost solid enough to be seen.

——Hayakawa, in *Films & Filming*, Feb 62

Sterling H A Y D E N [John Hamilton]
Born 1916 in Montclair, New Jersey; soon employed on various boats and ships before his "discovery" by Hollywood. A crucial point in his film career was John Huston's successful test of him for The Asphalt Jungle (1950):

`. . . I step on the butt, take several deep breaths, and advance toward no-man's land. Huston intercepts me, throws an arm around my shoulder, and walks me around the stage. His voice is urgent, but I'm thinking about the scene. When we stop we're next to the camera. . . .

A girl named Jean Hagen sits on a high stool. She is a redhead with a glorious smile, pretty but not too pretty, fresh from Broadway, and set to play in the picture. . . .

"Kid," [Huston] says, "play it the way it feels best. Lie down, sit up, walk around, do any damn thing you please. Wherever you go, we'll follow. Take your time. Let me know when you're ready." He drops in a canvas chair and starts to read a book. The girl smokes, not looking at me just yet. It is absolutely silent.

Have I got the words, I wonder. Just like old times. I mess around with my shirt, trying hard to concentrate. I sit on the edge of the cot and clutch at the cage of my ribs. A minute passes, maybe more. Huston has closed the book. Our eyes meet and I nod.

——Hayden, in *Wanderer* (NY, 1963)

On the first day of shooting [*Dr. Strangelove*, 1963] I found that I just couldn't handle all the technical jargon in my lines. I was utterly humiliated. Stanley [Kubrick] told me, "The terror on your face may yield just the quality we want and if it doesn't, the hell with it, we'll shoot the whole thing over. You and I both know that is something that can happen to anyone." He was beautiful. A lot of directors like to see actors wallow. Stanley isn't one of them.

——Hayden, interviewed for *Newsweek*, 3 Jan 72

Edith H E A D
Born 1907.

Well, I can go back to Mae West or right forward to Paul Newman. I was the first one to put clothes on Mae.

I remember she said to me: "Fit it tight, honey, I want them all to know I'm a girl from every angle." But it didn't work with Anita Ekberg.

There was so much of her that kept falling out.

I'm a camouflager. I can transform anyone into anything they want to be. You want to be Casanova or Jack the Ripper?

Okay, suppose it's Casanova. I just open up your collar, put in a silk muffler, narrow your pants.

She [Bette Davis] acts them [her costumes] out—I've had her rolling around on the floor more than once to see if they're okay to die or get hysterical in.

I give them what they want, as long as it is right for the part. I tell them, "If you need more bosom I can give it to you. If it wants hoisting, I can hoist it. If your derriere is too big, I can sink it in for you. But don't ask me to reconstruct your body."

——Head, interviewed for *The Daily Mirror*, 2 Nov 70

I dressed Swanson for *Sunset Boulevard* [1950], 25 years ago, and in *Airport* ['75, 1974] she plays a movie star, too, so I asked her what *she'd* wear, if she'd come from dinner and boarded a fast plane to make an appointment in another city. That's what she came up with, so she really dressed herself. The rest of the people in the picture, well, most of them look awful, they look real, you know. . . .

I always work with Hitchcock, except for his English productions, of course. We understand each other. He hates bright colors, feels they're obtrusive, too eye-catching, so I don't use them.

——Head, interviewed for *The Globe & Mail*, Toronto, 14 Sep 74

Ben H E C H T (1894–1964)
Born in New York City. Career as reporter and journalist begun in Chicago in 1910. Foreign correspondent in 1919. First film work: the story of Underworld *(1927).*

One of my biggest Hollywood victories is that I didn't go to the hospital writing *Design for Living* [1933]. Lubitsch went. I had figured out a way to confuse him. I always handed him 4 or 5 versions of each scene. Having to tear into these sapped his strength. He sneaked off to Harkness Pavilion, pretending he had the flu. While he was laid up, I finished the scenario. . . .

[For *Gone With the Wind*, 1939] Selznick and Vic Fleming appeared at my bedside one Sunday morning at dawn. I was employed by Metro at the time, but David had arranged to borrow me for a week.

After 3 weeks' shooting of *Gone With the Wind*, David had decided his script was no good and that he needed a new story and a new director. The shooting had been stopped and the $1,000,000 cast was now sitting by collecting its wages in idleness.

The 3 of us arrived at the Selznick studio a little after sunrise. We had settled on my wages on the way over. I was to receive $15,000 for the week's work, and no matter what happened I was not to work longer than a week. I knew in advance that 2 weeks of such toil as lay ahead might be fatal.

David was outraged to learn that I had not read *Gone With the Wind*, but decided there was no time for me to read the long novel. The Selznick overhead on the idle *Wind* stages was around $50,000 a day. David announced that he knew the story by heart and would brief me on it. For the next hour I listened to David recite the story. I had seldom heard a more involved plot. My verdict was that nobody could make a remotely sensible movie out of it. Fleming, who was reputed to be part Indian, sat brooding at his own council fires. I asked him if he had been able to follow the story David had told. He said no. I suggested we make up a new story, to which David replied with violence that every literate human in the United States except me had read Miss Mitchell's book and we would have to stick to it. I argued that surely in 2 years of preparation someone must have wangled a workable plot out of Miss Mitchell's Ouida-like flight into the Civil War. David suddenly remembered the first treatment, discarded 3 years earlier. It had been written by Sidney Howard, since dead. After an hour of searching, a lone copy of Howard's work was run down in an old safe. David read it aloud. We listened to a precise and telling narrative of *Gone With the Wind*. . . . We worked for 7 days, putting in 18 to 20 hours a day. Selznick refused to let us eat lunch, arguing that food would slow us down. He provided bananas and salted peanuts. On the fourth day a blood vessel broke in Fleming's right eye, giving him more an Indian look than ever. On the fifth day, Selznick toppled into a torpor while chewing on a banana. The wear and tear on me was less, for I had been able to lie on a couch and half-doze while the two darted about acting out the story. Thus on the seventh day I had completed, unscathed, the first 9 reels of the Civil War epic. . . .

———Hecht, quoted in *Film Comment*, Winter 70–71

Buck HENRY
Born 1930.

Q. In directing *Taking Off* [1971] Milos Forman says that he didn't give the actors the complete script. He gave it to them page by page, or scene by scene. As the star of the picture, did you ever see the screenplay?

A. No, I never had anything to read. Ever.

Q. Is that an effective way for you to work as an actor?

A. Oh, I think it's terrific. One, having been an improvisor, it's second nature. Some actors don't like it. But I think it's sensational and I think Forman's films are their own proof of the technique. He hates acting. I mean "acting," which is why he avoids, if he can, faces that are well known; he likes for the audience to have no references, except what is happening there on the screen. He's only interested in behavior. It's interesting to go from someone like Nichols to someone like Forman because Nichols, too, is only interested in behavior, but he can't always get it because of the structure of some of his films. There is almost no behavior in *Catch-22* [1969], which drove him crazy. The people don't behave because of the mood, because of the style, because there are so many events crammed into such a short space. His talents were stretched to their limit, I think, in finding areas for behavior. Because that's one of the things Mike does as well as any other director in the world. It's to get people to behave. But in a Forman film all you can do is behave because he constructs both the script and his system of shooting in such a way that nothing is important. Like life, the important things happen almost by accident, from moment to moment. And no one scene is the scene that says now I'm going to tell you what this is all about, I'm going to laugh, cry, or give a speech in such a way that everything is tied up in this one scene. His films are really an accumulation of every scene and every piece of behavior that happens. It's quite a different system.

Q. But he starts with a complete screenplay?

A. He starts with a total screenplay, every single word. I know this secondhand, of course, because I, being an actor, never saw the script. But I know he'll come in with it completely rewritten on the page in his own illegible handwriting or completely rewritten in his mind. Or sometimes the actors will take him in a direction that doesn't exist on the written page. . . .

———Henry, interviewed for *The Screenwriter Looks at the Screenwriter*
(NY, 1972)

Audrey H E P B U R N [Edda Hepburn van Heemstra]
Born 1929, of Irish-Dutch parentage. Trained as dancer. This interview was given during the production of How to Steal a Million (1966):

Willie [Wyler] came along and liberated me [in *Roman Holiday,* 1953]. He uninhibited me. He gave me confidence where before there was only a sort of numbed fear. He taught me what it was all about, showed me the way, and turned me loose.

We are in such close communication we hardly have to talk. I *know* when he feels it's wrong.

———Hepburn, interviewed for *The Daily Express,* 1 Oct 65

Katharine H E P B U R N
Born 1909 in Hartford, Connecticut; a career on the New York stage before her film debut in A Bill of Divorcement (1932).

My career almost ended just before I did *The Philadelphia Story* on stage. I couldn't get a job for peanuts. I had done a lot of bad pictures, and I just couldn't get a job. So I went back to New York and got *The Philadelphia Story* to do. I was to have a marvelous entrance, after 5 minutes or so of talk; but I said to Phil Barry, "Please don't give me an entrance. I'll die. I'll be standing off stage dying. Write a nice dull scene for me at the beginning where I can be mean to my mother, so that they can see I'm not trying to cotton up to them, that I'm just as horrible as ever, even though I can't get a job, which they all know." So he did. I was rude about a wedding present and then left the stage. Well, Erik Charell was in the audience and came to see me afterwards, and said he had been in fear and trembling because he knew I had a lot at stake. "But you came on and you sat there and you spat right in the audience's face and then left the stage. And I was so happy. I thought, 'Good Kate, she's going to be as rude as ever.'"

[For *The African Queen* (1951)] we were shooting on location in Africa, way down out of Ponteville in the Belgian Congo. I had played the first scene, in which I bury Robert Morley. And the next morning John Huston came waltzing up to my hut. I said, "I hope you're not planning to have breakfast with me every day, because I rather prefer to eat alone." And he said, "No, no. I'm just coming in for a minute."

Now you know, I've a sort of hollow face and a sort of a jaw, and my mouth goes down, and when my face is serious it is very on the down side. If I can smile I've a lot of nice teeth. I can cheer everything up quite a lot. So John sat down, and he just said, "Did you ever see Mrs. Roosevelt visiting the soldiers in the hospitals?" And I said, yes, I did; I did see that movie. And he said, "Well, I think of her a little bit as Mrs. Roosevelt." Then he drifted off.

Well, it was the most brilliant suggestion. Because she was ugly so she always smiled. So I smiled. Otherwise he said very little to me on the set. But it was an awfully clever piece of direction, wasn't it? Very bright. . . .

All actors are different, of course. For instance, I don't agree with the notion that the best acting comes from the first few takes. But Spencer Tracy was violent on that. He said that the first 2 takes are always the best, and I think that they were with him. But I think I can still go pretty well on that 23rd take. . . . And you know, it's interesting that all the times Spencer and I worked together, we never rehearsed together before shooting. Never. Not ever. . . .

———Hepburn, interviewed for *The Times Saturday Review*, 24 Nov 73

I know I'm the drawing-room type—but I did make two Westerns before, you know, *Spitfire* [1934], and *Sea of Grass* [1947]. Spencer and I wanted so much to make *Sea of Grass*. It was a great book. But it was loused up being done on a sound stage instead of location. We were both tremendously disappointed with it. . . .

I've just come from doing a TV special with Larry Olivier in England, a show called *Love Among the Ruins* [1974].

I've known Larry for years, but never worked with him. He was great, of course—and I was just adorable. So sweet and lovable . . . [she laughs]. And now I'm working with John [Wayne]. I always feel you deserve one final enormous spree before you pass on.

——Hepburn, interviewed for *The Toronto Star*, 5 Oct 74

Robert H E R L T H (1893–1962)
Born in Wriezen.

The hall in *Tartuffe* [1925] consisted merely of a wall: its dimensions were suggested by the shape of Jannings walking up and down with his breviary in his hand—all that was needed was an effect of relief. Depth of field, which all the specialists made such a fuss about at that time, was to us, in this particular case, immaterial.

The prologue and epilogue preceding and following the "Tartuffe plot" were created entirely by means of perspectives.

In *Tartuffe*, everything was done to heighten the black-and-white effects. The rooms were small and round, with smooth, creamy white-painted walls devoid of detail or ornament. All the molding was done by hand. The costumes, too, were designed for graphic effect. . . .

But Murnau's perfectionism made even the simplest thing a problem. I had designed an interior for *The Last Laugh*, in which a gaslight burned over a sofa. We experimented with that lamp for weeks: the difficulty then was to create a lighting effect that was at the same time a real source of illumination. . . .

I still remember how we had the idea of the mobile, or as it was then called, *"entfesselte Kamera."*

We were making *The Last Laugh*, this time without Röhrig. Erich Pommer had told us to "try to invent something mad!"

So far we hadn't succeeded, in spite of nights of brain-racking. We were using the cloakroom set, and Murnau was making preparations for the scene in which the millionaire gets the poor cloakroom attendant (not yet cast as Jannings) to light his fat cigar. The millionaire goes out through the door, which swings to slowly; I had made it 2 meters high so that it would take a long time to close. The attendant was supposed to sniff the cigar smoke after the millionaire had already departed up the stairs.

At this point Murnau said, "No, that doesn't work."

"Why not?" Karl Freund and I asked.

"Because you don't see anything—it doesn't have any effect," answered Murnau emphatically.

"What are we to do then?"

"We need something more intense—if only we could fly with the smoke."

"What? . . ."

"The stairs . . ." said Murnau.

"With the camera?" asked Freund.

"Of course—what else?"

"We'd need a fireman's ladder," I said timidly.

Everyone laughed at the idea of a ladder.

I stuck to my guns. Freund looked at me, then tossed his head, which meant that he agreed.

We didn't realize that we were already assuming the existence of a mobile camera; for us it was the stairs that presented the difficulty. We had made the first step without knowing it.

Someone was sent for a ladder, the camera was fixed at the top, and the not insubstantial Freund took up his position. We removed half the set and moved the ladder slowly towards the stairs; the camera followed the smoke, rising with it up the stairs as the ladder was wound upwards.

"We've got it!" cried Murnau.

After this there was no stopping us.

——Herlth, trans. in Eisner's *Murnau* (Berkeley 1973)

Bernard HERRMANN (1911–1975)
Born in New York City, and studied composition at New York University and the Juilliard School. He formed the New Chamber Orchestra and introduced important modern works to America, before becoming staff conductor and composer for the radio dramas of CBS. In 1936 he was assigned to Orson Welles's weekly program, "The Mercury Theatre on the Air," and accompanied Welles and the Mercury group to Hollywood.

I worked on the film [*Citizen Kane*, 1941], reel by reel, as it was being shot and cut. In this way I had a sense of the picture being built, and of my own music being a part of that building. Most musical scores in Hollywood are written after the film is entirely finished, and the composer must adapt his music to the scenes on the screen. In many scenes in *Citizen Kane* an entirely different method was used, many of the sequences being tailored to match the music.

This was particularly true in the numerous photographic "montages" which are used throughout the film to denote the passing of time. When I first saw the picture, I felt that it might be interesting to write complete musical numbers for these montages. In other words, instead of a mere atmospheric or rhythmic cue, a brief piece would be written. Welles agreed, and once the music was set, cut many of his sequences to match the length of the pieces.

The most striking illustration of this method may be found in the breakfast montage between Kane and his first wife. Here, in the space of 3 or 4 minutes, Welles shows the rise and fall of affection between two married people. The setting is a breakfast table. The young couple enter, gay and very much in love. They talk for a few seconds, then the scene changes. Once more we see them at the breakfast table, but the atmosphere has changed. Discord is beginning to creep into the conversation. Brief scene after brief scene follows, each showing the gradual breakdown of their affection, until finally they read their newspapers, opposite each other, in silence.

For this montage, I used the old classic form of the theme and variations. A waltz in the style of Waldteufel is the theme. It is heard during the first scene. Then, as discord crops up, the variations begin. Each scene is a separate variation. Finally, the waltz theme is heard bleakly played in the high registers of the violins. . . .

Leitmotifs are used in *Citizen Kane* to give unity to the score as a whole. I am not a great believer in the "leitmotif" as a device for motion picture music—but in this film it was practically imperative, because of the story itself and the manner in which it is unfolded.

There are two main motifs. One—a simple 4-note figure in the brass— is that of Kane's power. It is given out in the very first 2 bars of the film. The second motif is that of Rosebud. Heard as a solo on the vibraphone, it first appears during the death scene at the very beginning of the picture. It is heard again and again throughout the film under various guises, and if followed closely, is a clue to the ultimate identity of Rosebud itself.

The motif of power is also transformed, being a vigorous piece of ragtime, a hornpipe polka, and at the end of the picture, a final commentary on Kane's life.

In handling these motifs, I used a great deal of what might be termed "radio scoring." The movies frequently overlook opportunities for musical clues which last only a few seconds—that is, from 5 to 15 seconds at the most— the reason being that the eye usually covers the transition. On the other hand, in radio drama, every scene must be bridged by some sort of sound device, so that even 5 seconds of music becomes a vital instrument in telling the ear that the scene is shifting. I felt that in this film, where the photographic contrasts were often so sharp and sudden, a brief cue—even 2 or 3 chords—might heighten the effect immeasurably.

In orchestrating the picture I avoided, as much as possible, the realistic sound of a large symphony orchestra. The motion picture sound track is an exquisitely sensitive medium, and with skillful engineering a simple bass flute solo, the pulsing of a bass drum, or the sound of muted horns can often be far more effective than half a hundred musicians playing away. Save for the opera sequence, some of the ballet montages, and a portion of the final scene, most of the cues were orchestrated for unorthodox instrumental combinations.

——Herrmann, in *The New York Times*, 25 May 41

[For the disastrous opera debut in *Citizen Kane*] we needed something that would terrify the girl and put the audience a bit in suspense. I wrote the aria in a very high key which would make most performances sound strained. Then we got a very light lyric soprano and made her sing this heavy dramatic soprano part with a very heavy orchestration which created the feeling that she was in quicksand. Later on, that aria was sung many times by Eileen Farrell, who had the voice to sing it absolutely accurately in that key, and it sounded very impressive. Some writers have said that the singer in the film performed it deliberately badly, but that's not so. She was a good singer performing in too high a key.

——Herrmann, interviewed for *Sight & Sound*, Winter 71/72

. . . In *The Devil and Daniel Webster* [*All That Money Can Buy*, 1941], we recorded telephone wires singing at 4:00 in the morning to characterize the Devil (Mr. Scratch) and when he plays the violin at a barn dance we had a single violin playing 6 different variations on the same tune, each more complex than the last, and then superimposed all the tracks—so that we got solo violin music of a sort that no human violinist could possibly have played.

. . . In the RKO orchestra in the 'fifties there was a very fine viola player, Virginia Majewsky; and so for a picture called *On Dangerous Ground* [1951] —about a blind girl—I wrote for the now almost obsolete viola d'amore, which has a lower compass and a more refined tone than the standard viola. It had a veiled quality that was just right for the girl. Yet when I came to *Psycho* [1960] I went back to the clear cold classical sound of the string orchestra. You'd be surprised at the number of people who wrote in to find out what it was—they'd never heard it on a film sound track before and, in fact, I don't know of any film which had used it before.

The last film Hitchcock and I worked together on was *Marnie* [1964]. We fell out over *Torn Curtain* [1966]. The executives—the truly great men of the film business, creative geniuses every one of them—had the gall to pressure him into putting a pop score into the picture, because they no doubt figured that a pop tune would sell 10,000,000 records. No artist of Hitch's stature should allow himself to be dictated to by contemptible Philistines, whose only concern is lining their own pockets, and I'm afraid I wouldn't go along with him as long as he went along with them. And this is the general trend in films today. You're only as good as the number of records you sell. Experience, technical know-how, great professional skill—all that goes for little or nothing now.

——Herrmann, interviewed for *Crescendo*, Apr & May 73

Charlton HESTON
Born in Evanston, Illinois, 1923. Brought to Hollywood after his appearance in a 16 mm version of Julius Caesar (1949), *produced at Northwestern University and directed by David Bradley.*

Monday, April 14th [1958]: With family happily settling into plaster palazzo, went to [Cinecitta] studio where I'll be spending best part of the year [on *Ben-Hur,* 1959]. Very elaborate outside, fairly adequate inside. Met Yakima Canutt, ex-greatest stuntman in world, in charge of training drivers and setting up chariot race. Set, representing great Circus at Antioch, not finished; but we have large practice track (very muddy) to train on meantime. Over hundred horses brought here from Yugoslavia for race; met 4 white studs I'm to drive . . . very beautiful, also very mean-looking. If he's going to teach me to handle them, Yak had better be the best!

Saturday, May 17th: Spent morning rehearsing Christopher Fry's rewrite of crucial quarrel scene with Messala. Indeed, this is crucial scene of whole first half of story since it motivates everything that follows. Christopher's version vast improvement over script, and Willy [Wyler] has brought out its virtues in his usual manner as we worked . . . picking, carping, nagging, fiddling; a reading here and a gesture there until you are trammeled and fenced in by his concept . . . which you then realize is excellent. Rehearsals not nearly as trying, however, as dinner interview with one of those lethal London journalists who strain everything you say through an acid ear . . . they seem to take actual delight in being loathed by everyone they write about. Was able to skirt his more obvious pitfalls, but would not call it relaxed meal by any means.

Saturday, June 21st: Steve's [Boyd] eyes still bad, so we switched to first scene with Esther. Haya Harareet, I think, will be excellent in part, though today she had little to do but stand silent while Judah questioned her. Willy tough for me to please today. My problem seems clearer: In these delicate scenes must simply play with enough conviction and belief in the early takes before he fences me in with so many physical cues to the conviction that I can't reach it completely. Willy beyond question toughest director I've ever worked for . . . but I'm inclined more and more to opinion he's also the best.

Friday, June 27th: Still on Stage 1 trying to escape from that damned prison cell. We did, in all, 30 takes of fight with guards and attempted escape. At lunchtime, Willy came up with really brilliant idea that escape at this point should only be attempt that fails. Audiences have seen Errol Flynn do too many spectacular escapes in old Warner movies to try that one again. Today, he didn't like it early, Lord knows, but he liked it a lot when we finally got it. He even, surprisingly, asked me for idea on how to manage fight. I left a lot of sweat, not to mention drop or two of blood, on floor of that cell, though.

Wednesday, October 22nd: Today was gutbuster we all knew was coming when Willy got inside those caves where he wasn't dependent on sunlight to shoot by. Turned out very well finally . . . scene of Judah coming face to face with his mother went better than had been imagined possible, but it went till nearly 8:00. Felt very rebellious around 6:30 when he decided to put a 6-inch lens on a close-up of mine he had just shot, but then I realized again chance for final perfection such an approach gives me. Made me late as hell for dinner, though

Sunday, November 16th: Ty Power's shockingly sudden death on set in Spain yesterday made me suddenly aware of my mortality . . . appropriate time to think of it since we were shooting on our day off to take advantage of continuing fine weather. Probably that's why it seemed tougher day than usual; scudding clouds kept us trotting back and forth between setups that needed sun and those that could do without it. We did last close-up after sun had gone, really; I was perhaps too tired to react quickly in struggle with Roman legionnaire while trying give Christ water. Anyway, was flung heavily against well curbing on hip still unhealed from pirate scene and then clipped over the eye with spear. Neither blow disabling, but both gave me pause, thinking of Ty. This racket sure not padded refuge for idle boozehounds Hollywood novels make it out. Have been shooting 10- and 12-hour days, 6 days every damn week, not to mention a few Sundays, since May.

-——Heston, from his *Ben-Hur* diary, in *American Film*, Apr 76

Orson has a marvelous ear for the way people talk. One of the many things I learned from him was the degree to which people in real life overlap one another when they're talking. In the middle of somebody's sentence you will, in fact, apprehend what he's talking about and you will often start to reply through his closing phrase. People do that all the time. Orson directs scenes that way—to a larger degree than most directors do.

There's a marvelously counterpointed scene in *Lady from Shanghai* [1949] in which the people sit in the dark—obviously he doesn't want a visual image to intrude—and you hear 2 conversations interwoven. . . .

-——Heston, interviewed for *Take One*, July–Aug 71

. . . I feel at home in "wardrobe"—but it's important to get used to it. I think many film actors wearing complicated or unfamiliar period "wardrobe" make a great mistake in taking as much of it off as quickly as they can. Some will get out of it between shots. I think what you must do is wear it as much as you can. I often wear the base of it, the breeches and boots, home at the end of the day in the car. And I dress in it in the morning to come to work. It's important, you see, to feel what it's like. If "wardrobe" cannot become clothing —if it remains "costume"—then you fail with it in your work. Obviously there are certain impositions of social responsibility that restrict you in some cases; but when I'm doing a Western, for example, almost all of them are done on location mostly, and you're living off in a motel somewhere where you don't see anybody, I often wear the "wardrobe"—and I think it's very important to wake up in the morning and see the clothes lying in the corner where you kicked them off the night before. They're clothes. The trap most actors fall into is to regard the "wardrobe" as a costume—dress-up clothes. And if they think that way, it's liable to look that way.

——Heston, interviewed for *Films & Filming*, May 72

Alfred HITCHCOCK

Born in London, 1899. Educated in a Jesuit school and trained as an engineer specializing in mechanical drawing. His first films were made in 1925 for an English unit working in Berlin and Munich. First film to draw notice was The Lodger (1926), *and his sound film,* Blackmail (1929) *attracted international attention. Between 1934 and 1938 (when he left to work in America) made a series of commercially successful thrillers that established his place in English and world cinema. From 1955 Hitchcock alternated filmmaking with half-hour films for television, perfecting this film-novella form.*

In his interviews he is inclined to sacrifice accuracy for effectiveness, but the following extracts (mainly from interviews of February 1963 and 1967) seem to define his attitudes frankly.

The Lodger is the first picture possibly influenced by my period in Germany. The whole approach to this film was instinctive with me. It was the first time I exercised my style. In truth, you might almost say that *The Lodger* was my first picture. . . . I took a pure narrative and, for the first time, presented ideas in purely visual terms. We took 15 minutes of a winter afternoon in London, starting about 5:20. We opened with the head of a blonde girl, who is screaming. I remember the way I photographed it. I took a sheet of glass, placed the girl's head on the glass and spread her hair around until it filled the frame. Then we lit the glass from behind so that one would be struck by her light hair. Then we cut to show an electric sign advertising a musical play, *Tonight, Golden Curls*, with the reflection flickering in the water. The girl has drowned. She's hauled out of the water and pulled ashore. The consternation of the bystanders suggests that a murder has been committed. The police arrive on the scene, and then the press. The camera follows one of the newsmen as he moves toward a telephone. He isn't a local reporter but a wire-service man who is calling his office. And now I proceed to show everything that happens as the news spreads around. First, the item is typed out on the wire-service machine so that we are able to read a few sentences. Then it is forwarded on the teletypes. People in clubs learn the news. Then there is a radio announcement. . . . Finally it is flashed on an electric news sign—you know, like on Times Square. And each time, we give additional information, so that you learn more about the crime. The man murders only women. Always blondes. . . . Through all the different means of communication, the information begins to spread, and finally, the evening papers are out on the street. Now we show the effect on various people. Fair-haired girls are terrified. The brunettes are laughing. Reactions in the beauty parlors or of people on their way home. Some blondes steal dark curls and put them under their hats.

———Hitchcock, interviewed for Truffaut's *Hitchcock* (New York, 1967)

There are 2 primary uses of cutting or montage in film: montage to create ideas—and montage to create violence and emotions. For example, in *Rear Window* [1954], where Jimmy Stewart is thrown out of the window in the end, I just photographed that with feet, legs, arms, heads. Completely montage. I also photographed it from a distance, the complete action. There was no comparison between the two. There never is. Barroom fights, or whatever they do in Westerns, when they knock out the heavy or when one man knocks another across the table which breaks—they always break a table in bars—they are always shot at a distance. But it is much more effective if it's done in montage, because you involve the audience much more—that's the secret to that type of montage in film. And the other, of course, is the juxtaposition of imagery relating to the mind of the individual. You can have a man look, you show what he sees, you go back to the man. You can make him react in various ways. You see, you can make him look at one thing, look at another —without his speaking, you can show his mind at work, comparing things— any way you run, there's complete freedom. It's limitless, I would say, the power of cutting and the assembly of images. Like the man with no eyes in *The Birds* [1963]—zooming the camera in—the staccato jumps are almost like catching the breath. Is it? Gasp. Gasp. Yes. Young directors always come up with the idea, "Let the camera be someone and let it move as though it's the person, and you put the guy in front of a mirror and then you see him." It's a terrible mistake. Bob Montgomery did that in *Lady in the Lake* [1946]— I don't believe in it myself. What are you really doing? You are keeping back from the audience who it is. What for? That's all you are doing. Why not show who it is?

You've said that your pictures are finished before you set foot on the set— that is, once the script is completed. What is your working process with the writers?

In the early days—way, way back in the English period, I would always work on a treatment with a writer who would be a plot maker, or story man. I would work weeks and weeks on this treatment and what it would amount to would be a complete narrative, even indicating shots, but not in the words of long-shot or close-up. It would have everything in it, all the details. Then I used to give it to a top writer to dialogue it. When he sent in his dialogue, I would sit down and dictate the shots in a complete continuity. But the film had to be made on paper in this narrative form. It would describe the film, shot by shot, beginning to end. Sometimes with drawings, sometimes without. I abandoned this method when I came to America.

I found that American writers wouldn't go for that sort of thing. I do it verbally now, with the writer, and then I make corrections and adjustments afterwards. I work many weeks with him and he takes notes. And I describe the picture for the production designers as well. . . . I would say I apply myself two-thirds before he writes and one-third after he writes. But I will not and do not photograph anything that he puts in the script on his own apart from words. I mean any cinematic method of telling it—how can he know it? On *North by Northwest* [1959], Ernie Lehman wouldn't let me out of the office for a whole year. I was with him on every shot, every scene. Because it wasn't his material.

> ——Hitchcock, interviewed for *The Cinema of Alfred Hitchcock*
> by Peter Bogdanovich (NY, 1963)

When I look back [at *Rope*, 1948], I realize that it was quite nonsensical because I was breaking with my own theories on the importance of cutting and montage for the visual narration of a story. On the other hand, this film was, in a sense, precut. The mobility of the camera and the movement of the players closely followed my usual cutting practice. In other words, I maintained the rule of varying the size of the image in relation to its emotional importance within a given episode.

Naturally, we went to a lot of trouble to achieve this, and the difficulties went beyond our problems with the camera. Since the action starts in broad daylight and ends by nightfall, we had to deal with the gradual darkening of its background by altering the flow of light between 7:30 and 9:15. To maintain that continuous action, with no dissolves and no time lapses, there were other technical snags to overcome, among them, how to reload the camera at the end of each reel without interrupting the scene. We handled that by having a figure pass in front of the camera, blacking out the action very briefly while we changed from one camera to the other. In that way we'd end on a close-up of someone's jacket, and at the beginning of the next reel, we'd open with the same close-up of the same character.

Joseph Valentine, who photographed *Rope*, had also worked on *Shadow of a Doubt* [1943]. When I saw the initial rushes, my first feeling was that things show up much more in color than in black and white. And I discovered that it was the general practice to use the same lighting for color as for black and white. . . . I especially admired the approach to lighting used by the Americans in 1920 because it overcame the two-dimensional nature of the image by separating the actor from the background through the use of backlights—they call them liners—to detach him from his setting.

Now in color there is no need for this, unless the actor should happen to be dressed in the same color as the background, but that's highly improbable . . . now that we work in color, we shouldn't be made aware of the source of the studio lighting. And yet, in many pictures, you will find many people walking through the supposedly dingy corridors between the stage and dressing rooms of a theater, and because the scene is lighted by studio arc lamps, their shadows on the wall are black as coal. You just can't help wondering where those lights could possibly be coming from.

I truly believe that the problem of the lighting in color films has not yet been solved. I tried for the first time to change the style of color lighting in *Torn Curtain* [1966]. Jack Warren, who was on *Rebecca* and *Spellbound* with me, is the cameraman who cooperated.

——Hitchcock, interviewed for Truffaut's *Hitchcock* (NY, 1967)

The rhythm of the cutting in *Rear Window* [1954] speeds up as the film goes on. This is because of the nature of the structure of the film. At the beginning, life is going on quite normally. The tempo is leisurely. There's a bit of a conflict between the man and the girl. And then gradually the first suspicion grows and it increases. And naturally as you reach the last third of your picture, the events have to pile on top of each other. If you didn't, and if you slowed the tempo down, it would show up considerably. In the film *Psycho* [1960], you start off with just a sack of money and a girl who is suddenly murdered in a shower. The shower scene was made very violent because of what was to follow. The pattern there was that events again increased, but I'd transferred the violence from the screen to the mind of the audience. . . .

. . . To the question of color, again it's the same as the orchestration with cutting. If you noticed in *Rear Window*, Miss Lonely Hearts always dressed in emerald green. To make sure that that came off, there was no other green in the picture because we had to follow her very closely when she went across the street into the café. So I reserved that color for her. In *Dial M for Murder* [1954] I had the woman dressed in red to begin with and as the tragedy overtook her she went to brick, then to gray then to black.

——Hitchcock, in an Academy discussion of *Rear Window*; published in *Take One*, Nov–Dec 68

When Joan Fontaine fainted at the inquest in *Rebecca* [1940], I wanted to show how she felt that everything was moving far away from her before she toppled over. I always remember one night at the Chelsea Arts Ball at Albert Hall in London when I got terribly drunk and I had the sensation that everything was going far away from me. I tried to get that into *Rebecca*, but they couldn't do it. The viewpoint must be fixed, you see, while the perspective is changed as it stretches lengthwise. I thought about the problem for 15 years. By the time we got to *Vertigo* [1958], we solved it by using the dolly and zoom simultaneously. I asked how much it would cost, and they told me it would cost $50,000. When I asked why, they said, "Because to put the camera at the top of the stairs we have to have a big apparatus to lift it, counterweight it, and hold it up in space."

I said, "There are no characters in this scene; it's simply a viewpoint. Why can't we make a miniature of the stairway and lay it on its side, then take our shot by pulling away from it? We can use a tracking shot and a zoom flat on the ground." So that's the way we did it, and it only cost us $19,000.

Truffaut: [With *North by Northwest*, 1959] it seems to me that there were many trick shots in that picture, lots of them almost invisible, and also many special effects, like miniatures and fake sets.

Hitchcock: We had an exact copy made up of the United Nations lobby. You see, someone had used that setting for a film called *The Glass Wall* [1953], and after that Dag Hammarskjold prohibited any shooting of fiction films on the premises.

Just the same, while the guards were looking for our equipment, we shot one scene of Cary Grant coming into the building by using a concealed camera. We'd been told that we couldn't even do any photography, so we concealed the camera in the back of a truck and in that way we got enough footage for the background. Then we got a still photographer to get permission to take some colored stills inside, and I walked around with him, as if I was a visitor, whispering, "Take that shot from there. And now, another one from the roof down." We used those color photographs to reconstitute the settings in our studios.

———Hitchcock, interviewed for Truffaut's *Hitchcock* (NY, 1967)

Bogdanovich: How do you feel, on the whole, about trick effects and process shots?

Hitchcock: It is a means to an end. You must arrive at it somehow. A very important thing about *The Birds:* I never raised the point, "Can it be done?" Because then it would never have been made. Any technician would have said "impossible." So I didn't even bring that up, I simply said, "Here's what we're going to do." No one will ever realize that had the pioneering technical work on it not been attempted, the film would not have been made. *Cleopatra* [1963] or *Ben Hur* [1959] is nothing to this—just quantities of people and scenery. Just what the bird trainer has done is phenomenal. Look at the way the crows chase the children down the street, dive all around them, land on their backs. It took days to organize these birds on the hood of the car and to make them fly away at the right time. *The Birds* could easily have cost $5,000,000 if Bob Burks and the rest of us hadn't been technicians ourselves.

Bogdanovich: How do you work when you are shooting?

Hitchcock: Well, I never look through the camera you know. The cameraman knows me well enough to know what I want—and when in doubt, draw a rectangle and then draw the shot out for him. You see, the point is that you are, first of all, in a two-dimensional medium. Mustn't forget that. You have a rectangle to fill. Fill it. Compose it. I don't have to look through a camera for that.

———Hitchcock, interviewed for *The Cinema of Alfred Hitchcock* (NY, 1963)

When I made *Psycho*, I made it in black and white for the very simple reason that I didn't want to show the red blood flowing down the bathtub into the drain. The whole scene in the shower was shot as a concept of imagining this woman's being stabbed to death. But if you examine the film frame by frame, you'll find that no knife ever touched the woman's body. The whole structure of a film like *Psycho* is based on giving the audience an early sample of violence. As the film went on, however, I reduced the violence on the screen— but increased it in the minds of the audience.

I don't know whether it was widely noticed, but I also did some experiments with sound in *Frenzy* [1972] which I had never attempted before. If you remember in the early part of the story, two men are talking at the fruit stand and the police sergeant comes up and begins to talk about the latest murders. Rusk says, "Sergeant, have you met my friend?" And he turns and there is no one there. At that point I cut all the sound off, except for the footsteps of people going by. All the roar of the market was gone; I took it out arbitrarily to emphasize the man's disappearance. . . .

And I used it in reverse: When the camera retreated down the stairs after Rusk took the girl to his room. It went out into the street, and I brought up the traffic to a tremendous roar so that an audience would subconsciously say to itself, "Well, if the girl screams, no one's ever going to hear it."

———Hitchcock, interviewed for *Oui*, Feb 73

George HOELLERING
Born near Vienna 1900. Worked in film production in Austria, Germany, Hungary and England; has been director of London's Academy Cinema since 1937.

Q. Could you tell us how the film *Kühle Wampe* [1931] came to be made and about your role as producer?

A. There was a film company which distributed Russian films and produced a variety of social documentary films, called Prometheus-Film. The leading figure in it was a Mr. [Emil] Unfried. . . . Although we didn't know it, at that time Prometheus-Film was in financial difficulties, but they hoped to save themselves by making a positive film on the *Jugenbewegung*, the youth movement—a very optimistic youth film that would glorify sport for the workers. Unfried was very close to Robert Scharfenberg, who had been responsible for the script of *Mutter Krausens Fahrt ins Glück* [1929]. . . . He interested [Slatan] Dudow . . . [who] talked about it to Brecht; Brecht and Dudow were great friends and had a great respect for each other, but Dudow knew exactly how to use Brecht. . . . Dudow was the driving force behind the film and I think the greatest credit belongs to Dudow, rather than to Brecht. Brecht of course was responsible for all the texts, everything written was by him.

. . . I was asked by Prometheus if I would help in this production— Dudow had not had a great deal of experience in the cinema. I was fascinated by the idea of working with Brecht and accepted, subject to my being allowed to control the technical side of the production, in particular having a good cameraman and sound man. My conditions were accepted. I got Gunther Krampf, the best Austrian cameraman of the period. . . . The whole setup was not a collective, in the sense that everything was discussed beforehand by everyone at meetings—anyway, I would not have been a party to anything like that as you would never have got a film made that way.

———Hoellering, interviewed for *Screen*, Winter 74–75

Dustin HOFFMAN
Born 1937.

Q. Is that you on the screen in *Lenny* [1974], or is that Lenny Bruce?

A. Well, it's me. It looks like me up there. I think it's me.

Q. Who is on the screen if that's Dustin Hoffman?

A. It's always me on the screen if I do a role. You just can't divorce yourself from it, nor do I want to. What you do is a distortion always, in the sense that art is a distortion. If you say, Is that Truffaut in *Day for Night* [1973]?, yes, that's Truffaut, but it's also a distortion, it's a subjective feeling he wants to present as a director. What you see on the screen, let's say, in *Lenny,* is simply myself playing this role as I learned to see it over a period of little less than a year, giving the material I was given, arguing with certain aspects of it, having to compromise in certain ways. It is a collaborative business, an art form. You give and take with the director, writer, etc. Also, it's a point of view I felt strongly about. It's, I'm sure, a flawed piece of work. It is not a documentary. It is certainly not Lenny Bruce. It is me doing a certain feeling I have about him, as I learned him or studied what I could.

——Hoffman, interviewed for *Off Camera* (NY, 1975)

Carl HOFFMANN   (1881–1947)
Born in Silesia. Entered film industry in 1908.

In order to suppress the noise which the picture camera produced, very simple means were used at the beginning. Camera and cameraman were wrapped in woolen blankets which muffled the noise: a rather primitive and complicated procedure that limited the efficiency of the camera. The next step was to put camera and cameraman into a big box. Finally the box was equipped with rubber tires which conveyed more mobility to it. Meanwhile the camera manufacturers had intensively and constructively dealt with the problem of the "noiseless" camera. A recording box camera was built which was as easy to handle and as mobile as the small camera. Although working with it implied still some difficulties, it represented an obvious progress. Subsequent ameliorations and functional new constructions led to the camera we use now. It weighs about 300 lbs., functions absolutely without noise and controls its space on its noiselessly gliding undercarriage.

——Hoffmann, in *Die Filmwoche*, No. 10, 1932

Ralph HOGE
Worked 20 years with Gregg Toland and was the head grip on Citizen Kane (*1941*).

Perry Ferguson, the art director, deserves a lot of credit for the success of *Citizen Kane.* It was he who devised important scenes merely by using a hunk of cornice, a fireplace in the background, and a foreground chair. By using such props and Gregg's [Toland] depth-of-focus lens, Orson [Welles] could create the illusion of a huge set. Obviously we couldn't afford to duplicate the grandeur of San Simeon, so it was done by suggestion.

——Hoge, in *Action*, May–June 69

William H O L D E N [Beedle]
Born 1918 in O'Fallon, Illinois.

Movie acting may not have a certain kind of glory as a true art, but it's acting, and it's damn hard work. You kiss your wife good-bye at 8 in the morning, and an hour later you're on a set pretending to be killing somebody or whispering sweet nothings into some glamour girl's ear. It's a terrible emotional drain. It's devastating. The most demanding thing about it is that you must keep up the level of your performance. The way I do it is to think of myself as a reporter. My job is to portray the character and bring it to the audience in a way that will enable them to involve themselves emotionally. I read a script and analyze it. I find that if you develop an attitude toward the character, the mannerisms for it come later. You attempt to stay as detached as possible. Then there's a kind of final melting in your mind about a week before the picture is supposed to start. Once you're in it, you're involved in how you're going to develop the character. Once I'm fairly entrenched, I find that the character almost takes care of itself. Then the demands on you are the demands of a particular day of work. It's terribly exhausting. My most difficult roles have always been ones that are unlike me. Still, I've been able to find their motivation acceptable. If you're going to be Gillis in *Sunset Boulevard* [1950], for example, you must get it across that there but for the grace of God go I. I may not be able to understand Gillis, a gigolo, but I can sympathize with him. I've found that sympathy is about all you need if you want to act a different kind of person from your real self.

    ——Holden, interviewed for *The Player* (NY, 1962)

I talk of retiring all the time, but I'd like to go out with a bang. *The Christmas Tree* [1969] was a whimper. And the one before that, *The Wild Bunch* [1969] really started something new for me. It was the film in which I decided not to take it anymore—to use, or try to use, my liabilities as advantages: the lines around the eyes, the beer belly. I don't *look* like I can get the girl anymore, and I don't take roles like that anymore.

    ——Holden, interviewed for *The Village Voice*, 5 Aug 71

Dennis H O P P E R
Born 1936, in Dodge City, Kansas. Lives in Taos, New Mexico.

I edited [*Easy Rider,* 1969] for a year, and then Bert Schneider decided he didn't like it the way it was at that time. He came in himself and did some things on it. Jack [Nicholson] did some things on it. Henry Jaglom did some things on it. Bob Rafelson did some things on it. There were quite a few different people who worked on it. . . .

    I wanted to use a real Texan [for the role eventually played by Jack Nicholson]. Rip [Torn, who was originally signed to the part] and I had a fight, and he wanted some rewrites, and I said "Screw you.". . . And Bert Schneider, who was giving us the money, said, "I haven't asked for anything," which he hadn't, and he said, "I want Nicholson to play the part," and I

fought it and said that I didn't want him because I wanted a Texan. But I'm really glad that Jack did it, because he was great. . . .
. . . The whole "Nic, nic, nic, fire. Nic, nic, nic," thing was [Jack Nicholson's]. We had a biker working with us, who every time he couldn't start a bike he went, "Nic, nic, nic," you know, and did one of those for the crowd, and Jack picked that up. The scene that most people think was improvised, the thing around the campfire with all of us getting high, I wrote that. And that was word for word out of the script, except for the "Nic, nic, nic, fire."
———Hopper, interviewed for *Jack Nicholson, Face to Face* (NY, 1975)

William HORNBECK
Born in Los Angeles in 1901.

. . . By the time the [First] war was over I was editing. If it hadn't been for the war, it could have taken me years. By the time I was 20, I was head of the department [at the Sennett Studio].

The man who taught me most about editing was F. Richard Jones, an extremely fine editor who later became an important director and producer and made feature pictures for Sennett like *Mickey* [1917] and *The Extra Girl* [1923], both with Mabel Normand. . . .

A 2-reel picture would take much longer in those days than you'd think— often up to 3 or 4 weeks to shoot. We had 8 or 10 companies to keep up a schedule of one picture a week. We had to get that one picture out, or else we didn't get paid.

The person who really had to know his business was the cameraman. He had to be very skillful with his grinding speeds. Cars had to race through at the right pace, while in fact they might be moving very slowly. Dick Jones was very interested in camera speeds and how they can help a scene. He would try an action at varying speeds; 14 frames a second, 12, 10, 6. . . .

We had our own laboratory. They would screen the rushes first for the director; then Sennett would get a special running, either at the studio or at his home, in the evening, where he had projection equipment. The editor would then take it and go to work. . . .

On the Friday night, or the Saturday, when we had finally cut the work print, all the cutters would go over to negative cutting. . . . We would try to finish before midnight on Saturday night, when we had to ship the negative to New York. We got close to missing once or twice. Sometimes it would be early Sunday morning, but we always got it on the train. . . .

Mack Sennett supervised his pictures all along the way. But he couldn't afford to reject any; good or bad, the pictures had to go. A lot of them weren't quite up to standard, but they went.
———Hornbeck, interviewed for *The Parade's Gone By* (NY, 1968)

Harry HORNER
Born 1910 in Czechoslovakia. A graduate of Max Reinhardt's Theatrical Seminary in Vienna, he came to America in 1935.

The fact that there was only one important set [in *The Heiress*, 1949], namely, the house on Washington Square, made it necessary that the house should have a personality of its own which, in different ways, would affect those inhabitants with whom the story deals and also would impress the character whose visit to the house plays so vital a part in the drama. . . .

There had to be room for a dramatic staircase which was to play an important part in the story. One of the old houses of downtown New York gave me an idea for a staircase which was laid out so that from one vantage point three flights of stairs could be seen—with the father's bedroom on the second floor and the girl's bedroom and guest room on the third floor. There had to be room for an interesting arrangement of hall, dining room, front parlor, back parlor, study, and so on. All this we built in the studio, with the sliding doors placed so that certain vistas into rooms became dramatically important. The father's chair in the back parlor, for instance, dominated the house, and a direct view to the entrance hall was possible. . . .

But there was yet an obstacle before those sets could be called ready. This obstacle, so different from those of real life or of the stage, was the camera itself, with the sound boom. Proportions of rooms had to be carefully thought out so that they would photograph: not too high, or too much of the ceiling would be lost outside of the range of the lens; and not too low, of course, or there would be lost the typical architectural proportions of elegance and period. And, what was more important, all those walls and ceilings had to be constructed so that they could come apart—they had to be made "wild" as the technical expression goes—to make elbow room for the cameras.

——Horner, interviewed for *Hollywood Quarterly*, Fall 50

Edward Everett H O R T O N   (1888–1971)
Born in New York City. Moved from theater into films in 1918.

. . . I was invited to be in the second talking picture, a 6-reel, 100 percent–Warner Brothers Vitaphone talking picture. It was called *The Terror* [1928]. . . . The producers didn't seem to know what they had since *The Jazz Singer* [1927], which was really the third feature-length talkie, hadn't come out yet. In those days, there was no boom that followed you all around. The microphones hung down, all wrapped around with material to make them look like part of the backdrop. We had 3 or 4 cameras. In a great big ensemble scene these cameras were sort of coffins covered with tarpaulins so that you couldn't hear the buzz of the cameras. . . . We were instructed not to talk until we felt ourselves in the center of the camera [frame]. . . . We didn't think anything could be better than that. It was the last word in progress. . . .

The Merry Widow [1934] stands out above all in my memory. It was filmed on a gorgeous set at MGM. Never was there a set like it, with a palace and all that sort of thing. Chevalier and Jeanette MacDonald were the leads. I played the Baron Popoff. In the Lubitsch version, there was a king, and I played the prime minister. Anything I did that the king approved of prompted him to pin a little medal on me. If something happened that he didn't approve of, he'd take the medal off. No great reaction of any kind. But very amusing. Well, when we finished the scene, we'd all retire. Chevalier and MacDonald would go off with the French actors Chevalier had brought over with him, the French director, and the French dialogue director. MacDonald wasn't allowed to say a word that wasn't passed. It had to be excellent French. Then we'd watch them doing the scene that we did. They had a king and a prime minister, and whenever Popoff did anything that the king liked, the king would kiss him on both cheeks. Then, when he did something wrong, there was a terrible scene and you'd think a revolution had started. Lubitsch used to look at me and say, "Why? Why all that?"

——Horton, interviewed for *The Real Tinsel* (NY, 1970)

John H O U S E M A N [Jacques Haussmann]
Born c. 1903 in Bucharest.

My second assignment was to work with Alfred Hitchcock. It was no secret that all had not been roses between him and David [Selznick] during the making of *Rebecca* [1940], to which Hitch had attempted to apply the very personal creative methods that had made him world-famous. These methods were profoundly repulsive to David O. Selznick, who belonged to the school of the well-made, producer-controlled, strictly-adhered-to shooting script and who, besides, was determined on this, Hitch's first American picture, to assert his producer's position of power. With the success of *Rebecca* all had been forgiven, but a residue of hostility and suspicion remained. I was instructed to use my British background, as well as my cultivation and charm, to establish good personal relations with Hitch and to cajole and encourage him into conceiving and preparing an "original" screenplay for his second American film.

Rebecca had been a distasteful experience for him. Anxious to get started on a new and more individual film, he came up with a notion for a picaresque spy story—a U.S. version of *The Thirty-nine Steps* [1935]—with a transcontinental chase that moved from coast to coast and ended inside the hand of the Statue of Liberty. He called it *The Saboteur* [1942], and we outlined it to Selznick, who thought it was terrible but gave us the go-ahead—the quicker the better.

Working with Hitch really meant listening to him talk—anecdotes, situations, characters, revelations, and reversals, which he would think up at night and try out on us during the day and of which the surviving elements were finally strung together into some sort of story in accordance with carefully calculated and elaborately plotted rhythms.

——Houseman, in *Run-Through* (New York, 1972)

For all our planning and precaution it was inevitable, in making such a picture [*Julius Caesar*, 1953], that new problems should have been encountered right through to the last phases of editing and preparing the film for release.

We soon found that a Shakespearean scene, no matter how conventionally shot, is not subject to the normal laws of film cutting. With the intuitive skill of a sensitive editor watching new film running through his moviola, Jack

Dunning soon discovered that a Shakespearean scene had certain general rules of its own, differing from those of other movies.

The reaction shot, for instance, which has long been the basis of dramatic cutting in both silent and talking pictures, becomes a tricky thing to use in editing Shakespearean dialogue. Silent reactions, even when carefully planned by the director to fall in predetermined places during a long speech, were rarely used by the editor, who developed a strong reluctance—born not of veneration for the classics but of sound cutting instinct—to interrupt the line and cadence of a speech in the mouth of one character, by cutting away to the reaction of another. It struck him as arbitrary and false. And he was right. The film, as he worked on it, developed its own proper cutting-rhythm and form. The result was no less sharp.

——Houseman, interviewed for *Sight & Sound,* July–Sep, 53

. . . I think Pauline [Kael] overwrote ridiculously. The whole argument is foolish because [*Citizen Kane* is] Orson's movie. He took the material that Mankiewicz wrote and that I helped to edit, and he made it his own, just as he took a wonderful cameraman and used him, and Bernard Herrmann wrote him a wonderful score, and he used that, and he made a wonderful movie, so I don't know what the hoopla's about except that it's Orson's own fault for wanting all the credit for everything. He did exactly the same thing with "The War of the Worlds." I mean there was a writer [Howard Koch], but I think Orson in his own mind honestly believes that he wrote every word of it. There are those megalomaniacs for whom other people do not exist. . . .

. . . Howard Hughes came in, bought the studio, was determined nothing made before he'd arrived would be shown, took *They Live by Night* [1949] and locked it in a vault where it stayed for 2½ years. So I'd had one picture that I liked very much which was a commercial disaster, and another picture I adored locked up in a vault, and I got very depressed about the picture business and I rushed back to New York and directed *Lute Song* with Mary Martin simply to save myself. That's happened so often. As insurance against failure in one place, I do something some place else.

——Houseman, in *The New York Times,* 21 Apr 74

Leslie H O W A R D   [Leslie Howard Stainer] (1893–1943)
Born in London, of a Hungarian family. Killed by enemy action.

Q. And the next venture is *Pygmalion?*
A. Yes, and this time I am going to have a hand in the direction. Anthony Asquith and I will co-direct, and I will play Professor Higgins. It is still difficult for an actor in Hollywood to take any real part in the production. Every aspect of production is so self-contained, and there is so little come and go between writers, directors, and editors, that the best they can do is to become as expert as they can in their own limited field. It is the only way they can make any impression on the finished picture. And the same is true of the actor. The only impression he can make on a film is through his acting. He can have little effect on the people who work in these other airtight compartments. But in England

production is not so rigid, and I am going to try to contribute something more than I can through just acting.

——Howard, interviewed for *World Film News*, Feb 38

James Wong H O W E [Wang Tung Jim] (1899–1976)
Born Kwantung Province in China. In 1904 brought to the United States with his family, who lived in Washington and Oregon before moving to California. His first job in a film studio was at Paramount as assistant to Alvin Wyckoff; after 3 years he became a first cameraman. In addition to his contract years at MGM and Warner Brothers, he has done his most original and creative work on independent productions.

Well, the picture, *Transatlantic* [1931], was something remarkable. I used wide angles, deep focus throughout, long before *Kane*. Eighty percent of the picture was shot with a 25 mm. lens. . . . I carried focus from 5 feet back to 20, 30 feet. I argued with the art director, Gordon Wiles: I wanted ceilings to give the claustrophobic feeling of a ship. He did full ceilings and half-ceilings for me, and I used special lights in the engine room to give an illusion of depth, with special sets of machinery one behind the other. . . .

[For *Walking Down Broadway*, 1933] we had a dime-a-dance hall in it. [Stroheim] said, "Jimmy, I want a dancing camera." I told him I didn't know what he meant. He said, "A camera I can move around the floor with, like a dancer." I was baffled. Finally he grabbed hold of a light stand and said that we could set a camera on it. I told him it wouldn't stay on, it was too heavy, so I had a heavier lamp stand made up. The effect was wonderful. . . .

We had a tiny apartment in *He Ran All the Way* [1951], exactly copied from a real one; we put the camera in a wheelchair and pushed the cameraman around. On *Body and Soul* [1947] I myself got on roller skates to shoot the boxing scenes and they pushed *me* around. I wanted an effect where the boxer is knocked out and he looks up into a dazzle of lights; with a heavy, fixed camera, you'd never get that.

——Howe, interviewed for *Hollywood Cameramen* (London, 1970)

This question of backlighting in color is another thing that demands modification of usual techniques. In black and white we use back light and rim light to outline our characters so that they will stand out from their backgrounds. This is seldom necessary in color, for we have inherent color differences to serve the same purpose.

In one sequence of my present picture [*The Adventures of Tom Sawyer*, 1939] we had a scene showing young Tommy Kelly, who plays Tom Sawyer, walking atop a picket fence balancing a feather on his nose, to impress his sweetheart. The camera angle was such that Tommy's head moved against the open sky. In monochrome, the boy's hair and the sky would be rendered in very similar shades of gray.

Instinctively as we prepared to photograph the scene I arranged back lighting to outline the head and separate it from the sky. After the first take, it suddenly dawned on me that this was a color picture, and on the screen the sky would be blue while the boy's hair would be light brown, giving a natural separation. In the next take I eliminated the rim lighting. On the screen this latter take was far more pleasing.

———Howe, in *American Cinematographer*, Oct 37

John H U B L E Y (1914–1977)
Born in Marinette, Wisconsin. Left the Walt Disney studio in 1941.

I was with Disney from 1936 to 1941. I worked as an assistant art director on *Snow White* [1937], and associate art director on *Pinocchio* [1939], parts of *Fantasia* [1940], *Bambi* [1942] and *Dumbo* [1941]. They were days of terrific technical development, and the Disney studios were a wonderful school. There were classes in every phase of cartoon and animation work. It was only in my last year or so there that I began to feel the restrictions of Disney's production methods. The trouble was the depersonalized *horizontal* system—a sort of conveyor-belt idea. The marvelous training developed your imagination and ideas, which were then inhibited by the need to conform to a standardized style. We just got so sick of humanizing pigs and bunnies. We wanted to do films about human characters and real-life situations. And we wanted to do satire, which is natural material for the cartoon.

———Hubley, in *Sight & Sound*, Winter 61–62

Valentine H U G O

[While working on *La Passion de Jeanne d'Arc*, 1928] At all times we suffered the enveloping sense of horror, of an iniquitous trial, of an eternal judicial error. ... I saw the most mistrustful actors, carried away by the will and faith of the director [Dreyer], unconsciously continuing to play their roles after the cameras had stopped. A judge, after a scene in which he appeared moved by Joan's suffering, mumbling, "At heart she's a witch!" he was living the drama as though it were real. Another, boiling with rage, hurls a string of invective at the accused and finally interjects this apostrophe: "You are a disgrace to the Army!" ... [It was] particularly moving the day when Falconetti's hair was cropped close to her skull in the wan light of the execution morning and in the total silence on the set. We were as touched as if the mark of infamy were truly being applied and we were in the grip of ancient prejudices. The electricians, the mechanics held their breaths and their eyes were full of tears. [Falconetti herself cried.] Then the director slowly walked towards the heroine, caught some of her tears on his finger and touched them to his lips.

———Hugo, in *Ciné-Miroir*, Nov 1927;
repr. in Sadoul-Morris, *Dictionary of Films*, p. 17

John H U S T O N
Born in Nevada, Missouri, 1906. Son of Walter Huston. Random education. Worked as boxer, actor, cavalryman, writer, painter, reporter. First film work in 1931 as scriptwriter for William Wyler.

It's not often that I look through the camera. I know what lens they're using, and I know what it's going to look like. . . . I direct actors about as little as possible. The better an actor, the less I have to direct. I want to get as much out of the actor himself as I can. Because wonderful accidents occur. I guide an actor rather than direct; expand a performance or reduce it. So far as the mechanical element goes—why, that's just being a traffic cop. . . .

Now Paul Newman [in *The Life and Times of Judge Roy Bean* (1972) and *The Mackintosh Man* (1973)] is full of innovation. He has wonderful immediate ideas. Very often supplements mine, or has something better than my notions. Some action, perhaps. The very best actors, the ones that fill me with admiration, are those that furnish surprises. You don't know—I doubt that they do either—where it comes from. They reach down into some remote cavern and come up with something that reveals a principle, something mysterious and new.

—Huston, interviewed in *Sight & Sound*, Winter 72–73

Sam Goldwyn brought me to Hollywood in the early thirties on the strength of some short stories that I had published in *The American Mercury*, but I was a dismal failure trying to write scripts for him. . . .

Once I had become established as a screenwriter at Warners, I got a clause put into my contract that if I stayed on there they would give me the chance to direct. . . . After Allen Rivkin and I finished the screenplay of *The Maltese Falcon* (1941), I asked to direct it.

Before I started shooting [*The Maltese Falcon*] I made drawings, setup by setup, of the action. I discovered that about half the time the actors automatically fell into the blocking that I had worked out in my drawings, and the rest of the time I would either bring them into line with my original conception of the blocking or let them work out something for themselves. . . .

The color process in which [*Reflections in a Golden Eye*, 1967] was originally shot was the result of considerable experimentation, and was perfectly suited to this study of a group of neurotic people. This color process basically had a golden amber quality to it; other colors, toned, impinged on the screen, as it were, from behind this golden hue. This served to separate the audience somewhat from the characters, who were in various ways withdrawn from reality, and to make their story a bit more remote and exotic. I got the concession that the film would be released initially in this special color process in key cities, but the response wasn't good. Prints in Technicolor had also been processed at the same time the original prints were made, and it is the Technicolor prints that have been in circulation ever since.

—Huston, interviewed for *Film Comment*, May–June 73

Q. What caused all the trouble [on *A Farewell to Arms*, 1957]?
A. For one thing, they kept rewriting the script all the time. We had agreed to leave the script alone at a certain point, but [Selznick] kept going on with the changes.
We didn't see eye-to-eye on the script. Then just before the shooting be-

gan I received a 16-page single-spaced memorandum from David. It was the damnedest thing I'd ever read.

He told me what he thought of me and what I should think of him. After going into a long song and dance about what a wonderful producer he was and how he made such a success of *Gone With the Wind* he told me if I wanted to quit, he would accept the responsibility. The memo left me no choice but to leave.

———Huston, interviewed for *The Washington Post*, 7 Apr 57

Lighting is almost completely up to the cameraman, who of course must be in complete sympathy with the director. The setup is something else. Then you're telling the story, the composition will appear on the screen, also the movement of the camera. The variety of material to be included in the shot, and its displacement, those are the things I try to control. Again, when I decide about these things, I go by the rules that are imposed upon me by the central idea, by what I'm trying to say, and how I've decided to say it. And I choose setups and the camera angles that will tell my story as quickly and as strongly and as surely as possible.

Artistically, I am most concerned with controlling the color [of all the elements of filmmaking]. Some films would suffer from being in color. Color, like camera acrobatics, can be a distraction unless it's functional in the film. Both are important; black and white and color film. Artists have pigments but they continue to draw. Certain subjects are better in one and others in the other medium. I would have never made *Freud* [1962] in color. There was a certain projection of a unilateral thought, the development of a logic. Color would only have distracted. I wanted the audience to follow the logic that was as real as a detective's pursuit of a criminal, without distraction by visual elements. And by the same token, I would never have made *Moulin Rouge* [1953] in black and white. And in *Moby Dick* [1956] I tried to combine both by inventing a technique of printing both types of film together.

———Huston, interviewed for *Film Quarterly*, Fall 58

[On *Moby Dick*] we were dismasted 3 times. It was, I think, the worst winter in history of those seas and at least once I was sure we were on our way to the bottom, but were saved by a masterpiece of seamanship.

Q. Is it true that you actually lost the whale at one point?

A. We lost 3 whales. And the reason we'd lose them was there'd be a choice whether to save the personnel or the whale. And for sentimental reasons we'd pick up the humans instead of the whale. Three times warnings went out that these great structures of about 60 feet long made of steel and wood given a rubber skin were adrift and a danger to shipping. I think one ended up in Holland, but each time of course it was awful so far as we ourselves were concerned because, we'd have to then stop everything and make a new whale.

Q. In *Moby Dick* you used that special color process—why was that?

A. Well, I wanted to avoid the prettiness that Technicolor, on its own, is heir to. I didn't think it was right for this particular subject and so we, what amounted to, made a wedding between black and white, which fortified the color and gave it strength and body.

Q. There was something like that going on in *Moulin Rouge* too, wasn't there?

A. Not like that. Ossie Morris, by the way, who was the cameraman on *Moby Dick* and *Moulin Rouge*, used filters which before that had only been used out of doors, and we used smoke in the scenes in the Moulin Rouge. The effect, to flatten out instead of breaking up the color to make it a local color and make flat planes of color, was rather similar to the posters of Lautrec.

Q. And how about *Reflections in a Golden Eye?* Isn't that special color?

A. Yes. That had to be done in the lab itself, and I had a bit of a struggle with the studio because we shot it with that intention; worked for weeks on developing the technique. The lab was experimenting—the Tigan lab—and eventually we came up with this particular formula which I felt was quite right for the picture. Then I entered into a big struggle with the Warner Brothers at that time. It too has changed, there've been several turnovers since then, who believed in the old Technicolor process. Half the prints were made in my color and half in theirs.

[In *The Bible* (1966)] the animals are superb actors if you understand them. You can pretty well foretell what they are going to do. I remember the scene in which all the animals two by two filed into the Ark; well, it was the opinion of most trainers this couldn't be done. But finally I found a trainer that said it could and he devised a way and it worked and it took some weeks—it was done at enormous expense. We first built a road that led through the ark and ditches on either side of the road. First the animals were led singly just around this circuit to the Ark and then his mate, two animals would be led, and then finally when they had become used to this, nylon lines were attached to bridles and the men led them within the ditches and then they would add another pair of animals and each pair had been worked separately, at first singly and then in pairs, and then we added to the pairs, and finally came the time when the bridles were taken off and the animals walked altogether two by two around into the Ark.

———Huston, interviewed at the National Film Theatre, 14 Sep 72

Let me tell you about Tennessee Williams on *Night of the Iguana* [1964], which he generously lent himself to. Tony Veiller and I had a pretty good scene written where [Richard] Burton is alone in his room in a fever and in a drunk, and all these things are going on inside of him. The girl, Sue Lyon, comes in and tries to seduce him and he is doing everything in his power to keep away from the girl. Well, we gave the scene to Tennessee to see what he thought of it. The only change he wrote was the thing that made the scene. When the girl opens the door suddenly, a glass falls onto the floor leaving broken bits of glass scattered about the room. When the scene is played, both of them are barefoot. Burton walks on it and doesn't even feel being shredded. The girl sees this and joins him walking barefoot across the glass. It was the difference between an extraordinary scene and a pedestrian one. It's also an example of Tennessee's extraordinary powers of dramatization. It certainly was a welcome idea.

———Huston, interviewed for *Action*, Sep–Oct 72

I

Kon I C H I K A W A
Born 1915, in Ujiyamada. Worked in drawn and puppet animation before first
fictional film in 1948.

When I know what I want to do, then I sit down and study it for months. I
have to digest the whole thing, or live the whole thing before it will come out
as a film. [Ichikawa almost invariably works with his wife, Nato Wada.] We
usually read a book we like or are given a book the company has bought, or a
story or something, and we both read it carefully and then we start to work.
But the work isn't sitting down and writing, it's—well, it's sort of like living
with it, bringing it into the house as though it were a pet or a child. We are
very close and we communicate through good-mornings and what-do-you-want-
for-suppers and the script gets done page by page, a word here, a sentence
there, without our thinking too much about it. It is she who finally sits down
and writes it all up. Then if there is something I don't agree with we can talk
some more. But I usually agree: after all, it is just what we said it would be.
Her influence is absolutely crucial, I think. Without her there wouldn't be any
Ichikawa film. She says no, says I am the kind of director who transforms everything, and when the film is done she can seldom see any of her own work in it.
———Ichikawa, interviewed for *Sight & Sound,* Spring 66

Tadashi I M A I
Born in Tokyo in 1912, son of a chief priest. Arrested for radical activity while
in college. In 1943, he left his studies for a continuity job with J. O. Studios in
Kyoto and became a scriptwriter before directing Numazu Military Academy
(1939).

During the first 3 years of the occupation, America, through MacArthur, had
a plan to spread "democracy" in Japan, and many so-called leftists worked in
[the Civil Information and Education Section of the American army]. Anyway,
the CI&E film division dispatched several officers to the large Japanese film
companies. The directors and scenario writers were gathered together and we
were ordered to make 6 kinds of films. I have forgotten what the 6 were, but
they included (1) movies criticizing the Japanese imperial system, (2) movies
attacking the activities of the Japanese *zaibatsu* [giant industrial and financial

conglomerates] or cartel families during the war, (3) autobiographies of Japanese revolutionaries who were annihilated, like Takeji Kobayashi, who was tortured and killed by the police during the war, and Hidemi Ozaki, (4) films encouraging and urging coal miners and other sectors of labor to expand economic production in Japan so that Japanese industry might recover. I cannot recall the last two categories. But anyway, in accordance with these guidelines the companies summoned many young film directors and instructed them to carry out these projects. I was still a beginner at Toho at that time, and they made me do *An Enemy of the People* [*Minshu no Teki*, 1946]. I am sure you know *Waga Seishun ni Kuinashi* [*No Regrets for Our Youth*, 1946] of Kurosawa. He made this film based upon the life of Hidemi Ozaki, one of the persecuted revolutionaries of Japan. No one had the guts to make a film critical of the emperor, so we tacitly dropped this and made films that fit into the permitted categories. It seems somewhat funny in retrospect. Several officers gathered together the board of directors of the company, directors, scenario writers, assistants, everybody, and gave us a few long speeches. They threatened us, saying that if we didn't cooperate, they would immediately shut down the place. We cooperated.

——Imai, interviewed for *Voices from the Japanese Cinema* (New York, 1975)

William INGE (1913–1973)

Born in Independence, Kansas. Attended University of Kansas and Iowa State College. Without the transition of adapting his successful plays for film production, Inge surprised his friends with a first original film script, Splendor in the Grass, *produced in 1961.*

That was my first film, written after I did *Loss of Roses*. We did the whole thing in the East. It was the first time I had the desire to write for films. I was so accustomed to the theater that it was hard for me to adjust to the freedom of the cinematic medium. But I wanted to write about the transition from the high financial prosperity of the late twenties to the Depression—the social transition. It was something I had lived through. I couldn't get it on stage and was having real difficulty conceptualizing it for film until I remembered Chris Isherwood's *I Am a Camera* [1955]. That's literally what I did: I identified totally with the camera.

Q. Did it reach the screen the way you had anticipated?

A. It was about 350 pages originally. But Kazan and I wanted to remain independent in production, and the studio would back us only if we stayed within 2 hours. So we cut my panorama script. The boy and girl were originally just incidental. They had this youthful desire for one another but as time passed, it was ironically lost, just as the golden prosperity of the twenties was lost. They had to face realities as real people. Unfortunately, the film came off a bit like saying, "If you don't give in to the sex urge, you'll go crazy." Which is not quite what I had intended. . . .

I didn't want to adapt my plays for movies. I just wanted to learn more about writing for the theater. . . . Then in 1959 I was down in Florida, where

I wrote most of *Splendor* on vacation. I brought it back to Kazan, who was quite surprised because he thought I was writing a play.
———Inge, interviewed for *Transatlantic Review* (1967)

Rex I N G R A M [Reginald Ingram Montgomery Hitchcock] (1892–1950)
Born in Dublin. Studied sculpture at Yale School of Fine Arts. Began film work as actor and scenarist.

While good atmosphere gives an air of reality to a picture, the most convincing and engrossing atmosphere is often far from realistic. This is so because the aim of the director should be to get over the effect of the atmosphere he desires, rather than the actual atmosphere which exists in such scenes as he may wish to portray, and which, if reduced literally to the screen, would be quite unconvincing. . . .

Whether a scene is being made of a beachcomber's shanty, an underworld basement saloon, a pool hall, a ship's cabin, a shoe factory or a smart restaurant, not only should the aim be to convince the audience, but enough study should be given to the subject in each case to convince the habitués of any of these places that they are in familiar surroundings.

One of the most interesting sets that I have ever handled from an atmospheric standpoint was the interior of a derelict ship, beached, and become the hangout of beachcombers, in *Under Crimson Skies* [1920], a production some years old. Conrad, the master writer of the sea, never offered a more wonderful opportunity for color than did this episode in the story provided by J. G. Hawks, with its thrilling climax in the battle in the surf between the white man and the black giant.

In *The Four Horsemen* [1921], the basement resort of the Buenos Aires *bocca* or river front hangout furnished plenty of chances to make colorful pictures—yet had I been literal in the way I handled it, the effect would not have been anything as nearly realistic. For I doubt if anything just like that dive ever existed in the Argentine, or anywhere else for that matter.

The set was a Spanish version of a bowery cellar saloon that I used in a picture which I made several years before and re-created to suit the episodes suggested in the great Ibanez novel. The signs on the wall, the types of men, in fact all the bits of atmosphere in the place were the results of painstaking efforts to get "color" and local atmosphere into the set. In one corner a sign hung which was the advertisement of a notorious crimp, a sailor's boarding-house keeper, whose establishment was on the *bocca* for years. An old sailor who was working in the scene and who had lived in Buenos Aires came to me and said: "I've been shanghaied by that blood-sucker."

I have gone so far as to have my principals speak the language of the country in which the picture is laid. Few of them like to go to this trouble but it helps them materially in keeping to the required atmosphere. The results on the screen are so encouraging that after they see what it has done for them the players don't mind the extra study that this course entails.
———Ingram, contribution to Peter Milne's *Motion Picture Directing*
(NY, 1922)

Otar I O S E L I A N I
Born in Tiflis, 1934. Studied mathematics at Moscow University and composition at the Conservatory before joining the direction courses at the Film School.

Q. How did you prepare the filming [of *Once There Was a Singing Blackbird,* 1970]? Did any difficulties arise during that period?
    A. The fundamental difficulty stemmed from the fact that the film had to be shot very quickly. We started production after a great delay—in May 1970, and we were obliged to complete all work on the film and turn it in before the end of the year. That is why the preparation period had to include some of the basic work. It was necessary to decide all questions in a very short time; we depended on improvisation, on luck and fortunate accidents that were difficult to calculate in our plan. . . .
    Of course it is pleasant to film by improvising on the set something you thought of on the way that morning, changing the *mise-en-scène,* the background, the dialogue. But for that it is necessary to be *without* a timer at your ear.

                ——Ioseliani, interviewed for published screenplay of
                Once There Was a Singing Blackbird (Moscow, 1974)

Joris I V E N S
Born 1898 in Nijmegen, Netherlands. His family's photo-supply shop in Amsterdam, plus a film society formed with his friends, resulted in the production of experimental films that were shown throughout Europe. As he developed politically his subjects grew bolder and more ambitious, and he is today the best-known of international documentary filmmakers.

The second film I [left unfinished in 1928] was called the *I* film. This may be worth mentioning for anyone who wants to make a real experimental film or attempts such a film. In any case it's a fascinating subject to talk about: the camera has to be completely subjective, not just moving freely in space observing action as a third person. It must be the first person, the protagonist of the action. The lens becomes the human eye. It's as if the hero of a story becomes the writer of the story. . . .
    Our first experiment was: *"I" drink a glass of beer.* I see the glass of beer on the table, I pick up the glass with my right hand, I bring it to my mouth (the glass is brought forward to a little below the lens-eye, the lower half of the frame contains the upper half circle of the glass), over the glass I see the café, I drink the beer (the beer is poured out the same distance below the lens as my mouth is below my eye). We thought the subjectivity of this sequence could be increased by previously establishing the sensation of thirst; for example, shots of a hot desert, of a man lying on the sand panting for water. Followed by the "beer-drinking camera" this would achieve a strong physical effect on the audience. . . .

    The documentary film has always one great force, individual styles notwithstanding—that is, that it is taken on the spot. This gives an authenticity it must always have—too much emphasis on reenactment can be hazardous. Sixty percent of a normal documentary film has nothing to do with acting. *New Earth* [1934] had no acted-out sequences; *Borinage* [1933] had only a few brief ones. There will always be certain themes which will be best carried out in a purely documentary style. There are others that demand considerable reenactment, and by reenactment I mean the reconstruction of an emotional situation, not merely re-creating a familiar act.

Here we come to a problem with which I have fought for many years: the handling of non-actors. In reenacting a situation with a group of extremely pleasant persons, who for your purpose have become actors in a documentary film, there is the danger of falling back into an easy naturalism if the non-actors are allowed to do what they like. As location work progresses, the non-actors become the central figures in the film, creating problems that temporarily force all the others into the background. The Rural Electrification film *Power and the Land* [1940] depended largely on the non-actor and upon reenactment. . . .

My experience in directing non-actors who are playing together has shown that it is sometimes desirable to explain the action to each of them individually, so that a certain amount of unrehearsed reaction and surprise can be counted upon. To get natural reactions we played tricks similar to those Pudovkin describes in his book *Film Acting.* In our picture the father was filmed receiving a notification from the dairy that his milk was sour: he expected to unfold and pretend to read a blank piece of paper. But instead he read a startling message from me on the official stationery of the creamery department, complaining about his sour milk in no uncertain terms.

In general my method was to give precise directions to the non-actors, telling them what had to be done without acting it out for them.

—Ivens, *The Camera and I* (Berlin and New York, 1969)

J

Glenda JACKSON
Born in Birkenhead, England, 1940.

. . . [Ken Russell] just thinks that if you do it for real, it's that much better . . . which, of course, is ridiculous. But he's never very specific. He just creates a strong atmosphere, which is fine for intensely emotional scenes—what Ken does best. Really, I don't think he's very interested in actors. . . .

He's a very romantic man. Things enrage him, it's genuine. He's not doing it, thinking, "This'll bring 'em in, this'll make more money." He's exorcising demons of some kind. I was talking to Susan Sontag about him, and she thinks he may be the last great misogynist. It's probably true. I wouldn't for one minute presume to say that he beats Shirley or is a vile husband, but he does genuinely feel what's in his films.

———Jackson, interviewed for *Esquire*, May 72

[I] loathed and detested doing [*Marat-Sade*]. I couldn't wait for it to end. The cast was in hysterics. One of the actors who played in a straight-jacket had rheumatism at the end of the run; another developed a permanent crossed eye and today suffers from horrible headaches. Then we all did the film [1966] for Peter Brook and it was a shattering experience. People twitching, slobber running down their chins, everyone screaming from nerves and exhaustion.

———Jackson, interviewed for *The Toronto Star*, 23 Jan 71

What's remarkable about *Sunday Bloody Sunday* [1971] is that the characters don't automatically opt out and commit suicide, as in most films about unhappy love affairs. . . . With *Sunday Bloody Sunday*, which requires such specific things, the choices may be manifold, but you have to make the right choices. The dialogue was incredibly good, it was modern without being color supplement—and all that boring stuff. We improvised scenes working with John [Schlesinger] and Penelope [Gilliatt], but one knew the sort of person the character was before shooting started.

———Jackson, interviewed for *The Globe & Mail* (Toronto), 30 Oct 71

Miklos JANCSO
Born in Vác, Hungary, 1921. Studied law and ethnography, then transferred to the Budapest Academy of Theater and Cinematography, where he graduated

in 1950. His first film work was in newsreels. His first fictional film was The
Bells Have Gone to Rome (1958).

Anything I can say is only a working hypothesis. This film [*The Red and the
White*(?)] is also an experiment, and it is by no means certain that the final
effect on the screen will be what we imagined. In *The Round-Up* [1965], for
instance, the interrogators—the men with black cloaks—are always different
persons, not to flood the film with a sort of Kafka mysticism, but because if we
chose one single man to personify the oppressors, then the whole thing would
lose point, it would simply become a personal drama—whereas it is not the
person of the executioner that is interesting, but the mechanism of the system
itself. *The Round-Up* retained 2 of the 3 classical unities—the unity of place
and time—it was only the story that broke the uniformity. The new film
ignores all three of them, and we are dispensing with the *résoneur* as well. We
think this is a rather daring experiment, and that's not the least reason why the
job is so exciting.
    . . . And there is one more, apparently secondary factor, which has pro-
foundly determined the scenario: the zoom. Up to the present I have never
been able to work with them because Hungarian film studios don't have the
equipment. The classical visual composition of *The Round-Up* is chiefly the
result of the fact that the zoom was not used; we had to compose the successive settings throughout. This new film will have—not least on account of the
zoom—a completely different visual and dynamic composition.

——Jancso, interviewed for *Filmvilag;* trans. in
The New Hungarian Quarterly, Autumn 67

. . . The main reason [I postsync my films] is that I constantly talk to the actors
during the shooting to direct them, just as the cameraman directs his team, so
that when we are doing a tracking shot, we are constantly talking. . . .
    Maybe I should experiment with [a synchronized camera] but I think I
would need a special theme. My themes depend on the illusion that there is no
filming taking place, like drama or real life. That I am not present with the
camera. Perhaps that is why they say my films are so cold. There is a certain
restraint in the whole thing. My films all have the same style. If I used direct
sound, I would either have to change my method and not talk to the actors
during the shooting or I would have to use a theme that I am included in,
where the audience would know that I am making a film and there would be
several transferences of identity.

——Jancso, interviewed for *The Image Maker* (Richmond, 1971)

With my friend, the writer Hernadi, I have been trying to find a less theatrical
form of expression. We've studied Antonioni's style, Bergman's, and Heming-
way's, as a writer. We were looking for a colder style, but at the same time we
found that one utilizes the actors, the personalities on the screen, without making them act as they would in a Hollywood film. I adore Antonioni. He's my
master. But in each film of his there are always some sequences which are more
boring than the others. This is why we found we couldn't work in that style.
To avoid this problem, we could only make action films, showing the characters in conflict—fighting, debating, defending themselves. . . .

In real life there is always discussion. But this was my way of saying that in our country, opponents of the regime accepted oppression and repression without fighting against it, because things were tricky for them. For some years—in the time of Stalin—it was really tricky, especially for those who were opposed to popular democracy, but also for others. Silence was the only possibility. I wanted partly to explain that silence. Not outright. It is always important to be precise but in a film it doesn't work. I find that my films are little essays on certain questions. In a novel you can study all the aspects of a question, but I don't want to say in any single film what I have to say about politics, about life, about the future of humanity. If anyone wants to know what I have to say, he'd have to see all my films.

[Nudity and undressing] are a sign of inhumanity. If you do violence to someone, it always involves stripping him. I was just rereading Julius Caesar's History of the Civil War and in that just the same things happen. The conquerors make their defeated enemies take their clothes off. It's a sign of oppression and, philosophically, if you like, it's the same with women. But it's crueler because historically women have always been more oppressed than men.

————Jancso, interviewed for *The Times*, 16 May 70

Maurice J A U B E R T (1900–1940)
Born in Nice. Killed in action.

Unfortunately, most writers of music for films have already become enslaved by the usual requirements of producers, and have evolved a kind of film-music language, which combines the least suitable Wagnerian clichés with the smooth facility of imitation Debussy.

They should be reminded that we do not go to the films to hear music. We want music to give greater depth to our impressions of the visuals. We do not want it to explain the visuals, but to add to them *by differing from them.* In other words, it should not be *expressive,* in the sense of adding its quota to the sentiments expressed by the actors or the director, but *decorative* in the sense of adding its own design to that proper to the screen.

Finally, film-music must in nature be recorded, so that, however perfect the means of recording, the composer should never forget the special qualities of the microphone or the possibilities of re-recording and the cutting bench.

To give a personal example, in Vigo's *Zéro de conduite* [1932] I had to write music to a procession of small boys by night, the occasion being a dormitory rebellion. The sequence in itself was highly fantastic and shot in slow motion. In order to follow out this atmosphere of unreality, I recorded my music and then reversed the sound track. The effect of running it backwards was to retain the broad outline of the melody, but as each single note was heard backwards an atmosphere of strangeness was achieved.

————Jaubert, in *World Film News,* July 36

Henry J A W O R S K Y [Heinz von Jaworsky]
One of the mountain-film cameramen who joined Leni Riefenstahl's large crew for the Olympics film shot in 1936.

Q. How did she work with her cameramen?

A. . . . As I remember we were a total crew of about 40 cameramen, including assistants. I'll tell you one thing. After a 16-hour day's work—she had rented a summer castle, those were our headquarters not too far away from the stadium—after a 12- to 16-hour day, she would get the whole gang together around a big table. We were all falling asleep. She had been with us all day long. But that woman was full of energy she would knock the table and say, "Gentlemen, two weeks from now you can sleep. Right now we think about tomorrow." And she would tell every single cameraman—may he be a big old-timer with a famous name or a newcomer like myself—I was a cameraman by now—she would assign you to your position. She would tell you what lens you use, what focal length, she would tell you how many frames you run, 16, 24, or if it's high speed of 72 frames, she would tell you what filter to use. She would go into minute detail—and no contradictions, you do this.

Q. She told me about Zielke. He lives in Berlin.

A. Is he alive? He was very clever. When the war started he went insane and went to an asylum and was completely schizophrenic. When the war was over he was good again.

Q. There is a film by him called *Das Stahltier* [1936], distributed by the Germany embassy here.

A. This film was fantastic. I mean I was in the business and I was shaking from excitement. It was called *The Steel Beast* in English, *Das Stahltier* in German, which he did for the German railroads, which were government owned. *Das Stahltier* was a masterpiece, I must say. And Zielke managed to do the whole picture without interference; they didn't see a foot until he was finished. When the directors of the railroad saw it, they said—Oh, my God! This is horrible—we want a picture that makes people like the railroad. They're never going to ride the railroad again—because all kinds of accidents happen and the engines look like big monsters. *Das Stahltier* was a fantastic thing of cinematography but for advertising it was bad. So the producer came to me and said, "We have to reshoot scenes, I hate it." I said, "No, I don't do that. I don't want to have any part in it."

Q. But she had close technical supervision throughout the entire production [*Olympia*] about what she wanted?

A. Absolutely. And during the day she had special steel towers, portable towers: she had them designed before. And she placed the towers and as I told you, she would tell every cameraman what to shoot and how.

Q. She would come to them directly at times during the day, during the shooting?

A. She would rush around from one cameraman to the other like a maniac and say "How are you doing, how are you doing? How about this and this?" Screaming and hollering—oh, she was an absolute maniac, she was wild. But we all are—either you are crazy in this business or you don't get anything done.
———Jaworsky, interviewed for *Film Culture*, Spring 73

Norman J E W I S O N
Born 1926, in Canada. Graduated from University of Toronto and joined BBC as a scriptwriter.

The Cincinnati Kid [1965] was the first film that I did as a free choice. It was my decision. I had creative control—I had that written into my contract with Martin Ransohoff, the producer. I was wary of producers. . . . This was the result of my introduction to the old Hollywood, which has kind of disappeared. I've been very happy with this United Artists and Mirisch-UA setup.

. . . I was under contract to Universal at the time that I read the book by Nathaniel Benchley . . . called *The Off-Islanders.* I only liked the first chapter, which described the stranding of a Russian submarine off Cape Cod. It was an idea—and we [with William Rose] departed from the book completely. But it was hard to get anyone to back it because most of the studios just threw me out and said we couldn't make a film about a bunch of communists.

That's a typical American attitude. This is what brought me together with UA and Mirisch, who decided that they would take a chance on what was, for American cinema at that time, a rather outrageous story [*The Russians Are Coming, The Russians Are Coming,* 1966].

——Jewison, interviewed for *Films & Filming,* Jan 71

[In *The Cincinnati Kid,* 1965] I took out all the primaries. There were no reds, greens, yellows, whites, or blues in the film outside of the red cards and the blood of the cockfight. Now, in *Gaily, Gaily* [1969], we sat down with Robert Boyle, the art director, and with the costume designer, and we all sat down and we looked at film for about 3 or 4 days, various films on periods. This is why I threw out the Panavision lens, because I firmly believe that period is not as clear to us as our contemporary world. I think our life, or the life about us, when one just looks with one's eye, is very clearly focused. I think when you look back into a period, things become slightly fuzzy. And possibly this is because all our references to a period are from old daguerreotypes. This is 1910 in America. And I wanted to capture the mood of America in 1910 much as maybe Tony Richardson captured Hogarthian London in *Tom Jones* [1963]. Therefore, I thought it was going to have a great deal to do with color, and when we finally decided that we should shoot the whole film through fog filters, in varying degrees, and Dick Kline has been very courageous I think as a cameraman in agreeing to do this, because it means it's going on the negative. Then on top of that we decided this is a story of a boy coming from a small town. It's a loss of innocence. It's the Horatio Alger story—the American dream. It's a morality play. That's what it really is. It's snatches of Ben Hecht. Now, therefore, we decided, well, Chicago should be dark in blacks and browns and grays and earth tones and sooty, and therefore, all of our scenes in Chicago must look like that, even if we have to paint the streets. The small town of Galena, where he comes from, should be all pastoral and soft—whites and beiges and soft tones. But there should be no stark white, and there should be no bright red except for the flags in the film. There should be no bright yellows. There should be no bright blues, except the opening on July the Fourth in Galena.

——Jewison, interviewed for *Directors at Work* (NY, 1970)

Quincy JONES
Born in Chicago, 1933, trained at the Berlee School of Music.

As [*The Pawnbroker*, 1965] was my first film, I wasn't sure whether to use the music to define a third dimension for a dramatic premise or to follow the old school technique—I call it show-and-tell—of repeating musically what you're seeing visually. The mousing technique: right-up-the-stairs music, hit music, jump-out-the-window music. . . .

The cut in *The Pawnbroker* was so tight I just constructed the music to match what was up on the screen. It was never a question of recutting the scene to match the music. The only thing that worried us was how to score the subliminal flashbacks. They only lasted a twentieth of a second, and the dumbest thing in life would have been to try to catch them in the music. That would have made them look like some of the commercials you see. But since I didn't have any music scoring experience to relate to at the time, I wasn't really sure what to do. But Sidney's [Lumet] instincts were right, and he said we would make everything too ponderous if we attempted to change the music to match the flashbacks. . . .

To get the score exactly the way they want it to be, the really good directors don't let themselves get hung up on the time or money that are going into it. If they have to, they'll come back in and do a whole session over just to get one cue right. I haven't run into too much of that, but sometimes we might get inside of a cue, and I might not get the attitude exactly right. It might be a little too heavy. The textures might be too light or too strong, and I may have to pull the volume up or thin it down, say, the way Lumet likes it. Some directors may like mushy strings; Lumet doesn't. He likes them all vibrato-less, soft, and kind of detached because that seems to absorb better what's on the screen. Rather than tell the audience what to feel, this kind of treatment lets them read the feelings into the scene, and a Lumet might suggest that I handle a particular cue this way. Directors who ask for understatement are usually right. The screen absorbs understatement best, and you usually screw up when you get heavy-handed or too busy. . . .

——Jones, interviewed for *Movie People* (New York, 1973)

Claude J U T R A
Born in Montreal, 1930. Attended University of Montreal, then medical school, during which he directed amateur shorts in collaboration with Michel Brault.

. . . A *tout prendre* [1963] was made with total freedom, and also with teamwork. That film was made under conditions, which I will never know again. It was really quite an experience, because everybody was working on it for free and people would lend me equipment. I remember Michel Brault and Jean-Claude Labrecque both shot about half of the film each. I would call them in the middle of the night and say, "Hey look there's this thing happening; come quick and shoot it, man." They would grumble a bit but they would be right there in a few minutes. And everybody was doing that, because they all wanted the film to be made. You know, it was important that a film be made then, that kind of a film, a fiction, feature film, and I was the one who was doing it; they had confidence in me and they just worked for the hell of it. For the sake of making the film and also because we were really having a lot of fun doing it.

And there were no contracts signed, no obligations of anybody towards anybody else, and that in itself was something really extraordinary. It very seldom happens, I'm sure. But I don't have a fixation on the *A tout prendre* way of making films. I know it was beautiful, but that's not the way it works, normally, and I don't mind having pressures put on me, as long as I can control them to a certain degree and select them in another way.

——Jutra, interviewed for *Cinema Canada*, Apr–May 73

K

Garson **KANIN**
*Born in Rochester, New York, 1912. An artist of varied skills in theater and film
—writer, director, producer, with a background in music and acting. Brought
to Hollywood by Samuel Goldwyn in 1936. His first film direction, A* Man to
Remember *(1938), established a long film career, chiefly in comedy.*

. . . There were Warner directors, for instance, who never got near a script. It's
no secret that Michael Curtiz sometimes started shooting a script without reading it. He would make about 4 pictures a year, which at those studios wasn't
unusual. They would be prepared almost entirely by the front office, they'd be
cast and the sets would be designed. And then they would say, "Well, Mike
Curtiz, he's finishing Thursday. . . . Do you want him to start on Monday?" . . .
Frequently a director at Warners wouldn't even see his assembled stuff. It was
all organized, assembly-line stuff, and I think that's one reason why the general run of pictures was so bland. . . .

 [Preparing to leave RKO] I went back to the studio each evening to sort
out the stuff in my office, and across the hall there was a guy working every
night, banging a typewriter. One night we happened to stop at the same time
and introduced ourselves, and this was how I met Dalton Trumbo. He told me
about the story he was working on, using the skeleton of a John [Lionel] Barrymore picture about a country doctor [*One Man's Journey*, 1933] they had done
at the studio a few years before. We started talking . . . and after about 3 weeks
we had something we thought was pretty good. Together we took it to Bob
Sisk, a B-picture producer on the lot and a very nice man. He liked the *A
Man to Remember* script enormously. "The only trouble," he said, "is that I
don't know what kind of money I can get you to make it, or even if they would
want to make it. But if it can be done very quickly and cheaply, we might be
able to make it before they get wise." . . . The picture had an 18-day schedule
but it was shot in 15 days—mainly out of terror.

———Kanin, interviewed for *Sight & Sound*, Summer 72

The surprising aspect of their joint success was that they were so different.
Kate's working method and approach was opposite to Spencer's. She is a careful, thorough, methodical, analytical, concentrated artist. She reads and studies
and thinks. By the time she was ready to begin shooting *The Lion in Winter*
[1968], for example, she knew enough about Eleanor of Aquitaine to write a

master's thesis on the subject. She loves to rehearse and practice and try things and make just one more take. Spencer, conversely, was an instinctive player, who trusted the moment of creation, believed it was possible to go stale by overrehearsing, and usually did his best work on the first take. He was a firmly rooted subjective artist.

[When pressed for his opinion on acting] "It's taken me forty years of doing it for a living to learn the secret. I don't know that I want to give it away." Urged, he relented. "Okay, I'll tell you. The art of acting is—learn your lines!"

———Kanin, in *Tracy and Hepburn* (NY, 1971)

Boris K A U F M A N
Born 1906, in Bialystok, youngest of the 3 Kaufman brothers (see Dziga VERTOV and Mikhail KAUFMAN). His first noticed work was the photography in France of experimental films made with Jean Vigo, Jean Lods and Eugène Deslaw in the mid-1920s. Before emigrating to U.S.A. in 1940, he photographed a number of studio films for the Paris studio of Paramount. After photographing On the Waterfront (1954) *he became the most relied upon cameraman for the increasing number of independent films made on the East Coast.*

[For *L'Atalante* (1934) Vigo] used everything around him: the sun, the moon, snow, night. Instead of fighting unfavorable conditions, he made them play a part.

———Kaufman, quoted in Sadoul-Morris, *Dictionary of Films*, p 17

. . . [In *On The Waterfront*, 1954] On the rooftops, in the scene with the pigeons, I had to shoot against black tarpaper, black hatches, black dull metal, soot-covered pigeon coops, some TV antennas, and chimneys. So to bring it to life I used smoke, water, and a little paint—the last in order to break this blackness and bleakness of tarpaper. I also employed unusual filters and diffusion to maintain consistency within the changing conditions. Another example was the scene in the park. There were some leaves burning in the basket when we arrived. So I seized it as a possible source of drifting smoke. I sent for some smoke-pots and I let artificial smoke drift across the field. This device enabled me to continue the sequence through a different park which followed the first one, and to make it flow. In other words, I tried the smoke over, and I cleared only when we came to the iron fence facing the river. This is an example of positive exploitation of conditions. I used the smoke not as an artifice but because I found justification for it: the mood of the scene and the need for maintaining continuity. Also some interiors made in small tenement apartments were a challenge because of the physical smallness of the place into which my crew, the sound crew, and the actors had to be squeezed. The camera had to be mobile and the lighting keyed with precision.

———Kaufman, interviewed for *Film Culture*, Summer 55

Mikhail K A U F M A N
Born in Bialystok, Russia, in 1897. Served in Red Army. After demobilization 1922 worked as cameraman-collaborator with his older brother, Dziga Vertov,

on their Kino-Pravda *series and all other works of the Kino-Eye group. Last collaboration in the Ukraine:* Man with Camera (1929); *its sequel,* In Spring (1929) *was made by Kaufman alone.*

At one of the October celebrations I had the occasion to take, with a sloweddown camera, the passing of the procession. The accelerated movement obtained gave the impression of the movement of a human stream.

In the film, *In Spring*, I caught the long, slow-moving funeral service by slowing down the shooting, and in this case gave the impression of a glimpse of a puppet show—a way to present religious rites in general.

In such cases the camera helped to investigate a life-phenomenon by means of mechanically assisted vision, as a microscope discloses to us phenomena unseen by the unaided eye.

——Kaufman, in *Proletarskoye Kino*, No. 4, 1931;
trans. *Experimental Cinema*, No. 4, 1932

Elia K A Z A N [Kazanjoglou]
Born in a suburb of Istanbul, 1909. Greek parents emigrated to New York in 1913. Worked in New York theater and in 1932 joined the Group Theater.

When I started to make a film of that play [*A Streetcar Named Desire*, 1951], I thought in the usual terms. I thought we'd better open the play up, move it around a bit, make it pictorially more varied and so on. After all, I thought, film is a visual medium. We had better play some of the scenes somewhere else. So I worked with a writer for about 7 or 8 months on an "opened-up" script. I thought it was pretty good, put it away for a few days, then read it again, and found it a total loss. I realized the compression in *Streetcar* is its strength. So I went back and photographed the stage play as written. I think that particular play merited that treatment and I thought the film came off pretty well.

——Kazan, interviewed for *Directors at Work*, (NY, 1970)

The only truly correct thing on the visual side of *A Tree* [*Grows in Brooklyn*, 1945] was the face of the little girl, Peggy Ann Garner. Because her father was overseas in the war, because her mother had problems, because she herself was going through a lot of pains and uncertainties, Peggy's face was drawn and pale and worried. It looked exactly right. She was not pretty at all, or cute or picturesque, only true. It was my idea not to have any background music but just source music—the sound of an organ-grinder and so on. But my luck on this film was to have this congenial, affectionate, mutually trusting relationship with [Louis D.] Lighton.

Nick Ray was some kind of an assistant during the shooting. He hung around, took notes. He edited them for himself and gave me a copy. A lot of them were influenced by Lighton and others were my own thoughts or things I said. Nick liked that kind of generalization on aesthetics, etc. He is a dear and sweet man who has had a hard life. . . .

[*Boomerang*, 1947] was the first film I made in my own way; there were 5 professional actors—the others were non-actors. It was entirely made in Stamford, Connecticut, 30 miles from my house. We shot day and night in that city. . . . There are people from Hollywood, people from the Group Theater, people from the town, Arthur Miller, whose play *All My Sons* I had just produced, and even my uncle Joe Kazan, the hero of *America, America* [1963], then an old man.

Gentleman's Agreement [1948] was such a big hit . . . that Zanuck naturally said, "Let's do it again with a Negro." And this time he got Ford to direct it [*Pinky*, 1949]. Ford started it and shot about 10 days. He hated Ethel Waters and Ethel Waters hated him. He did not like the way the picture was turning out. So he went to bed, called Zanuck, and said to him, "I'm sick. I've got shingles." Zanuck told me later that Ford didn't have anything wrong, he just didn't want to make the picture. Zanuck called me up in New York. . . . We started from scratch. I worked the best I could but again it is a total dodge. It is not about a black girl but about a charming little white girl. All the unpleasant parts of the subject matter are eliminated. . . . Again everybody is very nice-looking, and clean, and neat. It's not a favorite of mine!
Q. Why didn't you take a black actress for Pinky?
[Jeanne Crain] was cast already and I had to take it or leave it. . . . She was the blandest person I ever worked with. She had no rebellion in her whatever. . . . She must have had things happen to her but she was very controlled about them.

I had made up my mind not to be bound by the script [of *Panic in the Streets*, 1950]. It is the first time I threw the script over. We had a property truck with a typewriter on the back of it, on the tailgate. Every morning the writer [Richard Murphy] came to work with me . . . we would redo every scene—that way we were able to use the terrific color and richness of New Orleans. We shot on the whorehouse streets, in the low bars, in the wharfs. I kept the whole process of picture-making creative instead of rigid devotion to a script. . . . I enjoyed that picture much more than any picture I had made up to then. I picked up people in the street. . . . I sort of felt liberated on that picture. It is much better than *Boomerang*. There is more flavor to it.

Viva Zapata [1952] was a terrific experience for me. It changed a lot in my life and films. . . . I was influenced by Eisenstein and Dovzhenko, but now it was a digested influence, I never thought about them while shooting. I used the long shots that I had discovered in Ford, but creatively, whereas I had used them mechanically in *Panic in the Streets*. Because with *Zapata* it was a subject matter I liked.

Q. Much before *On the Waterfront* [1954] you were thinking of doing a film about the docks?
A. Yes, that was in 1951, before *Zapata*. I spoke with Arthur Miller. There was a struggle within the Longshoremen's Union at that time, and Art knew a lot about longshoremen. He worked in the Brooklyn Navy Yard . . . during the war, before he could make his living as a playwright. He knew the waterfront, and I think the idea of a film was his. I was very enthusiastic about it. He began to work on a script; it was called *The Hook* . . . the script was completed, and we arranged the financing from Columbia Pictures. Then I got a phone call from Art saying that he had decided he didn't want to do

it. I still don't know why he did that. . . . I think Art saw the Un-American Activities Committee coming, and there was something that had suddenly developed in his personal life that made him not want to have that film done. Things were much touchier then; people were threatened and on trial. . . .

In *On the Waterfront* we had a beginning crew, a crew that had not worked together. They were not coherent, and they were not very friendly towards Boris [Kaufman]; I was protecting him all the time. They disliked him—he was a foreigner, he seemed to fumble; he didn't express himself in a forthright manner, but like an artist, in subtle things. This annoyed the fellows who had come out of television and commercials, mostly. I thought, well, Kaufman is the best cameraman I've ever got, so I'm going to stay with him. I did *Baby Doll* [1956] with him. In that film, I thought, the photography was even better.

I think the best color I ever had was at the end of *East of Eden* [1955] . . . I used a lot of greens. Everybody said, "Don't use green, green comes out black, you can't light green." . . . There's a lot of green in that picture. And I thought, it's verdent, it's a valley—and Steinbeck's description of Salinas: Green, green, green. The old man dies in green: a death's version of his valley, that was the idea.

Anyway, I worked it out carefully, and I had help on that from a wonderful cameraman, Ted McCord, a terrific, mean old man. People didn't like to work with him. He was pigheaded, bullheaded. But boy, when you talked to him, he *worked*. He really tried to give you his equivalent for what you wanted. He had a lot of guts. I got Ted because I liked *Treasure of the Sierra Madre* [1948], which he had photographed.

——Kazan, interviewed by Michel Ciment for his
Kazan on Kazan (London, 1974)

You're right. *The Visitors* [1971] is a home movie. My son Chris wrote the script and co-produced it with Nick Proferes, the cameraman on both this one and my wife's movie *Wanda* [1970]. We literally made it at my home in Connecticut, and put it together right here at my house in New York. We shot in 16mm, using only Nick and three friends on the crew.

Four of the five cast members had never been in a movie before. I picked up the guys in various acting classes and at the Actors Studio; the girl [Patricia Joyce] was a senior at Yale. Everybody lived in my house for eight weeks.

. . . It was like going back to my starting days as a director, when I was making left-wing documentaries. It's been a wonderful experience. It changed my life.

. . . I'm 62 years old now, and I'm just beginning.

——Kazan, interviewed for *The Toronto Star*, 12 Feb 72

Stacy K E A C H
Born 1941.

So much of what [John Huston] does isn't to do with words, but with feelings. He makes you, as an actor, feel very comfortable, also very concerned with every facet of the character you are playing.

He gives you tremendous freedom, but is always watching out so that you don't go over the top.

Most of all, however, is the fact that he's concerned with positive energy. He's very open, and he needs to feel that he's not stifling other people's creative energies, which, I think, is the mark of a good director.

He has a great love and a great passion for detail, and I love that. And he takes little incidents in life and thinks, and treats them, as though they are no less significant than the big ones.

———Keach, interviewed for *The Evening Standard,* 17 March 73

Q. Huston also claims that he likes to give the actor a lot of freedom in his creation of a role and a scene. Was this reflected in your work with him in *Fat City* [1972]?

A. Very much so. It was probably the most productive relationship that I've had with a director in the sense that we discussed the alternatives for a scene. We never made any hard and fast resolutions. I think that's an important point a lot of directors get stuck on. A lot of them think there's one and only one possible way for a scene to be done, and that can produce a feeling that's so airtight it's almost stultifying. I think it's better to give the actor alternatives so that something can happen spontaneously during a scene that is not the manifestation of a rehearsal. But Huston does rehearse a lot. He walks through the scene many times and works with the cameraman and the actors. But he sort of lets the actor stage the scene himself. He brings the camera in and lets the actor show him. Then he'll bring in his suggestions— something that might spice up a moment or change the rhythm or the tempo of a scene. It's a real collaboration in the best sense of the word.

———Keach, interviewed for *Filmmakers Newsletter,* June 73

Buster K E A T O N [Joseph Francis Keaton] (1895–1966)
Born in Pickway, Kansas, in a family of vaudeville acrobats. Brought into films by Roscoe Arbuckle.

By the time we were ready to start a picture, everyone on the lot knew what we'd been talking about, so we never had anything on paper. Neither Chaplin, Lloyd, nor myself, even when we got into feature-length pictures, ever had a script.

After we stopped making wild 2-reelers and got into feature-length pictures, our scenario boys had to be story-conscious. We couldn't tell any far-fetched stories. We couldn't do farce comedy, for instance. It would have been poison to us. An audience wanted to believe every story we told them. Well, that eliminates farce comedy and burlesque. The only time we could do something out of the ordinary had to be in a dream sequence, or in a vision. So story construction became very important to us.

Somebody would come up with an idea. "Here's a good start," we'd say. We skip the middle. We never paid any attention to the middle. We immediately went to the finish. We worked on the finish and if we get a finish that we're all satisfied with, then we'll go back and work on the middle. For some reason, the middle always took care of itself.

———Keaton, interviewed for *The Parade's Gone By* (NY, 1968)

Q. About the dream sequence in *Sherlock Jr.* [1924], was this something that you thought of on the spur of the moment, or something that had been planned out ahead?

No, it was planned out ahead because we had to build a set for that one.

Q. How was that done—did you have an actual screen beforehand on which the characters were appearing?

No. We built what looked like a motion picture screen and actually built a stage into that frame but lit it in such a way that it looked like a motion picture being projected on a screen. But it was real actors and the lighting effect gave us the illusion, so I could go out of semidarkness into that well-lit screen right from the front row of the theater right into the picture. Then when it came to the scene changing on me when I got up there, that was a case of timing and on every one of those things we would measure the distance to the fraction of an inch from the camera to where I was standing, also with a surveying outfit to get the exact height and angle so that there wouldn't be a fraction of an inch missing on me, and then we changed the setting to what we wanted it to be and I got back into that same spot and it overlapped the action to get the effect of the scene changing.

——Keaton, interviewed for *Film Quarterly*, Fall 58

Gene K E L L Y
Born 1912 in Pittsburgh. Education interrupted by Depression but graduated from University of Pittsburgh in 1933. Opened dancing schools and worked in nightclubs.

... Fred [Astaire] and I are very different performers. He went in for the sophisticated bit; top hat, white tie, elegant cane and tails, while with me it was just the opposite.

Instead of a dress suit, which I looked terrible in, I wore sweat shirts or sailor's gear ... more easy and more casual. Only once did Fred play a part which was meant for me, and that was as a result of an accident. It was when we were making *Easter Parade* [1948] with Judy [Garland] and Peter Lawford, and I got hurt playing softball with a group of kids.

Naturally, I couldn't tell my boss, Louis B. Mayer, how I'd injured myself. So I told him I'd hurt myself rehearsing one of the dance numbers from the movie and suggested they replace me with Fred Astaire.

Well, Louis B. agreed and Fred was delighted. And, as you know, the show was a great success. Still, whenever I see him and darling Judy singing "A Couple of Swells" together, I still get a twinge of regret.

... Judy Garland, I think, was the most extraordinary of all. She was like a computer, that girl. She could hear a song once, and she'd know it by ear; the same with dance steps. She'd pick 'em up like that.

Trouble with Judy, though, she would always arrive late. It was a sickness; a disease—a lot of women seem to have it, you know. Otherwise she was the most professional performer I've ever known.

Barbra Streisand in *Hello, Dolly!* [1969] was the same. Very professional, but infuriating in that she never arrived for work on time—and costly.

——Kelly, interviewed for *The Sunday Express*, 1 Nov 70

Singin' in the Rain [1952] is the best example of our musical group coming together. All we began with was this old skit—it wasn't even long enough to be called a sketch—about a silent movie actor becoming a sound star. We all charged around the studios asking everyone what it was like in the old days, to get background information. Believe me, all those fantastic stories in the film are true.

———Kelly, interviewed for *Radio Times*, 19 Oct 72

When we went to New York for location shots for *On the Town* [1949], they thought they were throwing their money away, but at least, when I insisted, they let me go ahead. There again, that picture is very dated now, but at the time it was another breakthrough. We did things with cutting that had never been done before, and several of the young French directors have since told me that they were influenced by it. It still remains my favorite because I know it had this kind of effect. It wasn't the best picture I ever did, that was *Singin' in the Rain*, but whatever you did in those days you had a real chance to experiment and push your ideas through no matter how tough the opposition.

———Kelly, interviewed for *The Guardian*, 12 Nov 73

To me, dancing is basically a three-dimensional art and loses a lot when put on film. The camera sees with a single eye and loses in environment, the background and, most of all, the kinetic forces that make dance exciting to an audience which sees it live. However, much can be done cinematically to overcome this.

To pluck an example from my own experience, one can dance down a real street in a real rain [*Singin' in the Rain*]. That can't be done on the stage. . . .

———Kelly, in *Action*, Mar–Apr 69

Kay KENDALL [MacCarthy] (1927–1959)
Born in Hull, Yorkshire. Daughter of a dance team.

I am sick, sick, sick and tired of those frothy comedies. It is tremendously hard work, and no one outside the acting profession appreciates it. The public thinks you're having a joyous time. It really is desperately difficult being light and gay at 9:00 on a Monday morning in a cold film studio. And when you've acted your heart out, people come up and say, "It's simply you, darling."

I mean, really, I don't see the point in worrying oneself to a standstill, and people turn round and say, "Darling, what gorgeous fun."

It isn't fun, believe me. Remember that scene in *The Reluctant Debutante* [1958] when I tripped down the stairs?

I told Vincente Minnelli, the director, a dear sweet man, that I couldn't do it. It was much too difficult.

I was almost in tears with frustration and anger trying to get it right. Ten times I did it. Ten times. Nothing very gay about that, is there?

I suppose I sound pompous and idiotic talking like this. But I do feel rather strongly about it.

Oh, I know there is a lot to be said for a performance which completely fools the public. And, of course, there is a lot of personal satisfaction to be had from it all.

------Kendall, interviewed for *The Daily Express*, 16 Jan 59

Janos K E N D E
Born 1941 in Marseilles. In Budapest graduated the cameramen's course at Academy of Dramatic and Cinema Arts in 1965. After assisting Somló and Sára worked as director of photography on Jansco's Silence and Cry *(1968).*

Q. What influenced the visual style of *Red Psalm* [1972]?

In addition to the combination of the earlier mentioned fahrt-crane-zoom, the television impact which first appeared in the Attila film made for the Italian Television. The producer wanted us to use many close-ups. In this film, we tried to further improve this style: retaining the technique of long shots, the alteration of close-ups and totals represented an especially exciting assignment together with the variations within the long shots.

Q. In your opinion what is the up-to-date modern camera style?

I have no idea! In my opinion, there are no camera styles; there are directors' styles, and the camera can serve them in a better or worse manner. Perhaps, I could list the outdated camera styles. Gianni di Venanzo's style meant an enormous revelation in this time—the tones, the lighting technique, and the camera movements—or the solutions in the films of Alain Resnais, I did not experience any significant innovations since. However, the last example, that of Resnais, indicates that one cannot speak about independent cameramen. The camera style of a film is determined by the technical means, the possibilities of the raw material, and primarily by the style of the director.

------Kende, interviewed for the press release for *Red Psalm*, 1972

Deborah K E R R [Kerr-Trimmer]
Born 1921 in Helensburgh, Scotland. Stage career in corps de ballet began in 1938, and film roles were offered immediately. Her first large expedition film was King Solomon's Mines *in 1950.*

Our safari was believed to be the biggest Africa had ever seen. It consisted of 102 people—50 actors and technicians and 52 Africans to carry supplies, set up camp and handle cooking and laundry.

There were 7 trucks to carry cameras and sound gear, electric generators, and wardrobe. Two of them had refrigeration units to protect our film from the heat. Another had a bulldozing unit and 2 more had winches for towing in case equipment became bogged down in the steaming jungle.

Before we arrived in Africa preparations for making the film had gone on for more than a year. Our directors, Compton Bennett and Andrew Marton, and our cameraman, Robert Surtees, had made a 45,000-mile trip to pick their locations.

The itinerary they decided on was to keep us in Africa for 5 months, taking us sometimes by plane or by boat, more often by truck, oxen-pulled wagons, horses or even by foot to the remote, fascinating lands of the Belgian Congo, Ruanda-Urundi, Uganda, Kenya, and Tanganyika.

Color film requires a low, even temperature. Ours, which was stored in the refrigerator trucks, made the 12,000-mile journey back to the studio in huge cans packed with ice. . . . There were 5 re-icing stations en route to make sure the precious film was always cool.

Filming on the exposed plateau at the top of [Murchison Falls] was like acting on a gigantic hot-plate. The temperature soared to 120 degrees at midday. As our boys held palm leaves over our aching heads they kept muttering in Swahili, "Bad land, very bad land." It was an understatement.

——Kerr, in *The Star*, 1, 2, 4 Jan 51

I only made one movie with Jack [Clayton], *The Innocents* [1962], but we're just on the same wavelength. I used to say, "I'm skating on thin ice here. You tell me. This woman, is she quite mad or perfectly sane? Do those things really exist or are they in her mind?" The way he governed me was marvelous. I was his instrument. Which is the way I like it to be. I want to be the jelly in the mold. You're safe within the realm of what you want to do. You feel that the inner you is being used without you having to be too aware of yourself.

Zinnemann's good at that, too. He really brings out of me—in a completely different way—an awful lot that perhaps I'd never have the courage to lay bare, to open up. He just knows how to get you to do it, to bring out some inner quality. I always like to cut out words if I possibly can. Why do I have to say anything? You know, just look at someone and it says it. . . .

. . . [Elia Kazan] has a kind of incredible instinct with people. He's so in sympathy with all the fears and frights of actors, through having done it himself. And he's got a personal magic that you have certain moments of feeling "Maybe I should do that?" and he'll pull it right out of you if it's right, and yet if it's not right he'll never hurt you or embarrass you or make you feel a fool.

. . . I thought I'd got such a hell of a nerve to think that maybe I could do [her role in *From Here to Eternity*, 1953]. But with Zinnemann the guidelines were right. The whole movie was a coming together of parts and personalities that together had a magic. Sinatra's emotional life was linked up with the playing of the thing, and he was a bit on the down. His voice had left him, and he went down on bended knees to get the part. But he was born to play it. And when I watched Monty Clift . . . I used to feel that the day when Prewitt is shot, Monty is going to die. I'm going to feel that he's really dead. The intensity of the way that boy lived that whole part was hair-raising. He tortured himself. He suffered so.

——Kerr, interviewed for *The Times*, 2 Sep 72

Masaki KOBAYASHI
Born in Otary, 1916. In 1941, began at Ofuna studios of Shochiku as assistant director.

I had some of the same experiences during the war as Kaji [in *The Human Condition,* 1958–61]. I wanted to bring to life the tragedy of men who are forced into war against their will. Kaji is both the oppressor and the oppressed and he learns that he can never stop being an oppressor while he himself is oppressed. Of course I wanted to denounce the crimes of war, but I also wanted to show how human society can become inhuman.

——Kobayashi, quoted in Sadoul-Morris, *Dictionary of Films*
(Berkeley 1972), p. 246

In that scene [the harakiri scene in *Harakiri,* 1963], there was no alternate method than to plunge the bamboo dagger into the stomach. I did not have the slightest intention of depicting brutality for brutality's sake. There was no other way to make Hanshiro's entry into the Iyi household more effective.

Q. We hear you used real swords in this picture. Is this correct?

A. Most of the fighting in samurai pictures in the past was more like a dance. Therefore, the swords were all swung with only the hands. In reality, when using a real sword, you cannot cut anyone without the use of the hip movement. Because the real sword is so heavy the actor must out of necessity use his hip movement. Moreover, if the actors used real swords when they carried them on their hips, the weight would make them make movements like the samurai of olden days. That is why I used real swords throughout the entire picture, even in the sword fight scenes.

——Kobayashi, interviewed for the *Asahi Weekly,* 12 Oct 62

With *Kwaidan* [1964] I tried to reach a stylization of color in the function of the story. This story, or more exactly, these 4 stories—you saw only 3 of them, as I had been told it might appear a little long, if I put all the 4 together; however, I would gladly organize the projection of the fourth for you—are fantasy novels which my country has inspired to the American writer Lafcadio Hearn and which Yoko Mizuki has adapted for the film.... We could speak about all that, if you want, although I am at the moment working on another project, a film on China and its history of 2,000 years ago which I am going to shoot soon in the People's Republic.

How do you place *Kwaidan* in your work?

Well, 2 years ago I noticed here in Cannes the international audience of *Harakiri* [1962] and I concluded that the wall between Asia and the Occident was not anymore insuperable, at least at a certain level of expression. Before that I did not have any personal experience of this phenomenon. This time, I deliberately wanted to make a very international film and to reveal tentatively through *Kwaidan* to the Occident the mystery of the Japanese tradition. Furthermore, I wanted to express indirectly the theme which you will easily recognize in *A Cup of Tea* and other stories: men, in their actual civilization, let their human aspects dim. They have lost their faculty of wondering and their ability to recognize the soul.

You are speaking about the mystery of the Japanese tradition. Why are you looking for it in the work of an American?

It does not matter that he is American. I am also searching through myself. And besides, I wanted an occidental version of Japan, as I told you....

It is of no importance, because I have constantly searched for stylization, not realism. And, to start with, the subject matter of these novels allowed me to reach for the theme I wanted to express. Besides, I always thought that strangers living in a country sensed things more acutely, their conscience being purer and their eyes more perceptive, not yet deformed, and that their intelligence, stimulated through discovery, compensated their lack of knowledge in depth which is often only a knowledge conveyed by habit. Therefore, this author just must have a feel for Japan, and maybe he has a more intense awareness of it than a Japanese. All the more as it concerns medieval Japan. . . .

How was your work received in Japan?

Up to now 6 weeks of exclusive shows in Tokyo.

Was the shooting very long?

A little more than a year. It was heaps of work. I like long periods of work. Let's say about 15 months.

Did you have considerable material means?

No. It was an independent production of a small producer, the Ninjin Club troop. We did not have any studios. Shigeru Wagatsuki, the director of Ninjin, and I borrowed an industrial plane plant—where we located the sequences to be shot, where we built up the settings, installed the platforms and boxes, the makeup places, etc. . . . This location was not convenient at all. Nevertheless, 99 percent of the film was shot inside, i.e., realized in these stores.

——Kobayashi, interviewed for *Séquences* (Montreal), Apr 68

Howard KOCH
Born in Kingston, New York, 1902. Came to Hollywood from radio, where he had written the script of "War of the Worlds" for Orson Welles's Mercury Theatre of the Air. His first employer was Warner Brothers, and his first screenplay, The Sea Hawk (1940), for Michael Curtiz.

With the deadline [for the beginning of *Casablanca*, 1942] creeping up on me and with Mike Curtiz asking when was he going to get pages, a kind of paralysis came over me. . . . Finally, in desperation, I decided to forget there was no story line and just start writing scenes as they came to me and using the Epstein material wherever it fitted in. I had only the vaguest notion where each scene was leading, just hoping that it would lead to another scene and another and that the sum total, if I lived that long, would add up to a film that wouldn't be bad enough to end my brief career in Hollywood. . . .

Two weeks away from the scheduled shooting date, I recall taking stock of where we were (the "we" including the Epsteins, whose material I used in the sequence along with my own). Numerically, we had about 40 pages, a quarter of the eventual screenplay. They were typed and sent to Curtiz, who quickly responded with enthusiasm, although I think Mike was so worried and hungry for a script that any pages would have looked good to him. The 40 pages were mimeographed and sent to the various departments—casting, camera, set construction, montage, location, music, and special effects—that were assigned to the production.

——Koch, in *Casablanca: Script and Legend* (NY, 1973)

[Max Ophüls] had a deep respect for what other talents contributed and, particularly, for the film's basic content as expressed in the screenplay, a quality understandably endearing to a writer. This may come as a surprise to some critics who praise Max, and justly, as a superb stylist but, from my observation, his style was invariably related to content, never at its expense. . . .

John Houseman came to see me. He brought with him a short story by Stefan Zweig entitled *Letter from an Unknown Woman* which he wanted me to dramatize for the screen. He had been engaged to produce the picture by Joan Fontaine and William Dozier, then husband and wife, who had formed their own company within the framework of Universal Studio. . . .

At the first reading I was not impressed with the story as picture material. It was entirely subjective with only fragmentary incidents. Besides, it was in the highly charged romantic tradition of Vienna at the turn of the century— definitely not the kind of story Hollywood did well. . . . Then I thought of Max Ophüls. Possibly he could bring it off, as he, like Zweig, was steeped in the romantic tradition. The upshot was that I agreed to write the screenplay if the studio would accept Max as the director.

. . . Houseman had seen *Liebelei* [1932], Max's most admired European film, an exquisite piece of romantic nostalgia, also set in Vienna. He agreed that Max was ideal for *Letter,* but he had to sell the idea of a foreign director they scarcely knew to Joan and Bill Dozier who, in turn, had to convince the Universal executives. Since Joan Fontaine was then their most important star, Dozier was able to obtain their somewhat reluctant consent.

At this point it was my function to plot a story line [continuity of scenes] that would carry the emotional progression of Zweig's story. Then followed the usual conferences with Max and Houseman and, after some revisions, with Joan and Bill Dozier. Everyone had criticisms and suggestions but, happily, no ego problems intruded, so that each contribution could be accepted or rejected on its merits. At this stage, Joan's ideas in relation to the central character of Lisa were especially helpful, since she would be on the screen almost constantly and needed actable situations in which to convey her feelings for the man (now a pianist) at the 3 periods when he entered her life. It was a difficult role—starting as the ardent, hero-worshipping girl of 14, then the young woman in her twenties when they had the affair, and finally the mature, love-crossed woman of middle age. Joan Fontaine was one of the few actresses capable of making the intensely romantic Lisa a credible character, and I still regard the performance she eventually gave as one of the most brilliant I've ever seen on film. . . .

Our departure [for the East] was a mistake. While we were away, the studio executives came into the projection room with their sharp knives and slashed away at the film to "make it move faster." Since they are mostly occupied with the business end of picturemaking, this is their one opportunity to be "creative" and also to exercise their authority over the film's real creators.

When Max and I returned to the studio, we were told that 20 minutes had been taken out of the film's running time. We ran the reedited print in shocked silence until it was over and then we exploded. Instead of "moving faster," the picture now seemed interminable. . . .

Houseman agreed with our objections. It took all his powers of persuasion to keep Max from invading the inner sanctum of Universal's top brass and telling them exactly what he thought of them—which, of course, would only have made them more obdurate. When the Doziers finally threw their weight on our side, we were able to replace the cut footage and reinstate the original version.

———Koch, in *Film Comment*, Winter 70–71

Alexander K O R D A [Sandor Kellner] (1893–1956)
Born in Turkeye, Hungary. Began film career in Budapest. Worked in European and American studios before his British achievements. Knighted in 1943.

[Speaking of *The Private Life of Henry VIII*, 1933] An outsider often makes the best job of a national film. He is not cumbered with excessively detailed knowledge and associations. . . . I know there are people who think it odd that a Hungarian from Hollywood should direct an English historical film, but I can't see their argument. . . . The basic formula of the *Private Life* idea was probably derived from the Lubitsch films of the early twenties.

———Korda, interviewed for *Cinema Quarterly*, Autumn 33

Ted K O T C H E F F
Born 1931, a Canadian with Bulgarian-Macedonian parents. Began his film work in England before returning to Canada.

You're just floating around. . . . Do you consider yourself a Canadian?
Yes.
How do you feel as a Canadian working "in exile" most of the time—self-imposed or otherwise?
People seem to forget, conveniently, that in 1957 when Arthur Hiller, Norman Jewison, myself . . . and all those people left, it wasn't some act of betrayal—turning our backs on "little provincial Canada." We all wanted to be film directors, and there was no film industry here. It wasn't dreamed of; it wasn't even a gleam in anybody's eye in 1957. We didn't want to wait around to be 95 before we directed our first film! We were full of burning aspirations and so we were forced to go abroad. Some went to Hollywood—Norman and Arthur—others went to London like myself. Originally a lot of us thought we were going for a fairly short time . . . but we stayed longer and there seemed to be little reason to come back if you wanted to work in films.

In effect what you're saying is that this country has a real identity problem: they look like Americans, they talk like Americans, they dress like Americans, they read American magazines, they drive American cars, they watch American television. So what are they? "They're north of the 49th parallel." And that's when you become a Canadian. . . . "What's the distinguishing characteristics of a Canadian?" "That he has no distinguishing characteristics." I keep fighting those notions. I think there is a Canadian quality and that I'm a Canadian and that we have to find out what it is. But we can't just say, "As soon as you leave the country, you're not Canadian."

———Kotcheff, interviewed for *Cinema Canada*, June–July 74

Q. Were there any sequences in the novel that you shot for *The Apprentice-ship of Duddy Kravitz* [1974] which you regret don't appear in the finished film?

I only missed 2 things in the film which I threw out. In the bar mitzvah scene which is in the middle of the film, there was a wonderful, very funny sequence with Joe Silver who plays Farber, the scrap dealer. He gets drunk at his son's bar mitzvah; it was hilarious. I was sorry that had to go, but the bar mitzvah scene I felt just went on too long, so I trimmed it down. Another scene I really regret and felt should have stayed in, but I took it out—a very funny scene where Duddy Kravitz is in the schoolroom writing the final exams at high school. It was a very funny scene where everyone is writing studiously but Duddy is looking bored and is not doing anything. The teacher wanders slowly around and as soon as he turns his back to Duddy and opens the window, Duddy quickly rolls up his sleeve and the whole of his arm is covered in facts and figures. He furiously scribbles them all down but suddenly the teacher sees him and advances towards him. As soon as he sees the teacher coming, he licks his arm clean. The teacher rushes up, grabs his arm, looks at it, and there's all these wonderful blue smears. So, Duddy looks up at him with absolute innocence and says, "Oh, what did I do, why are you grabbing me?" And the teacher just looks at him and says, "You'll go far, Kravitz, you'll go far." I did regret cutting that scene because it was so wonderful. I always did like funny scenes anyway. But I felt that at the beginning of the picture that it held up forward progress.

——Kotcheff, interviewed for *Cinema Canada*, July–Aug 75

Grigori KOZINTSEV (1905–1974)
Born in Kiev. With Leonid Trauberg and Sergei Yutkevich founded FEX (Factory of the Eccentric Actor). First film in 1924 continued the eccentric methods of his theater work. At the time of his death was planning 2 films, a fantasy of themes and figures from Gogol, and The Tempest; *the following is from his notes for the latter:*

Not a comedy, but a tragicomedy. A tragic grotesque, but not a pastorale.

The donning of the robes—film it in reverse. In slow motion. First appearance of color. The brighter the better.

Prospero wears a half-mask—theatrical—made of birds' feathers. He is a theatrical magician. Art—is his magic.

The robes are woven of living flowers; they dissolve before our eyes (animation) into butterflies, dragonflies.

And finally, before our eyes, everything grows, blossoms, dies.

The magic robes—that is what Marcel Marceau wears.

Caliban—his first appearance is horrifying. In a huge mask and dressed in rustling reeds.

A la Artaud.

Witchcraft—memory of Sycorax (whenever he pronounces her name, he puts on the mask—it hangs behind him).

Or, on the contrary, he is a pure-blooded Aryan with a 2-centimeter forehead:

Heil Hitler! (possibly with appropriate gesture). *A Clockwork Orange.*

But what if [Prospero] should cast away the magic wand at the end—quite unidyllic?

No "idyll" or féerie or pastorale.

It's about art. The magic of art. From which the artist must turn—for life.

End: far below we see a city. Characters exeunt in that direction. The last to leave is Prospero.

His cave—a tower of elephant hide; Gordon Craig's "Goldoni Arena."

[for graphic style:]
Méliès? Pirosmani? Rousseau?

The great magician Prospero (I hear the truly magic voice of John Gielgud on the record, "The Ages of Man," that Lindsay Anderson gave me) achieving the highest power and deciding that the hour of farewell has struck.

This film can be made if the fantastic (idyllic) element can be replaced by "magic realism."

Not a desert island but the broken cities of Peru.

Prospero learned to read their language.

And the "masque" is not a mannerist ballet, but a "tropical carnival," and the day for remembering the dead in Mexico.

Something akin to the imagery of the Cuban film *Day of Waters.*

Look at the work of Glauber Rocha!

An island in memory of humanity. Here everything is memory, everything is death.

A "masque"—but in the art of our century.

Gonzalo—Yarvet? The ideal is somewhere between Montaigne and Tolstoy.

Prospero—Dvorzhetsky (but only without the slightest demonism!) or Grinko—with something of Quixote in him.

Scofield!!! Olivier!!!

Caliban—Dzhigarkhanian?

Prospero on his island? Eisenstein receiving the boxes of his books in Alma-Ata.

The heroes (especially Miranda and Ferdinand) live on two planes: asleep (when the magic robe is over them)—a pastoral love; and complete reality—it is by no means a pastoral love that Caliban and Ferdinand and Miranda slide into.

One of the key phrases, such as "To be or not to be," is spoken by Miranda, "O brave new world, that has such people in't!"

And Prospero's answer, " 'Tis new to thee . . ."

——Kozintsev, notes for The Tempest,
posthumously published in Iskusstvo Kino, Aug 75

Hans K R Ä L Y (1885–1950)
The scenarist in Germany for Ernst Lubitsch, who brought Kräly to Hollywood when he came to work there in 1922.

It is a hard craft, to write the story of the picture. Me, I am one of the slowest workers in Hollywood, I believe. Weeks, months, before the story finally satisfies me. There are many days when I do not work at all because the right thoughts will not come. But one can not write a good novel in a few weeks, or a great play for the stage. Why, then, should one expect to write a good screen story in a shorter space of time?

The difference between American stories and those of the Continent? A matter of personal experience, I believe. In Europe life is sterner. People learn living in a harder school. A tragic ending is acceptable if it is realism, true to life as they know it. Here in America romance is the keynote.

———Kräly, interviewed for *The Motion Picture Classic*

Stanley K R A M E R
Born in New York City, 1913. Worked as assistant producer at MGM before becoming an independent producer in 1948 with So This Is New York.

Then there was *The Pride and the Passion* [1957]—which was my first and probably my last, epic. You know what happened on that one? Sinatra jumped the picture a month before the end. He just took off. We never saw him again.

Cary Grant had to do all the final close-ups talking to a clothes hanger. I don't know why he stood for it, but he did. No: I'd never work with Sinatra again.

———Kramer, interviewed for *The Sunday Express*, 15 Feb 63

No company would insure Tracy, so Katharine Hepburn and I put our salaries in escrow so that would be the first money tapped if anything happened before the picture [*Guess Who's Coming to Dinner*, 1967] was completed.

Tracy knew this, of course. We worked out an agreement that he would be on the set only between 9:30 A.M. and 12:30 P.M. The other leads agreed to play close-ups over the back of a stand-in the rest of the time.

———Kramer, interviewed for *The Globe & Mail*, Toronto, 25 Sept 71

Stanley K U B R I C K
Born in New York City, 1928. Worked 4 years as photographer for Look *magazine. Made documentary short films for RKO. In 1953 made his first film independently,* Fear and Desire. *Now lives and works in England.*

Dr. Strangelove [1963] came from my great desire to do something about the nuclear nightmare. I was very interested in what was going to happen, and started reading a lot of books about 4 years ago. I have a library of about 70 or 80 books written by various technical people on the subject and I began to subscribe to the military magazines, the Air Force magazine, and to follow the U.S. Naval [Institute] proceedings.

I was struck by the paradoxes of every variation of the problem from one extreme to the other—from the paradoxes of unilateral disarmament to the first strike. And it seemed to me that, aside from the fact that I was terribly interested myself, it was very important to deal with this problem dramatically because it's the only social problem where there's absolutely no chance for people to learn anything from experience. If it ever happens, there may be very little of the world left to profit by the experience. So it seemed to me that this was eminently a problem, a topic to be dealt with dramatically. This was the background to *Dr. Strangelove*. Then I was talking one day with Alistair Buchan from the Institute of Strategic Studies and he mentioned the novel *Red Alert* which was published in 1958. I read it and of course I was completely taken by it.

Now *Red Alert* is a completely serious suspense story. My idea of doing it as a nightmare comedy came when I was trying to work on it. I found that in trying to put meat on the bones and to imagine the scenes fully one had to keep leaving things out of it which were either absurd or paradoxical, in order to keep it from being funny, and these things seemed to be very real. Then I decided that the perfect tone to adopt for the film would be what I now call nightmare comedy, because it most truthfully presents the picture.

——Kubrick in *Films & Filming*, June 63

It was a novel thing for me to have such a complicated information-handling operation going [on *2001: A Space Odyssey*, 1969], but it was absolutely essential for keeping track of the thousands of technical details involved. We figured that there would be 205 effects scenes in the picture and that each of these would require an average of 10 major steps to complete. I define a "major step" as one in which the scene is handled by another technician or department. We found that it was so complicated to keep track of all these scenes and the separate steps involved in each that we wound up with a 3-man sort of "operations room" in which every wall was covered with swingout charts including a short history for each scene. Every separate element and step was recorded on this history—information as to shooting dates, exposure, mechanical processes, special requirements, and the technicians and departments involved. Figuring 10 steps for 200 scenes equals 2,000 steps—but when you realize that most of these steps had to be done over 8 or 9 times to make sure they were perfect, the true total is more like 16,000 steps. It took an incredible number of diagrams, flow charts, and other data to keep everything organized and to be able to retrieve information that somebody might need about something someone else had done seven months earlier. We had to be able to tell which stage each scene was in at any given moment—and the system worked.

——Kubrick, interviewed for *American Cinematographer*, June 68

The only sets in [*A Clockwork Orange*, 1971] are the Korova milkbar, the prison reception area, a mirrored bathroom and a mirrored hall at the writer's house. These were built because we couldn't find any suitable locations. I tried to be systematic about the location search. We wanted to find modern and interesting architecture, and it seemed that the best way to do this was to buy 10 years of back issues of 2 or 3 architectural magazines. I spent 2 weeks going through them with John Barry, the producer designer, and we filed and cross-referenced all the interesting photographs that we found. This proved to be a much more effective approach than just having a couple of location scouts driving around London. As it worked out, most of the interesting locations we finally chose originated from this sifting through the architectural magazines.

It's very simple now filming in even the most confined interiors. One has a very wide choice of fast, wide-angle lenses. For example, in the record boutique we shot with a 9.8 mm lens, which has a 90-degree viewing angle. Another very fast lens, the f0.95, made it possible to shoot with natural light in room interiors, late in the evening. It allows you to shoot in 200 percent less light than the normal f.2 movie lenses.

——Kubrick, interviewed for *The Saturday Review*, 25 Dec 71

[To do the subjective shot of Alex's suicide attempt in *The Clockwork Orange*] we bought an old Newman Sinclair clockwork mechanism for £50. It's a beautiful camera and it's built like a battleship. We made a number of polystyrene boxes which gave about 18 inches of protection around the camera and cut out a slice for the lens. We then threw the camera off a roof. In order to get it to land lens-first, we had to do this 6 times and the camera survived all 6 drops. On the final one, it landed right on the lens and smashed it, but it didn't do a bit of harm to the camera. This despite the fact that the polystyrene was literally blasted away from it each time by the impact. The next day we shot a steady test on the camera and found there wasn't a thing wrong with it. On this basis, I would say that the Newman Sinclair must be the most indestructible camera ever made.

——Kubrick, interviewed for *Sight & Sound*, Spring 72

Lev K U L E S H O V (1899–1970)
Born in Tambov. Began film work as assistant and designer to Eugene Bauer.

In making this film [*The Project of Engineer Prite*, 1917] I took into account a whole series of peculiarities proper to cinematographic montage. Let us suppose that in a certain place we are photographing a certain object. Then, in a quite different place, we film people looking at this object. We edit the whole thing, alternating the image of the object and the image of the people who are looking at it. In *The Project of Engineer Prite*, I show people looking at electric pylons in this way. It was thus that I made an accidental discovery: thanks to montage, it is possible to create, so to speak, a new geography, a new place of action. It is possible to create in this way new relations between the objects, the nature, the people and the progress of the film.

What I think was much more interesting [than the "Kuleshov effect"— the montage of the same shot of the actor Mozhukin in quite different contexts, producing contrasting situations] was the creation of a woman who had never existed. I did this experiment with my students. I shot a scene of a woman at her toilette: she did her hair, made up, put on her stockings and shoes and dress. . . . I filmed the face, the head, the hair, the hands, the legs, the feet of different women, but I edited them as if it was all one woman, and, thanks to the montage, I succeeded in creating a woman who did not exist in reality, but only in the cinema.

——Kuleshov, interviewed (in 1965) for *Cinema in Revolution*
(London 1973)

We were not only cold, but hungry, as well, in 1920–21, learning "to film without film," and to pick up a little extra cash, we took out our classroom *études* to concerts. We'd go to these affairs with our own costumes and properties, made by the students and instructors out of any sort of rubbish that came to hand or could be brought from our homes. We carried our equipment to and from the concerts on children's sleds—the trams weren't running, and we didn't have enough money to hire an *izvoshchik*.

Thus we prepared cinematographers, thus we taught others, and taught ourselves.

——Kuleshov, in *Iskusstvo Kino*, March 40

Akira KUROSAWA

Born in Tokyo in 1910, his father a severe military educator. Studied to become a painter. In 1936 answered a newspaper advertisement for an assistant film director. After working and studying with Kajiro Yamamoto, Kurosawa made a great success with his first film, Sugata Sanshiro (1943):

Actually, [*No Regrets for Our Youth,* 1946] wasn't much of a production— the labor unions got in the way, for one thing. Still, it was the first film in which *I* had something to say and in which *my* feelings were used. Everyone disagreed. They said I should go "back" to the style of *Sugata....* If you are only concerned with how you say something, without having anything to say it won't come to anything....

Nothing could be more difficult for me than to define my own style. I simply make a picture as I want it to be, or as nearly as possible for me to do so.

I got the idea for [*One Wonderful Sunday,* 1947] from an old D. W. Griffith picture [*Isn't Life Wonderful?,* 1924].... Though this film won me a prize for the best director of the year I don't think I made it nearly freely enough. I had a lot of things to say and I got them all mixed up—it certainly is not my favorite film. But I remembered, and in *Drunken Angel* [1948] I kept my eyes open.

[In *Drunken Angel*] Shimura played the doctor beautifully but I found I could not control Mifune. When I saw this, I let him do as he wanted, let him play the part freely ... I did not want to smother that vitality. In the end, though the title refers to the doctor, it is Mifune that everyone remembers.

... Just as an example, his reactions are so very swift. If I say one thing, he understands 10. He reacts extraordinarily quickly to the director's intentions. Most Japanese actors are the opposite of this and so I wanted Mifune to cultivate this gift.

Uegusa and I rewrote [Shimura's] part over and over again, and he still wasn't interesting. We had almost given up when it occurred to me that he was just too good to be true. He needed a defect. . . . That is why we made him an alcoholic. At this time most film characters were still either all black or all white. We made the doctor gray.

[The script of *Rashomon*, 1950] was a bit too short . . . but all of my friends liked it very much. Daiei, however, did not understand it and kept asking, "But what is it about?" I made it longer, put on a beginning and an ending—and they eventually agreed to make it. . . .

We were staying in Kyoto, waiting for the set to be finished. While we were there we ran off some 16 mm prints to amuse ourselves. One of them was a Martin Johnson jungle film in which there was a shot of a lion roaming around. I noticed it and told Mifune that that was just what I wanted him to be. . . . Mori had seen a jungle picture in which a black leopard was shown. We all went to see it. When the leopard came on, Machiko was so upset that she hid her face. I saw and recognized the gesture. It was just what I wanted for the young wife.

Making [*The Idiot*, 1951] was very hard work. It was extraordinarily difficult to make. At times I felt as though I just wanted to die. Dostoyevsky is very heavy, and now I was under him. I knew just how those enormous *sumo* wrestlers feel. All the same it was a marvelous experience for me. . . . If I do say so myself I think that after making this picture my own powers increased considerably.

I usually write with someone else. If I work by myself it tends to get lop-sided. . . . The way we work is that we all sit at a big table but a bit away from each other. Uegusa, or Hashimoto, or Oguni, and myself, we all write. Then we show each other what we've written. It is a real competition. Then each takes the other's and rewrites it. Then we talk about it and decide what to use. Even for a talented scenarist, this is very hard work.

In *Ikiru* [1952] it was Oguni who had the best ideas—and he wasn't even writing. He sat in the middle [between Hashimoto and Kurosawa] and gave suggestions and asked for more copy.

After *Rashomon* I wanted to do something with Shakespeare's *Macbeth*, but just about that time Orson Welles's version was announced, and so I postponed mine. . . .

There are very few close-ups [in *Throne of Blood*, 1957]. I tried to do everything using full shots. Japanese almost never make films this way, and I remember confusing my staff thoroughly with my instructions. They were so used to moving up for moments of emotion and I kept telling them to move back.

[*The Bad Sleep Well*, 1960] was the first film of Kurosawa Productions, my own unit which I run and finance myself. From this film on, I was responsible for everything. Consequently, when I began, I wondered what kind of film to make. . . . At last I decided to do something about corruption, because it has always seemed to me that graft, bribery, etc., at the public level, is one of the worst crimes that there is. These people hide behind the façade of some great company or corporation and consequently no one knows how dreadful they really are, what awful things they do.

... But even while we were making it, I knew that it wasn't working out as I had planned and that this was because I was simply not telling and showing enough ... maybe the picture would have been better if I had been braver.

After finishing *Sanjuro* [1962] I started looking around for something else to do, and quite by accident picked up *Red Beard* by Shugoro Yamamoto [author of the *Sanjuro* novel]. At first I thought that this would make a good script for Horikawa, but as I wrote I got so interested that I knew that I would have to direct it myself.

The script is quite different from the novel. One of the major characters, the young girl, is not even found in the book. While I was writing, I kept remembering Dostoyevsky and I tried to show the same thing that he showed in the character of Nelly in *The Insulted and Injured*.

Before I decide how to photograph something, I first of all think about how to improve whatever it is I'm photographing. When that is done, then I think how it can best be photographed, from what angle, etc. And each technique I use necessarily differs according to whatever it is I'm taking a picture of. . . . It is always I who frame the shot, who design the movement— though I usually also take the advice of anyone who happens to have a better idea than I do.

——Kurosawa, interviewed for and quoted in Richie's
The Films of Akira Kurosawa (Berkeley, 1969)

L

Hedy L A M A R R [Hedwig Kiesler]
Born 1914 in Vienna, of Czech parents.

Remember, I was only 15 [in *Ecstasy* (1933)] and eager to make good. I worked hard and everything went smoothly until nearly the end of the picture.

The director [Gustav Machaty] now insisted on changing a scene from the original script I had signed. He wanted me to be photographed openly in the nude, whereas originally I was to have undressed behind some bushes.

When I objected, he claimed that if I did not do the scene this way, he would not be able to finish the picture and I could be responsible for the cost of all the work that had already been done.

Not knowing my legal rights, I gave in. So the famous—or infamous—scene was done. And to this day people have not let me forget the mistake I made twenty years ago.

——Lamarr, in unidentified English newspaper, 27 May 56

Evelyn L A M B A R T
Born in Ottawa. Entered film work in 1942.

A great part of *Begone Dull Care* [1949] was done on a running moviola. A little pad was inserted in the gate of the moviola, in order to make the film bypass the intermittent mechanics, and run at a constant rate. We put the paint on an artificial sponge (celluloid sponge) and applied it to the running film at the point where the pad was placed in the moviola. This gives a fairly even coat of paint side by side on the original sponge; the stripes can be made to swing from side to side on the film by moving the sponge from side to side over the running film; in fact you can turn the sponge right around; you can cut a piece out of the sponge and get a clear stripe on the film, or you can cut lots of little nicks out of the sponge; you can vary the pressure, or anything you can think of; different treatments give different effects. It is really easy to make all sorts of beautiful things; the difficulty lies in selecting ones which will make a film. We painted about 1,200 feet when doing *Begone Dull Care*.

——Lambart, notes on *Begone Dull Care* (1949?)

Burt LANCASTER
Born in New York City in 1915. Studied physical education at New York University. Acrobatic career ended by injury.

I'll tell you how I got the part [in *The Leopard,* 1964]. Lombardo, the producer, came to Los Angeles to talk about an adventure story. But somehow we got round to *The Leopard,* and I told him what a wonderful book it was and how much I'd like to do the film. He went back to Visconti and he said, "No, that's ridiculous. He's a cowboy . . . a gangster." After he couldn't get the Russian actor he wanted for the part, he signed Olivier, though he wasn't absolutely happy with him. Eventually it was discovered that Olivier wasn't available at the right time because of his commitments in England and it just happened that Visconti saw *Judgment at Nuremberg* [1961].

Working on [*The Leopard*] was a completely different experience for me. Visconti took endless pains to get everything right. He was a perfectionist. Yet he had this amazing way of trusting you. He wouldn't tell you how to play a scene. He'd let you do it your own way, once he saw you knew what you were doing. I worked on the screenplay with him, too. He imparted this tremendous confidence, and you couldn't help but share it with him. But everything had to be exactly as he wanted in other departments. He wouldn't work unless it was. We once arrived at a Sicilian village to do some shooting, and found some of the houses had television aerials on them. He just said, "I want them down. Every one of them. When they are down we will shoot. You will find me in my hotel!" They came down okay.

We got slaughtered by the British press for sacking Sandy [Mackendrick, from *The Devil's Disciple,* 1958], because he had such a great reputation over here after *Whiskey Galore* [1948] and *The Lady Killers* [1955]. But we had no alternative.

Sandy was a very clever director and a very nice guy. But he took one helluva lot of time. He would get hold of a scene that was 5½ pages long and attempt to do it in one take by moving the dolly around and through his characters—an incredibly difficult task. We would arrive on the set ready to go at 9 in the morning and we'd be hanging around till 3 in the afternoon rehearsing the moves we had to make. Then we'd shoot, and sometimes he'd say, "No, I don't like that much. Let's do it a different way."

Well, we got through *Sweet Smell* [*of Success,* 1957] somehow. But when it came to the Shaw film, which my company produced, we realized there might be difficulties. We only had a certain amount of money and 48 days to shoot the whole thing. So we asked Sandy whether he could do it in the time. He insisted that he could, and we went ahead. At the end of the first week, we ended up with 2 days of film. It was impossible to continue like that. Let me add that what he shot turned out to be the best part of the movie, because Sandy was a very brilliant man. But we hadn't the time or the money for him. That's the truth.

———Lancaster, interviewed for *The Guardian,* 4 Aug 72

Fritz L A N G (1890–1976)
Born in Vienna, he later attended Vienna's Realschule studying architecture, but his real interest was painting; he went to 2 art schools, first in Vienna and then in Munich. In the First World War, was wounded 3 times and received 4 decorations. He became interested in films and found his first work as a screenwriter while in the hospital. He began to direct in 1918.

I learned a great lesson from a German writer, who worked in Germany in the 1900s. He said, "Fritz, when you write something for silent pictures, say to yourself, 'One sees,' and then start to write." So in those days, because we didn't have words, we tried to use camera movement almost as a dramatic point. Once, in *Metropolis* [1926], I had to make an explosion. Now, before you can see an explosion, you feel the impact, the blast—you are thrown back —and then maybe you see the flames or whatever. So in *Metropolis* I put the camera on a swing (the cameraman [Karl Freund] had it tied on his chest) and we swung it toward the actor [Gustav Fröhlich] who was experiencing this blast. He started to fall back the moment the camera swung toward him, and he pressed himself against the wall; then the camera went back into first position and you had the feeling of an explosion.

. . . Erich Pommer offered me *The Cabinet of Dr. Caligari*, which I was eventually unable to do. It was really the work of 3 painters [Hermann Warm, Walter Reimann, Walter Röhrig] who wanted to make a kind of an expressionistic picture; the whole story had been written, and the only contribution I made was that I said to Pommer, "Look, if the expressionistic sets stand for the world of the insane, and you use them from the beginning, it doesn't mean anything. Why don't you, instead, make the prologue and the epilogue of the picture normal?" So the film begins in the garden of an asylum and is told normally; then, when the story is told from the viewpoint of one of the inmates; it becomes expressionistic; and at the end it becomes normal again and we see that the villain of the picture, Dr. Caligari, is the doctor of the asylum.

I remember for *M* (my first talkie), I needed a boom. There was no boom. Nobody had ever heard about a boom in Germany. I explained it to a very intelligent worker, a craftsman who had great artistic qualities (he had built, by himself, the dragon in *Die Nibelungen*). So, for *M*, he took a kind of a chassis—on 4 wheels—and put a 2 x 4 on it 20 feet long. On one end stood the camera, and on the other end sat 4 or 5 heavy-bellied workers. And that was my boom.

In the studio, I first rehearse the whole scene so that every actor knows exactly what he has to do and how he will act; then I shoot everything in one direction, for which the lights have been set. Then I throw the whole thing around—180 degrees—and shoot in the other direction. I save a lot of time this way, and it's only possible when I have everything already written out in the script. I don't mean every shot or close-up, but the main movements. I make notes for myself—"This line is important," "This is a close-up." I usually say, "I'm through with the picture when I am through with the work at my desk."

Now, one might ask, how could you write [*Fury*, 1936] when you didn't even speak English very well? Well, by now I'd been here a year, I had learned a little, and I followed a habit I had in Europe (and still have) of collecting newspaper clippings—I have used them for a lot of my pictures. We found a lynching case that had happened in San Jose, California, a few years before I made the film, and we used many newspaper clippings for the script.

———Lang, interviewed for *Fritz Lang in America* (London, 1968)

[In *Le Mépris*, 1963] Godard adores improvising whereas I like to know, very exactly, when I arrive on the set, what I'm going to do. . . . It's the only way I can work. Sure, I give my actors maximum liberty, but Godard goes further: he only gives them the idea they must portray, leaving them to utilize their own vocabulary. Godard, who has never had the silent film experience, improvises the scene, and not only the dialogue: he invents the scene at the moment of shooting!

———Lang, interviewed for *Take One*, Nov–Dec 68

I don't know really what I did in those first few months [in Hollywood]. I worked on this and then on that, but nothing ever came of the stories. I wrote one about a fire aboard a liner at sea, but they decided it might offend one of the steamship companies. Always they were afraid that someone might object.

The secret of making good pictures, in my opinion, is to create situations that will cause a clash between characters whom filmgoers will like and those who will evoke hatred. Once established as a sympathetic character, a screen player may commit any evil on the calendar without losing the audience's respect.

The murder of the prison chaplain by Henry Fonda in *You Only Live Once* [1937] is so outrageous—so shocking—that we were tempted to change the story for fear of alienating audiences. But that would have weakened the irony of our story; so we chose another course. We justified his crime. To do this we had to present him as a victim of circumstances—a helpless boy caught in the meshes of the law, convicted for a murder of which he was innocent.

It was a car crash [in *Spione*, 1927] and I wanted to escape from the conventional treatment of long shots of the car, close-ups of the driver, and then a long shot of the car crash.

I wanted my audience to be behind the wheel of the car—not sitting at the side of the road. So I placed my cameras in strange positions. Rushing towards the car on each side of the road were tall trees in unbroken rows. As the speed of the cars increased, the trees swept by faster and faster, losing their identity and becoming threatening blurs of black and white.

Suddenly they appeared to shift the direction of their flow and loomed ahead at a crazy angle. One huge tree dashed straight into the camera, its trunk filling the entire screen. A quick cut to the terrified face of the driver then instant blackness. It was much more effective, I thought, than a conventional crash.

———Lang, interviewed for *Film Pictorial*, 5 June 37

I think some people overrate the power of a film director. It is a teamwork. But a director *does* have powers. Let me tell you a story. When *Fury* was finished, the producer [Joseph Mankiewicz] came out of a preview and called me to his office and accused me of changing the script. I said, "How could I change the script when I can't even speak English!" So they went and got a copy of the script and he read it and he said, "Damn you, you're right; but it *sounds* different on the screen." Perhaps it did—to him.

———Lang, interviewed for *Films & Filming*, June 62

Angela LANSBURY
Born 1925 in London.

Cukor is a man who doesn't mince words, and he told me that he wanted [in *Gaslight*, 1944] a very blowsy performance, rather loose. And he certainly coached me and got that out of me. I can sort of see him now, sitting there and saying, "You know, she's rather dirty and sleazy and she excites this man because she is so young and so aware of her sexuality, and she knows that he is aware of it too." I understood that. Some men are able to describe that kind of a girl in no uncertain terms and you can imagine why: I mean, Cukor himself wouldn't have liked such a girl—she would be distasteful to him, and yet he would think she was terribly funny. George would roar with laughter at me, in everything I did in the role that appealed to him. If it was something I thought of, and he liked it, he would scream with laughter.

———Lansbury, interviewed for *Films & Filming*, Dec 71

For a rather tense action piece like *The Manchurian Candidate* [1962], John Frankenheimer can pluck from me a whole lot of things that another director wouldn't know existed or wouldn't know how to use or wouldn't know how to challenge me to produce. Then you get into something like *The Dark at the Top of the Stairs* [1960], and you have Delbert Mann, who's an enormously sympathetic, mild man who wouldn't do a subject like *Manchurian Candidate*, but who knows how to unlock other doors with me or produce out of me facets of my abilities that Frankenheimer doesn't know about and probably wouldn't be interested in. So if you get the wrong director for the wrong film, you're in deep, deep trouble.

———Lansbury, interviewed for *The Times*, 29 Jan 72

Rod LA ROQUE
Born in Chicago, 1898. First film work at the Chicago studio of Essanay.

There were spectacular events [in *The Ten Commandments*, 1923]—like the opening and closing of the Red Sea. We had a technician, a miniature specialist, Roy Pomeroy, who was really fantastic. You wouldn't believe how he did the Red Sea scene. Two blocks of Jell-O, carved with waves, were set on a huge table which was split in the center. These 2 blocks were held together with water rushing over them. On cue, things on winches turned the blocks and separated them as water came over the edge. With the screen Jell-O shimmering and going away, they ran the thing forward, and it closed. When it was reversed, it opened. We had double exposures which were so realistic that we were hounded by the Society for the Prevention of Cruelty to Animals, who wanted to know why we had treated the horses so cruelly. Chariots, horses, and riders had tumbled into the Jell-O. Mr. De Mille asked these people, "Aren't you worried about the human beings at all?" They were only concerned about the horses. When we proved that it was double exposure and a trick, all was forgiven.

——La Roque, interviewed for *The Real Tinsel* (NY, 1970)

Walter L A S S A L L Y
Born in Berlin, 1926. Came to England in 1939; after war's end took several menial film jobs before recognition of his camera talent.

Q. How do the preparatory stages in a film go? How much time do you have to discuss a style?

A. Well, there are a lot of discussions with the director and also with the art director and the camera operator. On *Tom Jones* [1963] it was decided that, if the staging was impeccably in period, then the camera technique could be absolutely modern. There were a lot of discussions about the color, which we wanted very soft, and we made tests of different ways of shooting and of how different costumes would photograph. The whole photographic style was established within certain limits that would leave leeway in executing it. With *A Taste of Honey* [1961] we aimed for as rough and realistic a look as possible. We decided that it shouldn't look like a staged film, a studio film, and so in many sequences one was aiming at a newsreel sort of photography. A lot of cameramen couldn't conceive that this kind of roughness could be a deliberate stylistic effect. They just thought that it was incredibly sloppily photographed and that I didn't know any better. But, of course, the public accepted it. They know what real life looks like when it's photographed: they see it on television every day.

In *Loneliness of the Long Distance Runner* [1962], we shot the scenes in the Borstal in a tiny prefab up in North London, with no walls removed or anything like that. There were about 20 of us, actors and unit, all jammed in there. It's quite a job, but it works and it gives an atmosphere. Up to a point, such limitations are healthy because they force you away from the familiar pattern of lighting which arises from having it everywhere you want it. If you've got the whole set ringed with lamps and you can move them infinitesimally right or left, then you can do whatever you want. But this also leads to a kind of slackness, so that you don't, in fact, light it like real life. Limitations act as a good discipline. You are stimulated to work in a different way and you get a different look to the picture.

——Lassally, interviewed for *Sight & Sound*, Summer 65

Philip L A T H R O P
Born 1916. After service in the Second World War became assistant and operator to Russell Metty for 10 years.

[In *The Cincinnati Kid*, 1965] Before the marathon card game begins, putting the brash pretender up against the king of stud poker players, we see the story told in allegory in a vicious cockfight.

And although the picture is photographed in color, this scene is almost colorless, except for the scarlet dress worn by Ann-Margret. Everything else was down at the low end of the scale, in dark grays, browns, and blacks, with the costumes essentially in monotone.

I further built the mood of this clandestine affair through the use of a lot of bee smoke, which gives an overall beige cast to the scene.

Smoke is awfully hard to control. It's unpleasant for both cast and crew, and it's a lot easier to get roughly the same effect with a light fog filter. . . .

But the smoke has an overall tone, and provides subtle effects of light and shadow which are possible in no other way.

——Lathrop, in American Cinematographer, Nov 65

Charles L A U G H T O N (1899–1962)
Born in Scarborough, Yorkshire. Attended Royal Academy of Dramatic Arts.

I was assigned the part of Nero in *The Sign of the Cross* [1932]. Cecil De Mille, the director, saw Nero as a robust, domineering personality. I visualized a type exactly the opposite—a man whose preciousness would heighten the horror of the orgies staged for his pleasure.

After a long but friendly dispute between myself and De Mille—it lasted for a week—I was ultimately permitted to play the character in my own way.

Then came the problem of make up. Nero had a Roman nose. Mine has a wayward course of its own.

Walter Westmore, the chief make up man of the firm, was given the job of building the nose. He did so marvelously.

Although I must tell you this—the darned thing cracked one day unnoticed by any of us, and we had to retake yards of film. That episode cost £ 500. Expensive nose.

It was [Alexander Korda] who eventually conceived the idea of doing Henry VIII. When it looked as though he would succeed in bringing about the making of the film, he tried to cast the whole play in a way that would give me the greatest possible scope for my interpretation of the great character. . . .

I shall never forget the day I was lifted on to my horse with my 90 pounds of trappings. When I finally came to rest on the saddle without any trouble, the jeers from those boys made the taking of the sound film a difficult business. Walking through Long Crendon dressed as Henry VIII was much worse than walking down Oxford Street in tights.

I cannot quite say how I got my conception of Henry VIII. I did not take any historical acceptance of the man.

I suppose I must have read a good deal about him, but for the rest I spent a lot of my time walking around the old Tudor Palace at Hampton Court, getting my mind accustomed to the square, squat architecture of the rooms and the cloisters.

I think it was from the architecture of the houses and the rooms that I got my idea of Henry.

——Laughton, interviewed for The Sunday Express, 3–10 Dec 33

Stan L A U R E L [Arthur Stanley Jefferson]   (1890–1965)
Born in Lancashire. As music hall performer, brought to America in 1910. On second American tour, remained in U.S.A.

You have to learn what people laugh at, then proceed accordingly. First of all, you should start out, I think, with a fairly believable plot no matter how broad it is, and then work on from there. But you've got to *learn* how to go on from there. Nobody's going to teach you. That's why one of the best ways for a young comedian to learn his trade is to get as much repertory as possible, changing parts, being in different situations, over and over again until he learns the "feel" of different audiences. . . . You develop an intuition after facing various types of audiences. What one will laugh at, another won't. . . . One day you'll know. Then, you're in business.
——Laurel, interviewed for *Mr. Laurel & Mr. Hardy* (New York, 1961)

John Philip L A W
Born in 1937. Most of his film experience in Italian films. First American success in The Russians Are Coming, The Russians Are Coming *(1966):*

The kind of thing Norman [Jewison] gives you is the feeling that you've got a good solid production team behind you, doing their best to get the best out of you, and giving you every opportunity: good lighting, good sound and so forth. My experience on certain other [Italian?] films has been that they're in a hurry: they're losing light, they're late, they want to get the shots done, so they try to cut corners and get it done as quickly as they can and still turn in a creditable job. But from an actor's point of view, it's much better to have somebody who will take that little extra bit of time and energy to try and give you every possible break. When that happens, it opens an actor up. He's not on the defensive, fearing that something is going to be terrible on account of somebody else's neglect. He's trying everything he can to give the director something a little extra, something to choose from. With somebody like Norman, that's what happens.
——Law, interviewed for *Films & Filming*, Apr 72

John Howard L A W S O N
Born 1894; graduated from Williams College and served as an ambulance driver during World War I.

The fact that many stars talked with a foreign accent or had inadequate voice training was less threatening than the probability that spoken words—almost any words, could tear the whole fabric of a film like *Love* [1928].
    In my first contact with Thalberg I confronted this perplexing question. I was asked to write a sound sequence for a silent Garbo and Gilbert picture, *Flesh and the Devil* [1927]. It was already finished but talkies had become so popular that it seemed risky to release it without enough sound to permit it to be described as a film "with sound." The difficulty hung like a sword of Damocles over the first conference in which I participated: Gilbert and Garbo were not ready to undertake the ordeal of speech. But beyond this was the

larger possibility that words would annihilate the pictorial magic. (This happened when Garbo spoke in *Anna Christie* in 1930, but O'Neill's play solved the problem of content by giving Garbo a more realistic character and situation, with an atmospheric background of fog and sea.)

Since the stars could not speak, I prepared a fantastic dream sequence for *Flesh and the Devil*, with sounds and voices coming from a void. The director glanced at the script and tossed it aside. But Thalberg read every word, slowly, and then spoke with genuine surprise: "There's an idea in it." The scene was not used, but my future at MGM was assured.

Thalberg had a naïve but genuine respect for ideas. He used to call the writers together—there were 60 or 70 of them at the time—and plead with puzzled urgency, "Why are there so many writers and so few ideas? Perhaps you don't care about your work. You must realize that the studio cannot live without ideas." The writers would listen respectfully and return to their cubicles. Thalberg had forgotten, or pretended to forget, a simple economic fact: the writers, with few exceptions, were paid by the week and everything they wrote belonged to the studio. It would not be good business for a writer with a fresh idea to give it to the studio and lose a possible sale.

——Lawson, in his *Film: The Creative Process* (NY, 1964)

Richard L E A C O C K
Born 1921 in London; grew up in the Canary Islands, where he made his first film. Came to America in 1938; Army cameraman in the Second World War.

As I remember, the first Soviet documentary film that I saw was *Turksib* [1929]. I think I was 11 or 12 at the time—this was 1932 or 1933. It may have been because this was one of the first films of any sort that I had then seen that made it particularly impressive to me. In any case, if you look at my first film, *Canary Island Bananas* [1935] you can see the very obvious influence of *Turksib*, even to the split titles at the end. In general, I was impressed by the idea of filming processes, people doing things in a way that we could watch what was being done. And machines, too, for that matter. People and machines working together: pumping water, planting bananas, wrapping them—and drilling oil wells, as in *Louisiana Story* [1948]. It wasn't until easy do-it-yourself sound recording was developed that I moved on to being interested in filming people in their interactions. Before that it didn't seem possible. But it was *Turksib* that stimulated my first years of filmmaking.

——Leacock, from a letter of 23 Feb 67

The problem of film journalism arose and became acute to me long ago. I started in film very young, as you know, in documentary film. Already when we were working on *Louisiana Story* I saw that when we were using small cameras, we had tremendous flexibility, we could do anything we wanted, and get a wonderful sense of cinema. The moment we had to shoot dialogue, lip-sync—everything had to be locked down, the whole nature of the film changed. The whole thing seemed to stop. We had heavy disk recorders, and the camera that, instead of weighing 6 pounds, weighed 200 pounds, a sort of monster. As a result of this, the whole nature of what we were doing changed. We could no longer watch things as they developed, we had to impose ourselves to such an extent upon everything that happened before us, that everything sort of died. . . . Only recently, with all sorts of technical developments, we came to the verge of having equipment light and flexible enough to enable us to observe and record with a minimum of interference into what's going on. . . .

In theater, or in controlled filming, when you see it, as the end result, you can always question it. For instance, there was a film on racing. The driver burst into tears. The audience was perfectly justified in questioning the development of this situation, in doubting the writer, the director, and the actor. Would this happen, or wouldn't it? they asked. The questions are bound to arise. But when we are filming—and this is the basic difference between our cinema and the controlled cinema—when we are filming an actual driver, and when he bursts into tears, the doubt never arises: he did it. The ultimate fact, that this did happen, is fundamentally different from anything you can do in theater or in controlled cinema. Many filmmakers feel that the aim of the filmmaker is to have complete control. Then the conception of what happens is limited by the conception of the filmmaker. We don't want to put this limit on actuality. What's happening, the action, has no limitations, neither the significance of what's happening. The filmmaker's problem is more a problem of how to convey it. . . .

. . . The stuff we did with Godard [1 A.M. (One American Movie) 1969] . . . was a strange situation, because we really had no idea of what was going on in Godard's head. I was trying very hard to oblige the man, but he would always give you these very inhibiting injunctions, like don't zoom too much, don't do something else too much. He was that sort of director, but then you're in a half-assed position—it's the impossibility of the cameraman. You're sitting there thinking instead of saying to yourself, "Wow! Look!" You're thinking what does the man want? Does he want this, does he want that, and what am I supposed to do? The only reason you go on shooting is not because you're interested in what's going on, but because the man said shoot. You may be bored stiff, but you're in this ridiculous position, so I tend to think in my mechanical way that if you're going to direct a film, for Christ's sake direct it, and tell the cameraman exactly what you want. . . .

Now, the way he films in La Chinoise [1967] or Weekend [1968], the camera is a colossus. It's completely controlled. It's completely automatic. It's just like a great big shotgun. Fine, but then in a sense he's controlling it. Being the cameraman—someone says start and stop, and I don't like being a cameraman. When you're making your own film, it's different. But this, you're second-guessing somebody else. You're an engineer, or some thing.

———Leacock, interviewed for *Documentary Explorations*
(Garden City, 1971)

David LEAN
Born in Croydon in 1908. After working as camera assistant, cutting-room assistant, and assistant director, became editor in 1930 of Gaumont and Movietone News.

Robert Bolt had done the screenplay [for *Lawrence of Arabia,* 1962]. We talked a lot about it; but it is virtually his own construction. . . . The script is essentially Bolt's conception of Lawrence. It is very close to my own conception of Lawrence, too. . . .

It is remarkable that Bolt has scripted nothing before, although his plays *The Flowering Cherry* and *A Man for All Seasons* indicate the depth he can bring to character. It was our producer, Sam Spiegel's idea that he write the script. Although he has a great visual sense, I don't think there is a single scene that is there just for an "eyeful." For my part I would not have been happy filming the Lawrence story in black and white on a small-screen ratio. Lawrence was bitten by the desert and by the people of the desert; and if you are going to show that, it must be in the best possible way, and there is nothing like this big screen process for showing it.

Q. Has it been a difficult film to make?

A. Peter O'Toole has the most difficult part as Lawrence. He's seldom off the screen. Other characters with new interest value pop up around him; but he has to carry the drama from start to finish. . . . By moving from location to location we had to shoot hopelessly out of continuity and this was difficult for both Peter and myself.

The film has been shot on 65mm. stock in the Panavision process. All the material we shot in Jordan we could not see until we returned to Britain. I sat in a projection theater and saw it all in 3 sessions of 3 hours each, 9 hours of material from that location alone. Fortunately, with a cinematographer like Freddie Young, I could be certain of the material I was getting.

Q. You started your career as a film editor. How does this affect your approach as a director?

A. I supervise the editing myself, particularly the tricky action sequences. As I was an editor, it is hard to keep my hands off the celluloid. Nobody can prophesy at the script stage how a thing is going to be cut; but I try to shoot with a plan of the cutting in my mind. I try to get the shots that I know will be wanted, moving the artists from here to there and not repeating the action all over again from another setup.

———Lean, interviewed for *Films & Filming,* Jan 63

Christopher L E E
Born 1922, of Italian ancestry. Has played most of the film monsters.

The Dracula subject is played out. I have no intention of playing the character again because I'm increasingly disenchanted with the way he has been presented. Bram Stoker's book has never been done in its entirety on the screen. They write stories into which they fit the character, and that simply doesn't work.

Dracula has never been done properly. Basically it would cost an enormous amount of money. There'd have to be shipwrecks, craggy mountains, many varied locations, special effects, etc. Bits and pieces of Stoker's book have been presented on the screen.

With [my] first *Dracula* in 1957 I came fairly near it, except for the physical appearance of the character which in Hammer pix has been wrong.

If I was offered Stoker's story exactly as he had written it, I'd do it again, for the last time. I've only played it 6 times in 15 years. I've done Frankenstein's monster once, and never again.

——Lee, interviewed for *Variety*, 4 July 73

Fernand L E G E R (1881–1955)
Born in Argentan, France. With the advice of Man Ray and the photography of Dudley Murphy, Leger made his only film, Ballet Mécanique (1924), *possibly the most important experimental film made in France:*

The idea for the film came to me in order to be certain of the plastic possibilities of these new elements expressed in movement. The repetitions of shapes, of slow or rapid rhythms, allowed extremely rich possibilities. An object could become, all on its own, a tragic, comic or spectacular sight. It was an adventure in the land of wonders. I would have liked to use fragments of objects. But it would have become too abstract an experience, inaccessible to an ordinary audience. For this reason the editing alternated fragments and ordinary reality. True cinema is the image of the object totally unknown to my eyes.

——Leger, quoted in Sadoul-Morris, *Dictionary of Films*, p 22

Vivien L E I G H [Vivian Mary Hartley] (1913–1967)
Born in Darjeeling, India. Educated in England, Italy, Germany and France.

I'd never have been able to get through [*Gone With the Wind*, 1939] without the book and George Cukor. I'd keep the book beside me and look up each scene as we filmed it to remind me where I was supposed to be, and how I should be feeling, until Selznick shouted at me to throw the damned thing away. On Sundays, when we didn't shoot, I'd steal over to George Cukor's and discuss with him the bits we'd be working on the next week. It was probably terribly irregular, but I couldn't have finished it without him.

——Leigh, interviewed for *The Observer*, 7 Jan 68

Then I was offered the film [of *A Streetcar Named Desire*, 1951, after doing it on the stage in London, directed by Laurence Olivier] and I traveled across America with the director Elia Kazan, discussing the script and how it should be played. Kazan saw Blanche differently from me; he was irritated by her. I could not share his view, and I knew how it should be played after 9 months on the stage. I did it my way, and Kazan and I were finally in complete agreement. It took 3 months to make the film, and I loved every second. I couldn't wait to get to the studio every morning and I hated to leave every night. The script stayed exactly as it had been written without changes, and everyone knew it and wanted to help. Right down to the prop man who used to say to me, "What sort of things do you think Blanche would have on her table next to her bed?" . . . Brando was rather strange at first. I thought he was terribly affected. He used to say to me, "Why are you so damned polite? Why do you have to say good morning to everyone?" and I'd say, "Because it is a good morning and anyway it is a nice thing to say, so why not?" . . .

I got to understand him much better as we went on with the filming. He is such a good actor and when he wants to he can speak excellent English without a mumble. He is the only man I have ever met who can imitate Larry [Olivier] accurately. Larry is awfully difficult to imitate. Brando used to do speeches from *Henry V* and I closed my eyes and it could have been Larry.

Brando also has a nice singing voice; he sang folk songs to us beautifully.
——Leigh, interviewed for *The Daily Express*, 16 Aug 60

Margaret L E I G H T O N   (1922–1976)
Born near Birmingham, England, where she began her theater career at the age of 15.

Joe [Losey] was marvelous to me during [*The Go-Between*, 1971] because I had a bad arm and a bad leg. I was lame and halt half the time. But he never minded. I had never acted a Pinter script before, and I had to learn never to get one word wrong. Every word had a meaning. And this is what made it interesting where other films are not. The precision of the script. It had to be accurate.
——Leighton, interviewed for *The Evening Standard*, 27 Aug 71

Mitchell L E I S E N   (1898–1972)
Born in Menominee, Michigan. Began his film career as a costume designer and set decorator with C. B. De Mille. He worked for De Mille on almost 30 productions from 1919 to 1932 and directed his first film in 1933.

The shot where Douglas [Fairbanks] and Julanne Johnstone rode through the air [*The Thief of Bagdad*, 1924] was not a trick shot at all. The carpet was on top of a big steel plate suspended 30 feet off the ground by 4 piano wires. There were 3,000 people below, and Doug and Julanne were really riding the thing; we didn't use doubles. To make the carpet fly, the boom just swung across the set and the camera was right behind on the same boom, getting it all. Four piano wires, that was all!

The effect of Death being transparent [in *Death Takes a Holiday*, 1933] was very difficult to do because we wanted to do it right in the camera instead of having the lab put it in, and we had to keep him within 2 or 3 feet of Sir Guy Standing, who had to remain solid. We duplicated certain pieces of the set in black velvet. Then we put a mirror in front of Freddy [March] that was only 30 percent silvered so that you could shoot through it. In order to make him transparent, we simply lit up certain portions of the black set which reflected in the mirror superimposed over Freddy, giving the appearance that he was transparent. Shooting through the mirror had a tendency to make a slightly soft focus, but soft focus was considered very artistic at the time.

The costume was many layers of chiffon from charcoal gray to black. His face was made up like a skull, and there were tiny lights under the hood to light up the face. The shadows hovering over the ears were printed in by the Special Effects Department.

It was very difficult working with Technicolor [*Frenchman's Creek*, 1944] because you didn't get color rushes and you never knew what the colors would be. They sent 3 frames of each take in color and that was projected along the side while the film ran in black and white. We cut it in black and white, and then Technicolor made the first color answer print. The color would be way off, and then you'd start fighting them, sending the scene back over and over until they finally balanced it in the printing.

————Leisen, quoted in *Hollywood Director* (NY, 1973)

Richard L E I T E R M A N
Born in 1935.

I think these are the key words in the kind of shooting we were doing [*A Married Couple*, 1969]: "Will it develop into anything?" and secondly, "Can you possibly use it for a cutaway, or maybe just a silent music-over sequence?" Are they doing something alone which can be used to show something significant about their joint lives; or can it be used as just a simple little sequence by itself of something beautiful and softening. So you take it from there. . . . It's a matter of anticipating a movement, anticipating what's going to come next, where your dialogue might come from. . . . But it's hard because you're not ready most of the time. You just try to outguess them, or first-guess them. . . .

During the first few weeks, Allan [King] was around the house quite a bit, and he would sometimes go down to the office and screen the previous day's rushes. When he was actually in the house, just sitting in the living room or dining room trying to be inconspicuous, it became very difficult for him because he was just sitting there; he had nothing to hide behind—he wasn't doing anything. He couldn't make himself useful in any way and was just an extra person. Chris [Wangler the sound man] . . . could sneak behind his Nagra or fiddle with it; . . . I was behind my camera, . . . but Allan's presence was a bit inhibiting to Billy and Antoinette because he had nothing to do except just be there, kind of observing. And because he had nothing to do, he was more liable to be brought in or looked at in a way that asked, "Are we doing the right thing now?"

————Leiterman, interviewed for *The New Documentary in Action* (Berkeley, 1971)

In retrospect, was it a good working arrangement?

Oh, absolutely. Absolutely. Otherwise we'd get caught. They'd be looking to us for some kind of reaction. They'd be playing more to us. They might say —you know, after the first day, or something—they'd say, "Well, how did it go?" And I might have said, "Well, we could do with a little more from you." And then we would find that there'd be some playing. And it was hard enough in the first little while to stop them from playing up to the camera. Any closer relationship would not have been good. Unlike a lot of cinéma vérité, or portraits of people. Mailer, in the film we did on Mailer a few years ago, for example, was one where we tried to get closer to him by being friendly, by talking to him, by drinking with him, and by whatever.

Did that work out?

Oh, yeah. In that case it certainly did. Each thing has to be looked at in a different way as to what you want. Had we not said anything to Mailer, we would have got nothing from Mailer. But first of all, we had to be taken into his confidence, more or less. We had to be sure that we were going to do the right thing, and that he was going to be portrayed in the right way. And it was more of a case of—except when we were actually shooting a sequence, or an incident—of being friends. We were friends, and could talk.

——Leiterman, interviewed for *Cinema Canada*, Mar 72

Claude L E L O U C H
Born in Paris in 1937. Amateur filmmaker from the age of 13. Professional from 1956.

Never will I make a picture with more than a 6-man crew. I don't want all those people around my stage. I want to be alone with my actors. For *A Man and A Woman* [1966] I paid 11 people just to stay home and do nothing, because the unions demanded it, and those I had left I kept hidden so as not to interfere. With too many people around, it becomes cinema, not life.

For example, when I signed Anouk Aimée and Jean-Louis Trintignant for my film, I didn't tell them what it would be about, I simply asked them whether they wanted to work with me and then, when they said yes, we talked about price. That's all. Then I kept them, actors and crew, working sometimes 15 hours a day, because once you've got life going, you don't want to stop.

Before each scene I would take each actor aside and tell him what he was supposed to say, but I wouldn't tell him what the other person would say. Thus it was like a real conversation—like you and I now, neither one of us knowing what the other will say next. If we needed a second take, I would change the dialogue completely.

——Lelouch, interviewed for *Variety*, 13 July 66

Jack L E M M O N
Born in Boston, 1925.

Billy Wilder is demanding to this extent: he's very easy and he's an undidactic director. Many directors are what we would call strong directors and there is a lot of hollering and definite "I want this" and "It's *got* to be that" and so forth . . . to me that shows a sign of insecurity. Billy will take all the time in the world; he is terribly aware of actors and their problems and completely understanding. He doesn't mind how long it takes you to get what he wants, but he will not settle for less, which I think is wonderful. And he's quite willing to let an actor take all the time in the world until he feels right, let him try anything under the sun, any kind of different ideas or anything else, and very often he'll use those ideas.

He doesn't impose his own thoughts of what the scene should be even though he wrote it. As a director he will never impose the content of a scene on an actor's performance before the actor has also brought what he can bring to it.

——Lemmon, interviewed for *Films & Filming*, Nov 60

If I'm attracted to a part and it's really worthwhile, I don't know how to play it while I'm reading the script. If you know how to play it immediately, then either you've done it before or else it's rather shallow. The deeper and the more there is, then the more you have to dig in a part, and it seems like there's an acre between each line. What it really boils down to is selectivity, because there may be 20 or 30 different ways you can play a character at any given moment in a scene, but one or 2 of those will be much more exciting and legitimate.

So that's the "delicious hell" as I call it—digging in a character to figure out who he is and *why*. It really isn't what he says or does, but *why* does he behave that way? Once you know that, then you know the character. And in knowing him there is no one way he'll walk, no one way he'll do anything—all of that is just surface; you can make him behave the way you want to once you understand the mind, how he thinks and why he thinks that way, what has conditioned him, what is his background, everything. It's more or less drudgery, it really is hell, researching in your own mind, going back and digging, figuring the character out. Very often you have to make things up for yourself, just to feel complete.

I've seen Billy Wilder take suggestions from a prop man, and I don't know a stronger director than Billy as far as being very definite about what he wants, especially since he's also the author. But he'll listen and let you try. That's the important thing, to at least let others try their ideas, and then say no or yes.

——Lemmon, interviewed for *Film Comment*, May–June 73

Mervyn LEROY
Born in San Francisco in 1900. After being director, became a producer.

I believe in good scripts—I never start until I have the first and last page. And I always tried to help young players—Clark Gable would have been in *Little Caesar*, but front office thought his ears were too big.

It was difficult to find directors who could do fairy story fantasy. Victor Fleming, who gets final credit [for *The Wizard of Oz*, which LeRoy produced, 1939], was the third director I hired.

——LeRoy interviewed for *The Scotsman*, 27 Oct 70

I had heard that [John Ford] was ill, which was why Warner and Hayward had to make a change [of director on *Mister Roberts*, 1955]. They called me that Sunday morning, and then they came over to see me and brought the shooting script. They explained that Ford wouldn't be finishing the picture. Would I come in the next morning and take over? I said I would, and I stayed up all night to read both the script and the original stage play, which I had seen twice.

When I got to the studio the next day, it was rough. Right away, there was a big scene. I looked at the rushes Ford had shot, and decided on a few different approaches. The original play, as I had seen it in New York and read it the night before, was far superior to the script Ford had been using. I called the actors together and said we were throwing away the screenplay and going back to the Broadway play. Leland Hayward and Jack Warner went along with me.

The character William Powell was playing, Doc, had been changed by Ford. He had made him a drunk. I made him sober, as he had been in the original play. There was a fine cast already assembled. . . . They all pitched in to help. It is never easy for a director to step into a partially finished film, but this one was particularly rough because of the short notice they had given me. . . . I would estimate that I shot 90 percent of the finished product. I insisted, however, that the credits read: "directed by John Ford and Mervyn LeRoy."

——LeRoy, interviewed for . . . *The Fabulous Fondas* (NY, 1976)

Richard L E S T E R
Born in Philadelphia, 1932. Came to films from television work in U.S.A. and England.

I never direct an actor by *showing* him what to do, not being an actor myself, but I try to lead him into creating my own idea of a character without being too specific. The Beatles were very carefully manipulated in their 2 films because they had no acting experience. None of them had more than one line at a time. I do very little rehearsal—never before we get to the spot and never before the actual take. I merely see that the actors know what they say and where they are. This is because something exciting and unexpected may happen at any time and I don't want to lose it. I'm always prepared for the happy accident. It's for this reason I always leave blank spaces in my otherwise fairly complete scripts—room for improvisation. For instance, the moving bed sequence in *The Knack* [1965] was described in a couple of lines only: "The bed goes through a car wash" or "down the river." Everything else was ad lib.

——Lester, interviewed for *The Making of Feature Films* (London, 1971)

. . . If you take the *Hard Day's Night* [1964] field sequence, it had to be the result of a buildup of scenes which were constructed to create claustrophobia; scenes in trains, in cars, surrounded by people, which was very much like the life of the boys at that time, and then in the field sequence, I tried to get an explosive breakout . . . of freedom in space. It said in the script, "The boys go through a door and play about in a field." Then I shot it on 3 successive days— no, 3 days over 3 weeks in 3 different places. There was nothing planned. There was nothing specifically scripted. I went up in a helicopter after 3 sentences to the boys—"You can do this, this, or this; in any order you like. We'll find you. Just keep going," until they dropped.

——Lester, interviewed for *Directors at Work* (NY, 1970)

Joseph E. LEVINE
Born in Boston, 1905.

Any commodity has to be sold. You don't back a cigarette without making that cigarette available to as many people as possible without staging a big campaign.

Films are no different. Just a different merchandise. Possibly there are some pictures which don't need help, but I don't believe it. I invented the slogan "Wherever you are, you won't be far from *Hercules Unchained.*" That sums up the whole thing.

Get the picture into as many cinemas as possible in as short a time as possible, and spend as much money as possible in as many advertising media as possible. That's the method!

I've written a lot of my own ad copy. See, I bought this picture *Ravaged Earth* made by a Shanghai businessman [*Fight to the Last* (?), 1938(?)]. "See it!" I wrote. "It will make you fighting mad! Jap Rats stop at nothing! See the Rape of China!"

About my method. You can't do it with every picture. No, sir. You can't do it with *Sodom and Gomorrah* [1962] which I've just produced in Italy. I had artistic control on that picture. The cost of *Sodom and Gomorrah* is so great—$6,000,000 already—it wouldn't be economically feasible to use saturation tactics.

Up to now I've been trying to inject spectacle and adventure into my pictures. Color! Scope! That's what the public wants. But don't get me wrong. I've handled so-called Art films all my life. I distributed *Bicycle Thieves* [1948], one of the greatest pictures ever made. It didn't make me rich. But I enjoyed it!

See, the public's taste is changing all the time. I'm going to produce 6 pictures a year. I want to get into this so-called Art thing, see.

—Levine, interviewed for *The Daily Mail*, 31 July 61

Albert LEWIN (1902–1968)
Born in New York City. Studied at New York and Harvard Universities. Taught English at Missouri University. Began in films as reader for Samuel Goldwyn.

I wanted to get some experience in the cutting room. I didn't even ask for that job. The cutters were all my friends. I just went to work and didn't tell anybody. It was about 6 months before anyone found out. I was still on the payroll as a script clerk, but I cut and patched film with a razor blade the way they used to do it. I learned, and to this day, I'm a hell of a good cutter. I admit it. I know how to edit films from practical experience. It's tremendously important. And I think it important that you know what to do with a film that's been shot.

Irving [Thalberg] was also a great editor. He was a perfectionist. If we had an extremely successful preview, as we often did in those days, most people would pat themselves on the back and be awfully satisfied. He would tear the picture apart and improve it. He would push and push to get the very last bit of excellence into a production. After you've seen a picture with an audience, it's amazing what you can do. Sometimes three or four days of re-takes will improve a picture enormously, and Irving never hesitated to spend the extra money. His successors were not like that.

I wanted to direct, so I went back to Metro. I directed *Dorian Gray* [1945] for them, which didn't make anybody rich. It cost $1.8 million. It grossed $3 million, got some Academy Award nominations, and won an Oscar or two. Since I had done *The Moon and Sixpence* [1942] fast and cheap, Metro had the feeling that when I was spending their money, I did it slow and dear. It looked that way. But *The Moon and Sixpence* had a slashing dramatic design and the detail was less important, whereas *Dorian Gray* was merely a story of an exquisite character, and I got involved with making the picture exquisite. I really went to town on every set-up. When you have 2,000 setups in a picture, it can take rather long. I was even careful about the table linen and the cutlery and whatever was on the wall. All the upholstery was built for me. I decided that everything was going to be black and white because of the good and evil symbolism.

——Lewin, interviewed for *The Real Tinsel* (NY, 1970)

Jerry L E W I S [Levitch]
Born in Newark, New Jersey in 1926.

There is a classic tradition in speechmaking which has a direct relationship to comedy. It is known as the rhetoric structure: Tell the audience you are going to do something; do it; and then let them know it is done. The rule applies to comedy.

A comedian is walking boldly across a field. We see him in a knee shot, cockier than ever, but don't orient the audience to the fact that he's walking into an excavation. Dropping back to a wider shot, we see he's looking around and that his left foot is over the hole. Then to a closer cut, and he's yelling, "Ooooooh-whunk!" But until we see him flat on his ass in the excavation, the scene isn't resolved. . . .

So the basis of all the countless variations of visual jokes is the banana peel. If the audience is not told it is there, they are busy trying to figure out what happened as the comic reacts. The thought cannot be put in their minds at the point the laughter should prevail. If they have to say, or think, "Oh, it was a banana," the laugh is gone. They must laugh as the backside hits the pavement.

It is as important to punctuate a joke as it is to punctuate a point in drama or suspense. Use of the various lenses in comedy is just as necessary as it is in high drama. The same problems and benefits of camera movement apply to both. Dramatic sequences in comedy build specifically toward the punctuation of the comedy. . . .

In each film I attempt to apply substance to The Idiot's character some-where, sometime. The serious side of his character development cannot take place early in the film. Audiences will not accept it. But once The Idiot has made them laugh, once he is communicating clearly with them on the level of laughter, he can develop substance. Audiences then not only accept it but want it. They want him to be a little more than an idiot because in some of his entanglements he strikes awfully close to home. . . .

————Lewis, in his *The Total Film-Maker* (NY, 1971)

Robert LEWIS

Chaplin, as a director, is superb. He only talked to me about the *interpretation* of my character as M. Verdoux's friend, Maurice, the village apothecary. "He's the kind of bore who lectures when he talks," Charlie might say, never once "Say it like this" or "Go faster or slower" or any of the kind of external manipulating to which actors are often submitted.

Not that his directing technique is always the same. I have seen him with an amateur give every move and inflection because he had chosen the person not for his acting ability but because of a certain quality that Chaplin needed for that moment. He knows that the quickest way to get his result in this case is through imitation. Watching him direct a five-year-old child, I realized why *The Kid* was so wonderful. He makes the whole thing a game for the child, popping out from behind the camera and indulging in all sorts of shenanigans to keep the child's reactions spontaneous.

————Lewis, in *Theatre Arts Monthly*, June 47

Val LEWTON [Vladimir Leventon] (1904–1951)
Born in Yalta, in the Crimea; family emigrated to the U.S. in 1909. His mother and he worked in the story department of M-G-M's New York office. As a producer, established an original form of horror film at RKO.

Our formula is simple. A love story, three scenes of suggested horror and one of actual violence. Fadeout. It's all over in less than 70 minutes. We tossed away the horror formula right from the beginning. No grisly stuff for us. No masklike faces hardly human, with gnashing teeth and hair standing on end. No creaking physical manifestations. No horror piled on horror. You can't keep up horror that's long sustained. It becomes something to laugh at. But take a sweet love story, or a story of sexual antagonisms, about people like the rest of us, not freaks, and cut in your horror here and there by suggestion, and you've got something. Anyhow, we think you have. That's the way we try to do it.

————Lewton, interviewed for *The Los Angeles Times;* quoted in Joel Siegel's *Val Lewton* (NY, 1973)

Harold LLOYD (1893–1971)
Born in Nebraska, the dream of acting filled his childhood and youth, and it was inevitable that he would find some sort of work, any work in the mushrooming studios of prewar Hollywood. He and Hal Roach worked as extra players before trying to sell comedy ideas (and themselves as comedians) to the Keystone and Essanay companies. At Pathé they devised a series based on a character called "Lonesome Luke" (played by Lloyd and directed by Roach);

by 1917 Lloyd felt the character was too dependent on Chaplin's ideas and that Luke was too unreal.

I wanted to make comedies where people would see themselves and their neighbors. It was then that I hit on the straight make-up with the glasses. . . .

I had to direct the first few glass-character pictures myself. I didn't intend to. I didn't even intend to do the first one [*Over the Fence*, 1917]. I hired a director for it—J. Farrell MacDonald, who had directed pictures Roach and I were extras on. He had never directed comedy. He would say, "Harold, how do you want this scene?" I had to tell him exactly how the scene should go, and he would go in and tell the people. . . .

As a rule, when I put on the glasses, I never did anything you couldn't believe in. It may be a little improbable, but you could figure it could happen. In *Get Out and Get Under* [1920], I did something I very seldom did, but it was quite funny.

I was fixing my Ford, and I had the hood up. I had my head inside, then my shoulders went in, then half of me was in the car, and pretty soon my feet disappeared inside the engine. We were treating the picture as a satire. In those days, you felt the Model T could run without anything. . . .

When Hal and I started, we had to think up our own gags. When Hal went off to direct Toto, and I started my first picture with glasses, I had to think up all the gags myself. As the pictures began to make money, I hired as many idea men as I could get that I thought were good. . . .

Sometimes I felt fit to send them out alone, to work by themselves, or in pairs. Or divide them up, and let them work that way. You have a scene—say it's the magician's coat in *Movie Crazy* [1932]. We're starting to build that, and we've arrived at the point where I am to dance with the wife of an important personage. It is vital that I make a good impression. Of course, I don't know that I have a magician's coat on, full of white mice and doves, nor does she. So how are we going to fill that out? I send the boys out to work on ideas. . . .

We had no script, but we made minute notes of the particular sequence that we were going to shoot. We would even suspend work for three or four days to work out exactly what we wanted. But when we finished shooting, the result might be completely different from our original idea. . . . This way we built as we went along, like building a house. Building was of great importance.

We'd have a certain number of pieces of business, gags, that we knew we were going to do. They were called "islands." We knew we had to go there. But whatever we did between those was up to us. We would ad lib, and make it up as we went along.

. . . Generally, the takes we kept building turned out to be the best. You may start with only one or two little ideas. By the time you finished, you had ten ideas in the scene, none of which you had even conceived in the gag room.

———Lloyd, in interviews (1963–64) for *The Parade's Gone By* (NY, 1968)

. . . In the first place, we used 4 buildings [for *Safety Last*, 1923]. We picked out a structure we wanted for the actual building, then we chose a two story, four story, or whatever height building we needed. Then we built our own sets on top of them.

We started the film with a one-story building and built our set right on the edge of the real building's roof. We built it so that we could put platforms out and constructed the scaffolding on the side so that the cameraman could be up there and shoot down. I remember how we had to put the platform low enough and narrow enough so that the cameraman could miss it when he was shooting down at an angle.

The platform would be 14 feet or so below us. From above it looked no bigger than a postage stamp! It was loaded with mattresses in order to break our fall if we did slip as we went through our antics. We didn't want to commit suicide just to make somebody laugh. But we were always in danger despite this precaution. Falling even a short distance was no small matter. Besides, we could easily roll off the platform because it didn't have any railings around it.

In those days, we didn't want to divulge how we performed our stunts. We didn't want to give away any of our techniques for fear of making the public disillusioned with the thrill of it all. Looking back, it seems strange that we would have this worry, for the thrills were far from artificial. The danger, while not as great as it might appear to the public, was nevertheless still very real.

———Lloyd, in *Harold Lloyd's World of Comedy* (NY, 1964)

Barbara L O D E N
Born in Marion, North Carolina in 1937. As an actress, she has worked exten-sively in the theater and her films include Wild River [1960] *and* Splendor in the Grass [1961]. *In 1970, she directed her first film:*

At that time, when I was hawking the script [of *Wanda*, 1970] around I was seeing a lot of movies that were simply manipulating audiences. Saying "here you should think this or that; now weep, now laugh." I've no real filmic sense, but I didn't think that would be good enough. Maybe *Breathless* [1959] in-spired me, and perhaps Zola. Whatever it was I gradually reckoned that I'd better make the damned thing myself.

Harry Schuster, a producer friend of mine, eventually lent me enough money to make it very cheaply, so we got a non-union crew together—very small and everybody was doubling up jobs—and went off to Carbondale, Penn-sylvania, a little strip-mining township. Michael Higgins and I were the only two professionals in the cast. The rest were Carbondale people we'd persuaded. It took 10 weeks and nearly killed me. But we made it in the end.

———Loden, interviewed for *The Guardian*, 9 Dec 70

Joshua L O G A N
Born 1908.

[*Bus Stop*, 1956] took about three months to shoot. But we had a couple of months of preparation in Hollywood before going on location. The costume designer came with sketches and Marilyn and I both felt they were too fancy, not right for the pitiful comic character she was playing. She said the only thing you have to do around Hollywood is go to the wardrobe department, find some old things and put them on. That's what she did. I said, "Well you've got to have some kind of a coat but it's got to be thin enough that it won't protect you from the cold so that Don Murray can offer you his big, woolly cowboy coat, in a sense like Sir Walter Raleigh being very much the gentleman, which is what he is at the end of the picture." So we found a threadbare, old, wrinkled green-gold lamé coat which was as sad as could be, put some terrible little rabbit fur around the edge of it, and that was her main costume in the film. She had extraordinary taste. She knew exactly what this girl should wear and what she shouldn't. And Milton Greene had worked out a fantastic make-up for her because he had a feeling that she had always been too honey-colored and it didn't suit the character at all. This little nightclub singer, Cherie, stayed up all night singing and drinking with the cowboy and went to bed probably at six or seven—never saw the sun. So Milton had a very pale, pearly makeup arranged for her which I thought was just marvelous. It was not only beautiful, charming and sweet but also it wasn't slick, it was sort of clownlike which gave her performance a little more pitiful look—just that little white face. Marilyn was excited by it and by the costumes. . . .

. . . For the last scene in the film, I had been in the bus stop such a long time, that I wanted to have some visual effect that would give the ending a little extra. I had been asking my cameraman, Milton Krasner, if we couldn't get even closer to Marilyn. We'd only been able to be about as close as 8 feet. We were shooting in Cinemascope and Cinemascope is long and there were no lenses that could get very, very close. Yet I had seen one shot in a Disney picture, 20,000 *Leagues Under the Sea* [1954], where all I saw was James Mason's eye. "Well what about that, how did they get that? There must have been some lens." After a lot of talk and a lot of argument, they finally came up with what they called a diminishing lens or a series of diminishing lenses. And for the first time in Cinemascope we were going to get the kind of big head closeups that I used to see of Greta Garbo and Dietrich in the old shape. Marilyn was *thrilled*—anything new, anything different just pleased her to death. It was Marilyn Monroe's production so she was proud of it. Well, first we lined up on Don Murray because it wasn't quite as wrong if his head was distorted by being so close. It was only about 4 or 5 feet from Don's face and Paul, the operator, was looking through and he didn't want to make a mistake. It was all a big thing. The whole front office had heard about it. It was enor-mous. Marilyn was dancing around happy as she could be. The first decision about whether or not it was going to work was up to Paul and he leaned over and said, "I can't see the top of his head." And Marilyn said, "Well everyone knows he's got one. It's been established." We burst out laughing. It was a wonderful remark.

——Logan, in *Show*, Sept. 72

. . . [In filming *South Pacific*, 1958] the dialogue should increase in emotion, and in height, until there's a feeling that the moment has come when there's nothing else to do but sing. In addition to that, the preparatory music leading towards the song would start so far back during the dialogue that the audience does not really expect a song until that song takes place; but at that moment, they welcome it and feel that it is right for the character who has been speaking to progress into song. And the color goes with this. I always thought that, just as we dimmed our lights down on the stage for a song, we could also do a similar thing on the screen. Because we did have strange purples and deep orange tones in the shadows of the stage, when the spotlight is on the face of the singer while the background changes its color. Nobody has ever objected to that in the theater, but they did object to it on film in the case of *South Pacific* because they just had it fixed in their heads that film was a realistic medium.

—Logan, interviewed for *Films & Filming*, Dec 69

Gina LOLLOBRIGIDA
Born in Subiaco, Italy, 1927.

I love working with Vittorio De Sica. He is a wonderful person and we are also very much alike in temperament. We were both born in the same district—in neighboring small towns not far from Rome—and we think the same way. Often he doesn't need to tell me what to do. I know instinctively what is in his mind. Also he is an actor so he can show you exactly what he wants. It makes acting easy: all you have to do is to copy him. He could make a dog act.

Now, Soldati is different; he is a good director but a bad actor. If he shows you what he wants it is important not to look, only listen. His acting is terrible, and if you did the same the effect would be quite wrong. . . .

The kind of partner one has on the screen is of the utmost importance. Good actors are very generous; they help by taking part in a scene, and emoting even if their faces are away from the camera. . . . The two partners I like best are Mastroianni and Sir Ralph Richardson. Oh, that Sir Ralph. He is marvelous. His voice is so rich and he is a great actor and very generous. He is simple, modest and extremely thoughtful. . . .

I made my first Hollywood film with [Frank Sinatra] and it was disastrous because my English was not good then. When I am acting in Italian I can improvise, but in another language I must learn my lines so well that I can forget the words. In this film it was impossible. Every night they rewrote the script so it was impossible to learn by heart and Sinatra, too, was liable to put in his own words. I made mistake after mistake, and there was always several takes for every scene. Sinatra was very kind and never said anything, but I could tell he was annoyed and irritated, though he did his best not to show it. The strain on me was so great that when the film was finished I had a nervous breakdown.

—Lollobrigida, interviewed for *The Times;* repr.
in *The Globe & Mail* (Toronto), 3 June 67

Anita LOOS
Born in 1893 in Sisson, California. Daughter of a San Francisco theater owner, her first scenarios were written for the Biograph Company, and when she visited the company during their last California winter, her acquaintance with D. W. Griffith led him to absorb her into his more ambitious production plans.

I worked in the scenario department. I *was* the scenario department. There was nobody else on the lot who was writing. Fine-Arts used to buy scenarios, and I think there were 2 or 3 writers who sent things in rather regularly, but I don't remember anyone being right there on the lot but me. . . .

I would sit on set during rehearsals, and if one particular actor showed special talent, I could put something in for him . . . I'd be there during shooting and I'd be around at the cutting stage, putting in the titles. . . .

It was all very easy in those days. We had so much fun that I don't really remember when the work got done.

——Loos, letter to Kevin Brownlow (1964) for
The Parade's Gone By (NY, 1968)

I knew exactly it wasn't my cup of tea to write a soap opera [*The Struggle,* 1931]. I tried to make him put Jimmy Durante in the lead and make a comedy of it. He considered that for quite a while and then decided I was wrong and went on and made it as he first conceived it. Well, it was a debacle—a terrible movie. The movies had gone far beyond Griffith and he had taken to drinking and I think his talent had dissipated through alcoholism.

——Loos, interviewed for *Take One,* Sep–Oct 73

. . . In *San Francisco* [1936] there was a scene where Clark Gable hauled off and socked a priest, played by Spencer Tracy. The Johnson Office said you cannot have Clark Gable sock a priest, it's unthinkable. So I went away and got to pondering about how I could fix the scene. So I decided to show at the beginning that the priest could floor Gable any time he wanted to, that he was a much cleverer boxer than Gable. That proved that when Clark hit him, he (Tracy) could have killed Clark, but he didn't do it, which made his character stronger as a priest, and it was accepted by the censor. In order to prove this situation, I opened the picture with a scene of two men boxing and you saw Spencer Tracy sock Gable and knock him out. And then when they got dressed you saw that one of them was a priest. That scene wouldn't have been there if I hadn't had to outsmart the censor.

Q. When you subtitled *Intolerance* [1916], did you know what D. W. Griffith's conception was?

A. I didn't know what it was about. When I saw it, it rather startled me. I was terribly confused by it. I must have run it 50 times while I was writing the titles. By the time I finished the titles I had a feeling of what he was trying to do. When it was completed I had a great admiration for him.

——Loos, interviewed for *Film Fan Monthly,* March 67

Sophia L O R E N [Scicolone]
Born 1934 in Rome.

. . . I hate to hear actors say things like "When I play a king, I become a king," because to me this is really phony talk. You feel what the character you play feels, but not completely. You never lose control. When you kiss on the screen, you don't really kiss.

I am good-natured when I work, and I do not mind working very hard. I do a lot of dubbing for my pictures. For example, I dubbed my own English for *Two Women* [1961], which was made in Italian. When you dub, you do not have as much feeling as you had when the movie was originally shot, and it is hard work. After I have been dubbing, I eat and then go to bed right away, because it is so tiring. I never rehearse a part in front of a mirror. It is phony, I think, to do that. I want to get it the way it should be when I am on the set, in front of the camera. Before I start to work on a part, I read the script, but when shooting starts, I like improvisation right on the set. Even when I'm not consciously thinking about a part, I'm really thinking about it all the time. When I get to the set, I sometimes know suddenly what I will do. I didn't rehearse at all for *Two Women*.

—Loren, interviewed for *The Player* (NY, 1962)

Peter L O R R E (1904–1964)
Born in Rosenberg, Hungary. Best known theater work in Berlin, with Brecht.

It just so happened that one night—I was what you would call a very hot star on the stage in Berlin at that time—a man named Fritz Lang, a director, came to see me and said, "If you wait for my first talkie, you'll do the first talkie." He didn't know what at that time, and personally I didn't think that my puss could be photographed. I thought the longer the better. In the meantime, the Dusseldorf murders happened, and I made the picture *M* [1931] for him.

Q. Did that call you to America? Was *M* the only picture you made in Europe?

No, the funny thing is I went back to the stage. I had Hollywood offers but it didn't mean anything to me at the time, because you're very locked in if you're on the stage and you don't think anything else is important . . . that's how it should be. Actually, Hitler chased me out. I got away 3 days before the Reichstag sprung.

[*The Maltese Falcon*, 1941] was one of my happiest memories, a very nostalgic one, because for a few years we had a sort of stock company, an ensemble there [at Warner Brothers]. We were a ball team.

. . . Each one of those people, Claude Rains, Greenstreet, Bogart and so on, there is one quality in common, that is quite a hard quality to come by, it's something you can't teach, and that is to switch an audience from laughter to seriousness. We can do it at will, most people can't.

—Lorre, interviewed for "Assignment," CBC, 29–31 May 62

Joseph L O S E Y
Born 1909 in LaCrosse, Wisconsin. Work in the New York theater and in short films led to his first long film.

I was petrified. [Dore] Schary, to my eternal gratitude, called me up to his office the day before we started shooting [*The Boy with Green Hair*, 1948]. I told him I was absolutely petrified and didn't know what I was doing. He said, "Look, whatever your opening shot is, take as long as you like, take all day if you like lining it up, or take half an hour, get it right as far as you can, or don't get it right, it doesn't matter. But when you shoot it, say 'Print' on the first take. I guarantee if it's not right we'll do it again. But if you print your first take on your first shot on your first picture, everyone will think you know what you're doing." I did just that, and he was right—it made an enormous difference to that picture and every other one I've made. I still do it sometimes when I don't know what I'm doing, it makes quite an incalculable difference to the morale of the crew. This is one of the great burdens of filming: you have all those people round you who are great in their own jobs and who have to believe you know what you are doing.

The soundtrack of *Accident* [1967] is an exceptionally good one. . . . However, I feel the sound of the car is a failure. . . . Harold Pinter and I planned to sustain the crescendo of the car over a longer period of time than a film sound track can accommodate. Ideally, if I had all the money in the world, I would have shot the opening sequence with a helicopter a little ahead of it and not much above it, and then have lost the car and come down into a static position on the house just before the crash is heard. That way there would have been an increasing excitement and crescendo, which I don't think sound alone can do because both the decibel range and the reproduction range are too limited. Anyway, we had to cheat a bit on the car. We used a high-powered sports car rather than a vintage high-powered one—technicians will recognize the difference, but the real thing simply didn't work at all.

The sound track is precisely the same at the end as at the beginning, and it was started over the cloister. In fact I took the music and the bells out over the cloister completely, so there would be no doubt in anybody's mind that this was not intended as a realistic effect. How could there be the sound of an approaching car about to crash over an evening cloister in Oxford, which then crashes in the afternoon by a countryhouse? I also thought the two tracks would be recognized as identical. Obviously I overestimated what people remember of soundtracks and what the ear absorbs when they are also seeing something visual and are not particularly concentrating on it.

. . . I know very well that as soon as a print gets a little bit old and brittle, or conversely if a film is "green" and not sufficiently used or if there is any inaccuracy in threading a print, you will get a quaver or wow in the sound. Therefore it is extremely dangerous to use string instruments, to use even a solo piano or a solo violin, or a reed instrument. For *Accident* I wanted very much—and I am sure it was right for this picture—to use 2 harps. They are fairly safe because they're slightly untrue. But I wanted against this agony and wail of the saxophone, which John Dankworth played himself—and by the way the score was mostly improvised though carefully prepared. John and I talked about it, and the exact combination which finally emerged was his. I had originally suggested it should maybe be only one instrument or two: I was afraid we might be running a risk with the saxophone. He said no. Well, 90 percent of the times I have seen *Accident* projected, the score has had a wow; in other words it's gone flat, it's gone sharp, and it drives me out of my mind, though most of the people probably don't notice. I'm never going to make this mistake again; I'm never going to make this sound mistake either. If I want to do this kind of sustained crescendo sound effect, then I will have to find some way of complementing it in terms of image without destroying the plan of what I'm doing. When I told you how I would have shot it if I had the money, this is an after-thought. But with the helicopter I could have started before the titles and behind the titles, and still have managed to land the helicopter in position to get the static shot of the house; I wouldn't have been able to move in, excepting possibly with a zoom.

——Losey, interviewed for *Losey on Losey* (London, 1967)

On *M* [1950] . . . I was bound to the structure of the original picture and script because this was a condition made when the film was passed—I don't know whether it was then the Breen Office, or still the Hays Office, but they said they would pass *M* provided it was a remake of what they considered to be a classic, so there had to be a certain adherence to the original, although the intent and the point of my film was entirely different. I'd seen *M* [1931] in the early thirties; I saw it again, once, in a very bad copy, just before I made it. I never referred to it. I consciously repeated only one shot. There may have been unconscious repetitions, in terms of the atmosphere of certain sequences, but essentially Lang's villain was my hero.

——Losey, interviewed for *The Cinema of Joseph Losey* (London 1967)

Bannion [in *The Criminal*, 1960] was modeled after someone that I know who is very active in the so-called underworld. And a man who, if his life had taken another direction, could have been a great executive, could have done anything he wanted to, because he has brains, he has humor, he has power. . . . And this is what I tried to present in Bannion, that this is waste, that the prison system hasn't changed, that it doesn't help, that it is a reflection of the society outside, that it has its own organization, its own immediate parallels. It is at once more loyal, more sentimental, more violent, but it's the same thing and one creates the other.

——Losey, quoted in Sadoul-Morris, *Dictionary of Films*, p 38

I like to shoot in extreme long shot and extreme close-up and to avoid the medium shot wherever possible. I also like to avoid cutting except where cutting has its own particular stylistic value.

In *The Servant* [1963] there are a lot of sustained shots, shots that run up to 5 minutes without any intercutting at all. There's a great deal of camera movement—most of *The Servant* takes place in one house, but by no means all of it. In taking place in one house, obviously one is going up and down stairs and looking at things from different angles. But I don't think there are any angles for the sake of angles—the angles have some real motivation, as the movements have motivation, which I hope is often subtle enough to disguise the movement. . . .

I always do as much rehearsing as I can. It's usually very hard to get the money or to get the actors for it, but beginning with my very first film, *The Boy with Green Hair*, in Hollywood I rehearsed. On *The Prowler* [1951] I had a composite set which was built before we shot, I had floor plans all laid out on the stages before we shot and had a week of reading, then a week of rehearsals on the set with all the technicians. The result of that was that *The Prowler* was shot in 23 days. . . .

I'm much more concerned with how a set looks than I am with how it works. Obviously it has to work, too, but I never, or rarely, design a set for a particular shot. I'm more concerned to get the set right for the background for the screenplay and the actors, and then figure out how to make it work.

I think it's enormously valuable to use real locations wherever you can; to accept their limitations, excepting in instances where obviously you can build them much more easily and efficiently on the stage. But wherever I can shoot location I do. In *Eve* [1962], for instance, many of the interiors were location, in fact there were only two sets, all the rest was location. That is, I haven't been to see the version shown in England, so I don't know how much there is on the screen, but of what I shot there are only two.

———Losey, interviewed for *Films & Filming*, Oct 63

We shot *King and Country* [1964] in 18 days—that is, a working 3½ weeks. We had about 10 days' rehearsal beforehand—or rather, reading not rehearsing as we had no sets or anything. The whole project took an even 3 months from the go-ahead signal to the first print. I like to shoot fairly fast—most directors hate to get stuck on a long schedule—but I've never shot as fast as this. *The Prowler* was shot in 19 or 20 days, but then we'd rehearsed for several weeks with sets, cameramen and everything, and there was no limit to overtime in Hollywood in those days. *King and Country* wasn't an easy film to shoot. The set was a horror to get around, we all got stuck in the mud and after a week the smell was terrible: it was very hot, and we had those rats and the dead horse. . . . By the end of the film we hated it and each other, which may have got into the picture and helped the atmosphere. I learned a lot I didn't know before about the war. Did you know something like a quarter of a million men died by just disappearing into the mud? . . . We set it in Passchendaele, as I needed the mud as a unifying theme.

There isn't a single setup I shot for *King and Country* that isn't in the final picture. I myself cut 3 scenes out of *The Servant*: I was intimidated by people telling me the film would be too long, but now I rather regret it. I think it would have seemed shorter with the scenes in.

———Losey, interviewed for *The Sunday Times*, 29 Nov 64

The Burtons are petrified about starting a film. So am I. Elizabeth's experience in Hollywood has distorted her. She had a very rough time—unforgivable things were done to her under the studio system in those days. It has given her a deep-rooted mistrust of American directors.

"I'm not an American director," I told her, but it's no good. One has to wait till she gets over the suspicion. She'll make life hell as a way of testing you—it's a common thing with all the indestructible Hollywood stars. They want to find out your breaking point.

Elizabeth was belligerent towards me at the start of *Boom* [1968] in which she played Mrs. Goforth, the world's richest woman, dying in luxury and awaiting the Angel of Death, played by Burton, to release her from life. Unless she trusts her director completely, to film her is useless. She didn't know what I was doing and it was a struggle to simplify the conception of the part she plays. We toned down her makeup, simplified her hairstyle—it looks much better when she wears it down, not up on her head. All except in the death scene, where she is dressed overall in her jewels. We tried to eliminate color in *Boom*. "Wear one color," I said to Elizabeth. "I'll wear no color," she said, meaning an all-white costume, and thus improved on the idea 100 percent.

The toughest scene was the one where Mrs. Goforth is talking about her 6 husbands. Elizabeth fought me when shooting it. "I can't film that scene again," she said. "It's a funny scene, Elizabeth," I told her, "but not as you're playing it. You should be able to see the funny side of it." I made a bad mistake there. She looked up at me and she snapped, "I do not find such a life funny." We finally compromised. I played the scene and then she followed me—and she was wonderful. As she was throughout the whole picture. On *Secret Ceremony* [1968] she was so patient, generous, helpful to Mia Farrow. She consoled her over her marriage troubles and on the screen she is so unselfish that it almost hurts her own performance. Mia plays the girl in the film. When she was suggested for the part, I didn't go for the idea, I'd only seen her in *Peyton Place* [TV series, 1966–68], and frankly, thought she held nothing for me. . . .

——Losey, interviewed for *The Times*, 5 Sep 70

The events [of *The Go-Between*, 1971] aren't really seen through the boy's eyes, but through those of an old man recalling an adolescent experience. What we're trying to do in the film is to scramble the past and present and give the impression they're continuous. There's no artificial framework of Then and Now. The old man appears throughout the film in scattered, nonchronological cuts. You get old voices over shots of him in his youth; you get voices from the past over shots of the present day; you also get places that are seen in a neutral light so that you can't immediately tell whether they belong to past or present. I hope ultimately this will convey a sense of the wholeness of one life. I want to stress as well that the film won't be a piece of picturesque Edwardian nostalgia: it's a cruel, strong story with a sour, hard core. It won't be a pretty film, but it'll be a handsome film.

——Losey, interviewed for *The Times*, 5 Sep 70

Bessie L O V E [Juanita Horton]
Born 1898.

One of Mr. Griffith's directorial staff [at Triangle]—John O'Brien, Lloyd Ingraham, or Christy Cabanne, for instance—would rehearse the film, and Mr. Griffith himself would take the final run-through before shooting. And when he came along, of course, the whole production came to life. I know of no other studio in my experience where this method was employed.

——Love, interviewed for an unidentified English newspaper of 1956

Myrna L O Y [Williams]
Born 1902, in Helena, Montana.

One night, the director Edward Griffith saw me doing the usual half-caste in a film, and sent for me to take a test for Evie in an Ina Claire film called *Rebound* [1932]. I got the part. Evie was a little snob from the social register, but thank goodness, not a half-caste. I owe more to Griffith than all the others. I would never have been given my role in *Animal Kingdom* [1932] but for him, and it was that picture which proved to be the turning point in my career.

Rouben Mamoulian was another who helped me. I heard he wanted me for Maurice Chevalier's picture *Love Me Tonight* [1932]. It was a small part, but at least I was permitted to wear sensible modish clothes. It was my first comedy role. I was a personality not a type any longer.

——Loy, interviewed for *Leader Magazine*, 4 Dec 48

We made [*The Thin Man,* 1934] on a small budget and 21 days of shooting, but it was such a hit we went on for 10 years and made 5 sequels. . . . [Asta, the dog] was a wire-haired terrier, and they were not popular at all at the time. His name was really Skippy, and he was highly trained to do all his tricks for a little squeaky mouse and a biscuit. He'd do anything for that reward. But the minute his scenes were over, it was definitely verboten to hug him or have any further contact with him off the set.

[In *The Mask of Fu Manchu,* 1932] I carried around a pet python and whipped a young man tied to a rack and all sorts of dreadful things. Now I had been reading a little Freud around that time, so I called the director [Charles Brabin] over one day and said, "Say, this is obscene. This woman is a sadistic nymphomaniac!" And he said, "What does *that* mean? I mean, we did it all before these kids today ever thought of it, and we didn't even know what we were doing."

——Loy, interviewed for *The New York Times,* 13 Apr 69

Ernst L U B I T S C H   (1892–1947)
Born in Berlin.

[The late Victor Arnold was my teacher.] He had a great influence on my entire career and my future. Not only did he introduce me to Max Reinhardt, but also was responsible for my first success in pictures in getting me the part of the apprentice in *Die Firma Heiratet* [1914].

Although being starred in the next picture, *Der Stolz der Firma* [1914], and despite its success, my picture career came to a standstill. I was typed, and no one seemed to write any part which would have fitted me. After two successes, I found myself completely left out of pictures, and as I was unwilling to give up I found it necessary that I had to create parts for myself. Together with an actor friend of mine, the late Erich Schoenfelder, I wrote a series of one-reelers which I sold to the Union Company. I directed and starred in them. And that is how I became a director. If my acting career had progressed more smoothly, I wonder if I ever would have become a director.

Die Austernprinzessin [1919] was my first comedy which showed something of a definite style. I remember a piece of business which caused a lot of comment at the time. A poor man had to wait in the magnificent entrance hall of the home of a multimillionaire. The parquet floor of the multimillionaire's home was of a most complicated design. The poor man in order to overcome his impatience and his humiliation after having waited for hours walked along the outlines of the very intricate pattern on the floor. It is very difficult to describe this nuance and I don't know if I succeeded, but it was the first time I turned from comedy to satire.

In a completely different style was *Die Puppe* [1919]. It was, like *Die Austernprinzessin*, a great success from every angle. It was pure fantasy; most of the sets were made of cardboard, some even out of paper. Even to this day I still consider it one of the most imaginative pictures I ever made.

Of the historical and costume period of my pictures, I would say that *Carmen, Madame Du Barry* [1919] (*Passion*), and *Anna Boleyn* [1920] (*Deception*) were the 3 outstanding pictures. The importance of these pictures, in my opinion, was the fact that they differed completely from the Italian school, then very much en vogue, which had a kind of grand-opera-like quality. I tried to de-operatize my pictures and to humanize my historical characters—I treated the intimate nuances just as important as the mass movements, and tried to blend them both together.

The picture *Die Bergkatze* [1921] was a complete failure, and yet this picture had more inventiveness and satirical pictorial wit than many of my other pictures. Released shortly after the war, I found the German audiences in no mood to accept a picture which satirized militarism and war. . . .

In my silent period in Germany as well as in America I tried to use less and less subtitles. It was my aim to tell the story through pictorial nuances and the facial expressions of my actors. There were very often long scenes in which people were talking without being interrupted by subtitles. The lip movement was used as a kind of pantomime. Not that I wanted the audience to become lip readers, but I tried to time the speech in such a way that the audience could listen with their eyes.

——Lubitsch, in a letter to Herman Weinberg, 10 July 47; published in *The Lubitsch Touch* (NY, 1968)

It is my idea to work with the scenario writer from the very beginning and as I do so I build up in my own mind exactly how I am going to direct the picture. When the scenario is finished I know just what I want. It is important that a scenario should be a good manuscript, as it is essential in the directing of a picture. You have to know before you start "shooting" what to do in every scene. Some scenes are taken according to necessity and not according to their continuity. You may begin work on the last scene and then skip to the middle of the production. Therefore, how can one start at the end without having mapped out carefully beforehand every detail of direction of the production?

Then, I try to exclude titles wherever possible. I want all action, where it is feasible, to explain itself without titles to interrupt the suspense, which is so often killed by the insertion of words. For a modern realistic drama, we must have spoken titles, but even these should be made to read just as one speaks in real life, and not according to the stiff conversation of books. The ideal manuscript is one without titles, but it is not for today or tomorrow, but in a couple of years or infinitely longer. This has nothing to do with pictures as they are produced nowadays. In our titles we borrow from the stage or the novel. Later we will have discovered the motion picture style.

It is very interesting to have every scene speak for itself and what I talk about in this regard may not happen for 50 years. In the painting you understand what it means without titles. All the great masters explain themselves. In my last picture I experienced a great change in my career, as it is the first time I have made an important modern drama. I have gotten away from spectacles, as there are only 5 characters in this film, which is called *The Marriage Circle* [1924]. It is a very intimate drama. Even the script of the story was different, and I never got so close to real life as I have in this picture. . . .

Yes—yes—I do believe that some time in the future stories will be written direct for the screen. I prefer a manuscript for the screen by somebody familiar with the dramatic construction of a picture.

As far as I can, I try to keep the action going without tiring the players, I think over my medium shot when I am making my long shot, and I am ready for what I want when it comes to a close-up. I don't want to get the actors fatigued, and only when it appears absolutely necessary do I insist upon going over the scene 3 or 4 times. You lose the feeling when you do. A player may have just the expression you want, but on the fourth or fifth attempt he is too sure of himself.

——Lubitsch, interviewed for *The New York Times*, 16 Dec 23; repr. in *Spellbound in Darkness*

For myself, I do not believe in this present craze for covering a set with directors of dialogue, directors of dancing, directors of music, and all the other would-be directors who are interfering with the Director's work. I would not make a picture that way, for it could not be a satisfactory picture with so many minds trying to govern it. . . .

Our art directors [in Germany] are a much more intimate part of the production than they are here [in the U.S.A.]: they stay right with the picture from start to finish, even being on the set with us while we are shooting, ready to make any repairs or alterations that may be needed. Over here, there is a separate man for all of these duties—a separate mind to interpret the original design in its own way. Only once over here have I been able to have my art director work through the picture with me as we did in Europe: that was in *Lady Windermere's Fan* [1925], a picture which I think had the most perfect sets of any I have made. . . .

——Lubitsch, interviewed for *American Cinematographer*, Nov 1929

George L U C A S
Born in Modesto, California, in 1945.

Q. How did *American Graffiti* [1973] grow and develop?

A. It started at the beginning of 1971. I had an idea for this movie about life in my home town when I was 18. So I sat down with Bill Huyck and

Gloria Katz . . . and we worked on the idea together. Then they had to leave because Bill had the chance to direct a film.

I then wrote a whole screenplay based on our discussions. United Artists had been interested up to that point, but they decided they didn't want to do the film. I took the script around and tried to sell it to other studios, and this took me about a year. Finally I took it to Universal. But they weren't totally happy with the script. A rewrite was needed, but by that time I was written out on the subject, so I turned it back to the Huycks and—with me looking over their shoulders—they did the final draft that became the movie.

———Lucas, interviewed for *The Toronto Star*, 25 Aug 73

Bela LUGOSI (1882–1956)

. . . My childhood in the Black Mountains was the usual husky, healthy every-day life of any country boy. My father, Baron Lugosi, was engaged in the practical and profitable business of banking, and there was nothing weird or extraordinary.

It is my particular pride that even in the most fantastic of my film roles I do not use makeup. Instead of depending upon masks, casts, court plaster and false features, I create the illusion of a terrifying, distorted or uncanny makeup by an appeal to the imagination. An evil expression in the eyes, a sinister arch to the brows or a leer on my lips—all of which take long practice in muscular control—are sufficient to hypnotize an audience into seeing what I want them to see and what I myself see in my mind's eye. In like manner, by the way in which I use my fingers and gesticulate with my hands, I give the illusion of their being misshapen, extra large, or extra small—or whatever the part requires. And I consider it part of an actor's art to be able to shorten or lengthen his body or change its very shape by the power of suggestion, without false paddings or other artificial aids.

———Lugosi, in press-book for *The Raven*, 1935

Sidney LUMET
Born in Philadelphia, 1924. From childhood acted on stage and in television before his first film direction, Twelve Angry Men (1957).

The closeness in the work with the actors is the heart of the picture [*Long Day's Journey Into Night*, 1962]. Like all good working experience, I think we emerged from it totally close personally, a complete connection for all of us. That was accomplished, really, in the prerehearsal period in quiet conferences between ourselves. Then in rehearsal itself.

What was fascinating was that each of the actors worked very, very differently. Ralph Richardson works on what amounts to a musical basis. I finally found a shorthand with him of "Ralph, a little more bassoon, a little less violin, a little more cello, a little tympani here," literally in those terms. It was immediately picked up and translated into acting.

Dean [Stockwell] worked very internally, needed total discussion. . . . Strasbergian analysis of each moment in him, in the character.

Jason [Robards] likes to think of himself as an out-and-out technician. Of course, he's not. He's a totally inspired artist. With Jason, as always when we've worked together, one doesn't talk about the most profound elements of it or the most moving. They are somehow understood between you. One deals largely on a technical level with him.

Katie [Hepburn] was a fascinating factor. Because I'd never worked with her before, I let her go. In the first 3 days, she took off with that extraordinary instinct, that incredible energy of hers. On the third day of rehearsal she panicked because, as so often happens on a great role, instinct isn't enough. It only lasts for a short while and then starts collapsing under the weight of the emotional demand. It became necessary to search for it elsewhere. Searching for it someplace else meant, at certain times, sheerly technical adjustments, on a level of "Let's get on with it. You're taking too long with this speech. Don't try to stretch the emotion. Let the words carry it," that kind of thing. Too, really profound, close, personal discussions between the two of us, of that character, of O'Neill.

A question of collaboration between a director and a cameraman is always such a highly individual one. Boris [Kaufman] and I have done, as you know, 8 pictures together, and it's always a very close relationship. The choice, the selection of a shot, I guard jealously. And that is my prerogative. The 360-degreer was mine, the final pullback was mine, the shooting plot of the picture was mine. But I don't in any way mean to denigrate Boris's contribution [on *Long Day's Journey Into Night*]. Where he begins, and this becomes an enormously vital element, is in the lighting. In black and white, particularly, the light is one of the key ways in which one extracts the meaning of the drama. Boris's triumph, from a lighting point of view in *Long Day's Journey*, lies in the fact that if you take the same close-up of Ralph Richardson from Act One, and a close-up of Ralph Richardson from Act Four, the exact same size, and put those two faces next to each other on the screen, they will look like a different man. It'll almost be hard to think the same actor is in both shots. That is Boris's triumph, and it's a tremendous one, through the use of light.

———Lumet, interviewed for *Film Quarterly*, Fall 71

People have told me, "You can't keep that music at the end [of *The Pawnbroker*, 1965] because it is so loud." I know what they are complaining about but it was a deliberate intent on the part of the composer [Quincy Jones] and myself. I don't want anybody to cry; I don't want that kind of sentimentality on it. The kind of insane joy that starts with the music at the end with its wildness, is joy in the sense that Sol's alive again . . . and in my eyes it's a happy ending! We worked very hard and specifically with that final result, so as not to give the audience the conventional catharsis, not to let them off the hook in the sense of "Have a good weep . . . but now let's go and have a cup of coffee, fellows." . . .

Unfortunately, I had come into the project rather late, in fact only 2 weeks before it was due to shoot. It had originally been offered to me by the 2 men who produced it, Roger Lewis and Philip Langner, who at the time had a deal with Metro. Metro had wanted to do it as an Eady plan picture, with a script where it all took place in Soho, to be shot in England! It was ridiculous. I had read the book before, loved Wallant's work, and was furious at the kind of treatment it had been given, so turned it down. Then the producers took the property to Ely Landau (at the time I was doing *Fail-Safe* [1964]) and another director was assigned, another script was written, with the setting moved back to New York. Then literally 2 weeks before shooting the other director had to leave because he was physically ill. So I came in 2 weeks before the film was due to be shot.

The only actor who had been set up to then was Rod Steiger as Sol. I cast everyone else and found the location in just 2 weeks . . . thankfully it is an area I know. When you go for unnatural-naturalism, as I have in the film, it is very important when casting to get artists most people don't know about. So the problem was to find people who had not worked that much, and in fact for about 20 of the people it is their first film, like Jaime Sanchez, who plays Jesus Ortiz.

The technique we used for showing the intrusion into Sol's memory of the horrors of the concentration camp he was in, the way he lost his family and his hopes, is based on quick shock cuts. For me it works marvelously— it is not used as a technique just for the sake of itself. I began with the basis that for Sol the past is not past, it is much more present than what is going on at the moment around him. This is a man who is in such agony that he must feel nothing or he will go to pieces. Then, knowing the way my own memory works, when it is something that I do not want to remember I will fight it and fight it; but it keeps intruding itself in larger and larger bursts, and if it is important enough it finally breaks through and takes over completely, and then recedes in the same way. These sequences are laid out using one-frame, 2-frame, 3-frame cuts of increasing rapidity finally up to 6-frame cuts and then eventually into a sequence.

The old idea was that it took 3 frames for an image to register on the eye, that the eye could not retain an image of less than 3 frames. So the first time we used this quick cutting device was where it was a question of taking an idea and moving it from an intellectualization to a good technique, to make it something that will work for an audience. In the first sequence the cuts are not nearly as short as later; they are 6 frames because I knew that the first time I used it the shock to an audience would be enormous anyway, and clarity was the important thing; the following time I used 4, then 2 frames, and by the third sequence I was using just 2 and one frame cuts . . . and you *see* it, which shows that the eye can absorb this if it is led into it gently enough.

——Lumet, interviewed for *Films & Filming*, Oct 64

. . . I think that an actor like Brando can give you certain moments that have nothing to do with any director, have nothing to do with any script, have nothing to do with anything aside from his own talent. When you work with Marlon, you have only one job: release him, get him moving, get him un-afraid . . . get him functioning. Now that doesn't mean you simply let him go. You must stay within the confines, heading toward an objective.

Marlon is a fascinating man. Like many great actors, he is also a very suspicious man. He likes to test his directors. In the first 2 days of shooting, he will do 2 takes that may seem identical, but one is full and the other is only technical. Then he will watch which one you decide to print, and on that decision lies your whole subsequent relationship with him, because if you don't know your job as well as he knows his, you've had it. In those performances where you have seen him just walk through a film, he made the test and the director flunked it.

——Lumet, interviewed for *Movie People* (NY, 1973)

Louis L U M I È R E   (1864–1948)
Born in Besançon, France.

It was at the end of the summer of 1894 that I was able to make my first film, *Workers Leaving the Lumière Factory*. As you may have noticed, the men are wearing straw hats and the women summer dresses. Moreover, I needed strong sunlight to be able to make such scenes, for my lens was not very powerful, and I should not have been able to take such a view in winter or at the end of autumn. The film was shown in public for the first time at Paris, rue de Rennes, before the "Societé d'Encouragement pour l'Industrie Nationale." This was on 22 March 1895. This showing ended a lecture which I had been asked to give by the illustrious physicist, Mascarat, of the Institute, then President of the Society. I also showed on the screen the formation of a photographic image in course of development.

——Lumière, interviewed for *Sight & Sound*, Summer 48

Len L Y E
Born in Christchurch, New Zealand, 1901. Came to England in 1926.

Although a strong sensation of color-flow was attempted in both the films *Colour Box* [1935] and *Rainbow Dance* [1936] there are differences in technical and pictorial treatment between the two. *Colour Box* was painted straight on to the film celluloid and printed in the Dufay colour system direct from this "master"; *Rainbow Dance* is a combination of black and white photographic records equaling densities of colour which are printed on Gasparcolor film stock. In pictorial treatment, the differences lie in the use of color. Color was used in *Colour Box* in an objective way, and in *Rainbow Dance* in a subjective way.

In *Colour Box* the color was "on the surface" in an arabesque of color design (apparently motivated by the light arabesque quality of the simple dance music [La Belle Creole] it accompanied). Whatever movement occurred was color movement alone.

In *Rainbow Dance* the color is used in a "spatial" way so that it comes up to the eye or recedes from it or vanishes and reappears in definite color rhythms. In fact, color is made to turn inside out in movement regardless of the movement of the object or objects on which it is seen. Here the color movement is a form of counterpoint to the movement of the object carrying the color—often this counterpoint of color-flow dominates the movement of the object to such an extent that the object becomes merely an element of the color movement, instead of the usual circumstance of color being merely an element in an object enacting a strong literary role. In other words, the color movement dominates all other movement, *both* pictorial and cinematic.

——Lye, in *World Film News*, Dec 36

M

Shirley M A C L A I N E   (Shirley Maclean Beaty)
Born 1934, in Arlington, Virginia.

Billy Wilder's very dominating. He knows what he wants and he's absolutely certain. It's not that he leaves the actor out of it. We can discuss things with Wilder and come to some kind of an agreement. Once you get on the set the important things for Wilder are the script and the first preview. What happens on the set is unimportant compared to the other two, because the script is such a polished product that he knows exactly how it will work.

Q. Wilder then has a complete blueprint for his film before he starts shooting?

A. *Billy* yes. *Willy* Wyler, no. Willy Wyler does as much as can be done, and you think nothing more can be done with the script, but he will find something. And once you get on the set that's the beginning. He will try maybe 12 different ways. For instance, in *The Children's Hour* [1962], which I have just finished with Willy, as far as my role is concerned (and my role is the one of the guilty party), he was not sure exactly what he wanted on the screen. And the way he wanted the audience to think. So Willy had maybe 2, 3 or 4 different ways for each scene.

——MacLaine, interviewed for *Films & Filming*, Feb 62

Ben M A D D O W
Born 1909 in Passaic, New Jersey. Part of his experience in Hollywood was as an unhappy ghost writer:

X: Have you ever tried a western?

I hadn't, but on Monday I brought him an idea that tried to look like a treatment.

X: Fifty-fifty—OK?

Without looking at it X picks up the telephone to call Warners: I've just sold a great western novel to Simon & Schuster—what will you give me for it?

A very large amount is agreed upon, and a very satisfied X puts in a call to Simon & Schuster: Warners has just bought my new western novel—are you interested?

I now saw the plan, and how simple it was, and I was too aghast to stop the machinery. Besides, I knew what should be in the bank that week, and wasn't.

X (still to Simon & Schuster): I'll let you see it first. What are you paying these days? (Aside, to me: Is four weeks enough? It's the only way to make the Warners deal. I nod Yes.) Fine! Warners made some suggestions, so I'll have it re-typed and bring it in to you next month.

A useless thought in the front of my mind: Is this the way things are done?

Yes, I got the 50% on the script, and I delivered the novel it was supposed to be based on—for which I got nothing.

Three years later, my wife, in a London bookshop, noticed a paperback by X with a familiar title. It was the book I wrote to make the Warners deal possible.

————Maddow, in an interview, Apr 74

Anna MAGNANI (1908–1973)
Born in Rome. Entered films in 1934.

[Marlon Brando] is great, and he's half-crazy. But to work with—impossible.

He wanted to be the big star all the time. Always the prima donna, trying to put everybody else on edge and make them feel small. It was an unhappy film altogether [*The Fugitive Kind,* 1960]. The subject was perfect, but the producer was never sure of himself, the director [Sidney Lumet] used no imagination . . . and there was Brando.

So pretentious he was. Running round playing with the lights when you wanted to discuss a scene, or suddenly stopping and staring at a hole in the wall at some big dramatic moment. Then the next minute—all over you.

How does he need all those silly little things? He is such a great artist and I have such admiration for him.

The last day was terrible. By then the whole unit was reduced to such a nervous state that I turned on him and gave him such a roasting that he couldn't sleep for 3 nights.

After that we met at a farewell party for the film and made it up. When all the tension's over it's easy to forgive a "character" like that. I still say better a hundred Brandos any day than one nice, dull negative man.

————Magnani, interviewed for *The Daily Mail,* 28 Apr 61

Norman MAILER
Born 1923 in Long Branch, New Jersey. Twenty years after his successful first novel, The Naked and the Dead, *he began directing films with* Wild 90 *(1968).*

If you don't have the material at *all,* then you're dead. But the art of cutting is to find material where no one else can find it. It's a little like a detective story. You can cut something out of nothing, almost. In *Maidstone* [1969], we have 12-minute reels, and these are a unit in a way, because that's what a cameraman sticks in his Arriflex magazine. We shoot until the reel is empty. We look at the reel in the projection room and we all groan. There isn't a thing in it that has any life. It's dead, it's horrible.

Suddenly you take out the sound in a place and then you look at it and it's not a bad piece of film without sound. And then you see another piece 5 minutes later on which has a relation to this piece. Or you might get 30 really good seconds out of that 12-minute reel if it's hopeless, and it'll have an artistry and elegance to it. So that afterwards, you'll say, "How the hell did you ever get that?"

———Mailer, interviewed for *The Film Director as Superstar* (NY, 1970)

Dušan MAKAVEJEV
Born in Belgrade, 1932. Trained in psychology. First experimental films made in 1955–58.

Q. *WR: Mysteries of the Organism* [1971] is a film that deals with heterogeneous materials dialectically organized. Can you talk about this structuring of WR and its political content?

A. I find I am using more and more heterogeneous material. It is not true that you cannot mix different materials. And when you do this, a number of things reveal themselves—style, for one thing. And style is always a very specific artistic expression. You bring together films of different genres. And at each place where you jump from film to film, you have jumped from one level of reality to another. So, first the illusion of reality is destroyed and second, the fictionality of the moment is revealed even if you are speaking about documentary intersection. A film that deals with different materials is more documentary than any other film because each piece in a sense becomes the documentary of something else. This interrelationship of different materials creates a rich spiritual field. Each separate mono-stylistic point is a layering that only film can create. So you have a complete web of interrelated associations that can be political, sociological, psychological.

———Makavejev, interviewed for *University Film Study Center Newsletter*, Dec 75

Louis MALLE
Born in Thumeries, France, 1932. After war and IDHEC, assisted Cousteau and Bresson.

The initial idea of *Place de la République* [1972] was to try to break down the boundary between fiction and documentary, to show how one can move gradually from direct cinema and over towards the cinema of fiction. I had a few actors, playing the role of *provocateurs*, intervene in this reality of the street—for example, a couple arguing in a car in the middle of the traffic, or a man staggering and falling on the sidewalk with the passersby stopping. . . . But that didn't really work and I took out all of these interventions in order to leave just the unknowns of the street. We then adopted the principle of a more straightforward contact between the camera and the passersby: we filmed and the people came along. . . . But once the film was shot we found again the initial design: bordering on a strong impression of fiction, with people seeming to act, although we thought we had erased the acted parts. Which proves that the separation between documentary cinema and cinema with a scenario is more and more difficult to establish. . . .

Calcutta [1969] has already been very much attacked in this sense: no ready-made ideological schema can, it seems to me, apply itself to the Indian situation. But the public generally refused this freedom which was left to it, taking for indifference that which was obviously only a false neutrality. . . . And already in Calcutta I had envisaged not using any commentary, but the very particular situation of this artificial colonial city necessitated, just the same, a minimum of information. On the other hand, the procedure was reversed for the series Phantom India [1969]—seven 50-minute films for television and the American university circuit—where I adopted the form of a first-person travel journal. . . .

It was parallel to the editing of these 2 films that I wrote, with Patrick Modiano, the scenario of Lacombe, Lucien [1974]. . . . It seems to me that, although Lacombe, Lucien is a film for which a fiction was fabricated, I had the impression of shooting in the same spirit as the two preceding films: with the same distance, the same refusal to comment on Lucien as on the work on the assembly line [in Humain trop humain, 1973], and perhaps with the same pessimism which comes, without doubt, from the vision the world today gives us, but which also comes from the fact of our only having shown a part of the epoch. We supposed as implicit for Lacombe all that which took place around it—the Resistance, the heroism, etc.—which it wasn't my purpose to show, since the point of view adopted was to follow Lucien from his village to his flight and to remain with him without knowing what was taking place outside.

It was always obvious to me that the interpreter of Lucien could only be a nonprofessional: who, in fact, in the French cinema could play a 17-year-old peasant? But in seeing the images from Place de la République, I was struck by the enormous acting talent of these amateurs who could be used as models in a dramatic arts course. And this delicate shooting, with this daily effort to break the wall of indifference, of silence in the contacts with strangers, helped me a great deal in my relations with the actors of Lacombe: everything in the two films was done to put its interpreters at ease, professionals or amateurs, to shoot in the freest possible way in relation to the technique. Lacombe was filmed two-thirds by hand, with the new Arriflex portable 35 mm synchronous camera which allows one not to constrict the actors.

It is this feeling of much greater freedom which ties together Humain trop humain, Place de la République and Lacombe, Lucien. . . . With Lacombe, a step forward was made on the level of style, and it marks for me a departure towards another cinema.

——Malle, interviewed for Écran, 25 May 74;
trans. in Thousand Eyes, June 76

Rouben MAMOULIAN

Born in Tiflis in 1898, he attended the Universities of Moscow and London, and the Vakhtangov Studio of Moscow Art Theatre, before coming to America in 1923. He was solely a stage director until 1929 when his first job of film direction was Applause.

You have no idea how cumbersome sound and camera equipment was in the beginning. It was like walking around with a bungalow on your back. The camera had to be enclosed in a booth so that the whirring of the motor didn't get on the sound track, and the sound technicians kept telling you that "mixing" was impossible. For a certain scene in *Applause*, I insisted on using two separate channels for recording two sounds: one, soft whispering; the other, loud singing; which later would be mixed, so that the audience could hear both simultaneously. It seems funny today when we use a multitude of channels that this was a revolutionary breakthrough. I had to fight for every innovation, for every camera movement. In those days, a scene was shot with 3 cameras; 2 for close-ups, one for long shot. And then into the cutting room to intercut the 3. I insisted on a fluid camera which would pan freely, as well as move in and out of a scene. George Folsey kept telling me that it couldn't be done, but we did it, and he [the cameraman] was very proud of it.

As you remember, the whole last sequence in *Queen Christina* [1933] is practically silent. It consists of a rhythmic progression of graphic images (ship sails, faces, pantomimic action) ending with Garbo's close-up. I was sure that the dramatic effect of this silent sequence would produce a feeling of exaltation, the classical catharsis. My trump in this was the final close-up of Garbo's face, which began with a long view and ended with an enormous close-up that ran for 85 feet. I gambled much on this last shot. Again, the technicians said it couldn't be done. The dilemma was that the long shot at the start required a wide-angle lens, while the close-up at the end called for a 4- or 6-inch lens. It was obvious that I had to use a wide-angle lens which would have to come within a few inches of Garbo's face to achieve the final close-up. For this, I needed a device which would progressively modify the degrees of diffusion as the camera rolled in. There was the run—no such device existed at that time. (Today, of course, it is child's play.) We were stuck. Suddenly an early childhood memory popped into my mind when my parents gave me a magic lantern for Christmas. I thought of that long glass slide on which there were 4 separate pictures that could be projected on a white sheet or a wall by gradually moving the glass slide in front of the lens. That was it—all we needed was a similar piece of glass on which, instead of pictures, there would be graduated diffusions. The laboratory went to work and the new gadget was ready by 5 o'clock. Garbo always stopped shooting at 5; this time, however, she stayed until 7. We made two takes: one was no good; the other was perfect. The rest, as we say, is history.

———Mamoulian, interviewed for *Interviews with Film Directors* (NY, 1967)

Garbo asked me, "What do I play in this scene?" [the end of *Queen Christina*]. Remember she is standing there for 150 feet of film—90 feet of them in close-up. I said, "Have you heard of *tabula rasa*? I want your face to be a blank sheet of paper. I want the writing to be done by every member of the audience. I'd like it if you could avoid even blinking your eyes, so that you're nothing but a beautiful mask." So in fact there is *nothing* on her face: but everyone who has seen the film will tell you what she is thinking and feeling. And always it's something different. Each one writes his own ending to the film; and it's interesting that this is the scene everyone remembers most clearly. . . .

Color cinematography tends to brighten and cheapen natural color. The problem was to counteract that. I realized that color in films is nearer to painting than to the stage. Now if you look, for instance, at a crimson cloak painted by El Greco, you'll find that what first appears as a mass of color is in fact a subtle blending of all sorts of shades, with patches of pink and blue and purple and green. So I treated the color [in *Blood & Sand*, 1941] the way a painter would. I devised what came to be known as the Mamoulian Palette. Beside me on the set I had a huge box of scraps of material—scarves and handkerchiefs and so on, in all colors—so that if a costume or a set needed a bit more of a particular color—a color accent, as it were—I could put it in myself. And I had a collection of spray guns beside me, so that I could spray color on a costume or set or even an actor. The art director had made me a beautiful chapel; and he was very upset when I sprayed everything with green and gray paint. Then again, there's a banquet, which was done entirely in black and white. There were flowers on the table and (naturally) the leaves were green. I think when they saw me painting them black they went and told Mr. Zanuck I'd gone out of my mind. . . .

———Mamoulian, interviewed for *Sight & Sound,* Summer 61

. . . In the ballroom scene in *Becky Sharp* [1935], on the eve of Waterloo, the dancers were gay and carefree when news of Napoleon's approaching army came to them. The alarm spread and they went into a panic, with the women rushing to escape and the men hurrying out to their horses to join their troops. Now, if I had thrown the colors in the scene together, I would have had a jumble. I had to arrange my shots so that each had a dominant hue, running first to the weaker tints and later to the powerful ones. I took my groups in this order—dark blacks and blues and greens, then lighter greens, yellows, orange, purple and finally scarlet. In life it would have been unreal for them so to select themselves, but on the screen the color logic is so undeniable that it is completely convincing.

———Mamoulian, interviewed for *The New Movie Magazine,* Sep 35

Henry MANCINI
Born 1922. Began his musical career as an arranger for Glenn Miller.

You want to know how I go about scaring people? Really, it is a matter of colors. Of using the orchestra in various combinations to create tension. *Frenzy* [1972] is a very low-key picture about a necktie murderer, and what I have done is to just cut off the orchestra around middle C. There is no high; there are no violins nor high flutes; it is all from there down with 10 cellos, 10 violas, basses, horns, bassoon, and bass flutes . . . none of the screeching, high, intense sounds that would be thought a little melodramatic today. It is very sparse . . . there's not a lot going on, but what there is will, I trust, sound pretty spooky.

———Mancini, interviewed for *The Guardian,* 29 Dec 71

Francis M A N K I E W I C Z
The first film by this refugee from a distinguished Hollywood family was made for the National Film Board of Canada.

The first thing I did on arriving at the set, *Le Temps d'une chasse* [1972] in the morning would be to have a reading session. We'd read the scene we were doing that day with the actors. We read it together, talked about it a little, and then I'd ask them to just act it out whichever way they felt. Move, and do whatever they felt like. While they were doing that, Michel Brault and I would look at it and decide on the angles. It was very close. Once we figured out an angle and the actors had rehearsed it, we might find that the action wasn't quite right for the camera. So we changed the action a bit to fit better with the camera position. It's sort of like a sculptor who starts with a block of rock and chips it down to get a general shape, chips it a little more to bring out different features, and finally polishes it. Every scene was built that way. The camera and the actors worked very closely.
———Mankiewicz, interviewed for *Cinema Canada*, Apr–May 73

Herman M A N K I E W I C Z   (1897–1953)
Born in New York City. Foreign correspondent and drama critic before collaborating with Tod Browning on story for The Road to Mandalay (1926).

... You don't really need to be a writer, in the accepted sense of the word, to write for pictures. Some of the best scenario writers in Hollywood can't write at all. They simply have a flair for ideas, for situations; these, in turn, suggest bits of business; then they tie dialogue onto the business, or hire someone to do it for them. ...

In the movies, for the most part, there is no such thing as individual creation. No one person makes a picture. It is the blend of the work of from 5 to 10 people—each one of whom is boss of his particular field, each one of whom has to be satisfied. And if it takes 10 writers to satisfy the real bosses, what difference does it make, as long as the picture is good?
———Mankiewicz, interviewed for *Theatre Arts Monthly*, June 37

Joseph L. M A N K I E W I C Z
Born 1909, in Wilkes-Barre, Pennsylvania. After Columbia University, followed his brother Herman to Hollywood.

I remember [Fritz Lang] had pieces of paper on his office wall, marked in different colors to distinguish each character [*Fury*, 1936]. The story of *Fury* came from an idea Norman Krasna had for a play. He told it to me and said that he thought I could write it better. This was just after there had been a lynching in northern California, which was unusual because evil things mostly happen in southern California. Anyway, he based his plot on that, and some time went by, and one day I told the story to Louis B. Mayer, who said he'd let me make it. He said also that he would spend as much money on exploiting it as he was spending to exploit *Romeo and Juliet*—the Norma Shearer and Leslie Howard one, just to prove to me that even with all this publicity *Fury* could never be a big smash hit. Well, Fritz Lang was on the point of leaving MGM, because he'd been brought over and had been around for some time with nothing to do. So he was about to go back to Germany[?]. But he stayed for this.

———Mankiewicz, interviewed for *Films & Filming*, Nov 70

Anthony M A N N   [Emil or Anton Bundsmann]   (1906–1967)
Born in San Diego, California; acted in theater before joining the Selznick organization in 1938. First films directed in 1942.

I watched Preston Sturges work on *Sullivan's Travels* [1942]. He let me go through the entire production, watching him direct—and I directed a little. I'd stage a scene and he'd tell me how lousy it was. Then I watched the editing and I was able gradually to build up knowledge. Preston insisted I make a film as soon as possible. . . . He said it's better to have done something bad than to have done nothing . . . so the first picture, good or bad, that came along, I decided to do. And this was *Dr. Broadway* [1942].

I remember very warmly the cameraman, an old-timer name of Sparkuhl who had done many films for UFA and Lubitsch, and he was a great help. Nobody else cared a damn about the picture. They said, "Don't build sets, don't do anything. You have to get finished in eighteen days and, if you don't, the cameras are taken from you and OUT."

. . . [Sparkuhl] was doing nothing at that time so the studio let me have him. He didn't care how many hours I spent at night with him, discussing how to shoot the scene next morning. This was Macdonald Carey's first film, too, and you see the problem of a young director? They give you every obstacle in the book. They say, "Give him fifteen days, give him no actors at all, only people who've never been in front of a camera before; God help him, and let's see what happens." And that's the way you generally start.

. . . It was only through [William Cameron Menzies's] ability that we were able to achieve any style, feeling or period [in *Reign of Terror*, 1949]. For instance, we were faced with the problem of re-creating the Commune, which was supposed to be packed with thousands and thousands of people. And the money we had could only get us 100 people for one day. So Menzies devised a scheme whereby for that day we put all these people on a platform like a football or baseball field, but straight up so it would be square. And we sat the 100 people, crowded into this small space, put the camera so they would just fill the frame, and John Alton lit it with some shafts of light at different angles, so we'd have light and shadow, and so some of the people would be seen and some would be shadowed. And then for a day, I shot all the reactions to all the speeches of Robespierre and Danton and so forth.

Then, we took it, and multiplied it 20 times, projecting it on a rear-projecting machine so that we no longer had 100 people; we had 2,000. It was on a rear projector and all we had in the foreground was a big, big door, with guards standing on duty. As the door opened Robespierre walked in, and the people rose, the 2,000 people against this background. And then for all the speeches, we just went into a big close-up of Robespierre against this background of people who were screaming and yelling. We were able to achieve this tremendous effect with only 100 people. And this was conceived completely by Cameron Menzies. . . .

—Mann, interviewed for *Screen,* July–Oct 69

Fredric M A R C H [Frederick Bickel] (1897–1975)
Born in Racine, Wisconsin.

There's so much mumbo-jumbo about acting. Spencer Tracy, one of the finest actors of our time, once told me, "I just learn my lines." Laurette Taylor really explained the way it is for actresses when she told me, "I just pretend." . . . I learned about the importance of relaxation when I started making pictures. The director of *The Marriage Playground* [1929], Lothar Mendes, was the first person to mention it to me. He said, "Freddie, when I say 'Camera,' all it means is—relax."

—March, interviewed for *The Player* (NY, 1962)

Mae M A R S H   (1895–1968)
Born in Madrid, New Mexico.

When Mr. Griffith began rehearsing a picture called *Man's Genesis* [1912], I got my first chance for a lead role. In the film a girl had to wear a grass skirt which would show all her limbs. Mary Pickford didn't want to do that. "Give the part to the little girl. She doesn't mind showing her limbs." In those days, they wore skirts down to the ankles. You couldn't show the calf of your leg. And I said, "Oh, yes, I would like to do it." It was immaterial to me whether I showed my limbs or not.

I received $5 a day when I worked on *Man's Genesis*. Mr. Griffith would tell me exactly what to do. On the first day, he explained, "I want you to sit on that rock wall over there. This boy you're sitting next to, you're very, very much in love with him. Have you ever been in love?" And I said oh yes, which I hadn't. He said, "Just think that you're terribly in love and look up at him shy-like." So I did, and then he said, "Look up at him again and then put your head down," which I did. Then he said, "Now get up and run away." So I got up and ran away. That was my first acting part. I loved it. I said to Mr. Griffith, "When am I going to do it again?" He said, "You've done it once. You can't do it again. That was fine. Maybe you can do something else tomorrow."

—Marsh, interviewed for *The Real Tinsel* (NY, 1970)

Lee M A R V I N
Born 1924 in New York City. Stage work before his film debut in 1951.

[John Boorman] and I . . . worked together on *Point Blank* [1968]. The two of us kind of wrote that while we were sittin' around in England. Bill Stair, he's a friend of John's who—I don't know exactly what he does. He invents crazy games, you know—challenges for the mind. So he came along to the States with us on the project as the art director. Stair got into color and everything. I mean, we started the film in kind of a prison gray and then went to a warmer gray and then got into the blues and went on through the whole color spectrum—I'm talkin' about backgrounds, parkin' lots, everything.

——Marvin, interviewed for *Rolling Stone*, 21 Dec 72

Groucho [Julius Henry] M A R X
Born in New York City, 1895.

Didn't S. J. Perelman write for you?
Not a great deal. There's a strange thing about that man. When he was riding high on *The New Yorker,* and anybody asked him if he'd worked with the Marx Brothers, he'd say, "A little bit, not very much." Now that he isn't so successful any more, and his name isn't front page, when he gives an interview he says, "Oh yes, I wrote pretty near all of two of their movies," which is a goddamned lie. As a matter of fact, he worked in conjunction with 4 other writers, and he wasn't very good for us.
Why not?
He wasn't a dramatist. He could write funny dialogue, but that's very different from writing drama. For that we needed a different kind of writer, like Kaufman and Ryskind. . . .
Did you write most of *Animal Crackers* [1930]?
No, we had Kaufman and Ryskind. I added stuff to it, but every first-class comedian is supposed to be able to do that. Otherwise you're just a schlump, you're not a comedian.

——Marx, interviewed for *Take One*, Sep–Oct 70

Samuel M A R X
Born in New York City. Headed Story Department at MGM in its heyday.

. . . I observed the forlorn figure of D. W. Griffith on Hollywood Boulevard; the once-great director had been neglected by the industry he had served so well. It was obvious he needed a job, so I went to Thalberg about it, but he shook his head. No amount of argument, including the reminder that he believed "Once a champion, always a champion" would sway him. "I could never work with Griffith," he said, "nor he with me."

——Marx, a footnote in his *Mayer and Thalberg* (NY, 1975)

James M A S O N
Born 1909 in Huddersfield, England. Trained as an architect, and a graduate of Cambridge University, he began a stage career in 1931; his first film role was in Late Extra (1935).

Marlon Brando . . . is quoted as saying that when he is playing opposite another actor he has no need to draw anything at all from him. . . . Brando would rather look into space, and use his own imagination to feed him. I, on the contrary, like to receive whatever is available from the actors around me: I find the personal exchange very often of the greatest possible help. In *The Seagull* [1968], for instance, not only did I receive the most wonderful assistance from Vanessa Redgrave's speaking of her lines and from the way she reacted to mine, but also she was entirely unpredictable herself, constantly expressing thoughts with her eyes or her manner of speaking to which I could react in an altogether fresh way myself.

——Mason, interviewed for *The Making of Feature Films* (London, 1971)

Marcello MASTROIANNI

Born 1924 in Frosinone, Italy. Studied acting at Rome University's Centro Teatro. Has been in films since the 1947 version of Les Misérables.

Fellini is one of the few directors who really like actors, and an actor feels this and responds to it—in other words, he is happy. And he is convinced that every time he opens his mouth he is saying everything splendidly. That is a great secret. Fellini is very crafty in his dealings with actors, very crafty indeed. I say this because, when I have been with other directors who, like Fellini, really direct the acting, I have always been afraid of going wrong, but with him I always feel I am being marvelous . . . the truth is that I have never worked so happily as in *La Dolce Vita* [1960]. I have never enjoyed myself so much, and I really mean enjoyed. For 6 months I really felt that I was an exceptional man, so that everything was bound to go right.

——Mastroianni, interviewed for *Bianco e nero*, Feb 60;
trans. in *Fellini* (NY, 1969)

Louis B. MAYER (1885–1957)

Born in a village near Vilna, in Lithuanian Russia. Family left for Canada in 1888.

The final script of *Song of Russia* [1944] was little more than a pleasant musical romance—the story of a boy and girl that, except for the music of Tchaikovsky might just as well have taken place in Switzerland or England or any other country on the earth.

I thought Robert Taylor ideal for the leading male role in *Song of Russia*, but he did not like the story. This was not unusual as actors and actresses many times do not care for stories suggested to them.

At the time, Taylor mentioned his pending commission in the navy, so I telephoned the Secretary of the Navy, Frank Knox, and told him of the situation, recalling the good that had been accomplished with *Mrs. Miniver* [1942] and other pictures released during the war period. The Secretary called back and said he thought Taylor could be given time to make the film before being called to the service. Accordingly, Taylor made the picture.

——Mayer, in testimony (1947) before the House Committee on
Un-American Activities

But Garbo could never appeal to the masses—just the middle and upper strata. We also had Andy Hardy—young Mickey Rooney. I was the daddy of the Andy Hardy films. What made the money—Garbo with the ribbons or Andy Hardy, which the critics tore to ribbons?

I'll tell you. Andy Hardy. There were difficulties. In one film [*Judge Hardy and Son,* 1939] Andy Hardy's mother is dying. The writer asked me what Andy should do in the scene. "Make him pray," I said. The writer said he couldn't write a prayer. I urged him to. He made Andy Hardy talk about God and chariots and love. They filmed the scene with Andy Hardy standing up. Standing up in prayer! I warned them. "Audiences will laugh when they see it," I said.

We went to a cinema and ran the film. The audience laughed. They reshot it then. With Andy Hardy kneeling. I told them what the prayer should be. Something simple—from the heart. . . .

Andy Hardy said, "Please God, don't take mother away from us—we can't do without her." Simple—direct. The audience cried. The film made more money than Garbo. . . .

I saw Judy Garland when she was 12. Wonderful voice. I signed her. What a girl—all the talent in the world. Like my own daughter she was to me. But then she got sick.

It became too much to ask my producers and directors to work with her. She had to go. It broke my heart. She had to go.

———Mayer, interviewed for *The Daily Express,* 14 July 55

Ken MAYNARD (1895–1973)
Born in Vevey, Indiana. Rode in circuses and Wild West shows before entering films in 1924.

I started out full of pep and did the trick as I had been taught, that is, with grace. But it looked too easy and what was my chagrin to have letters suggesting that it had been faked. It sure had me sore. So I began to wobble and half lose my balance, and then everyone thought I was great.

The other stunts that I used to risk my neck doing had to be too quickly done for the camera to pick up, so they didn't mean a thing.

———Maynard, interviewed for *Screenland,* July 1929

Jim McBRIDE
Born in New York City, 1941; attended film school at New York University.

It's a very mysterious process, how you get a film. It starts out for me as just a need to make a film. And then it comes to images, obsessive images. And because I was so involved in movies, there was always in my mind an image of a guy with a camera on his shoulder filming himself in a mirror. And that image seemed terribly profound to me. I'm not sure I could explain why. . . .

But it's just those random images and obsessions that suddenly come together. If you take the image of a guy filming himself in a mirror and you put that together with the other elements that I mentioned, you come up with a diary as a logical form.

This particular film [*David Holzman's Diary*, 1967] had about a 3-year gestation process, from the time the original idea occurred to me until the film was made. In all that time I was thinking about it. Images were coming to me and it was like fitting a puzzle together. I think you *discover* a film. There's something there in the original intention, the original idea. Then apparently irrelevant things come to you from somewhere else, and all of a sudden you discover they all fit in. . . .

[Kit Carson] and I spent a week together before shooting. We sat down in a room with a tape recorder—and I think this is the way Brian [De Palma] got the idea to do *Greetings* [1969]. I would say, "This is what happens in this scene. This is what I want you to say." As you know, most of the film's dialogue is in direct confrontation with the camera.

So I would tell him what I wanted and he would do it. He'd put it in his own words and throw in new things of his own. Then we'd listen to the tape together and I'd tell him, "I don't like this. You missed this. I've got an idea; put this in." He would do it again and together we refined each scene. We didn't transcribe it. We just listened to it, again and again, until we both had a fairly clear idea of what was going to happen when we were actually pointing the camera at him.

It never got down to a word-by-word situation. And when we started shooting it was always better than it had been in the taping sessions. He always threw in a little zinger for me that he hadn't told me about.

———McBride, interviewed for *The Film Director as Superstar* (NY, 1970)

Leo McCAREY
Born in Los Angeles, 1898. First film job, script clerk for Tod Browning. From 1923 to 1929, directed and supervised films for Hal Roach, including the first films that teamed Laurel & Hardy:

At that time comics had, for the most part, a tendency to "do too much." With Laurel and Hardy we introduced a nearly opposite comic conception. I tried —we tried—to direct them in such a way that they showed nothing, expressed nothing, which had the consequence of making the public, which was waiting for the opposite, laugh. We restrained ourselves so much in showing the actors' feelings that the public couldn't hold back its laughter, and laughed because we remained serious. . . .

Q. What was Laurel's role on the crew? It is said that he was very inventive. . . .

A. He was one of the rare comics intelligent enough to invent his own gags. Laurel was remarkably talented, while Hardy wasn't. This is the key to the Laurel-Hardy association. Throughout their lives (I was one of their intimates), Laurel insisted on earning twice as much as Hardy. He said that he was twice as good and twice as important, that he wrote the film and participated in its creation, while Hardy was really incapable of creating anything at all—it was astonishing that he could even find his way to the studio.

———McCarey, interviewed for *Cahiers du cinéma*, Feb 65;
trans. by Rose Kaplin for *Cahiers du Cinema in English*, Jan 67

Malcolm McDOWELL [Taylor]
Born in Leeds, England, 1943.

[Lindsay Anderson and Stanley Kubrick] work from totally opposite directions yet they have the same total control. That's the only way to make a film. If the director is not strong there is no style to the film. Stanley is a great technician, Lindsay is great talking to the actors, getting an ensemble feeling into the work.

Kubrick has complete control. If he hadn't been a film director he would have been a General, Chief of Staff of the U.S. Forces. He's sort of H.Q. No matter what it is—even if it's a question of buying shampoo for your hair—it goes through him. It has to be okayed by H.Q. He just likes total control. He learned his lesson the hard way. With one early film he had no legal control and he had a hard time.

We never talked about the character of Alex [in *A Clockwork Orange*, 1971]. I was really worried. In the end you just did it. Alex is a pure evil force. Kubrick's way is to rehearse all day from 7 and then shoot the scene around 4 or 5 in the afternoon. By then he had it right and he saved film.
——McDowell, interviewed for *The Evening Standard*, 31 Dec 71

I went to see Stanley and he said, "I've got this book for you. . . ." When I read the book I found it very hard going, first time. I thought, what is all this "malenky" and "droogies" nonsense. . . . We didn't start shooting till September, and I went out to his house pretty well every day from June on, played about a million games of table tennis. . . . We talked a lot about costume. I'd bought some makeup and lashes to try and find the futuristic bit. I was putting on one pair, and he said, "Let's just take a still of that." Saw the still and that was it. I said, "That's all Alex wears, none of the colors, that, only that." He said, "Oh, would you like black lips or something?" I said, "No, just the one eye, 'cause when they see the face, there's something wrong, and they're not quite sure what it is at first." I was very pleased with that.

The "Singin' in the Rain" sequence was extraordinary. We had come to this set, looked at it, sat down for the whole day, said nothing, did nothing, nothing happened. The next day, the same. On the third day Stanley said, "You come in, kick the feller down, can you dance?" So I came in, kicked the feller down the stairs, suddenly went into . . . "Doobie-do-dah-bah-doobie-do . . . I'm Singin' in the Rain . . . Just singin' in the rain." And it just went through, like that on a rehearsal, right the way through to the end . . . on the phone to the New York office, "Get me the rights." Sat there for an hour waiting for the return call, $10,000 to use it for 30 seconds. That was it, end of our problem.

The thing with Stanley is that you have to be on form, bouncing with vitality at 8 in the morning—there's no walk-through rehearsal with him, you have to zing it—and over 7 months, every day, work. . . . There was quite a lot of ad libbing in the film. The psycho test, where they show you the inkblots and ask you to do the first thing that comes in your head. What you heard on the film were the first genuine things that came to mind.
——McDowell, interviewed for *Rolling Stone*, 2 Aug 73

Norman M c L A R E N
Born in Stirling, Scotland, 1914. Trained at the Glasgow School of Art, where he became interested in animated and abstract films. After filming The Defense of Madrid *(1936), he joined the GPO Film Unit in London. Since 1941 he has worked with the National Film Board of Canada.*

This technique used in my film *Neighbours* [1952] (sometimes referred to as "pixillation") consists of applying the principles normally used in the photographing of animated and cartoon movies to the shooting of actors; that is, instead of placing drawing, cartoons or puppets in front of the animation camera, we place real human beings.

The technique is not new, its origins go back to the early French movies of the Méliès epoch, when the camera was stopped in the middle of shots to produce trick effects, and the same principle has since been used occasionally in films by experimentalists like Hans Richter, Len Lye, Richard Massingham and many others. But on the whole, the technique has never had the exploration it deserves, nor has it had this in the film *Neighbours* or *Two Bagatelles* [1952], where only a few of the possibilities have been applied, and rather crudely at that. None the less, as a result of working with this approach I have jotted down the following observations.

In essence, any technique of animation consists of stopping the camera between the taking of each frame of film, instead of letting it run on relentlessly at normal speed. Once it is assumed that the actor being photographed by a movie camera can stop between any or every 24th of a second, a new range of human behaviour becomes possible. The laws of appearance and disappearance can be circumvented as can the laws of momentum, inertia, centrifugal force, and gravity; but what is perhaps even more important, the tempo of acting can be infinitely modulated from the slowest speed to the fastest.

At the outset of shooting *Neighbours,* our conception was to get all action by taking a single frame at a time throughout each shot (having the actors move in small amounts, between frames); but after some experimenting it became apparent that the single-frame approach was best only for certain types of shot.

To meet all our requirements, we decided to use a whole gamut of shooting speeds, from one frame every 5 minutes to one frame every 1/16th of a second, depending on the nature of the shot, so we would select the most desirable shooting speed. Within one shot we might often vary the shooting speed if different parts of the action demanded it.
———McLaren, in *Canadian Film News,* Oct 53

[*Pas de deux,* 1967] goes back over 20 years. I was in France in the late forties or early fifties and saw a 10-second commercial advertising women's corsets. The commercial consisted of a woman running in slow motion across the screen from left to right against a plain background. There were 6 images of the woman, each staggered and delayed a bit—and that was all. It immediately occurred to me that there were all sorts of possibilities in the technique; and as so often in the past, I tucked it in the back of my mind knowing it was the seed of a new idea. Years later, around 1961, I got excited about the possibility of this kind of "stroboscopic" effect in film. I had no idea of a theme but many ideas of a technical nature, and so started shooting experimental takes of Grant Munro and myself walking, running, and playing leapfrog.

I also had another technical idea that I thought would make it very easy to convert the material into a stroboscopic effect and, in fact, I think this was why I got excited about the whole project. If you print from a negative to a positive on a standard laboratory printer and both of them are in loop form, and if the negative loop is a few frames shorter than the positive loop, then each time they come around the image will be delayed or "staggered." We tried it in the lab and the results were wonderful. We now had these running, walking, and leapfrog shots considerably multiplied, while in some cases the image repeated itself 34 times giving a fantastic visual flow. . . .

Before we did the running and leapfrog tests, I multiplied some stock shots of a man walking through a kitchen. It was all utterly confused, because the background cluttered up the action, and I realized it was best to do without background in shots intended for multiplication. I also noticed from the kitchen scene that normal front lighting creates confusion when the images overlap, and that what was needed was mere edge lighting, either on one edge of the figure or on both edges. . . .

It seemed clear that I could use acrobatics or some kind of sport or dance for this technique; but since I didn't have a theme, I did nothing about it at that time. Three or 4 years later I felt I would like to try it with ballet movement, so I approached the directress and the choreographer of a Montreal ballet company and showed these running and leapfrog tests. I told her that I wanted to investigate a number of fairly standard ballet movements. . . .

It would have been impossible for the dancers to dance to music of any kind which could have been used in the final film, because although the initial shooting was straightforward, the multiplied images extended the length of almost every action by varying amounts. Thus, we only had precise timing and measurements when we had finished making the visual part of the film.

Then came the problem of sound. I had some idea of music for male and female voices without actually using words. . . . I . . . showed the film to several people at [the National Film Board of Canada] to get their suggestions for music. Eventually, Maurice Blackburn saw the film and proposed using a particular recording of Romanian panpipes which he had. . . . When we tried the disk the tempo was right and the mood very appropriate, but it was only 2 or 3 minutes long while our film ran for 14 minutes. Maurice, however, had a solution. He recorded the disc a number of other times, fragmented it, and re-edited it to fit the picture. In the original recording there is a sustained orchestral drone in one key behind the melody which continues throughout. What Maurice did was record additional material of the same chord played on a harp in the low, middle, and high registers. He then cut the recorded tape into a number of different loops each of slightly different lengths. The first 3 or 4 minutes of the film has nothing but this chord changing its texture, color, and register. Then one gets fragments of the panpipe melody from the original disk, and gradually these fragments become complete until the entire melody is played at the end.

——McLaren, interviewed for *The New Documentary in Action* (Berkeley, 1971)

Narcissus [his next project] denies love. The film for me is a kind of reflection that I'm coming to the end of a whole span of my life. I'm not depressed by the thought of death. I realize I have been very narcissistic myself—at one level, though not on the surface. Once I had many potentialities, but the one that developed was narcissism. And maybe that wasn't so bad. Every artist must be somewhat narcissistic.

——McLaren, interviewed in *Weekend Magazine* (Montreal), 30 Mar 74

Alexander M E D V E D K I N
Born 1900 in Penza (Russia), in the family of a railroad engineer. Joined Budyonny's cavalry, became a political instructor. Demobilized in 1927.

The end of the twenties. . . . The tenor of life had been upset throughout the huge country, changing the destiny of people; everywhere there was a severe struggle of the new with the old, but in the evenings (if nothing disturbed the peace!) over the screens of film theaters moved the flat shadows of "heroes," infecting the spectators with the poison of bourgeois happiness. . . . Of course there were also films that conveyed the pathos of revolution. But contemporary life, the burning life of today was left almost completely un-reflected on the screens; instead we got tearful melodramas. In those years many filmmakers threw themselves headlong into the fight, some even denied the right of existence to acted films, fiction films, with plots.

With a group of like-minded comrades I opposed the bourgeois cinema, openly declaring war on it for crowding out genuine, revolutionary art. It seemed to us that it required only one powerful blow to knock the breath out of the bourgeois "illusions." *What* we wanted to destroy was clear. But *how*. . . ? I felt that I knew exactly *what* and *how* it should be done in films. (Every beginner in films then, and today, too, knows "exactly" how "to beard the gods.") . . .

Our group proposed the production of short satirical films. . . .

——Medvedkin, contribution to *A Life in Films* (Moscow, 1971)

Michael M E D W I N
Born 1923. Actor, writer, producer in English films.

[Lindsay Anderson] cares about actors. His great love is the actor. All actors are terribly vulnerable and insecure. The one thing that they really do demand of a director is that he knows what he's doing better than they do. With Lindsay, one is in the safest hands. He's such a stunning psychologist, it's unnerving. He's quite a wonderful director for actors.

——Medwin, press release for *O Lucky Man*, 1973

We went into action, got everything crewed up and ready to start, and then CBS decided to cancel. They never told us why. Perhaps they finally got round to reading the script. This was about 6 weeks from shooting. Paramount threw us a lifebelt. In 48 hours they said they would do it, and saved the situation totally. Otherwise *If . . .* would perhaps have never been made.

With the Newsom report coming out and the whole future of public schools under review, the climate was a very delicate one vis-à-vis the public schools. Also with the budget that we had, we needed to have the facilities practically given to us. We needed a lot of boys as well as a school.

——Medwin, press release for *If . . .* , 1969

Jonas MEKAS
Born in Lithuania, 1922. One of his many contributions to the American independent cinema was a filming of the Living Theater's production, in 1964, of The Brig:

The theater was already locked up by the owner. We got the cast and the equipment into the theatre through the sidewalk coal chute, late at night. (We left the place the same way at 3 or 4 in the morning.) . . . The lighting remained the same as during the regular stage performance. I placed two strong floods on the front seats of the theatre so I could move freely around without showing the seats. I had three 16 mm. Auricon cameras (single-system, with sound directly on film) with 10-minute magazines. I kept changing cameras as I went along. The performance was stopped every 10 minutes to change cameras, with a few seconds overlap of the action at each start. I shot the play in 10-minute takes, 12 takes in all.

. . . My intention wasn't to show the play in its entirety but to catch as much of the action as my "reporter" eyes could. This kind of shooting required an exhausting concentration of body and eye. I had to operate the camera; I had to keep out of the cast's way; I had to look for what was going on and listen for what was said; I had to make instantaneous decisions about my movements and the camera movements, knowing that there was no time for thinking or reflecting; there was no time for reshooting, no time for mistakes. . . .

——Mekas, in *The Village Voice*, 24 June 65;
repr. in his *Movie Journal* (NY, 1972)

Georges MÉLIÈS (1861–1938)
Toward the end of his life Méliès wrote his memoirs in the third person, calling it "La Vie et l'oeuvre d'un des plus anciens pionniers de la cinématographie mondiale—Georges Méliès, créateur du spectacle cinématographique." It was first published in Georges Méliès, Mage *(1945 & 1961) by Maurice Bessy and Lo Duca.*

Having filmed in the studio a number of short comic or artistic scenes, Méliès wanted to take some sea views on the spot, in order to enhance his program with some scenic views, or documentaries, as we call them now. Very determined, he left for Trouville and Le Havre, loaded like a donkey. Two excruciating working days were in store for him. A storm was raging, as Méliès had chosen on purpose a period of bad weather, so as to obtain more attractive effects. His camera could hold only 20 meters of film and films could not be inserted or removed in the open air, therefore he had to spend the whole day in gymnastics, taking down his setup after each shot, carrying all his equipment to a photographer's shop to get it ready for his next shot. As he was alone he did not dare to leave anything on the shore, being afraid that somebody might touch his equipment and perhaps take away parts of it. It is easy to imagine the fatigue produced by such maneuvers, especially if they are repeated 20 times in a day, usually walking miles on sandy beaches into which he often sank up to his knees, heavily loaded as he was. Nothing could stop him, however, as he was dedicated [*avait le feu sacré*]. He was tired when he came home, but he triumphantly brought back to Paris about 15 glorious shots which had a prodigious effect on the spectators. Nothing of that kind had ever been seen before; the assault of raging waves on the cliffs of Sainte-Adresse, the foam, the seething waters, foam sprayed into the air, the eddies and spindrifts which were flitting about—as banal as all this might appear today, it fascinated the public then, as it was used to standard representations of the sea in the theater which was realized by means of painted canvas surfaces shaken by kids crawling underneath it. It was the rigorously exact nature representation—a complete novelty at that time—which thrilled the public. The ones who were familiar with the sea exclaimed, "That's it, exactly!" and the ones who had never seen the sea felt they were standing on its shore.

——Méliès, memoirs in *Georges Méliès, Mage* (Paris, 1945)

Jean-Pierre M E L V I L L E   [Grumbach]   (1917–1973)

Q. How long do you take to prepare a film?

A. A long time. I have spent many, many months on *Le Cercle rouge* [1970]. I first began writing it in March 1968, and then having completed the first draft, I destroyed it. I wrote a second draft but I was still not satisfied so I tore that up. Then I began for a third time . . . when I had completed this final draft I showed it to Alain [Delon]. This is what we are shooting.

Q. Is it just a dialogue script that you write, or do you break it down into individual shots?

A. I plan everything on paper, all the camera angles and movements are written down. I find it absolutely impossible to have imagination when actually on the set.

Q. You are the complete *auteur* of your films. Which stage of production do you like working on most?

A. I like it in the middle of the night when I am writing . . . completely alone in my room at 3 in the morning. This I enjoy. And I love cutting. I have an assistant but I actually do the editing myself. What I do dislike is coming on to the set and shooting the film. You know, if there was another "me," a twin brother, I would ask him to take over the work of actually filming the script.

——Melville, interviewed for *Films & Filming*, June 70

Adolphe M E N J O U
Born 1890 in Pittsburgh, of French and Irish parents.

In the cast of *The Marriage Circle* [1923] were Marie Prevost, Florence Vidor, and Monte Blue. Ernst Lubitsch was the director. They say that he was influenced by Chaplin's direction of *A Woman of Paris,* but I doubt this because the latter film had not yet been released; however, he may have seen it at a private showing before release. . . .

Lubitsch, as a director, had the same regard for realistic and subtle touches as Chaplin, but his methods were entirely different. Lubitsch planned everything very carefully in advance; he knew the content of every scene before he began shooting, and he acted out every part in rehearsal. I discovered in this picture that all I had to do to make Lubitsch happy was to step before the camera and mimic every gesture he gave me. The Lubitsch method produced some very good pictures, for he was a fine director; but Chaplin taught me much more about my business.

———Menjou, in *It Took Nine Tailors* (NY, 1948)

Ernö M E T Z N E R (1892–1953)
Born in Hungary, where he studied architecture and design. Best-known work for G. W. Pabst.

. . . A moving camera shot Mr. Pabst ordered to be constructed in the film *Westfront* [1930]. The scene showed soldiers proceeding through an entanglement. Mr. Pabst wanted to photograph the people from below while they were working their way through the [barbed wire], he wanted to track with them to their new shelter. At the end of the track when the soldiers arrive in a shell crater, the camera is to look down into it from above. Thus the ways of the actors and the camera have crossed: while the camera was digging its way deep into the earth, the actors were crawling along the surface. At the end of the drive the camera reached the surface of the earth, and the actors are deep in the earth at the bottom of the crater.

———Metzner, in *Close-Up,* June 33

[In *Kameradschaft,* 1931] the impression of reality and genuineness of the decor and its occupants is augmented by heaping up buckets of coal-dust, fine as flour. Actors and staff are black to the base of their lungs. One reason why the realism of these sets must be carried to extremes is that the spectators can watch the actor with anxiety and alarm only if the supposed danger becomes credible and imminent by the utmost truth to life. Rocks that had been cast in real mines and copied in plaster of Paris, genuine coal, wood and coal-dust, engines, lorries, windlasses, and machines taken from mines, support the illusion which, scantly lighted, has been caught by [Fritz Arno Wagner's] camera in a masterly way.

———Metzner, in *Close-Up,* March 32

Mr. Pabst's fundamental idea for his production [of *Atlantis,* 1932] was that the film should strike the mass of spectators as a description of real occurrences; the more clever ones in the audience, however, should recognize that the events only happened in the imagination of the hero suffering from tropic delirium. The sets had to support this objective, on the one hand they must give the impression of complete reality, on the other hand this reality must be rendered improbable. The task is an interesting one, it stimulates the imagination, and while the expedition had been working already for quite a long time in Africa, I myself in my studio in Berlin tried to find the way which would combine African reality with the imaginary realm of Atlantis. . . .

Some time ago the camera would not have registered much of the many lights and mystic illuminations. For only recently has been brought out a new negative sensitive to yellow and red rays, and therefore able to photograph the small dancing flames. This negative is very sensitive and enables the cameraman to light the actors sufficiently with little light only, thus allowing the delicate lights of the oil lamps to be visible as light sources.

——Metzner, in *Close-Up*, Sept 32

Vsevolod [Karl Theodor] M E Y E R H O L D (*1874–1940*)

Recently, more and more scenarios have been based on novels. In adapting a novel for the cinema, the problem lies in transferring to the screen not only the plot but the whole atmosphere of the work; somehow the screen must be permeated with the entire spirit of the novel. Nowadays, films are being made of Dostoevsky, Turgenev, Przybyszewski, Wilde, and so on. The manner in which the plot is realized on the screen should vary according to the author. The plot of a novel by Dickens should be filmed with an eye to the style of Dickens. If the cameraman disregards this when setting up the lighting, his task becomes simple; but in lighting first a picture by Wilde, then one by Dostoevsky, he should consult with the director and the designer in order to establish the extent to which his approach must vary. . . .

Even a simple move from a door to a chair, from a chair on to the fore-stage has its own precise allocation of time. Turns, exits, and entrances are particularly difficult on the screen. In the scene where Dorian gives the servant the letter, I asked him to start the gesture, then stop and hesitate slightly. In this way, the phrase, "Wait a moment" creates a psychological impression: the audience waits, wondering what will happen next.

——Meyerhold, a lecture of 1918; trans. in *Meyerhold on Theatre*
(London, 1969)

In producing a film adaptation of Przybyszewski's novel [*The Strong Man*, 1917] I wanted to carry out the same ideas which I attempted to realize in *The Picture of Dorian Gray*. I wanted to bring to the screen those specific acting gestures that respond to the laws of rhythm and to utilize in the fullest way the light effects that are natural to the cinema. My work in the field of light effects, to which I ascribe great importance, was considerably hindered last year by a cameraman who couldn't be persuaded to leave his conservative notions. This time, the firm has given me a more experimental cameraman [Samuel Bendersky] with more understanding. The technical side of the cinema plays a great role, but is far from completely known. As to the settings of the film I found a real artist and an inventive collaborator in Vladimir Yegorov. We agreed to show in the film not whole scenes, but only sharp fragments of the whole. We've cast out a mass of unnecessary detail in order to focus the audience's attention on the highest moments of the rapidly developing film. . . . As to the acting itself I want to point out that my aim was to avoid any excessive accents, the moving-picture apparatus being over-sensitive in catching and reproducing even the most subtle gestures.

———Meyerhold, interviewed for *Teatralnaya Gazeta*, 7 Aug 1916

Lewis M I L E S T O N E [Milstein]
Born in Odessa, Russia, 1895. Educated in Russia, Germany, Belgium; emi-grated to the U.S. in 1913.

You hear a lot of picture people yelling that there is too much dialogue. Well, perhaps they are right—too much dialogue of the kind we have been given in our stories.

But . . . let me go on record right now with this . . . I maintain that we can hold a screen audience for 2 hours with a screenplay that is filled with conversation just as easily as you can hold them in the theater of the spoken drama with a play of conversation. However, the dialogue, in conversation, must be scintillating. Scintillating conversation can hold and entertain just as well as action, many times better. Take the plays of Shakespeare, for an example. They have come down through the years because of the scintillating conversation. So with the screenplay. If an audience in the legitimate theater can be held for 2 hours with the brilliant lines of a Shaw, Molnar, Chekhov or a Coward play, the same can be true with the screen. In everyday life we enjoy listening to a brilliant conversation by the hour, but we are bored to tears if the conversation is stupid. So it is with pictures.

I am not attaching undue importance to dialogue. In *All Quiet on the Western Front* you will recall that I depended mostly on action and psychologi-cal reactions. But when the characters spoke they had real thoughts to utter. Remarque put them there.

In *Front Page* [1931] which I am doing now, I must depend upon dialogue more than action. With the brillance, virility and humor of the lines, and with the advanced sound technique to use, the responsibility for its success or failure rests upon my own shoulders.

———Milestone, interviewed for *American Cinematographer*, Jan 1931

Arthur C. M I L L E R (1895–1970)
Born in Long Island, New York. First important camera work for New York Motion Picture Company in 1909.

Our first movie [for Edwin Porter's Defender Company in 1910] was called something like *Russia, Country of Depression,* and the only exterior scenes in the picture were shot on Staten Island. Those scenes showed Russian Cossacks riding full speed through the countryside in search of peasant cabins. The alarm shown by the peasants inside the cabins, or sometimes a spoken title mentioning their fear of the Cossacks at the door, was a trick used to avoid the necessity of building a cabin outside. Sometimes the peasant would open the door fearfully; if not, it would be broken down. Once inside the cabin, the Cossacks would beat the peasants with their whips and depart. We changed the dressing of the set and used different actors to make it appear that the Cossacks had visited several cabins. It was a horrifying subject for a picture and the expectation that fast-riding Cossacks would create the same colorful excitement as cowboys and Indians did not materialize.

From Gasnier's talk, I gathered that they had finished half of the first episode of a serial they intended to make. At this juncture, he sent me downstairs to tell Mr. Franconie that I was no longer in the news department but would be working upstairs in the studio. Louis Gasnier also informed me that my next assgnment was to photograph their new serial, with Harry Wood as my second cameraman. Early in April 1914, I started shooting the first episode of a serial that became well known as *The Perils of Pauline*.

The man in full charge of *Pauline* as well as of the Pathé studio was Louis J. Gasnier, who directed the first 10 episodes but then turned the director's job over to Donald MacKenzie. Donald MacKenzie had played the part of a pirate in one of the early installments. Shooting scripts were written by George B. Seitz and Bertram Millhauser. Seitz always cut the finished episodes. Contrary to many serials produced afterwards, each installment was completed separately. Later, many were made as one picture, shooting every location, from the first to the last episode, in one visit. The interiors were handled in the same manner—serials produced on a sort of production-line basis. . . .

The very nature of the serial called for peril and dangerous situations, and frequently required extra cameras to shoot several angles of a particular stunt. Cameramen working at the studio who happened to be between assignments operated the extra cameras.

We used negative film manufactured by the Pathé company. Gasnier viewed the developed negative on the screen and chose the desired take of each scene.

Toward the end of the serial, Spencer Bennett, now a director, was made an assistant to Donald MacKenzie and also played parts when called upon. The principals in the cast, of course, were Pearl White, Crane Wilbur, and Paul Panzer, who played the villain.

——Miller, in *One Reel a Week* (Berkeley, 1967)

[John Ford was] the director I liked working with better than anybody in the industry. You'd only talk, I think you might say, 50 words to him in a day; you had a communication with him so great you could *sense* what he wanted. He knew nothing of lighting; he never once looked in the camera when we worked together. You see, the man had bad eyes, as long as I knew him, but he was a man whose veins ran with the business. He had a tremendous memory; he could come up with an idea from some picture he had made 30 years before, and suggest you did that.

I've had people offer me money to give them the formula that Jack Ford used to direct. But he had no formula. . . .

——Miller, interviewed for *Hollywood Cameramen* (London, 1970)

When we go outdoors on location . . . I always scrim the direct sunlight from Shirley [Temple]. And as even experienced adults dislike facing reflectors I do all my modeling with artificial light. Usually I employ Solarspots and baby spots.

On [*Wee Willie Winkie*, 1937], we have one location representing a cantonment in India. Here we've had the problem of suggesting heat without building up unduly "hot" light levels. One sequence, for instance, takes place on the veranda of an officer's bungalow. I needed plenty of light in that porch to balance the strong sunlight outside. Ordinary inkies weren't adequate, and the sun men wouldn't let us use a generator big enough to power arcs. So I used one of the big Senior Solarspots—and the trick was done.

In one sequence of the last picture, *Stowaway* [1936], I also made good use of these larger units. The set represented the deck of a steamship, and I needed a strong, uniform key-light to represent sunlight. The answer was 3 Seniors lined up outside, overlapping at the stanchions supporting the upper deck. The effect could not have been more convincing had I used arcs— and it was obtained easily and economically.

——Miller, in *American Cinematographer*, Mar 37

Victor MILNER

Born in New York City, 1893, began his film career as a projectionist in New York nickelodeons, before training himself in film photography. His first professional film was Hiawatha (1914), *filmed with Seneca Indians playing all roles. Then he joined Pathé News as one of its five cameramen before the First World War. In Hollywood he worked as assistant to Joseph August and John Seitz before beginning his Paramount contract in 1924.*

I have photographed many of Ernst Lubitsch's sparkling comedy-romances, and more than a few similar stories directed by other directors. Few, if any, directors can impart to action and dialogue the peculiarly brittle brilliance which characterizes Lubitsch's work; and where one might stress the romantic phases, requiring much softer lighting and photographic treatment, and another might play everything for broader comedy, requiring more conventional, highly keyed lighting, Lubitsch's own style demands an equally distinctive, scintillating brilliance in photography and lighting which is rarely applicable elsewhere.

——Milner, in *American Cinematographer*, Jan 35

I have filmed scores of productions—important and otherwise—but in only one of them has such an ideal state of preproduction planning been realized. This was in the making of *The General Died at Dawn* [1936], in which I was immensely favored by being able to work with two exceptional artists— director Lewis Milestone and writer Clifford Odets—who worked with me beforehand, carefully planning direction and dialogue for the camera, and striving at every turn to inject visual mood into the scenes. But this was an exception: one production in a hundred.

——Milner, in *American Cinematographer*, March 38

Liza MINNELLI
Born in Los Angeles, 1946. Her Broadway debut was at the age of 19, and her
film debut was in Charlie Bubbles *(1967).*

[For *Cabaret,* 1972] Bob Fosse wanted the cabaret set to be authentic, and
authentic meant smoky. So he built a completely enclosed set, 4 walls, no
walls down for the camera to shoot from or anything phony. We almost got
acute asphyxiation ever time we did a number.

I had to do my own makeup for *Cabaret*—there wasn't much money,
so we had to do everything ourselves and it's fantastic . . . and Fosse made us
dress for every rehearsal. Nothing slapdash about it, I can tell you. We rehearsed for 3 or 4 weeks before we ever saw a camera. That picture is really
authentic. I mean Fosse wouldn't even let the girls shave under their arms,
and they just hated it! That's how you can tell that I'm the star, because I'm
the only one who doesn't have hairy armpits.
                                                          ——Minnelli, interviewed for *Impact,* Mar 72

Vincente MINNELLI
Born in Chicago, 1913. Family ran a touring tent show that collapsed under
competition with film theaters. Brought from designing film "presentations"
and Broadway shows to a long Hollywood career.

Judy [Garland] reported to Dotty's [makeup] department with her own gear:
rubber discs which were inserted to change the shape of her nose and caps
to disguise her slightly irregular teeth. "What are these?" Dotty [Ponedel]
asked. Judy explained.
    "You don't need all this junk," Dotty said. "You're a pretty girl. Let's
see what we can do."
    She didn't do all that much, Dotty recalls. "I raised her eyebrows a bit,
and gave her a fuller lower lip. I put on a makeup base that was pretty to
the eye. I knew it would be pretty to the camera, too. I tweezed out some of
the hairline." And that was that.

Monstrous stories have been told, accusing some Lucifer at the studio
of starting Judy on this tragic, gradually accelerated treadmill. I don't believe
them. Why would anyone want to make a nonfunctioning player out of a very
important star?
    The way it happened wasn't nearly as nefarious. The unions, during
Judy's early days at the studio, weren't as powerful as they later became.
Everyone put in long hours. Some fellow actor, trying to be helpful, probably
offered some amphetamines to Judy during one of those especially long days.
It probably wasn't long before she herself was seeking them out to see her
through her many 14-hour work days. The pills probably left her wide awake,
unable to sleep, so somebody else probably offered her sedatives. Few people
knew about the long-range effects of such drugs at the time.
    By the time of *Meet Me in St. Louis* [1944], the working conditions at
Metro were more humane, and Judy shouldn't have needed them any longer.
But she continued using them.

The standout scene of the picture [*Madame Bovary*, 1949] was the waltz. The dance was new to the period, and the sequence conveyed all the giddiness that enveloped Emma at the ball.

I told composer Miklos Rozsa what I wanted to create for the scene, and he wrote a neurotic waltz with an accelerating tempo that would work well with what we had in mind. All the action of the scene was shot to his pre-recorded music.

As Emma swirled around, the baroque mirror and chandeliers swung around with her. The camera movement suggested her dizziness and breath-lessness and explained why the host ordered the breaking of the windows, an action we retained from the book. At the same time, the husband is in the billiard room, getting cordially drunk. The sequence, shot in February 1949, was among the most difficult I'd ever directed.

... I'd noticed that Eastman negatives, in which Metro's color pictures were then being shot, didn't have the subdued tones that would be needed in a film about Van Gogh [*Lust for Life*, 1955]. The color process had origi-nally been developed for Twentieth Century–Fox's production of *The Robe* in 1953, and the palette was straight from the candy box, a brilliant mixture of blues, reds, and yellows that resembled neither life nor art. Since that time, Cinemascope and Eastmancolor had become [inseparable]. I insisted the picture be shot in Ansco film. But that company, having conceded to the popular taste that the best was the brightest, had stopped producing its line of color negatives. We badgered, cajoled, wheedled, and bullied, and Metro finally saw it our way. The studio bought 300,000 feet of Ansco film, the last remaining inventory, and persuaded Ansco to open a special laboratory to process what we shot. It was to prove to be the most important victory of the many battles John [Houseman] and I fought during the making of the picture. Joe Ruttenberg was sent ahead to film the fruit trees in blossom. For on the night Van Gogh first arrived in Arles 60 years previously, he'd opened the shutters of his room and saw the trees in a blaze of color. They were the first objects he painted there.

——Minnelli, with Hector Arce, in *I Remember It Well* (NY, 1975)

Howard G. MINSKY

I didn't think the first part [of *Love Story*, 1970] was quite right; Erich [Segal] had made the girl Jewish. I thought we should have the girl an American Italian, a Catholic, so that we could make a thing visually out of the cross she wears. And I wanted the mother out earlier, so that we could have an interesting father-daughter relationship.

I told Erich it had to be in hardback. I didn't want it in flashy paperback first; I wanted those hardback reviews for the prestige. Erich said it was too short an idea for a novel, then he worked on it and he did a fine job.

——Minsky, interviewed for *The Guardian*, 9 Feb 71

Robert MITCHUM
Born in Bridgeport, Connecticut, 1917.

Q. Did you value [*The Night of the Hunter*, 1955] highly when you did it?

A. Yes. Charlie Laughton sent me the book and he said this is the story of a real, you know, monster. . . . I said yes, I'd like to do it—the book was really a good book . . . he directed and put together dramatized and also wrote the screenplay for *Night of the Hunter*—it was the first time he'd ever done that and unfortunately he also cut the film and it was a bit much you know for him to do it and just too much for him to do. He was very fond of me and he didn't want people dragging their children in off the streets so he kind of introduced a sort of a fairy-tale atmosphere a children's book atmosphere in the film just so that people wouldn't think too unkindly of me and I thought that was really contrary to my thought because I thought that the mother should be a solid strangler all the way.

——Mitchum, interviewed at the National Film Theatre, 7 Sep 72

Subrata M I T R A
Born in 1931.

I had had no training. When I was in school I saw good films and good photography. That got me interested, and I sort of decided to be either a cameraman or an architect. Later on in college, I decided on cinematography. At that time there were no film schools in our country. . . .

In 1950, Jean Renoir came to India to shoot *The River;* his cinematographer was Claude Renoir. I left college, and although I didn't work on that film, I watched the entire shooting. You could really say that was my first real experience because I watched a great director and a great cameraman working together. During that period I met Satyajit Ray who also came to watch the shooting, usually only on weekends because he was working as an art director in an ad agency.

. . . When Mr. Ray was ready to start shooting [*Pather Panchali*, 1955], one day he asked me to photograph it. To be frank, I had never touched a movie camera before. But Mr. Ray pointed out that I had done still photography, and it was practically the same thing.

Later on, of course, I came to know it's not the same thing. . . . I had to learn cinematography while shooting my first film. So *Pather Panchali* was sort of my film school.

——Mitra, interviewed for *Filmmakers Newsletter*, Jan 75

Tom M I X (1880–1940)
Born in Mix Run, Pennsylvania. In 1911 served in the U.S. Cavalry. From 1913 worked as actor for Selig Polyscope in one- and 2-reelers.

Well, what with my early youth having been spent on one of these hitting-the-high-spot cattle ranches, and what with my butting into 5 different wars; I was pretty well able to handle any kind of proposition by the time I arrived on my aforementioned visit of inspection in movieland.

A bit critical I was, too, you can guess. So when some fancy-looking dude from the East, who was playing hero, decided that he couldn't take any risks with his precious face, I pushed myself forward in my usual modest way, and whispered, "Say, boss, I'll do them horse-jumps for you!"

And that was the way I broke into the movies!

For the director accepted my offer, and I did several "doubling" stunts. And, by the way, that's the only sort of "doubling" I've ever experienced. Nobody does my hard bits for me now that I'm a hero myself.

——Mix, in *Pictures*, 19 March 1921

Kenji MIZOGUCHI (1898–1956)
Born in Tokyo.

The producers did not know that the script [of *Tokai Kokyogaku*, 1929] was based on works of extreme left-wing writers. If they had, they would never have approved the project. We had great difficulties with the police when the film was finished. We shot it in a very lawless section of the city and were obliged to disguise ourselves as workers and hide the equipment.

This film [*Saikaku Ichidai Onna*, 1952] was very close to me ever since I went to Kyoto. It is a true maxim that "If you want something badly enough, you will get it." It is essential that one should reflect for 5 or 6 years before beginning to film. Films produced quickly are never very good. Among the books of Saikaku are many others I would like to film because it would allow me to depict men and women as part of the social system of the time.

——Mizoguchi, quoted in Sadoul-Morris, *Dictionary of Films*, pp 377, 322

Jean-Pierre MOCKY [Mokiejewski]
Born in Nice, 1929. Studied law and drama; acting in films since 1944.

Ten days before we were due to start production [of *La Tête contre les murs*, 1958] we had a setback, when the producer died. His associates were against doing the film because they thought it was not commercial. They also did not want me to direct as I had not directed before and said I was too young. . . . The producers agreed to make the film with Franju directing, and I took the lead part and engaged Charles Aznavour for the other main role, that of the man who commits suicide.

When the film started it became a fight between Franju and myself. When I wrote the script I planned camera movements and everything, and he wanted to change many things. He is a poet and he made some of the scenes very slow, for instance he dwelt a lot on the decor of the asylum more than was necessary and treated it as documentary. This made a sudden change in pace of the film, because the opening is very fast moving and strong, like the films of James Dean, but then it suddenly becomes poetic and loses impact.

——Mocky, in *Films & Filming*, Oct 61

Hal MOHR (1894–1974)
Born in San Francisco, where he built his own camera for newsreels. His first Hollywood job in 1915 was as a film cutter at Universal, before he directed

and photographed comedies for Hal Roach. Returned to newsreels (for the army photographic service) during the First World War, in Europe. Worked for Mary Pickford and Douglas Fairbanks, and photographed Stroheim's Wedding March.

We did rather well, if you recall, with *Watch on the Rhine* [1943]. For me, it was just a case of engineering. The first thing I said to Shumlin was, "Please rehearse the scene exactly as you did it on the stage. Let me watch." The sets were more or less like the stage sets. He would rehearse; I'd take a script clerk and break it all down. As he did a scene I would say, "There is the camera, and we'll move it across to here," without changing his action at all. In this way, I wrote my own shooting script. Shumlin would rehearse and leave the set. I'd mark the camera positions, mark the stand-in positions, call Shumlin back, show him exactly what I intended to do, and he'd give me the go-ahead.
———Mohr, interviewed for *The Real Tinsel* (NY, 1970)

Ivor M O N T A G U
Born in London, 1904; after a scientific education at Cambridge, became interested in films. A founder of the Film Society, an associate producer with Michael Balcon (helping Hitchcock at two critical periods of his career) and a lifelong friend of Eisenstein and Chaplin.

Mick [Balcon] asked me to see *The Lodger* [1926] to consider editing and titling it. . . .
    Hitch had made 3 pictures [for Gainsborough]. The first they wouldn't show because they didn't think it was good enough; the second the same. . . . Then he had done *The Lodger*. And they wouldn't show that either . . . [Adrian Brunel] must have suggested [me]. They said would I do it and if necessary reshoot it, or arrange with Hitch for things to be reshot. Hitch was awfully nice about it, he could have been very bad-tempered and irritated, but he wasn't. He did reshoot one or two shots and I completely retitled it, without any original thoughts, but simply pinching ideas from other pictures [*The Gold Rush*, 1925, and *Schatten*, 1922] and things like that; after all, most original ideas have just been pinched unconsciously.

    Q. At what stage was *The Man Who Knew Too Much* [1934] when you became involved with it? I mean had Hitchcock decided already to make that?
    A. No. That was really an original of Hitchcock's. You see Charles Bennett had the credit for story-making in that, but you see what happened with Hitch's stories was that he would want an amanuensis. He originally used Alma Reville on a lot of these things. He would have the idea, but I don't mean to say at all he couldn't, he wouldn't, it wasn't his style of work, to put pen to paper. He wanted a screen writer to talk to. . . . The screen writer and the associate producer who was me or anybody else we brought in would throw out ideas. Hitch would go around London and he'd see something from a bus, he would go, for example, to the Albert Hall. We would work these into the stories. . . . The writer would be given the credit because Mick wouldn't allow associate producers to have any credit at all.

. . . What really made *Blackmail* [1929] what it was was the fact that it became a talkie halfway through, so that what he had to think of was ingenious ways of saving the silent picture with a certain amount of talk and it became the best talkie to that date, because it was the only one in which the whole picture wasn't shot in blimp—that really was the accident that gave it its character.

————Montagu, interviewed for *Screen*, Autumn 72

William P. MONTAGUE
Assignment Editor of Paramount News.

A few weeks ago I had a phone call from our Chicago cameraman. He was about to leave for Indianapolis along with the rest of the opposition cameramen to cover the big auto races. They are always a sure-fire thrill and good entertainment and, as you know, practically routine coverage for every newsreel. Our cameraman wanted to go along with the gang—it's always a swell party—but he did begrudgingly mention that he had been out at the Republic Steel plant that day and things looked tough. Well, it was quite a gamble to take, but we pulled him off those auto races and sent him back to the steel plant. . . .

Well, we made the riot story, screened it, and immediately realized the problem on our hands. Several paths were open to us. We could have killed the story and no one would have been the wiser. Newsreel film is tricky stuff to work with. Quite a lot is often no good and if it had been reported technically defective we would have been out of the jam. . . .

Instead, we got socially conscious. We realized that we had to assume the obligations of a news organization. We had to act as editors and consider the ultimate consequences of what we released. We had to remember what had happened when we released that [San Jose] kidnapping picture. . . .

Paramount did not suppress the Chicago riot pictures. Instead, it voluntarily turned them over to the LaFollette Senate Committee investigating the situation, to make what use it could of them in behalf of public welfare. They immediately became part of the record of the proceedings, but in a way that insured no harm to the general public.

Senator LaFollette expressed his appreciation for the stand that Paramount had taken, and finally after the film had been used as evidence, recommended the release of the pictures. By that time the industrial situation had quieted down and there was no danger of riots developing, and Paramount sent the complete and unexpurgated pictures out to every one of its exchanges.

————Montague, statement repr. in *World Film News*, Feb 38

Agnes MOOREHEAD (1906–1974)
Born in Clinton, Massachusetts, daughter of a Presbyterian minister.

Orson [Welles] believed in good acting, and he realized that rehearsals were needed to get the most from his actors. That was something new in Hollywood: nobody seemed interested in bringing in a group to rehearse before scenes were shot. But Orson knew it was necessary, and we rehearsed every sequence [of *Citizen Kane,* 1941] before it was shot.

——Moorehead, in *Action,* May–June 69

Jeanne M O R E A U
Born 1928. From 1948 to 1952 in the company of the Comédie Française.

... Each time Antonioni came to Paris we met—about once a year. It was a period in which he had great difficulties. He told me repeatedly, "Someday we will make a film together." ... Then he initiated his adventure with *L'Avventura* [1960], which lasted ... a very long time, and while he was shooting it, he wrote to me. Sometimes he really went through moments of desperation. It was in this period that he formulated the wish to make a film with me which he had already conceived and which turned out to be *La Notte* [1961].

Then *L'Avventura* had the success you know, and Antonioni became famous and created *La Notte,* the shooting of which was long. Extremely long. Many nights. About 40, I think. We lived in an absolutely abnormal rhythm. We were shooting even on Sunday nights. It was quite horrible. We were like fish in an aquarium, in this famous bay of Barnasina where we were shooting. Even food was of no importance. Nothing was important, except sleeping. In the few hours that remained for sleeping I think that everybody was having nightmares about being prevented from sleeping. ...

The atmosphere of the film deteriorated for this reason. People did not like each other very much. Furthermore, Antonioni is very distant. "Distant" is not really the right term, because he is related constantly to the others, but he keeps always a certain ... distance. He is not a director who gives the impression that you can touch him. I was a close friend of Marcello Mastroianni and nobody's enemy, but beyond that, quite solitary.

We all were physically weakened at the end of the film. It was a devouring film. ...

Being an actor one witnesses many things, on all levels, and even the electricians' and mechanics' mood is of some importance. The successful films reflect generally a good atmosphere. In *Eva* [1962], e.g. some people could not stand the director [Losey], Heaven knows why. These people indulged in a systematic destructive action which involved the producer, the stage director, and the manager. Furthermore, the director was an American working with an Italian crew, which meant that it was difficult to communicate. At times I served as interpreter and I realized perfectly that the team had no consideration for the boss who directed them, which creates inevitably a horrible atmosphere. To make things even worse there was antagonism between the director and the first cameraman [Gianni Di Venanzo], although he happened to be an excellent cameraman. This factor, added to the others, made the atmosphere worse and worse.

Furthermore, this film—a difficult one in any respect—was shot in Venice in bad weather conditions, with temperatures reaching 10 degrees C. below zero. There was also a schedule problem. In France, even with a small crew, the producer always grants the workers at least a 10-hour rest, knowing that the electricians have not finished their work once the shooting is stopped, as everything has to be repacked and sometimes transported. In Italy, on the contrary, one does not care about that, and a crew works frequently 12 to 14 hours steadily. In our case, this had an influence on the moods, and the antagonisms became sharper. In a film all this is reflected; you can sense it in the quality of the light, as well as in the framing and everywhere. It has to be admitted, it was a failure on the human plane and I was convinced that Losey would give up.

When the film was stopped, many things had not been shot, but the systematic destructive action did not stop at that point. Then came the editing. . . .

How easy it is to spoil something! . . . without any open opposition, trimming everything, nibbling away, gradually. A film is not only a matter of money. That which matters is the atmosphere in which things happen. Great films have been realized with little money and in our case there was no lack of money. Simply, there was a terrible squandering of human beings.

———Moreau, interviewed for *Cahiers du cinéma*, Jan 65

With Peter [Brook] I am always like a baby. He creates great confidence and a great sense of life. He knows exactly what he wants. The part I did in *La notte* with Antonioni, I couldn't do it again. It was absolutely exhausting. You had no feeling that you as a human being were important at all. It did not matter whether you were happy or not. I was not. The exercise was fascinating, but I wouldn't do it again.

———Moreau, interviewed for *The Times*, 7 Jan 67

How was it for her, after so many years of acting, to direct for the first time [*Lumière*, 1976]?

All the pains and anxieties were expected. Every time I made a film I realized what the director went through. And on this picture I remember 2 nights before the shooting started waking up in a state of fear.

It was like a vision. I remembered Joseph Losey's allergy just before shooting. He couldn't breathe. I remembered at the beginning of *Jules and Jim*, in the little hotel we stayed at, hearing Truffaut walking up and down in his room all night. I remembered Buñuel's rigor, just before shooting, when he would touch everything, each object to reassure himself.

With me what was unexpected was the exhilaration when I got on the set. It's like being in battle. You have all the actors and crew waiting for you. You feel alone and selfish; you don't care about anyone's problems, you only care about your film. You are like the spider in her web, drawing everything to her.

———Moreau, interviewed for *The New York Times*, 30 June 76

Oswald MORRIS

Born in Ruislip, Middlesex in 1915, he began his career in films at age 16. Before the war he worked in sound departments and as a camera assistant and operator. During the war he was a bomber and transport pilot, and in 1949 became a director of photography.

Moulin Rouge [1953] broke every rule in the book. We used very strong light-scattering filters on the camera which had never been used before, and we also filmed every set full of smoke so that the actors always stood out from the background. It was a monumental job but every minute of it was worth it now, looking back. We used to color the smoke with back-lighting—the colors that Toulouse-Lautrec used to use—and we colored the shadows and the filter lights for the various characters so that José Ferrer who played Lautrec always had a blue-green filter light on his face and Colette Marchand, who played the part of the prostitute, a sort of purple-violet light which Lautrec had used in his paintings, while Suzanne Flon, who played a very honest, nice person, had a pink fill light. And, with the colored smoke behind, this gave a most extraordinary effect. That film is always remembered for its visual quality, but every rule was broken. We were just doing everything to destroy what lens manufacturers, laboratories, and film stock manufacturers were trying to achieve.

Knave of Hearts [1954] was the first time we'd gone in the streets and wrapped cameras up in paper. René Clément was a great pioneer of that kind of photography. And with an actor like Gérard Philipe, who was so used to working that way, there was a great understanding between them. We went to the craziest of places to film—Charing Cross Station in the rush hour, filming there with Gérard Philipe, and Piccadilly Circus, playing scenes right round Eros! No English producer or director would have dared to do that. I used to have a newspaper with me all the time and my operator would wrap the camera up in a brown piece of paper and he would have it just behind me by my right shoulder; I would be reading the newspaper and then just at a given cue I would drop the newspaper and the camera would turn over. Clément was wonderful at putting decoy cameras out—if he thought we'd been discovered, he would set up a decoy camera say 200 or 300 yards away and leave our location for 20 minutes. And it always worked. . . .

Sidney [Lumet] wanted *The Hill* [1965] to look a pretty rough, rugged, documentary type of picture so we decided we'd go out to the location in Almería and I took 6 different sorts of black-and-white film stock and we tested this material with a small camera in all sorts of ways—over exposing and underdeveloping and underexposing and overdeveloping. We brought them all back, had them processed, and obtained some most exciting effects. We narrowed the choice down to two styles, one of which we were going to shoot on exteriors, the other on interiors. Nothing in *The Hill* was processed normally but we think the effect that we got was just right. Now, as far as camera movement was concerned, we went out of our way to mess about with the tracks and the dollies—I mean, if we laid a track down of boards on the sand, we got it roughly level and then we threw sand and lumps of rock all over it so that, when we dollied across it, the camera bounced all over the place. If that film had been photographed in a smooth, slick, sophisticated way, it wouldn't have had half the strength.

I didn't photograph [*Reflections in a Golden Eye,* 1968] from the beginning, but I was asked to take over a little way through. John Huston, with the previous cameraman, had evolved a very extreme system of color desaturation (toning down the colors) which we could only do at the end, apart from the early tests—the final result could only be done when the negative was cut because it was quite a costly and complicated system. It was filmed pretty near normal but with very strict color control but when the answer print was produced the distributors thought it was too extreme and too way out, and I think only one desaturated copy was made and the rest of the copies were printed normally. It was almost a complete desaturation and that one copy will be a museum piece because it really was quite extraordinary.

We experimented quite a bit with this on *Moby Dick* [1956]. It was a period film, and modern colors gave it a veneer, a gloss, which was completely bogus. You could not believe these whaling men were really suffering in those boats because the colors were too lush and glossy. So we evolved a system of desaturation there—not as extreme as in *Reflections*—but we found that it desaturated the blacks and it became wishy-washy and anemic and not masculine—and it was a very masculine picture—so to reinforce the black we added a gray image (black and white) onto the desaturated colors and that brought the contrast back without bringing in the colors. That was a completely fresh breakthrough but this system has never been used.

——Morris, interviewed for *Focus on Film*, No. 8, 71

Photographers get typecast sometimes, like stars. I suppose Figueroa's lush, luminous lightings for a lot of minor Mexican films made Ford, say, pick him to do the same in *The Fugitive* [1947]. But for all I know he may resent this enormously. You notice that when he is working with Buñuel, a director who obviously knows just what he wants and is determined to get it, Figueroa uses the same tremendous technical know-how, but the style is bare, harsh, totally different. This is what I prefer myself, and I think all photographers prefer it: a director with a strong personality and a very clear idea of what he wants the photographer to do. Even if you think he is quite wrong, any strong line is better than no line at all.

[*Indiscretions of an American Wife*, 1954] was a special case: the director wanted to make a neo-realist film, the American producer wanted a glossy romantic drama, and I got caught somewhere between the two. And of course, you find that the importance of the photographer's role in the creation of a film varies enormously from film to film, director to director.

Tony Richardson, for instance, is extraordinarily open to suggestion: he makes it almost a principle not to make decisions in advance, to go too deeply into the subject he is treating, since he feels that this is liable to make the film go dead during the shooting. Consequently, you find that his films take color very much from the particular group of collaborators he has round him at any particular time. Now Jack Clayton, on the other hand, is at the other end of the scale: he prepares everything meticulously in advance, and has the whole film laid out in his mind before he shoots an inch. I am happier myself with the latter approach: I have a great love for what one might call the classical, well-made cinema style. And yet both *The Pumpkin Eater* [1964] and the two films I made with Tony Richardson would come in my short list of the films I have been happiest with, so I suppose one can achieve what one wants within all sorts of discipline.

——Morris, interviewed for *The Times*, 22 July 67

Ivan MOZHUKHIN (1889–1939)
Born in Penza. The most popular actor in pre-revolutionary Russian films.

. . . One day [Yevgeni] Bauer had the idea of entrusting to me an important and very dramatic role in a film whose title I have forgotten [probably *Life in Death*, 1914]. In the course of the plot a woman, whom I was supposed to have loved, died, and I had a long scene of despair beside her body. Up to then, when an actor was given a scene of this sort, he expressed his grief with much wringing of hands, attitudes of dejection, facial contortions practiced at great length before a mirror, and glycerine tears. In a complete break with this tradition, already entrenched in our studios, I contented myself with playing the scene in an absolutely motionless position, gradually bringing myself to the point where tears—*real* ones—suddenly welled up in my eyes and trickled down my cheeks. . . . What made me more happy than the success of the film was that I felt I now understood cinema.

———Mozhukhin, memoirs in *Pour vous*, 1 Feb 39

Paul M U N I   [Muni Weisenfreund]   (1896–1967)
Born in Lwow, Poland. Actor parents emigrated to U.S. via London, 1902.

. . . I would certainly say that the theater is a much better medium for the actor than the film, if for no other reason than that he goes through at one fell swoop with the whole plot, so that he doesn't have to chop things up into little things. And there are other reasons. The mechanical business of sticking a camera into your face, if they're going into a close-up, and you have to concentrate on the scene, and it's devilish and difficult to try to make yourself believe that there isn't a camera in your face. And you're talking into a lens and you're supposed to be talking to another human being and you know bloody damn well you're talking to a lens. And to be able to so metamorphose yourself into the sense of making yourself believe that it's not so, is a tough job. You try to do it, but you succeed only partially.

Q. What was the satisfaction from *Pasteur* [1935] and from *Zola* [1937]

Muni: They were just well written, but we actually had quite a hassle with this fellow—Hal Wallis . . . and Jack Warner. They said, "What kind of a picture is that?" They didn't want to do it. We sneaked in *The Story of Louis Pasteur* on them. . . .

Actually, they fought us on it and it so happened that I was fortunate. I held the thing up at that time because of a contract that I'd made. Again it's the rigidity about that contract that they couldn't make me do any picture unless I okayed it, and when I okayed it, it had to be substantially as it was written. They had to do it. They sent me script after script which were so terrible that I just couldn't accept them. They were supposed to send me 3 scripts, and if I didn't like theirs, I was to send them 3 scripts. And the other arrangement was that if I didn't accept their 3 scripts and they didn't accept my 3 scripts, they'd have to pay me a half-salary and I wouldn't have to do anything. . . .

I had made one picture after another that was considered very arty. I don't know how much money they made. Like *The Good Earth* [1937], *Pasteur*, and *I Am a Fugitive from a Chain Gang* [1932], and *Scarface* [1932]. They knew that so many studios were out to get me to sign, and all that, so they wanted to keep me there and they gave me leeway, a lot of things that normally an actor wouldn't be able to get. So, therefore, we practically pushed it down their throats. They just didn't want to do *Pasteur*. . . .

You know what they spent to make *Pasteur?* . . . $260,000!

Mrs. Muni: In five weeks they made it. Anyway, with this protest from Wallis and Warner, and all of that, well, finally, they sold it at a smaller percentage to the exhibitors because they didn't think they had a picture. And it opened in a second-run theater in Chicago, and then all of a sudden this thing went, you know, and with the Academy Award, and so forth. Then later that year, the following year, they submitted some story to Muni, and I don't remember what it was, he did not want to do it. And Jack Warner called him up to the office to try and persuade him, and he said, "Muni, for God's sake, why don't you listen to me? After all, I gave you *Pasteur*."

Muni: And then he said, "This has got social consciousness in it."

——Muni, interviewed for *Actors Talk About Acting* (NY 1961)

When First National assigned me to the role [of Emile Zola] I began collecting all the material bearing on Zola's life and times that I could lay hands on. I read the man's own books; I read personal reminiscences of him by friends and fellow authors; I read half a dozen biographies.

When I felt sure of my background, I began to study the physical appearance of the man, I looked over innumerable portraits, some of them life-size, some mere sketches. Out of them I got a good mental picture of what Zola looked like and then I began several weeks of experiment with makeup until I approached that appearance as closely as it was possible.

For the voice part, I used a dictaphone arrangement. I would read the lines several ways, then play them back so I could judge what was the most effective way of delivering them. And I practiced walking with a stoop as Zola himself did. I found it exhausting often, because I had to hold it and sometimes I almost forgot I was Paul Muni and not Emile Zola.

——Muni, in press sheet from Warner House, London, 1937

Andrzej MUNK (1921–1961)

Born in Cracow, studied architecture before entering cinema, first as cameraman, then as director. Died in an automobile accident before completing The Passenger.

What is the subject of my new film [*The Passenger*, 1961]? It goes back to the war years and Nazi occupation, but the action takes place in the present. The events happen as if on 2 levels: today on board a luxurious ocean liner, and 20 years ago in the occupation period.

The main problems of my film? Those of the limits of human endurance and the conflict of moral responsibility. There is also the personal problem of a German woman who did not torture a woman prisoner but was trying to fight her on moral grounds by bribing her with a privileged position in the camp. She knew that the prisoner had a fiancé in the camp, and she used him as her weapon.

The past events to which the film refers took place in Auschwitz. We had a difficult problem to solve here: How to show Auschwitz without employing the method of a realistic documentary. In such a verisimilar art as a film is, realism would be unbearable. There were minor obstacles, too: how to find such faces today, such famished people.

Auschwitz is shown in the film through 2 filters: as viewed from 20 years' perspective, and as seen through the eyes of a German S.S. woman whose narration is cool, whose conscience is clear.

But let us go back to the problem of the imagination of the film audience. Making this film I am aware of certain dangers. As an example: We show the death block just before the execution. A black van appears in the empty yard. An S.S. man is loading his gun, stripped people are standing [in] the corridor, some are just taking off their last pieces of clothing. Then we enter the same yard after the execution. We can see a little cart loaded with the prisoners' clothes and a big black van. We guess that inside are the killed people. A Kapo is washing the wall with a hose pipe. This is probably where the execution has taken place. Another Kapo is raking the lawn. There has not even been a sound of shooting.

We did not manage, however, to avoid the scenes of torturing or beating prisoners throughout the film. But even if any such scene occurs, we can see neither the one that is beating, nor the beaten. This is left entirely to the imagination. We are trying to dispense with all direct portrayals of brutality.
——Munk, interviewed for *Polish Film*, Sep 61

Friedrich Wilhelm M U R N A U   [Plumpe]   (1888–1931)
Born in Bielefeld, Westphalia. First film work in Switzerland during the First World War, making propaganda films for the German embassy.

A film is nearly always finished before one has had time to get the actors to forget the bad habit of "giving a performance." If only our actors could learn to act like the Swedes. German actors don't get any artistic satisfaction out of their work nowadays. They are too businesslike, and in too much of a hurry to go from one film to the next.
——Murnau, interviewed for *Film Kurier*, 1922;
trans. in Eisner, *Murnau* (Berkeley, 1973)

The present machinery of the studios will not be enough for the director of the future. Even now I ask that they make me especial equipment so that I can get my camera where I want it.

The picture I am working on now is a circus story [*Four Devils,* 1928] and naturally the camera must not stand stock still in one spot in such a gay place as a circus! It must gallop after the equestrienne, it must pick out the painted tears of the clown and jump from him to a high box to show the face of the rich lady thinking about the clown.

So I have had them build me a sort of traveling crane with a platform swung at one end for the camera. My staff has nick-named it the "Go-Devil." The studios will all have Go-Devils, some day, to make the camera mobile.
——Murnau, in *McCall's Magazine*, Sep 1928

N

Conrad NAGEL

Born in Iowa, 1897; began stage career in 1914 with a stock company of Des Moines; first film appearance 1920: The Fighting Chance, *for Lasky.*

It took a lot more time to make a talkie, and it was a lot more expensive than to make a silent film. The studios began to overwork their actors. You'd work until midnight and be back on the set at 9:00 the next morning. You'd work all night Saturday because you could sleep on your own time on Sunday. Very often you'd work on Sunday, particularly if you were on location. Then when the Screen Actors' Guild finally got organized, they set out to define a working day. They established the working day and judged everything on the basis of the free-lance player, not by the contract player. The contract player was getting paid week after week whether he worked or not. The Screen Actors' Guild helped to eliminate many abuses. For instance, if a director didn't know what he wanted, he would experiment, try a thing 50 different ways, all on the actor's time, and run until 7:00 or 8:00 at night. But when he knew he could only have an actor 8 hours that day, he'd do his homework and make things a lot easier for the actor. Then, of course, the 5-day week finally came in. That was a bit of a struggle because once a picture is started, the overhead continues 24 hours a day, whether you're shooting or not.

——Nagel, interviewed for *The Real Tinsel* (NY, 1970)

Ronald NEAME

Born 1911 in London; educated at University College School, London. First job in industry was as assistant cameraman for Hitchcock's Blackmail, *1929.*

As for how I came into the business, I was practically born in a film studio, so my future was inevitable I suppose. My mother [Ivy Close] was an actress, and my father [Elwin Neame] was a stills photographer and later a filmmaker. He was making feature films around 1911, when a big feature film would run for only 10 minutes or so. He made one film starring my mother, *The Lady of Shalott* [1912]. That was a single-reeler, and was sold outright for £70 to the Coronet Cinema in Notting Hill Gate. . . .

By and large the cameraman does what I ask him to do, but that doesn't mean I am arbitrary in trying to tell him, say, how to light a shot; I tell him the effect I want and he creates that effect. The actual movement of the

camera—whether it pans or tracks, whether it zooms or cuts or whatever—is an absolute directive from me, because the director is the only person who knows how all the bits of the film are going to be cut. I do a tremendous amount of cutting of a film when I'm on the set, in my mind, while actually making the film. I don't believe in master shots; I don't believe in playing sequences all the way through in medium shot, then in close shot. I believe in cutting in the camera, before going into the cutting room. The result is that I usually have a first cut of any film I make within a few days of finishing shooting, because it's virtually already there before it goes into the cutting room.
——Neame, interviewed for *Amateur Photographer*, 28 Mar 73

Jean N E G U L E S C O

Born in Rumania, 1900; educated Liceul Carol University of Rumania. Served as technical director, assistant producer, assistant director; directed first film for Universal, Crash Donovan, *1936.*

[In *The Mask of Dimitrios*, 1944] I allowed Lorre complete freedom to improvise. Sometimes he went too far, and then I think it's the role of the director to step in and say, "I think it's wonderful, it's very funny, but it's not in keeping with the mood and style of the rest of the film." Something similar happened in *The Mudlark* [1950] with Alec Guinness, who was so good, so different, that the rest of it was thrown a little out of balance.

But it's generally a good idea for an actor to improvise, because it keeps him thinking about the role; he stays at home with it, he wants to improve it. And, because a modern actor who has achieved a certain standing in the industry is a human being who reads and collects and listens to music, he has certain valid notions about his part or about the significance of the picture.
——Negulesco, interviewed in *The Celluloid Muse* (Chicago, 1969)

Ralph N E L S O N

Born in New York City, 1916; producer, director, playwright, actor 1933–41; interrupted to serve in the Air Force.

The multi-image screen is a new advance in story telling. It can be used to good effect in collapsing story points and generating excitement. It can also be used in conventional scenes. For instance, I had a sequence in *Charly* [1968] where the boy and the girl were talking together. I wanted to avoid the usual method of cutting back and forth between the two faces, so I put both of them on a split screen. Thus you could see both the action and the reaction; the audience itself does the cutting. Stirling Silliphant, who was the writer, didn't think it would work. But now he says he wouldn't want to go back to the usual way of filming a conversation.
——Nelson, in *Action*, Nov–Dec 68

Paul N E W M A N

Born in Cleveland, in 1925. After his navy service, his G. I. Bill schools brought him closer to the stage and in 1952 he joined The Actors' Studio.

A plus about making pictures is that you learn something new on every one, whether it's a good one or a stinker. If nothing else, you meet new people. I didn't want to do *Exodus* [1960], for example. I thought it was too cold and expository, and actually I tried to get out of it. But I did get to know [Otto] Preminger.

He's got the reputation of being such a fascist asshole, when he is on the set. I mean, he can pick out the most vulnerable person and then walk all over him, you know. He could walk down a line of 200 people at a fast pace and pick somebody out and make lunch out of him. Off the set, though, I found him articulate, informed, funny, absolutely lovable. . . .

Good scripts are damn scarce. I recall I wanted to do *The Hustler* [1961] with Bob Rossen from the word go. That picture was something special for Rossen, who was already terminally ill, because he was familiar with the world of pool and that whole hustler era, and he just pulled himself together to do the film, and he was incredible. I blame the blacklist in part for Rossen's death. I think the second he succumbed to that, he hurt his pride to a fatal extent.

There was one scene in *The Hustler*, though, that I always had a big quarrel with—the scene on the hillside where Eddie tells the girl what it's like to play pool, right? Well, the way it was originally written, I thought it was a nothing scene—it just wasn't there, it had no sense of specialness. So I told Rossen he ought to somehow liken what Eddie does to what anybody who's performing something sensational is doing—a ball player, say, or some guy who laid 477 bricks in one day.

Well, we were shooting on 55th Street in New York, and Bob listened to what I said, and we walked into his office, and it couldn't have been 6 minutes later that he came out with the 4-page scene that was in the film. He was that type of artist. He did the whole goddamn thing.

———Newman, interviewed for *Rolling Stone*, 5 July 73

When I begin working on a part, I find that the first things I do are usually wrong. After rehearsals start, however, I find that I get rid of the wrong things bit by bit, until I get the part so that it feels fairly comfortable and fairly right. Nowadays, for movies, I always give a director or a producer 3 or 4 weeks for nothing, in order to have a rehearsal period. I won't ever do anything again without rehearsals. For *The Hustler*, we had 3 weeks of rehearsals, using television technique, where you lay out tape on the floor to mark the sets. The motion-picture business is unlike any other in the way it forces you to walk into tight personal relationships and direct, close contacts for a period of 3 months, and exactly 3 months, and then—boom!—it's over.

———Newman, interviewed for *The Player* (New York, 1962)

. . . I'd also made up my mind I didn't want the film [*Rachel, Rachel*, 1968] to be tricky. The function of the camera was simply to eavesdrop. I made it a rule that the actor would never have to go to the camera: the camera would always come to him. It was rather like the old days of live television. At the same time it was a film where everyone was expected to make large contributions: I don't understand those directors who want to cut their own pictures all the time. There was some talk at one stage of shooting the film in California, but we finally did it in Connecticut, because I very much wanted to contrast the schoolteacher's rather arid, dry existence with the lush, verdant spring background—it would have been far too obvious to have placed a barren life against a barren setting.

———Newman, interviewed for *The Times*, 8 Feb 69

Fred N I B L O   (1874–1948)
Born in York, Nebraska. Began acting career in 1890 as a vaudeville entertainer. Joined the Ince Company in 1917.

Many a time since, in my work in Hollywood, I have seen this ability to keep on grinding in the face of the unexpected prove a vital aid to both director and cinematographer. In *Ben Hur* [1925], for instance, the greatest thrill in the chariot race sequence was secured because the cinematographers kept on grinding while an entirely unscheduled accident occurred before them. In making these scenes we knew that we had but a single day to work in, on account of the tremendous expense of the thousands of people employed. Therefore Percy Hilburn, who was in charge of the photography of the sequence, took pains to place expert cinematographers at every conceivable vantage point. When his plans were perfected, there was not an inch of the vast set which was not under the eye of at least 2 or 3 of the 42 cameras he used. This careful planning would have been amply repaid in the normal course of events, but when the unexpected happened it enabled the cinematographers to bring one of the outstanding moments of the completed picture to the screen. Everyone who has seen the picture remembers the thrilling scene when one of the chariots unexpectedly loses a wheel, and the chariots following behind crash into it at breakneck speed. This occurrence was in no way staged, but, though it was unexpected, Mr. Hilburn's plans were so well laid that no fewer than 6 cameras caught the crash. And through it all, the 6 cameramen, though as surprised is we all were, kept their eyes glued to the finders, and their right hands revolving regularly, so that every split-second's action was captured.

———Niblo, in *American Cinematographer*, July 1930

Dudley N I C H O L S   (1895–1960)
Born in Ohio; studied journalism at University of Michigan. Went to Hollywood in 1929, where he began as a screenwriter on Men Without Women.

Symbolism is only good when the audience is not aware of it. So when we had to deal with a character like Gypo [in *The Informer*, 1935], who was a traitor out of ignorance, out of smallness of mind, we thought we would make it the state of his mind . . . as the story progresses he is overtaken by conscience slowly working up out of his unconscious mind. We gave that a symbol of a blind man. So that when Gypo first gets his money, his £20, as he starts away, as he comes out he sees the blind man, seizes him by the throat, and realizes he is blind. It is as if he has seen his own conscience. . . . He passes his hand over his eyes and hurries away and always the tapping of the blind man's stick is behind him.

———Nichols, interviewed for *National Board of Review Magazine*, Mar 36

Unthinking people speak of the motion picture as the medium of "action"; the truth is that the stage is the medium of action while the screen is the medium of reaction. It is through identification with the person *acted upon* on the screen, and not with the person acting, that the film builds up its oscillating power with an audience. . . . At any emotional crisis in a film, when a character is saying something which profoundly affects another, it is to this second character that the camera instinctively roves, perhaps in a close-up; and it is then that the hearts of the audience quiver and open in release, or rock with laughter or shrink with pain, leap to the screen and back again in swift-growing vibrations. The great actors of the stage are actors; of the screen, reactors. . . .

Sound is a magic element, and part of your design as a screenwriter or director has been the effect of sound. In the case of *This Land Is Mine* [1943] . . . one of the focal points of the drama was a railroad yard, and as we could not shoot the action in an actual railroad yard we determined to create it largely by sound. We spent endless days gathering sound tracks and trying to orchestrate our sounds as carefully as if they were music.

——Nichols, in *Great Film Plays* (NY, 1959)

Mike N I C H O L S [Michael Igor Peschkovsky]
Born in Berlin, 1931. First theatrical work at University of Chicago, where he formed an experimental comedy team with Elaine May. This led to successful direction on Broadway and in Hollywood; his first film was Who's Afraid of Virginia Woolf (*1966*).

The end originally planned for the film [*The Graduate*, 1967] was that they [Katherine Ross and Dustin Hoffman] would get on the bus, turn, laugh, she would say, "Benjamin." He would say, "What?" which is all he ever said. She would kiss him and the bus would go off. I never questioned it. But something very odd happened to me the day we were shooting that scene. I was rotten to the two of them, really rotten. And I told them—and I don't usually do this —I said, "Now, listen, it's a big deal and we've stopped traffic for miles and we've got a police car. You get on that bus and you better laugh. You hear me?"

They had tears in their eyes, they were so terrified. They got on the bus and they tried to laugh, and we kept rolling, and they tried to laugh some more. And then they finally gave up, and they thought, "I don't know what the hell he wants me to do." And we rolled and we rolled and we rolled and we drove for miles. Then when I saw those rushes, I thought, "That's the end of the picture. They don't know what the hell to do, or to think, or to say to each other."

——Nichols, interviewed for *The Film Director as Superstar* (NY, 1970)

The Graduate wasn't really about any aspect of carnal knowledge or sexuality. It was more about trying to free yourself from being possessed by possessions and about the way that a generation that had a difficult time and tried to do its best for its children maybe enslaved them in a way that it didn't intend. Benjamin's flight to Mrs. Robinson was a deliberate act of iconoclasm and self-destruction, which had very little to do with the kind of score-keeping sportive, pseudo-sexuality that the men in *Carnal Knowledge* [1971] find themselves engaged in. But it's perfectly possible that one makes the same movie over and over, which wouldn't be bad at all.

He [Jules Feiffer, scenarist for *Carnal Knowledge*] brought me something that in large part contains the dialogue that's presently in the picture, and then we worked together for several months on the form of it, thinning it and simplifying it out. I wanted it and he happily agreed to make it more spare and with more jumps in it, more holes, fewer things explained. . . . Just as in the lives of friends and acquaintances, everything isn't explained. You have to guess.

It was the happiest working experience I've had because we tried an experiment. I wanted to take the actors away from their lives and their friends and going out to dinner, so we went to Vancouver, where none of us knew anyone and we all lived together—not all in the same house, though sometimes that, too—and we all became very close. Not in any encounter group sense—there were boundaries. But we were dependent only on each other and we started to live as a kind of surrogate family for one another. . . . Jack [Nicholson] and Art [Garfunkel] did room together and Jack was instructing Art. He helped him all the time about acting because he'd only acted once before, and that briefly. And they started—not in any Pirandello-esque way—to live the relationships between the characters. One of the things I'm pleased with is that there's a very thick feeling of intimacy between the people, even when they're at odds with each other, even when they're separated. They've somehow got knowledge of each other, which was real, which they got from living together.

——Nichols, interviewed for *The Times,* 15 Sept 71

Jack NICHOLSON
Born 1937.

Roger [Corman] had just made *The Raven* [1963] for A.I.P., and they had built some terrific scary-Gothic sets for him. After he finished the picture, Roger kept looking at those sets, trying to figure how he could make another quick buck out of them before they were torn down. He was able to rent the sets for just 2 days. Then, after he had hired Boris Karloff to play the lead, he just barely had enough money for those 2 days of shooting with a union crew. I was in the picture, too, playing a young officer from Napoleon's army who gets lost on the Baltic coast and ends up in Karloff's castle. . . . Roger shot nonstop for 2 days in the A.I.P. sets, and we still had a lot of outdoor scenes to do. He had no money left for union crews and, as a member of the Directors Guild, he couldn't use cheaper *non*-union crews. So the wily bastard went to all the young nonunion guys he knew who *wanted* to be directors but weren't yet members of the guild. He asked them if they'd like to direct a day here and a day there, and he ended up with Francis Coppola, Monte Hellman, Jack Hale, and Dennis Jacob working with the nonunion crews. He even came down to using *me*, directing myself in the final sequence. The picture [*The Terror,* 1963] looked like a lot of separate components pasted together with Band-Aids, but it had Boris Karloff and it was scary-funny—and it made a potful of money.

——Nicholson, interviewed in *The New York Times Magazine,* 28 Dec 75

I almost always grow with [a part] during the filming. One of the things that was wrong with my work in low-budget filmmaking was that you always shot them in 2 weeks. I've noticed that my own rhythm in a movie that's shooting 8 to 12 weeks, which is average, I'm really not in to the character for the first week and a half. I've got it, and I know where I want it to go in my mind, and so on. I don't have this diamond-hard gem carved out, but I've got all the impulses. You tend to overcharacterize when you first step into a part. You tend to show it. You know, this guy's got a limp or he doesn't like dogs. Where once you've done it for a while, you know the actor's thinking about it all day long, you get with it much more. In a 2-week picture all you've done is that early stage of overshowing a character.

[*Five Easy Pieces*, 1970] had lots of endings. Bob [Rafelson] likes to work with lots of endings. He doesn't like to know the ending while he's shoot-ing it. He likes to feel like something's going to happen. He usually ends up shooting the ending that he had.
——Nicholson, interviewed for *Jack Nicholson, Face to Face* (NY, 1975)

In [*The King of Marvin Gardens*, 1972], I consider the character I played a one-roomer, which is what Kafka was, a man who lives in one room—that's a very specific image, and one that relates to more people than we would care to think about. When I act I try honestly to represent the peer-group, and that's what the peer-group is there. But we don't like to look at them in life, so you can't expect a film audience that is used to riding the back of a hero, or reveling in the audacity of a villain, to identify with these people in a con-ventional way. But at the same time, this doesn't mean that the film shouldn't be widely available to people who might want to see it. It's a process, really, of educating the audience as you go. . . .

. . . Antonioni's basic approach to his actors is "Don't act, just say the lines and make the movements." He doesn't make dramatic constructions, he makes configurations. And the simpler you can be, the clearer will be the configura-tion. If you mess the interior up, and so break up the interior part of your character, you will in fact be working at cross-purposes with him, because he is looking for clarity in that area, so that the configuration can be seen. If you break that up, you are working against the style in which he is working.
——Nicholson, interviewed for *Sight & Sound*, Summer 74

Rudolf N U R E Y E V [Hametovich]
Born 1938.

There were many technical flaws in this *Don Quixote* [1974]. We had to film everything in an airport hangar and the light wasn't too good. But I made sure of everything else, each camera lens, each angle, everything. When I got back to London, I did all the editing in my bedroom, in the morning before I go to class and in the evening after a performance. So I had a firm control and I think it shows. I am a dancer and I can create ballets and I know how to film them—it's as simple as that. But you know, even after all that, the producers

managed to add some things to the sound track that were offensive. So now I know. Next time I not only have to lay all the eggs. I have to hatch them, too.
——Nureyev, interviewed for *The Globe & Mail*, Toronto, 9 Feb 74

Sven N Y K V I S T
Born 1923. Studied photography, worked as assistant cameraman, worked for a year at Cine-Citta before becoming Bergman's cameraman.

[Bergman] is definitely the stronger man, and I am the weaker; we've fought very little in recent years simply because we now understand each other so well. Also, as I've gotten older I've become less interested in the prestige of winning arguments. You know, if the director doesn't have the support of his cameraman he's the most lonely and unhappy man in the world. I found this out when I myself directed a film.
——Nykvist, interviewed for *The New York Times*, 25 Apr 76

Q. Your last 3 films for Bergman, *Scenes from a Marriage*, *The Magic Flute*, and now *Face to Face*, have all been shot for TV and film. Can you discuss the problems involved?
A. It's very difficult. If you make a picture for television and film you have to compromise. At first, for television you have this 1:33 ratio, and then when you show it in the cinemas in Europe, we use 1:66 and in America it's 1:85, so at the same time we have to shoot it for all three formats which is terrible. I don't like having to compromise. So I put in the viewfinder a red filmstock so I can see all the formats. If you are shooting just for television you have to use very very soft lighting, almost flat lighting, that's not good for film. So I had to decide that the most important thing was the film. So I made film lighting with a little more contrast, then I work more on the print for television. But as a cinematographer I don't like this, I think it should be shot for television or film. But it's a question of economics.
——Nykvist, interviewed for *Millimeter*, July–Aug 76

O

Clifford O D E T S   (1906–1963)
Born in Philadelphia; worked on New York stage with Theater Guild and the Group Theatre.

Early in 1943 I was due to go into the Services, and I asked my agent if he could find something for me to write in Hollywood so I could earn some extra money for my family. He came up with *None But the Lonely Heart* [1944] which one of the studios wanted adapted.

Well, I read it, liked it, and took a train for Hollywood. When I arrived I asked who they had in mind for the lead and they said Cary Grant. There was silence for a moment and I asked if anyone *read* this book. It seemed no one had. Well, it's about a 19-year-old boy with pimples whose two desires in life are to have a girl and get a new suit of clothes. Are you sure it's right for Cary Grant?

Well, it seemed they were so I had to change the concept of the book considerably. When I met Cary for the first time he said that he'd like me to direct him in the movie, too.

I explained that I'd never directed a film before—let alone Cary Grant—but he told me if I could write the words I should certainly be able to direct their use. Well, I did. He's a fine man. If he believes in you, he'll gamble his entire career with you.

———Odets, interviewed for *The Sunday Express*, 11 Oct 64

Laurence O L I V I E R
Born 1907, in Dorking, Surrey. On stage, London, New York since 1925. First appeared in film in As You Like It, *1936. Was made a life peer in 1970.*

Looking back at it, I was snobbish about making films. Then I had the good luck—but what hell it seemed at the time—to be directed in a film by William Wyler, *Wuthering Heights* [1939]. He was a brute. He was tough. I'd do my damnedest in a really exacting and complicated scene. "That's lousy," he'd say, "we'll do it again." At first we fought. Then when we had hit each other till we were senseless we became friends.

Gradually I came to see that film was a different medium, and that if one treated it as such, and tried to learn it, humbly, and with an open mind, one could work in it. I saw that it could use the best that was going. It was for me a new medium, a new vernacular. It was Wyler who gave me the simple thought—if you do it right, you can do anything. And if he hadn't said that, I think I wouldn't have done *Henry V* [1946] 5 years later. . . .

Take the film *Henry V*. I thought of the production against say, Kenilworth Castle. Wonderful castle, wonderful battlements. You might be forgiven for thinking it the ideal background. Very real. Yes, so real and so familiar that the audience would ask at once, "Why are they talking so funny?" No good. At least I'd seen that. On the contrary, I came to the conclusion that only against some kind of unreal background could the verse be made to sound real. The next problem was what I thought would be the audience's need to be helped to accept his conception, in the simplest possible way. One day I was coming back from somewhere or other . . . in a taxi with Puffin [Anthony] Asquith. We were talking about this problem of mine. Suddenly I saw the solution. I have always seen my films from the last shot backwards and was trying out on Puffin the idea that the first time we saw the Chorus, who up to now would have been merely an off-screen commentator, would be for the last speech, when we would discover that we'd been in the Globe Playhouse all the time.

I had no sooner said this to him than I saw immediately that the Globe Playhouse was to be the frame—with its actors employing a highly rhetorical method that would most felicitously set the central idea.

———Olivier, interviewed for *The Observer Review*, 9 Feb 69

Ermanno O L M I
Born in Bergamo, 1931.

. . . When we were looking for an old man of indefinable age for *I Recuperanti* [1970] we had great difficulty. Somebody suggested taking one of those amateur dialect actors who abound in the Veneto. But that would have meant using someone who maybe was a bank clerk during the day and put on a wig and makeup in the evening, and I didn't want this kind of phony intermediary.

One day when we were looking for locations we went into an inn on the outskirts of one of those lonely mountain villages, a place we thought would be useful for the film. And there sitting in a corner was Toni Lunardi, celebrating his eightieth birthday, drinking happily by himself. He didn't ask who we were, naturally he hadn't any idea we were film people. He talked to us willingly, told us things about himself and his life in the mountains. We realized immediately that Toni was just the person we were looking for. He had lived in the mountains all his life, had himself worked for years as a scavenger. He had that baggage of experience which the character we had "invented" in our script should carry with him. The real Toni then took over from our literary creation. Of the thousand things he said ad lib as we were shooting maybe only a dozen were used in the final track, but they were elements which added richness because they came from the truth of his life.

———Olmi, interviewed for *Sight & Sound*, Summer 70

Marcel O P H Ü L S
Born 1927 in Frankfurt, where his father Max Ophüls was working in the theater.

My father was a man of great prestige; he really shone, so one can perhaps talk of atavism. But all the same I think I came into the cinema world in spite of him. He had such a hatred of nepotism, that though his name may have helped me, he certainly did not.

Jeanne [Moreau] decided she would help me to make my first film. We had two projects in mind: *Les Platanes* and *Three Rooms in Manhattan*. But we couldn't get them off the ground. Meanwhile, I directed a short film about Matisse, a sketch in *L'Amour a vingt ans* (*Love at 20*, 1962) and happened to read *Peau de banane* [1963]. I was captivated by the novel, and I told Jeanne so, who promptly bought the film rights. I owe her everything: I work slowly, but Jeanne was always patient. For 5 months I worked with Claude Sautet on the adaptation, and Jeanne was financing us all the time.

——Ophüls, in a press release

Q. Do you have a particular thesis in mind while shooting. . . ?

A. The answer is "No," although persons always bring to bear conceptions based on their own background, education, and experiences. One of the disciplines in this type of filming is to rid yourself of these biases as you work. It's a good policy on this kind of adventure [*America Revisited*, 1971] not to prescript, nor to pigeonhole people.

That doesn't mean that I didn't have a basic structure to hang my coat on. In this particular case, it was the business of coming back to America and looking up my family and old friends. In *The Sorrow and the Pity* [1970], the gimmick is Clermont-Ferrand, the choice of one town. And even then, I didn't stick to it. Once in a while I broke out.

My films are poststructured. That's why they are such edited works. That's where my point of view and creativity come in. Before that, I'm in a much more passive position.

Q. But how can you remain so utterly calm when interviewing, especially when those to whom you talk say such outrageous things?

A. Whatever anger I feel is pushed into the background by my professional reaction telling me, "Well, I got it." I laugh on the inside thinking, "That's going in the film." Even when interviewing Lester Maddox in *America Revisited*, I didn't get mad at him, because I knew I had him.

——Ophüls, interviewed for *The Velvet Light Trap*, Summer 73

Q. In view of its American producers, etc., was *Sense of Loss* [1973] made with an eye out particularly for the American market?

A. No, I have no principal eye for any particular market. This is one of the influences my father had on me. My father's opinion was that the most decent, the most democratic way to operate in this profession is to try to do things which you find convincing, which you find make sense, with the hope that your likes and your opinions will meet with popular approval. Because of the basic belief that—mainly on the level of sensitivity—there is such a thing as universality.

Q. So if you strike the universal within yourself you will automatically . . .

A. . . . transmit it.

——Ophüls, interviewed for *Critic*, Nov–Dec 72

Max O P H Ü L S [Maximilian Oppenheimer] (1902–1957)
Born in Sarrebruck. Came to films from the theater (as actor and director).

[In *Liebelei,* 1932] I saw the opportunity of making a picture with young
people as yet unspoiled by stardom. Not an easy task, certainly, but fascinating. I believe that most young actors have to be steered through great dangers.
Wealth, publicity, a higher standard of living—it all happens far too quickly.
The shyness and reserve that constitute the appeal of youth, are easily lost. . . .
   [After three idle years in Hollywood] my chance came unexpectedly,
when Preston Sturges one day by accident came across *Liebelei* and redis-
covered me. I was first assigned to the scripting of Prosper Merimée's *Colomba*
for Howard Hughes (a picture unfinished yet, as far as I know), then worked
for Douglas Fairbanks [Jr.] on *The Exile* [1948]. Then I made *Letter From
an Unknown Woman* [1948] for Universal-International, *Caught* [1949] for
Enterprise, and finally *The Reckless Moment* [1949], produced by Walter
Wanger for Columbia, which . . . led to the project of *La Duchesse de
Langeais*. I actually came to Paris to shoot this famous novel [by Balzac]
with Greta Garbo and James Mason. As nothing came of it, I finally got tired
of drawing my salary in idleness and I enthusiastically seized the chance of
filming another famous Schnitzler subject: *Der Reigen* [*La Ronde*, 1950], a
favorite story of mine.

—Ophüls, interviewed by Francis Koval, 1950; repr. in
Masterworks of the French Cinema (London 1974)

Mr. Deutschmeister, the man who owns the best production company in Paris
has the intention to do *The Magic Mountain.* . . . It was once Mann's desire
that I should direct the picture. . . . Deutschmeister was in Hollywood to look
for a co-production and met Bill Dozier. And Bill . . . accepted under the condition that the picture should be done by our team. I think this is a nice proof
of friendship, and you should drop him a line. . . . But this is all you *should*
do [now], because for the moment I have to get the rights away from your
friend Wolfgang Reinhardt.

—Orphüls, letter to Howard Koch, 5 Sep 56

Arthur O R N I T Z

In *Serpico* [1974] we had a problem. We were shooting in July and August,
yet many of the scenes were supposed to be in winter, with the police in their
heavy coats. And they couldn't sweat, couldn't do this or that, and had to
look blue with cold; you had to be able to see frost on their breaths.
   So we developed a technique with [Sidney] Lumet. Right at the beginning we decided that this was going to be one of our key problems: that
the winter should look cold and heavy and the summer should look a little
idyllic and hazy. That came from Serpico himself. He loved the streets and
felt that as a policeman his duty to the community and the streets were where
his work belonged.
   But we didn't always want the streets to look as ugly as they really were.
There were *certain* times when we did, but Sidney and I worked at it so that

in handling those various situations we used certain treatments to maintain a mood. For instance, we always knew that the mood in the Serpico home (there was more shot in the Serpico home than there is in the finished film) should always be home base, should always have a warm, warm look.

We knew that in his pad in Greenwich Village there should be a changing look and various moods, because he lived there many years and went through various torments there. And all of this had to be worked out in terms of color values, in terms of the kinds of lighting and lighting techniques that we used.

——Ornitz, interviewed for *Filmmakers Newsletter*, Feb 74

Peter O'TOOLE
Born 1932 in Ireland, a bombed and evacuated childhood in North England; entry in 1952 into the Royal Academy of Dramatic Art. Extensive and heavy repertory jobs, with small film roles to bolster income. Comfortable theater and film fame since 1959.

My trick [in preparing a film role] is to vanish for 2 weeks. Be alone. And I have a set routine of reading the script and working on it that seems to work . . . the script perks you. You get such perks constantly. They lead me on to my own loves which are archaeology and history. I play Henry [II in *The Lion in Winter,* 1968] and that leads me to histories of Henry and Eleanor, and that leads me to where he lived and was born, and that leads me to the groundworks about him and his influence upon other people of the time.

——O'Toole, interviewed in *Show,* Jan 73

Don't play small parts in highly exposed places, because that will make you a small-part actor. Play leading parts anywhere—in rubbish—but play leading parts.

——O'Toole to Michael Caine, quoted by him in *Time,* 17 Feb 67

Maria OUSPENSKAYA (1876–1949)
Born in Tula, Russia. Entered Moscow Art Theater in 1911; when it toured the United States in 1924, she remained to teach and act.

In the United States life has been very pleasant. I have never had more than one fight at a time. Usually that fight has had to do with typing me. On the stage and screen, they are always and forever wishing to make me a grandmother or a trainer of pigeons or a titled, decadent lady. I refuse to be typed. What can I learn if I am always a grandmother. . . ? After all, I am not happy unless I am learning something. . . . After *Dodsworth* on the stage and screen [1936], I was offered contracts from practically every motion picture company—to play grandmothers.

——Ouspenskaya, interviewed for *Screen & Radio Weekly,* 1939

Don O W E N
Born in Toronto, 1933.

I proposed it as a kind of half-hour story film, and on the original budget it's a half-hour story film called *First Offense*. I started shooting and in the first 3 days we shot almost half our budget of film and I was already into deep trouble because we were doing something that hadn't been done before, certainly not at the Film Board anyway. . . .

. . . And I kept on ordering more film. It so happened that all the people were away so that in fact there was nobody at the NFB to say don't send any more film. They kept on sending film and I kept on shooting and the story kept on getting more elaborate and more elaborate, and I added scenes —the great thing about improvising is you're really writing the script while you're shooting—so the thing grew. And when I came back to Montreal 4 weeks later, I was then something like $10,000 over budget, and I shot 50,000 feet of film instead of 25,000 feet, and I said, "I shot a feature [*Nobody Waved Goodbye*, 1964]."

———Owen, for *Cinema Canada*, June–July 73

When I was making *Nobody Waved Goodbye* I shot it chronologically, for one thing. But all the way during the shooting I was thinking to myself, "Have I still got the viewers with me? Are they still there?" I wasn't making the film only for the audience, I was following something in my own head while I was making it. But I was also taking cognizance of the audience. I was thinking to myself, "Well, I'll get it straight from this situation; this scene has to work; this is a turning point in which the audience will come back into the story with greater strength if I do this." It's manipulating all the time. It's manipulating that you have in your head in such a way that you hopefully are communicating it to other people.

———Owen, in *Canadian Cinematography*, Jan–Feb 67

Yasujiro O Z U   (1903–1963)
Born in Tokyo, entered film industry in 1923 as assistant director; directed his first film in 1927.

The company [Shochiku] kept after me. They said the film [*The Brothers and Sisters of the Toda Family*, 1941] would never be ready in time. You have to finish shooting today, they said. I had only 2 hours of shooting time left and lots of long scenes to do. I felt bad about not working this out, but most people, I guess, didn't notice the difference. I liked the film; any film I enjoyed making I tend to like, whether it is any good or not.

———Ozu, quoted in Richie's *Ozu* (Berkeley, 1974)

Miyagawa, the cameraman [on *Floating Weeds*, 1959] took a lot of trouble and tried a lot of different things in this film, so I began to understand what a color picture is. For example, it is necessary to give the right amount of the right kind of lighting to a certain color in order to prevent it from turning out different from what it looks like to our eye. Therefore, when you try to shoot two different colors with the same amount of lighting, one is destroyed. So you must choose which color you want to be faded. This is what I learned for the first time.

——Ozu, quoted in *Cinema,* Winter 72–73

P

Georg Wilhelm P A B S T (1885–1967)
*Born in Raudnitz, Bohemia. Began theater and film work as actor; assisted
Carl Froelich on 2 films before directing his first film,* Der Schatz, *in 1923 for
Froelich's company.*

Every cut [in *Die Liebe der Jeanne Ney*, 1927] is made on some movement.
At the end of one cut somebody is moving; at the beginning of the adjoining
one the movement is continued. The eye is thus so occupied in following these
movements that it misses the cuts. Of course, this was very difficult to do.
——Pabst, interviewed for *Close-Up*, Dec 1927

The future of sound is one of the problems that remain to be solved. In my
new film, *Herrin von Atlantis* [1932] I have used sound very sparingly, and
chiefly to form a sharp contrast to the background of the Sahara, whose long
stretches of sand, sometimes rippled like the wave, sometimes swirling like
the wind, express in themselves the agelessness of the desert, the timelessness
of a city hidden and buried whether this be under the surface of what was
once a sea or only in the imagination of a fevered brain.

There is little speech save to break the tension of high dramatic moments
of sudden action. For instance, a name reiterated and echoing down monotonous empty, narrow streets conveys the horror of a man searching for his lost
comrade far more subtly than any agonized monologue or convulsed features
of a close-up; there is no need for the question and answer of dialogue to
express more. Symbolism combined with sound comes to the producer's aid
when use is made of an old-fashioned gramophone with a long trumpet,
played by Arabs sitting around in stately circle, to introduce the idea of a
Parisian civilization that was—the Paris of the can-can days.

Here the shrill raucous sounds convey the jarring note of two conflicting
races, centuries, and ideas. While the type of instrument alone tells the
audience it was the Paris of yesterday. . . .
——Pabst, interviewed for *The Times*, 1932

Al [Alfredo] P A C I N O
*Born in 1939, of New York/Sicilian descent. Theater experience before enter-
ing film in 1971.*

Q. Why was *Godfather II* [1974] so oppressive?

A. I became physically exhausted and got bronchial pneumonia. It was frightening. This had to do with a combination of nervous exhaustion and my own need to get away, to pull out. I'm not very fond of doing films—it's wear and tear on me. I have a very strong musical sense in me. In a movie, there's not a chance for that rhythm to build. . . . That's why I fear doing things in translation, because words are notes to me and I play them. This is an area of myself nobody knows about. Michael Corleone didn't have many words.

——Pacino, interviewed for *Off Camera* (NY, 1975)

Genevieve P A G E
Born 1931.

I have a lot of trouble with my hands. I move them a lot and they quiver. [In *Belle de Jour,* 1966] Buñuel knew this but he made me do a scene over and over again where I had to pour a drink with my left hand. I was furious and all the shots were wasted, but he got what he wanted in the end.

——Page, interviewed for *The Sunday Times,* 4 Aug 68

Marcel P A G N O L   (1895–1974)
Marseilles's chief contribution to the French theater and cinema.

I learned about the cinema from Alexander Korda. It was he who directed *Marius,* in 1931. In those days Paramount had come to Joinville to make French films. Sound films had just come in (in France). Korda was a Hungarian and spoke very good French, so while we at first thought that no one from Hollywood had any business making a film about Marseilles it worked out very well.

Not only did I not think *Marius* would not be a success with the Americans, when I wrote it as a play I did not think it would even go down well with the Parisians. I wrote it for Marseilles. But it made a fortune. So did *Fanny* [1932]. Then I began to make films myself—*Angèle* [1934]; *Joffroi* [1933] *César* . . . How much did it cost? *César* [1936] cost me about 1,500 English pounds. Remember I had my own studios and laboratory. Our own carpenters. We paid Raimu £300 for his 3 weeks' work. . . . It is strange to think that since his death he has performed more than he ever did in his lifetime. . . .

I miss the actors most. They were all my friends. That is the inconvenience of living a long time, you outlive your friends. I was the youngest of them. If Raimu and Charpin were alive today, they would be 90. No, I never go to see the films now. Imagine that 7 of the actors in *Marius* are dead. To see them again, still joking and playacting would be difficult to bear.

——Pagnol, interviewed for *The Guardian,* 16 Apr 69

Jack P A L A N C E   [Walter Palanuik]
Born in Lattimer, Pennsylvania, 1921. Seriously burned in World War II.

I was taught to draw ... like every Hollywood actor ... by a character named Ron Red Eagle. And he taught me for my part in *Shane* [1953] to draw so fast that I should be able to beat the kid by so much that I would be able to laugh at him and then shoot him. By doing that it made me a more evil character.

—Palance, interviewed for *The Guardian*, 22 July 71

Lilli PALMER [Maria Lilli Peiser]
Born in Posen, Germany in 1914. Appeared on German stage before going to London in 1934 and acting in the film Crime Unlimited (1935). *One of her American films was* But Not for Me, 1959:

What impressed me most about [Clark Gable] was his sturdy "pro" mentality. Every morning on the stroke of 9 he entered the set, knew his lines to perfection, nodded to the director's suggestions, never disputed them, and carried them out. His contract stipulated that he could go home at 5:00. At 5 minutes to 5 he would glance at his watch and call out a calm, firm "Five more minutes, boys!" into the air, not caring if anybody heard him or not. On the dot of 5 he would get up and leave. Sometimes we were in the midst of a take, and I pleaded with him to let us finish, but he shook his head. "If I stayed on for a couple of minutes just one single time, that would be the thin end of the wedge. I work eight hours a day, like everybody else. No more."

—Palmer, in *Change Lobsters—and Dance* (NY, 1975)

Robert PARRISH
Born in Columbus, Georgia, 1916. Edited Ford's Battle of Midway *and Toland's* December 7th. *After his Navy service edited* Body and Soul (1947) *and* All the King's Men (1950).

Early in 1941 John Ford had the foresight to form a voluntary Navy Photographic Unit made up of artists and technicians from the Hollywood film industry....

Ford also realized that, first of all, a photographic unit should have cameramen and that the number of competent cameramen was limited; so he decided to train his own. He enlisted the help of several top directors of photography for this job. The first two volunteers were men who had worked with Ford—Joe August (*The Informer*) and Gregg Toland (*The Grapes of Wrath* and *The Long Voyage Home*). All the volunteers were top men in their field and all gave freely of their time to try to pass some of their valuable knowledge along to Ford's group of eager recruits....

A few days after the Japanese attack on Pearl Harbor, we were summoned to Washington as an active duty photographic unit, and assigned to the Office of Strategic Services. At that time, Toland was a lieutenant in the U.S. Naval Reserve and Commander Ford gave him the difficult assignment of heading a unit which was to proceed to Honolulu to make a complete photographic report of the Japanese attack. He organized his unit quickly and efficiently and left Washington in February 1942 for Hawaii. While there he photographed and directed a full length film, *December 7th*, in which he used many of the new ideas in photography and presentation that he had been working with as a civilian, but which had never realized their full potential until he was given this assignment. Because much of the material in *December 7th* was secret and for military use only, the picture was never given a public release.

————Parrish, letter to *Sequence*, Autumn 49

Pier-Paolo P A S O L I N I (1922–1975)
Born in Bologna; an established poet and novelist before working as film scenarist (since 1954). His first film was Accattone (*1961*).

The idea [for *The Gospel According to St. Matthew*, 1964] began a few months ago when I was a guest at a Roman Catholic Study center in Assisi. The priest there received people of all religious and political beliefs. I was there for one of the congresses they organize occasionally.

One day the Pope arrived in the city. The whole place was in a ferment. I didn't fancy going out in all that confusion and decided to stay in my room. Not knowing how to pass the time, I picked up a copy of St. Matthew's Gospel. I was remarkably impressed and enthusiastic.

When I returned to Rome, I spoke to producer Alfredo Bini about it. I told him I wanted to make a film out of the Gospel. He was so excited about the project that he jumped out of his seat.

————Pasolini, interviewed for *Scene*, 19 Feb 63

Not desiring to reconstruct settings [for *The Gospel*] that were not philosophically exact ... I was obliged to find everything—the characters and the ambience—in reality. And so the rule that dominated the making of the film was the rule of analogy. That is, I found settings that were not reconstructions, but were analogous to ancient Palestine. The characters, too—I didn't reconstruct characters but tried to find individuals who were analogous. I was obliged to scour Southern Italy because I realized that the preindustrial agricultural world, the still feudal area of Southern Italy was the historical setting analogous to ancient Palestine. . . . The Apostles for example, belonged to the ruling classes of their time, and so obeying my usual rule of analogy, I was obliged to take members of the present ruling class.

————Pasolini, quoted in *Studio International*, March 69

. . . My ambition in making films is to make them political in the sense of being profoundly "real" in intent; in choosing the characters, in that which they say and in that which they do. That is why I refuse the political fiction film. One of the least appetizing things of the past few years are precisely those fashionable political films, these fictional political films, which are films of half-truths, of reality-unreality, of consolation and of falseness. They are made to pacify the consciousness. Instead of arousing polemics they suffocate it.

When a spectator has no doubts and can recognize at once, in accordance with his own ideology, on which side he is meant to be in the film, that means all is calm. But that is the definition of fiction! I avoid fiction in my films. I do nothing to console, nothing to embellish reality, nothing to sell the goods. I pick actors whose sheer physical presence suffices to convey this sense of reality. I do not pick them at random but in order to offer examples of reality. From *Decameron* [1971] on, the personaggi of my films are exactly the opposite of the ones you find in television or in the so-called escapist cinema. And that is only on the level of the figurative aspect. From here on in, that is what counts: this physicality of the characters, imposing itself, whereas in *Accattone* there was present, too, an ideological thesis which carried me through *Uccelacci e Uccellini* [1966].

—Pasolini, interviewed for *The Guardian*, 13 Aug 73

Ivan PASSER
Born in Prague, 1933. The following interview was given in Paris, where Passer had come to see the first French showings of his first film, Intimate Lighting *(1966):*

What is most vital for me in the cinema is not the story or the action, it is the intonation. The intonation, the expression, the movements of the people. Obviously you cannot get this in literature or even in the theater. You can get it on the street, but there you cannot select. I don't understand why people use real streets and real houses to film in and then use actors. Actors don't have style. Real people with a developed personality, or a developing personality, have style. They can give you an experience of life. Actors often don't know who they are.

—Passer, interviewed for *The Guardian*, 4 Mar 67

Gregory PECK
Born in La Jolla, California, 1916; trained at Neighborhood Playhouse School of Dramatics, performed extensively on stage prior to film debut in Days of Glory *(1944).*

Exposition . . . is always very hard. You always get patches of it, and writers are rarely skilled enough to camouflage it. . . . I can't remember the number of times I've stood in front of a body of men and said something like: "Now we're going to raid a ball-bearings factory in Frankfurt and this is what I want you to do." What can an actor do with stuff like this? The only thing possible is to invest it with some kind of feeling by making it seem important to yourself. . . . Well, as you probably know, [Hitchcock] once said that the important work in filmmaking is done in the office—directing the actors is simply like getting the cattle into the corral. He wasn't by any means as cruel to actors as this suggests, but I wish I hadn't worked with him quite so early on in my career. I remember, for instance, when we were making *Spellbound* [1945], he suddenly asked me at one point to drain my face of all emotion. One was immediately required to produce a certain effect without being told why: a director like Kazan, on the other hand, would have given one some clue as to what the character was supposed to be thinking. After all, what Bogart said about screen acting is basically true: if you think right, then you look right.

—Peck, interviewed for *The Times*, 9 Nov 68

To Kill a Mockingbird [1962] is a special memory. It was so easy for me to do. It was just like putting on a comfortable well-worn suit of clothes. It was never any strain. I identified emotionally with everything that happened in that story. With the character I played and with the children in the small-town life. There was something about it. It was as if I were born to do it. . . . Yet, it was more like a gift from Harper Lee—the author. I feel I was lucky to be there at the right time. And to be her idea of the best man to play it.

I've worked much harder, and have even felt I've done better acting in less successful pictures. . . . Sometimes you do your best work in mediocre films because you're calling on all your ingenuity, all the tricks of the trade to bring out truth, reality and ideas that will lend excitement to an unexciting scene—and sometimes you even get away from it.

———Peck, interviewed for *Marquee*, June–July 76

Sam PECKINPAH
Born 1925 and raised in the mountains above Fresno, California.

Q. What came next—*Major Dundee* [1965]?

A. Yes. Columbia wanted a picture to be made under $3,000,000 to fulfill a commitment they had with Chuck Heston. They had a script of sorts—something that Chuck and I both saw potential in providing I could do some rewriting. The producer assigned to the picture, Jerry Bressler, gave his blessing to what we wanted to do—though when it came time to shoot, he double-crossed us by ordering 15 days cut from the schedule.

Q. Was this when you were actually shooting the picture?

A. No, 2 days prior to starting. I said what he was asking was impossible, that I would rather leave the picture there and then. To which he replied, "Look, I'm acting under instructions from New York; leave it to me, I'll take care of it." But he never did. When I saw the final release print, which is to say Columbia's final release print, not mine, I was sick to my stomach. I tried to have my name taken off it, but by this time the machinery was too far along. What I had worked so hard to achieve—all of Dundee's motivation (what it was that made him the man he was)—was gone. This was material I'd both written and shot and cared very much about, but which Bressler or Columbia had thought unnecessary to the total effect of the film.

———Peckinpah, interviewed for *Films & Filming*, Oct 69

Q. How much actual visual planning do you do? Do you try to conceive all of the shots very carefully before you get to the set?

A. Every one. I'm up at 4 in the morning, looking at my day's work, which I've already sketched in before, and I go over it again and again. Light changes, action, something may come up, so I try to know every single possible approach, and then I pick up the one I want. I always prepare. That's why I lose 15 to 20 pounds on every picture, it's like an endurance race or something. No, I don't like to go on the set and start "creating." We do that before in rehearsal. But we know our work so well that if some new idea does come up, we've gone through everything else, and we know exactly where to go. For example, the exit from the village in *Wild Bunch* [1969] was not in the script. I shot that in less than a day, and it's one of the high points in the picture. All of a sudden we knew the picture needed it. But that couldn't have happened unless we'd been so well prepared.

——Peckinpah, interviewed for *Film Quarterly*, Fall 69

... When you get shot by one of those guns, it's a mess. They blow a bloody big hole in a wall, let alone a human and if you pretend otherwise you're working in another medium. . . .

One of my chief purposes in making *The Wild Bunch* [1969] was to show that people we identify with, even approve of, did some terrible things. Those old boys who bring tears to the eyes were real bastards—unchanged men in a changing land. But the law, too, was a bastard. You had to question both sides, and you can't do it properly unless you show what both were really like.

... During the shooting someone was trampled on by a horse that got out of control. The cameras were going at the time, and it's in the picture. It was a ghastly moment, and just because it was so awful it seemed to last forever. Must have been 15 seconds really. But it seemed like 5 minutes. That's what I was trying to get over. It wasn't pretty at all to me. It was a ballet perhaps, but murderous. . . .

... I'm not a pessimist, but I've learned to question. That's what most of my films are about, *The Wild Bunch* particularly. We really lived it. It was that important to us. I think it turned out more or less right. I just wanted 2 more weeks on it really but there wasn't the time. It's always like that.

——Peckinpah, interviewed for *The Guardian*, 27 Oct 69

I want to rub their noses in the violence of it [*Straw Dogs*, 1971]. I regard all men as violent, including myself. I'm not cynical. I still believe, and I still want everything to work out, but it never does. When you see the degree of violence in men, you realize that we're still just a few steps up from apes in the evolutionary scale. . . .

It was a phony Hollywood fallacy to have people get shot and not seem to be dead at all. I don't mind saying that I myself was sickened by my own film. But somewhere in it there is a mirror for everybody. If I'm so bloody that I drive people out of the theater, then I've failed.

——Peckinpah, interviewed for *Time*, 20 Dec 71

Arthur PENN
Born in Philadelphia, 1922. Demobilized from U.S. infantry in 1946 and attended Black Mountain College, then Universities of Perugia and Florence.

Q. Did you consciously try to match known photographs of, say, Billy the Kid in *The Left-Handed Gun* [1958], or Bonnie and Clyde?

A. Yes, there's one known photograph of Billy the Kid holding a rifle, and it was part of it, yeah, to get him [Paul Newman] to get the look very much of that one photograph. And the same was true of Bonnie and Clyde: their public character, their photographic character, it seemed to me was very important to their whole role.

——Penn, interviewed in *Take One*, Sep–Oct 68

. . . Film offers the opportunity for constant contradiction between what is said and what is done. It's closer to how we really experience life. I'm saying *that,* but I'm really feeling *this.* And these two things are going on at once. Ambivalence is closer to the human feeling than the simple Eugene O'Neill statement: "My father was a bastard." That sort of statement that says everything and says nothing. Well, film is the exquisite medium for expressing ambivalence. A man says one thing, but his eyes are saying another thing.

. . . Nothing can match the cinema. I didn't understand that, however, at the time I was making *The Miracle Worker* [1962]. I went to see it the first time and sat there smothering myself in self-congratulations on doing this marvelous transition to the screen. And everybody was delighted. Anne Bancroft and Bill Gibson (the author) had come to see a rough cut and just hated it. I told them to wait until I finished it and they'd change their minds. They had no choice, of course. But they were suffering. Then they saw the finished print and said it was the best film they'd ever seen. But about the third time I saw it, it jumped off the screen at me as a near-disaster. We got away with it because there was just about 9 minutes or so of cinema in the whole picture. . . .

I learned two things [from *Mickey One,* 1964]. I learned how to work with Warren Beatty, which is no simple problem. I don't mean to suggest anything pejorative. Warren is a covert personality. There's a distinct quantity of him that's hidden. It took a whole film for him to trust that he could be bad on film and that I would take it out. The other thing I learned was the alternation of emotions and moods on the screen. I feel that *Mickey One* was boring. *Bonnie and Clyde* [1967] was a distinct and conscious effort not to be boring, by alternation of effect. The unexpected in the sequence of scenes is as important as the unexpected in affect and behavior.

. . . Historically, there is an existing body of norms in Hollywood for the levels of light. So, in a way, the cameramen themselves are really interchangeable. The technique is constant from film to film. The lab can take up Burney Guffey's work and Ted McCord's work and put them together and there's almost nothing to distinguish them. Because they stay within the same foot-candles, essentially they follow the same simple ideas. What is the light source? What is the secondary light source? They're pretty simpleminded formulas.

For years they've been the Hollywood norms. And the cameramen have been ignoring the fact that film has gotten so much faster, that still photography has advanced into a completely new direction. Indeed, *cinema* has advanced. [Henri] Decae and [Raoul] Coutard and [Walter] Lassally have broken new ground in cinematography while Hollywood has stayed in the same place as before. So when I would see Burney Guffey lighting a set, I would say; "Hell, Burney, do we need all these lights?" And he'd say, "Well, if you don't want them, we don't need them." I didn't want them. So I'd say, "Let's turn them off." And that's the way we did it [on *Bonnie and Clyde,* 1967].

———Penn, interviewed for *The Film Director as Superstar* (New York, 1970)

Violence is like sex: it was going on for centuries long before anyone ever started turning a camera. But I'm less obsessed with it than some critics think.

It's always in my films for a reason. When I made *The Left-Handed Gun* [1958] I was appalled by the clean violence of the traditional Western: in that film you had a feeling that you didn't just pull a trigger and a man fell off a horse, but that it also blew a hole in him. In *The Chase* [1966] I tried to show that you can't have it both ways: you can't have that American legend of killing someone leaving a man 10 feet tall without its having an effect on community life. In *Bonnie and Clyde* [1967] I showed how violence was translated into myth; a process, incidentally, helped by the law. There were 87 distinct hits on the bodies of the 2 gangsters when they were found, and the popular legend was instantly nourished. The capture was more than efficient: it was symbolic. A kind of overkill.

————Penn, interviewed for *The Times,* 10 Apr 71

I'm afraid I do lean on a script, and probably that's where my mark gets left for better or worse, probably with varying responses from the authors in terms of how intruded upon they feel. Calder Willingham and I worked together on the screenplay of *Little Big Man* [1969] over a period of several years, although he did all the writing. I don't mean to suggest that I had any hand in the actual writing. But I did have a say about the techniques that we would employ in the film, and then eventually in the construction of certain scenes. I acted selectively, as it were, over the material he provided—saying what ought to be emphasized and what might be omitted. Since we were working from an enormous novel, it was important to choose the material we would dramatize from it.

With *Bonnie and Clyde* there was a completed screenplay by David Newman and Robert Benton in existence when I started to work on the film. There was a reorganized screenplay by the time we actually began to shoot—considerably reorganized, with quite a number of changes made. I labored over several months with the writers. On the whole, I don't make changes in the course of shooting—although I have done so in a couple of cases where I've decided that something need not be shot, because several scenes that had already been made had covered exactly the same points. That happens very rarely, though. It happened in *Alice's Restaurant* [1969]. But I do very little makeshift work on the set. I like to go in with a strong script and adhere to it pretty closely.

————Penn, interviewed for *Films & Filming,* July 71

Sydney Joseph P E R E L M A N
Born 1904 in Brooklyn, moved to Rhode Island, where his father was for a time an unsuccessful poultry farmer. He graduated from Brown University and was first interested in becoming an artist, then moved into cartoons, and then into writing. After his first novel in 1929, and some writing for Broadway revues, he was hired by Paramount to write for the Marx Brothers.

I had a tentative acquaintance with Groucho, in that he apparently liked my writing for *Judge* and *College Humor* in the twenties, and when my first book was published, he supplied an arresting blurb, which ran like this: "This is a marvelous book. From the moment I picked it up to the moment I laid it down, I was suffused with laughter. Some day I intend reading it." Anyway, my wife and I had a couple of ducats to see the Marxes' Broadway musical, *Animal Crackers,* and we were so diverted by this that we sent a card back-stage at the interval, announcing the fact.

Well, we were invited to go round and meet the artists, and my wife was rather unhorsed by what she saw, because the Marxes were running around in their undershorts and goosing showgirls, and that was a scene she wasn't very well clued into. This was the era of the great radio comedians; Eddie Cantor, Ed Wynn, Fred Allen, Jack Benny, and so on. They were all making a great deal of money, and the Marxes, being avaricious, wanted some of this loot, and the substance of this visit was that they wanted me to think out some radio programs for them.

They coupled me with a New York newspaper man called Will Johnstone, and the two of us sat about trying to scratch up some idea for a radio program, and the only thing that occurred to us was that the brothers might be stowaways, each in his own barrel, on a transatlantic liner. Beyond that, our inspiration failed, and for 2 or 3 days we just sat there. Then to our horror, the Marxes bade us to lunch at the Hotel Astor, where we showed up, and rather gingerly presented our idea. And to our great surprise, Groucho looked at Chico and said, "This isn't our radio program, it's our next picture." And they took us both by all hands and led us down to the Paramount Building. . . .

As far as temperaments and their personalities were concerned, they were capricious, tricky beyond endurance, altogether unreliable, and treacherous to a degree that would make Machiavelli absolutely kneel at their feet. They were also megalomaniac to a degree which is impossible to describe, despite the fact that they were not what they were to become after these pictures.

I did 2 films with them, which in its way is perhaps my greatest distinction in life, because anybody who ever worked on any picture for the Marx Brothers said he would rather be chained to a galley oar and lashed at 10-minute intervals until the blood spurted from his frame than ever work for these sons of bitches again.

————Perelman, interviewed for *The Guardian,* 30 Nov 70

It's a not inconsiderable achievement to have worked on 2 of their pictures. . . . During *Monkey Business* [1931] Chico made several well-documented attempts to have me fired.

Groucho felt I was overliterary. I felt he had a wonderful talent for parody and literary turns of speech.

For example, in *Monkey Business* we had a love scene in a conservatory, with Groucho reclining like Mme. Récamier. I wanted him to leap to his feet and say "Come, Kapellmeister, let the violas throb, my regiment leaves at dawn," and then go into a parody of *The Merry Widow* [1925] which was playing everywhere with Mae Murray.

Groucho left in the "Come, Kapellmeister" line but cut *The Merry Widow* reference as too literary. He claimed this would be incomprehensible to what he called the barber from Peru—by which he meant Peru, Indiana—whom he conceived of as a mindless cretin.

————Perelman, interviewed for *Herald-Tribune* (Paris), 31 May 67

Anthony PERKINS
Born in New York City, 1932, son of Osgood Perkins; studied at Columbia University and Rollins College before working in theater and television. First film role in The Actress, 1953.

... Of course, [Hitchcock's] been quoted many times either correctly or incorrectly, that he thought of actors as cattle. When we started [*Psycho*, 1960] I had actually never met him but once, and I was very apprehensive about making any statements about what I thought what I felt about the character and about different scenes. But, even as the first day proceeded I could see he wanted to know what I thought and what I wanted to do and I was really very surprised by this. I kind of tentatively made a small suggestion about something I might do. He said, "Do it." And later I suggested changing a "but" to an "and." He said, "Go ahead." I got to relaxing more with him and making more and more suggestions and ideas. At the end of the picture, I realized I'd worked with THE director who had been more open to the actor's suggestions and ideas than any I'd ever worked with before, with the possible exception of William Wyler. Since that was the reverse of what I'd expected of Hitchcock, it came as a great surprise.

——Perkins, in *Cinema*, Mar–Apr 65

I enjoyed making *Psycho*. In fact, I accepted the film before I'd even read the script. That's the kind of reputation Alfred Hitchcock has in Hollywood. You hear he's planning a film, you say yes—and then you read the script.

We got on very well, and he let me make several changes and suggestions. It was my idea that I should eat candy throughout the film. I thought it would be more interesting if the killer were a compulsive candy eater.

——Perkins, interviewed for *The Sunday Express*, 11 Sep 70

... I think the role in *Psycho* is one of the greatest gambles I've taken because if that picture hadn't worked, if the public's acceptance of the role hadn't been as complete as it was, it might have been a very disadvantageous thing for an actor to play. I discussed this question very frankly with Hitchcock. He agreed that it was a gamble, he had no idea of the real possible success of the picture, but he suggested that I give it a try anyway. Luckily, I think that most of the people who saw the picture enjoyed it in a very good warmhearted way. When they were frightened, they were pleased that they were frightened.

I'm very grateful to Hitchcock for the quality that this picture had. ... He did it in a very clever and subtle way; after every scene of horror, fright, and shock there is always a gag of some kind. In the fade-up after the fade-out on the scene of shock, there is always something funny happening, and this reduces the audience to very generous laughter, and I think that the times that it happens helps the picture very much, to make it palatable rather than unpleasant. It doesn't have to be too terribly funny because the audience is already so keyed up and tense that even a minor joke will seem like major humor.

It was one of those crazy unplanned things that I came to do *The Trial* [1963]. I got a call from Litvak saying, "Orson Welles wants to get in touch with you." . . . he acted as a kind of go-between between Welles and my-self. . . .

The biggest problem for me on that film was the simple technical one that I don't like to work at night, and I do my best work, my best scene or shot is always before noon and from then on till 6 I'm all right but . . . the earlier the better. Orson doesn't really feel like doing it until after dinner and from then on until dawn. He himself has told me many times that he doesn't really like to go to sleep until he can see the outlines of buildings against the sky as morning is breaking. This to me is a horrifying idea and it was very hard to stay with it all night—we frequently shot through all night long.

Q. How was Welles to work with?

A. Absolutely great. He'll listen to any suggestion, he'll take it very seri-ously, he's extremely patient with the actors, he never loses his temper, never becomes impatient. Even with the greatest problem—it may be a financial one—on the picture where the assistant director tells him, "We've got to be out of here in half an hour," and we have still 4 setups to do, if the actor needs something Orson will always, always, supply it.

He can speak to the actor in any way that the actor responds to—if it's a physical, mental, Stanislavski, personal or emotional way, Orson will direct the actor in the vocabulary that the actor responds to. It is a very distinct trait which few directors have: Hitchcock has it, so does Wyler, Bob Mulligan, and Jules Dassin. . . .

Q. How does it work for the sequences in which Welles was himself acting in front of the camera; for instance, the bedroom sequence in which Welles's face is obscured by the towel and cigar?

A. Well, I kind of directed that scene! It was the scene in which Orson was wrapped up and I more or less stood behind the camera. He'd say "Is that all right?" After we'd done about 5 takes I said, "No. The towel has to be hotter because we're not seeing the steam rise off your face. We have to do it again Orson." "All right." So we got a hotter towel. . . . Actually, in that entire scene we don't play opposite each other, because we shot his close-ups after.

Q. How many of the actors did Welles in fact dub himself?

A. I can hear at least a dozen. Orson probably dubbed more than that.

Dubbing is a fantastic art. In *The Trial* there wasn't one line of original track. Orson's theory, and it's one I wholeheartedly subscribe to, is that the very least you can expect in dubbing is as good as the original. I hated dub-bing until I did *The Trial;* then I realized the possibilities of it.

——Perkins, interviewed for *Films & Filming,* July 65

Eleanor P E R R Y
Born in Cleveland, Ohio.

Q. How has your writing changed since your earlier films? Do you feel you have had an opportunity to probe deeper into subjects that interest you?

A. My experience is probably different from that of most screenwriters since I was never employed by studios or Hollywood producers. Frank [Perry] and I employed me (on speculation, I might add), thus I was able to choose only subjects which interested us and to probe into them as deeply as we wanted to. Even after our initial success I was rarely asked to write what might be called a "Hollywood" film, so I have never really suffered from any kind of restrictions. Except for *The Swimmer* [1968], when we signed away our controls over the film in order to get it made (a great mistake), we are responsible in our films for whatever worked and whatever was flawed. The major way my writing has changed is that it has simply become better with more experience, more appropriate to the film medium, leaner. . . .

A. Directly after the success of *David and Lisa* [1962] I was offered several jobs. The novels all dealt with retarded or mentally ill adolescents or were sappy, soapy stories which the producers called "women's pictures." The term infuriated me then and still does when I read it in the trades: "for the femme audience"—always referring to some sentimental tripe. We were so unhip at the time that the kind of thing we wanted to do was *The Fall* by Camus. . . . Our second picture, *Ladybug, Ladybug* [1963], an anti-bomb, anti-war film got clobbered (this was 7 years ago!), so the offers stopped coming.

The next project I really wanted to do, *The Swimmer* by John Cheever, met intense resistance not because it was an 8-page story with metaphysical overtones which no one at all believed would make a movie. (Finally Sam Spiegel thought so, but only on condition that he had complete control over script and production and that he had final cut and a male superstar as the lead.)

——Perry, interviewed for *Film Comment,* Spring 71

The only reason I wanted to co-produce [*The Man Who Loved Cat Dancing,* 1973] was to have some clout, the way I used to with Frank [Perry] when we would consult about the script and casting. But I never had one approval! I never knew what was happening. I'd go to a party in Beverly Hills on the weekend and someone would say, "I hear Jack Warden's in your picture," and I'd say, "He is?" I learned about all of the casting at parties.

I didn't go to location shooting in Gila Bend, Arizona, and one day I got a telephone call from there and my associate said George was rewriting his scenes. I said, "George who?" and he said, "George Hamilton. He's playing Catherine's husband." After that, I didn't have much to do with it.

There was talk that Burt Reynolds was dissatisfied with the script. I said, "I'm a writer, why don't I meet with him?" My associate said, "He doesn't want to work with you. He wants to work with a man." My associate kept implying that I didn't know Westerns, as though there was something mystical about Westerns, that only jocks can write Westerns. I can write this sagebrush crap; I know the proper curse words. Finally one night after a long drink, I called Burt and he said, "What do you mean? I wondered why you weren't here. Why weren't you here?"

Then my associate told me that Richard Sarafian, the director, didn't want to work with me, he wanted to work with a man. I started to scream, "If I ever hear that again, I don't know what I'm going to do." When I finally saw Sarafian, he said it wasn't true, and we got along very well.

——Perry, interviewed for the *International Herald Tribune,* 2 Aug 73

Gérard PHILIPE (1922–1959)
*Born in Cannes. A popular figure in the Paris theater before entering films.
The following memoir concerns the filming of* Une si jolie petite plage, *1948:*

It was a question of 2 characters on the beach who, with the camera tracking
back away from them, would be reduced to 2 tiny points on the sands, opposite the sea. Yves Allégret wanted a helicopter for the shot, but could only get
an ordinary trolley. So he had to adapt the technical idea to the means at his
disposal. But the trolley left tracks in the sand. The whole idea was abandoned,
when suddenly Arignon thought it would be possible to get the shot by having
a track forward, with the characters walking backwards, and the film running
upside-down in the camera.

Thus the resources of several technicians were necessary to obtain the
shot imagined by Sigurd. But whatever the difficulties of shooting, it is primarily to Jacques Sigurd that one owes the remarkable ending of *Une si jolie
petite plage.*

——Philipe, in *L'Écran français;* trans. in *Sequence,* Spring 49

David PICKER
*Born 1931 in New York City. Entered movie business in 1956 as sales-promo-
tion liaison for United Artists. President of Paramount Pictures.*

In the late 1950s Jules Dassin wasn't working in the United States. One day
he called us from Greece, saying that he needed $140,000 to make a movie.
"It's about a hooker. She's very happy with what she's doing, until this American comes over and tries to make her know the truth. Eventually, he discovers
that she is truth and that he doesn't know anything. It's called *The Happy
Whore* [*Never on Sunday,* 1960].

Well, we knew that Jules Dassin had made *Naked City* [1948], *Brute
Force* [1947], and a lot of other good pictures, including *Rififi* [1956]. So we
gave him the $140,000 he needed. Eight weeks later he called us again to say
he had the entire $140,000 committed and didn't have a cent left for a leading
man. We literally told him to play the part himself—which he did, much to
his own regret. When he completed the picture, he wanted to scrap it and
make it all over again with somebody else in the male lead.

——Picker, interviewed for *Movie People* (NY, 1973)

Mary PICKFORD [Gladys Marie Smith]
*Born in Toronto, Canada, 1893; her family moved to New York City, where
Gladys got her first theater work at the age of 5. In 1909 extra money was
made in "picture work," a career where her unusual talents for acting and
business made her the best-known and best-paid actress in world cinema.*

I went into pictures in 1909. I refused to exaggerate in my performances, and
my brother Jack wouldn't either. Nobody ever directed me, not even Mr.
Griffith. I respected him, yes. I even had an affection for him, but when he
told me to do things I didn't believe in, I wouldn't do them. I would *not* run
around like a goose with its head cut off, crying "Oooooh . . . the little birds!

Oooooh . . . look! A little bunny!" That's what he taught his ingenues, and they all did the same thing.

"I'm a grown girl. I'm sixteen years old. I won't do it!" I said. . . .

But he taught me a lot. For instance, in one picture I was a poor little girl, and I had this miserable little coat on, with a moth-eaten fur collar, and a funny little hat with a bird on it. I came into my room, threw the hat on the bed, and threw my coat on top of it. Griffith stopped the camera.

Now to stop the camera in those days, with film costing something like two cents a foot, was unheard of. He walked over to the set and said, "Pickford, you'll never do that again. You'll never come in and throw your hat on the bed and put your coat down without shaking it. You must take care of your clothes. No heroine is untidy."

I said, "Yes, sir."

"Now, Pickford, you go back and come in again. Camera, Bitzer."

I thought, "Mr. Griffith's right." So I went outside and came back in, took my coat off, shook it, brushed the fur, fixed the little bird on the hat, put it down on the chair, and put my coat carefully on the back.

Mr. Griffith said, "Very good."

That was the way he directed me. He once said that he could sit back of the camera, think something, and I'd do it.

——Pickford, interviewed (1965) for *The Parade's Gone By* (NY, 1968)

I was given the leading role opposite Owen Moore in *The Violin Maker of Cremona* [1909]. I shall never forget that moment when Owen Moore put his arms around me. My heart was pounding so fast from embarrassment that I was sure he could hear it.

Making a picture in those days generally took one day indoors and one day outdoors. *The Violin Maker of Cremona* was apparently successful, and Mr. Griffith seemed to be very happy over his latest acquisition. In fact he announced to the heads of the Biograph Company that he intended to put me under contract at a guaranteed weekly salary of $25 dollars for the first 3 days, and $5 for the remaining 3. The Biograph people were thunderstruck.

" 'Forty dollars a week for that kid!' " Mr. Griffith told me they shouted. "You're out of your mind." He, in the meantime, had talked me out of the $10 a day with a promise of a guarantee.

In a chorus they demanded to know just what I had that entitled me to $10 more a week, on the average, than the others in the company. A very heated argument ensued, and Mr. Griffith told me it ended in his threatening to leave the company unless they agreed to engage me at the figure. Under vehement protest, and with dire predictions of bankruptcy, they agreed. . . .

Mr. Zukor took me to a restaurant on Broadway, across the street from a theater where they were showing my latest film, *Hearts Adrift* [1914]. After we had sat there some time, Mr. Zukor said:

"Mary, I want you to know that your happiness means everything, not only to me personally, but to my pictures and to my company as a whole."

He paused a moment, then:

"You asked me for more money. How would you like to have your salary doubled?"

I told him that was a very generous offer indeed, and I must have beamed unashamedly at the prospect of $1,000 a week.

As we talked over our tea, my eyes would catch the title of the film through the window of the restaurant. I soon began to wonder why Mr. Zukor didn't suggest leaving after we had finished our tea and talk. It began to get dark, and then suddenly I saw it, one of the most thrilling sights of my whole career: my name blazing on the marquee of the Fifth Avenue Theater! That was the first time I saw my name in electric lights. That dear, sweet man had planned his surprise with such loving care, and I had repaid him by asking him for a raise! The respect and thoughtfulness of Mr. Zukor, the patient eagerness to share with me that moment of excitement and accomplishment. Such things endeared Adolph Zukor to me forever.

It was while working on *Poor Little Rich Girl* [1917] that the advantages of using artificial light from below first dawned on me. I was powdering my nose in the large mirror of the dresser when a small hand mirror lying at an angle caught the glow of the early morning light and reflected it flatteringly on my face. I went to the studio bursting with my discovery. The moment I arrived I asked my director, Mr. Tourneur, if he would have the cameraman place one of the spotlights down low. Mr. Tourneur laughed at me, enumerating several reasons why it wouldn't work.

"All right," I said. "Let's first take the scene the usual way, and then shoot it the way I suggest. You'll decide for yourself when you see it."

"Just to make you happy," said Mr. Tourneur with a sigh of resignation, "we'll make the experiment."

We did, and the difference was so great that ever since that day they have used the low-lying light to reflect back into the actor's face.

——Pickford, in *Sunshine and Shadow* (Garden City, 1955)

Frank PIERSON

Q. As a writer, is there a drawback in that usually when you write a script you don't know who's going to be playing it?

A. Well, I've never felt so, because I've never been able to write for somebody in any conscious kind of way. When I was doing *Cool Hand Luke* [1967], Paul Newman asked me how many of his films I'd seen before and I said, "I've seen quite a few." And he said, "You're not writing this for me, are you?" I said, "I'm not trying to, but how does it strike you?" "Well, I have the feeling that you're writing this too much for me. Give me something that goes against the image; don't write for it." "Believe me, if I'm doing it, I'm doing it unconsciously." In fact, I don't think I was, because when I saw the finished picture I felt there were a number of places where Paul played differently to what I had in mind. There was a tendency, particularly towards the end of the film, to sentimentalize things which I had intended to be read against the intrinsic sentimentality of the words and the scene, and instead Paul and the director were with the sentimentality.

——Pierson, interviewed for *Films & Filming*, Sep 69

Harold PINTER & Clive DONNER

Q. How did the idea of making *The Caretaker* [1963] start?

Pinter: Donald Pleasance had a great deal to do with it. But we all had it in mind, and then Donald, Bob Shaw, and myself discussed it, and finally Donald got on to Clive about it.

Donner: Yes, Donald asked me whether I thought a film of *The Caretaker* could be made, and how, and what it would cost. I said I thought a film could be made with a very economical budget, shooting on location, with very little adaptation, very little expansion of the play. As far as the budget was concerned, I said we could make it for £40,000. In fact it cost £30,000.

Q. Does that mean that in effect the initiative came from the actors and yourself?

Donner: Yes, in a sense. . . .

Q. Had you been approached to make adaptations of your own work before?

Pinter: Yes, but I'd never agreed to anything.

Q. Why?

Pinter: The circumstances didn't seem right. I thought there were all sorts of things needed for film production which I wasn't prepared to deal with. And I was extremely reluctant to make a film of *The Caretaker* because I thought I couldn't possibly get anything fresh from the subject. I'd been associated with the play, you see, through various productions in London and New York for a couple of years.

Q. What persuaded you this time?

Pinter: It might have been something about . . . I don't know, the general common sense and relaxation of the people I met. I put up a lot of defense mechanisms about it, and said I couldn't possibly even write the draft of a screenplay, couldn't do anything at all, and then someone said, "You don't have to do anything" (though it turned out I did) . . . and I let myself be won over. I was behaving rather like a child about it.

Donner: I think it's slightly unfair to say that you've been behaving like a child. I think you were expecting a more conventional approach to the adaptation of the work. . . .

Q. Did you ever think you might do it in a studio?

Donner: No, never!

Pinter: I wish the actors were here to ask, but I'm sure that for them it was tremendous—I'm sorry to say this, it sounds rather strange, almost as if I'm asking for realism, which I'm not—but I think it did an awful lot for the actors to go up real stairs, open real doors in a house which existed, with a dirty garden and a back wall. . . .

——Pinter and Donner, interviewed for the *Transatlantic Review*, 1963

Donald PLEASENCE

Born in Worksop, Nottinghamshire, 1919; first stage appearance in London in Twelfth Night; *film debut in 1953.*

I try not to use artificial aids in my performances, unless they are essential. You must bring a great deal of yourself to any part you play. If you can't find something in yourself with which to play the part, then you are going to have a disaster. I sometimes play parts in which I cannot find anything within me. When the two lines meet, that is yourself and the part you are playing, somehow that becomes truth. It doesn't happen often, but when it does it is exciting. I don't think false noses, beards, or moustaches have anything to do with it; I don't like external acting.

I don't mean that you should not try to find something in yourself that is exactly the character you are playing. For instance, with Davis in *The Caretaker* [1963], I think there is a great deal of Davis in everybody and a great deal of him in me: the obsessions, the petty pride, the ingratitude and so on. If you can find these things within yourself, you can use them in the part you are playing. The end product may bear no relation to you, yourself. I say "you," but I should say "I have got to find these things within myself"; because there are many ways of acting and this is my way. I have to know, if I am going to do something seriously, how this character would behave under any circumstances. It is perhaps a bit along the lines of the Method; but I am not a Method actor.

———Pleasence, in *Films & Filming*, Aug 62

[*Fantastic Voyage*, 1966] was a lovely film to make; it went on a long time, much over schedule and I wonder now whether it could happen in these days of spare budgets and shorter schedules. Four stages at 20th Century-Fox in Hollywood were employed and . . . we were lucky if we got 3 setups a day because all of the artwork was done after the film was finished so they had to get everything exactly in position for the people who were going to paint in all the livers and kidneys and whatever it was, I was never quite sure where we were in the body.

. . . I remember my funniest moment was when I was eaten up by antibodies at the end of the film because predictably I turned out to be the Russian agent who was trying to run them down in some attempt in the minuscule microscopic-sized submarine when they were trying to rescue the great scientist by burning out his blood clot with a minuscule laser beam and of course the submarine, I think began to leak and the antibodies began to creep in and I was swallowed and eaten up by them and thus they came out by the eyeball, which is as good a way to get out as any, I suppose, if you happen to be there at the time, but anyway we spent 2 days trying to work out what it would be like, cinematographically, to be eaten up by antibodies, and we tried all kind of things, y'know like porridge and polycell and anything, you name it we tried it y'know blancmange, custard, I forget what we finally settled for, haggis or something, anyway every time we tried this and all this goo poured over my head, I was in this body molded rubber suit and sitting there looking mad and Communist and wicked and all that trying to mow down these people and I would always have to go off and shower and come back and have some more different goo, pancake mixture poured down me; it was a hilarious 2 days, actually.

———Pleasence, interviewed at the National Film Theatre, 18 May 72

James P O E
Born in Dobbs Ferry, New York, 1923.

[*They Shoot Horses, Don't They* has] been a favorite [book] of mine since 1940. I tried to buy it in 1949. The price was $3,000 for all rights. McCoy was alive then. I didn't have $3,000. A friend of mine borrowed $3,000 from Chaplin and proceeded to try to get a script out of it—he was the first of many. It then traveled around from hand to hand like an unwanted child. No one could come up with an acceptable screenplay. I finally bought it in 1966. The price had gone from $3,000 to $50,000. It took a year to do my research and write a screenplay that was workable. . . .

The ABC agreement was that there would be mutual artistic control and consultation and agreement and so forth. After a lot of discussion we decided to make the picture in Hollywood. Actually it could have been made anywhere in the world because I had written a one-set picture which was entirely interior, which could be shot by day or by night. I wanted to use the original ballroom, which was on the beach, and we made an arrangement to use what had formerly been the Bon Ton Ballroom in the twenties and through the years gone downhill, had been a roller skating rink, for a long period it was Lawrence Welk's stronghold, and at this time it had just finished a psychedelic trip as The Cheetah. It was a sensational set. Dick Sylbert, an old friend of mine, looked at it and told me how we could dress it for the picture with very little money. A sound man scared ABC. He said it was too noisy. I thought that was fine. My script anticipated that. It was jammed with noise. It used the surf continually, the way McCoy had in the book. In addition to that the foot noises of the dancers, the crowd noises, the music track (which was to run throughout the picture)—for the most part, scratchy 78 rpm records. I even put the floor men on roller skates. What I wanted to do was get away from the Hollywood thing of total silence during shooting. ABC didn't go for it, and this meant calling in an art director. Harry Horner, who's one of the best I know, read the script, was enthusiastic, and agreed to do it. He designed a facsimile of the ballroom, and it was set to be built at Warners. At the same time there was a problem of casting. I wanted the picture made without names. . . .

But there was a lot of pressure for a star. . . .

I was reluctant because I could feel what the addition of a single star would do. A star usually calls for a co-star. That meant I'd have to get a name for the boy. If you had two, you had to get important people for the supporting roles and so on and so on. At this point the only important name I had in mind was for the part of Rocky. I'd written that part for Lionel Stander, who hadn't been seen in America for a dozen years. The part of the Sailor I'd created around an old actor named Allen Jenkins. You may remember him from the old Warner Brothers pictures of the thirties. I went to France and saw Fonda on her farm outside Paris. She was pregnant. This meant 8 months' delay. I felt she could handle the part, and she felt I could handle the picture from what she knew of me and the script, and we agreed to go ahead. . . .

. . . Later I was fired. The reasons for the firing were somewhat nebulous. The general feeling seemed to be that my picture, which seemed to cost in excess of $4,000,000, was not to be entrusted to someone who hadn't directed before. It was a total violation of trust and faith; and I looked at the contract, my lawyers looked at it, and they said that as long as ABC paid me off, there was nothing we could do. . . .

————Poe, interviewed for *Film Comment*, Winter 70–71

Sidney POITIER

Born in Miami, Florida, 1924; and grew up in the Bahamas and Nassau. Some success in the New York theater brought him to films in the early 1950s.

For the most part, my work in movies, especially over the last few years, has brought me diminishing creative satisfaction. To get pleasure out of being in a movie, I have to work with a director who is able to inspire me. If the director knows more than you know and can find a way to bring out what is in you to be brought out, then you come alive. But if you know in your heart that the director is making a mistake, or maybe that a whole movie is a mistake, it's like going up a dead-end street. You keep looking and hoping for a little opening in the fence where you can slip through, but you never find it. That's what happens when you try to make a film with people who are not essentially filmmakers. I have tried to do the best I could with every picture I've been in. But all my experience has taught me is that films, to be any good, should be made by filmmakers. . . . A filmmaker is somebody who is able to exercise complete authority over the film he is making.

————Poitier, interviewed for *The Player* (New York, 1962)

Q. What sort of instructions do you give your cinematographer?

A. I worked with Don Morgan the last trip out. How do I work with him? I like to tell him what my feel is for the scene, what I want to accomplish in this scene. He, then, lights accordingly. Almost without exception, his lighting would complement the mood I wanted. When it doesn't, it's usually just a matter of a few adjustments here and there. He's a very low-key lighting man, as you have probably noticed. He likes to go for deep, rich colors. I find that cool, except for certain parts of comedy. As a result, in *Let's Do It Again* [1975], I had him come up more. I needed a bright rather than *deep* color.

Q. Did you spend time with him before shooting, discussing camera angles and so forth?

A. Oh, yes. As a matter of fact, I let him sit in on my wardrobe selection, so that he could see the colors he would have to deal with. And at times, he would say, "I would prefer that that actor have a different color." I've changed suits for actors, I've changed dresses for actresses—if they've created a problem for him. I would take him with me to the set designer, and the set designer would tell us what color he was going to use on the set. Morgan then had an idea of the color of the sets and the color of the costumes of the actors. He then knew if it was a night shot or a day shot, and he could then make suggestions. It's too late to change, after the damage is done, when you're on the floor ready to shoot.

Q. As a practicing actor, how do you find yourself working with actors when you're on the directing end?

A. Actors are very sensitive instruments, and I never give an actor instructions that other actors can hear, unless it's a general instruction. I find that if I'm given a specific instruction—and this may be my neurosis as an actor—on the floor, where everybody hears the instruction, then all those people become arbiters as to whether I did or did not fulfill the instruction, which is inhibiting. It puts an unnecessary—unintended, but unnecessary—pressure on the actor.

I speak in private, by going up to the actor and moving him a step away from the other actor. I'll talk in his ear and tell him what I need. If there are two actors involved, I can get them to work in concert, without telling one actor what the other guy's instructions are. By so doing, I find that my actors are completely confident. They will try anything, because there are no judges except me—and, probably, themselves. I did a picture some years ago for a director who had the habit of giving instructions very loudly and very clearly—even the most intimate instructions. I found I couldn't work.

————Poitier, interviewed for *Dialogue on Film* in *American Film*, Sep 76

Roman P O L A N S K I
Born in Paris 1933; educated in Poland; studied at art school in Cracow, State Film College at Lodz. Wrote, directed Two Men and a Wardrobe *while at college.*

Practically every director in Poland goes through one of the film schools, because that is how he qualifies for entry into the industry. In a school you have to make at least 2 shorts as part of the course and I did so; indeed, I made 6 shorts altogether before *Knife in the Water* [1961], one in France and the rest in Poland, besides acting in a number of films. But the main thing was that I was assigned as assistant to Andrzej Munk on *Bad Luck* [1960]. Everyone thought I would be a terrible assistant, and so I would have been with anyone else, but Munk was a remarkable man. He left me alone for much of the time: he would set up the foreground action and hand over the background to me, saying, "Do what you like with that," and then just accept what I did without demur. This was marvelous; I was happy and did a good job, and so everyone was pleasantly surprised and the result was that I got the chance to make *Knife in the Water* much earlier than would normally have been the case.

————Polanski, interviewed for *The Times*, 8 Apr 64

[After Munk's death in 1961] I wrote 3 pages of a story which was called *A Knife in the Water,* not yet, then, later, and I submitted it to the director of the company saying that I would like to make my first film, and he contracted me to write a script. That's how it functions, or how it did function, these production groups. At that time there were 8 of them of different sizes, different names; ours was called Camera. They have power to develop a project up to the script stage then they have no power to make a film unless it is approved by a board. This board consists of the directors of all this unit plus some writers, some film directors and a representative of the Ministry of Culture. They rejected *A Knife in the Water,* I went to France for about a year, 2 years, and then they suggested that since the atmosphere had changed politically a little bit, they said that there is a better moment to submit it once again, so I did, came back to Poland and it was accepted.

———Polanski, interviewed at the National Film Theatre, 10 Feb 72

I have been asked why I chose to work in Britain for a company that has made a lot of money out of some very commercial films. All I know is that they are the first people I have made a film with who did not interfere while I was working.

Repulsion [1965] is a shocker. I mean it will shock some people, jolt them. What interested me in making it is the study of a girl's disintegration; withdrawal turning to violence. I'm concerned with showing something; exposing a little bit of human behavior that society likes to keep hidden, because then everyone can pretend it doesn't exist. But it does exist, and by lifting the curtain on the forbidden subject, I think one liberates it from this secrecy and shame.

———Polanski, interviewed for *The Guardian*, 10 May 75

Well, when I read a book, I *see* it. I just took the book [*Rosemary's Baby*] and wrote the screenplay straight from it. I tried to follow the book as closely as I could. I didn't see any reason for changing it. I assumed that the writer was right even in the choice of the color of a tie. I just tried to be as close to it as possible. I wrote a very detailed script where everything was written except for any camera indications or movements. Technical things I just don't put in a script. I don't even know where the camera will be put when I'm driving to the studio. . . . [After I rehearse with the actors (I rehearse before each shot, each scene. I rehearse the whole scene. . . .) then I break it down into shots]. . . .

It's difficult to shorten a book to acceptable length, because the film would have to be 5 hours long if you just went straight through the story. But I tried to do it by just eliminating a few things, rather than major cuts. I think it's difficult for someone who has read the book to find out what changes I made in it. The first cut of the film ran nearly 5 hours, before I got it down to the 2½-hour running time.

In this particular case, I had to leave a lot of decisions for the last moment. I shot a lot of scenes even though I knew they might not get into the picture, because I wasn't sure they were the ones I should eliminate right away. And that gave me, also, the chance to eliminate the ones that were weaker, that just didn't come out right for one reason or another.

And this is because this film has such careful construction, for the sake of suspense, where you don't really play on the mood so much, or on some sort of poetic approach. You just have to tell the story well. I never made a film like this before. I shot it and cut it very deliberately this particular way.

———Polanski, interviewed for *The Film Director as Superstar* (NY, 1970)

Sydney POLLACK
Born in South Bend, Indiana, 1934; served as assistant to Sanford Meisner at Neighborhood Playhouse. Appeared as actor on Broadway and TV. Directorial début in 1960.

The shooting [of *They Shoot Horses, Don't They*, 1969] went smoothly. Because it was necessary to capture the gradual deterioration of each of the contestants, we shot in continuity: we began on page one and continued in sequence right to the end. This is almost never done in making films, for economic reasons too complicated to get into here. But the luxury of shooting in this way contributed greatly to everybody's sense of involvement. As we worked on, you could see the fatigue come over the actors as they entered the set. For 63 days we worked in the same surroundings, indoors, on the dance floor, with the same band. The dancers began to melt into each other, each learning the most comfortable position to assume in relation to his partner. After the first few weeks you could feel the depression and it became impossible for me to tell sometimes whether it was made-up or real exhaustion. The work was certainly very far from glamorous.

———Pollack, foreword to screenplay, *They Shoot Horses, Don't They?* (NY, 1969)

Eddie P O L O
Born in an Italian family and grew up in a circus. His adventure films were extremely popular in England (Queen Mary was one of his fans) and the Continent.

Here let me say to those of my British correspondents who have written to me for my advice that there has been practically no faking in my feats on the film. Let me add that many are the dangerous experiences and the trying anxious moments that one has to go through before the film camera. And one does not always succeed at the first attempt.

A stay or a nut may work loose, a rope or a chair may give way, an incident ill-timed or delayed, all mean a great uncertainty to the performance.

I do not like writing about these "slips," but as your representative has expressly asked me to do so, let me relate a few of them.

At one time, I remember, I had to jump from a high pier into a passing barge. Now, that doesn't sound difficult, does it?

But supposing you miscalculate, or the current of the river being strong carries the barge a little out of your reckoning, you have jumped short. And there are 3 ribs broken, a jaw fractured, and 14 teeth missing, as was once my lot.

Then, again, during the filming of *The Circus King* [*Lure of the Circus*, 1918], I was bound by ropes to the connecting rod coupling up the driving wheels of a locomotive that is shifting along at high speed. That sounds a little more thrilling, doesn't it?

Yet, should the rope get chafed as the wheels revolve and you are hurled up into the air, as from a catapult, something may happen even though you have planned this ordeal.

Nor is fighting a lion out in the open air a very desirable occupation. Granting that help is at hand should the King of the Forest wish to "cut up rough," then there is a nasty gash awaiting one.

On another occasion I had to jump on horseback from a very great height: the horse was killed, but, strange to say, I escaped uninjured.

———Polo, a letter to *Cheerio!*, published 3 Sept 1919

Abraham POLONSKY
*Born in New York City, 1910; taught at City College of New York from 1932
until World War II; wrote novels and screenplays.*

Q. Are your films preconceived and prerehearsed or does the image-word-actor
tie-up result from the editing process?
    A. The film scripts pretty well suggest the kind of film it's going to be.
The style that I used in *Force of Evil* [1948] is not my habitual writing style,
but one that I thought was appropriate for that film. It's partly based on the
way the book is written, but it's different also. What I did was have Wolfert
write the first-draft screenplay after we had discussed it. I wrote the second
draft myself and asked him how he liked it. . . .
    The director must edit his film. Obviously he must edit it with an editor.
. . . I work very closely with the editor; I take all the suggestions and consider
them, but then I take the suggestions from everyone who works with me—
my cameraman, my actors especially, obviously, my costumer, my makeup man,
and art director. Everybody is very creative and full of talent, but it's my film
they're making, and in that sense I think the editor is part of a director's filmmaking process. . . .
    I worked in a kind of strange way in *Force of Evil*—I didn't know what
was going on. I told the composer what I wanted, and left it up to him.
Raksin's score is excellent, but it's not my idea of what music should be in
films. It's what people who like movie music like. I mean people who really
like it for its good qualities. In *Willie Boy* [1970] it was demonstrated when I
went off to Paris . . . and talked to a composer. . . . I wanted Dave Gruson to
begin with, but he was busy. . . . [I] told him [the other composer—here name-
less] what I wanted—and I left him just the way I left Raksin; the only difference is that Polonsky who came back from Paris is not the Polonsky who
walked in on *Force of Evil*. Polonsky knew what he wanted by now. I listened
to the score and it was terrible because it was telling me about the movie and
that's not the role of music in a movie. It had already been recorded, and this
cost about $75,000. I raised my complaints, and they just took it away. They'll
use it in some other picture I suppose, because in Hollywood you can always
find a use for music. Then I got Gruson. I sat through the film 3 times with
him—and he went and composed a few themes. We discussed the orchestration
and the role of the music in the film and had 10 electronic musicians, carefully
selected by Gruson. He handed them bits of paper, and they practiced a little,
and then we ran the film and then he would improvise along with them, along
with the film, and I would be sitting there saying, "Too much—No! Very good!
It sounds too much like music!" Gruson is totally conscious of what his music
is doing. He worked out all kinds of effects and strange things. You've heard
the recorder before, but have you heard it with a girl soprano singing in unison?
That's what makes that queer sound—that's Gruson's contribution to it. I was
the audience who if he didn't applaud had his way. That's the difference between the two scores. Raksin's score is absolutely first-class—I like it—but
Gruson's score is part of the picture.
                        ——Polonsky, interviewed for *Screen*, Summer 70

What particularly interested me [in making *Tell Them Willie Boy Is Here*,
1969] is the fact that the Indian is a kind of exile in his own country, and so

am I—or was—for a brief period: for 20 years. I thought my reaction to his problem might be interesting in terms of my reaction to my own.

Strangely enough, the real-life incident on which the story is based took on the shape of the Western myth. Filmmakers have celebrated our heroic Western myth with great nostalgia and warmth and I have loved their films. But it was genocide for the Indians.

——Polonsky, interviewed for *Morning Star*, 24 Jan 70

Gillo PONTECORVO
Born in Pisa, 1919. Worked as Paris correspondent for Italian journals, and as assistant director in films.

Q. What part did editing play in *The Battle of Algiers* [1966]?
A. A very small one, although it turned out to be a difficult task. The editor we started out with wanted to do a classical cutting job, while I wanted it to look as though it had been "stolen" from reality. We couldn't agree, so we ended our collaboration. Next, we de-edited and re-edited with Mario Morra, who today is one of the best in Italy. At that time he was a young editor just starting out, and *The Battle of Algiers* was his first important project. ... Thanks to him we were able to edit the movie in a way which corresponded with the screenplay, the shooting, etc....

——Pontecorvo, interviewed for published screenplay of
The Battle of Algiers (NY, 1973)

Edwin S. PORTER   (1869–1941)
Born in Pittsburgh, Pennsylvania. Electrician, U.S. Navy, film salesman. Toured a film show through Caribbean Islands in 1897; showed advertising films on New York buildings; joined Thomas Edison as cinematographer.

When forty- or fifty-foot lengths was the vogue, I often wondered why it was not possible to produce a dramatic story in motion pictures. At this period I was chief producer of the Edison Company and it seemed peculiarly proper to me for the Edison Company to inaugurate this innovation. Accordingly, I conceived and prepared a story called *The Life of an American Fireman*, [1903] a complete 800-foot story based on a fairly good dramatic element and introducing the fireman's life in the engine house and in his home. The subject became instantly popular, and continued to run for a longer time consecutively than any film production previously. Encouraged by the success of this experiment, we devoted all our resources to the production of *stories*, instead of disconnected and unrelated scenes.

——Porter, in *The Moving Picture World*, 11 July 1914;
repr. in Koszarski's *Hollywood Directors*

Albert PRÉJEAN
Born in Paris, 1893. His light acting style often used by Clair.

. . . A piece of advice given me once by Feyder [during the making of *Les Nouveaux Messieurs*, 1928]: "When you don't feel you're in character, stay neutral."

——Préjean, in *The Sky and the Stars* (London, 1956)

Otto PREMINGER
Born in Vienna, 1906; student at University of Vienna. At 17 joined Max Reinhardt troupe as actor before he began directing; 1935–40 stage work in New York.

. . . I think this sort of film [*Porgy and Bess*, 1959] calls for the smell of reality. The set was designed by a stage designer [Oliver Smith]; it was very difficult to work in. The cameraman [Leon Shamroy] and I got together and repainted it every night, and when Goldwyn would come in he was appalled that the color had been changed. This designer was a very good stage designer, but he does not understand films. For example, he designed in perspective; the windows became smaller as they went up. But that doesn't work in films because the camera has its own perspective. When the people looked out the window I had to have them on their knees, because there was no room for them to stand.

——Preminger, interviewed for *Movie*, Nov 62

Robert PRESTON [Meservey]
Born in Newton Highlands, Massachusetts, 1918; studied at Pasadena Playhouse before his motion picture debut in King of Alcatraz (1938):

[In *King of Alcatraz*] Lloyd Nolan and I played two sailor buddies, brash young guys, on leave. It was a good part for me, and I was lucky to have a good man to act with. Nolan is generous and kind, both as a man and as an actor. We spent 18 days shooting the film. By the second day, I felt so much at home I forgot all about the camera. . . . For me, the acting in the movies was the same kind of acting I'd always done. The main difference was that I had to learn how to stay within range of the camera. Acting wasn't a big problem then, and, actually, I've never made a big problem of it. In the early days, there was nothing to fear. You'd usually have another movie to make after you'd finished one. In my early movies, there wasn't much difference between me and my parts. In *King of Alcatraz*, Lloyd Nolan and I were rivals for the hand of Gail Patrick; we went ashore, went to a bar, got drunk, returned drunk to our ship, and were chewed out by the captain, played by Harry Carey. As an actor, I was simply the author's means of getting to an audience. I knew what my character said and thought and did, because I knew what I said and thought and did.

——Preston, interviewed for *The Player* (NY, 1962)

I'll never forget that first day on the set [of *Union Pacific*, 1939]. It was the toughest sequence in the entire script, and I couldn't understand why Mr. De Mille wanted to shoot it first, me being so jittery and more apt than not to set the whole company off on the wrong foot when the cameras began to grind.

Somehow I managed to go through my part well enough to satisfy Mr. De Mille. The reason he selected the toughest sequence first, he explained to me when he finally okayed the shooting, was because he knew I was as high-strung as a fiddle string, a state of mind and of nerves demanded of me by the sequence, and he was afraid I'd never be able to whip myself into this particular tension later on. Which was pretty slick of him, don't you think?

——Preston, interviewed for *Screenland*, Oct 39

Jacques PRÉVERT
Born in Paris, 1900; poet and songwriter.

. . . We have just brought out *Paris la belle,* a short subject on Paris linking up an old film we made with Man Ray in 1928 with a color film we shot last year. Then I wanted to do *The Playboy of the Western World.* I discovered that the Finistère district of France was an ideal substitute for the West of Ireland. I wanted to adapt *The Playboy,* but it fell through. The producers wanted Fernandel in the part.

In 1932 [his first feature-length film] was called *L'Affaire est dans le sac.* I wrote the script and my brother Pierre directed. I still think it's my best film. There was a group of us living in the Rue Dauphine that time and we used to rehearse in our rooms. Then one of the technical directors at the Billancourt studios, Charles David . . . got us permission to go into the studio at night and use the decor they had set up for another film they were shooting. I wrote the script in 8 days and the shooting took only 7.

. . . In those days, we had the splendid privilege of being despised by the elite. . . . We worked like good tradesmen and enjoyed ourselves. Nowadays the directors take themselves too seriously; they are too solemn.

——Prévert, interviewed for *The Guardian*, 7 Mar 61

André PREVIN
Born 1929 in Berlin, in a musically cultured family. After the family moved to California, André (a child prodigy pianist) joined the California Youth Symphony and drifted into work at MGM, first as a ghost-arranger for musically illiterate composers, and then as a successful composer of film music. He now resides and works in England as composer and conductor.

Aaron Copland won his Academy Award for the score to *The Heiress* [1949], and a wonderful score it was, too. However, William Wyler, who produced and directed, thought Aaron's title music too harsh and dissonant and wanted it rewritten based on a tune called *Souvenir d'amour.* Copland refused, of course, and his music was thrown out. Two arrangers were called in, they wrote a nice orchestration of the desired tune, and when you next see the film on television, take notice of a musically wild first 5 minutes; after a few declamatory seconds of Copland comes a very soupily sentimental arrangement of an awful melody; then quite suddenly, after perhaps 3 minutes, Copland's unmistakably personal music shines through again. In those days, composers had rather unprotected contracts, and any mayhem could be committed on their music.

——Previn, in *Music Face to Face* (London, 1971)

They had to have a scary kind of score [for *See No Evil*, 1971]. They had to have one because the picture is a bloodbath. I hadn't done a film score in 8 years . . . but here was this film that Mia [Farrow] did, a small thing shot quickly, and they wanted a particular kind of score. I looked at the film, an unpretentious but quite nice thriller . . . for the sheer fun of scoring a film it's always better to have a scary film. It's nicer to do a score for *Psycho* than for one of the "Carry On" series.

As far as I know, the film has so far had 4 titles. When I saw it first, it was called *Bluff;* then they changed it to something else, and now it's called *Blind Panic,* except that in the United States it will be called *See No Evil*. It was one of my conditions to do the score with the [London Symphony Orchestra] and they agreed to that. They decided it was worth the extra expense. . . . I wrote a fairly relentless score, and I also used a synthesizer to make some especially eerie electronic sounds, but merely within the orchestra as another instrument.

I wrote the score, and we recorded it, but at the recording sessions neither the producer, Leslie Linder, nor the director, Richard Fleischer, bothered to come. . . . Never in my experience of the 57 film scores which I have written have I recorded for 3 days without either the producer or director being there at all, but Mr. Fleischer was filming in Spain, and Mr. Linder was skiing, so there was nothing we could do.

The next thing that happened was that various people returned. . . , saw the picture, and decided that the music was too harsh, too stringent, too ugly, too rough. They used every adjective except too "modern." I pointed out as gently as I could that the accompaniment to someone slitting 4 throats isn't Mantovani. They said, "Yes, but there isn't anything the kids can whistle."

Then they made suggestions. First to rewrite the score—which I couldn't do, because when I write I have already considered most of the alternatives and rejected them. Second, they said, "Let us take out the bits we don't like and get someone to rewrite the rest on the side, and you can keep the credits."

The albums aren't coming out, and I have asked for a tape of the score just for personal reasons, because I liked the music, but it doesn't exist anymore, and the score doesn't exist anymore, and so 45 minutes of original music has simply vanished into thin air, and that makes me rather sad. I should have liked to have heard it once.

It's taught me a good lesson. I never miss scoring films anymore, and if I do do a film in future it'll be for someone for whom I have worked before, and whose word I rely on and who relies on mine. If Billy Wilder or Bob Mulligan wanted me to score a film, and I had time, then I would always like to, but I shall never work again for someone whom I don't know.

———Previn, interviewed for *The Guardian,* 10 July 71

Vincent P R I C E
Born St. Louis, Montana, 1911; studied at Yale, University of London, Nuremberg University.

I work in a funny way. From the minute I found out that films were seldom shot in continuity, I have studied the entire script every night so I have a feeling of where I am, where I've been and where I am going. This way they can switch the whole schedule the next day and I will still be in continuity with myself. In working [Roger Corman] has a thing which he has so far been able to bring about, which is a 2-day rehearsal. This is not so much a characterization rehearsal—he just walks around the set saying, "Now in this scene this is what happens, then we move from here to there. . . ." so that you establish a continuity in your mind, and then you can break it up.

Where Roger and I have worked well together has been in the fact that I am a terrible stickler for explanations, motivations, if you want to call them that, although I really think they are explanations—why does a man do something? What should the audience know, see, feel or hear that makes the character do something preposterous? Roger is a director who loves to create a mood and who loves all the uses of the camera, or lighting, or effects. And the way we complement each other is in that where he may forget a story point, I don't. If I have to say, "Yes, but I loved her" on page one to explain what Roger is going to do on page 998, I'm going to do it because the audience can get terribly lost and also I could get lost as a character.

——Price, interviewed for *Films & Filming*, Mar 65

Roger has an extremely ambivalent attitude toward actors. Even on those tight schedules he'd make sure we rehearsed the film. We would come in on our own, you know, without pay or even a fixed starting date, and read it and then walk through it. This was terribly important. But on the other hand, he hasn't the slightest interest in makeup, which is a key factor in some of these Poe films. In *Usher* [1960], I bleached my hair white and wore pure white makeup with black eyebrows—I don't think anybody had done that since Conrad Veidt—there was this whole extraordinary thing that he [Usher] was ultrasensitive to light and sound, so I tried to give the impression he'd never been exposed to the light, someone who had just bleached away. Now Roger dug this entirely . . . he found it very exciting that the actor could bring it to a visual creation that complemented his. And again makeup was so vital in *Tales of Terror* [1962], the collection of 3 short stories. I was the only actor to appear in all 3, so I had to change the looks, change the characterization, in each one. Well, Roger couldn't have cared less about this aspect, it was my problem, but then he would come to you with all these deep and profound things which he feels underlies the stories. Personally, I think that Roger only three-quarters believes in them, and one-quarter uses them to prod the actor. I must confess that it's very stimulating and inventive to work with him.

——Price, interviewed for *Films & Filming*, Aug 69

Vsevolod PUDOVKIN (1893–1953)
Born in Penza, Russia. Studied in the physics-mathematics department of Moscow University and worked as a chemist. Fought in First World War and was taken prisoner. After the war gave up chemistry in 1920 to join the First State Film School, where he participated in production as actor, scenarist, assistant, and designer. In 1922 transferred to Kuleshov's workshop.

Editing is the basic creative force, by power of which the soulless photographs (the separate shots) are engineered into living, cinematographic form. And it is typical that, in the construction of this form, material may be used that is in reality of an entirely different character from that in the guise of which it eventually appears. I shall take an example from my . . . film, *The End of St. Petersburg* [1927].

At the beginning of that part of the action that represents war, I wished to show a terrific explosion. In order to render the effect of this explosion with absolute faithfulness, I caused a great mass of dynamite to be buried in the earth, had it blasted, and shot it. The explosion was veritably colossal—but filmically it was nothing. On the screen it was merely a slow, lifeless movement. Later, after much trial and experiment, I managed to "edit" the explosion with all the effect I required—moreover, without using a single piece of the scene I had just taken. I took a *flammenwerfer* that belched forth clouds of smoke. In order to give the effect of the crash I cut in short flashes of a magnesium flare, in rhythmic alternation of light and dark. Into the middle of this I cut a shot of a river taken some time before, that seemed to me to be appropriate owing to its special tones of light and shade. Thus gradually arose before me the visual effect I required. The bomb explosion was at last upon the screen, but, in reality, its elements comprised everything imaginable except a real explosion.

In my earlier film, *Mother* [1926], I tried to affect the spectators not by the psychological performances of an actor, but by plastic synthesis through editing. The son sits in prison. Suddenly, passed in to him surreptitiously, he receives a note the next day he is to be set free. The problem was the expression, filmically, of his joy. The photographing of a face lighting up with joy would have been flat and void of effect. I show, therefore, the nervous play of his hands and a big close-up of the lower half of his face, the corners of a smile. These shots I cut in with other and varied material—shots of a brook, swollen with the rapid flow of spring, of the play of sunlight broken on the water, birds splashing in the village pond, and finally a laughing child. By the junction of these components our expression of "prisoner's joy" takes shape. I do not know how the spectators reacted to my experiment—I myself have always been deeply convinced of its force.

——Pudovkin, in *Film Technique* (London, 1933)

It is of interest to mention here that Baranovskaya in *Mother* categorically declared to me (we were then about halfway through the film) that she could not act unless I were in my accustomed place beside the camera. I cite this declaration as further confirmation of the fact that the presence of the director responsively reacting to the actor's acting is an organic necessity for the latter. I recall that I have invariably tried to establish the most intimate personal relationship possible with all the actors playing principal roles in my films before the actual work of shooting began. I have always regarded it as important to win in advance the deep-seated trust of the acting ensemble, so that later the actors could fall back on this trust and not feel solitary.

——Pudovkin, in *Film Acting* (London, 1935)

You will know that for our film industry too these difficulties have been very great. When the war began, Ukrainian and Byelo-Russian studios had to stop work. Several of the factories producing films were in occupied territory. . . .

Like many other important war industries, our industry has moved to new locations. . . . We had to start from scratch on a new site. There was nothing even faintly resembling a studio in Alma Ata. We were given an ordinary theater building and it took much effort and ingenuity to go on. But we had no right to suspend our work for even the shortest time. Millions of people were waiting for new films about the war. . . . It was in surroundings like this that Eisenstein started his monumental work on *Ivan the Terrible* [1944].

——Pudovkin, interviewed for Moscow Radio, 18 Apr 44; printed in *Documentary News Letter* No. 3, 44

R

Martin R A C K I N   (1918–1976)
Born in New York City. Screenwriter and producer.

I think we pulled something off that has never been pulled off before. Our film
[*The Revengers,* 1972] was the first "for real" Mexican-American co-production
in that it was mostly Mexican financed, filmed in Mexico, and using a Mexican
crew. . . .

In Mexico you must hire a complete crew. For years everybody has gone
to Mexico and the only things they didn't take along were a couple of carpenters. My *Two Mules for Sister Sara* (1970) was also made in Mexico, and
that was when I realized the full potential of the country.

. . . Today every secretary has been to Mexico City or to Paris or wherever.
They won't accept the fake backlot painted scenery any more. It has to be
authentic. They've been there and they know.

Anyhow, Mexico City is only 3 hours from Hollywood and that's not like
shooting a Mexican film somewhere in Spain is it? Mexican technicians are
good, and they're getting better every day. So I decided it was right to go to
Mexico and make a friendship deal.

On *The Revengers* everybody behind the camera was Mexican. The only
ones we took with us were our director, Daniel Mann, our cutter, the first
assistant director, and an American manager (who worked hand-in-hand with
the Mexican production manager). And we also took along a Titan boom as
we weren't sure whether Churubusco Studios would have one.
————Rackin, interviewed for *Variety,* 26 Aug 72

George R A F T   [Ranft]
*Born in New York City, 1903. Boxer, night-club dancer and member of Capone
gang.*

Owney [Madden] had backed a Broadway show called *Diamond Lil,* and I
went to the theater every Saturday night to collect his share of the investment
from the star and her managers. Her name was Mae West, and I admired her
unique talents.

Eventually, when I was starred in a picture called *Night After Night*
[1932] and was allowed to choose my own leading lady, I sent for Mae West.

It was her first screen appearance, and her cleverness on stage was a new kind of thievery to me. She stole everything but the cameras, and I never made another picture with her. I knew she had me licked.

——Raft, in *The People*, 17 Nov 57

RAIMU [Jules Muraire] (1883–1946)
Born in Toulon, where his stage career began at the Toulon Casino.

The older I get, the more difficult I like my subject to be. That is why I have recently left pure comedy for roles like that of Aimable in *La Femme du Boulanger* [1938] where comedy borders on tragedy at moments.

Soon I shall be making films of pure comedy because comedy is so necessary in everyday life. I love to make people laugh and that is a difficult thing to do without distorting the truth. Marcel Pagnol's genius lies in his ability to take the public from laughter to tears and back again in a flash. That is why I like working with him.

——Raimu, in press release for *La Femme du Boulanger*, 1938

Yuli RAIZMAN (or Reisman)
Born in Moscow, 1903. First film work in 1924 as literary consultant at the Mezhrabpom Studio. In 1927 became an assistant director and director.

I recall the disappointment on the faces of those who saw the screened rushes of the scenes of preparation for the decisive offensive against Berlin—I mean those of us who had not been eyewitnesses of these scenes.

The shots did not seem very vivid—platform cars loaded with tanks, a forest road hidden beneath a huge camouflage net, sappers putting a bridge across a river, trucks fueling up from a petrol pipeline, another column of trucks concealed in tree branches and moving into the mist at the river-crossing just built.

Our companions in the projection room found this material commonplace and even boring, while it told us a great deal; for we realized the vast scope and scale that these shots indicated, and we were able to appreciate the thoroughness and precision with which the whole operation had been planned and executed.

We were able to edit this material so that spectators would sense what we had seen, thought, and understood out there, at the front. . . .

We did *Berlin* [1945] in 16 days. Towards the end of May material was still coming in from the laboratory. We aimed the general release for June 22, the day when the session of the Supreme Soviet of the U.S.S.R. was to open, the fourth anniversary of the outbreak of war. And 2 days later, on June 24, was to be the V.E. Day Parade. The film was ready on June 17.

——Raizman, in *Cinema Chronicle*, July 45

Samson RAPHAELSON
Born in New York City, 1896. Taught English at University of Illinois before branching off into advertising, police reporting, and writing of every sort.

Lubitsch prepared a foolproof script that you'd say almost any director could direct. That's not true, of course, but it's comparatively true. Seventy-five per-cent of his work was done when that script was done. And he already had the performances in mind and they weren't just performances that he superimposed on actors, they were performances that he knew those actors could give. . . .

So whatever it was that he contributed, whether it was to inspire me or actual writing . . . whatever I contributed . . . and, good God, how could you help, over a period of 9 pictures, how could I help not contributing *some* shots that were known as "Lubitsch shots"? And how, in God's name, could this very, very, *very* talented man not help but contribute some goddamn good lines of dialogue? Or concepts of dialogue? It ultimately becomes a question of: in which field is which man more likely to contribute; which is his speciality? . . .

I couldn't tell you [whose idea it was to open *Trouble in Paradise* (1932) with the garbage-gondola]. If it were a clean-cut Lubitsch inspiration, I would remember. If it were a clean-cut inspiration of my own, I would remember. In other words, there were times when Lubitsch would say, "Sam, here's how ve get into dis. Listen to dis!" And I'd say, "Wonderful!" This wasn't one of those times. We labored for 3 days and we had terrible ideas and we had almost-ideas and then the minute we got this one, whoever got it, we knew we had it . . . but I have no idea now beyond that.
———Raphaelson, interviewed for *The Lubitsch Touch* (NY, 1968)

Nicholas R A Y   [Raymond Nicholas Kienzle]
Born in LaCrosse, Wisconsin 1909 or 1911. Won Frank Lloyd Wright architec-tural fellowship while at University of Chicago. Wrote and directed CBS Back Where I Come From *series with Office of War Information. Produced and directed in New York before entering movies.*

I began shooting *Rebel Without a Cause* [1957] in black and white and then changed over to color. I have my own ideas about the psychological values of color. There's no really authoritative piece of literature on it. I do not feel that not only story points can be made but emphasis can be put on scenes where you want emphasis to be put on them. In *Rebel*, Natalie [Wood] and Jim [Dean] kneel over Sal [Mineo] and notice for the first time that he has one red sock and one blue sock on: that helps in the most external way to say to the audience quickly that he's had a pretty confused day, he woke up confused.

I would take Gavin Lambert with me after the day's shooting [of *Bigger Than Life*, 1956] to the home of Clifford Odets [neither is credited with the script] who was an exceptionally good man on construction and for this par-ticular kind of story. He was working on another film and as a favor he would stay awake nights. I would take my tape recorder and discuss the problems that I had coming up, and Clifford would give us some ideas. Then Gavin and I would go over those ideas and try to execute them until we couldn't stay awake any longer, and then start shooting again the next morning at about 8 or 9. Usually 4 to 4½ hours' sleep maximum. But when we came to the ending, I just didn't have an ending and I had to shoot it the next day. I had an ending I didn't believe in at all, nobody else believed in it. I called Odets and said,

"Clifford, I'm going into the ending tomorrow, I need some help tonight," and Clifford said very sleepily, "I've just taken two sleeping pills. I didn't realize you were going into it this soon. I'll be up and I'll be on your stage at eight in the morning. Try to find something else to do first so that we can talk and I can do something." Well, I had a couple of process shots to do, so I lined those up and Clifford arrived on the set at 8:30. . . . He sat in the back of the property truck writing the ending and page by page I would take it, edit it, give it to my secretary to type and make copies to give page by page to the actors. That's how we did the last scene.

———Ray, in *Movie*, May 63

Satyajit R A Y
Born Calcutta, 1921; a graphic artist working in illustration and advertising. His determination to make films was strengthened by a meeting with Jean Renoir while making The River *in 1950.*

When I was at Keymer, I was doing book illustrations, book covers, book design, and typography for a publisher on the side. Around 1949, the publisher asked me to do illustrations, for a new edition of *Pather Panchali*, a novel by one of the best-known Bengali writers, Bibhutibhushan Bannerji. . . .

While illustrating the book, I got the idea of turning it into a film, and I did a few rough drawings. *Pather Panchali* is not the kind of book that most directors and producers would think of making into a film. It hasn't the dramatic structure, the single, unified episode. It has loving descriptions of rural life, of little, subtle relationships among brother, sister, parents, and an old, unwanted aunt. . . .

I went to England for 6 months, and in that time I saw about 95 films, I made a point of seeking out all the films by the big names in postwar Italy, acted mainly by nonprofessionals, out on the streets without any makeup. On the boat on the way back from England, I wrote a proper scenario of *Pather Panchali*, hoping to do it on the same lines as the Italians. For a year and a half after I came back to Calcutta, I went around to producers. Nobody showed any interest in filming the story, or in me as a possible director. So I took a loan of 8,000 rupees from my insurance company and started shooting. I had a cameraman new to films, Subrata Mitra. . . . I had Banshi Chandra Gupta as my art director. For my film editor I had Dulal Dutta, who had just started editing films. The 3 have been with me ever since. We were all in our twenties. I still had my job at the advertising agency, so we could shoot only on Sundays and holidays.

———Ray, interviewed for *The New Yorker*, 21 Mar 70

I chose *Pather Panchali* [1954] for the qualities that made it a great book: its humanism, its lyricism, and its ring of truth. I knew I would have to do a lot of pruning and reshaping—I certainly could not go beyond the first half, which ended with the family's departure for Benares—but at the same time I felt that to cast the thing into a mold of cut-and-dried narrative would be wrong. The script had to retain some of the rambling quality of the novel because that in itself contained a clue to the feel of authenticity; life in a poor Bengali village does ramble.

Considerations of form, rhythm or movement didn't worry me much at this stage. I had my nucleus: the family, consisting of husband and wife, the 2 children, and the old aunt. The characters had been so conceived by the author that there was a constant and subtle interplay between them. I had my time span of one year. I had my contrasts—pictorial as well as emotional: the rich and the poor, the laughter and the tears, the beauty of the countryside and the grimness of poverty existing in it. Finally, I had the 2 natural halves of the story culminating in 2 poignant deaths. What more could a scenarist want?

What I lacked was firsthand acquaintance with the *milieu* of the story. I could, of course, draw upon the book itself, which was a kind of encyclopedia of Bengali rural life, but I knew that this was not enough. In any case, one had only to drive 6 miles out of the city to get to the heart of the authentic village.

While far from being an adventure in the physical sense, these explorations into the village nevertheless opened up a new and fascinating world. To one born and bred in the city, it had a new flavor, a new texture; and its values were different. It made you want to observe and probe, to catch the revealing details, the telling gestures, the particular turns of speech. You wanted to fathom the mysteries of "atmosphere." Does it consist in the sight, or in the sounds? How to catch the subtle difference between dawn and dusk, or convey the gray humid stillness that precedes the first monsoon shower? Is sunlight in spring the same as sunlight in autumn? . . .

The more you probed the more was revealed, and familiarity bred not contempt but love, understanding, tolerance. Problems of filmmaking began to recede into the background and you found yourself belittling the importance of the camera. After all, you said, it is only a recording instrument. The important thing is Truth. Get at it and you've got your great humanist masterpiece.

But how wrong you were! The moment you are on the set, the three-legged instrument takes charge. Problems come thick and fast. Where to place the camera? High or low? Near or far? On the dolly or on the ground? Is the 35 okay or would you rather move back and use the 50? Get too close to the action and the emotion of the scene spills over; get too far back and the thing becomes cold and remote. To each problem that arises you must find a quick answer. If you delay, the sun shifts and makes nonsense of your light continuity.

——Ray, in *Sight & Sound,* Spring 57

The only answer [to street crowds] is to shoot very fast and use unknown actors as I did in *The Adversary* [1971]—the star is an amateur, you know. To film those outdoor sequences we used to get together in the park, choose our moment carefully, dash out into the street, shoot the scene in three minutes flat and then drive quickly away.

Even the villages are becoming impossible. I'll have to shoot my next film, [*Distant Thunder*], about the 1943 Bengal famine, in Bangladesh where the villages are more pristine and the people more cooperative.

——Ray, interviewed for *The Times,* 22 Jan 73

Robert REDFORD
Born Santa Monica, California, 1937. After teen-age travels in Europe living off his art (painting), he returned to the U.S. and studied at the Pratt Institute and American Academy of Dramatic Arts.

I never thought of myself as a glamorous guy, a handsome guy, any of that stuff. Suddenly there's this *image*. And it makes me very nervous, because it keeps people from judging you on performance. When I made *The Candidate* [1972], people said, "Yeah, sure, slick, handsome guy, the part's just right for him." When I made *The Way We Were* [1973], they said, "Yeah, Ivy League WASP jock. The part fits him like a glove." But I had to fight to get *Jeremiah Johnson* [1972] because it didn't fit the *image*.

And I think a lot of the knocks I took for *Gatsby* [1974] were because of image. Critics said Redford was too good-looking, Redford was awkward with the language. . . . *Fitzgerald* never said Gatsby wasn't good-looking. He said Gatsby was a fine figure of a man, an elegant young roughneck. He said Gatsby's language *was* awkward, bordering on the absurd. That was a key to the character. That was a quality I *worked* for. I mean, didn't they read the book?

——Redford, interviewed for *The New York Times Magazine*, 7 July 74

George Roy Hill is a crazy bastard. And a *military* goddamn director. Oh, you can fight with him, you can have an idea about something, but you'd better have about four reasons to back it up, and be able to fight for it, because he will fight like hell.

——Redford, interviewed for *Esquire*, Oct 70

Lynn REDGRAVE
Born 1944, the younger daughter of Michael Redgrave.

I don't think many actresses would have gone as far as I did for *Georgy Girl* [1966]. I put on a lot of weight and looked pretty awful. So it did hurt my pride after being interviewed on the set to find myself described as some sort of plea for the plain girl.

The funny thing, of course, is that the part was first offered to Vanessa, who turned it down.

——Redgrave, interviewed for *The Sunday Express*, 13 July 69

Michael REDGRAVE
Born Bristol, England, 1908, in a theater family. Started stage career in 1934 with the Liverpool Repertory. In 1938, signed a long-term contract with Gainsborough.

I've known Mickey Anderson a long time and watched him develop. And now I regard him as one of the finest directors in the business. Filming is a tricky game. You've got to rely on strength as well as understanding from a director if you're to give of your best. Constant praise—the sort of "Thank you, Redgrave, that was wonderful" after each shot—is as irritating as it is useless. But with Mickey Anderson you know that he understands what you're trying to do, and you know he can help you to do it.

It's so different on the stage. There you've got full rehearsals—time to "play yourself in" to a part. Of course you can play a scene a dozen times before a camera and choose only the best strip of film, but it is impossible for you to sense the whole. And when it's done—it's done. All in a tin can—no chance of pulling together in a second performance.

—Redgrave, interviewed for *The Evening News*, 30 July 55

. . . But I confess that many of the pictures I have made I have accepted because the money they brought me helped me to choose in the theater only the parts I liked. *Dead of Night* [1946] is one of the films that many people, oddly enough, seem to remember me for. I played the role of a mad ventriloquist. The director of my sequence in the film was Alberto Cavalcanti, and something happened, the kind of thing that happens when a particular actor meets a particular director who excites his invention in a particular part and works with him on a give-and-take basis. Perhaps it's too easy an answer, but I've always believed to a certain degree that the effectiveness of a film part depends on whether you can say in one sentence, or on a postcard, what the part is. For example, about my part in *Dead of Night* you can say, "It's about a ventriloquist who believes his life is controlled by his dummy." And everyone then is able to say "Ah!" I don't think you can describe Hamlet on a postcard. A film has a more immediate impact than a stage play, which is not necessarily an advantage for the actor.

—Redgrave, interviewed for *The Player* (NY, 1962)

Vanessa REDGRAVE
Born in London, 1937, to Michael Redgrave and Rachel Kempson; early career with Royal Shakespeare Company.

I'd made a stinker of a film [*Behind the Mask*] years before with my father and I never got asked to do another. Tony Richardson and I talked about doing a film sometimes but I'd been so frightened by that first experience that I didn't really think I was cut out for film work.

It's hard to describe how dreadful my debut was! In close-ups they made me move my eyes like this. Or they told me to turn my head 2 centimeters to the right and they were a lot more interested in how my lipstick was on than they were in anything else. It was old-fashioned filmmaking. In *Morgan* [1966] I worked for the first time with people who made films as films should be made.

After the baby was born, Karel [Reisz] came to see me at the nursing home and he persuaded me to do *Morgan*. I was—and this is an understatement—very, very nervous. It was a real case of once burned. I could not get over that first film disaster.

He explained to me that in filming each individual scene is a whole unit, and its own value must be found, unlike a play which has a single value and climbs to it from start to finish. I'm sure he used clearer words than that, but however he said it I understood him.

We rehearsed a bit too. I was very nervous and I overacted terribly, which was what he wanted me to do, to clean myself out. Of course, working with David Warner was marvelous. He was smashing. I hate to use words like this but he was, how else can I say it? Sensitive.

Morgan changed a lot as we went along because of the people in it. Karel let it grow. He had to tell me an awful lot of things—technical things and things about acting. But electricity did happen among the three of us. David's interpretation of Morgan, for instance, was so delightful and charming that I became sure that Leonie had to have a side that loved him deeply, always would love him, in spite of not really understanding him.

—Redgrave, interviewed for *Radio Times,* 30 Sept 71

Carol R E E D   (1906–1976)
Born in a well-to-do Putney family. Began as a stage actor and director in 1924. From 1942–45 director of Army Kinematograph Service. Knighted in 1952.

Orson suddenly turned up one morning [on the set of *The Third Man,* 1949] just as we had set up our cameras in the famous sewers. He told me that he felt very ill, had just got over a bout of influenza, and could not possibly play the role. . . . I entreated him, in any case, just to stay and play the scene we had prepared, where he is chased along the sewers. . . . Reluctantly he agreed. "Those sewers will give me pneumonia!" he grumbled, as he descended the iron steps. We shot the scene. Then Orson asked us to shoot it again, although I was satisfied with the first "take." He talked with the cameraman, made some suggestions, and did the chase again. Then again. The upshot was that Orson did that scene 10 times, became enthusiastic about the story—and stayed in Vienna to finish the picture.

—Reed, quoted in Sadoul-Morris, *Dictionary of Films,* p 373

[In *Oliver!*] I enjoy working with children. Of course it can be tedious, but it can also be exhilarating. The trick is to try to start off every scene with the child. That way the little boy gets his lines over first, and the adult actors in the scene relax knowing that the boy isn't going to spoil the scene for them. Another trick is to do a child's scene over as many times as you need to without pausing in between takes. I just keep the camera running and gently tell the child that he's doing fine, but just do it once more. It is very important, too, that children do not get nervous; they must think of filming as a game. Therefore you must never let them see that you are worried or that tension is gathering. It is also important for your relationship with the child to be exactly right, not too friendly because then he will take advantage of you, but not too formal because in that case he will be afraid of you.

—Reed, for the *Oliver!* souvenir book (London, 1968)

Lotte R E I N I G E R
Born in Berlin, 1899. Began her animation of jointed silhouettes in 1916.

At that time animation was in its infancy, there was just Felix the Cat, Fleischer's cartoons and some others. Mickey Mouse hadn't arrived. Nobody had thought of making a full-length cartoon. Animated films were supposed to make people roar with laughter, and no one dared to try this for more than 10 minutes. Everybody in the industry was horrified. But we didn't belong to the industry—we being me and my husband Carl Koch. We had always been outsiders and done what we wanted to do. A Berlin banker asked me to consider making a full-length film and installed us in a studio above the garages of the house in Potsdam.

The studio had a low attic roof and the animation rostrum looked like a four-poster bed with the camera supported by wooden beams which we could adapt for special effects.

———Reiniger, interviewed for *The Guardian*, 13 Feb 73

First of all, when I have decided upon a story, I make lots and lots of rough sketches to find out how I can tell it in pictures, what characters and backgrounds will be needed, and how the action could be broken up in a flow of different scenes. Then I can decide what the hero of the story should look like and how the figure has to be constructed to fit the action it has to perform.

When I have found the right shape, I take my scissors and cut the figure out of black cardboard and thin pieces of lead, limb by limb, joining the limbs together with wire hinges. I don't have to invent a difficult mechanism to hold up the figure against the screen, but can lay it out flat on a glass plate, covered with transparent paper to diffuse the light. I fix my lamps underneath that glass plate, and when every other light in the room is switched off the figure appears as a pure silhouette; all the joints and wire hinges are no longer to be seen.

The animation can now be taken over by the stop-motion camera and the hands of the animator. The camera is placed at a suitable distance above the glass plate, looking down at the picture. To that camera a motor is attached, which, when I press a button, will move the film in the camera just for one frame. The shutter is then closed and I can move the figure on the glass plate into the next position, press the button again, move the figure into the following position, and make the next shot. And so on.

———Reiniger, in *Radio Times*, 15 Jan 60

Karel R E I S Z
Born in Ostrava, Czechoslovakia, 1926. Work with British Film Institute and British Film Academy before beginning career as director and producer.

The whole technique of shooting, too, is completely different. A documentary is much freer; you just go off with a small group of technicians and film away and then shape your material. If you film, say, a sequence of 12 shots and 4 of them do not come off, you still have a sequence, though perhaps rather different from your first idea of it. On the other hand, in the feature film everything is much more prearranged, and if one shot out of a 12-shot sequence goes wrong, you have no sequence. It can all be very intimidating.

———Reisz, interviewed for *The Times*, 19 May 60

Lee REMICK
Born 1935 in Boston. Worked in summer stock before appearing on the New York stage.

It wasn't until *Wild River* [1960] that I was able to be more objective about myself. My part in that movie—of a raw mountain girl, warm and loving, who isn't satisfied with her life and who chooses to follow her own desires instead of what her family wants for her—was my favorite up to then. Working with Kazan on that part was a revelation. He has been an actor himself, and he knows how actors feel. He knows that anyone who is fool enough to get up on a stage or go before a camera is exposing himself in so many ways, and needs someone to give him support and confidence. Kazan always made me feel that I was the only person in the world who could do my part. There's so much to Kazan. He knows how to listen to actors; most actors love to talk, and never have a chance to say enough. He's observant of everything relevant to the actor. He's eloquent, and he knows how to extract the best performance from an actor. Actors confide in him. They tell him things they'd never tell another living soul. Then, whenever it's needed for your performance, he pulls something you've told him out of a hat and hands it back to you, and you know what to do in the performance. My interpretation of the role in *Wild River* was the truest in my experience, and it was Kazan who enabled me to make it true. In one scene, for example, it's raining outside, and I'm in my house waiting for Montgomery Clift, the man I'm in love with. Kazan suggested that I have a towel in my hands while waiting. He wanted me to give the towel to Monty in a certain way. Kazan kept telling me, "It's wet outside, wet and muddy, muddy and wet, wet, wet, and as soon as Monty comes in you'll want to give him the towel." Then, when Monty came in, I don't remember how I did what I did, but somehow I was feeling Monty's wetness. There was a certain feeling in it that couldn't have been there without Kazan.
———Remick, interviewed for *The Player* (NY, 1962)

Days of Wine and Roses [1962] called for a kind of research . . . so, [Jack Lemmon and I] went off to A.A. meetings, and I, of course, had the general idea that a lot of people have, that A.A. meetings are all a lot of sort of derelict drunks sitting around looking red eyed and shaking in awful hovels in the Bowery in New York. So the author of the piece, J. P. Miller, took us to a meeting . . . on 64th and Park Avenue where all these lovely people were drinking coffee, shaking a bit, to be sure, but it was a marvelous experience in a strange way, it's a wonderful thing that they do. Anyway, we watched that one, then went down to see another sort on the Bowery in California. I went to a few, to listen to these people talk and tell why they did what they did, what it meant to their lives and then I also went unhappily to the jails in Los Angeles to the drunk tanks and things, late at night watching them bringing in people they would have picked up off the street from doorways and things and that was very very upsetting, revealing and helpful in so far as the way people looked physically what happened to them, the way they talked, it was very depressing.

Paul Newman is a director with whom I hope I will work again (having worked with him on *Sometimes a Great Notion* [retitled *Never Give an*

Inch in Britain, 1971]). He's an absolutely marvelous director, he's worked with Kazan and so he and I had that sort of common language to refer to, he would say, "Y'know what Gadge would say in this kind of instance?" and we would both think, "Well, what would Gadge say?"

[Montgomery Clift] was not very well at the time, when we were working together [on *Wild River*], but he did inspire such love from everybody. He was really like a wounded bird, he really was. He cared an awful lot about what he did, he was meticulous, absolutely, but I mean meticulous to the point of, if he had a scene to play sitting in this chair and he would finally settle himself in . . . and he'd say, "That okay?" He was convinced that everybody hated him and he was hopeless and awful and he would fall apart if you said, "No, it's not quite right at all." "Why isn't it all right?" and he'd shuffle himself around, "Now, there, is that okay?" Every little move was so carefully, painfully, and painstakingly worked out, I adored him, I really did love him.

––––Remick, interviewed at the National Film Theatre, 15 June 72

Jean RENOIR
Born in Paris, 1894, son of Auguste Renoir. Wounded in service in First World War. Began film career in 1924.

It was Werner Krauss who taught me to understand the importance of actors. I greatly admired him and that is why I asked him to play the part of Count Muffat in *Nana* [1926]. My admiration dated from *Caligari*. I had also seen him in other films and in a stage production of Ibsen's *Wild Duck*. What impressed me about him was in the first place his technical skill, his knowledge of makeup and the use he made of small physical peculiarities. After a number of experiments he devised a Count Muffat which was not Werner Krauss and yet was him. Later on I was to realize that this skill in the physical presentation of a character is not the root of the actor's business, and that although a convincing outward appearance is certainly a help, it can never be more.

Werner Krauss was at the height of his fame. He had already become what he has since remained, the finest actor in the German language. He took pity on my inexperience, treated me with friendship and understood my problems. After we had been working together for some weeks a great degree of frankness had sprung up between us. He admitted to me that he made use of clichés. In particular he had invented his famous walk seen from behind. To the enthusiastic audience, that bowed head and those drooping shoulders, laden with all the cares of the world, were the expression of their own unhappiness. The director had to find an excuse for using that walk in all his films, and I did not fail to do so in *Nana*. . . . "At the beginning of my career," Werner Krauss said to me, "that walk was entirely spontaneous. The movement of my legs and the forward droop of my body were prompted by the fact that I really did feel the sorrows of the character I was playing. Now I put it on in the way one does an old coat; but I can do so honorably because I forget about it as readily as one forgets an old coat. I use it as a prop. It isn't what really matters. What really matters is what I feel, and that is expressed by reactions of which I am not the master." But he genuinely believed that audiences were charmed and delighted by the clichés. The public looks for a particular reaction on the part of an actor in a given set of circumstances, and if it is not humored, it resents it, and the actor may fall out of favor.

There is not a yard of dubbed film in *La Chienne* [1931]. When shooting out of doors we sought to damp down background noise with hangings and mattresses. We tried the experiment of attaching a microphone to the projector. Hotchkiss, the manager of Western Electric, was passionately interested in these experiments. He took a hand in them, realizing that my achievement might extend the range of the talking film. At that time we had not thought of recording sound on location, particularly not in a town, where the street noises are so loud that they may swamp the dialogue. But on the other hand I did not want to shoot street scenes in the studio. I wanted the realism of genuine buildings, streets and traffic. I remember a gutter whose waters rippled in front of a house which was to serve as background for an important scene. The microphone made it sound like a torrent. It must be borne in mind that in those days we did not possess directional microphones. I solved the problem by taking a close-up of the gutter and thereby justifying the noise it made. . . .

After the shooting, the editing of the film was accomplished without incident. Pierre Braunberger, who had closely followed the shooting, was delighted. Richebé, who had been away, had it run through for him. Since he had expected a comedy he was very much put out, but he thought that by editing he could make it into the kind of film he wanted. He asked another director, Fejos, to take charge of the operation; but when the latter heard that I did not agree he refused to do so. Richebé then passed the film over to an accommodating lady named Madame Batcheff. I protested, but in vain. "It's for your own good," people who witnessed this act of robbery told me. "You've been living with the film for months. What it needs to make it really first-rate is a wider perspective—a fresh eye." I have heard that talk about "a fresh eye" many times; it is simply a euphemism designed to reconcile a filmmaker to the theft of his work. [*La Chienne* was recut, but Renoir was allowed to restore it before its release.]

[For *Une Partie de campagne*, 1936] We selected a site only a few miles from Marlotte, where I had made *La Fille de l'eau* [1924]. My script was designed for fine weather, and I wrote it with scenes of brilliant sunshine in mind, although there were one or two cloud effects. But the wind changed and a large part of the film was shot in pouring rain. Either we had to give up or the script had to be altered. I liked the story too much to give it up, so I adapted the script. This turned out to be all to the good. The threat of a storm added a new dimension to the drama. When the shooting was over, Braunberger, who was producing, was so pleased with it that he proposed that I should turn it into a full-length film. But I could not agree. To do so would have been contrary to Maupassant's intention and to the intention of my own script. Jacques Prévert, who was consulted, agreed with me. In any case, I had to give it up in order to make *Les Bas Fonds* [1936] I left the film in the hands of Marguerite [Renoir], my friend and film editor. Then the war broke out and I went to America. Marguerite did the editing on her own. Braunberger brought out the film after an interval of 10 years [1946]. As I had foreseen, they had found it impossible to make it into a full-length film.

Toni [1935] has often been described as the forerunner of the Italian neo-realist films. I do not think that is quite correct. The Italian films are magnificent dramatic productions, whereas in Toni I was at pains to avoid the dramatic. I attached as much importance to the countrywoman surprised while doing the washing as to the hero of the story. I had various thoughts in mind. For one thing, a number of carefully selected close-ups seemed to me a way of depicting my characters that was abstract and even stark; and also the use of natural backgrounds enabled me to achieve a realism that was as little distorted as possible.

Now, after a lapse of time, when I can see things a little more clearly, I think I may say that what characterized Toni is the absence of any dominating element, whether star performer, setting or situation. My aim was to give the impression that I was carrying a camera and microphone in my pocket and recording whatever came my way regardless of its comparative importance. Nevertheless, I had given myself a framework. Toni is not a documentary; it is a news item, a love story that really happened in Les Martigues and was told to me by my friend Jacques Mortier, who at the time was chief of police in that small town. I scarcely needed to adapt it for the screen.

At the beginning of the shooting of La Grande Illusion [1937] Stroheim behaved intolerably. We had an argument about the opening scene in the German living quarters. He refused to understand why I had not brought some prostitutes of an obviously Viennese type into the scene. I was shattered. My intense admiration for the great man put me in an impossible position. It was partly because of my enthusiasm for his work that I was in film business at all. Greed [1923] was for me the banner of my profession. And now here he was, my idol, acting in my film, and instead of the figure of truth that I had looked for I found a being steeped in childish clichés. I was well aware that those same clichés, in his hands, became strokes of genius. Bad taste is often a source of inspiration to the greatest artists. Neither Cézanne nor Van Gogh had good taste.

This dispute with Stroheim so distressed me that I burst into tears, which so affected him that there were tears in his own eyes. We fell into each other's arms, damping his German army-officer's tunic. I said that I had so much respect for his talent that rather than quarrel with him I would give up directing the film. This led to further effusions and Stroheim promised that henceforth he would follow my instructions with a slavish docility. And he kept his word.

——Renoir, in My Life and My Films (NY, 1974)

When I made The Rules of the Game [1939], I knew what I was doing. I knew the malady which was afflicting my contemporaries. This does not mean that I knew how to give a clear idea of this in my film. But my instinct guided me.

My awareness of the danger we were in, enabled me to find the right situations, gave me the right words, and my friends thought the same way as I did. How worried we were! I think the film is good. But it is not very difficult to work well when your anxiety acts as a compass, pointing you in the right direction. . . .

Of all the films I have made, this one is probably the most improvised. We worked out the script and decided on the places we were going to shoot as we went along. We only gradually discovered the true theme of the film. But each day we were absolutely immersed in a particular situation—influenced by the decors, by the locations and by the woods surrounding the chateau, all of which made a strong impression on us.

You know there are a lot of filmmakers who use exteriors just in order to show some beautiful scenery on the screen. I think, however, that that aspect is totally unimportant. One shouldn't make use of scenery just for the sake of having some beautiful landscapes or merely to add a touch of realism to the film. Its real function is to plunge us into a particular atmosphere. When we are placed within a particular landscape, we become actors. And this was very necessary in *The Rules of the Game,* for, as I have already pointed out, it is a film which we came to understand only gradually, in the process of making it. . . .

The swamps and landscapes played a very important part in *The Rules of the Game,* not only in the planning of the film but also in the shooting of it. The swamps are, in a way, the essence of Sologne. When I think of Sologne, I think of the reeds, the colors—which are extremely pure—and I think of the mist which you get some mornings. I wanted all that to play a part in the film.

And I wished to capture that strange kind of poetry, both calm and dramatic at the same time, which emanates from the landscapes of Sologne— I wanted it to have just as important a part in the film as one of the characters. For this reason I tried to modify my technique. For the exterior scenes in *The Rules of the Game* I used a very simplified technique. I tried not to move the camera too much; I had very few panning shots and avoided high angle shots, and other unusual angles, as much as possible.

I also wanted to use lenses that would capture the pure and revealing qualities of the Sologne countryside. I wished to show that depth of characterization cannot be separated from the setting of the film, that the characters must be considered as part of an entire world—each element in this world influences all the other elements. . . .

——Renoir, interviewed for French television, 1961;
trans. in published screenplay *The Rules of the Game* (NY, 1969)

The basic principle which was to govern my use of color was to avoid laboratory effects. The problem is to put in front of the camera a landscape or set of the kind that best suits the scene that is being played. In other words, no special filters or retouching. My second rule was to avoid landscapes with too delicate shades of coloring when shooting outdoors. Although our eyes are far superior to the most perfect manufactured lens, we still have difficulty in distinguishing all the shades that Nature offers us; and the artificial eye which is the camera can only work satisfactorily if we set it simple problems. The countryside of the Île de France, for example, contains a myriad blended tints, of which the camera can bring us only a garbled representation. But tropical vegetation, on the other hand, offers us a limited range of colors; its greens are really green and its reds really red. That is why Bengal, like many tropical countries, is so suited to color photography. The colors are neither too vivid nor mixed. Their lightness puts one in mind of Marie Laurencin, or Dufy, or I venture to add, Matisse. The green and red of the Indian flag are different from the green and red on the flags of other nations.

While we were shooting *The River* [1950] we watched out for half-tints. Lourié went so far as to have the lawn in one of our scenes repainted green. Nothing escaped our notice—house, curtains, furniture, clothing. In the case of the latter it was an easy task: the Indians have a fondness for white, that ideally simple color. But the river itself, of course, was outside our control: we had to arrange the close-ups to suit the background.

The part of La Pericole [in *Le Carrosse d'or*, 1952] was played by Anna Magnani, and many people were astonished that an actress famous for her portrayal of stormy emotion should have been used in a piece more suited to a Milanese puppet show. If I had been dealing with a bourgeois type of actress, the film would have risked lapsing into affectation: the danger with Magnani was that it would go too far in the direction of what is called realism. Her dazzling interpretation forced me to treat the film as a light comedy. Another gift which she brought me was her natural nobility. Although she was accustomed to playing women of the people torn by passion, she was perfectly at her ease amid the subtleties of a court intrigue.

The studio's working hours were from midday until 8 in the evening. At first Magnani never arrived before 2. I explained to her that this added greatly to the cost of the production, but she was quite unmoved. I said that it was not a nice way to treat her fellow actors, who turned up on time and then had to wait. Finally I took her aside and declared that I would rather drop the film altogether than keep everyone hanging about. This really did shake her; she promised that from then on she would be punctual, and she kept her word.

Another problem with Magnani was to persuade her to spend the night in bed and not in nightclubs. She turned up worn out, with bags under her eyes and incapable of remembering any of her lines. My nephew, Claude [Renoir]; pulled a face at the thought of having to photograph her in that state. She would start by saying that she couldn't go on, that she looked foul, like an old beggar woman; a string of excuses while she sat shivering in a huge mink cape chain-smoking cigarettes. I insisted on her letting herself be made up and then rehearsed her on the set. At the same time I asked Claude to switch on the lighting so that she could feel the warmth of the lights. Within 5 minutes the bags under her eyes had vanished, her voice had cleared and she looked ten years younger. She had become La Pericole.

——Renoir, in *My Life and My Films* (NY, 1974)

Q. I believe you've kept on with the techniques of your recent films, *Dr. Cordelier* [1961] and *Le Déjeuner sur l'herbe* [1959]. Does this mean shooting with 3 or 4 cameras simultaneously?

A. Generally 3. And we've mostly recorded direct sound. There's nothing dubbed in the film—oh, yes, there is one scene, a short one, where it was raining so hard that you couldn't hear the words.

Q. When you're using this number of cameras, does it make difficulties in the editing, in matching shots? Are there different light levels, for instance.

A. No, we take all that into account. I'm working with Renée Lichtig, the same cutter who helped me on *Dr. Cordelier* and *Le Déjeuner sur l'herbe*, and she's used to this sort of juggling about. In fact, with this method of shooting, the editing becomes essentially a matter of selection and assembly. I'm not faced with a mountain of film which can be so reconstructed in the cutting that something which started out as a comedy can end up as a tragedy.

Q. What struck me about *Dr. Cordelier* was the extraordinary freedom your methods seemed to give the actors.

A. Here too, I hope, here too. I haven't used the identical technique because the subject doesn't lend itself in the same way. Not all subjects do . . . I can't see Jean Rouch, for instance, going off to make one of his African films with half a dozen cameras. He obviously needs one camera, and needs it in exactly the right place. But there are no theories, no general rules. All one can say is that with some scenes and subject it's an unbeatable method. You get this freedom for the actors, and you get a kind of emotional progression.

Q. But I suppose you have to rehearse very carefully just the same?

A. Of course, you always have to rehearse; and you rehearse even more thoroughly when there are several cameras, in order to pin down an emotion and even quite simply to follow through on physical movement. It is easy to lose time on this business of matching shots, even when you're just trying to match physical continuity. You take a close-up, and then comes the medium shot which is to follow it in the montage, and which is filmed the next day, and everyone on the set is asking "Was he like this; wasn't his voice sharper; no, not at all, it was less sharp . . . I promise you it was exactly like this . . . I had my elbow bent just this way. . . ." And the cinema finally becomes a job for the continuity girl, and then a job of composition and inspiration. For myself, I'd really rather call a truce to all these problems and shoot the scene in one go.

Q. I read recently something you were reported as saying . . . I can't quote it exactly, but it seemed to me marvelous. You said something like this: "I'm not ashamed of changing my mind, at least I'm not afraid of setting out, looking for something, without knowing where I'm going. . . ."

A. Well, what matters is the action, not the target. Of course one needs general ideas, but they must be so deep-rooted, so profound, that one hardly knows one has them. You have to start out in a certain direction and keep to it, but in the way that migratory birds follow a line instinctively, without knowledge. I believe the artist ought to be like that. And then the conscious part of his mind goes into the detail, into action, into doing. An 18th- or 19th-century idea which has caused immense trouble is this one of targets: "Do this and you will be rewarded," "Work well and you will have money for your old age." It ought to be done for the pleasure of the moment, the pleasure of working well.

——Renoir, interviewed for *Sight & Sound*, Spring 62

Q. [What do you think] about the recent American trend towards documentary realism?

A. That is nothing new, I shot most of *La Bête humaine* [1938] on
location in Le Havre. I built very few sets for *The Southerner* [1945]. But I
am not dogmatic about it. I think a set is a useful and necessary thing at
times. And in any case, if the people don't behave in a realistic manner there
is no point in having them perform against real backgrounds. I have also
heard theories about nonprofessional actors. This I don't understand at all.
Can you think of a non-actor replacing Raimu or Gabin? I can't. Personally, I
have a great respect for the acting profession.

——Renoir, interviewed for *Sequence*, New Year 50

Alain RESNAIS
*Born Vannes, 1922. Began film career with short films on the arts, and as
editor of 5 fictional films (including* La Pointe courte *in 1954).*

[I work closely] with my scriptwriters and with actors and technicians too. I
always work with an original script. The writer and I talk it over and prepare it for months in advance. Even now during the editing [of *Last Year at
Marienbad*] we still keep closely in touch. Then when we assemble the cast
and technicians we talk over the ideas. Everyone has a right to make a
suggestion. I don't want to make out that we use a kind of demagogy [democ-
racy?] with people raising their hands to vote, but we do want everyone to
understand what they are doing. We want everything clear and simple.

——Resnais, interviewed for *The Guardian*, 14 Mar 63

Every time I make a film I discover that one can't allocate gestures or words
to the characters just as one pleases. There was a moment, during the preparation of *Marienbad*, where I arrived with my little black notebook and
suggested to Robbe-Grillet that we should introduce the real world under the
guise of conversations concerning a political problem, which would be in-
soluble, at least for those who were interested in it. But we realized that the
real world would be introduced by the spectators themselves as they watched
the film, and that it was impossible to include them in it. . . .

For me, shooting is elucidation. I do make small sketches beforehand
but for the sake of peace. . . . I still study them. It helps in my relationships
with the actors and the cameramen. They save the actor from getting panicky 8
or 10 days before we shoot. If he has read the shooting script and has a clear
idea of it, and then, while shooting, I place him in a position or composition
which hasn't been foreseen, he is apt to worry. And as I like everyone to be
as relaxed as possible on the set, I prefer arguments to be over before shooting. I'm all in favor of rehearsing the entire film before shooting begins.

For *Marienbad* we drew up a complete chronology on squared paper.
And before beginning any scene with the actors, we said, "In the editing this
scene follows such and such a scene, but, in actual chronology it follows another scene, which will appear much later in the film." I frequently recorded
a fragment of the preceding scene, so as to work from the continuity rather

than the cue. This chronological chart was drawn up after the scenario was finished. Obviously, all the changes of costume correspond to different "layers" of time.

——Resnais, interviewed for *Cahiers du cinéma;* trans. by Durgnat for *Films & Filming,* Feb. 62; repr in *Film Makers on Film Making,* 1967

R-G: The genesis of the film, *L'Année dernière à Marienbad,* is particularly illuminating. When Resnais and I had our first discussion, we found we had both conceived a cinematic "form" of the same kind. I knew that all my ideas on the cinema would somehow suit whatever Resnais would set out to achieve from then on. It so happened that he wanted to make the kind of film I had been thinking of. I didn't actually produce 4 outlines in 3 days for him, but I have written 4 projects each about 1½ pages long, which I have had in mind for a long time.

R: When I had finished reading his work I said to myself: we've already made one film together—*Toute la mémoire du monde* [1956].

R-G: That doesn't stop us from having different ideas about all his films or my novels. But we do seem to have a world in common, which we can both inhabit. There was never any question of compromise between Resnais and myself, but of a common "form" which functioned in the same way for us both, although it's not certain that we both give the same importance to the details.

R: We don't have the same tastes, and we sometimes disagree violently about a book, a film, or a way of life. . . .

R-G: All the same, we are constantly having the same intuitions. For example, I was explaining a camera movement, and Resnais said, "Don't worry, it's the movement I would have chosen in any case." Still, it is quite possible that *Marienbad* isn't exactly the same film for Resnais as it is for me. We must see the world around us rather differently, although it's the same world. . . .

Q. To return to *Marienbad,* there is one curious phenomenon. One can say equally well: it's a Resnais film or: it's a Robbe-Grillet film. But it's no secret that there are a few minimal differences between the very detailed shooting script and the finished product.

R-G: In the scenario I handed over to Resnais there were already numerous specifications as to editing, composition, and camera movement. But I had no notion of the technical terms used in the cinema nor of its real possibilities. I described a film which I saw in my imagination and in very naïve terms.

——Resnais and Robbe-Grillet, interviewed for *Films & Filming,* March 62

My great hope in making *Muriel* [1963] was to save time by not having any camera movements, and when they asked me how many feet of track rails I was going to need, I said, none at all. I wanted to see if I could make a film without using a single tracking shot. . . . But in spite of this, the shooting went more slowly than ever. Mind you, we did pan and tilt, but the camera didn't actually move except in the final scene. *Harry Dickson* [unrealized], on the other hand, would have been done in 70mm. with the actors always framed full length—head to toe—throughout the film. A little like Feuillade, perhaps. But I would have been able to take advantage of the high definition and absolute clarity as well as the absence of depth of field that only 70mm. can give you. That way, I would have been able to show the characters full length without sacrificing any details or facial expressions.

In both cases, of course, the formal structures were suggested by the subject matter. *Muriel* had to be a mosaic. I mean, Cayrol and I didn't just decide to make a film which would be shot this way or that. It all began with an idea: one day on the stairs, Cayrol said, "I've got an idea you might like, a film about provincial life. Wouldn't you like the idea of a movie about a kind of double city—prewar and postwar, with people who can't find their way anymore because the new streets don't follow the lines of the old ones?" Of course, I was interested.

——Resnais, interviewed for *Sight & Sound*, Summer 69

Q. Could your film [*La Guerre est finie,* 1966] in any way, be described as propaganda or do the political events simply provide a background for a portrait of Diego?

A. It is difficult to separate the two—I mean that the background of political events go a long way towards explaining Diego's character. What I am trying to show is the lack of coordination and contact that exists in the antifascist organization. Inevitably, this leads to misunderstanding and inefficiency.

Q. How did you come to work with your scenarist Jorge Semprun?

A. As usual, with the help of friends. Somebody suggested that I should get to know Jorge because our work has certain elements in common. . . .

Q. Are the scriptwriters present during the shooting?

A. Never. Before, during the preparatory phase and afterwards during the editing, but never during the shooting.

Q. You once said that the film is a living material that is constantly being shaped and changed—does that mean that you improvise during the shooting?

A. Yes, but not too much because it's expensive and the producer starts to worry. Usually, I rehearse the scenes with the actors, get the script girl to check dialogue and am then ready to begin shooting.

——Resnais, interviewed for *Films & Filming*, Oct 66

John RICHARDSON

I should think we used about 8 gallons of makeup blood [for *Straw Dogs,* 1971], the best; Sam [Peckinpah] is very funny about the color and look of the blood he uses. The special glass (in fact, a plasticized resin) broken in the siege of the farm cost about £2,000 and 20 pounds of cheap off-cuts from a local butcher were used to add realism. Sam's a hard man to work for, he likes total realism; in the end we took everything to him, as you could never tell how he'd react. . . . We had small charges in the coats [to simulate shotgun wounds] to blow holes in the material; we had to be careful because the artists were actually wearing the coats.

When Major Scott was being shot, we had to devise a platform for him to stand on. He had a button in his hand to fire the shotgun and the charges in his back—and to work the device which threw him backwards through the air for 10 feet. On that occasion we used a stunt double. We did the shot 5 times on a cold damp night on top of a hill in Cornwall. . . .

I was horrified sometimes at what we were doing [on *The Devils*, 1971]. But seeing the picture I wasn't at all offended by it, it all had a rightful place in the film.

———Richardson, interviewed for *The Times*, 7 Dec 71

Tony [Cecil Antonio] R I C H A R D S O N
Born Shipley, Yorkshire, 1928. Attended Oxford where he directed plays for the Dramatic Society; began career with BBC–TV.

I asked first for permission to go into one of the institutions and make the picture [*The Loneliness of the Long Distance Runner*, 1962] there. This was refused. Then I asked if I could visit one or two of the places to get the atmosphere. I got another refusal. In the end I managed to get into 3 Borstals under an assumed name and posing as all sorts of things, such as Richardson, the prisoner's friend.

So I've decided that, apart from the major roles, I shall cast the whole film with ex-Borstal boys just to annoy the commissioners. I've spoken to quite a few lads and they are very keen. But I shall put an advert in *The Times* to make sure of a lot of applications. I imagine a lot of readers . . . are former Borstal boys.

———Richardson, interviewed for *The Daily Mail*, 13 Sept 61

Martin R I T T
Born New York City, 1920; started on New York stage as an actor in Golden Boy; *studied with Elia Kazan; acted, directed for TV before beginning in film with* Edge of the City, 1957, *as a director.*

I used Orson [Welles] in *The Long Hot Summer* [1958]. Twentieth Century–Fox warned me about him, and were against his being in the picture. Too much temperament, they said. And his temperament, they said, had once run up the cost on, I believe, a Henry Hathaway film. But I wanted him so I got him.

For the first scene, we had to wait around a few days until the sun was just right. He got upset just sitting around and not being called to shoot, so when it's finally time I find him just sitting and reading a Spanish-language newspaper. He's not prepared for the scene. I'm pretty mad so I tell everyone. "That's it. Let's strike the setup. We'll shoot something else."

That night Welles calls me and says, "Marty, why'd you do that? You humiliated me in front of everyone!" "I humiliated you? What the hell do you think you did to me?" Then I told him the facts of life. We got along fine after that.

———Ritt, interviewed for *The Toronto Star*, 11 Dec 65

Part of the attraction of *Hud* [1963], was that it told the truth about the West as it was. Most Westerns are mythic, which really means that they tell out-and-out lies. But in *Hud* I wanted to make a film showing that the Gable character who always turned out to be a golden-hearted fellow in the end was really addicted to his own appetites and was a no-good. In my new film, *The Molly Maguires* [1968], we're trying to deal with the truth about that situation, too, and with the right of a man to make his own sound. Whether one agrees with men like Eldridge Cleaver and Rap Brown or not, one should allow them the chance to make their own sound. If you can view the picture historically, there is something heroic about those miners. Finally, to die for something one believes worthwhile is a good definition of a hero.

——Ritt, interviewed for *The Times*, 18 Mar 69

Hal ROACH
Born Elmira, New York, 1892. In 1912 worked as cowboy at the Universal Studio. Produced his own films in 1914, employing Harold Lloyd.

[In 1914] cinemas showed one 5-reel drama, one 2-reel comedy, a newsreel and another short in each program, and the 2-reel form was almost the ideal length for a comedy on one situation—the comedian had time to milk it for as much humor as it would yield without having to devise a more elaborate plot framework or outstaying his welcome (even in those days, long before television, there was the danger of overexposure to be considered). But then the vaudeville houses took to showing 5-reel films to complement their live bills; at first any old films which came along so as not to detract from the live shows, then, when they realized that films were an attraction in themselves, the best films they could get. To compete with this the full-time cinemas had to show double bills, and the days of the 2-reeler were over.

Many good reliable comics who just did not have that extra something to carry a full length feature-film—Charlie Chase, Thelma Todd, Zasu Pitts— slipped from their places at the top right away, and others hung on for the moment with the risk that fairly soon they would work themselves out or the public would get tired of them just from seeing too much of them.

Of course the coming of sound hastened the process, because anyway filmmakers became obsessed with the idea that if you were making a talking picture all the humor must be verbal too, and so the more visual comedians got pushed into the background but a lot of them had probably already passed their zenith. Chaplin, for instance, was the greatest clown we have ever had, but he had his head turned by the reverence with which people received everything he said at the height of his career (when, after all, he was the most famous man in the world) into believing that he had the answers to the world's problems and it was his duty to put them over in his films instead of just making people laugh. Keaton, to my taste, was funnier in his 2-reelers than in his feature films.

Harry Langdon, who was in his day the nearest thing to Chaplin, was another spoiled by his own success with the critics. He became obsessed with the idea that his main talent was that he could sustain a scene longer than any other comic on the screen, and no one could reason him out of it; he would do everything at snail's pace, whether it was suitable or not, and though he was naturally a slow comedian this killed all his effects because the film would come to a stop just when it should have been hurrying through the linking passages to the next key scene. Harold Lloyd was rather a different case. I made practically all Harold's films, and basically he had not a funny bone in his body, but he was such a good actor that if you gave him a good script, he could play it to the best advantage for laughs. The only trouble was that his character could not age; he concentrated so much on the dopey but likable young man who always wins out in the end that he just could not carry it over into middle age.

——Roach, interviewed for *The Times*, 17 Aug 61

This is the way we made those one-reelers: Monday morning I would bring the group in and say, "You make up as a cop, you make up as a garbageman, you make up as a pedestrian." We'd go out in the park, and we'd start to do something. By that time, I'd have an idea of what the sets were going to be. By noon, I would tell the set man what I wanted, and he would go back to the studio to get them ready.

I don't think we ever had anything on paper until we started making 2-reelers with lights. Nobody but me had any idea what the hell we were going to do. We'd try one thing, it wasn't funny; we'd try something else.

——Roach, interviewed for *The Real Tinsel* (NY, 1970)

In the early years there were no scripts. Scripts didn't come in until the early twenties, before that it was off-the-cuff. We just thought of an idea and went into certain sets and tried to get the comedians to do what we thought was funny. It was very broad slapstick at that time. You hit everybody on the head with a hammer, or a brick, and when they were knocked down they went sailing through at least 2 sets before they landed and all kinds of physical things. That, at the time, seemed very humorous to the audience. . . .

Laurel and Hardy were unique. They were two comedians that complemented each other. When Hardy fell in the mud puddle, you would cut to his expression of disgust because he fell into the puddle, then you cut to the bewildered Laurel looking at Hardy in the puddle, then back to Hardy; so actually you got 3 laughs where with a single comedian you'd only get one.

——Roach, in *Films & Filming*, Oct 64

What I did with Laurel and Hardy was in writing the themes. As a rule, I decided what type of picture it was to be and picked the locations. Then I'd pick out a couple of my writers or gag men sympathetic to this main theme— of course, there was no better writer than Laurel himself, with the possible exception of Chaplin. As for Chaplin, he killed more comedians than anybody else by writing, directing, and producing his own pictures. Everybody wanted to do that but he had 100 years of English music hall and pantomime to draw upon.

——Roach, interviewed for *Screen* (India), 7 June 68

Alain ROBBE-GRILLET
Born in Brest, 1922. An agricultural scientist before writing his first novel. His work as scenarist (Last Year at Marienbad, 1962) *has led to the direction of his own scripts.*

. . . What I've been trying to do is break away from the idea that a film must be based on an anecdote. I think a film needs to be organized according to cinematic logic and not any other kind, and it may be quite false, in terms of this cinematic logic, to stick to ordinary chronological time and sequence. On the screen there's no grammatical tense, everything is present, and ordinary sequence may have very little to do with how the hero lives through his experience, or how he looks back on it, or how the author himself originally imagined it.

I don't think either the cinema or the novel is for explaining the world. Some people believe there's a certain definite reality and all that a work of art has to do is pursue it and try to describe it. I don't think that at all. I don't believe a work of art has reference to anything outside itself. In a film there's no reality except that of the film, no time except that of the film. If people ask me, "How long did *Marienbad* take to happen? Two years. One? Two months? Three days?" I say, "No, an hour and thirty-two minutes." The duration of the film. The story of *Marienbad* doesn't exist apart from the way it's told. The only reality is the film's, and as for the criterion of that reality, for the author it's his vision, what he feels. For the spectator, the only test is whether he accepts.

——Robbe-Grillet, interviewed for *The Observer*, 18 Nov 62

Cliff ROBERTSON
Born in La Jolla, California, 1925. Acted on stage and for TV prior to films.

Emotionally, I'll always be terribly grateful that President Kennedy chose me for the role [in *P.T. 109,* 1963] That's the sole reason I played it. I had no misgivings about the script. I felt it regrettable that it didn't try to inspect the inside of what makes a man what he was, instead of just telling the physical exploits. I mean, it could have been about anyone.

President Kennedy had requested 3 things only about the movie. That it be historically accurate . . . that any money due to him from added sales of the book, film rights and so on, be given to the crew (or their dependents) of the P.T. 109 . . . and finally that he be allowed to select who would play him.

They tested a lot of actors at the Warners studio, and sent on the better tests to Washington. And whenever he had 2 minutes free, the president would stick his head into his cinema and look them over.

——Robertson, interviewed for *Photoplay*, July 69

People couldn't believe I would ever make *Charly* [1968].

It took me 7 years trying to get it off the ground. Everyone said it was too bold, too risky.

But in those 7 years I had the chance to do all the homework I needed

to be sure of the part. Not many actors get that chance. I knew Charly inside out. I digested the character as well as the words. I went to several retarded centers during that time, and studied the patients, but in fact playing the man in the early stages was easier than playing him as a genius.
————Robertson, interviewed for *The Evening News*, 15 Apr 68

Edward G. R O B I N S O N (Emmanuel Goldenberg) [1893–1972]
Born in Bucharest; appeared in U.S. theater and vaudeville before taking first picture role in The Bright Shawl, *1923.*

In late 1930 Hal Wallis asked me to his office to discuss my playing the role of Otero in *Little Caesar*—the best-seller by William R. Burnett. . . .

Yes, I said Otero. Not Rico (Cesare Bandello), the lead, but Otero, a minor part.

To this day I think it was a ruse. I think Hal had always meant for me to play Rico, and his ploy was to soften my rigid backbone. I've never asked him. . . . In his cool, offhand and peremptory manner he handed me the script of *Little Caesar*, pointing out that the part of Otero was exactly right for me. I took the script back to my dressing room, read it, and decided not only that the part of Otero was exactly wrong for me but that the script itself was a literal and undramatized rendering of the novel. . . .

So back I went to Wallis and announced pompously: "If you're going to have me in *Little Caesar* as Otero, you will completely imbalance the picture. The only part I will consider playing is Little Caesar."

. . . Hal listened carefully to my ravings, made a few notes, then reminded me that my contract gave me no approval of roles . . . Hal then said he would take the matter up with Mr. Warner, and within a matter of hours I was cast as Little Caesar.
————Robinson (with Leonard Spigelgass), in *All My Yesterdays* (NY, 1973)

Mark R O B S O N
Born in Montreal, 1913; studied at U.C.L.A. and at Pacific Coast University. Joined Fox property department in 1932; moved to R.K.O. (1932–43) editorial department before starting as a film director in 1943 with The Seventh Victim.

Q. *Bedlam* [1946] and *Isle of the Dead* [1945] were inspired at least in part by paintings, and in many of the films there are tableaux that look like reproductions of art works. How much of a part did art play in the [Val] Lewton films?

A. Before filming, we looked endlessly at books and books of paintings. This came out of Val's training with David Selznick. If there was a sunset, we looked at hundreds of paintings and photographs of sunsets. We looked at modern art and at 18th-century art to find the light and shadow of a painting.

Q. What more was involved in preproduction planning?

A. We thought everything out. We had to do this to accomplish what we did with such low budgets. Val emphasized detail. I remembered that Orson [Welles] had said that "Detail is the most important thing; the big things take care of themselves." Detail was very important in terms of the texture of these films. Also, we chose the sets very carefully, used them as modules.

Q. Was the low-key lighting attributed to low budgets?

A. Not really. It was attributed more to the desired mysterious look of the films. Of course, the streets we had in *The Seventh Victim* for instance, were studio streets, and the less light we put on them the better they looked. We would just suggest certain things on that street hidden in the darkness because the streets were architecturally wrong. We were interested in single-source lighting. We chose sets that were suitable for single-source. It made setups and characters very interesting. It was important for us to use light for dramatic purposes.

Q. How much leeway did the cameraman have?

A. In terms of camera movement, position, setups—none. In terms of light source, very little. We prescribed all the shots. The cameraman's job was to see that we captured the image on the negative with enough balance. He worked with us very closely, but he wasn't an inventor of setups or design.

My contributions to [*Cat People*, 1942] were editing techniques that were quite good. I did the editing of the echoes in the swimming pool sequence. Also, we developed a sharp cutting technique we later grew to call the "bus" and that is that from a close-up of a person in terror we cut to the impact of a bus (with the hiss of the airbrakes) coming to a stop. The sharpness of that cutting would knock people out of their seats in the theater.

————Robson, interviewed for *Velvet Light Trap*, Fall 73

[For *Isle of the Dead*, 1945] we had to do a number of battlefield scenes and of course we couldn't afford to build anything. But we managed to get our hands on some white muslin and some dirt and came up with a false-perspective landscape. Where the dirt and the muslin met we took as the horizon. We kept dressing the small set with different trees and wagon wheels to disguise the fact that, while we were trying to suggest the illusion of continuous space, we were actually using the same mock-up over and over again. We finally did the battle scenes with a total of thirty extras, basing their groupings upon Goya's Disasters of War. . . . Through each Goyaesque layout, we'd shoot tracks of Karloff wandering about the battlefield.

————Robson, interviewed by Joel Siegel for his *Val Lewton* (NY, 1973)

Glauber R O C H A
Born in Bahia, Brazil, 1938 [1939?]. Worked as journalist before directing his first short film in 1959.

I shot most of my newest film, *Cabecas Cortadas (Severed Heads)* [1970] in Barcelona. It is about a fictitious Latin American country under a dictatorship, told in a surrealist style.

When I returned to Brazil in 1969 I was thoroughly shattered by conditions there. Almost anybody who was anybody in the arts was abroad—if not worse. The great historian Caio Prado was in jail; economists and sociologists of the stature of Josue de Castro and Celso Furtado were teaching in foreign universities. The regime had truly taken to heart the famous fascist dictum, "Down with the intelligentsia.". . .

So, in April this year [1969], realizing I could not help a situation where even the Italian director Antonioni had been forbidden to shoot a film in Brazil, I decided that I, too, would have to choose freedom.

I have now been in Europe for some months, but have not yet quite made up my mind whether I defected or whether I was rejected; whether I left; or whether I was pushed out. But in one way or another I will continue using my camera as one uses a weapon. I will be fighting for the masses of Negroes and people of a lighter shade as well who have been so used to being exploited that they have hardly felt the difference in the various changes of regime.

——Rocha, interviewed for *The Manchester Guardian*, 1969

Joe R O C K
Born in New York City, 1893. Entered motion pictures in 1916 with Mont-gomery-Rock comedies for the Brooklyn studios of Vitagraph, before moving to Hollywood.

We made the first and second films. And the third. He [Stan Laurel] was appearing on time and was very cooperative. We would sometimes work all night trying to improve a gag. He would sit in on cutting. He wanted to sit in on the story. Oh, he was good, better than Babe Hardy when the two of them were a team. Babe didn't care. He came in the morning and left at 5:00 P.M. But Stan was interested. He knew cutting, and he'd tell you, "I think if we did this and this . . ." He was fine. And I had good men with me.

——Rock, interviewed for *The Real Tinsel* (NY, 1970)

. . . Although I had no intention of making them a team, I had wanted to use Babe Hardy in a number of the Stan Laurel comedies I made, but Stan always said no. Understandably, no top comic wanted to team with another comic unless that comic was willing to be either stooge, foil, or straight man—and whenever that kind of teaming was forced on comics—I mean equal teaming—it inevitably broke such teams up because of ego or jealousy problems. When I offered to bring Hardy into his pictures, Stan refused because he said that any heavy who played for laughs reduced the image of a heavy—and then really became a comic in competition with the star.

——Rock, interviewed for *The Comedy World of Stan Laurel* (Garden City, 1974)

Nicholas R O E G
Born in London, 1928. Began film career as cutter in the English studio of MGM.

In Dick Lester's *A Funny Thing* [*Happened on the Way to the Forum*, 1966], 68 pages of the script took place outside the door of a house. One opening shot and that finished it, then it would be entirely up to the actors. So we built a complicated set with back light and cross light, and the first shots we overexposed almost burning out everything except the shadow areas, then gradually the set became a recognizable entity, dazzlingly bright.

Far from the Madding Crowd [1967] was a very challenging film for me to work on, since Hardy's story is inseparable from the descriptions of the seasons and the Dorsetshire countryside. I had to find ways of weaving the passing of time and the twist of seasons into the action of the film, in order to create a sense of the pace of 19th-century rural England.

———Roeg, interviewed for *The Guardian*, 3 Apr 71

Will R O G E R S (1879–1935)
Born in Cologah, Oklahoma. Brought his own comedy style to his work in Broadway revues before entering films in 1918.

In "Jubilo" Ben Ames Williams wrote the finest story it was ever my privilege to work in. It was the only Story ever made out here [1919] where there was no Scenario made. We just shot the scenes from the various paragraphs in the Story in the Saturday Evening Post. When we took a Scene we just marked it off and went on to the next. I think, and Williams verified it, that it was the only story ever made that was absolutely filmed as it was written, and here is the big Novelty to it. We didn't change his main Title either.

———In *The Autobiography of Will Rogers* (Boston, 1949)

Sure; this is just up my alley, for talk is the way I've put over my gags. In the silents I'd do a scene and say what I thought was the right thing, but they'd always change it in the titles. For instance, in *The Texas Steer* [1927] I was a congressman, and one day I'm walkin' along a street in Washington—we shot it there—when I met a white wings cleanin' the street. I said to him: "Is yours a political job?" He looked at me in contempt. "No," he answers. "Civil Service. We have to pass examinations!"

That gag had meanin'. What do you think they changed it to? I say to the fellow; "One-horse town, what?" and he answers, "You wouldn't think so in my job." Smart crack instead of satire, and an old smart crack at that.

No, the best part of the talkies is that when I say somethin' I say it, and it sticks. There's no way of changin' it without cutting the whole sequence. In *The Texas Steer* they turned the titles of the picture over to a young smart-crackin' boy. They regret now that they did it. But in this I'm safe.

Furthermore, Frank Borzage, who's directing *They Had To See Paris* [1929], has a good subtle sense of humor. He doesn't make me do such broad comedy as I have had to do in most silent pictures. Also he lets me ad-lib, and that helps, for some of my best gags come to me durin' the action.

———Rogers, interviewed for *Screenland*, Oct 1929

Eric R O H M E R [Maurice Scherer]
Born in Nancy, France, 1920.

... I shoot the [Moral Tales] with the point of view of one of the characters. What he knows, we will know. What he doesn't know, we will never know. The husband, Frédéric, (in *Chloe in the Afternoon*, 1972), will not know what the wife did in the afternoon because he is not interested in finding out. He does not want to know. You, like Frédéric, may not be interested in the thing. You also have every right to guess. Maybe she was on an errand. Maybe it was something different. As far as I'm concerned, I don't know. In the Moral Tales I only ask questions; I do not give answers. It is only the drama that is exposed.

Q. For an actor to play a part, does he or she have to know what the answer to the question is, and if so, does he or she tell you?

A. That's precisely what I would never have dared to ask the actor. In that last scene in *Chloe in the Afternoon* when the wife comes in, I have the impression that the two actors did more than just merely play a part. I had a real husband and wife (Bernard and Françoise Vérley) play the parts of the husband and wfe, and that's what they told me. And when we shot that scene, I was almost embarrassed to sit through it even though I knew they were acting out. It was a scene we did only one take of and it would have been absolutely impossible to have done it over. I like it when in my films something happens that I am not forcing—that happens and I just have to film. My film is nothing of a documentary, nothing of a cinéma vérité film. It was written and well prepared. It was acted by actors. But there are certain moments, despite everything, when the actors forget they are actors, and I forget that they are actors too. And that's what interests me most in the films: to find these moments. But in general, I find them without looking for them. In *Chloe in the Afternoon* it happened at the very end and it was only then that I felt that I was happy with my film. Until then I was not very satisfied.

———Rohmer, interviewed for *Take One*, Sept–Oct 72

Owen R O I Z M A N
Born in New York City.

Q. After you read a script, how much time do you have for preproduction?

A. I usually get 2 to 3 weeks. What happens is that the production designer scouts the location according to the vision he has set up with the director. Once the director is locked into his locations, I go around and approve them from a photographic and technical point of view. Generally they're satisfactory.... There was only one location on *Three Days of the Condor* [1975] I suggested be changed into a set.... I looked at the location they had selected and said, "No way can we work here—no room, bad angles, a real hassle." I made my recommendation, they had a full-scale meeting ... and decided to build a set. Most people today think you can save a lot of time and money shooting on actual locations ... it's become a vogue to get that "real look," but there are times when a studio-built set can save you. You can work faster and cover many more set-ups per day. The entire interior of the house and room in *The Exorcist* [1973] was a studio set built right here in NYC. At times the flexibility of a movable set is advantageous. Actually Bill Friedkin wanted to shoot *The Exorcist* on location, like *The French Connection* [1971], but again I knew from the start that all those intricate special effects would demand a set that could be changed and moved at will.

———Roizman, interviewed for *Millimeter*, Feb 75

Mikhail R O M M (1901–1971)
Born in Irkutsk. Trained as sculptor, changed career to films at end of 1920s.
The following quotation concerns the preparation of Shchukin to play the role
of Lenin in Lenin in October, *1937:*

When I suggested that we should start "shooting" the first episode Shchukin
told me:

"You know, there is something I have not yet ascertained—how Lenin
laughed. I cannot act the part till I find out. Find someone who remembers
Lenin laughing, let him show me Lenin's laughter. It is then that a man's
character is revealed."

Finally we heard of an old Bolshevik, who was well known for his ability
to imitate Lenin perfectly. Even Vladimir Ilyich himself had asked for a
demonstration and had laughed uproariously when he heard "himself" talk.

When Shchukin and I learned about this man, we decided that we had to
get hold of him by all means.

Shchukin was made up, he had on his costume and waited, extremely
excited. Our guest arrived and inspected the makeup and the costume. We
asked him a few questions and then got down to the main question.

"Can you tell us how Lenin laughed?"

"He used to laugh in all sorts of ways," the old man replied. "Sometimes
he would laugh in a caustic, mocking way; sometimes kindly and good-
naturedly. There were times when his laughter was just like a child's."

"Can you show us how he did it?"

This was not so easy. He could imitate Lenin's voice, but laughter was
more difficult. To imitate the way someone laughs, you have to be a real actor.
Our guest tried to laugh but failed. The sound he produced was not natural.
He felt it himself and said, "I cannot do it."

"Then I will try." Shchukin suggested. He walked away from us to the
corner of the room, turned his back and was silent for a moment, thinking.
Then he turned round to face us—and I saw a different man. I saw Lenin. He
seemed to have become shorter, his eyebrows took on a different shape, his
face had changed, and his body had another bearing.

Then Shchukin took a step towards us and broke into laughter. Our guest
turned pale, obviously recollecting Vladimir Ilyich, and this caused him pain.

"It is just like him," he said. "I cannot teach you anything."

——Romm, in *Screen* (India), 29 Apr 60

For 2 years during my work on *Ordinary Fascism* [1965] I spent about 8 hours
every day looking at newsreel shots. Films long and short, shot at different
times, passed before my eyes, and gradually I noticed a curious effect upon
myself: after some time one's consciousness becomes attuned to acceptance of
genuine film documents, and when some studio fragment appears it is irritating, one rejects it as superfluous, one feels a sharp distinction between reality
and its copy.

Our cutting room was in a long corridor with another half-dozen cutting
rooms and 2 demonstration halls. For some reason each cutter likes to have the
sound on very loud, and going out into the corridor I would hear a well-trained
baritone speaking on an artificial, trembling note about love or building or the
romance of tourism, and alongside some woman's voice loudly proclaiming

something very dramatic. Those voices sounded very unnatural. They came from the world of acted films. To transfer oneself into the artificial acting world from the world of documentaries demanded very great effort.

This was not because I heard bad actors or fragments from bad films. By no means. I could bring vividly to mind fragments from my own feature films, and they had the same effect.

With regard to the general trend of cinematography, the most essential indication of its development is the change in the style of acting. The director working with the actor, and the actor himself before the camera, try to an increasing extent to avoid the "conventional" elements in acting which are inculcated from the first year in schools for actors.

——Romm, interviewed for *Soviet Film*, 4, 1966

Conrad R O O K S

Q. Would you like to talk a bit about your experience with Mrs. Gandhi?

A. I met with her twice—once in '67 and the last time in '70 or '71 . . . I was studying [in '67] with a swami. We talked about the possibility of making *Siddhartha* into a film; she had read the book and I wanted her blessing. She was very interested and said of course I hope you will try to depict Indian life in a way that is in keeping with your friendship for the country and not try to do a number on us. Which Louis Malle later *did* do to the country with his *Calcutta 71* [1969?]. And Malle really did make it difficult for any filmmaker who came after because he created a climate of extreme distrust for any filmmaker who tried to come out to India again. For instance, when I went there the first time and shot in 1964—when I was doing *Chappaqua*—I could do whatever the hell I wanted—just no problem whatsoever. The *next* time I went, after Louis Malle had done *Calcutta*, it was a much different ball game. And he did a great disservice to other filmmakers by doing that.

——Rooks, interviewed in 1973

Françoise R O S A Y [Bandy de Nalèche] (1891–1974)
Born in Paris, near the Place Pigalle. Appeared in films in 1913 and married Jacques Feyder in 1917.

I have been acting since I was 16—acting, I always like to think, with conviction.

I have played prostitutes, drug addicts and alcoholics, I have led a blameless life myself—I have been married once, to film director Jacques Feyder, and have 3 children.

So, monsieur, when I have to play the part I have to play I go into another world to gain the necessary background. Naturally, my late husband used to accompany me when I went in search of background. If I had to play a drug addict in a film, Jacques would say, "Ma chérie Françoise, I know just the place where the best drug addicts hang out."

When as a young actress I had to play prostitutes, Jacques would say, "Ma chérie Françoise, you cannot play these parts without knowing how these people live. We must find out."

——Rosay, interviewed for *The Evening Standard*
Saturday Magazine, 2 Jan 60

Charles ROSHER
Born in London, 1885; studied photography at the London Polytechnic and joined a firm of Court photographers. In 1908 visited the United States and in 1909 bought a motion-picture camera. His work with the Horsley Brothers took him to Hollywood in 1911 (their Nestor company was the first studio there) and his accumulating experience and reputation brought him a nearly lifelong contract with Mary Pickford.

Carl Hoffman photographed *Faust* [1926] and I learned a great deal from him. I took several ideas back, including the dolly suspended from railway tracks in the ceiling, which I adapted for *Sunrise* [1927].

That was a very difficult film, *Sunrise*. We had many problems. My assistant was excellent and very helpful—Stewart Thompson. . . . For some scenes, such as the swamp sequence, the camera went in a complete circle. This created enormous lighting problems. We built a railway line in the roof, suspended a little platform from it, which could be raised or lowered by motors. My friend and associate, Karl Struss, operated the camera on this scene. It was a big undertaking; practically every shot was on the move. . . .

I found it difficult to get Murnau to look through the camera. "I'll tell you if I like it in the projection room," he used to say. I would have continued to work with Murnau on *Four Devils* [1928], but I had to go back to Mary Pickford.

———Rosher, interviewed for *The Parade's Gone By* (NY, 1968)

[Murnau] would tell me, always holding the sketches [by Gliese] in his hands, what he wanted—camera angles and lighting. Then, during the shooting, he would say, "You know what I want." He had confidence in me, and as everything had been decided in advance there was no need for him to verify the picture in the viewfinder.

In the projection room, looking at the rushes, he would tell us if anything needed modifying. He was very fond of having the characters followed by the camera. But he preferred dolly shots to trolley shots—although the tram journey had all been filmed with a camera on a trolley. And whenever possible we used a camera suspended somewhere above the actors. . . .

I worked with a wide-focus lens of 35 to 55mm. for the scenes in the big café. All the sets had floors that sloped slightly upwards as they receded, and the ceilings had artificial perspectives: the bulbs hanging from them were bigger in the foreground than in the background. We even had dwarfs, men and women, on the terrace. Of course all this produced an amazing sense of depth.

———Rosher, interviewed for *Murnau* (Berkeley, 1973)

Roberto ROSSELLINI
Born in Rome, 1906. Father opened Rome's first modern cinema in 1919. Entered films as writer in 1938.

We began our film only 2 months after the liberation of Rome, despite the shortage of film stock. We shot it in the same settings in which the events we re-created had taken place. In order to pay for my film I sold my bed, then a chest of drawers and a mirrored wardrobe. . . . *Rome, Open City* [1945] was shot silent, not by choice but by necessity. Film stock cost 60 liras a meter on the black market, and it would have involved us in additional expense if we had recorded the sound. Also, the Allied authorities had only given us a permit to produce a documentary film. After the film was edited, the actors dubbed their own voices.

In order to choose my actors for *Paisa* [1947], I began by establishing myself with my cameraman in the middle of the district where such-and-such an episode of my film was to be shot. The rubberneckers then gathered around us and I chose my actors from among the crowd. . . . Amidei and I never finished our script before we arrived on location. We adapted ourselves to the existing circumstances and to the actors we selected. The dialogue and intonation were determined by our nonprofessional actors. . . . *Paisa* is a film without actors in the accepted sense of the term.
————Rossellini, quoted in Sadoul-Morris, *Dictionary of Films*, pp 317, 272

This film [*India 1958*] is very precious to my heart. I don't think it will be a success, but I shall never regret making it. . . .

I wanted to show the world the true India, the real people beyond the legend. So I went into the streets and the fields, and for each of my 4 unrelated episodes, I took one man out of a crowd. This is the way I like to work, without actors.

For days I would study my man, in a spirit of deep observation. I would see how he used his hands, how he turned his head; listened to the things he said, discovered the things that he did naturally. Then, when the time came, I told him what was happening in the picture—that could have been absolutely fatal!
————Rossellini, interviewed for *The Northern Chronicle*, 15 Mar 60

All the emotions come either from the screen or from you. What I try to do is to be very honest and so inside yourself you develop an emotion, there is nothing wrong with that. But I don't want to convey my emotions and I don't want to capture through emotions. It is a very subtle point, but very important. It would be easy to make people cry, I could have done it with the end of *Socrates* [1970]. To remain detached is very hard.

Q. Could you pinpoint how you achieve detachment?

A. For example the final sequence in *Socrates* is a distant shot of everybody together. If you use more of a microscope you can easily evoke emotions. The timing of the scene is all and it is chosen for clarity as I don't want to seduce.

. . . I have always done the editing, and I do it now too, it is nothing at all. I have a Moviola at home and in 2, 3 nights I cut the film. It is a very simple thing.

In *Open City* [1945] I made the scene in the end with the priest getting out from a little truck, walking and being tied to a chair. I did the whole shooting. At the time we had very little money so we could only buy the negative and had no money to process it. So I saw the shots only 3 months later. And when I was cutting the film there was very little material because from the beginning I have had a repulsion to do angles. I wanted to take risks, I like that. I felt that the whole scene was tremendously flat, something was missing. We were editing the film and missing the sound track and I was worrying about what to do. Just at the last moment I thought of giving the scene a certain kind of rhythm. It was very simple, we set up a microphone and with a finger I beat a chair, thump, thump, thump, and that little, nearly imperceptible noise completely changed the rhythm of the scene. So through that I have learned a lot and I know very well that the main thing is to find the right rhythm for what one is doing.

[Orizzonte 2000] is a company that we created to support us. We are a little group of people and we always work together. Mainly it is a family group; one of my former wives does all the costumes, my son, my sister, my nephew, my niece work with us. Other people do, too; it is not purely a tribe....

————Rossellini, interviewed for *Film Culture*, Spring 71

Q. Have you now become, then, more teacher than filmmaker?

A. Oh, I'm the same person that I always have been—filmmaking is simply a technique that I've acquired little by little. And the technique I use now, with the Pancinor camera that can zoom in here and pan out there, perfectly suits what I want the film to demonstrate. The dialogues could be filmed in other ways, but given the possibility of moving all the time with the zoom lens, I can add a lot of extra messages—reactions, backgrounds, feelings, distractions—to stir the audience to want to know more. It's an attempt to reproduce what happens in life, in conversation, when one's attention wanders around the subject, looks away, then returns from a different angle. I think that conventional filming of these sequences—long shot, close-up, close-up, close-up —would be intolerable. The challenge of filming them in an interesting way is something I find very exciting.

Q. Do these enormous speeches cause problems for your actors?

A. In general, with few exceptions, I give the scripts to the actors at the last minute, because I don't want them to prepare themselves mentally. Otherwise I may have to demolish what *they* think in order to get what *I* think is the correct sense of a scene. So they memorize what they can and they improvise the rest. I don't mind; I can profit from their improvisations. It's the way I've always worked, although in the case of *The Messiah* [1975] the texts had to be accurately taken from the Scriptures (mainly the Gospel of St. John). We shot the film in English, often with the actors not understanding a word they were saying, so I wound up with the same sense of spontaneity as usual....

————Rossellini, interviewed for *Sight & Sound*, Spring 76

Robert R O S S E N (1908–1966)
Born in New York City. Writing and producing plays led to employment at Warner Brothers in 1937 as scenarist. First film directed, Johnny O'Clock, *1947.*

Q. Concerning *Alexander the Great* [1956], was there any kind of conflict between what you wanted to do with this historical setting and what the studio demanded of you?

A. No, there wasn't any conflict. The only pressures—and I could have withstood them, I suppose, if I had been strong enough at the time—were pressures on cutting the film, on getting it down in size. You see *Alexander* originally was a 3-hour picture. I wanted it done with an intermission. They got very frightened at the length, and they finally wore me down. Actually, it's a much better picture in 3 hours than it is in 2 hours and 20 minutes, precisely for one reason. It unveils the various guilts Alexander felt toward his father much more deeply—for instance his chase of Darius. It is not just a simple chase to kill the Emperor of the Persian Empire. The chase for Darius is tied up with his tremendous feeling that as long as a father figure is alive in royalty, he has to kill him.

Q. *Body and Soul* [1947] and *The Hustler* [1962] came very much out of your background, didn't they?

A. Yes they did. I once wrote a play 30 years ago called *Corner Pocket*. It wasn't done; I didn't want it to be done, but everybody wanted to do it. It was a play about a poolroom. I spent a lot of my time from about 15 to 19 years old in a poolroom, so obviously I was attracted to it. But the aspect of poolrooms that I was attracted to was not in *The Hustler*. The aspect I was originally attracted to was my thought that pool halls, at a certain stage in the life of America, were a poor man's opium den. There was no place in the world where you could lie and be believed like in a poolroom; no place in the world where a guy who was running a laundry wagon you know, who was a shit, a nothing on the outside, suddenly walks in and shoots a good game of pool, and tells lies. He sits around and bullshits—it's a place to stay in, you know, till 3 or 4 or it's a place to go to at 11 in the morning. That was the basis of my play, but then I read this book and there were other things in it, which were also very valid, which I totally understood. The best kind of pictures you can get are films that are not at all intellectually constructed, but drawn out of your experience and senses.

I didn't know it but my star [in *Lilith*, 1964, Warren Beatty] almost killed me. I made a terrible mistake in casting.

A young guy who wants to do something good, who has all kinds of decent instincts, walks in there, totally well and as he gets into this world, he, too, begins to have doubts and he, too, on the basis of his own experience, begins to get entangled. But, you see, he never gave you the feeling of entanglement, because right from the beginning he belonged in that institution. He was psychotic from the start. . . .

You should have gotten the feeling that this American guy had gone through a war experience, come back with a new sense, didn't want to take that old crappy job they had around but was a guy who really meant what he said when he said "I want to do something." You never believed him for a moment. You see, it was wrong casting and there was nothing I could do. . . .
I liked the picture. I think what it had to say was an important comment to make for today's society, because I don't think it has even been touched yet—this whole question of inner life. I think there is only one man that I know of in films who really understands how to do it, and that's Bergman. . . .

I only had one set in the whole picture [*All the King's Men*, 1949]—the governor's mansion—that was the only set.

Q. But where was the judge's house?

A. An older house in Stockton, California. I shot the impeachment scene with Stockton lawyers and judges in the courtroom.

Q. And the crowd—all the scenes were natural?

A. Oh yeah, I even gave the cameramen phony cameras. I didn't even know what was going to happen.

. . . When it came to *Body and Soul,* I knew a lot about fighting. Jimmie Howe, who used to be the Dynamite Champion on the Pacific Coast, knew a lot of these guys, and he knew a lot about fighting so we decided that in the whole mishmash there would be absolutely no actors, and that's the way we shot it. For years Hollywood used to ask, "How do you get newsreel photography?" Well, we came up with an answer and it was so simple. You shoot it like a newsreel man. This was early stuff. Today it's taken for granted. You never use any lights, you don't have any filters. You have 6 Eyemo cameramen and you put "Newspaperman" on their hats, so they shoot right into each other's lenses. You get every conceivable angle you want—which you see in the newsreels and you get that wonderful grainy quality.

————Rossen, interviewed (Dec 65) for *Arts in Society,* Winter 66–67

Paul ROTHA [pseud.]
Born in London, 1907; studied at Slade School; entered films in 1928 with British International Art Dept.

The most disheartening thing is the number of marvelous shots one sees but cannot get. Whether you haven't got permission to film, or the sun is in the wrong place, or you haven't the time. When a plane stops at a place for only 10 minutes to refuel, there's no time to think of your script or your eventual editing. It's really newsreel work. The allocation of film stock is difficult. You shoot some cloud shots, say, between Galilee and Baghdad, and later see something much better but you have no film stock left. It is not possible to carry much stock with us because of its weight and the customs duty to pay from country to country. Imperial Airways in London could have done so much to help in advance.

Unlike Baghdad, Babylon was far from a disappointment. I had not expected it to be so large or in such a fine state of preservation. Wandered all over the ruins and got some good material of broken columns, animal bas-reliefs on the Ishtar Gate and the famous Lion. Had what could be a good idea when I saw some of the masonry crumble and fall of its own accord. In all shots thereafter I had our guide kick dust and stones down, he himself being out of picture of course. Perhaps in this way I can get the effect of the past crumbling before the future. The present being, of course, the airplane.

————Rotha, in *Documentary Diary* (London 1973)

Jean ROUCH
Born in Paris, 1917. An ethnographer who began using film in Nigeria and Senegal in 1947. In 1952 helped to establish an International Ethnographic Film Committee.

Africa: The films I realized in Africa were, as always, private productions. I use my own equipment, 25 to 30 spools of Ektachrome. When a subject appears, I shoot:

1st case: Of no interest; too bad, I lost the money the film cost.

2nd case: Of ethnological interest. The Ethnographic Film Committee produces the film in 16mm, thanks to a subvention obtained for each film.

3rd case: This film might appeal to a larger audience. I project it for producers who are friends of mine and I produce it together with them (blown up to 35mm). I like this system of chain production very much. I am the only one to take risks (most of the time I shoot on my own, together with an African sound assistant, Moussa). In other terms, I make a film only if I feel like it. Later on, the risks are shared by others (state or producer), but only for one film at a time and which is already shot.

———Rouch, *Cahiers du cinéma,* Jan 65

A lot of my films are suggestive. For example, the film I made about lion hunting [*La Chasse au lion a l'arc* (1958–65)] is much less the lion hunt as it actually exists than myself faced by this phenomenon. That's the reason that the commentary is very important. I've wanted to, but haven't finished researching this—how to make films without a commentary, which is almost impossible, precisely because of this subjective outlook.

You could say that a particular shot, let's say of the crowd in the streets of Paris, is significant in itself. But it's not true; it's dependent on the context, and therefore there is something to say. The solution is to do what I'm doing now, the fiction film, if you like. This is, invent a story which is also in great part improvised but which is meant to illustrate an aspect of something. Say to people, for example, "You're going to be such a character, a plausible character, and you're going to act as if you were that plausible character in a given situation," which is to my mind a psychodrama, if you like, and one of the ways to rediscover the truth. To do that I've made many films, fiction films in fact, on real subjects, and which are much more real than I myself would have been able to make. I did a film called *Jaguar* [1958–67] about migrant laborers who work in West Africa, in Ghana, and at the same time I did a sociological, ethnographic investigation. Well, the only objective document is the film, which is, however, a fiction film, acted by people playing plausible roles. Why? Because they show what an investigation would never show, that is, the context: how it happened, where it happened, the relationships between people, their gestures, their behaviour, their speech, etc.

———Rouch, interviewed for *Documentary Explorations* (NY, 1971)

Miklos R O Z S A
Born in Budapest, 1907. Studied in Leipzig and Paris.

... In *Double Indemnity* [1944] I introduced certain asperities of rhythm and harmony which wouldn't have caused anyone familiar with the "serious" musical scene to bat an eyelid, but which did cause consternation in certain musical quarters in Hollywood. The musical director of Paramount—a former café violinist—couldn't stand the score from the beginning, and told me so. Did I really have to have a G sharp in the second fiddles clashing with a G natural in the violas an octave below? In his opinion the place for such eccentricities was Carnegie Hall, not a movie studio. I thanked him for the compliment, and he assured me it wasn't meant as such and that the score would be thrown out lock, stock, and barrel after the sneak preview. In fact, everybody liked what I'd done and the score was used, but the story gives you some idea of how difficult it was to maintain any decent level of musical integrity in the Hollywood of those days. People with a "serious" musical upbringing such as myself, Hermann and Korngold were the exception rather than the rule.

If a song such as "Yes, We Have No Bananas" is used in a picture about the twenties, painstaking research ascertains the date of publication, but no one seems to care much if early Christians in the first century sing "Onward, Christian Soldiers" by Sir Arthur Sullivan, composed a mere nine hundred years later! Of course compromise is involved, since what is stylistically accurate isn't necessarily dramatically practicable, and I've made a point of taking each picture on its own terms. In *Plymouth Adventure* [1952], the story of the Pilgrim Fathers, I used as the main theme a melody from the one book with music the Pilgrim Fathers had on board when they sailed: Henry Ainsworth's Psalter. Elsewhere I imitated the manner of the 17th-century English lutenists. In this way I could get a convincing sense of period atmosphere and at the same time make the music do what dramatically it had to do. In *Quo Vadis* [1951] I used fragments from contemporary Greek and early Christian sources, but in *Julius Caesar* [1953], where the focal point is the Shakespearean drama, not the setting, I made no such attempt. I simply wrote interpretative incidental music in my own idiom, as for a modern stage production. I don't think I have the reputation of being difficult to work with, although I did have to put my foot down over *Ben Hur* [1959] when I was expected to use "O Come All Ye Faithful" for the Nativity scene, "because it was the first Christmas." They also wanted me to use my theremin for Christ, but I opted for something much less arty—soft organ chords and high strings—and I have a feeling it worked.
——Rozsa, interviewed for *Music & Musicians*, Dec 72

Q. What was your most difficult problem in scoring *Ben Hur?*
A. The music to depict the presence and influence of Christ. Although he is never fully seen, he is shown from behind, and I finally decided to employ an organ to convey his presence. In the scene of the Sermon on the Mount, naturally William Wyler could not use any actual speaking voice, so I took the St. James version of the Sermon, put it to music and then played the music alone to impart something of the spirit of the Sermon.
——Rozsa, interviewed for *Record & Show Mirror*, 14 Nov 59

Albert S. R U D D Y
Born Montreal, 1934.

Six months before filming started [on *The Godfather*, 1972] the Italian-American community held a rally in Madison Square Garden, with Sinatra singing, and raised $600,000 for the sole purpose of stopping *The Godfather*. Then when we actually got down to shooting there was a lot of political pressure on me and on Paramount not to continue with it. I had letters from Senators—

one of them a presidential candidate, would you believe?—imploring me not to go ahead because the film would defame Italian-Americans. . . .

We didn't draw up a contract, we just made an agreement [with Colombo, that the words Mafia and Cosa Nostra be dropped from the script]. And believe me, I kept my word. But so did Colombo and, all of a sudden, the opposition to the film stopped and all the things we wanted came to us. . . . On account of my deal I almost got fired twice and, at one time or another, I had the Senate rackets committee, the FBI and the New York Police Department on my back.

——Ruddy, interviewed for *The Times*, 19 Aug 72

Ken RUSSELL

Born Southampton, 1927. Dancer, actor, photographer, director of advertising films before establishing his reputation with 33 BBC-TV films on composers.

Glenda Jackson I'd never heard of. When she walked into the room I found myself watching her varicose veins more than her face and only later when I saw her in the movie of *Marat/Sade* [1966] did I realize what a magnificent screen personality she was. I couldn't quite understand it. Sometimes she looked plain ugly, sometimes just plain and then sometimes the most beautiful creature one had ever seen. For the role of Charlotte Corday she'd worn a long dress and the veins were not in evidence, but our film was set in the Twenties with plenty of ankle and a good deal more. Glenda is not one to let a few veins stand between her and stardom so out they came.

We started shooting [*Women in Love*, 1969] on September 25th and, because it was rather later than we wanted, shot most of the exteriors first. I was very glad we did. In most of my films I try to do the physically difficult bits first, because it breaks down any preconceived notion the actors may have about his or her solipsist self-importance. On *Song of Summer* [1968], for instance, I thought: it's all very well to have them sitting comfortably in the paralyzed old man's sickroom *talking* about taking him up the mountain to see his last sunset before blindness overtakes him, but I'm going to make them carry Delius up that mountain in the very first sequence we do. And we did, for shot after shot all day long in the freezing cold, to telling effect. One of the first scenes we did with Glenda in *Women in Love* was the island sequence with Gerald and the cattle. The operator did his version of the shot of Gudrun falling at Gerald's feet, which was hand-held, and though I thought what he was doing might be marvelous I said "Do you mind if I try?" (One doesn't just snatch away the camera and do it willy-nilly.) In the end we used my version in the film, mostly because I turned the camera sideways, which he wouldn't have done, being of the old school, and you can see all of her. The fact that the light was fading, that she knew I was operating the camera and probably doing it badly, and that she didn't get on with Oliver [Reed] anyway and hated the cows and was cold—these took the starry quality out of her and made her real. If they're cold and walking through slush and mud, it humiliates them a little and shows them they're at the mercy of the elements, and of me.

——Russell, interviewed by John Baxter for *An Appalling Talent*
(London, 1973)

It [*The Devils,* 1971] was pretty gory, but they knew what they were getting into. I never force my actors to do anything they don't want to do, but English extras are the lowest form of animal, the dregs of the underworld, and they manhandled two of the girls a bit harshly and the whole orgy scene got out of hand. Some of the electricians were running off the set from nausea. Then Actors Equity got into it and there was a fracas in the papers. But actors love me.

They forced me to make 23 cuts in America and the ones who made the biggest fuss were atheists—movie moguls who give some of the wildest orgies in Hollywood. Hypocrites! Some of my best scenes had to be cut. It was glorious stuff.

The church has always been appalling. I'm an ordinary run-of-the-mill sinner who only pays lip service to the church, but I was trying to tell the truth about how it uses totally illiterate people to seduce everyone through terror.

——Russell, interviewed for *The Toronto Star,* 4 Dec 71

You get a nod when you come in and then you're ignored while you wait your turn. Eventually Harry [Saltzman] said to me: "I liked your Debussy film very much. I'm setting up a consortium of young directors." (I was young then—comparatively.) "People like Tony Richardson, Karel Reisz, half a dozen others. You'll make 3 films each and the profits will be divided equally among all the members, and so will the losses. But you'll be able to make the films you want. What films do you wanna make?"

I said, "Well, I'd like to do a film on Nijinsky and then on Tchaikovsky...." "You can't do Tchaikovsky," he snapped. "Dimitri Tiomkin's gonna do that *and he's already writing the music*"—which is almost my favorite Saltzman story. But he said, "The Nijinsky idea sounds good, though no film on a dancer ever made money." Then he started thinking about it. "Yeah, fantastic. We'll call it *The Dancer.* We'll shoot it in Paris."

"Why don't you try this Harry Palmer film with Michael Caine?"

"Well, I'd rather do the Nijinsky."

"Yeah, but that will take time to set up. We've already got the rights to *Billion Dollar Brain* and it's hot. But you can get your writer to work on the script of the Nijinsky film while you're doing it." I thought: maybe he's right. Melvyn Bragg began the Nijinsky script, and John McGrath and I started to think about *Billion Dollar Brain.*

——Russell, interviewed for John Baxter's *An Appalling Talent*
(London, 1973)

We were thinking of a parallel to the Fascist force invading Russia, and thought of the logical way it would have to go—across the ice. Then I realized that the American "invaders" of *Brain* are the German knights of Eisenstein's film, and the whole thing fell into place.... Filming in Finland was pretty rough. We had a petrol motor attached to the camera all the time, running a generator to keep the temperature even. And you try loading and unloading a camera in thick woolen mittens....

The end sequence, on the ice, we filmed on the Gulf of Finland, and in places the ice was so soft we were in slush up to the axles—the water half a mile deep beneath us, and ships passing less than 50 yards away.

——Russell, interviewed for *The Guardian*, 26 Oct 67

Rosalind R U S S E L L   (1911–1976)
Born in Waterbury, Connecticut. First film in 1934.

Q. About this time you got into your career-women era.

A. Yes. Those parts went on and on! I played 23 different career women. If you need an operation, I am capable, you know! I have played a doctor, a psychologist, a newspaperwoman, a nurse, a head of an advertising firm, an actress, a professional pilot, a lady judge, and so on. . . .

Q. Most of your career-women pictures were made at Columbia, right?

A. Right. I had the same office set in I don't know how many pictures! Ten or fifteen! The same cameraman, Joe Walker, and the same propman named Blackie. The opening shot was always an air shot over New York. Then it would bleed into my suite of offices on the fortieth floor of Radio City. I would have the same desk and the same side chairs and bookcase. Out the window behind me was always a view of the Empire State Building, in order to identify the setting. I used to say to Joe Walker, "Joe, where was the Empire State Building in the last picture?" which had only been a couple of months before. He would say, "I had it a little to the left." I'd say, "Well, this time throw it over on the right."

Another Englishman I liked working with was Ronald Colman. *Under Two Flags* [1936], that was Ronnie. He was charming, but he never would kiss you on the mouth. He always got over on the corner of your mouth because of the better camera angle. He knew the camera better than any actor I have known. He also played a little bit to your ear, never looking you in the eyes, so that his face would be more turned toward the camera. That was always a little disconcerting. After I couldn't find his eyes, those beautiful orbs of his, I asked, "What is he doing?" And I learned something. It was only my third or fourth film.

Q. Do you think he was just being aware of how he should be photographed, or was that his way of trying to steal the scene?

A. No, that was the way he worked with everyone. He couldn't have been more polite. He was the essence of good manners.

Q. But I suppose you have had experiences when somebody tried to steal the scene.

A. Oh, that's useless with me, kid! No, no. Those people are easy to put down. Anybody starts to upstage you, you simply turn your back to the camera, then the director has to come around to take a close-up of you. It's a technical thing. The director *must* do it.

——Russell, interviewed for *Hollywood Speaks!* (NY, 1974)

Walter R U T T M A N N   (1887–1941)
Born in Frankfurt, Germany. Served as lieutenant on the Eastern Front, 1914–1918. Painting led him to abstract films, which in turn led to Berlin, Symphony

of a Big City (*1926*) *and to experiments in editing and sound. Died on the Eastern Front in World War II.*

Since I began in the cinema, I had the idea of making something out of life, of creating a symphonic film out of the millions of energies that comprise the life of a big city. The possibility of such a film arose the day I met Karl Freund, who had the same ideas. During several weeks, as early as 4 A.M., he and I had to photograph the dead city. It is strange that Berlin tried to escape my efforts to capture its life and rhythm with my lens. We were constantly tormented by the hunter's fever, but the most difficult parts were those of the sleeping city. It is easier to work with moving things than to give the impression of absolute repose and the calm of death. For the night scenes, the chief cameraman, Reimar Kuntze, developed a hypersensitive film stock so that we could avoid using artificial light.

——Ruttmann, quoted in Sadoul-Morris, *Dictionary of Films*
(Berkeley 1972) p 31

Chishu RYU

As to Mr. Ozu's way of direction, he had made up the complete picture in his head before he went on the set, so that all we actors had to do was to follow his directions, from the way we lifted and dropped our arms to the way we blinked our eyes. That is, we hadn't to worry about our acting at all. In a sense, we felt quite at home when we were playing in his pictures. Even if I did not know what I was doing and how those shots would be connected in the end, and when I looked at the first screening I was often surprised to find my performance far better than I had expected. He paid this minute attention not only to the actors' performances but also to stage settings and properties, and sometimes even painted appropriate pictures on the sliding doors used for the set. Therefore, what was called Mr. Ozu's production was, I think, the film produced by himself.

Kenji Mizoguchi's way was quite the opposite of Mr. Ozu's. He just gave hints to the actors, who had to make every effort to obtain the best effect, whereas Mr. Ozu worked over his ideas in advance from the beginning to the end and fixed each actor into each shot.

Mr. Ozu looked happiest when he was engaged in writing scenario with Mr. Kogo Noda, at the latter's cottage on the tableland of Nagano Prefecture. By the time he finished writing a script, after about 4 months' effort, he had already made up every image in every shot, so that he never changed the scenario after we went on the set. The words were so polished up that he would not allow us even a single mistake.

He told me that he was happiest when a scenario was completed. He also told me in jest that he had often been disappointed to find those images broken as he cast the parts and went on the set. He was always ready to go location-hunting and walked the narrow lanes and back streets all day long in search of the places which would best fit his images. He was such a good walker and had such enthusiasm that the cameraman, who accompanied him, used to be tired out first.

And once a film was completed, even if the actors' performances were poor, Mr. Ozu never complained of it. Even when we were sure that he must have had complaints in his mind, he took all the responsibilities on himself and never spoke of them to others. This, alone, gives one some idea of his character.

————Ryu, in *Sight & Sound*, Spring 64

S

Leontine S A G A N   [Schlesinger]   (1899–1974)
Born in Austria. Worked in the theaters of Germany, England and South Africa.

Every film director, I imagine, would prefer to work with trained actors. It is the ideal. But they ought to be trained, and not routine actors. If an actor has no knowledge of the art of acting, he has such difficulties that he cannot express himself freely. . . .

I am a great believer in rhythmic and dynamic effects, as I had an opportunity of showing in *Maedchen in Uniform* [1931]. But there I had the advantage of [a] preceding stage production, and knew already where the effects lay. If I could do *Men of Tomorrow* [1932] again, I suppose I should do it quite differently.

——Sagan, interviewed for *Cinema Quarterly*, Spring 33

Dominique S A N D A   [Varaigne]
Born 1948.

I like Robert Bresson's films a lot. All the same on the set of *Une femme douce* [1969] I had a fight on my hands, trying not to be just an object in his hands. I tried to give Dostoievsky's heroine a real full-fleshed existence of her own.

After working with Robert Bresson I moved straight on to Maximilian Schell's adaptation of Turgenev, *Premier amour* [1970]. Then there was Vittorio De Sica's *Le Jardin de Finzi-Contini* [1971] and Bertolucci's *Le Conformiste* [1970]. There was such a warm atmosphere of friendship on the set that I felt able to give of my best. Bernardo Bertolucci tries to understand you and to help. You don't have the unpleasant feeling of being an object and nothing more. You discuss things between you and try to work out the best way of approaching the part. I like surprises and Bernardo was full of them.

——Sanda, interviewed for *Unifrance*, July 71

Maria [Margarete] S C H E L L
Born in Vienna, 1926.

For the first 2 or 3 days, in making a movie, my body still hasn't experienced all the thoughts, feelings, and images, and I am slow and awkward, but then it begins to happen, and I can make the image live. Movies are a wonderful medium. Through a close-up, you can say something with your own heart that is the equivalent of the monologue on the stage. However, in films the image is very fragile; it can be easily disturbed if you don't work toward giving it form. The way I have found to strengthen the image for a movie is to write on the script what the author did not write about the character. In films, I cannot rely on my intuitive feelings of the moment, which may mislead me. I can't talk to myself. I can't rehearse with myself. So I write out my thoughts until the image becomes more and more clear.

——Schell, interviewed for *The Player* (NY, 1962)

John SCHLESINGER
Born in London, 1926. Apprenticeship in short films before directing A Kind of Loving (*1961*).

One of the most vital things in making the film, *Billy Liar* [1963], was to keep the fantasies arising spontaneously from the real moments, and this demanded a high degree of collaboration between Tom Courtenay and myself. He is a natural actor, who likes to work instinctively. Often his early and unrehearsed takes are the ones we use in the final film. (There were, on the other hand, certain scenes which needed very careful rehearsal, and we only got what we finally wanted after several takes.) The shooting of one of my favorite moments in the film comes to mind—when Billy practices giving in his notice to the empty chair of his boss. He starts by saying, "Mr. Shadrack, I feel it is necessary for me to give in my notice, because I have been offered a job in London . . ." and then everything starts to build up in Billy's own mind . . . "it's very nice of you to offer me a partnership, thank you very much, but . . ." and this develops further into a play with words, and into the expression of a power complex, of frustration and hate against someone who is supposedly sitting in the chair across the desk from him. This was one of the most difficult scenes for Tom Courtenay to do, and it was necessary to do it in one continuous take. We rehearsed it many times, but it was eventually the first (and longest) take that we decided on. I do not in any case like too much pre-rehearsal on the set—there is something very inhibiting about the atmosphere created by all the technicians standing round watching. I prefer to rehearse in dressing rooms, or in odd corners away from the general activity.

——Schlesinger, interviewed for *Films & Filming*, May 63

I like to have a script pretty well set before shooting. . . . I think it's ridiculous to regard the script as the final, absolute blueprint. I believe that a film has to grow as you're making it, and you should be able to alter things accordingly. Of course, if one had a Pinter script which was very economically worded, then it would be extremely difficult and not very valid to take that and say, "Now, let's improvise round it." The thing you can do, in improvisation with actors, is to free them up so that they know more about each other and about the characters, and the way to act with each other, before you come eventually to the technical business of putting it all down on film, when of course by totally artificial means one achieves a sequence.

You can only really do it with actors who are free enough to work together in this way. It would probably be hopeless to expect a traditional older actor to be able to do that. In the case of *Midnight Cowboy* [1969], I happened to have two quite exceptional actors to work with, Jon Voight as Joe Buck and Dustin Hoffman as Rizzo, who knew each other and worked extremely well together. And therefore we used one week's advance rehearsal, rather than plotting everything accurately (which I think is a waste of time), just finding out how far beyond the scripted material the actors could go. In other words, I had them read the scenes, play them a bit, and then I'd say, "Look, we've left something out; what else would these characters be discussing?" When Joe and Rizzo had got to know one another and were holed up together in that condemned tenement, one wondered what they would talk about. And how would they talk? Maybe they would talk about their own sexuality. Had he ever had it? Did he ever change his underwear? Why was he so secretive about doing this or that in front of the other? We threw this growing familiarity between them into an improvisatory area. We had a tape recorder. The writer [Waldo Salt] of the screenplay was there. And by working with the two actors in this manner, we expanded both the film and their performances. We took the tape and examined what they had said, and considered what areas were missing from the script, and reshaped it accordingly. It was a very worthwhile method of working.

——Schlesinger, interviewed for *Films & Filming*, Nov 69

[*Midnight Cowboy*] wasn't an easy picture to make. It wasn't even particularly enjoyable to make. In fact, I was miserable. I don't like New York enormously and somehow one was always confronted by something worse on the street than one was putting into the film. There wasn't anything in the movie that I hadn't somehow seen in some way somewhere. People said, "Isn't it a bit much having a man lying on the sidewalk outside Tiffany's?" I said, "Why?"

. . . The woman who was on a strange "trip" with that mouse was something we actually saw in Los Angeles. Horrifying.

When we were working on the script, we'd motor thousands of miles in Texas having a look at it and getting ideas.

[*Sunday, Bloody Sunday*, 1971, was] the most difficult film I've ever made in that it's all understatement. I knew it had to be made with kid gloves but it's a bit of a strain wearing kid gloves for months on end. That's why on the set itself I tried to keep up an atmosphere of considerable levity.

But we weren't trying to make a film about the two aspects of sexuality. The film is about the different emotional stages that people go through and about the business of coping with life. Both the girl and the doctor are approaching middle age and both are concerned with external responsibilities— to their families and their work, and their affair with the boy. We've also started at a deliberately static time in the relationship instead of trying to explore its origins. Right from the start the idea was not to make a great dramatic film about the subject but to delicately expose the moments of pressure.

——Schlesinger, interviewed for *The Times*, 30 June 71

I hated a lot of things that went on in the unit [of *Midnight Cowboy*]. I felt it was full of graft. . . . There was a lack of real enthusiasm from certain quarters, which you don't find in a really good British unit. On [*Far From the*] *Madding Crowd* [1967] for 6 months we'd been working as a community, really, in Dorset, with people who were totally committed to what they were doing. But to find that camera operators and so forth wanted to be paid overtime to come and see rushes depressed me, and finally angered me considerably, because I didn't think their work was of a high enough standard to warrant that kind of high-handed attitude. I don't say that it's like that all through. For instance, I had a designer and a group of craftsmen working with him who were absolutely committed to the film and did do a really beautiful job. But in other areas I think we fell badly short and therefore it was for me a difficult and unhappy experience, except with the actors, who were very good to work with.

——Schlesinger, interviewed for *Screen,* Summer 70

When I first brought the property [*The Day of the Locust,* 1975] to Paramount there was not too much enthusiasm about it, but Waldo [Salt] and Jerry [Hellman] and I went on pretending that it was all going to happen and Waldo and I continued improving the script. Bit by bit the script for *Locust* got better and better, and the studio got more interested. The first real indication that we got that the production was going to go ahead was when the studio had our offices redecorated.

Shooting on location can be very expensive—trooping around with all that equipment and all of those people. I am leaning more and more toward doing as much in the studio as I possibly can, because there you can get total concentration. That is why we have built a Los Angeles street on the Paramount backlot for *Day of the Locust* . . . even though we are working in Los Angeles.

——Schlesinger, interviewed for *Film Comment,* May–June 75

Maria SCHNEIDER

Brando gave me his blah-blah once the first day [of *Last Tango in Paris,* 1973] and tried to be very paternalistic with me. But I kept him laughing, and it really wasn't any father-daughter relationship. Brando is a man who is still a child—a bit ambivalent. He senses he's getting old. He keeps an eye on his makeup. And he can be slow, too. He'd improvise and then go back to his dressing room to find his intensity again. But he is instinctive and so am I. Bernardo is not. So there was a good balance.

——Schneider, interviewed in *Newsweek,* 12 Feb 73

[I was] full of [Brando's] vibrations. That heavy, very slow movement. His ability to size up a scene in an instant and then do it perfectly naturally. In the movie, his character takes that girl and teaches her a lot of things, makes her stretch, makes her explode. That's what he did to me as an actress.

——Schneider, interviewed in *Time,* 22 Jan 73

Eugene SCHÜFFTAN
Born in Breslau, 1893. An international cameraman and inventor.

I did my composition [for *Mademoiselle Docteur*, 1937] not only with the actor and the movement and the set; for me the value for composition is the light. Because the light must be at the point where the action is, so that the spectator knows where the action is. One picture changes to the next terribly quickly, so you have to be precise . . . when you look at a Rembrandt picture, mostly the light is not directly centered on the action; only in the neighborhood of the action. The action sort of continues the light. That's what Pabst likes very much, and I always tried to do it for him. Immediately when we saw the first rushes he saw that what he had wanted had come out. Lighting is the main thing.

He works his scenes out very clearly, and perhaps you think he is too theoretical in the first moment, but then you find out in the studio that he is very intuitive. It is always like that with an artist; he has to prepare his work very carefully beforehand; then when he is on the spot he can be direct and quick.

——Schüfftan, in publicity for *Mlle. Docteur*

Budd S C H U L B E R G
Born in New York City, 1914, son of B. P. Schulberg, producer. Joined Paramount in 1931 as a publicist; began screenwriting in 1932.

During the 1952–53 period when I was preparing the screenplay [*On the Waterfront*] I was fully aware that the wholesale crimes of the waterfront were not to be explained merely by the prominence of certain gentlemen from Sing-Sing and Dannemora in positions of authority on the docks. The shipping companies and the stevedore management had accepted—in some cases encouraged—the thugs for years, and in many cases city politicians were nothing less than partners of the longshore union racketeers. It was this unhealthy axis, I knew, that made it so difficult to bring any real democratic reform to the graft-ridden docks. I even discussed with my film collaborators scenes that would dramatize this civic blight. Those scenes were not eliminated through any cowardice or fear of censorship, as some critics have suggested. No it was another tyrant, the 90-minute feature form, that lopped off their heads.

. . . In the novel I found my opportunity to put Terry Malloy in proper focus. It only required retelling his story from another point of view, and with a different end in mind. I mean this literally and figuratively. Terry's decision, even his fate, became subordinated to the anxious balance and the fate of the waterfront as a whole. This demanded an entirely different ending, as well as fuller development of characters who were secondary figures in the film. So Father Barry, the "waterfront priest," is brought to stage center, is allowed to share the action with Terry and to dominate the thinking of the book. As a curate in a poor parish he must take grave chances if he is to follow Christ. The film had no time for this sort of thing. The novel has not only time but the obligation to examine this with great care. This searching becomes, in fact, the stuff of the novel, and the violent action line of Terry Malloy is now seen for what it is, one of the many moral crises in the spiritual-social development of Father Barry.

——Schulberg, in *The Saturday Review*, 3 Sep 55

Paul SCOFIELD
Born in Kings Norton, Warwickshire, in 1922.

Perhaps you remember the scene [in *A Man For All Seasons,* 1966] that I had with Susannah York on the beach, which is the real crunch of the action of ideas, when the daughter comes to her father and seems to oppose him as an intellectual equal, using her wits that he had helped form, against him. Now, Susannah was marvelous, but she did that scene at first all supplicating and feminine; not as an equal, which was the way I knew that Robert Bolt had intended it. So I thought that she should be told this and all he said was, "I can't do that" and would not be involved. I had to suggest the idea to her myself and I think it worked out quite well.
——Scofield, interviewed for *The Guardian,* 4 Aug 71

It took me a long time to get Sir Thomas More in *A Man For All Seasons.* He is a very difficult man to show because he was a family man and he liked good living, but at the same time he was a lawyer and an aesthete and he had spiritual and intellectual lengths which I couldn't really understand.
So it was very difficult to do and get right. I had to use a special voice . . . an accent that was a bastard thing of my own. His dryness of mind I thought led him to use a dryness of speech, so I would flatten or elongate vowels in a certain way to get the effect I wanted.
——Scofield, interviewed for *The People,* 12 Feb 67

Martin SCORSESE
Born New York City, 1942. First film experience, directing and editing short films; taught editing for 3 years at New York University.

Q. What about the issue of directing autobiographical material? Did you consciously want to get away from doing things that were derived from your own life?
A. Yes, *blatantly* from my own life: you know *Mean Streets* [1973] is Scorsese when he was a kid. *Alice [Doesn't Live Here Anymore,* 1974] is from my own life, it's just not blatant. I guess you could say that anything you get involved with is from your own life—particularly if you work the way I do, or work the way an actress like Ellen [Burstyn] works, or an actor like Harvey Keitel.
Q. You seemed to use the hand-held camera a great deal . . .
A. The hand-held camera was used in *Alice* for two reasons. First, because we were shooting on location and sometimes the rooms were very small and I had a lot of action going on in them, so the camera *had* to be hand-held. It also meant that the whole scene had to be hand-held because I don't like intercutting tied-down shots with hand-held. The second reason was because I wanted to suggest a psychological uneasiness in the character or drop a hint of what was coming in order to make the audience feel subconsciously uneasy. For example, the sequence of Harvey breaking into the room really begins with Tommy sitting down at the table with his mother and saying, "You're going out again tonight." . . . Normally, that scene would have been done with

a simple master and a two-shot, a close-up and a close-up—and all done with a tied-down camera. Instead, we moved the camera all in one take and panned over everything hand-held . . . it was done to create a little tension.

———Scorsese, interviewed for *Filmmakers Newsletter*, Mar 75

It's true that some films will involve me more than others. It's also true that I might never have made *Taxi Driver* [1975] were it not for the success of *Alice*. The question of commercialism is a source of worry. Must one make a choice, must it be a matter of either setting your sights on winning an Academy Award and becoming a millionaire, or making only the movies you want to make and starving to death?

. . . [For the new film, *New York, New York*] I wanted to make a big, commercial Hollywood movie, and still get my theme across. We'll start off with aerial shots of New York, the way they did in all those movies in the 40s, but everything else will be shot in the studio. Even the cars won't be real cars. But the people will be real, the couple will be real. . . .

[*Taxi Driver*] deals with sexual repression, so there's a lot of talk but no sex, no lovemaking, no nudity. If the audience saw nudity, it would work like a release valve, and the tension that's been building up would be dissolved. The valve in *Taxi Driver* is not released until Travis finally lets loose and starts shooting.

———Scorsese, interviewed for *The New York Times Magazine*, 8 Feb 76

George C. SCOTT
Born in Wise, Virginia, 1927; from 17 to 21 served in Marine Corps; attended University of Missouri.

I've always been rather a cold actor, I think, certainly in films, so what I am trying to say crudely is that I've never had any compunction about examining and analyzing myself in films. Some actors suffer terribly at seeing themselves. Some actors cannot look at rushes and so forth. I've never been that way, either happily or unhappily. The problem seems to be that my mind is so active and buzzing with so many details that I find that I have a tendency to let the acting sort of go by itself and hope for the best.

I did rewrite the script [*The Savage Is Loose*, 1974] a great deal, I have to confess. Our friends who wrote it, Max Ehrlich and Frank Felitta, had written a very, very fine script—unique, I thought—and yet I had to make a number of changes that I really didn't want to make but I found them necessary. There was no one else to make them and the responsibility is mine for doing that.

The writers had a tendency to duplicate—I'm speaking technically now— so that where we had one scene, we always had two of the same or essentially the same thing. Conflicts were avoided even more than they are in the film. In point of fact, what I did was telescope what was in the textual material. I eliminated very carefully any kind of gratuitous violence that was in the script. There was a huge scene, a fight scene, between the father and the son in a stream; I took it out entirely because I thought that it stole from the ending, bled from the ending. Foremostly and furthermore, I didn't want to see them in a Rod Cameron–Forrest Tucker knock-down-drag-out-bullshit encounter too soon, you see, which was going to go nowhere, because I wanted the encounter to be final, not melodramatic.

I turned in the director's cut of [Rage, 1972] to Warner Brothers. The film was produced by a team that is now defunct; Fromkess and Getty were the producers of the film. At that time, there were two factions at Warner Brothers—one was the Zanuck-Brown faction, the other was the Ashley-Calley faction. There was a great deal of internecine warfare going on administratively and every other way as far as I know. I turned the picture in. Fromkess and Getty couldn't agree about it; it was a dead certain cinch that the Calley-Ashley faction, as opposed to the Zanuck-Brown faction, was not going to agree about it. I got word that they wanted to cut the picture further and I said, "No." They said, "Yes, we're going to." I said, "Bye!" I left the lot and I've never been back and I've never seen the picture since that moment.

Well, working with Mike [Nichols] is a magnificent experience, because he's a magnificent human being and a very bright man, an extremely generous human being. We had some script problems. Trish [Van Devere] and I sat down with Mike here in Hollywood before we ever wafted to the Bahamas. We asked that the script be changed; Mike said it couldn't be changed. . . .

Q. He liked the script?

A. He never admitted to liking it. . . . I'm not saying he said that. He said, "Really, this is what we've got and this is what we've got to go ahead with. Are you on or off?" We said, "We're on." So we had problems in reconciling that. I felt that—and Trish felt the same way, I'm sure—that had we stuck with the magnificence of these creatures and the incredible desire to communicate and to build the characters between the animals and the people, we might have had an interesting movie. When we started blowing up the president's yacht and that kind of bullshit, I was bored to tears and so was she. But we were into it and there was nothing—you know, you don't tell the director what to do with his movie. What you do is show up on time, maybe, and sober and you do the job. As far as working for Mike goes, he does one thing as a director that no other director I've ever worked with does. He creates the most magnificent atmosphere in which actors can function and get along and really create. It's a wonderful, wonderful quality and one that all directors should emulate. Few do to his degree.

[John Huston] has extensive rehearsals; not too long but enough. He has a very efficient mind. When you watch him talk to an operator or a cameraman, you see that he is picking every shot along with his floridity. He's picking it all the time. The lighting people are going ape, you know, and the cameraman is saying, "John, we can't do that." And he's saying "Oh, it's all right; it's all right, kid. We'll find a way, kid." That's the way he talks to everyone. Somehow he manages to do that and the essentials are there but, of course, he's been at it for quite some time; a very gifted man.

I did a great deal of research because it was a real person. Patton [1969] was the only biographical piece that I had done and I felt that it deserved a great deal of authentic attention so I read about 13 books on him and had about 3,000 feet of documentary film that I ran at my house every night for a couple of months. I really got into it.

—Scott, interviewed for *Dialogue on Film*, Jan 75

Peter SELLERS

Born 1925 in a theatrical family. After his army service found work in the music halls and on the radio—"The Goon Show," where his talents for impersonation and satire were prepared for a sudden and successful film career in 1958.

Clouseau [in *The Pink Panther*, 1963] is really a lot more than he appears to be; a guy who falls over things. He's really a very tragic character. It is in fact that he has an impediment. I always use that word "impediment" because his proneness to accidents is a form of impediment you know, like he can't do anything without his going wrong. Well, that is what he obviously is on the set. Things happen to him. Other people are like this in life, but with Clouseau it's, you see, he knows but he doesn't want anyone else to know it— he knows he can't help this sort of thing and he tries to hide it by being one up all the time, being very suspicious or trying to be officious another way to hide it. . . .

Q. What about that scene at the billiard table with George Sanders where you play with all these cues that are the wrong shape? Was all this written or did you work that out with the director?

A. Well, as with all Blake's [Edwards] things, they are partly written and the rest we sort of improvised, you know. That was mainly written.

—Sellers, interviewed at the National Film Theatre, 19 Oct 72

David O. SELZNICK (1902–1965)

Born in Pittsburgh, son of the producer, Lewis Selznick. All the following documents are drawn from the remarkable reconstruction, Memo From: David O. Selznick.

To: Mr. B. P. Schulberg   October 8, 1930
I have just finished reading the Eisenstein adaptation of *An American Tragedy*. It was for me a memorable experience; the most moving script I have read. It was so effective, that it was positively torturing. . . . As entertainment, I don't think it has one chance in a hundred.

. . . Is it too late to try to [dissuade] the enthusiasts of the picture from making it? . . . I think it an inexcusable gamble on the part of this department to put into a subject as depressing as is this one, anything like the cost that an Eisenstein production must necessarily entail.

If we want to make *An American Tragedy* as a glorious experiment and purely for the advancement of the art (which I certainly do not think is the business of this organization), then let's do it with a [John] Cromwell directing, and chop $300,000 or $400,000 dollars off the loss. If the cry of "courage!" be raised against this protest, I should like to suggest that we have the courage not to make the picture . . . with a million or more of the stockholders' cash.

Let's try new things, by all means. But . . . let's not put more money than we have into any one picture . . . that will appeal to our vanity through the critical acclaim . . . but that cannot possibly offer anything but a most miserable two hours to millions of happy-minded young Americans.

To: Mr. [Louis B.] Mayer   September 6, 1933
I have arranged with Ben Hecht to do the final script of *Viva Villa!* [1934, at first directed by Hawks but completed and signed by Jack Conway]. My arrangements with Mr. Hecht . . . are as follows:

He is to receive $10,000 for the job, plus a $5,000 bonus if it is completed to my entire satisfaction within 15 days.

I expressly included the time element because this is, at the moment, as important to us as the quality of the work, since we plan on having Howard Hawks leave for Mexico in 2 weeks, and I want to be sure the company is on the ground and working on [Wallace] Beery's return from Europe. On the quality we are protected not merely by Hecht's ability but by the clause that the work must be to my satisfaction. It may seem like a short space of time for a man to do a complete new script, but Hecht is famous for his speed, and did the entire job on *Scarface* [1932] in 11 days. I do not think we should take into consideration the fact that we are paying him a seemingly large sum of money for 2 weeks' work, because this would merely be penalizing him for doing in 2 weeks what it would take a lesser man to do, with infinitely poorer results, in 6 or 8 weeks.

To: Mr. Richard Boleslawski [Director of *The Garden of Allah*] April 14, 1936
Incidentally and confidentially, [Charles] Boyer told me this morning, before leaving, that [Marlene Dietrich] had kidded a couple of the lines to him and he had said—and very properly—that any line could be misread to make it sound comical; so apparently you can count on him in this, as well as every other, respect. . . .

When I had finished with Boyer . . . I asked Marlene to come over, and gave her a last-minute pep talk. I pointed out to her that our budget was fantastically high and put it more or less on a personal basis that it was up to her to keep it from going higher. I told her once more, frankly, about the tales around town about what she goes through between takes with her makeup, costumes, etc.—and as before, and curiously I believe in her sincerity—she told me this was all nonsense and that she *never* indulged in such carryings on and certainly would not on this picture.

TO: MESSRS. [John Hay] WHITNEY AND [John] WHARTON   June 29, 1937
I SPENT A LONG TIME WITH COOP [Merian C. Cooper] TODAY AND . . . FEEL VERY STRONGLY, AS I EXPRESSED TO COOP, THAT WE MUST SELECT THE STORY AND SELL IT TO JOHN FORD, INSTEAD OF HAVING FORD SELECT SOME UNCOMMERCIAL PET OF HIS THAT WE WOULD BE MAKING ONLY BECAUSE OF FORD'S ENTHUSIASM. I DO NOT THINK WE CAN MAKE ANY PICTURE BECAUSE OF ANY DIRECTOR'S ENTHUSIASM, AND IF THIS MEANS WE ARE TO LOSE FORD, I WILL SUPPLY COOP WITH AS FINE A DIRECTOR AS POSSIBLE. I SEE NO JUSTIFICATION FOR MAKING ANY STORY JUST BECAUSE IT IS LIKED BY A MAN WHO, I AM WILLING TO CONCEDE, IS ONE OF THE GREATEST DIRECTORS IN THE WORLD, BUT WHOSE RECORD COMMERCIALLY IS FAR FROM GOOD . . . I THEREFORE FEEL THAT WE

MUST DISMISS FORD AS A MAN WHO IS NO MORE SURE-FIRE THAN IS CUKOR. BOTH ARE GREAT DIRECTORS AND BOTH HAVE TO HAVE THEIR STORIES SELECTED FOR THEM, AND PRESUMABLY FORD NEEDS THE SAME GUIDANCE IN SCRIPT THAT CUKOR DOES. . . .

To: Mr. [Daniel T.] O'Shea   February 28, 1947
After seeing tonight's tests and the previous day's work [on Hitchcock's *The Paradine Case*], I am more than ever disturbed about the enormous waste and overshooting. . . .

    I think it would be most useful if for once we followed the efficient methods of the German studios, where there isn't an angle wasted, or even the methods of a competent craftsman like Milestone, who prepares for his staff and crew a complete blueprint of each day's shooting, showing exact angles to be made on each scene, and the exact portions of each scene to be used in these angles, and who has every part of a sequence or sequences that is necessary on each camera setup, instead of going back again and again to the same moving of the cameras with the enormous waste each time the camera is moved back to a position it has been in formerly, or something extremely close to it. . . .

Dear Bill [Paley]:   August 9, 1956
My people inform me that the deal is concluded with your company for our stock film, which should be of enormous value to CBS for many, many years to come and should add production values to both your live and your filmed shows that could not possibly be obtained in any other way. . . .

    When we first [1935] formed the old Selznick International company, I started assembling a Trick (Special-Effects and Optical) Department. Forgive me if I say that one of the many fields in which the Selznick International pictures were way ahead of the rest of the business was in their enormous use of matte shots, optical effects, etc. Whereas other producers use these only when necessary, I made it part of my business, in the creation of scripts, to look for and to conceive opportunities for furthering the spectacular values and improve the production design of our films through the use of this equipment and the services of talented special-effects creators.

    When *Gone With the Wind* [1939] came along, it became even more apparent to me that I could not even hope to put the picture on the screen properly without an even more extensive use of special effects than had ever before been attempted in the business; and, consistent with this, we made huge investments in this equipment. . . . There were substantially over 100 shots [using special effects] in *Gone With the Wind* which were so effective that to this day I would defy even the greatest experts in the picture business to spot more than half a dozen of them. . . .
                    ——*Memo From: David O. Selznick* (NY, 1972)

Ousmane S E M B È N E
Born in 1923 in southern Senegal.

I became aware of the fact that using the written word, I could reach only a limited number of people, especially in Africa where illiteracy is so deplorably widespread. I recognized that the film on the other hand was capable of reaching large masses of people. That is when I decided to submit applications to several embassies for a scholarship to pay for training in filmmaking. The first country to respond favorably was the Soviet Union. I spent a year at the Gorki Studio in Moscow, where I received a basically practical instruction under the direction of Mark Donskoi.

Our situation as black African cinéastes is extremely uncomfortable. African cinema cannot and must not remain dependent upon the "good will" of French sources . . . We are caught in a web of contradictions . . . Some trouble-makers reproach me for having shot [*Mandabi*, 1969] with French money . . . namely an advance against future profits granted by [French Minister of Cultural Affairs André] Malraux . . . I agree that that is indeed a contradiction. But I had no choice: between two contradictions, one must choose the lesser one. I had two options: take this money . . . and make my film, or refuse it and not make a film. . . . If an African country had proposed a budget to me, I would have accepted joyfully. That was not the case. I take money where I can find it. I am ready to ally myself with the devil if this devil gives me the money to shoot films.

———Sembène, interviewed for *L'Afrique littéraire et artistique;*
trans. by Robert Mortimer in *African Arts*, Spring 72

Mack S E N N E T T [Michael Sinnott] (1880–1960)
Born in an Irish family of Richmond, a small town in Ontario. Came to New York as a singer in musical comedies and drifted into work at the Biograph Studio in 1908, just at the time that D. W. Griffith was taking his first important steps there in the development of modern film technique. Sennett learned quickly, as scenarist and as comedy actor and director, and his first large responsibility, was as organizer, producer and leading director of a new comedy firm, Keystone, in 1912. Here he founded the traditions of the American slapstick comedy, and a large number of actors, actresses, directors and writers received their first training and experience in his methods. He transferred his activities to other studios, yet kept his individuality, even after the introduction of sound. In 1913, when Chaplin, then an English stage comedian, first came to work in films under him, Sennett described his method:

We have no scenario—we get an idea then follow the natural sequence of events until it leads up to a chase, which is the essence of our comedy.
———Sennett, quoted in Chaplin, *My Autobiography* (London 1964)

We heard our first picture before we saw it, although sound didn't arrive in motion pictures until 15 years later. A Shriners' parade, stepping to oom-pah and brass, was marching up Main Street. . . .
The parade was a whopper and it would take a long time to pass a given point. A given point in my mind was a free lunch or wherever I could set up the camera and shoot unpaid actors.
"We got us a spectacle, kids." I said. "Bauman and Kessel are always hollering about costs. Look at that crowd scene—all free!" . . .

"What's the story, boss?" Pathé [Lehrman] asked.

"Got no story. We'll make it up as we go along." I said. "Pathé, run over there to the department store and buy a baby doll. . . . Jim, you get the camera set up on the corner. Ford [Sterling], you put on a tall overcoat and make like an actor."

Mabel Normand could throw herself into any part instantly, even into a part that didn't exist. . . .

Mabel put on the comicalest act you ever clapped eyes on, pleading, stumbling, holding out her baby—and the reactions she got from those good and pious gentlemen in the parade were something you couldn't have caught on film after 6 days of D. W. Griffith rehearsals. Men were horrified, abashed, dismayed. One kind soul dropped out and tried to help Mabel.

"Move in, Ford," I told Sterling. Ford leaped in and started a screaming argument with the innocent Shriner, who didn't know he was being photographed to make a buck for Keystone.

The police moved in on Ford and Mabel. Ford fled, leaping, insulting the police, and they—God bless the police!—they chased him. I helped the cameraman and we got it all.

The Shriners were good, but the best scenes ~ nabbed were the running cops. . . . They were the original Keystone Cops.

Since I did produce the Keystone Comedies, it turns out that I have been credited with considerably more inventiveness than I actually possessed. For instance, historians of the drama put me down for the creation of what was once a distinguished facet of cineplastic art—pie-throwing. I'd be glad to claim this honor, if I could claim it honestly, since a pie in the face represents a fine, wish-fulfilling, universal idea, especially in the face of authority, as in cop or mother-in-law. Also, these sequences in which we started building from the tossing of one pie, quickly increasing the tempo and the quantity until we had dozens of pastries in flight across the screen simultaneously, were wholesome releases of nervous tension for the people and made them laugh. But honor for the pie is not mine. It belongs to Mabel Normand. . . . Worse luck for scholars, I don't remember the name of the picture in which the first custard was thrown. The date would have been sometime in 1913. . . . It became, in time, a learned routine like the pratfall, the double-take, the slow burn, and the frantic leap, all stock equipment of competent comedians.

Harry Langdon actually was as innocent as an infant. He had his routines, well learned in vaudeville and he could do them on demand, but he seldom had the mistiest notion of what his screen stories were about. Like Charlie Chaplin, you had to let him take his time and go through his motions. His twitters and hesitations built up a ridiculous but sympathetic little character. . . . Like Charlie, Harry was a slow starter. Even after we learned how to use him—I mean, saw what his essential character was for screen purposes—we had to give him 100 feet of film or so to play around in, do little bits of business, and introduce himself. The two were the same in their universal appeal.

——Sennett, in *King of Comedy* (with Cameron Shipp, NY 1954);
repr. in *Film Makers on Film Making* (1967)

Leon S H A M R O Y   (1901–1974)
Born in New York City; studied mechanical engineering at Columbia University before turning to cinematography.

Perhaps the major problem [in *Porgy & Bess*, 1959] was getting the illumination in various scenes just right so there would never be a sharp difference in the skin tones of the light-skinned Negroes compared with the dark. To keep contrasts here to a minimum, I used a great deal of yellow light in such scenes as the saucer funeral sequence and in other scenes where there were large numbers of players. This was a bit difficult because colored people do not reflect light as do white people. The problem was to equalize, as much as possible, the extremely dark with the extremely light when both appeared together in scenes. To accomplish this, I used a substantial volume of warm fill light on the players' faces.

This problem of contrasts was forever present in the scenes in which Dorothy Dandridge and Sidney Poitier played together. Miss Dandridge's skin tone is quite light, while Poitier's is quite dark. In no instance did I gauze the light on them. Instead, I used colored gels on the lights which gave a mellow quality to the lighting and this produced the desired equalization of skin tones.

————Shamroy, in *American Cinematographer*, Aug 59

Omar S H A R I F   [Michel Shahoub]
Born in Alexandria, Egypt, 1921. Attended Victoria College in Cairo where he was president of the Dramatic Society. Prior to Lawrence of Arabia *(1962) he was in 21 Egyptian and 2 French films.*

[Fred Zinnemann] does a scene, then he discusses it with you. He lets you bring out your own ideas which he later incorporates into his final instructions. When it's all over, you realize that he has really guided you into expressing his own ideas, but he has done it so subtly, and with such respect for his actors, that we think we have done it ourselves. He has a marvelous rapport.

————Sharif, interviewed for *The New York Herald-Tribune*, 9 Aug 64

Lawrence [of Arabia] was banned by the Arab League of all Arab countries. They didn't consider the Arabs were well represented in the film. Sam Spiegel rang me in Cairo and asked if I could do anything—so I arranged for President Nasser to see it.

He liked it, fortunately, and ordered the film to be released in Egypt without cuts. It broke all records there. Nasser had once before reversed an Arab League ruling [over *Judgment at Nuremberg*, 1961] so I knew he could do it if he chose. . . . No one else dared defy the ruling, so *Lawrence* was not shown in any other Arab State.

————Sharif, interviewed for *The Sunday Express*, 12 Feb 67

Esther S H U B   (1894–1959)
Born in the Ukraine. Before 1926 prepared 200 foreign films for Soviet distribution.

But to get a chance to put this idea [of editing archive footage] into practical actuality was not so easy. It was long before the Sovkino administration would consent to approve my application to make such a film on the tenth anniversary of the February Revolution, and it was not until August 1926 that I began work on my first independent large work—*Fall of the Romanov Dynasty*. . . .

This and my following 2 films filled 3 years with the joy of searching, finding, "opening" historical film-documents—but not in film-libraries or archives, for there were no such things then. In the damp cellars of Goskino, in "Kino Moskva," in the Museum of the Revolution lay boxes of negatives and random prints, and no one knew how they had got there.

———Shub, in *Sovietskoye Kino*, Nov–Dec 34

At the end of summer, 1926, I went to Leningrad. It was even tougher there. All the valuable negatives and positives of wartime and prerevolutionary news-reels were kept in a damp cellar on Sergeievsky Street. The cans were coated with rust. In many places the dampness had caused the emulsion to come away from the celluloid base. Many shots that appeared on the lists had disappeared altogether.

———Shub, in her memoirs, *In Close-Up* (Moscow 1959)

Vasili SHUKSHIN (1929–1974)
Born in an Altai mountain village. An immensely popular writer who worked in films as writer, director and actor. The following is quoted from a discussion of his last film, The Red Guelder Rose (1975):

As soon as I get down to work—to write a story or to shoot a film—I am faced by two problems: the depicting of a man's outer life (his words, deeds, gestures) and the depicting of his inner life (his secret thoughts, his pain, his hopes); both aspects are perfectly real and concrete; the difficulty lies in bringing them together, discovering the logic of their coexistence, and besides drawing a definite "conclusion." I don't give up, I struggle with the problem. I am more interested in the "story of the soul," and for the sake of revealing this I deliberately delete much from the external life of the individual. I have found critics calling me a writer concerned with "daily life." Good God! In some of my stories it is hard to tell whether they take place in summer or winter! I do not mean by this to assert that I am something quite different (I haven't the slightest idea what I am), but surely I am not a writer interested first and foremost in the daily round; it is only fair to set this straight. Not that I look on "daily life" as something vulgar and beneath me. Not at all. The truth is of value wherever it is to be found. But it is also to be found deep down within us, and there it is usually harder to get at.

Yegor Prokudin is undoubtedly a strong personality. I like strong personalities. In the film-story I wrote with satisfaction that in his worst moments he only ground his teeth and cursed himself for being unable to cry; crying might bring relief. When I began unrolling his life day by day, I realized that in the film-story I had been false, had grasped no more than the general idea, had not plumbed the whole truth of his nature. I do not suppose that I plumbed the whole truth in the film, but I do think I got rid of the cliché of "a strong personality." . . . It seems to me that the moment [Yegor] saw his mother he realized he would never enjoy that holiday of peace, never would be able to atone for the wrong he had done her, always be tortured by his conscience. Let me say something even more strange: I believe he sought his own death. I simply lacked the courage to state this outright, I allowed myself the loophole of incongruous chance, of the evil vengeance wreaked by his criminal associates. I foresaw the discontent such an ending would arouse and supplied circumstances justifying it. It needed no justification: according to the laws operating within this particular character, life had lost its meaning. In the future I must be more bold. An artist's intuition must not be ignored.

———Shukshin, from discussion published in *Soviet Literature*, Sept 75

The subject that Shukshin most wanted to film was Stepan Razin, the 17th-century rebel. Though his scenario was published, the film was not realized.

Work on the scenario, *I Came to Give You Freedom*, has gone on for 4 years. One thing is certain—the film will be made. In the people's legends of Razin he is a great warrior, endowed with remarkable strength, beauty and cunning. I see him as a man of middling physical attributes, an ordinary man. So the question arises: what brought him to the fore? His head, his wisdom and good sense. . . . In studying the materials on Razin, I learned that not only did he capture cities, but some cities surrendered to him. . . .

What was ever dear to me in Stepan Razin was the naturalness and simplicity with which he treated his fellow champions, and the manliness with which he bore himself in captivity and punishment. Three things one needs to know about a man: how he is born, how he marries, how he dies. . . .

———Shukshin, posthumously in *Sovietsky Ekran*, May 75

Don SIEGEL
Born in Chicago, 1912. Studied at Cambridge University (Jesus College) and at the Royal Academy of Dramatic Arts. In 1933 joined Warner Brothers as an assistant film librarian, then an assistant cutter and head of the insert department.

I worked 14 years for Jack Warner, a man whom I considered a monster. I actually shot more film for Warner Brothers than any of their highly touted directors but when I went to Jack Warner and said I wanted to be a director directing my own films, he said, "Look, I can get directors a dime a dozen. But who am I going to get to do the action sequences, the inserts and the montages?" So I said, "Fine, pay me what you pay the directors and I'll carry on doing that stuff for you." But he wouldn't listen. He wouldn't let me direct either.

———Siegel, interviewed for *The Times*, 15 Sep 73

. . . I was working with Sidney Greenstreet and Peter Lorre [in *The Verdict*, 1946], who were absolute opposites in their approach to their roles. If you so much as changed a comma, Sidney was upset, particularly if it was the last word in an exchange. He wanted to get his cues down to the word, and he studied his part very carefully. On the other hand, not only didn't Peter study, but he would come on the set as if he didn't even know what studio he was in.

[In every confrontation] I've had with a star, I've always realized that if it came to a choice of one of us going, the studio would always boot out the director. Once you start shooting, it costs a tremendous amount of money to replace a star because you have to reshoot everything you've done. If you fire the director you may suffer, but you don't have to reshoot. On the other hand, a director who walks away from a confrontation with a star is lost. If he is to retain his respect, the director must stand up for what he thinks is right. Actors know this, and respect a director who is willing to risk his job over an aesthetic point.

One problem [in *Madigan*, 1968] was that he [producer Frank Rosenberg] had us start work by shooting the last scene in the picture, the scene in which Inger Stevens screams at Fonda, calls him names, because her husband has been killed. I got along very well with Inger and we both realized it was going to be very hard to do this emotional scene on our first day of work. So, I said to her, "Inger, this shooting schedule was the idea of our distinguished producer. Make it work for you. In the scene, pretend you're talking to the producer, not Fonda." She did, and the scene was excellent. . . .

. . . You always have the feeling, in looking at my pictures, that there's a great deal more violence than there really is. The violence is imminent, latent. At some stage the violence is tremendous, so that you know it's going to explode, rather than to have every sequence with people getting senselessly beaten up. A good example is the scene [in *Dirty Harry*, 1971] where the black beats up the psychopathic killer. The way the beating was written every blow was seen, along with the result of every blow. We could have done it, but it would have meant a makeup job after each shot. . . . I shot it in such a way that you're unable to tell what damage is being inflicted. Yet I think the effect is terrific, even more so than if you were to see the most gratuitous kind of violence, violence for violence's sake.

———Siegel, interviewed for *Take One*, Mar–Apr 71

I ask Siegel how he and Wayne got along [on *The Shootist*, 1976].

I would say, from my standpoint, Wayne got along with me better than 95 percent of the other directors he's worked with since the great Mr. Ford. Duke happens to be extremely knowledgeable about the making of movies— he has many excellent ideas which he doesn't hesitate to tell you about. I do know that there was a great deal about my style of shooting that puzzled him, but to my surprise he was quite familiar with my films. He couldn't believe that I was actually the guy who had made all those tough, violent pictures. That really confused him. You know I'm only 4 or 5 years younger than him (most of the other directors he's worked with recently have been much younger) so that he respected me. And the fact that I have a following, a cult, also kind of impressed him.

———Siegel, interviewed for *Millimeter*, July–Aug 76

Simone SIGNORET [Kaminker]
Born in Wiesbaden, 1921; her father in the French army of occupation.

I knew [Luis Buñuel] before we made the picture [*La Mort en ce jardin*, 1958]. He likes to make pictures with friends. He doesn't care if you're not exactly the character. He wants to have fun making films. He cannot work with people he doesn't like, or with people he doesn't have fun with.

La Mort en ce jardin belongs to one of the Buñuel periods when he didn't care much. He didn't care for 5 years; but he certainly cared for *Viridiana* [1961] . . . and it shows. I remember he was laughing at me when I was conscientiously dirtying my face for my part in *La Mort en ce jardin*. "Look at her," he said. "It doesn't matter. Nobody takes any notice of continuity in pictures."

Henri-Georges Clouzot is quite the opposite. He is concerned with every detail, almost to an obsession. He cannot work in peace. He has to work in a constant ambience of crisis. He has to be furious, he has to be depressed and he has to be sad. And he expects all his artists and technicians to share his sorrows completely. It is very tiring. Besides that he is tyrannical. He does not ask you to do things, he demands that you do things. It is no use your trying to explain that you would prefer to do something another way. He tells you, "Do what I tell you and shut up."

I was not very happy when I was doing *Les Diaboliques* [1955] for him.

But in making *Les Diaboliques*, he was right to behave that way. He used to tell me all the time we were shooting, "I should never have let you read the final pages of script." I was at first very hurt, because I thought he regarded me as an idiot. He wanted me to play this criminal as though she was not a criminal, so that the twist at the end was very convincing. But as I knew she was the criminal, the whole time I was making the film I had a tendency of having a double-attitude which he was constantly fighting; and which in any other script would have been good (because when you do a scene at the beginning you cannot completely forget what you are at the end) but it was not good for this kind of story. It was a few months after finishing the picture that I realized how right he was. . . . Clouzot does not really respect actors. He claims that he could make anyone act. So different to Jacques Becker who loved actors in a similar way to Renoir, who delights in the whole mystique of acting. Becker could say to a horrible actor, "That was good" and have him start the scene again and again, perhaps 15 times, never getting what he wanted, but still complimenting and progressively leading the actor to the point that he wanted. Making *Casque d'or* [1952] it was so easy. Actors need to be given confidence, but they also need to feel that they are interesting the director. There is nothing worse for an actor than a director who doesn't appear to be interested in what you have been doing, or trying to do. And that goes for big parts, less big parts and particularly the small parts; Becker would take infinite pains with these "little" people.

——Signoret, in *Films & Filming*, June 62

When you start to dress the character, it starts to live. Dressing a character is already working on the character. Even before you've started filming, the moment you've said yes to a character, your life changes.

If tomorrow I were playing an ambassadress, I'd start to walk on the Faubourg St.-Honoré. I'd buy *Vogue*. I'd look at things differently. If I played a pediatrician I wouldn't study medicine but I would go to hospitals. With

Stanley Kramer for *Ship of Fools* [1965] we spent the day at Synanon seeing drug addicts. I didn't want to be ridiculous to my dope-addict friends.

The day you put on your clothes for the film, it's done. She is herself. You are her. And from then on, you mustn't think about it. In *La Veuve Couderc* [1971] I played a peasant woman in her late 40s. The film was set in 1934. The first day, when Alain Delon saw my clothes, I saw he was afraid. The producer, too. There was terror in their eyes.

Alain said, "You're going to look like that?" I knew he was thinking, what will people think of me, sleeping with that old bag? It took him a few hours, but it finally worked out and the result had a sort of quasi-maternal tenderness.

If I'd wanted to play it younger, it would just have been the story of an old tart after a young man.

—————Signoret, interviewed for *The Daily Mirror*, 24 Nov 73

My first real movie part was as a prostitute in *Les Démons de l'Aube*, made in 1945. I was married to a director, Yves Allégret, and was pregnant when I made the movie. When my baby, Catherine, was 21 days old, I was hired by Jacques Feyder to play with his wife, Françoise Rosay, in his movie *Macadam* [1946]. I will never be as happy as I was the night I was chosen for the part, when they called me and told me. Again I played a prostitute. Françoise Rosay is very handsome, very elegant, and very wonderful, and I was very much afraid of her. She took me aside and gave me some good advice: You can't act unless you know your lines upside-down. . . . Feyder taught me how to act with natural gestures and not fiddle with objects for no reason. He taught me how to be relaxed.

—————Signoret, interviewed for *The Player* (NY, 1962)

Robert SIODMAK

Born in Memphis, Tennessee in 1900, while his German parents were traveling in America. Childhood in Leipzig and Berlin; University of Marburg. Miscellaneous jobs in theater and films. Left Nazi Germany in 1933.

In 1943 I had been in Hollywood for 3 years, doing what work I could get. Then Universal sent me the script of *Son of Dracula*: it was terrible—it had been knocked together in a few days. I told my wife I just couldn't do it, but she said to me: "Look, they've been making these films for 20 years, they know just what to expect from a director and just how much they're going to pay him," (I'd been offered $150 a week for the 3 weeks shooting) "so if you're just that little bit better than their other directors . . . then they'll see right away and it'll lead to better things." So I took the job, and on the third day of shooting they offered me a contract, with options, for 7 years. I took it and our association was very happy: in fact, though my salary was supposed to rise gradually until I was earning $1,100 a week in the seventh year, if I lasted that long, in fact they tore up the contract and by the third year I was earning about $3,000 a week. As for *Son of Dracula*, we did a lot of rewriting and the result wasn't bad: it wasn't good, but some scenes had a certain quality. . . .

I think it's not widely know that the script [of *The Killers*, 1946] was in fact by [John] Huston. His name didn't appear on the credits because he was under contract to another studio at the time, but he wrote the script for us in his spare afternoons (with Tony Veiller cracking the whip occasionally). He was very pleased with the result and what we made of it. Hellinger was quite a reasonable producer, but with his journalistic training he always insisted on each scene ending with a punch line and every character being overestablished with a telling remark, which in my opinion took a lot of the reality out of the film. So I always cut out the punch lines when he wasn't looking: it drove him wild for a bit, but finally he got the idea. The robbery scene in one long crane shot was done in a single take: everything was very confused, with people not knowing where they ought to be, a car backed up wrong and left in the middle of the road, and so on, but curiously enough the result turned out to give just the right effect when we printed it.

———Siodmak, interviewed for *Sight & Sound*, Summer-Autumn 59

[Ava Gardner] had already been in three or four movies before *The Killers* but none of them were any good. Certainly she had not displayed any talent in them. But I think that *The Killers* was the first part where she was really noticed. There was one scene in the picture which I was very worried about. I thought she might not be able to do it. That's the scene toward the end when she gets hysterical. Every day on the set I would tell her, "If you don't do that scene right I shall *hit* you, I shall *kill* you." My intention was to frighten her. We shot this particular scene toward the end of the shooting. Every day for five weeks I would make her nervous about that scene. On the day we had to shoot the scene I looked at her like Frankenstein's monster and I said, "Ava, if you don't do this scene right, I shall *hit* you, I shall *kill* you." She was so frightened by then that she really did get hysterical and she did the scene perfectly on the very first take. But it took me 5 weeks to prepare her for that scene.

———Siodmak, interviewed for *Ava* (NY, 1974)

Douglas S I R K [Detlef Sierck]
Born in Germany of Danish parents in 1900, he returned to Germany to study first law, then philosophy. Leaving his university in 1922, he became involved in theater until 1934, when he directed his first short films at UFA. He became a director of features until his departure from Germany in 1937, and made 2 more films in France and Holland before coming to America in 1939.

When I came to America I found John Wayne being appreciated as the most wooden and incompetent leading man in pictures. No one ever had a worse press. He was taking one beating after another. In every picture, even if it might be by a great director like Ford or Hawks, he was panned by virtually every critic. I always thought he was a great movie actor.... And after only recently seeing him again in a picture I should like to call him an outstanding personage of undiminished power and simplicity—a simplicity not marred by any "acting" tricks.

Of course, there is always the danger of petrification, of sameness, of not reshaping your style. Because the only kind of style these actors have at their command is one of their personality. But don't forget that pertrification makes for greatness, sometimes. Petrification leads to being a statue of yourself.

Wayne is a great actor because he has become petrified. He has become a statue. You need an "auteur" theory on this, too. Because he has a very consistent handwriting, all his own. I enjoy seeing him: he has become a cipher, a sign in the cinema. Like Charlie Chaplin—he has become a cipher, too. You cannot talk about him changing, at least not basically.

[*A Time to Love and a Time to Die*, 1958] I think illustrates quite well a thing I maybe learned from Dreyer—slow cutting, holding a shot much longer than the average director does. I consider his late picture *Gertrud* [1964] a very great and subtle study. *Day of Wrath* [1942] I saw 3 or 4 times, and I thought it was fantastic. Before that, I was deeply impressed by *The Passion of Joan of Arc*. I learned from it the importance of certain hesitating cuts, which throw tremendous emphasis on a story. Dreyer has developed this slowness to an almost unbearable degree, but there is the whole Middle Ages in it —it's a slow, precise, and deadly way of thinking. It harbors a threat by being so slow. You can see it in some of my pictures.

——Interviewed for *Sirk on Sirk* (London, 1971)

Jerzy SKOLIMOWSKI
Born in Warsaw, 1938.

I always begin with a scene, a gesture, a word or a line from which all else follows. In this case [*Deep End*, 1970] it was an image of a girl screaming in an echoing, reverberating building which turned out to be an empty pool. I also had an idea for a scene in which a young boy, naïve and inexperienced would be in the hands of an older woman. She would be raping him through the words she used. For him it would be like a mad scene: for her it would be a ritual. I slowly created a story around these images writing the dialogue in Polish and then having it translated into English. Then 3 days before shooting, I sat down with the actors and we went through the script line by line discussing it and rewriting it. But I never ask the actors to learn the lines by heart: I fix the development of a scene and they improvise around this.

——Skolimowski, interviewed for *The Times*, 3 Apr 71

Douglas SLOCOMBE
Born in London, 1913, educated in Paris.

In my experience I have only met one instance of a director actually having a chance to approve the style of the lighting. That was on *Freud* [1962], where I did a month's tests before shooting. What John Huston wanted here was an overall style, and within that two separate styles, one for the dreams and one for the flashbacks, which would be so different that the audience always knew where they were. I used very sharp photography for the main part of the film, to give the clarity of steel etchings, and help the period feeling. For flashbacks I shot through a glass plate, treated to fuzz out all the details except those most clearly recalled by the patient. For the dream sequences I aimed for a very contrasty, grainy effect of extreme black and white, in which chalky faces and relevant details would stand out like luminous figures in tunnels of blackness.

——Slocombe, interviewed in *Sight & Sound,* Summer 65

We have little choice nowadays as to whether or not we photograph in color. Personally, I regret the almost total passing of black-and-white, though I admit that now the first frenzy has passed and techniques have improved, color can be used very dramatically. Restraint is the keyword. I was able to conjure up the cold, dank, gloomy atmosphere of a 12th-century castle for *The Lion in Winter* [1968] far more satisfactorily than I should have been able to do in black-and-white, even in the daytime. I carefully avoided any "pure" color here —it would have been an intrusion. I tried to let tints glow through palely. The secret is to photograph places and objects *less* colorfully than they would appear in real life.

——Slocombe, interviewed for *The Making of Feature Films* (London 1971)

But [directors] can only describe what they want in general terms, like moody, dark, airy. [For *The Lion in Winter*] Tony Harvey showed me a photograph of a nun in a cell. It had a cold atmosphere which he loved. That set me on course, so to speak.

The cameraman then can only produce his own effects—which people either like or don't like. The excitement of the job is that on the floor you're on your own in terms of the final visual effect. The director can't say anything until he sees the rushes next day. He doesn't know what film, what stock you're using, what it's being developed to.

For *Lion,* I think, one tried to give a tapestry feeling, and also very much a feeling of dreary, if you like, damp, dirty, unlit castle. One threw most of the sets into dark relief. For *Boom* [1968] one wanted this intense, almost mesmerizing sunshine, sunlit whites which daze the senses and accentuate a feeling of unreality. I originated a processing technique for [*The Servant,* 1964] which I had the laboratories carry out against their better judgment, and I changed certain lighting techniques on the floor. Altogether these changes increased the contrast on the film, and gave the shimmering highlights against those deep blacks.

——Slocombe, quoted in *The Times,* 16 Jan 69

Fred Y. SMITH

Q. Didn't Gaumont-British make trilingual films?

A. Yes. Each picture had an English, French, and German version. They used the same story, costumes, and sets and worked around the clock on 8-hour shifts with 3 different casts, directors, and crews! Sometimes my editing job took me to France or Germany. In Berlin in 1934 I met the head of the great film company UFA, Erich Pommer. He had been an editor and had designed and made up the first German cutting table. Pommer is the only producer I ever sat down with and made a suggestion for a cut who put the film on the table, executed the cut, and spliced the film himself. These specially

designed cutting tables from Germany and France have become quite sophisticated and are in popular use all over the world. I think, however, the Movieola is still the best editing machine being used.

——Smith, interviewed for *Hollywood Speaks!* (NY, 1974)

Lee S M I T H
One of Bitzer's assistants on Way Down East, *1920:*

Our first action was to establish an outpost far above the falls to watch the ice
for the breakup. There the cameramen were stationed with instructions to keep
their lenses trained on the river night and day. . . . We were 35 days on this
ice job and there were 4 to 14 cameras always on the job, which accounts for
the great variety of the ice scenes filmed and the perfection of the sequencs. . . .

Our first problem was to get the ice moving and Mr. Griffith hit upon the
idea of utilizing the mill race to the paper mill until the ice began to break up
in the river. It was in the mill race, therefore, that we got most of the rescue
scenes and the shots of Dick [Barthelmess] going to the rescue. The ice was
sawed up into large squares by professional icemen and the thickness of it
was dynamited to get open water to float the cakes carrying Miss Gish and
Dick. When the cakes were free we tied them together with wire cables so
that they would not float too far apart. The cameras were set up on the edge
of the ice as near the floating ice as possible as it was impracticable to use a
boat or a raft. . . .

——Smith, *American Cinematographer*, Vol. 2, No. 22

Michael S N O W
Born in Canada, 1929.

When I'm talking about my films it sometimes worries me that I give the impression that they're just a kind of documentation of a thesis. They're not.
They're experiences: real experiences, even if they are representational. The
structure is obviously important and one describes it because it's more easily
describable than other aspects; but the shape, with all the other elements, adds
up to something which can't be said verbally, and that's why the work is, why
it exists. There are a lot of quite complex things going on, some of which develop from setting the idea in motion. The idea is one thing, the result is another.

——Snow, interviewed for *Artscanada*, Feb–Mar 71

B. S O R E N S O N
One of the assistant cameramen on The Wedding March (*1926–28*).

Von has a sense of perspective that is so keen it creates amazement in our
minds. Every little thing, no matter how tiny, even to the number of candles
and their length, that were used in the cathedral. When a man's mind observes
minute detail such as that, larger things are like mountains to him. Everything

with him has to be right, not mediocre. It seems uncanny, when he has a dozen people working in one scene, that their every little movement would be observed.

As an actor, Mr. Von thinks himself of the worst. I can point out a dozen instances to prove this firm belief. On several separate occasions Stroheim was just getting ready to work when actors of noted ability and fame were shown on the set. They were asked to leave because of the embarrassment caused to Mr. Von by his attitude of self-condemnation and self-consciousness. His own way of expressing this is, "I am scared silly, my knees quiver and I shake all over the minute I step in front of a camera with the lights on, and I know I have to do something. I am like a kid—I forget everything—my mind becomes a perfect blank." At present he is working in scenes surrounded by capable people, and this disbelief in his ability is so pronounced that it is embarrassing to all of us. This concerns his acting only. He has a sneaking belief that his directing ability is on a par with anyone else's, and it is only through this weak belief in himself that he keeps on making pictures. . . .

One of his greatest assets is his adherence to realism. To get realism in his pictures I have heard him abuse everyone *often*. Some shots of himself have been postponed for days, because, as he expresses it, "I don't feel the thing, and unless I do, I know the audience won't grasp it." Many actors have come to him with marvelous opinions of themselves and their ability. All have had these opinions quickly changed because of their lack of realism, caused by too much acting. I have heard him plead for hours, "Please be yourself; don't act, just be natural, that's all I want. The instant you start acting, it shows. Now, try it again, please, and be your natural self." And unless they are natural, after many, many trials, he shouts, "Look out; don't get me sore again. If you can't be natural, say so; if not, we will get someone else. I am not running any school for actors. Try it again and do it as you would in real life." With his determination to have things right, he keeps rehearsing until they are. Coupled with this determination for realism is the good fault of being too analytical. Everything that is done is very carefully thought out. Many times we are asked what we would do if we were placed in the same place and under the same conditions. From Harry Carr I learned that during the writing of the script [*The Wedding March*, 1926–28] every scene had to have dozens of reasons before they would either be used or left out of the script. Every little detail was acted out, even to how a man should stand inside a room. All this, months before actual shooting began.

——Sorenson, in *Motion Picture Magazine,* July 1927;
repr. in *Spellbound in Darkness*

Marc S O R K I N
Associated with Pabst in the production of Die Freudlose Gasse *(1925), for which Pabst wanted an actress he had seen in* Gösta Berlings Saga, *1924:*

When the Trianon Company bought the picture, *Gösta Berling*, they gave Stiller money, and Stiller wanted to make a picture in Istanbul. So he went to Istanbul with Garbo, and while they were there, Trianon went bankrupt. Trianon's money was invested to build new [cinemas?] but they took the money to make movies. One day it was found out and the company broke up—and there was Stiller, in Istanbul with Garbo, and Hansen, the actor; with lamps, cameramen, and all the equipment. And they hadn't started to work. . . .

Q. So they sold the equipment in Istanbul?

A. Yes, they did. We knew they were in Istanbul, and we knew that Trianon was not well off, so Pabst went directly to Trianon in Berlin, and told them, "We know your people are in Istanbul, Garbo and Stiller and all; we want to use Garbo. Give us your contract with her." But they replied, "No, no, nobody can make a picture with her; it is only a rumor that you heard; we will make a big picture in Istanbul." And Pabst said, "That is impossible, I have heard the stories and I have their address"; and Trianon said, "You cannot get Garbo; look for another girl." It was a long story. In the meantime Stiller came back to Berlin.

——Sorkin, interviewed for *Cinemages*, 3, 1955

Wladyslaw S T A R E W I C Z (1892–1965)
Born in Poland. Continued his Russian film career in Paris.

The words, and very often the music, will be conventionalized. Let me explain. When, at the beginning of *The Tale of Renard* [1930], we see the frogs manifesting their joy at being present at the renewal of nature, we will hear the words "Lovely Spring! Lovely Spring!" spoken by a voice that somewhat resembles the croak of these animals. It will be the same for the musical accompaniment. When we see a dog which seems to growl, the spectator will hear a sort of roll of drums imitating the noise; the braying of Master Aliboron will be rendered by the notes of a cello; the surprise of Renard, by a saxophone, and so on. . . .

——Starewicz, interviewed in *Cinémonde;* trans. in
American Cinematographer, Feb 1930

Rod S T E I G E R
Born in Westhampton, New York, 1925.

I don't know what made that [the taxi scene in *On the Waterfront*, 1954] as good as it was. Maybe because it was made under peculiar circumstances. We were supposed to have back projection. It didn't happen. The director was forced to find a way to shoot in the cab. One of the stagehands said, "I was in a cab the other day—had a venetian blind." Kazan, who is no coward, said, "Get a goddamn venetian blind." So the scene became two close-ups, more or less. You never cut outside the cab because you couldn't. You had to keep going in.

——Steiger, interviewed for *The Times*, 31 Oct 70

I don't like Mr. Brando. I'll never forget, or forgive, what he did to me on [*On the Waterfront*]. We were doing that now-famous taxi scene. I did the take with him, when the camera was on him, but when it came for the camera to be on me—he went home! I had to speak my lines to an assistant director. It must have just burned him up that we came out even in that scene—despite what he did.

—Steiger, interviewed for *The Sunday Express*, 31 Oct 65

An actor must have patience. He must be able to turn things down. I remember how I used to say, "Boy, when I make it, by Christ, watch out! I'm going to do this, and I'm going to do that!" But first I made 9 films in a row. (I did do one smart thing: I refused to sign a long-term contract with a studio.) When I had finally done the 9 pictures, I figured, "That's it! Now I'll get the better scripts!" Did I know that we were going into a period when there would be no better scripts? . . .

I had to wait 2 years for a decent script. And while I was waiting I went into debt $14,000. . . .

A good director is like a good psychiatrist. He knows what conclusion he wants you to reach, but he lets you discover it for yourself. He acts as a guide rather than as a commander. . . . The good director functions like the father of a family. Now if a man is a good father, he knows that he can't get things out of his children by fear. He shouldn't spoil his children, but he should encourage them to make their own discoveries and then be able to tell them, "Oh, yes, that's right." The director must be able to lead the actor to a conclusion that proves to be correct in the actual performance of the scene. Then there is no argument. . . .

To get the same results, the director has to know how to work differently with different actors. If the actor works in images, as many actors do, then the director has to know how to evoke the right image to trigger the response he wants. . . .

. . . I remember a magazine review of *On the Waterfront* that called Brando's fight at the end of the picture a March to Calvary and analyzed the entire film in terms of how Kazan had been influenced by the life of Christ. Actually, this scene didn't appear in the original ending of the picture. It was to have concluded with a shot of the dead boy floating down the river. But the Hays office had called up and said, "Wait a minute. We have a rule: crime cannot triumph in films." Okay, they had a point. A lot of young people were going to see the picture. So in the middle of making the film, Kazan had to improvise a new ending. March to Calvary? We were just trying to get out of a hole. . . .

—Steiger, interviewed for *Movie People* (New York 1973)

Max S T E I N E R   (1888–1971)
Born and educated in Vienna.

I went to work for William Fox, who was one of the finest men the world has ever known. He was a truly wonderful person. I was the conductor at the Riverside Theater where we were showing a picture called *The Bondman*. I had an idea. Until about 1915 there was no special music written for motion pictures. We just used to take the albums publishers put out and would play "Hurry number 1, hurry number 3, love scene number 6." I said to myself,

"This is a lot of baloney. I'd like to do something new." I talked to Mr. Fox and told him I wanted to write music for the picture. . . .

And I went down and wrote the music for William Farnum's *The Bondman*. We put together another 110-man orchestra. The orchestra came from different theaters we owned, from Mr. Fox's circuit, Jack Loeb's, and others. We had a big opening at the 14th Street Playhouse, opposite the City Theater, which we owned, too. I was the boss and now I had 110 men, but what 110 did I have. They were put together from all the theaters we owned. But these theaters used to have 10 men in a band, 1 trombone, 2 trumpets, a piano, a fiddle, a banjo. Now you put 100 of them together and what do you get? Something that sounds like 100 banjos. I wanted to make it a symphonic orchestra. There was only 1 cello in the 10 theaters. Not much choice. Yet we were a success. The thing sounded like Sousa's Brass Band. When we accompanied a love scene, you never heard so many trumpets in your life. . . .

The way I approached writing music for films was to fit the music to what I thought the dramatic story should be and score according to the way a character impressed me, whoever he might be. He may be a bastard, she may be a wonderful woman, he may be a child. I write what I see. This is very difficult for anybody to understand. Especially for anybody with such bad eyesight as I have. But I see a character on the screen and that is what makes me write the way I do. That is also the reason that people enjoy what they hear because it happens to fit.

————Steiner, interviewed for *The Real Tinsel* (NY, 1970)

Josef S T E R N B E R G   (Vienna 1894–Hollywood 1969)
Supreme stylist of the American cinema, discoverer and exploiter of Marlene Dietrich, and infuriating autobiographer (Fun in a Chinese Laundry), *his youth was spent between Viennese and New York schools. His miscellaneous first film experience turned out of great value, especially his training in photography.*

. . . I asked him how such great cameramen as Lee Garmes were able to work with him when he controlled the photography.

"Lee Garmes did exactly as I told him to. Exactly. To the extent that I would always be beside the camera. No picture of mine has ever been independently photographed. I always liked the best man I could find—Lee Garmes was excellent. One of the best men I had was Bert Glennon. Every time I had a different cameraman. They were learning. They were pleased to be instructed."

"Where did you learn photography?" I asked.

"Photography is not an independent art."

"Lighting?"

"Is not an independent art. . . ."

"When I made *Underworld* [1927] I was not a gangster, nor did I know anything about gangsters. I knew nothing about China when I made *Shanghai Express* [1932]. These are not authentic. I do not value the fetish for authenticity. I have no regard for it. On the contrary, the illusion of reality is what I look for, not reality itself. . . .

"A landscape must be photographed in the same way as a human face. You have the hills, the trees, a lake if possible. I always gauze the sky at the top—I burn holes in the gauze with a cigarette to give me an irregular edge. . . . I always have a light in the frame, which is very bright. It can be any part of the frame. I place a light directly above a face so that the nose shadow is very short. I do not use fill light. Cameramen always want fill light. Why? . . .

"What script? There was no script. If I gave my actors a script they would spend all night rehearsing before a mirror, and it would be very hard for me to undo all that. . . ."

———Sternberg, interviewed for *The Parade's Gone By* (NY, 1968)

[In *An American Tragedy*, 1931] I eliminated the sociological elements, which, in my opinion, were far from being responsible for the dramatic incident [with] which Dreiser had concerned himself.

———Sternberg, quoted in Sadoul-Morris, *Dictionary of Films* (Berkeley, 1972) p 9

In *An American Tragedy*, I replaced the voice of the man who played the important part of the judge in the famous trial. This man was not a bad actor, but only too late did I discover that his diction betrayed an accent which was inconsistent with the intended portrayal. I was asked afterwards how I failed to notice this accent. I confessed my fault but pleaded that the actor had impressed me by not speaking when I met him. Rather than replace the actor himself and hurt his feelings, I replaced his voice, without anyone being the wiser for it, except the actor who must have experienced no mean surprise to see his mouth open and speak with a voice not his.

———Sternberg, in *Film Culture*, Winter 55; repr. in *Film Makers on Film Making* (1967)

George S T E V E N S (1904–1975)
Born in Oakland, California. Cameraman for Hal Roach, and then director of comedy shorts.

I took a look at the script [of *Gunga Din*, 1939] and there were no outside scenes. The only thing you saw was through the windows of the officers' barracks and a little area between buildings where some people would ride by occasionally. I was afraid it would be very dreary. So I told the studio that I would take it on but I would make a location picture out of it. I knew where the location should be, in California around Lone Pine. I took this on but I said I wanted another man so there would be 3 male characters—the reason being a simple matter of arithmetic. To keep a story like this going, a slight story having to do with action, cause and effect; action, premise, promise and result, that if you have 2 principal characters, they would be playing with one another and by the time you get to the next sequence you'd have to prepare it. So the third character, one of the essential characters, could alter-

nate and I could be preparing the next development of the story at the time this one was happening and nobody would really get a chance to think about it.
———Stevens, interviewed at The American Film Institute for
Dialogue on Film, May–June 75

James STEWART
Born in Indiana, Pennsylvania, 1908. Brought from Broadway to Hollywood 1935.

Mr. Aldrich rehearses all the time evidently, I'd never worked with him before. But we rehearsed [*The Flight of the Phoenix,* 1965] for a week, actually part of the week just as in a play, just reading the script around a table, getting familiar with the script. Then we got on our feet in a blocked-out area of the crashed airplane.

Q. [*Two Rode Together,* 1961] had one very long sequence of you and Widmark on a log by the river, in which the dialogue seemed "awkward," almost as though it were improvised! Was this completely intentional on Ford's part?

Yes, it was just all one take. It was early in the morning and he was sort of grouchy and he walked out and for some reason put the camera in the river. He didn't have to put the camera in the river, but I think he did it because that meant that all the crew had to walk out up to their waists in the river, he's like that, and it was terribly cold. Widmark and I did this, it was a long, long scene, we did it and left.

A script clerk is a completely frustrated person with Hitchcock because Hitch really doesn't care what people say, he looks at it visually and if the thing makes sense to him, and he hears what they say, that's it.

John Ford has the same thing, he has no respect for the spoken word. He loves to tear pages out of scripts, he likes to cut sentences down to phrases, and phrases to words. He'll spend an hour getting the wind at the right force, so that it blows the sand in the background just right. But if you don't have the dialogue right immediately he is ready, he is completely impatient.

———Stewart, interviewed for *Films & Filming,* Apr 66

George STONEY
Born 1916 in North Carolina. Gained a wide experience in sponsored films; the following interview concerned A Cry for Help (1959), *an instructional film for police departments.*

Q. How did you select your actors and work with them in their roles?

A. Most of the actors were collected around the police department, or around Northwestern University. The script called for types, very carefully worked out, and so I looked for types. I tend to cast from my belly. I look at a guy and if it clicks, he's in, because I realize that the audience is going to have exactly the same response. The only time I can get away from that is when I have a major character, when I have someone on the screen long enough to break the stereotype of immediate identification.

I very seldom talk with non-actors about motivation. I try my best not to show them the script, because then they start thinking in terms of ordinary acting. Many times I write out the dialogue fairly completely and then ask, "What would *you* say in a situation like this?" We talk it out, and often they finish up with almost exactly the words I have written but by that time it has come from them. For example, there is the case of the motorcycle cop who is contemplating suicide in the film. The cop didn't like me, and I knew he didn't like me. I weigh around 130 pounds, and I'm not particularly masculine as he sees it. I played into that, I admitted that I couldn't do all kinds of things he could do. I told him *I* wouldn't know what a man like this would do. "*You* would know. You tell me what the dialogue should be." You play into their ego structure. . . .

In most situations where you are doing dramatic films with non-actors, all the turmoil is happening beyond the camera; somebody fiddles with lights, somebody fiddles with microphones, and somebody else is fiddling with sets. Usually there is so much tension and argument behind the camera that you can forget what is happening in front of the camera.

When you have non-actors and there's that kind of turmoil behind the camera, it can so dominate your cast that they go to pieces. You have to build up the idea that the most important thing that is happening is what is taking place in front of the camera. The actor has to feel that he is the most important thing, not your lighting, not your sound, nothing. And everybody's ego feeds into that. You have to have an atmosphere where people can act and not feel self-conscious. Each of these people is living for one moment. You are getting the one characterization they can give.

—————Stoney, interviewed for
The New Documentary in Action (Berkeley 1971)

Harry STRADLING [Sr.] (1902–1970)
Born in England, began his camera career in the United States. Worked in Paris, Berlin and London before returning to Hollywood.

There are two facts that worked very much in my favor while shooting *Streetcar* [*Named Desire,* 1951]. One is the complete free rein given me by the production heads. I was encouraged to plan and execute the photography exactly as I saw it in terms of the script. My camera was not inhibited by any cut-and-dried rules. The second advantage was the 2 days of rehearsal shooting we did prior to actual production. The shooting done in these 2 days was not meant to be used in the picture. It was set up solely as a method of experiment, to try out effects and set a definite style. As a result, the actual shooting went much faster, and we weren't forced to do our experimenting while shooting for keeps.

—————Stradling, quoted in *American Cinematographer,* Oct 51

Barbra STREISAND
Born in New York City, 1942. Performed in New York nightclubs and then on Broadway (at age 20).

I just played Fanny Brice [in *Funny Girl*, 1968] as a part—I never studied her whole life. I felt that we were so instinctively alike that I didn't have to work to get her.

I love Willy Wyler.... He's not eloquent. He'll sit there and he won't know when it's quite right. He's not like a director who says "Print!" and that's it and on to the next. He'll print 5, 6 of them even when the first one was right. But he always knows in the end, d'ya know what I mean, and will always pick the right piece. And that's really what counts, because I guess that's what makes him a better director than most. I think he's tremendous, but he's not what I thought a director would be like.

———Streisand, interviewed for *The Sunday Times Magazine*, 12 Nov 69

Erich von S T R O H E I M (1885–1957)
There are discrepancies between the documents and Stroheim's own account of his early years in Vienna, but it seems that he did emigrate to the U.S. in 1909, where he took various employment before joining the small film colony in Hollywood.

Greed [1923] was, up to that time, and perhaps even to now the only film in which there was *not one* set in a studio used. I had rented an old uninhabited house on Gower Street in San Francisco, furnished the rooms in the exact way in which the author [Frank Norris] had described them, and photographed there with only very few lamps, and the daylight which penetrated through the windows. Of course this was not to the cameraman's liking, but I insisted—and we got some very good photographic results. In order to make the actors really feel the characters they were to portray I made them live in those rooms. . . .

At the time when I began [working on *Greed*] the slogan of the Goldwyn Company was "the author and the play are the thing," and I was given *plein pouvoir* to make the picture as the author might have wanted it. However, when—during the time I was cutting the film—the Goldwyn Company became Metro-Goldwyn-Mayer, with Irving Thalberg as the new general manager, their new slogan was "The *producer* is the thing." I soon realized that the change boded no good for me, as Thalberg and I had often crossed swords at Universal. Thalberg and Mayer, the head of MGM, did not care a whoop about what the author or I, or the former Goldwyn Company had wanted. . . .

When I got through making the film as written and okayed by Goldwyn, I found myself with 42 reels. Even if I wanted the film to be shown in 2 parts, it was necessary to cut half of it. This I accomplished myself. When I arrived at 24 reels I could not, to save my soul, cut another foot. But the new company insisted on cutting it down. Unknown to them I sent one print to my friend Rex Ingram, who worked at that time in New York, and begged him to cut it, if he could. He returned it in 18 reels . . . [and] sent me a telegram: "If you cut one more foot I shall never speak to you again." I showed the telegram to Mr. Mayer who told me that he did not give a damn about Rex Ingram or me, and that the picture would be a total loss to the company anyway and that the picture must be cut to 10 reels. . . . It was given to a cutter, a man earning 30 a week who had never read the book nor the script,

and on whose mind was nothing but a hat. That man ruined my work of two years.
—Stroheim, quoted in Noble's *Hollywood Scapegoat* (London 1950)

When I saw how the censors mutilated my picture *Greed*, which I did really with my entire heart, I abandoned all my ideals to create real art pictures and made pictures to order from now on. My film *The Merry Widow* [1925] proved that this kind of picture is liked by the public, but I am far from being proud of it and I do not want to be identified at all with the so-called box-office attractions. So I have to quit realism entirely.... When you ask me why do I do such pictures I am not ashamed to tell you the true reason: only because I do not want my family to starve.
—Stroheim, quoted in Jacobs, *The Rise of the American Film* (NY 1939)

Karl S T R U S S
Born in New York City, 1891. After studying photography at Columbia University for 4 years, he enjoyed a variety of photographic experiences before entering motion pictures in 1919.

Sunrise [1927] reunited me with Charles Rosher, who did *Sparrows* [1926] with me. Most of the time we worked together on *Sunrise*....Murnau left the whole visual side of the picture to us; he concentrated entirely on the actors. Of course, he'd see what size the image was, and he was interested in the permanently moving camera; he had a certain feeling.

One of the opening shots was in a village at sundown. We showed lights coming out of doorways; to achieve the effect of interior light coming out and the twilight, the soft light around it, we had to work without exposure meters; there weren't any then!

When you photograph someone and change them into something else without cuts or dissolves (as with [Fredric] March from Jekyll to Hyde), you have to put red makeup on the actor's face. Then, when you put a red filter on the camera, it doesn't show the red makeup at all. The lips of course remain the same, so they are painted a neutral grey. You move the filter up or down very slowly, and as it moves, you see the makeup emerge. I worked it out for Mamoulian. I thought they made a very bad mistake; the change from Jekyll should have been largely a psychological one, with subtle changes only in the makeup. But they foolishly changed the hair and put false teeth in, and made him look like a monkey. That was terrible.

In the late thirties, Charlie Chaplin's brother, Sydney, called me. His usual cameraman, Rollie Totheroh, couldn't handle *The Great Dictator* [1940] which Charlie was about to make, and so Sydney asked me to do it. Later, on *Limelight* [1952], they did start out with Rollie Totheroh and a top crew, but Rollie still didn't know how to light. So they called me in on that one, too.

Limelight was slightly the more interesting of the 2 films photographically. I wanted to use 2 cameras for every shot, which we had done on *Dictator*, but [Chaplin] wouldn't let me do that the second time. I thought

I'd help him, give him something to cut, because he had no knowledge of camera direction, his films were completely "theater." It was very routine work with him; you'd just set up the camera and let it go and he and the other actors would play in front of it.

——Struss, interviewed for *Hollywood Cameramen* (London 1970)

Chaplin was one director who left camerawork [on *The Great Dictator* and *Limelight*] entirely to me, although sometimes he would change things like setups, inconsequential things that he shouldn't have worried about. . . . The time that was lost to make the change wasn't worth it, but he wanted it. The kids, maybe my assistant and operator, sort of kicked, and I said, "Well, after all, who's got the four million?". . . He had the power to do it. . . .

Murnau was the only director who, right in the beginning, knew how to use the moving camera. He didn't use it as so many of them do that don't know what they're doing with it. He moved that camera so that it came to a climax at the end of the shot. And he stayed with that; he just didn't cut the moment it was over with.

——Struss, interviewed for *Karl Struss* (Ann Arbor 1976)

John STURGES

Born in Oak Park, Illinois, 1911. Entered motion pictures in 1932 with RKO-Radio Pictures as assistant in the blueprint department. After serving in World War II, returned to Hollywood.

The Old Man and the Sea [1958] was begun by Fred Zinnemann at Warner Brothers. Well, they made a whole bunch of mistakes. It's not snide of me to say so. It's obvious now. They got mixed up with reality and film. The fact that the story takes place in the Gulf Stream off Cuba doesn't mean that that's the right place to shoot it. It isn't. The Gulf Stream goes at 12 miles an hour and it's rough. They took a very realistic approach to the film. And if you're going to do that, then I don't think Spencer Tracy was a good choice. He's an actor of obvious skills and emotional power and all the things that make him such a great actor. But he's certainly not a starving Cuban fisherman. I think if you attack the picture that way you're in trouble. The plans they had to get the shark, the plans to get the fish, got all scrambled up and 50 sets of people came up with 50 sets of solutions and the first thing they knew was that they'd spent $3,000,000. Why I took it on I'll never really know. I knew Tracy well. The idea intrigued me, to play it as an exercise in imagination and emotion. A theatrical approach. Now if anyone objected to that, the hell with them, they weren't going to like the film. This approach I found interesting and I felt I could profit by the mistakes they'd already made.

——Sturges, interviewed for
Hollywood: The Haunted House (London 1967)

Robert SURTEES

Born in Covington, Kentucky, 1906. Entered motion pictures in 1927 as an assistant cameraman with Universal. Worked for Universal in Berlin, 1929–30, then returned to career in the U.S.

In April of 1950, Dore Schary gave the signal that started actual production of *Quo Vadis* on its way. I had just completed the photography of *King Solomon's Mines,* and within a week John Schmitz, my camera operator, and I were flying the Atlantic, bound for Rome and Cinecitta. . . .

Cinecitta had previously been stripped clean of all electrical equipment—even to the wiring—by the German army, which accounts for the necessity of having to ship so much from America. On arrival, we found much of the U.S. equipment badly in need of repair, so roughly had it been handled on the ship, and in loading and unloading. But Hamilton and Leonetti soon had their students sufficiently organized and advanced in their training to tackle the job of getting the equipment in shape and the studio in order for its use.

The first few days of production in Rome were "rough." We were able to secure only three or four setups per day. Camera motors broke down; sound equipment blew; the Italian electricians, new to their jobs, allowed lamps to go out during takes.

Novel shortcut methods were devised in the issuing and checking-in of costumes for the thousands of extras. When we worked the Arena set, 14,000 extras would have to be outfitted, and at the close of the day's work, all wardrobes had to be turned in. During the night, these were cleaned, repairs made where necessary, and all made ready for use again the following day. Besides the mechanics of issuing and retrieving costumes daily, McCoy's greater problem concerned the colors in the costumes. Here the technical requirements of the camera had to be considered as well as the pictorial composition of the photography. The rushes were carefully studied each day to make sure we were not getting too many people in blue or red uniforms in clusters in the vast assemblages. To avoid the problem of too many red-dressed players grouping together inadvertently in a scene—which would create a strong distracting factor—the red costumes were dyed in various shades of red, so that there would be little likelihood of too much of any one color tone appearing in any one spot.

As the picture progressed we changed our style of lighting. For the interiors during the burning of Rome we tried keeping all the highlights and kickers on the copper-toned side. We lit one sequence from units on the floor, with no overhead lighting whatsoever to make it look drab and foreboding.

As Nero's death approached we began the effect-lighting. It was done progressively, until at Nero's death we actually had a photographic climax too. . . .

We had no background projection equipment with us in Rome, so Tom Howard of MGM's London Studios introduced us to the blue-backing method. His own inventions for combining, in the printing, the background and foreground action, are without doubt the best in the entire world.

For example, we would make a running background as for ordinary back projection. Next, placing the chariot driven by [Robert] Taylor in front of brightly illuminated blue-backing, we would photograph his action. Then Tom Howard, in London, would combine the two negatives by means of his optical system of printing. You will see many of these shots in *Quo Vadis* and will marvel at the great depth of focus and the quality Howard secured so simply. For day scenes we lit the blue-backing with a smooth overall 750 foot-candle, and then the foreground objects with exactly the same amount of light. But for a night effect or a low-key shot, the backing was lit as for day, 750 foot-candles, but the lighting of the foreground action was reduced to 400 foot-candles. A register and definition chart was photographed on the front of each take.

All the composite and painted glass shots were finally combined by Howard, and without a doubt they're the finest of their kind I've seen since the ones he did for *Black Narcissus* [1947].

——Surtees, in *American Cinematographer*, Oct, Nov 51;
revised for *Films in Review*, Apr 52

Sometimes when you get on the set, even though you've rehearsed it and marked it on the floor, something doesn't work. And if the director is pig-headed and sticks to his plan, you're in trouble. You've got to be pliable and have something just as good in case the other doesn't work.

——Surtees, interviewed for *Action*, Jan–Feb 76

A. Edward SUTHERLAND
Born 1895, in Hollywood from 1914. Assistant to Charles Chaplin.

[In *A Woman of Paris* (1923) after the boy's suicide] Charlie wanted [Lydia Knott, who played the mother] to give a reaction of complete shock. As the Sureté asked her all the usual questions—"What's his name, how old was he?"—he asked her for a total dead nonreaction. He wanted the audience to supply the emotion, not the actress. I can't tell you how many times we shot it. She kept playing it as a sweet, smiling, courageous old lady. She was a very fine person, and very determined, so it was tough going. Charlie took it maybe 50 times. Then he told me to take over. I shot it about 30 times. Finally the old lady got so angry that she swore at us. "All right," she snapped. "If that's the way you want it. But it's not the way I am." And she went through the scene in such a temper that we got it. . . . It took nearly a week to get that one reaction. Lydia Knott was the only player I ever knew to argue with Chaplin.

It took us weeks to cook up the routine in *The Gold Rush* [1925], when Chaplin eats his boots. The shoelaces were made of licorice; so were the shoes. The nails were some kind of candy. We had something like 20 pairs of boots made by a confectioner, and we shot and shot that scene, too. . . .

With this basis of working, it took us about a year and a half to shoot *A Woman of Paris*. I left *The Gold Rush* after 18 months, and he was about two-thirds through. But of course he didn't shoot all the time. We'd shoot for 3 or 4 days, then lay off for a couple of weeks and rethink, rehearse, and rarefy the scene.

——Sutherland, interviewed (1964) for *The Parade's Gone By* (NY, 1968)

Gloria SWANSON
Born in Chicago, 1899. Worked for Essanay, Keystone, Sennett, and Triangle Studios before doing a number of films with Cecil B. De Mille.

. . . Not that it makes any difference to anyone now, but I was never a Mack Sennett Bathing Beauty, though all the lives of me say I was. For one thing, I couldn't swim, which oddly enough was a necessary qualification, and in fact I only once wore a bathing costume the whole time I was at the studio, when we took some publicity stills on the beach just before I left. . . .

We had a complete script [of *Queen Kelly*, 1928] which had been passed by the Hays office, and he [Stroheim] agreed to stick to this, which he did for a time. But then we got to the scenes in a brothel—well, in the script it was a dance hall, but Stroheim had other ideas, and proceeded to spend a fortune—of my money—shooting stuff I knew perfectly well would never get into the finished picture. I don't mind spending money on a film provided it all shows on the screen, but this was sheer waste and enraged me, so we halted the picture to see what could be done.

By that time sound was coming in, and we had shot only the first third of the film, so while we were considering what to do I made very quickly, with the English director Edmund Goulding, a talkie, *The Trespasser* [1929], and then somehow *Queen Kelly* just stayed on the shelf. Finally I myself directed a sort of patched-up last scene to tie the story and it was shown a little in Europe and South America, in places where they didn't yet have talking apparatus, and that was that. A year or two before his death Stroheim and I talked about it and wondered if we couldn't do something with it, but neither of us had time.

———Swanson, interviewed for *The Times*, 16 Oct 61

[Sarah] Blanche S W E E T
Born in Chicago in 1896. In 1909 joined the Biograph Company where she stayed for 4 years, thereafter continuing her successful career with other film companies.

I can remember *Oil and Water* [1913] because Griffith was trying for something, a characterization. You didn't usually have time for characterizations in pictures in those days, because you got through as quickly as you could do it adequately. I mean you did the best you could, but you couldn't take time. We had a system, if anything could be called a system in those days. For instance, we were supposed to do exteriors, and it was raining or snowing, and we couldn't do them. Then, we would take that day to stay inside and rehearse several ideas, not just one but several, so that we would have a backlog on which to draw when something happened like inclement weather. Then we could go right into shooting in the studio. I don't know if other directors did that or not, but that was his way of doing it.

———Sweet, interviewed for *The Griffith Actresses* (London, 1973)

I doubt if any of us wanted to leave because we were all devoted to [Griffith]. There wasn't a member of that company, male or female, who didn't love that man. It's difficult to explain this devotion. We had great respect for his ability and understanding as a director. He opened up vista after vista. He was a marvelous actor himself, although he didn't make good as an actor. One minute he was discouraging to you, and the next minute he was inspiring you. I say "discouraging to you" because if you weren't getting the scene as he felt you should, he would show you how it should be done. He'd show you so beautifully that you felt, "Oh, I'd never be able to do it that way."...

He was a one-man show. He had to do everything himself: develop the original idea, carry it through, do it his own way, spend what he wanted on it. He was never good at working with anybody else—except Billy Bitzer. They were like fingers on a hand, and they got along beautifully. But that was different because Billy wasn't in a position of control. He would have ideas and then bat them back and forth with Mr. Griffith—you couldn't really know whose idea it was. Often they didn't know themselves.

——Sweet, interviewed for *The Real Tinsel* (NY, 1970)

Max von S Y D O W

Born in Lund, Sweden, 1929. Traveled Europe on the stage before entering motion pictures in Wild Strawberries, *1957.*

I didn't decide to play Christ [in *The Greatest Story Ever Told,* 1965] for the money. George Stevens (the director) did not raise his first offer, which was large by our modest Swedish standards. But I was scared. It meant going to Hollywood, out of the security of our stock-company type of filmmaking.

It meant playing a whole role in English, and what a role! Not that I am against representing Christ in the flesh. But not being a deeply religious man, I felt I must show Him as a man of worldly powers before He had divine ones attributed to Him; and this carries a big risk. My Christ was a kind of cross-country preacher prepared to live, if need be, on the iron rations of his faith....

Unfortunately, the film had to take account of the sensitivities of Lutherans, Catholics, and Jews. That is what went wrong with it, I think. That and the fact that the characters in it behave as if they had read the Bible in advance....

Bergman's screenplays resemble short stories, except that very little is obvious in them. He gives his actors the meaning by the physical movements he asks them to make. He'll say, "Get up on this word," or "Sit down on that," or "Now you half turn away here." You have to have almost telepathic communication with Bergman.

——von Sydow, interviewed for *The Evening Standard,* 2 Sep 66

T

TAO Chin
From theater acting to film acting in Shanghai and Hong Kong. In 1956 directed his first film, Fifteen Strings of Cash:

Some say that opera films should be as stylized as possible. But what is stylization? In the theater it usually means no more than the application of exaggeration or an extra emphasis on a vivid romantic imagination. In directing *Fifteen Strings of Cash* I wanted its means to be more realistic. I thought this would bring its 300-year-old story closer to the film audience. I consider that its background and characters demand a realistic method. And we tried to give its designs a maximum simplicity.

In spite of our hard discussions I enjoyed working with the cameraman Huang Shao-fen—and we finally resolved all disagreements. We experimented with light and used stronger colors than usual.
——Tao, interviewed for *Dazhong Dianying,* No. 6, 57

Frank TASHLIN
Born in Weehawken, New Jersey, in 1913. First film jobs for Max Fleischer and Aesop's Fables.

Jerry [Lewis] never rehearses. Just one take and that's it. You rehearse with Jerry and you'll die. So you can't really do anything interesting with the camera—his habits dictate your style. Sometimes when I have to repeat a scene, he'll change it around and do something completely different. And that's his charm, you see—you never know what he's going to do next. He doesn't look at his dialogue until he walks on the set, and then he never sticks to the lines anyway—usually he makes them better. I just tell him roughly what the scene is and he does it, kind of hit-and-run, and it's very successful. But you get no credit for doing a Lewis picture.
——Tashlin, interviewed for *Pieces of Time* (NY, 1973)

Jacques TATI [Tatischeff]
Born 1908, in Pecq, France.

I don't like to say to people "This is funny," because they may find it only a little bit funny. So I don't like to shoot in close-up. I have no right to bang anyone's nose against the screen. Besides, comedians speak with their legs. I spent years in music hall, you know, and I realize therefore especially that you need legs. Music hall also taught me that it is often difficult to be funny without music, because being funny is like being on the high wire or juggling, so I try to have a tune in my head for actors.

... M. Hulot is beginning to disappear in the scheme of *Playtime* [1967], beginning to be not the hero—because *Playtime* is about everybody, I hope. It has no hero. It is another style for me. Necessary because I find we are making another style of city designing, in which the stars are everybody.... One has to look at the people on the streets. I am trying to defend them....

[While in music hall] I did some short films, which were very, very bad. They were so bad that they made even me laugh. The fourth short film [*L'Ecole des facteurs*(?), 1947] made me laugh in the right way. So it is worth going on, I thought. Then I began to make long films. I loved slapstick, but I wanted to find another sort of visual comedy. Not the ancient formula. I like using sound tracks in a way that I expect some people find to be odd. It is because I know you can't ignore the coming of the talkies, but not all sound is *talk*. I don't want people to say "What a wonderful picture": I want them to notice details.

Tati, interviewed for The New Yorker, 27 Jan 73

Chaplin is a gagman; he invents a gag and does it in front of the public. Hulot is not a gagman, he is not even an actor. I invented him because I wanted to find a man who would be simple and honest and also a little bit out of control.

His feet, you see, are always half on the ground and half in the air. I like him best from the back view, because you never know what he is going to do.

——Tati, interviewed for The Times, 15 Nov 71

I thought at first of giving it [*Playtime*] the French title "Recreation" ... but then I thought [Parisian] housewives shop at the *supermarket;* they go to *nightclubs;* there's a new French cigarette out called *Flash;* there's a magazine called *"Twenty,"* and a brand of drinks called *"Verigoud."* ... since my film is a parody of Parisian life today, I told myself this was certainly the moment for an English title for a French film.... I do an enormous amount of preparation. I search for my characters. I am a great believer in the importance of gestures, the way a man moves. With me, words don't count for much.

I just don't think, for instance, that an actor can cut a piece of meat as it should be done. To have a piece of beef properly cut, it's better to call in a butcher. I try to root comic effects in truth: for instance, if in *M. Hulot's Holiday* [1951] I'd put a star name into one of the beach huts, it wouldn't have improved the film, it would only have made people wonder why the star was on holiday at the same time as M. Hulot....

——Tati, press for Playtime, 1967

I rehearse all the movements. If the man has to go around the chair then I show him the way he has to go around the chair. And with each one I show them what I would like them to do. But then I put on the music so as to create an atmosphere so they are not afraid when the clapper-boy steps in front of the camera and begins the scene, and they freeze on you. When the music is on I go out into the set and talk to them about the scene and get them relaxed and involved. You see, in *Playtime,* what I want is *participation.* I don't say YOU MUST LOOK AT THAT; I try to open a window.... So I say, "Please look at that; if you find something funny, okay...."

Sound is very important in my films. I think that sound can bring out much more comedy in a film when it is used carefully with the image. In *Jour de fête* [1947], in the scene where you have the postman going over the bridge, you don't see him, you only hear the noise of his feet. Take Hulot's car, in *Hulot's Holiday:* the shape of the car is not as funny as the noise the car makes. So you know before you see the image that the car is coming by the noise the engine of his car makes....

...The sound is not more funny than the image but together they produce some very funny effects. That is why I spent some time with Buster Keaton. I will not say that he liked *Hulot's Holiday,* but he did like the way I used the sound in *Hulot's Holiday* and he asked me to do the sound for his picture [*Paradise for Buster*(?)]. For I know I did put in the sound effect, not to exaggerate the image or the movement (like in the Laurel and Hardy film, when they take off their hat you hear a whistle sound—and you hear a whistle sound when they put it back on). That is exaggeration.... I believe in using sound in a funny way but not in exaggeration....

———Tati, interviewed for *Take One,* July–Aug 69

Robert T A Y L O R   [Spangler Arlington Brough]   (1911–1969)
Born in Filley, Nebraska.

You can't imagine how the studios cosseted us in those days. They had to. If we weren't looked after and guarded the fans would simply tear us to pieces.

When they finally decided I was going to make it as a star, Louis B. Mayer, the head of the studio, called me into his office and said: "How's your wardrobe, son?" I told him I'd got a couple of £10 suits and he said that wasn't good enough. So he sent me down to his own tailor—the best in Hollywood, of course—and ordered me 4 new ones, together with some evening kit. And he had me in his office to inspect them.

He was entitled to that—after all, he was paying for them! Everything in those days was aimed at glamour. There was no such thing as an unflattering "still"—the studio just wouldn't release it. And I used to wear pounds of makeup—yes, even lipstick—when I was filming. On top of that they always photographed me softly to enhance the glamour.

It was the same with the women. Their dresses were always approved by the studio. I tell you, when women like Joan Crawford and Norma Shearer went out, you knew you were looking at stars. Walk down Sunset Boulevard today, and most of the actors look like bums. There's no glamour any more.

Once they'd built this big romantic legend around me the studio was furious when I said I wanted to get married [to first wife, Barbara Stanwyck]. I guess they figured it would destroy my image. Eventually, they gave in, of course, and masterminded the whole affair for me. The only thing I was allowed to do was to choose the girl and say "I do."

In those days, you know, the publicity department never stopped working. And when I came to England to make *A Yank at Oxford* [1938] they really excelled themselves. There must have been 30,000 women waiting for me at Southampton and Waterloo. And a big story broke about how 2 girls had smuggled themselves aboard the boat and hidden under my bed.

How do you think they ever got under my bed in the first place? The MGM publicity department put them there, of course. . . .

So MGM—very nicely, I thought—gave me a big private plane. Each time we arrived somewhere the pilot flew around several times before landing, and I could never figure out why so many people always collected. Then I discovered they'd painted a damn great MGM lion under the belly of the plane with my name in huge letters beside it.

——Taylor, interviewed for *The Sunday Express*, 12 Aug 62

Irving THALBERG (1899–1936)
Born in Brooklyn. At age 19 became private secretary to Carl Laemmle, head of Universal studios; at 20 became studio manager of Universal; at 23 became V.P. and Production Assistant of Mayer Co.; 1924 became 2nd V.P. and Supervisor of Production of MGM.

. . . One of my chief functions is to be an observer and sense and feel the moods of the public. When I am asked to pass on the expenditure of huge sums of money and decide whether one kind of picture should be made or another kind, the greatest problem to be settled is that of judging whether or not the subject matter of the story is topical. What is accepted by the public today may not be accepted tomorrow. One of the finest examples I can give you of this is that war pictures in one period and another, in order to be successful, have had to be presented in an entirely different flavor.

. . . We produced a picture called *The Big Parade* [1924] which to a great extent has made history along the lines of pictures, and the only difference between it and the other war pictures was the different viewpoint taken in the picture. We took a boy whose idea in entering the war was not patriotic. He was swept along by the war spirit around him and entered it but didn't like it. He met a French girl who was intriguing to him, but he wasn't really serious about her. The only time he was interested in fighting was when a friend, who was close to him, was killed. It was human appeal rather than patriotic appeal, and when he reached the German trenches and came face to face with the opportunity to kill, he couldn't do it. In other words, a new thought regarding the war was in the minds of most people, and that was the basis of its appeal. . . .

. . . King Vidor is as much a realist as Griffith is an idealist, and his pictures have been an attempt to mirror life of today as it really is. I have discussed scenes with him many times, and have asked him to do this or that to heighten the dramatic effect, and his worst fear has always been to make any character do anything that wasn't natural for him to do.

——Thalberg, a public statement on 20 Mar 29

MGM inherited [*Ben-Hur*, 1925], which had been started with great hopes by the Goldwyn Company.

But when we began to get the rushes of the picture in Hollywood, and ran them off in the cold, analytical, almost surgical atmosphere of the studio projection room, we decided that they were not getting anywhere at all. It was then that we made the decision, which was considered at the time a crossing of the Rubicon from sanity to insanity. We sent a new director and a new star to Rome. We junked a half-million dollars in completed film and started all over again. It was the only thing to do. . . .

. . . With a property like that on our hands, we had a duty not only to our stockholders but to theater owners and to the public as well, to make good. A poor picturization of *Ben-Hur* would have cost us in prestige far more than the half million dollars' worth of junked film.

———Thalberg, quoted in *Thalberg, Life and Legend* (NY, 1970)

J. Lee THOMPSON
Born in Bristol, 1914.

We wanted to film many important scenes [for *The Chairman*, 1969] in Hong Kong and Taiwan. We were going to Taiwan for 2 days, then to Hong Kong for another 8 days. Soon after we arrived in Taiwan we were told of trouble in Hong Kong with the threat of riots. The authorities in Hong Kong, however, said they would nevertheless support the film unit to the hilt.

Within 3 hours of receiving that message, they telephoned to tell us that they were not requesting us to stay out of Hong Kong, but that they were barring us from Hong Kong, adding, "How dare you put us in this position!"

Of course, there were violent demonstrations being held in Peking and other places. They burnt effigies of Gregory Peck and Lyndon Johnson. It was looking very ugly.

Of course we would not have dreamed of subjecting anybody to possible injury or even death. But we did give the statement out, which was correct, that we were in no way insulting to Mao, that the scene with Mao was treated with respect, which it is.

Well, after that statement, the Taiwan authorities said, "Oh, so it's not anti-Mao? We would not have allowed you in Taiwan if it was not anti-Mao. We will therefore confiscate your film." So there we were—caught between two factions.

Eventually we had to smuggle the film out of Taiwan. One of the members of the unit who hadn't dealt with the officials was sent, with the film hidden in a suitcase full of clothes, to Hong Kong. The case was then put on a plane to London. It was quite an ordeal. We took our own Mao posters on location. These had to be covered with white paper until we were actually ready to film the scene.

Nobody was allowed to take pictures unless he or she were members of the film unit. All the posters were kept under guard. At the end of filming they were all burned under supervision.

. . . One day one of the officials came up to me and said, "Take off the shoes of all those children, remove those girls, they're too pretty."

I must say that was the one time I really lost my temper. I said, "Do you really honestly believe that in Red China no children wear shoes, and that there are no pretty girls?" But they were adamant their orders be carried out. Since we were using Taiwan for Red China in the story of the film, then everything that went on the screen they wanted exaggerated as poor and dirty.

———Thompson, interviewed for *Photoplay*, Sept 69

Virgil T H O M S O N
Born in Kansas City, 1896.

Q. Do you take into account anything outside the dramatic and visual elements of the film sequence—for example, the level of musical understanding of the film audience?

A. I don't think it ever advisable to be obscure when writing for a large number of people and I do not think it advisable ever to write down to anybody. The only exterior circumstances I know of that need to be taken account of in writing music for films is the fact that the beginning and ending of a film are the time when people come and go and change seats. Consequently a soft beginning is likely not to be heard at all.

Q. Do you feel the need of unifying all the passages of music within a film as you would unify them in any other musical work? Have you found that the film permits this or prevents this?

A. I think the composer of film music and of theatrical incidental music achieves a better result when he gives to his entire score a certain unity or continuity, in spite of the interruptions, comparable to the unity and continuity he would endeavor to achieve in a continuous composition. There is no reason why this should be impossible to achieve with any film, but the degree of difficulty with which it is achieved will naturally depend on the director one is working with. The musical continuity in the scores I have made is not ideal but it is better than most.

Thomson, answering questionnaire in *Films*, Winter 40

Ingrid T H U L I N
Born in Solleftea, Sweden, in 1929. Her theater debut at the age of 15; entered films in 1949.

Our performances are agreed between ourselves and Bergman through an instinct, and this instinct would be spoiled if we had to keep stopping to talk about why we were doing what we were. It is how we are doing them that is important. The actors and Bergman are very emotionally involved for a short time, and when the film is made the spell is broken. . . .

What I wanted to show [in *The Silence*, 1964] was the strongest fear people in Scandinavia have: they are frightened of dying inside themselves. They do not believe in God and there is no idealism in the State, so people have only their own personalities to think about. In the film, Ester was an intelligent woman who began to lose the sensual side of herself and became desperate because there was nothing to take its place. She was tired of herself and tired of the attitudes conditioned by language—such problems are very real in Sweden and the disenchantment can become a kind of madness. The silence was silence from God. No Swede is shocked by this idea, but they might be frightened by it. I think it is poetical.

——Thulin, interviewed for *The Guardian*, 1 Apr 65

It is always amusing to play terrible women [Sophie in *The Damned*, 1970]. This woman has a taste for power, for her it is almost like lovemaking. There is a scene in bed like a love scene, but Sophie is thinking only of power. I think her feeling may be like Eva Braun's for Hitler—she stayed with him even if, as a lover, he was nothing because she had this other deep drive.

I don't know if all this will show, but it gives me a scale to work in. If you analyze too much it is bad—when I am doing these very strong emotions I prefer just to go on a mood. In films I haven't done too much with high points of emotion.

We started shooting [the remake of *The Four Horsemen of the Apocalypse*, 1962] in the Bois de Boulogne in November. Minnelli thought the leaves would stay on the trees as they do in California. When they didn't, he started nailing leaves on, but the gardien of the Bois wouldn't allow that, so he glued them. It was raining. Minnelli was so funny. He didn't like the leaves they bought, so he had them painted.

——Thulin, interviewed for *The International Herald Tribune*, 8–9 Feb 69

Dimitri T I O M K I N
Born in St. Petersburg, Russia in 1899. Came to U.S. as pianist in 1925.

I've often been criticized for starting a trend which has led to the pop-concert-style scores you get in many films today. But in *High Noon* [1952] the song was conceived as an integral part of the score. After that, I admit that there was strong financial inducement to fit my scores with theme songs that might sell in their own right. But I think it's fair to say that I never held up the action of any film to plug a song of mine; the song was always built into the score, then extracted and fitted with lyrics separately. And I certainly never put lyrics on the sound track itself unless they were directly relevant to the action on the screen—the songs for the unaccompanied chorus in *The Alamo* [1960], for instance, or the pianissimo chorus at the end of *The Guns of Navarone* [1961], where I did what I often wanted to in the early days but wasn't allowed to—end a picture on a dying fall.

——Tiomkin, interviewed for *Crescendo*, Aug 72

Edward T I S S E [pseud.] (1897–1961)
Born in Latvia. First film experience: newsreel cameraman on the Russian front.

In this film [*The General Line*, 1926–1929] we resolved to get away from all trick camerawork, and to use simple methods of direct filming, with the most severe attention to the composition of each shot. Only exception to this rule: when we sometimes employed artificial lighting in exterior scenes—and this was to gain more control over final compositional unity. This gave us the means to determine all degrees of light, from day to night, without resorting to a chemical process at the laboratory, to achieve such gradations. . . . Our aim in this film: to gain artistic and technical effects by entirely new methods of filming reality with simplicity.

————Tisse, in *Sovietsky Ekran,* 11 Dec 1926

Gregg TOLAND (1904–1948)
Born in Charleston, Illinois.

A fine cameraman begins his work long before the actual start of his photographic duties. In the case of *The Little Foxes* (1941), for Samuel Goldwyn, my work began 6 weeks before we shot the first scene. There were long conferences with the producer, with William Wyler, the director, with the architect who designed the sets [Stephen Goosson], with the property man and other artisans.

Discussions with the director involved a complete breakdown of the script, scene by scene, with an eye to the photographic approach, considering the various dramatic effects required. We built knockdown models of the most important sets and juggled the places to set up the camera. We took into consideration color values, types of wallpaper or background finishes, the color and styles of costumes to be worn by the principals, the furnishings and investiture. We set the photographic key for various sequences—the light or gay ones, dramatically speaking, in a high key of light, the more somber or moody scenes in a low and more "contrasty" key.

We determined that Bette Davis, the star, should wear a pure white makeup. This is revolutionary, but it is a potent device in suggesting the kind of character she portrays in the story—a woman waging the eternal conflict with age, trying to cling to her fading beauty. But because of the contrast between her makeup and that of the other principals, we had to discover exactly the balance of light which would illuminate both to advantage. Ascertaining this light balance required extensive makeup tests. . . .

In *Citizen Kane* we made 15 takes of a particular scene. Without obtaining one that was completely perfect. When the dialogue was right, the mechanics were off. Or it was the other way round. I suggested that we try to match the perfect sound track of one take with the flawless photographic mechanics of another. Orson Welles agreed. The experiment was a success. . . .

Color will continue to be improved but will never be 100 percent successful. Nor will it ever entirely replace black-and-white film because of the inflexibility of light in color photography and the consequent sacrifice of dramatic contrasts. Anything done in the gay, high-key light which color photography necessitates for its existence (such as musical comedies) will continue to be suitable as a subject for color film. But low-key, more dramatic use of light seems to me automatically to rule color out in pictures of another type. Paradoxically enough, realism suffers in the color medium. . . . Three prime colors are now utilized but not enough shades are possible with those three. More basic colors would involve too complex a problem to be economically practicable.

————Toland, in *Theatre Arts Monthly,* Sep 41

We had 12 cameras shooting simultaneously [on *The Trespasser,* 1929] to cover various setups, and we had 2 sound tracks going. In those days we didn't know how to cut sound, so we'd shoot the sound in one solid unit, and then cut the film from our 12 cameras to fit the track. Since all our cameras ran continuously, on some days we had 30,000 feet of rushes.

Wuthering Heights [1939] was a soft picture, diffused with soft-candle-lighting effects. I tried to make the love scenes beautiful in a romantic way. It was a love story, a story of escape and fantasy. So I tried to keep it that way photographically, and let the audience dream through a whirl of beautiful close-ups.

On the other hand, *The Grapes of Wrath* [1940] had to be a sharp picture. It was a story of unhappy people, people of the earth, who had real problems and who suffered. So we made it very sharp. There wasn't any makeup used. The picture had some extreme effects in low key but they were, I think, real. As I remember the camera moved only once—a long travel shot through the sordid streets of a Hooverville. It was what the occupants of the car, after the long drive to a promised haven, were examining. Photography such as we had in *Wuthering Heights* could ruin a picture like *Grapes of Wrath* completely.

Long Voyage Home [1940] was a mood picture. Storywise it was a series of compositions of the mood of the men aboard the ship. It was a story of what men felt rather than what they did. The camera *never* moved in that picture. . . .

I might add that one reason for many of the effects [in *Kane*] was a lack of money. We just couldn't afford to have an audience in the opera house when the camera was shooting from behind Dorothy Comingore, the singer. So we *thought.* I put up a series of baby spots in a black opera set and trained them at the camera. I believe that the ultimate effect was more desirable than an expensive audience of extra people. . . .

The Best Years of Our Lives [1946] was another experiment. But in a different way. [Wyler and I] . . . talked at length about the story and decided it demanded simple, unaffected realism. Willy had been thinking a lot, too, during the war. He had seen a lot of candid photography and lots of scenes without a camera dolly or boom. He used to go overboard on movement, but he came back with, I think, a better perspective on what was and wasn't important. Anyway, Willy left me pretty much alone. While he rehearsed, I would try to find a method of shooting it. Usually he liked it. When he didn't, he was the boss and we did it his way. However, at this point we understand each other pretty well and Willy knows that I will sacrifice photography and time if it means a better scene. I, in turn, know that he will listen to any suggestion. . . .

———Toland, interviewed for *The Screen Writer,* 1949

[Orson] Welles's use of the cinematographer as a real aid to him in telling the story, and his appreciation of the camera's story-telling potentialities helped me immeasurably. He was willing—and this is very rare in Hollywood—that I take weeks to achieve a desired photographic effect.

The photographic approach to *Citizen Kane* was planned and considered long before the first camera turned. That is also unconventional in Hollywood, where most cinematographers learn of their next assignments only a few days before the scheduled shooting starts. Altogether I was on the job for a half year, including preparation and actual shooting.

The *Citizen Kane* sets have ceilings because we wanted reality, and we felt that it would be easier to believe a room was a room if its ceiling could be seen in the picture. Furthermore, lighting effects in unceilinged rooms generally are not realistic because the illumination comes from unnatural angles. . . .

There were other violations of Hollywood tradition in the photographic details of *Citizen Kane*. One of them resulted from Welles's insistence that scenes should flow together smoothly and imperceptibly. Accordingly, before actual shooting began, everything had been planned with full realization of what the camera could bring to the audience. We arranged our action so as to avoid direct cuts, to permit panning or dollying from one angle to another whenever that type of camera action fitted the continuity. By way of example, scenes which conventionally would require a shift from close-up to full shot were planned so that the action would take place simultaneously in extreme foreground and extreme background.

——Toland, in *Popular Photography Magazine,* June 41; repr. in
Focus on Citizen Kane (Englewood Cliffs, 1971)

Citizen Kane is by no means a conventional, run-of-the-mill movie. Its keynote is realism. As we worked together over the script and the final preproduction planning, both Welles and I thought this, and felt that if it was possible, the picture should be brought to the screen in such a way that the audience would feel it was looking at reality, rather than merely a movie.

[Welles] instinctively grasped a point which many other far more experienced directors and producers never comprehend: that the scenes and sequences should flow together so smoothly that the audience would not be conscious of the mechanics of picturemaking. And in spite of the fact that his previous experience had been in directing for the stage and for radio, he had a full realization of the great power of the camera in conveying dramatic ideas without recourse to words.

Therefore from the moment the production began to take shape in script form, everything was planned with reference to what the camera could bring to the eyes of the audience. Direct cuts, we felt, were something that should be avoided wherever possible. Instead, we tried to plan action so that the camera could pan or dolly from one angle to another whenever this type of treatment was desirable. In other scenes, we preplanned our angles and compositions so that action which ordinarily would be shown in a single, longer scene—often one in which important action might take place simultaneously in widely separated points in extreme foreground and background. . . .

The majority of our sets for *Citizen Kane* had actual ceilings—in many instances even lower than they would be in a real room of similar style. Furthermore, many of our camera angles were planned for unusually low camera setups, so that we could shoot upward and take advantage of the more realistic effects of those ceilings. Several sets were even built on parallels, so that we could take up any desired section of the flooring and place the lens actually at floor level.

This, as may be imagined, immediately created a very interesting problem in lighting. Since the sets were ceilinged, not one of the 110 sets were paralleled for overhead lighting. . . . Everything in the picture was to be lighted from the floor. . . .

The next problem was to obtain the definition and depth necessary to Welles's conception of the picture. While the human eye is not literally a universal-focus optical instrument, its depth of field is so great, and its focus changes so completely automatic, that for all practical purposes it is a perfect universal-focus lens.

In a motion picture on the other hand, especially in interior scenes filmed at large apertures commonly employed, there are inevitable limitations. . . .

Now it is well known that the use of lenses of short focal length tends in itself to increase the depth of field. So, too, does stopping down the lens.

Since the introduction of today's high-speed emulsions, some photographers and some studios make it a practice to take advantage of the film's speed by stopping their lenses down to apertures as low as f:3.5 . . . when for some reason added depth may be desired for a scene. . . .

To solve our problem, we decided to carry this idea a step further. If using a high-speed film like Plus-X and stopping down to f:3.5 gave a desirable increase in definition, wouldn't it—for our purposes, at least—be still a better idea to employ a super-speed emulsion like Super-XX, and to stop down even further.

Preliminary experiments proved that it was. However, merely stopping down to the extent that would compensate for higher sensitivity of Super-XX was still not enough, though we were on the right track.

The next step inevitably was to stop down to whatever point might give us the desired depth of field in any given scene, compensating for the decreased exposure-values by increasing the illumination level.

This, especially on deep roofed-in sets where no overhead lighting could be used, naturally created another lighting problem. Fortunately, two other factors helped to make this less troublesome than might have been expected.

First, we were using . . . lenses treated with Vard "Opticoat" nonglare coating. . . . Depending upon the design of the lens to which it is applied, it gives an increase in speed ranging between half a stop and a stop, while at the same time giving a very marked increase in definition, due to the elimination of flare and internal reflections.

Secondly, due to the nature of our sets, and the lighting problems incident to our use of ceilinged sets, we were . . . making considerable use of arc broadsides. In addition to the greater penetrating power of arc light as compared to incident, this gave us a further advantage, for the arc is unexcelled in concentrating the greatest illuminating power into a comparatively small unit.

It was therefore possible to work at apertures infinitely smaller than anything that had been used for conventional interior cinematography in many years. While in conventional practice even with coated lenses, most normal interior scenes are filmed . . . within the range between f:2.3 and f:2.8. . . . We photographed nearly all of our interior scenes at apertures not greater than f:8—and often smaller. Some scenes were filmed at f:11, and one at f:16!

... This solved our depth-of-field problem.... Even the standard 50mm and 47mm objectives conventionally used have tremendous depth of field when stopped down to such apertures. Wide-angle lenses such as 35mm, 28mm, and 24mm objectives, when stopped down to f:11 or f:16, become to all intents and purposes universal-focus lenses.

But we needed every bit of depth we could possibly obtain. Some of the larger sets extended the full length of 2 stages at the RKO-Pathé Studio, and necessitated holding an acceptably sharp focus over a depth of nearly 200 feet. ...

——Toland, in *American Cinematographer*, Feb 41

[Haym] T O P O L
Born 1935.

We started [*Fiddler on the Roof*, 1971] at the beginning of August and finished in January, so we got all the seasons—heat, autumn leaves, and snowstorms, too.

Everything you see in the movie is natural. It is a very primitive country. The houses are real in the film, the barns had old wood, the manure we stepped in was not placed there just for the scene. It was there when we got there. We had no other choice but to step in it.

When I had to pull the cart, it was really hard because of the mud, so the strain on my face is not just acting. But I learned to love Yugoslavia. The soil is very fertile, but the people are very poor.

I am more interested in movies, but in a tiny country of 2,500,000 people, you can't make a lot of money. Israel will never have an important film industry because if you spend more than $250,000 on a film you never get your money back. So I must go elsewhere.

——Topol, interviewed for *The Toronto Star*, 13 Nov 71

Roland H. T O T H E R O H (1890–1967)
From California baseball to cameraman at the Essanay Studio in Niles, California was a transformation that Totheroh made with little effort.

We [Essanay] had two companies: Broncho Billy and making the Ramblers, and we were the comedy company, the Snakeville gang. [G.M.] Anderson used to make about 8 or 9 pictures a day. All the posse chases were left behind and Jess Robbins used to do them. Eventually that's how I got started as a cameraman. I helped, too. They'd take all of these wild chases, stagecoach chases, and everything else.

The first picture I shot [*The Dance at Eagle Pass*, 1911?] was for a fellow named Lloyd Ingraham. Before that I would do some of Anderson's chases. I'd make them very simple, of course. I'd shoot across from left to right on one side of the road without moving the camera around a lot; then I would have the posse come the other way. Stagecoaches used to knock me right off my tripod! I used to say, "Come as close to me as you can," and they would! ...

When we went on location, [Chaplin] used to come out and watch us. Finally, we shot his first picture [at Essanay, *His New Job*, 1915]. At that time used to help G. M. Anderson cut the pictures. The way he would cut was he came right up to a big close-up and roll his eyes around. There was no expression and he could use it anywhere. He just measured off the tip of his nose to the length of his arm and tear it off. That was Anderson's way of editing in a close-up!

After Charlie finished his first picture, he wanted to rest and go to San Francisco for a couple of days over the weekend. He was getting $1250 a week and he'd been on this one picture close to a month and the picture wasn't out yet. Anderson decided he was going to cut it so he got ahold of me and we went in and we started to cut on the first reel of Charlie's picture. Lo and behold! Chaplin didn't go to San Francisco. He decided not to at the last minute and came walking in on us. We were cutting the first reel, and Charlie said, "Take your hands off that." At that time we never had a print made; we used to do the cutting on negative. If we scratched it, it was just too bad. So Charlie said, "And furthermore, I want a print." At that time we had our own little laboratory, but we never had a printing machine because we never used it. Our laboratory man didn't know anything about a printing machine. So they had to send all the way back to Chicago to get one. . . .

They were going into the second month and the first film still wasn't out yet. So finally they got everything on schedule, and Charlie started getting his films done.

On a typical day, we'd shoot from around 8 or 9 in the morning right straight through till lunch. Of course, this was before unions. And a lot of times he'd want to shoot 2 hours after dinner. After we'd break for lunch or for dinner, we'd start up again. . . .

Pretty near everything prior to *The Great Dictator* [1940] was *ad lib*. He didn't have a script at the time, didn't have a script girl or anything like that, and he never checked whether the scene was in its right place or that continuity was followed. The script would develop as it went along. A lot of times after we saw the dailies the next morning, if it didn't warrant what he thought the expectation was, he'd put in some other sort of a sequence and work on that instead of going through with what he started out to do. We never had a continuity. He'd have an idea and he'd build up. He had sort of a synopsis laid out in his mind but nothing on paper. He'd talk it over and come in and do a sequence. In a lot of his old pictures, he'd make that separation by using titles about the time: "next day" or "the following day" or "that night"—these would cover the script gaps in between. . . .

——Totheroh, interviewed (1964 and 1967) for *Film Culture*, Spring 72

Jacques TOURNEUR
Born in Paris, 1904, son of Maurice Tourneur.

The Department of Justice asked Mr. Louis B. Mayer if he would make in his short subjects a 2-reel subject about the federal penitentiaries. So since I was doing shorts they sent me to 5 or 6 . . . all over the United States. Then Mr. John Higgins wrote a 2-reel *Crime Does Not Pay* story with actors about that.

The 2-reel thing comes out and Mr. Louis B. Mayer looks at it and says, "This is interesting. We're now doing featurettes, we're going to do 4-reel films to complete the program." They said, "Call back Johnny Higgins and write 2 more reels." So we had an awful time getting the actors together. They were all over the place. We had to wait a month or two before we could get them all together.

We cut that together—3 months go by—Mr. Mayer looks at it: "This is 4 reels—this shouldn't be a featurette—this should be 6 reels—and be a full-length feature." We wait, get all the actors together again and we finished with a full length feature called *They All Come Out* [1939], which unbelievably made good sense. Looking at it, you'd never think it was first 2 reels, then 4 reels, then 6 reels. It was a *tour de force* on the part of Mr. John C. Higgins and that's how I did my first feature at MGM.

—Tourneur, interviewed for *Films & Filming*, Nov 65

I don't believe in doing everything in advance, as Hitchcock does. I began working in France, and there everything is without a schedule. I'd go on the set and say to the cameraman, "Look, come on over here, and let's look at it from this point of view." That's how we worked! I believe great things come from that great reservoir we have within us of past experience, which is all available. But I do work very hard on the dialogue before we shoot, because I consider the poor actors; once you change the lines you throw them. I sometimes get new writers brought in, to ensure that the writing is quite perfect.

—Tourneur, interviewed for *The Celluloid Muse* (Chicago, 1969)

Robert T O W N E
Born in Los Angeles, 1935; studied English literature at Pomona College; first screen credit was The Tomb of Ligeia (1964).

Q. Did you rewrite the ending [of *Chinatown*, 1974] yourself?

A. More or less, though I was arguing while I was doing it. A very tricky thing happens when you're doing a film. A director comes along, and you recognize that a transference has to take place, and he has to conceive of the film as his film. You just hope that your visions will complement his and be consistent with each other. So I said "Okay," and the film ends the way it does. My own feeling is if a scene is relentlessly bleak—as the revised ending is—it isn't as powerful as it can be if there's a little light there to underscore the bleakness. If you show something decent happening, it makes what's bad almost worse.

For example, *The Last Detail* [1973] ends up badly, but along the way there is a certain amount of warmth, friendship, good times, a concern for each other, people being decent. This serves to accentuate that in the end all those things go by the boards. If there's going to be a light at the end of the tunnel, you want to have some light before you get there. In a melodrama, where there are confrontations between good and evil—if the evil is too triumphant, it destroys your ability to identify with it rather than if its victory is only qualified. I'm making no relationship to anything I've done, but if you read a great tragedy like *King Lear*, you see what makes it so effective are all the little kindnesses along the way, the Fool and Cordelia, the virtuous daughter. Ultimately, goodness gets destroyed, but its ongoing presence lends a reality to the presence of evil.

Q. Besides turning out original screenplays, you've also had a successful career as a script doctor. When you were brought in to doctor *The Godfather* [1971] script, were you given certain sections or the entire screenplay?

A. I was given certain sections. The main problem was that there was no final scene between Michael Corleone and his father. Since he was about 4 or 5 weeks into shooting, Francis Coppola didn't know what to do about it. He kept saying, "I want a scene where they say they love each other." I couldn't write a scene with 2 people saying they love each other. It had to be about something, an action. So that scene in the garden between Al Pacino and Marlon Brando is what I ended up doing—a scene about the transfer of power. There were other little things which I did, but they were inconsequential.

———Towne, interviewed for *American Film*, Dec 75

Spencer T R A C Y (1900–1967)
Spent many years on New York and touring stages before he was offered his first film contract. In Hollywood he became one of its most respected and private actors. He described the circumstances that made him consider the career of director:

I'll tell you when it all started. I was making that goddamn *Plymouth Adventure* [1952] and the ulcer was kicking up. I look lousy and I felt worse and one day I found myself out there in front of a great big process screen. I felt particularly fat that morning, and about 94. I'd seen myself in the mirror and thought I was like an old beat-up barn door. My face looked like it could hold 3 days of rain. Anyway, there we stood playing the scene and this lovely kid, Gene Tierney, had to look up and say to me, "I love you, John. I love you." And all of a sudden, I was embarrassed. I don't mean for myself. I was embarrassed for *her*. Here was this beautiful young actress trying to make her way, playing the parts she could get to play, and now they'd got her standing up against me making no sense at all. Later on I began to think, "What the hell will the audience make of this idiocy? This sensational young beauty looking up at this cranky old man and saying all this bullshit." It just didn't make any sense. The only reason she was saying it to me was because I was a big Metro star playing the lead in the picture. That was the moment I decided I ought to begin to think of packing it in as an actor.

. . . I never meant to direct *myself*. . . . If I ever did anything like that I'd have to look at myself up there, wouldn't I? At the rushes? That's something I've never done. Anyway, those guys [Olivier, Welles] are geniuses and I'm not. No, if I'm going to direct, I'll direct other people . . . I honest to God think I could help some actors, some I've seen.

———Tracy, in Garson Kanin, *Tracy and Hepburn* (NY, 1971)

Jean-Louis T R I N T I G N A N T
Born in Aix-en-Provence, France, 1930. Stage debut in 1951, films in 1955.

When we are about to shoot a scene, [Claude Lelouch] takes one of us aside and describes the situation. For example, he tells Anouk Aimée, my partner, the stage the story has reached, suggests some phrases she may use, emphasizing 2 or 3 key phrases which she must work in. But he does not tell Anouk what I am going to say to her; nor does he tell me what she is going to say. Then we act out the scene, without rehearsal. If it is good he keeps it, if it is not he shoots the whole scene over again with fresh dialogue.

——Trintignant, interviewed for *The Guardian*, 10 Feb 66

François TRUFFAUT

Born in Paris, 1932. As a teen-ager, he organized and ran small ciné clubs in Paris. This led to work in journalism, including Les Cahiers du cinéma. *In 1956 he became assistant to Roberto Rossellini.*

Having started out with a short subject titled *The Mischief Makers* (*Les Mistons*) I realized that I preferred to work with children than with adults. Initially, *The 400 Blows* was supposed to be a short subject, or perhaps the first sketch of an omnibus film about childhood; we had planned to call it *Antoine's Fugue*. Later on, in working out the story with Marcel Moussy, we decided to develop the story into a feature film. Our main purpose was not to depict adolescence from the usual viewpoint of sentimental nostalgia but, on the contrary, to show it as the painful experience it is.

It was from Jean Renoir that I learned that actors are always more important than the characters they portray, or, to put it in a different way, that we should always sacrifice the abstract for the concrete. It is hardly surprising therefore that from the day we started shooting *The 400 Blows* [1959] Antoine Doinel [the protagonist] began to move away from me to come closer to Jean-Pierre [Léaud, the actor]. . . .

Jean-Pierre turned out to be a valuable collaborator to *The 400 Blows*. He instinctively found the right gestures, his corrections imparted to the dialogue the ring of truth, and I encouraged him to use the words of his own vocabulary. . . .

One of my prime concerns was to achieve a maximum of truth, and it seemed to me that Jean-Pierre Léaud was not as natural and genuine as he had been in the 16mm tests we had made prior to the shooting.

It was this preoccupation that led to the creation of a scene that the critics later singled out as one of the highlights of the picture, namely, Antoine's session with the staff psychologist at the juvenile delinquents' detention center.

Initially, Marcel Moussy and I had written a normal psychological session, using the usual Rorschach tests, but at the last minute I changed my mind. A sound camera and a microphone were brought in and I asked the crew to leave the set. Seated across the table from Jean-Pierre, I asked him a series of questions of which he had no advance knowledge, leaving him free to answer as he pleased. This was relatively easy for him since we had almost reached the end of shooting and he was, by this time, thoroughly acquainted with his character. But even so, he was so spontaneous in his replies that some of them were based upon his own life; at one point, for instance, he tells all about a grandmother who never appears in the film.

——Truffaut, introduction to *The Adventures of Antoine Doinel* (NY, 1971)

The idea of the frozen frame [at the end of *400 Blows*] came to me in the cutting room, moving the film backwards and forwards and stopping and starting; that way you sometimes discover moments that would be lost if you ran them at normal speed. The real reason I used it was because the child didn't play the scene as I wanted. Jean-Pierre went towards the sea, and he was supposed to turn and come back, and what I asked him to do was just to look into the camera, to give almost the effect of a stage actor bidding farewell to his audience, as if he were coming down off the stage and drawing nearer to the audience. I wanted to be sure the audience would not think he was going to commit suicide in the water. I needed to establish beyond doubt that he wasn't going to do that. But when he came up to the camera, he moved his head around and didn't give that steady look. And then afterwards, while I was editing, I realized that I could get a good effect by stopping the film earlier. . . .

. . . I was very unhappy when I was making [*Tirez sur le pianiste*, 1960]. I found that I didn't like putting gangsters on the screen. It was for that reason that I decided to make it comic. I felt uncomfortable with gangsters, and I had no desire to influence the public to approve of gangsters. That, too, is probably because of my childhood, and the way I grew up. . . .

——Truffaut, interviewed for *Films & Filming*, July 72

I made *Jules and Jim* [1961] somewhat in reaction against mistreated scenarios. For example, I was told that I would have to modernize the period of the original book; and in substituting the Second World War for the First, the transposition would have been simple. But since the film was to be about a woman and love, I refused. I was anxious not to have my film be like all the rest made today on these particular topics: with a sports car . . . lots of scotch, and of course a high-fidelity set, as compulsory equipment. Had I done this, I would have been in complete conformity with the rules of the "nouveau cinéma." However I chose to remain faithful to the period of the book, and try and pattern *Jules and Jim* after some of the small films made by MGM during the forties, like *Mrs. Parkington* [1944] and *The Green Years* [1946]— films whose only fault was being conventional but films which succeeded marvelously in creating the mood of a huge 800-page novel of many years passing, of much white hair arriving. You see, I didn't want to follow the fashion, even a fashion that has produced so many films I love. . . .

——Truffaut, interviewed for *Cahiers du cinéma*, Dec 62;
trans. *Film Quarterly*, Fall 63

Q. It's 3 years since you gave up criticism to become a filmmaker. Have you changed any of your ideas about the cinema?

A. At that time I was very conscious of the gulf between the cinema as I saw it and the cinema as practiced by directors. Now I know that any film is abstract and even experimental, whether, like *Psycho* [1960], it pretends to tell a story, or whether, like *Marienbad* [1962], it doesn't even pretend.

The question which really interests me now is this. Should one continue to pretend to be telling a story which is controlled and authoritative, weighted with the same meaning and interest for the filmmaker and for the spectator? Or ought one rather to admit that one is throwing on the market a kind of rough draft of one's ideal film, hoping that it will help one advance in the practice of this terribly difficult art? . . .

Q. Your own heroes are almost always outsiders, people on the fringes of society. Is this deliberate on your part? Do you feel, like Chabrol, that one can't show a workingman on the screen?

A. It's true that we're all more or less anarchists, of the right or the left, and that our characters, like ourselves, tend to be unresolved. But the French cinema has scruples which you won't find, for instance, in the American. Many French filmmakers, Becker probably more than anyone, don't like dealing with subjects they don't know well.

In fact I did once work in a factory, as a welder, and I remember it well enough to show workingmen honestly. But what point is there in filming people who are engaged 8 hours a day on work they don't enjoy? It's hypocritical to exalt their work, and just as hypocritical to encourage their resignation to it. . . . At that period of my life, I used to try to "escape" by mentally re-creating the 3 or 4 films I'd seen on the Sunday; and, believe me, nothing on earth would have dragged me to a film about factory workers. There are half a dozen Communist directors in France and about 15 left-wingers. You should ask them to make these films about working-class problems.

———Truffaut, interviewed for *Sight & Sound,* Winter 61/62

I think very much about an audience's reaction. For me the cinema is a show. The characters in *Jules et Jim* are perhaps antisocial. In my treatment I have tried, little by little, to make the audience understand them, perhaps even love them. First, in a very simple way, by the use of comic effects. Later, the comic shell breaks away and the romantic progression of the characters becomes much more important.

The thing that surprised me with *Les Quatre Cent Coups* was that I did not realize that the audience would be with the boy against the adults. If I did the film again, the boy would become less endearing and the parents would be made more sympathetic.

Jules et Jim is much more complicated in its relationships because sex plays a much bigger part. That is perhaps why the film has a greater appeal to women than to men.

In tackling sex in the cinema, the director must always keep in mind that as soon as sex comes to the surface the public in the cinema respond like a lot of twelve-year-olds. So we have to make the film as though it was done for children, with all sorts of tricks. In *Jules et Jim,* when the dialogue is becoming very intimate, I knew the danger was that the audience would laugh. I used a helicopter shot, coming up from the human characters to take in a large aerial view of nature. It worked. It prevented people from laughing at the dialogue.

———Truffaut, in *Films & Filming,* July 62

Q. Do you ever work out shots or scenes very carefully and very precisely beforehand, the way Hitchcock does?

A. The only time I ever really worked out anything in great detail like that was in *Fahrenheit 451* [1966]. But I don't work like that for my French films. Obviously the form of the film and the script are there beforehand, but I like to work things out as I go. Or, for instance, I like to spend a Sunday working on the script for the next week's shooting.

Q. Then how do you handle your actors? Do you allow them great freedom for portrayal and improvisation, or do you control their every move...?

A. The treatment varies with each actor. For example, Valentina Cortese in *Day for Night* [1973] did some improvisation, but there was none at all with Jean-Pierre Aumont. On the other hand, Jacqueline Bisset was the first actress I'd worked with that I hadn't met before. So in her case I kept her role [dialogue?] very vague because I had to find out the kinds of words she could use and what she could say correctly in French. . . .

I don't look at what I am shooting through the camera very much, however I do talk things over with the cameraman and discuss the lighting and the framing. But I would much rather keep my eye on the acting and the actors than deal with the camera. And I never cover myself when I shoot. I take it only from one angle . . . I believe that every shot has only ONE angle, ONE lens.

——Truffaut, interviewed for *Filmmakers Newsletter*, Dec 73

Dalton T R U M B O (1905–1976)
Born in Montrose, Colorado, in a working-class family. Film career began at 31 in story department at Warner Bros. A successful screenwriter until jailed with the "Hollywood 10." The first to outwit the subsequent blacklist. His novel, Johnny Got His Gun, *was published in 1939:*

Q. When you wrote the novel, did you hope to make a film of it?

A. Well, I'd always wanted to have a film made of it but I never thought it could be done. I had received some offers for it but I said, "No, I don't know how to make it and I don't think you do either. I like the book, it's a pretty good book, and I don't want a bad movie made out of it." In 1964 I went to Mexico—where I had spent a couple of years just after I got out of jail in 1951—and Gustavo Alatriste, a Mexican producer who had produced Luis Buñuel's *Simon of the Desert*, decided that he wanted to do *Johnny Got His Gun* and wired and asked if I would do the script if Buñuel would direct it. I went down and had 2 delightful weeks—long Mexican lunches with plenty of wine, and Luis who is an enchanting man—and I came back and finished the script about 8 months later. It took me that long because I received no money for it; the money was if, when and how, and was to be on a 7-year lease if it went through. But by the time I had finished the script something had happened to the financing and we could not do the film. So Luis went to Europe and I put the script away because I didn't think it likely that anyone would care to make it. Then a friend of mine who was story editor for Campbell, Silver and Cosby asked me to send the script for their consideration. And I said—it was about this time that I first got the idea—"No, I won't because I would want to direct it myself, I would want control over every aspect of it and nobody but a fool would give me that, so let's not burden either of us with this discussion." He showed them the letter and called back to say that they still wanted to see it. So I said, "Well, then, we'll do it very simply. I'll send the script but tell them that I don't want to discuss it. The answer is either yes or no based on my previous letter." The answer was yes. When they began to seek financing for it, they were rejected by every studio—we have a total of 17 rejection letters. The firm itself dissolved, but I maintained the relationship with producer Bruce Campbell and about February or March of last year he stumbled onto the money and we began to work in July.

——Trumbo, interviewed for *Film Society Review*, Oct 71

Florence TURNER
Born in New York, 1887. Joined Vitagraph in spring of 1907 after working in vaudeville.

Those were the wonderful days when J. Stuart Blackton, Albert Smith, one director, one scenic artist, one property man and myself comprised the Vitagraph stock company, and put our shoulders to the wheel and helped to put the move in movie. We had no cameraman in 1907—Mr. Smith "took" the scenes and Mr. Blackton the "stills." It was a great life!

——Turner, quoted in *Early American Cinema* (NY, 1970)

u

Liv ULLMANN
Born in Tokyo, 1938. Studied drama in England and Norway before moving to Sweden.

Bergman taught me how little you can do rather than how much. I can now use much smaller means to express what I want to say. . . .

To me, he was God. I admired him so much, and I was scared to death of him. I was only 25—too young—and he was 46. When he spoke, I blushed. I remember that he was worried the first week of shooting *Persona* [1967]. But he trusts the people he picks, and the moment you open up he will be there to help.

——Ullmann, interviewed for *Time*, 4 Dec 72

Everything I know about films I owe to [Ingmar Bergman]. He is not a Svengali, he doesn't mold you. He encourages you to develop your own ideas, your own fantasies, about the role you are playing. He has a great interest in women, and I think he would rather work with actresses than actors. He believes that women are more free and less inhibited, that there are no limits to what they dare show of themselves, of their emotions. A woman is more like a whore in films in that she will do anything that is necessary.

——Ullmann, interviewed for *The Times*, 7 March 73

Peter USTINOV
Born in London, 1921, to Russian parents.

I like working with [Sophia Loren] enormously. Of course I was very flattered in a way because the suggestion of the film [*Lady L*, 1965] came from her. She had an obligation with Metro-Goldwyn-Mayer and they owned the property and she read it and said she would like to do it on condition I wrote it and directed it and that's the kind of temptation you will understand is very difficult to resist.

Obviously it's tremendously exciting to be in at the beginning of something like Terence Stamp because even finding Terence Stamp for the role of Billy Budd was quite interesting because he came into the office which I was using and was so nervous he could hardly get a word out and the more he became convinced it was a hopeless hopeless case, that he would never be considered, the more he started stuttering and stammering, the more convinced I became that if one could control this, this was it and there came a day when we decided to take the risk. The Americans wanted a name, of course, but I think it paid off. I think that you couldn't cast *Billy Budd* [1962] with a known actor because nobody's going to believe in the purity of somebody we all know.

———Ustinov, interviewed at the National Film Theatre, 21 June 66

V

Joseph V A L E N T I N E [Giuseppe Valentino] (1900–1949)
Born in New York City.

The whole of an actual town used for a movie set! . . . Intimate scenes, both exteriors and interiors, photographed against authentic backgrounds which would put to shame the best art directors' attempt at art realism!

That is the experience I have just had during four weeks of location work in Northern California filming Alfred Hitchcock's *Shadow of a Doubt* [1942].

After viewing the rushes I'm convinced "Hitch" has really started something in pioneering this idea. Not only have we given our picture its background on a scale that couldn't satisfactorily be reproduced in studio-made construction; we've captured a note of realism which also can't be reproduced in a studio. . . .

But today we *can't* build these sets. With a wartime ceiling of $5,000 on new set construction for an entire picture, the building of large sets like these is definitely out for the duration. Yet we still need those sets; so we must go outside and shoot the real thing.

Our Santa Rosa location was chosen because it seemed so typical of the average American small city. . . .

From the technical viewpoint most of our day exteriors were of a comparatively routine nature . . . and most of our problems in these scenes were the ordinary ones of rigging scrims and placing reflectors or booster lights where they were needed.

In some of the scenes around the house we had selected to represent the home of our picture's family, however, we had some problems in contrast. In building a set of that nature we are accustomed to placing trees and the like largely for decorative value. But here they had been planted to provide shade—and they certainly provided it! The troubles we had in controlling the balance between the brightly sunlit areas and the deeply shaded ones. . . !

The most spectacular part of our work was naturally the making of the night exterior sequences. . . . We lit up an expanse of four city blocks for our night-effect long shots!

Most of the credit for this must certainly go to the high sensitivity of the Super-XX negative I used throughout the production. In emergencies like this, Super-XX lets a cameraman get the maximum effectiveness out of every light; in this instance, we successfully lit up an area which only a few years ago would have demanded 4 or 5 times as much illumination to produce an inferior result. . . .

All of our night scenes were filmed actually at night [and did not employ the day-for-night technique of using infrared film]—and we just got under the wire, finishing the last one scarcely a matter of hours before the [Pacific Coast's] dim-out became effective.

——Valentine, in *American Cinematographer*, Oct 42

Helen VAN DONGEN

. . .With every shot that appeared [for *The Land*, 1939–42], I hoped [Flaherty] would tell me why he shot it, how he wanted it used, what it belonged with. . . .

I was too inexperienced in Flaherty's method of working to make head or tail out of any possible connection between his remarks and his film. After 3 weeks, I was at an utter loss. We screened the same material over and over again, but he never came to the point at which he would outline his story.

Went out yesterday to location [for *Louisiana Story*, 1948]. Saw place where cypress swamps were filmed earlier, and alligators 1 and 2's nest. Was expecting to be dragged into Louisiana wilds. Instead to Avery Island, Colonel McIlhenny's home, branched off to tropical jungle—park with mown lawns and beautifully cultivated flowers and bushes. So the camera never lies? Well, then the artistry of director and cameraman can darned well change location from an appealing jungle back to a foreboding, weird and eerie swamp. The cypress swamp, which looks so expansive and monumental on the screen in the rushes, is in reality nothing but a little pool with a few cypress trees!

. . . Difficulty of keeping film authentic; sequences such as the catching of the alligator, or J.C. disturbing the alligator nest, which are staged and planned by us, could be shot according to a preconceived shooting-script covering the action from every angle, with long shots, medium shots and close-ups, in order to have sufficient cutting material. When trying to do so however, it turned out that the sequence when edited told you that a camera had been ever present. No matter how naturally and beautifully played, the ever-present camera ruins the authenticity of the scene. Films like *Louisiana Story* should be shot in such way as if the camera were accidentally present to record the action while it happened without the subject coverage from every angle or with more than two lenses. Obviously this makes the editing of such a sequence sometimes extremely difficult.

——Van Dongen, quoted in *The Innocent Eye* (London 1963)

Willard VAN DYKE
Born in Denver, Colorado, 1906. Began career as a photographer during the early 1930's; began in films in 1935 and in 1936 served as cameraman for Pare Lorentz on The River.

Pare Lorentz's influence on me was enormous. But this was because he gave me complete freedom to do what I wanted as a cameraman. He never talked filmmaking to me. Instead, he would recount stories that would tell me what his aims and goals were.

Working on *The River* gave me confidence as a young, beginning camera-man. . . .

During the war, at the Office of War Information, we tried to find a way of using captured German film material to make anti-Nazi films. We had a fine-grain of all Leni Riefenstahl's work, and we used to sit night after night screening this material, trying to discover how to turn it against the Nazis. But we never could. The reason was that it was all spectacle, and there was simply no way to make it unattractive. . . .

Q. Many of your films have very successful musical sequences—the lunch-break section in *The City* [1939], for example. Or the marvelous balletlike sequence with the mill workers in *Valley Town* [1940]. How was this unity of image and music created?

A. The sequence in *Valley Town* came about as a result of watching Aaron Copland working on the score for *The City*. Copland brought a piano into the editing room next to the Movieola. He'd run a sequence, then try out an idea for it. By running a sequence over and over, he would work out his musical idea in a most direct way. He didn't just create a general character of music. Notes and visual images played in a counterpoint that could have been achieved only through this method.

But music had a more important role in *Valley Town*. Irving Lerner, who edited the film, suggested that I use Marc Blitzstein for the score. Marc had written *The Cradle Will Rock*, which also dealt with unemployment in a steel town. So music became a part of the conception of the film. In one sequence a steelworker is walking home after looking for a job. I had planned to use a thought speech over this section. However, Marc suggested we try a kind of recitative, as in opera, that would lead into a song once we got inside the man's home. We worked closely together this way—the director, the editor, and the composer—conceiving sections musically the whole time. This was especially true with the handmill sequence you mentioned. It was shot as a ballet, edited as a ballet, and scored as a ballet.

——Van Dyke, interviewed for *Film Comment*, Spring 65

Agnes VARDA
Born in Brussels, 1928. First professional work in Paris, as photographer.

I was 25, and was working as a still photographer. I wrote my first film [based on Faulkner's *The Wild Palms*] just the way a person writes his first book. When I'd finished writing it, I thought to myself: "I'd like to shoot that script," and so some friends and I formed a cooperative to make it. I'd never really been to the cinema before that age. Scandalous, wasn't it? Maybe I'd seen *Snow White* and *Captains Courageous*, but nothing much more. It was Alain Resnais who persuaded me to go. When he was editing the film, he kept on saying: "H'm, this bit's like Visconti," "Mm, this piece reminds me of Antonioni," until I got so fed up with it all that I went along to the Cinémathèque to find out what he was talking about.

I can do many things at once. Of course, it's sometimes difficult, but I don't make that many films. When I'm shooting, the rest of the family goes off to our seaside house in Brittany—Jacques [Demy] and the little girl, Michel Legrand and his family. Jacques says that his best work is done there, and it is better for me to be alone when I'm shooting. The work is so tough that it would be impossible to have the distractions and worries of running a home, or even to have people around. For the rest of the time, I can organize things so that when I come home, I become a pleasant woman once more.

———Varda, interviewed for *The Sunday Times Magazine*, 17 Jan 65

I had written the whole script of *La Pointe courte*. It was finished, on paper. I thought I would never shoot it. I thought I would put it in a drawer and look at it 3 years later saying, "Yes, at that time I was thinking about making a movie." And then a friend came to me and said, "Why don't you do it?" I said, "With what? How?" They said, "It's easy, let's make it." The problem was to find money, to get a crew, and to find people able to help me do it. We were all very young and had very little experience. But we lived together in a rented house. Everybody had to stay there and eat there because we had no money to pay individual expenses. We had to organize ourselves as a collective. And then we shot.

From the point of view of production, it was really something revolutionary in 1954. I didn't even have the right to be a producer. We have a professional hierarchy in France in which it's necessary to pass through the ranks, do 5 apprenticeships before making a film. And the same for the technicians. I didn't ask for my card. (It's very funny after all, because I only got my card entitling me to be a director 13 years after my first film.) I didn't bother with laws or unions, or get official authorization. It was a way of eliminating the "taboo" of cinema, of the closed world of cinema and its hierarchies. That's how it became a real film. I was so sure that it was a one-time thing—I never thought of myself as a filmmaker—I went back to photography after that, making money since the film didn't make any money. But, years later, someone asked me if I wanted to make films for the tourist office and I thought yes, it was another way of making money, and maybe later I will make other films. That's how I did the shorts—*O Saisons, O Châteaux* [1957], *Du Côté de la côte* [1958], and then *L'Opéra mouffe* [1958]. Then the desire came to make other movies; then I became a "filmmaker."

It took me 7 years to make another feature, *Cléo from 5 to 7* [1961]— because I could not find the money, because I had no time to write scripts. I was taking stills, not because I was a woman, but because I was writing the kind of films that are difficult to set up financially. When I did *Cléo*, which is about a woman, I really had in mind to make a film about a woman facing a great fear, and that fear makes her think about herself. She discovers that she is a little doll, manipulated by men, a little girl who makes no decision, who sees herself only through other people's eyes. And in that hour and a half she starts to relate differently.

———Varda, interviewed for *Women & Film*, June 74

Dziga **VERTOV** [Denis Kaufman] (1896–1954)
Born in Bialystok. One of three brothers, all of whom were to have distinguished film careers.

We had a basement in the center of the city. It was dark and damp, with an earthen floor and holes that you stumbled into at every turn. Large hungry rats scuttled over our feet. Somewhere above was a single window below the surface of the street; underfoot, a stream of water from dripping pipes. You had to take care that your film never touched anything but the table, or it would get wet. This dampness prevented our reels of lovingly edited film from sticking together properly, rusted our scissors and our splicers. Don't lean back on that chair—film is hanging there, as it was all over the room. Before dawn —damp—cold—teeth chattering. I wrap Comrade Svilova in a *third* jacket. The last night of work so that the next two issues of *Kino-Pravda* will be ready on time.

—————Vertov, in *Sovietskoye Kino*, Nov–Dec 34

King V I D O R
Born in Galveston, Texas, 1895. Educated in Texas and Maryland.

In the silent days, the players were supposed to know the characters they were portraying. Sometimes they didn't even read the script, but there was a thing that went on, almost telepathic, between the director and the actor. Things developed in scenes while the camera was going. And we had music on the set—that was very helpful to get the mood. In *The Big Parade* [1924], when Gilbert encounters a German soldier in the shellhole, that was ad-libbed. I didn't have a big voice; I might say "More," "Now," "That's wonderful," "That's great" . . . I wouldn't talk all the time and I'd get silent as quickly as possible. It was hypnotism.

Gilbert never read the script of *The Big Parade*, and there were other actors of the period like that. They had faith and confidence in you. They knew you had a way of transferring emotion to them. I can't rationalize it. It's like a love affair; you just can't describe it. I actually remember moments when I didn't say a thing. I'd just have a quick thought and Gilbert would react to it.

—————Vidor, letter to Kevin Brownlow (1962) for *The Parade's Gone By* (NY, 1968)

[On *La Boheme*, 1926] Miss [Lillian] Gish had a definite conception of her own regarding the love scenes between Mimi and Rudolph, and she set about to convince Jack [Gilbert] and me of its value and effectiveness. She believed that the two lovers should never be shown in actual physical contact. She argued that, if we photographed their lips coming together in a kiss, a great amount of suppressed emotion would be dissipated. She was convinced that, if we avoided this moment, a surge of suppressed romance would be built up and serve to heighten the final impact of the tragedy when Mimi dies.

She suggested love scenes in which two lovers were always separated by space: Mimi in a window above, Rudolph in the street below. Another idea of hers was to have them kiss with the cold barrier of a windowpane between them. . . . Throughout the entire action Mimi and Rudolph never entered into physical embrace; each aggressive advance on Rudolph's part was intercepted and turned into meanings more ethereal and poetic.

—————Vidor, in *A Tree Is a Tree* (NY, 1954)

I shot probably half [*The Crowd*, 1928] on location in New York: we went all around the city with hidden cameras. . . .

Those larger-than-life-sized sets in *The Crowd* were the work of the recently retired Arnold Gillespie, who was then in charge of MGM's trick department. He did them in association with the art director, Cedric Gibbons. I was probably influenced by the Germans on that, by such silent films as E. A. Dupont's *Variety* [1925] and Fritz Lang's *Metropolis* [1925].

For the scene in which the camera seemed to ascend along the outside of a building and then enter it through a window, Arnold Gillespie and his staff had to construct a whole horizontal 30-foot-long miniature building and then have a bridge with the camera on it roll up outside it. Today, of course, you'd have a zoom lens and it would be nothing.

But in those days we had no zoom lenses or booms and had to let the camera down on a movable platform with cables. As it went forward on a track it had to be lowered, and we went right up into a close-up with this thing. Later, on location for *The Texas Ranger* in the 1930s, I remember we constructed a boom out of a telephone pole.

Although *Hallelujah!* [1929] was my first sound film, much of it, including all the traveling shots, was shot silent and the sound dubbed in later. That gave us all the freedom of a silent picture.

At that time sound equipment was immobile. . . . I was so anxious to do this film that I just went ahead and shot it silent as I'd done all my previous pictures. If we'd been using synchronized sound, all those elaborate traveling shots would have been impossible.

Postsynching *Hallelujah!* was a madhouse. They had no equipment for doing it—Movieolas or things of that kind. We had to run the thing in a projection room equipped with a buzzer which, when pressed, flashed a light which acted as a signal to the operator to put a grease-pencil mark on the film.

Of course, by the time you'd pressed the button and the light had flashed on he'd put the pencil mark 4 or 5 feet away from where you'd intended. It was maddening. We did a lot of close-ups back at the studio because of that. I think the 6 months we spent postsynching the picture hastened the sound-cutter's death.

The crime of the early days of sound was that they thought you had to do stage plays and photograph them "straight." This practically set movies back 20 years, I suppose. So, when faced with the challenge of bringing Elmer Rice's one-set play *Street Scene* [1931] to the screen, I realized that you could make a terribly dull thing out of it by using uninteresting camera angles.

I didn't want to spoil the stage play by going into interiors or moving away from the front of the house, nor did I want to photograph it deadpan: that was the challenge. I wanted to preserve the play's purity and still have what used to be called "action."

My solution was to do it by change of camera setups, by change of composition: the composition became the action. We had a street built on the Goldwyn lot and didn't leave it at all except for one scene inside a taxi. . . .

This was a pure experiment—I didn't know if it could be done successfully—but it worked, as I confirmed just recently on seeing *Street Scene* again.

My original conception of *Duel in the Sun* [1946] was of an intense, *High Noon* type of thing: all that bigness and blowup was added later by the producer, David O. Selznick . . . he added the prologue, narrated by Orson Welles, he added a big spectacular opening, he called in other directors to shoot additional sequences, he had at least 3 cameramen at different times throughout the making of the picture, and he kept constantly augmenting the cast. . . .

Josef von Sternberg's contribution to *Duel in the Sun* was as a sort of general assistant. He suggested lighting, interviewed and tested actors, looked for locations—anything that Selznick and I wanted him to do. He helped in any way he could. . . . He might, for example, have made suggestions concerning Jennifer Jones's clothes or her hairstyle—things like that. . . . It's been claimed he had a lot to do with the picture's color design. Perhaps he did preliminary tests before I came onto it, but afterwards he certainly had little to do with that aspect of it.

The reason for the 3 accredited cameramen—Harold Rosson, Lee Garmes, and Ray Rennahan—was because we had a strike in the middle of the film and had to stop work for something like 3 to 6 weeks. Rosson was our original cameraman, but when we resumed it was with Garmes because Rosson was probably on another film. All those flamboyant sunset effects were done by Rennahan, who was Technicolor's man.

Jennifer Jones's climactic ride into the desert involved shooting directly into the sun, an idea inspired by Orson Welles's *Citizen Kane,* which had spotlights shining right into the camera. The aim of that was to accentuate the heat: the heat on the rocks, the heat on the desert, and the heat of the atmosphere.

———Vidor, interviewed in *The Celluloid Muse* (Chicago, 1969)

When *The Big Parade* first opened in New York, it was 12,800 feet in length. In the editorial process, we had pared the action to the bone. Each one of the several thousand scenes had been subjected to the closest scrutiny, trimmed to start as late as possible and end the moment the climax was reached while still preserving its full value. Nevertheless, the 800 feet seemed to bother the distributing company. They informed us that it made the first show begin too early and the last show too late. They told us that if the New York commuters came out of the theater too late, they missed the train departures and sometimes were forced to spend the night in a hotel in the city. I hated to sacrifice another foot of the film for the sake of eastern commuters, but I began to fear that if I didn't eliminate the 800 feet, someone with a less sympathetic pair of scissors might do it for me.

By this time I was directing another film, but I volunteered to take the picture home with me, all 13 reels of it, and each night after dinner I'd see what kind of loving surgery I could perform. I set up a cutting table in my living room, complete with rewinds and strong frosted backlight. It occurred to me after several evenings of getting nowhere that if I could cut 3 frames from the beginning and end of each scene (6 frames at each film splice) the total might add up to 800 feet, since there were thousands of splices in the picture. It took several nights and a whole Sunday to do this job. At its completion I still had 165 feet to go. I went back and cut out one frame on each side of each patch and the combined total of the many little pieces of cinema film added up to exactly 800 feet.

Miss Gish was an artist who spared herself in no way. She threw herself wholeheartedly into everything she did, even dying. She wanted to know well in advance when we would film her death scene in *La Boheme*. She wanted to get in the mood and stay in it. This caused me some alarm. Perhaps as a precautionary measure, I decided I had better schedule it on the last day of shooting. She asked for 3 days' notice, and Jack Gilbert and I watched Lillian grow paler and paler, thinner and thinner.

When she arrived on the set that fateful day, we saw her sunken eyes, her hollow cheeks, and we noticed that her lips had curled outward and were parched with dryness. What on earth had she done to herself? I ventured to ask her about her lips and she said in syllables hardly audible that she had succeeded in removing all saliva from her mouth by not drinking any liquids for 3 days, and by keeping cotton pads between her teeth and gums even in her sleep.

Finally the scene came in which Rudolph carries the exhausted Mimi to her little bed and her bohemian friends gather around while Mimi breathes her last. I let the camera continue on her lifeless form and the tragic faces around her and decided to call "cut" only when Miss Gish would be forced to inhale after holding her breath to simulate death. But the familiar movement of the chest didn't come. She neither inhaled nor exhaled. I began to fear she had played her part too well, and I could see that the other members of the cast and crew had the same fears as I. . . .

John Gilbert bent close, and softly whispered her name. Her eyes slowly opened. She permitted herself her first deep breath since the scene had started: for the past days she had trained herself, somehow or other, to get along without visible breathing. She had to wet her lips before she could speak. By this time there was no one on the set whose eyes were dry.

My first color film was *Northwest Passage* [1940] based on the book by Kenneth Roberts. Most of the scenes were about a group of rugged fighting men called Rogers' Rangers. The script called for the soldiers to be dressed in uniforms of an indeterminate green that would help conceal the men from their enemies' view as they walked or crawled through the mottled growth of the forest. When the production tests were made, I was surprised to see that what seemed an inoffensive shade to the eye appeared on the screen as a brilliant kelly green. I consulted the Technicolor representative, pointing out the great change that had occurred in the costumes on the screen. He said that he was aware of it, but that the Technicolor process was similar to lithography; as for this particular green, it was one that Mr. Darryl Zanuck liked and had selected for one of his Twentieth Century-Fox productions. With some argument and persuasion, we succeeded in getting the Technicolor company to mix up a new batch of green dye. I realized that the whole dramatic intent of a scene could, through the use of color, be heightened, diminished, or completely destroyed.

As late as 1956, during the shooting of *War and Peace* in Italy, the studio was unable to provide background projection for making traveling shots. The reason given was color and large-screen VistaVision. We had to mount the rear section of a period coach on a wheeled platform which was also large enough for an 800-pound Technicolor camera, 4 stage lamps, sound boom and operator, director, chief photographer, and camera operator together with an electrician or two. It was a real Rube Goldberg contraption. The foul-up occurred when I learned that there were only 40 feet of track available on which to move the oversized perambulator. In a single run of the track, we could cover a mere 2 lines of dialogue. Then we had to tow the platform back to the starting point, change the camera angle somewhat, and make another take of the next 2 lines.

Through the windows could be seen the residents of Moscow fleeing the city before the arrival of Napoleon. Instead of a projected background scene that could have been taken by a second-unit cameraman on a previous day, it was necessary to employ 600 extras and have them do their stuff over and over because only small areas were visible between the actors and the curtained windows.

———Vidor, in *King Vidor on Film-Making* (NY, 1972)

In Arkansas, across the Mississippi River from Memphis, we had photographed the climax of *Hallelujah*. This was a relentless, evenly measured pursuit through an eerie swamp which culminated in the Negro evangelist choking to death the two-timer who had taken away his lady love. In Arkansas we had worked, of course, without benefit of recording equipment.

Now we were faced with the problem of supplying the sounds. To a motion-picture studio in 1929 this was a fresh and unexplored adventure. We found ourselves making big puddles of water and mud, tramping through them with a microphone while a sound truck recorded the effect.

Never one to treat a dramatic effect literally, the thought struck me—why not free the imagination and record this sequence impressionistically?

When someone stepped on a broken branch, we made it sound as if bones were breaking. As the pursued victim withdrew his foot from the stickiness of the mud, we made the vacuum sound strong enough to pull him down into hell. When a bird called, we made it sound like a hiss or a threat of impending doom, rather than a bird call.

———Vidor, in *Films & Filming*, May 55

Luchino V I S C O N T I [Luchino Visconti de Modrone] (1906–1976) *Born in Milan.*

... *Ossessione* [1942] is characteristic. It was banned by the Fascists out of hand. The person who passed it was Mussolini. He had it screened in his own house.

The cinema then was an arm of propaganda. The government was naturally interested in giving a false idea of what society was like. Or perhaps it would be more true to say that Italian films then didn't give one any idea of modern Italy at all: they were all fake historical pieces or sentimental comedies.

The censors didn't suppose that anything dangerously Italian would come of it. When it was finished and they realized that I'd transferred the story to a depressed part of their own country, and given it very Italian sentiments, they jumped to the fact that it was revolutionary and banned it. . . .

Professionals can't help being aware of the camera all the time, like fashion models who look at themselves in mirrors and shop windows. The men in *La terra trema* [1947] were quite inarticulate and they had no conscious idea of the society they were living in, but they came out all the time with lines that were marvellously expressive. In the Sicilian dialect, some of the language sounded like Sophocles.

The Ministry of War couldn't stand the idea that the truth might come out about a century-old battle. The military were beaten in 1866 because the regulars refused to enroll the volunteers. This is the whole story of the Risorgimento: the Piedmontese ruling class was always opposed to the popular movement because the monarchy would have been thrown out. In *Senso* [1954] as I wanted to make it this would have been very plain. So it was hacked to pieces.

———Visconti, interviewed for *The Observer*, 10 Sept 61

I'm very German. I like the German cultura, German music, German philosophia, and also the origin of the Visconti family is in Germany. So, *a la lontana*, I am a little German. I want to ask in this picture [*The Damned*, 1970] where lay the responsibility for the Nazis in Germany. The most grave responsibility was with the bourgeoisie and the industrialists, because if Hitler had not had their help, he would never have arrived to real power. Books say that the Krupps paid Hitler, so I don't invent. And I like in all my films to have a *cellule* of humanity, a family, I try to explain in the development of this family the parallel of what happens in all Germany and later in all the world. That is all I try to say.

———Visconti, interviewed for *The Guardian*, 4 June 70

Monica V I T T I [Maria Luisa Ceciarelli]
Born in Rome 1931. During '50s dubbed other actresses' voices.

I went to England because I wanted to do a light comedy and I thought *Modesty Blaise* was just right. But Losey did not agree with me. He looked upon it as a spectacle—a kind of pop film. He seemed to think there was something immoral about making people laugh. . . .

We were filming [*L'Avventura*, 1960] on the island of Panarea, but we had no producer and Michelangelo soon ran out of money.

We were there for weeks. The last few days all we had to eat were eggs and vino that the peasants gave us.

It was wonderful. We were alone and penniless. Nearly everyone had deserted us. It was one of the happiest experiences of my life.
———Vitti, interviewed for *The New York Times International Edition,*
24 March 67

Up until *Modesty Blaise* [1966], I had done every long film with [Antonioni]. But I am an actress and I think that artistically a change is necessary. Humor is an important part of life, it is like a lens, and I have always wanted to make people laugh. That is why I decided to play Modesty. *Che disastro....*

He is my life. For 7 years I work only with him, turning down all other offers. When I am filming I need to love, esteem and understand the people with whom I work.

With Michelangelo this is possible. With others, no.

But Michelangelo say to me, "Go, you must work for others too." So I say yes and I go, but I do not like.
———Vitti, interviewed for *The Daily Mail,* 17 May 67

Jon V O I G H T
Born in Yonkers, New York 1938. Received BFA, 1960, Catholic University. Worked off-Broadway before entering films.

... I need discipline. John Schlesinger and John Boorman were good for me because they gave me lots of room. And they also gave me lots of help. Because you need to know when you're off. I like to be criticized when I work but I don't like to be told what to do. But I like to be helped because I can't see myself, I can't see what I'm doing.

I'll give you a good example. There was a terrific scene in [*Midnight Cowboy,* 1969], the crux of the film, really, when I come back with some stuff. I've just had a good night with that girl that I picked up. I made some money as a stud. I come back with all this stuff—pills and soup and clothes. I come back and Dusty's sitting on the bed. He's sick. And I come in and I'm real happy. I'm on top of it. Now, the way the scene was written, it was, "See, I've got some stuff for you, got this thing for you, Ratso, goddam, we're gonna make it, man." Then Dusty says, "I ain't feeling good, Joe," and I say, "Oh yeah, what's the matter?" We played the scene a couple of times. It was so sentimental, something was wrong. We were acting it well but something was wrong.

John couldn't figure it out. He called up Waldo Salt, the screenwriter. Waldo was asleep, but he says, "Yes, I'll be down." He comes down to the studio in an hour; we've closed it; we've rehearsed it every kind of way. Waldo comes in. We go through the scene and he says, "You've got to remember that Joe is very selfish. He wants to leave Ratso." Bing! Here we go. So I changed a few lines. I said, "Well, then I'll say, 'I've got some stuff in there for you too.'" I pulled out this stuff—I've got some socks. "Look at them socks, see? Ratso, I got some stuff in there for you too, boy; you're gonna to be all right." But I'm thinking, "I'm getting out of here in a couple of days because man, I'm tough stuff." I find him sick and it makes me angry. And then I don't know what to do because the responsibility is on me. And then the scene—"I'm going to get you a doctor," it's a tough thing for Joe. Joe has not made the move to go back to Ratso to protect Ratso or to get him to Florida. Joe has made the move to leave Ratso. And that's the beginning of a dramatic section that finally winds up with his decision to go with Ratso.

What we didn't get to [on *Deliverance*, 1972] was completion, in a sense. It wasn't complete work but it was good work. I didn't feel I completed it but I did what I had to do under the circumstances well and [Boorman] did what he had to do well. The best thing in the movie is the scene with the guitar. He was in top form. He knew exactly what he wanted to do and went in and shot it like that. With a kid who didn't play the banjo and all this stuff. Shot it like that. No problems. Then he gets to the end of the script and he's worked so hard and he just gets impatient.

I'll give you an example. We're on this river. There's this dam up above and the river is dry. We turn the dam on, open 2 gates; the river becomes a river—a huge roaring river. Okay, that's where we're going to shoot the scene and we're going to get everything ready and he's going to have the water come in and there's a 70-foot waterfall about 15 feet from where we're working.

So John [Boorman] says, "Let's get this shot." And usually we try to test the river. It takes 4 minutes for the gates to open and it takes so many more minutes for the river to fill up and then get to full height. He's looking at the sun and he's saying, "Open it up to 4! Open the gates up to 4!" I'm saying, "John, 4 is a lot of gates. How do you know what 4 is today?" We hadn't tried the river that day and one could be the same as 4, depending on the rainfall and stuff. But John's yelling, "Let's get it on. Jon, let's go!" He gets the megaphone. This is the scene where we're floundering around and Louis has gotten his leg broken. So the water starts coming down. We're making a lot of noise—boy, we're in trouble here. Vilmos Zsigmond is down there and the crew is there and they have nets to catch us from going over the 70-foot waterfall. And I'm standing there watching this crazy guy and he's got this dopey hat on. He's wearing this hat and glasses and he's looking and the water's starting to come and he's yelling, "Okay, just about ready to shoot! Camera rolling! Sound!" and the water's coming up and up and up and finally it goes right over the camera and he says, "This is filmmaking!"

——Voight, a group interview at the American Film Institute, 11 April 73

W

Andrzej W A J D A
Born in Suwalki, Poland, 1926.

What [Zbigniew Cybulski] was looking for from the director was first of all what every actor wants—to be looked at with approval. But then he also wanted to have his own inventiveness fired and strengthened. It was he himself who invented the way the Party Secretary, Szczka, died in *Ashes and Diamonds* [1958]. There was nothing in the script to say that he fell into Maciek's arms.

It was also the director's task to protect Cybulski from himself. He was involved with a number of student theatres, experimental groups and the kind of theaters that are concerned with problems of the day, and in filming he sometimes incorporated certain gimmicks, mannerisms derived from this kind of burlesque. These had to be watched and smoothed out.

———Wajda, interviewed for *The Times*, 27 May 72

Joseph W A L K E R
Born in Denver, 1902. Entered film industry in 1914; from 1927 to 1952 (when he retired to do research) was the chief cameraman for Columbia Pictures and Frank Capra. Developed the telephoto lens and the zoom lens.

One side of me is very technically inclined. I loved motion pictures, the camera and all that. The big Biograph camera sold me on the technical side, and I loved the challenge. . . . But artistically I wanted to be like Stieglitz. I wanted to try and do what I saw in still pictures. I wanted to try to get those wonderful effects onto this little film, which was practically then like taking it up to the corner drugstore. The film was slow, it was crude, it had nothing but black-and-white as a rule except Biograph, who had a way of getting some nice grays in there, and that was the challenge. That's what I felt I could do. And I figured somehow as I had no control over the developing, no control over the size of the film, and no control over the emulsion, what's left? The lens, the light, and the composition. So those are the things that I'd strive for.

———Walker, interviewed for *Karl Struss* (Ann Arbor, 1976)

Eli WALLACH
Born in Brooklyn, 1915. Acting at the University of Texas and some summer stock, prepared Wallach for his 1945 Broadway debut in Skydrift.

A fine director like Huston (Huston is an actor too!) guides you. For example, in *The Misfits* [1961] I had a scene with Clark Gable where we were supposed to be drunk. We sat around a table, and I kept drinking and all that stuff. . . . We did it several times: didn't work. While they were setting up and changing the lights, Huston walked over and said, "You know the drunkest I've ever been?" and I said "No." He said "Yesterday" (there was a camel race in Virginia City, and he raced on a camel and won the race), "that was the drunkest I've ever been." I said, "I had no idea you were drunk." "Oh," he said, "it's the worst I've ever been." I said, "Nonsense, John. I was there at the race." He said, "So help me, that's the drunkest I've ever been in my life." The technicians said, "We're ready, Mr. Huston." He got up and walked away from the set and I realized he's telling me you can be so drunk that no one knows it, you see. That was direction by indirection. And it's the sweetest way to elicit a performance from someone.

———Wallach, in *Films & Filming*, May 64

Raoul WALSH
Born in New York City in 1892; soon after his birth the Walsh family moved to Texas, where he grew up and found his first work in the theater. In 1909 looked for work in New York theaters, and soon was employed in films, riding for the U.S. studio of Pathé, for Griffith at Biograph, then assisting and acting for him in The Birth of a Nation.

Q. When did you first assist Griffith?
A. When we first went to California, about 1910 or 1911. I'm a bit hazy on the dates. If I was making one- or two-reelers, then someone else would be the assistant. But if I was at liberty, then I'd help. Usually if he had any horse action, then I was the assistant. "Mr. Walsh, would you kindly get those horsemen up here," or "Get that Indian off that horse." I might say, "He's all right. He can ride. He's just drunk." It was my job to round up the cowboys, who didn't have telephones. Griffith would say, "Mr. Walsh, I need 15 cowboys tomorrow morning at Newhall," which is a good 25 miles from downtown Los Angeles. I'd have to go down to where the cowboys were sleeping and in saloons and such at 2 or 3 in the morning, and get them on their horses. We'd be up there in the morning when the old man got there.
Did you assist him on *Birth of a Nation?*
Yes, off and on. The battle scenes and different things. . . .
Do you think you learned much from Griffith?
Oh, yes. Oh, yes.

———Walsh, interviewed in *Sight & Sound*, Winter 72–73

D. W. Griffith had a stock company—4 or 5 of us, 3 or 4 girls—and one day he asked me if I would like to go to Mexico and film some battle scenes. I said I would, and he said, "Well, you're going to go and meet a very notorious bandit. You're going to meet Pancho Villa. And I may as well tell you this: we've had a very sad experience. We had Villa under contract through Mutual, and they signed Pancho Villa up for $500 a week. So I must tell you that Mutual sent a Mr. Doaks or somebody down to meet Pancho Villa with a check for $500 and we never heard anything more from him."

So I said to Mr. Griffith, "What am I going there for—to find Mr. Doaks?" And he said, "No, no, no. You're going to meet a Mr. So-and-So at the Del Norte Hotel in El Paso and they will have $500 in gold for you to give to this bandit. . . ."

By the way, before I went down, Griffith told me, "You know, we have no story to do of Villa's life, so while you are on the train you will probably think up some story. Either that or get shot." So I kept thinking about stories on the way down. I had nothing else to do. I kept about 8 possible stories in mind until I could see this bum and see how he would react. They led me in to Villa, and he was sitting there with his goddamn big hat on and he was loaded with bullets and guns and he had a big black moustache.

The interpreter started palavering. "Why did you come?" he said. "With the $500," I said, and I opened the bag and showed it to him. Ah, they were tickled to death. And they came over and looked down and saw the money. Ah, yes, gold!

So then this fellow says, "What do you want to do with my general?" I said, "I want to make a story of the general's life," and he told that to the general and then he said, "The general is interested. Tell me the general's life —he wants to hear it, too."

Well, a couple of guards are at the door and a guard is at the window, and I thought, "Hell, I'm never going to get out of here. Why did I come?" So I told him the general's life. . . .

Then this handsome young boy, with this terrible calamity that hit him just in the prime of life—I said he stood there before his mother and vowed to kill Federal after Federal until the whole army was wiped out. And I said that from then on the general had hatred, nothing but hatred, for the Federals. And he decided to collect an army, and he went from town to town to tell them what these Federals did to his family, what they did to the poor, what they did to this, what they did to that, and I said that finally he got a great following of people. And I said that they're here in Juarez right now, and here is the general who accomplished all this. And he got up and shook hands with me.

We actually made the picture. It was called *The Life of Villa*, and I played the young Villa myself.

——Walsh, quoted in *Yale Alumni Magazine*, June 72

Charles W A L T E R S
Born in Pasadena, California. Began on the stage in 1934 with Fanchon & Marco shows. As a dancer, performed on the stage, then moved into movies as a director of dance sequences.

Q. How did a dance director function in those days [1940s]?
    A. We were dance directors plain and simple; choreography, a much

grander term, was only for ballet. Working in movies, particularly after the excitement of Broadway, seemed so mechanical. You simply took a number and blocked it out with dancers in a rehearsal hall. Then you'd try and get someone, preferably the film's director, to come and look at it. But by the time he was through shooting, you'd hardly recognize anything. You see, he had to change it to fit the camera, had to change theatrical dance style to play filmically.

Q. Weren't you there when it came to filming the number?

A. Not always—sometimes the director didn't want you around. And then if I was, I'd be over on the side somewhere—nowhere near the camera. "Get the kids up, Chuck," they'd yell. "Get 'em on." It was all somehow slapped together. . . .

. . . Gene Kelly was to have starred, and Vincente Minnelli was to have directed *Easter Parade* [1948]. Judy Garland was already set—and Bob Alton had been signed for the dances. The reason why Vince backed out was that he and Judy were going to the same psychiatrist who advised them against making the picture in that they shouldn't be together both day and night! So Vince went out and I came in. Then, while we were in rehearsal, Kelly broke his ankle playing football in his back garden. Arthur persuaded Fred Astaire to come out of retirement to do the picture. But if you look very closely, you'll see that the numbers don't really fit Fred. . . .

. . . I said, "Let's not tease the audience. Let's open the picture [*Torch Song* (1954), Joan Crawford's first musical in 25 years] with a number. Let's get a dancing Joan Crawford right out front." There's a marvelous conceit of mine in that picture. The script called for a party scene, and I thought "What sort of party would Joan Crawford give?" Then it came to me—all men, with nary another woman in sight! When you make a Crawford picture you've got to go all the way. She's the picture and she dominates. I remember stealing ideas from her personal life to fit the character in the picture. For instance, we had a bedroom scene where she draws the curtains—first the drapes, then the underdrapes, then the blackout material. Three layers of curtain in a bedroom! Well, that idea came from Joan's own room. That's the way she lives—like someone out of her own movies!

——Walters, interviewed for *Films & Filming*, Aug 70

Henry B. W A L T H A L L (1878?–1936)

As I sat there [at Biograph, waiting to deliver a message to James Kirkwood], Mr. Griffith came up to me and asked me whether I would like to try a picture with him. I told him I didn't think I could do it. "Just rehearse a scene for me," he urged, and before I knew exactly what happened I was playing an honest workingman who climbed out of a ditch when his little daughter—Mary Pickford[?]—brought him his dinner pail, and at her urging shared his lunch with a poor tramp [*A Convict's Sacrifice*, 1909]. As I left the studio, I was handed a five-dollar bill. Such reckless munificence made up my mind!

——Walthall, interviewed for *Motion Picture Classic*, Nov 1925

Walter WANGER [Feuchtwanger?] (1894–1968)
Born in San Francisco.

I think the first picture we made on Long Island was *Applause* [1930]. . . .
I brought Mamoulian from the Theater Guild. Our problem was that we knew
nothing about dubbing. We had this terrible problem of how to handle sound.
Mamoulian wanted to have the noise of a subway train pulling out of a station
while a girl is waving to a sailor on his way to enlist. I tied up the New York
subways for a whole day getting one shot. Nobody had ever heard of dubbing.
A man named Pomeroy was our sound expert. At that time, Western Electric
sent its technicians to us. They wanted to control all the cycles, to have everything perfect. They built a stage about the size of an average room and
wouldn't let us use the big stage. We had to work on their size stage, the
walls were thick, and there was no air conditioning. The stars would go in
with their makeup, which would be melted by the time the technicians could
shoot. Everyone was dying of the heat. You couldn't move the camera. We
were bullied like this for months. One day we said, "The hell with them,"
and threw them out. We just hung monk's cloth around the studio and shot
as we normally would shoot. Since then, we've done things in the way of
soundproofing, but nothing like what those technicians wanted.
——Wanger, interviewed for *The Real Tinsel* (NY, 1970)

David WARNER
Born 1941. First film experience in Tom Jones *(1963)*.

I'm not a perfectionist. I don't expect instant success any more than I anticipate total failure. Karel Reisz is a totally dedicated director, and if he believes
in the subject, then I'll certainly go along with him. Jack Gold, who made *The
Bofors Gun* [1968], wasn't looking for instant success, and the fact that the
film never got a proper release doesn't negate the value or integrity of the
enterprise.
    Who wants to go on an ego trip? Struggles for power are very boring and
have nothing to do with self-expression. I did a movie recently with Sam
Peckinpah [*The Ballad of Cable Hogue*, 1970] and although a lot of people
said it was one of the best Westerns for some time, that doesn't mean to say
that John Wayne is going to ask him to direct his next movie. . . .
——Warner, interviewed for the *Radio Times*, 30 Sept 71

H. B. WARNER (1876–1958)

. . . Mr. Warner thus describes his conversation with J. L. Warner, the vice-
president of Warner Brothers:
    "Why do you want me to play 'heavy' roles?"
    "Because you don't look like a heavy."
    And when I thought that over, I decided it was a good reason.
    If all villains looked the part, as they once did on the stage, there could
be little successful villainy. There would be no successful confidence men.
The real-life villain is often enough a peculiarly likable fellow, popular, genteel,

capable. I think sometimes a rascal is more interesting than a respectable citizen, often has more attractive qualities, often is a good fellow.

I'm interested in this new type of stage and screen villains. When my father played on the English stage and I was with him, there was never any doubt in the audience's mind as to which actor was the villain. We had regulation villain music. His entrance was always accompanied with minor chords; he wore certain distinguishing clothes. It seemed to be necessary to give him the mark of Cain before his first lines were spoken.

Of course, this is not a true nor lifelike characterization. Even a born villain has redeeming qualities as well as attractive angles.

———Warner, interviewed for *Screenland,* Aug 1929

Jack WARNER

The surviving brother of Warner Brothers was born in London, Ontario, 1892.

I first saw [Errol Flynn] one day in our London Studios, doing a bit in some film. I didn't know if the guy could act, but he was handsomer than hell and radiated charm. So I hired him, on impulse, for $150 a week. Back here in Hollywood he hung around for months doing nothing . . . we tested him for *Captain Blood* [1935]. I'd signed Robert Donat to the part, but we had a $20,000 misunderstanding about payment, and he turned it down. Good thing, too, because as soon as I saw Flynn's tests, I knew he had it. We gave him $300 for the part, and it made him a star.

When he was making *Montana* [1950], one of his last pictures for us, he got so crocked during the final scene he insisted on playing it on his back and he refused to kiss Alexis Smith. He left our lot soon after—without any farewell parties. We brought him back years later to play John Barrymore in *Too Much, Too Soon* [1958], but the experience was terrible. He was hung over every day. I couldn't bear to watch him struggle through take after take. He was one of the most charming and most tragic men I ever knew.

———Warner, interviewed for *The Canadian* (*Toronto Star*) 28 July 73

Peter WATKINS

Born in Norbiton, Surrey, 1935; trained in a London advertising film agency, from where he was employed by BBC. His first success and his first battle with BBC was The Battle of Culloden (*1964*), *an effective reconstruction of the final Scottish defeat of 1746.*

Q. Do you anticipate that *Punishment Park* [1971] will be as "effective" as your extremely-well-received first film, *The Battle of Culloden?* Based on pragmatic results so far—the initial audience and critical reaction—it looks as though it would not.

A. I think what you're talking about is what I would refer to as "populist" effect; I think it is relatively easy to say that it is effective because it is *comfortably* effective. I'm not negating the film, because I think it does work in certain areas, but it does not in my opinion even begin to measure up to the task that *Punishment Park* undertakes, which is the first stage of the philosophy of a self-examination on a very bleak level. *Culloden,* by contrast, can be responded to on the level of armchair, white-liberal discomfort at a historical event. It was not intended to be taken on this level, but I know that a lot of people accept it this way; that, I think, is the reason for its popularity. People can say, "*Culloden,* oh yes, that's a fantastic film, look what they did in those times, isn't war bad!" But although the film does affect us all—and I think all of us can see ourselves in the faces of those people at that time—I think there is a mental loophole so that you can also say that you don't. It just sits at that edge of the definition where a white middle-class liberal—and in fact a broader area even than that—can sort of indulge in the cathartic exercise of looking at something, getting a kick out of it, washing his guilt off, and then getting on with the dishes afterwards. I think that *Culloden—now—*fulfills that role. *Punishment Park* is light-years ahead of that, it does not play to that role. *Culloden* is mellow, you see, while *Punishment Park* is raw.

———Watkins, interviewed for *Film Society Review* (Mar-Apr-May 72)

I really think that a large proportion of the realism is due to the fact that I try to make my films provide a common experience for the people in them. Both *Culloden* and *The War Game* are films made in unusually adverse conditions. For me, they are practically pure conditions, as I think this is what film making is about. When you do a film like *Culloden* or *The War Game,* people have literally to stand in the gutters, in the howling wind for hours on end, fed probably on beans and a hamburger.

In *Culloden,* people were standing in fairly good reproduction Highland costume, which meant a plaid, probably a pair of jockey shorts underneath, and something on their feet—and that was it. They then walked for the best part of 2 weeks in the biting wind, in the rain, over moors more than a foot deep in water. And something built up between them. A similar kind of thing happened in *The War Game.* And all this is done out of enthusiasm. The people aren't paid, or paid only token amounts. . . .

You cannot just pull a man in from a job, and say, "Okay, fellow, I want you to suddenly become involved in a nuclear war, and I want you to give me a very stark realism which has to come smacking across as if you were actually caught in those circumstances." That doesn't just happen in 5 minutes. You have to get to know the chap, you have to pull him into the communal thing of making films. . . .

I must emphasize that there's no pat answer to this; it's part of a collective experience. It may have come from something generated for them over a couple of meetings or the collective thing of 2 or 3 weeks filming. What matters is getting people involved in a human experience or emotion, and letting it develop and flower in the particular way you need. I have also found that using nonprofessionals in this sort of film is usually a little better, because professionals often bring in a tremendous art and craft and technique which spoils the naturalism. But it's a difficult problem. There are no rules.

———Watkins, interviewed for *The New Documentary in Action*
(Berkeley, 1971)

James Sibley WATSON, Jr.

We decided to work first of all on scenery. *The Fall of the House of Usher* [1928] seemed to us to be a suitable story because its intense mood and atmosphere depended more upon background than upon good character drawing.

We first constructed a 30-foot mansion out of painted wallboard. This, of course, proved to be worthless, but it furnished us with one scene and some experience. After that we stopped painting wallboard and tinted the surfaces with light only. To make these surfaces more interesting, we break them up with various-shaped prisms. When we want a flight of stairs or a landscape, we introduce it by double exposure.

Films must have movement, of course. For movement we have the actors walk about, the camera moving on a rubber-tired truck and the scenery also in movement. This all requires expert timing and we are getting better at it with practice.

Sometimes we resort to double printing, but only when absolutely necessary. With a Duplex printer this is no joke. We do our own finishing—and our film looks it. The Standard Bell and Howell is one of the few cameras which will take backwards and still register perfectly. We are fortunate in having one available. As we are limited in our light power, we use a 43mm F.1.5 Ernemann lens for most long shots. We use arcs and Kirby lights, but not many at a time because of lack of juice. On account of the Kirby lights we use panchromatic film. . . .

———Watson, quoted in *Photoplay*, May 1928; repr. in
Spellbound in Darkness

Harry WATT
Born in Edinburgh, 1906; educated in Edinburgh. Joined the Empire Marketing Board's Film Unit in 1931.

After the basking-shark sequence [for *Man of Aran*, 1934] was finished . . . I began to get more and more restive. It was partly the dreary job I had so often to do. This was in the lab with John Taylor. When the thousands of feet of film from Flaherty's indiscriminate shooting came in, we two youngsters often had to work day and night in the smelly cold uncomfortable tin shed. This was boring enough, but it wasn't helped by the fact that often we knew that the stuff we were working on was repetitive or irrelevant. Without a tight script, there is always overshooting and waste on a film. This led me to my main discontent; I felt I was learning nothing. . . .

But what [Flaherty] was doing on *Aran* was not, again to me, documentary. It was a romanticized pictorial record of what may have been the island's way of life about 100 years back. That was all right, but when I realized that it was going to be presented to the world as the truth of that present day, and when I saw that the real life of the islanders was just as exciting and dramatic in a different, but much more human way, I decided to get out.

[Wright and Grierson] told me that they had decided to make a film [*Night Mail*, 1936] about a special mail train that ran nightly from London to Scotland, and that they wanted me to direct it. I was delighted and agreed at once, although, in point of fact, from the way we worked, it was an order. They told me something about the subject and showed me a rough outline that had been prepared. I was to go out and write a full script. . . .

An unexpected recruit joined us at the last moment. It was W. H. Auden, the poet. With our growing prestige and publicity, a number of the intellectuals of the time began to want to know more about this new art-form, and Grierson had quite rightly told Auden that he'd better start by working on a production. . . .

When I saw the credits of *Night Mail*, I was shocked. The main credit was "Produced by Basil Wright and Harry Watt." But I hadn't produced it, I'd directed it! I was by now determined to be a film director, and a good one, and I wanted this stated up on the screen for this film. Wright was my senior—he already had *Song of Ceylon* [1943] under his belt—and deserved the larger credit. But, even if it was in letters half the size, I wanted "Directed by Harry Watt."

I learned a great deal shooting *The Saving of Bill Blewett* [1936], because our only real professional, Cavalcanti, moved in and helped me when I started to get into a mess. From him I found that filming a story was quite different from our usual general sort of atmospheric shooting. Your audience is interested in your principal artists only and, through them, follows the story. When I started shooting, I would, for instance, have long scenes with my actors mingling with a crowd of others, all the same size on the screen. I imagined that the viewers would pick out our characters easily enough. But this is not so. If they have to search the crowd for the principals, there is an immediate impatience, and you lose the concentration that you must have to hold an audience. . . .

I also learned from Cavalcanti the gentle art of faking, because, of course, 90 percent of cinema is faked, in some way or other. When the sun moved off a scene, as it always seems to do at the crucial moment, he pointed out that a white fisherman's cottage round the corner, in full sun, exactly matched the one I was filming against, and all I had to do was move my actors 30 yards, place them in the same juxtaposition they were in before the shadows came, and carry on.

——Watt, in *Don't Look at the Camera* (London, 1974)

North Sea [1938] was, as always, based on fact, but numerous storm episodes and dramas were tabloided into the one story.

It was cast in the Labour Exchange in Aberdeen. We hired a derelict trawler and the cast worked the ship while acting in the film. We even fished and sold the catch towards the film costs.

We searched for bad weather and eventually weighed our ship down by the bows to get exciting effects.

The interiors were shot in our tiny Blackheath studio. It was so small that we couldn't move the camera, so we built the set on a saucer-shaped rocker and moved it around the camera.

One great advantage in casting a film like *Nine Men* [1943] is to have worked very closely on the script and dialogue. During all this you are creating the characters and personalities, and by the time you have finished you have a perfect mind picture of exactly what your character is like. You then go ahead and find the nearest human approximation to your imaginary figure. If you can get one that fits almost exactly, then you've won half the battle of getting the character on the screen. Your mind-man has walked, talked, and reacted to situations while you've been creating him. Just get your real character to behave in almost the same way, and you've got your script coming to life.

———Watt, for *Documentary Newsletter,* Feb 43

John W A Y N E [Marion Michael Morrison]
Born in Winterset, Iowa, 1907; entered films in 1931 in The Big Trail.

. . . Like most young actors, I did want to play a variety of roles. I remember walking down the street one day mumbling to myself about the way my movie career was going, when suddenly I bumped into Will Rogers. "What's the matter, Duke?" he asked, and I said things weren't going so well. "You working?" he asked, and I said "Yep." "Keep working, Duke," he said and smiled and walked on.

Once I was working in a movie with Harry Carey and his wife Olive, and I was complaining about being typed. "Duke," Ollie said, "look at Harry over there—would you like to see Harry Carey play any other way?" "Of course not," I said. "Well," Ollie said, "the American public doesn't want to see *you* any other way, either. So wake up, Duke! Be what they want you to be."

———Wayne, interviewed for *The New York Times,* 30 Dec 73

Roy W E B B
Born in New York City in 1888. Music training at Columbia University. Began work on Hollywood scores in 1929.

Max Steiner and I were friends for over 40 years; no one really escaped his influence in those early days, certainly not I. Many familiar workaday techniques were formulated by him and films such as *The Informer* [1935] and *King Kong* [1933] were signposts for all of us. We both of us had backgrounds in operetta and musical comedy, but because of the thoroughness of our original training, we found we were able to write dramatic "symphonic" music of the tune required, although there was plenty of scope for the lighter side as well. . . .

There was a constant stream of work coming in—in 1945 I took on a total of 12 films, several of them big jobs, and in 1939 I clocked up 25! Music had to be written at breakneck speed—I remember doing *Sinbad* [1958], which had over half an hour of music, much of it very fully scored, in a fortnight; and then after the first preview there would always be alterations to be made. I rarely had time to do all my own orchestrating, but I'd made very detailed sketches and was often complimented by my arrangers for making their job so easy. Men like Gil Grau and Maurice de Packh worked many times for me and got to know my style of doing things which, again, made the process that much less hectic.

When I had time, I would do my own scoring, of course, or else have my sketch so complete that parts could be made directly from it. At the sessions I very often shared the conducting with the musical director, Constantin Bakaleinikoff, but preferred to do it myself whenever there was anything I felt particularly strongly about.

——Webb, interviewed for *Crescendo*, March 73

Paul W E G E N E R   (1874–1948)
Born in Bischdorf, Germany.

... The possibility of a continuous change of focus for the spectator, the innumerable tricks through split-screen, mirroring etc. of the image, in short: the technique of the film must become important for the choice of the content. After some unsuccessful films about which I prefer not to speak arose my idea of the *Golem,* this strange mythical clay figure of the Prague Ghetto legends and the Rabbi Löw. With this figure I entered even more the field of pure film features in which everything is centered on the image, on a merging of an imaginary world of past centuries with contemporary life. The real predetermination of the film to seek effects only through photographic technique became more and more evident to me. Rhythm and tempo, light and dark, play a role in the film as well as in the music. As an ultimate goal I imagine some kind of kinetic lyricism in which one renounces totally any factual image.
——Wegener, *Sein Leben und seine Rollen* (Hamburg, 1954)

[George] Orson W E L L E S
Born in Kenosha, Wisconsin, 1915.

Q. Is it true that when *Citizen Kane* [1941] was being made, people actually tried to stop it being made; and is it true that Randolph Hearst the newspaper tycoon took it as being an attack on himself and tried to stop it when it was made from being shown?

A. To the first part of your question, there was indeed a very definite effort to stop the film during shooting by those elements in the studio who were attempting to seize power because in those days studio politics—particularly RKO and indeed many of the big studios in Hollywood—were very much like Central American republics and there were revolutions and counter-revolutions and every sort of palace intrigue and there was a big effort to overthrow the then head of the studio, who was taken to be out of his mind because he had given me this contract ... and stopping me or proving my incompetence would have won their case so it wasn't malice toward me—it was a cold-blooded political maneuver—having nothing to do with Mr. Hearst. That came later ... he had many hatchet men, editors and representatives of this great network of newspapers ... and to get in good with the Chief there was a good deal of very strong pressure including an effort to frame me, on a criminal charge, which a policeman was good enough to tell me about . . . but Mr. Hearst must be absolved.

Q. . . . Did you mean it as a social document or as a story?

A. . . . I must admit that it was intended, consciously, as a sort of social document—as an attack on the acquisitive society and indeed on acquisition in general, but I didn't think that up and then try to find a story to match the idea. . . .

. . . My contract was extraordinary in the control it gave me over my own material . . . according to the terms of my contract the rushes couldn't be seen by anyone, and indeed the film couldn't be seen until it was ready for release.

. . . In my case I didn't want money, I wanted authority, so I asked the impossible, hoping to be left alone and at the end of a year's negotiations I got it . . . my love for films began only when we started work.

I thought you could do anything with a camera, you know, that the eye could do and the imagination could do and if you came up from the bottom in the film business you're taught all the things that the cameraman doesn't want to attempt for fear he will be criticized for having failed. And in this case I had a cameraman who didn't care if he was criticized if he failed, and I didn't know there were things you couldn't do, so anything I could think up in my dreams I attempted to photograph.

Q. [One thing about *Kane*] which I don't think has been digested at all, is the notion of making a film with a team of actors who've been brought from one theater.

A. . . . Except the second girl and the wife . . . nobody had ever been in front of a camera before in the entire picture . . . that gives a kind of style, automatic style, to anything, just as a theater in which players live and work together for a certain length of time begins to make its effect . . . nobody else will make that sort of picture under those ideal circumstances until another man will give a studio and its facilities to an artist to make the film he wants to make. It sounds terribly simple but it literally never happens. . . . I've regretted early successes in many fields, but I don't regret that in *Kane* because it was the only chance I ever had of that kind.

Q. What was your father?

A. He retired!—early in his life, having been an automobile manufacturer as in *The Magnificent Ambersons* . . . he was also a playboy, *bon viveur*, he was a great friend of Mr. Hearst's—yes, and of Booth Tarkington who wrote the novel on which *The Magnificent Ambersons* [1942] was based. So there's a very close connection in both films to my father.

. . . *Ambersons* was a very happy experience for me because it's the only film I have ever made in which I didn't have to appear—it was a joy not to have to stand in front of a camera. . . .

I regard the whole bag of tricks of the cinema as being so petty and so simple and so uninteresting essentially—it's what a film says and its real, its real effect, rather than a question of cinematic style and plastic shrinery. . . .

——Welles, interviewed for "Monitor," BBC-TV, shown 13 Mar 60

Falstaff [1965] should be very plain on the visual level because above all it is a very real human story, very comprehensible and very adaptable to modern tragedy. And nothing should come between the story and the dialogue. The visual part of this story should exist as a background, as something secondary. Everything of importance in the film should be found on the faces. . . . I imagine that it will be "the" film of my life in terms of close-ups of all types, although I consider few theories as given and am for remaining very free. I am resolutely against close-ups, but I am convinced that this story requires them.

Q. Why this objection to close-ups?

A. I find it marvelous that the public may choose, with its eyes, what it wants to see of a shot. I don't like to force it, and the use of the close-up amounts to forcing it: you can see nothing else. In *Kane*, for example, you must have seen that there were very few close-ups, hardly any. There are perhaps 6 in the whole film. But a story like *Falstaff* demands them, because the moment we step back and separate ourselves from the faces, we see the people in the period costumes and many actors in the foreground. The closer we are to the face the more universal it becomes; *Falstaff* is a somber comedy, the story of the betrayal of friendship. . . .

I could never have done all that I did in *Touch of Evil* [1957] elsewhere. And it is not only a question of technique; it essentially concerns the human competence of the men with whom I worked. All this stems from the economic security they enjoy, from the fact that they are well paid, from the fact that they do not think of themselves as belonging to another class. . . .

[Herman Mankiewicz] wrote several important scenes [of *Kane*] . . . I was very lucky to work with Mankiewicz: everything concerning Rosebud belongs to him. I had . . . the good fortune to have Gregg Toland, who is the best director of photography that ever existed. . . . I could never have made *Citizen Kane* with actors who were old hands at cinema, because they would have said right off, "Just what do you think you're doing?" My being a newcomer would have put them on guard and, with the same blow, would have made a mess of the film. It was possible because I had my own family, so to speak.

Q. How did you arrive at *Citizen Kane*'s cinematic innovations?

A. I owe it to my ignorance. If this word seems inadequate to you, replace it with innocence. I said to myself, "This is what the camera should be really capable of doing, in a normal fashion." When we were on the point of shooting the first sequence, I said, "Let's do that!" Gregg Toland answered that it was impossible. I came back with, "We can always try; we'll soon see. Why not?" We had to have special lenses made because at that time there weren't any like those that exist today.

——Welles, interviewed for *Cahiers du cinéma;* trans. by Rose Kaplin for *Cahiers du Cinéma in English*, No. 5, 1966

William W E L L M A N (1896–1975)
Born near Boston, Massachusetts. Entered films when he returned to America from the Lafayette Flying Corps, an experience on which he based his best known films.

Camera movement I loved—and then I got awfully sick of it. I did the first big boom shot in *Wings* [1927], when the camera moved across the tables in the big French café set. Then everybody got on a boom, and both me and

Jack Ford got right off. We both agreed we'd never use the thing again. There's too much movement. It makes some people dizzy—it really does, and they become more conscious of the camera movement than they are of what the hell you're photographing. I don't know what made me begin to move the camera around. I'd seen fights, and wanted to get closer to them, so I'd run forward. Then I thought I'd do that with a camera. But what I loved most was composition. I used to get some wonderful odd angles, but then everybody started odd angles . . . so the idea was destroyed. Then I realized that the best thing was to make the picture the simplest way you could; if you wanted movement, or anything like that, use it where it really meant something, where it would help the picture. I used that theory completely in the last pictures I made.

———Wellman, interviewed (1964) for *The Parade's Gone By* (NY, 1968)

At the time we were making *Public Enemy* [1932], I was married to a beautiful blond aviatrix. She was really something to look at, but we couldn't get along. At breakfast that morning we had just had a row and weren't speaking to each other. I looked at the half-grapefruit on my plate, and I felt this overpowering desire to shove it into the lady's kisser. But I didn't have the nerve to do it.

Later that day I was preparing to shoot a scene in which Cagney, by sheer coincidence, was supposed to throw a grapefruit—THROW, not shove—across the room at Mae Clarke during an argument.

On the spur of the moment I changed the script and made them sit at the table, and gave Cagney new instructions. And when he bashed that messy thing up against Mae Clarke's face, so-help-me he was representing ME in the morning's argument with my own wife. I was getting back at her in my own way.

———Wellman, interviewed for *The Toronto Star*, 1975

Later on when I worked for [Zanuck] again, I got him to let me make *The Ox-Bow Incident* [1943]. I had bought the property from Harold Hurley, a producer at Paramount Studios, after he had gotten into some sort of a beef with the big boys and was relieved of his job. Things apparently had collapsed all around him, and I offered him 500 bucks more than he had paid for the book. This he gladly accepted, and then I went to all the producers for whom I had worked and got turned down. Zanuck was the only one with guts to do an out-of-the-ordinary story for the prestige rather than the dough.

Zanuck was in the army during the war, and this was the time of *The Ox-Bow Incident*. He was stationed in London, and the studio head was Bill Goetz. The production head, Bill Koenig, and Lew Schrieber did the dirty work.

I had the green light on *The Ox-Bow* and was working hard and fast to get it rolling before some of the principals might be called into service. The budget had been completed, and the estimated cost determined. That was it. When the unholy three heard the amount, they decided that it was a bad deal at the time and so prepared a cable to Zanuck, informing him in no uncertain terms of their opinions on the project. All emphatic nos. Goetz, being a fair and decent executive and an unusual one, called me in to his office and let me read the verdict and asked me if I wished to add my point of view. I thanked him and said I did, and I wrote, "This is to remind you of our hand-shake; regards, Bill Wellman." That's all. Next day they got word back. "Let Wellman go ahead." It was all just that simple.

Kind of nice, huh? When the picture was first released in this country, it fell flat on its face. . . .

Ring of Fear [1954] had already been completed. It was not good, so Duke [Wayne] and his then-partner, Bob Fellows, asked me to help them out and do a little doctoring on it. I had made enough for that year, so I consented, provided I didn't get paid and didn't get credit. That was agreeable to all, so I got me a couple of writers and went to work. . . .

[*Track of the Cat,* 1954] was a very intimate story with but a handful of characters. Practically the whole story took place in or around a ranch house, in the winter with snow on the ground.

This was it. The ranch house was painted off-white, the snow was white, the cattle and horses black and white or a combination of the two. The big pine trees I shot from the shady side so they photographed black. The characters were all clothed in black and white. The only splash of color was the red mackinaw that Mitchum wore and a little flimsy yellow silk scarf that Diana Lynn wore. Bill Clothier, than whom there is no better, was my cameraman. He shared my enthusiasm, and the result photographically was fantastic. Never have I seen such beauty, a naked kind of beauty. Bill and I saw the first print back from the lab. We sat there together, drooling. We had it at last. It was a flower, a portrait, a vision, a dream come true—it was a flop artistically, financially, and Wellmanly.

——Wellman, in *A Short Time for Insanity* (NY, 1974)

Lina W E R T M Ü G L L E R [Arcangela Wertmüller von Elgg]
Born in Rome in 1930. Beginning in 1952, worked in the theater as a writer and assistant director. Her film career started in 1963 when she served as assistant director to Fellini on 8½.

Q. Did you have trouble finding a producer willing to take on your first film, *The Lizards* [1963]?

A. Terrible problems. When I first proposed doing it everyone felt it was too regional. Instead, when it went to Locarno, to Canada—it toured the world—everyone saw that the problems it raised, those of false development, are everywhere. I mean the false development of humanity, which for me is the gravest problem of all. That is, the face this society puts on of having arrived at a grand level of civilization, but then in substance its base is imbedded in the fogs of injustice and ignorance.

The Lizards was my act of accusation against the bourgeoisie. It was set in a small town in southern Italy where only the few were able to continue their education. It was about one young man who seemed about to make it out of the stagnation of the life of the town, who could have made it, but then didn't.

——Wertmüller, interviewed for *Women & Film*, June 74

Mae WEST
Born in Brooklyn, 1893. Started on the Broadway stage at age 5. Was author, producer and star of Sex *on Broadway, also* Diamond Lil. *Joined Paramount in 1932 for her first film:*

In 1932 I was doing a play called *The Constant Sinner* on Broadway. We'd closed down for the summer and were planning to reopen in the fall— when I got an offer from Paramount. They wanted me for a picture, minimum of ten weeks at $5,000 per week. I didn't want to do it without seeing the script, but it hadn't been written yet. My agent felt it was foolish to turn down good money like that, script or no script, so I went.

When I got there, I sat around for a few weeks, doing nothing and collecting my salary. They do things like that out here, you know. The waste is unbelievable. Anyway, the script finally came through—and my part had absolutely nothing going for it! It was unimportant to the story and flatly written. I got very upset and offered to give them back all the money they'd paid me if they'd let me out of the contract.

William LeBaron, a fine man whom I'd known back in New York, was the producer. He saw I was quite serious and said I could rewrite the part anyway I wanted—which is exactly what I did. So I made the picture; it wasn't easy to get things the way I wanted them. Archie Mayo, the director, was all right, but he didn't know theater, pauses, the value of timing, that sort of thing. My first line in the film was in response to a remark about my jewelry. Someone said, "Goodness, what beautiful diamonds," and I was supposed to say, "Goodness had nothing to do with it, dearie."

I wanted the camera to follow me as I spoke the line, as I walked away from the person and up a stairway. I knew it was a great line, that it would break up the audience; it had to be protected with footage. There was a big row about that. Mayo wanted to cut away right after the line. It got so bad that they called in Emanuel Cohen, who was in charge of production at the studio. He told Mayo to shoot it my way, and if it didn't work at the preview they could take it out. So we shot it, and the preview audience went wild; the film went over. . . .

My Little Chickadee [1940] was all right; I think it's a good picture. But Bill Fields got co-script credit, which was a farce. He wrote one scene, between himself and another guy in a barroom. One scene! I liked Bill and all that, but he could be miserable when he wanted to be. I guess he hounded them and hounded them until they gave him screen credit just to get rid of him. I never saw the picture until after it'd been released, and by then it was too late to do anything about it. That irritates me.
———West, interviewed for *Take One*, Sept–Oct 72

Perc WESTMORE (1904–1970)
Born in Canterbury, England. Family moved to Canada and then drove to Los Angeles in 1920. Perc and his father George Westmore found jobs in a wig shop.

. . . So I sat down with the head of the studio, which was still First National, and I said, "I can tell you what the industry needs. I, as a hairdresser, see a player come in in the morning. One day she has on pink makeup and a bright red lipstick and blue eye shadow. Then another day she might come in with a different lip color and new makeup. What we need is a chart system and records on every player and what they wore and how they made up in each scene. Then, if we get that same player back in a future film, we can adhere to the way we know she has photographed before." With that idea they gave me a makeup department! The first in the whole industry. It was 1924, and I got a group of 12 character actors together who knew how to make up themselves from the basic stage makeup principles. I told them we were going to develop a profession known as the makeup artist. We got organized and even began training apprentices from among sketch artists, painters, and musicians. Anyone who had a touch of art in them. I trained all my brothers and brought them into the business. Wally just retired at Paramount after 38 years! Bud is still head of the makeup department at Universal.

Mr. Warner loaned me to RKO for $10,000, to him, to create the makeup for Charles Laughton in *The Hunchback of Notre Dame* [1939]. Laughton was in England when I went to work on my preproduction makeup experiments. I had a death mask of Laughton's face. I made 12 copies of it and molded 12 different makeup ideas for the character on them. One idea was that one eye would be grotesquely deformed and low on the cheek. Laughton arrived and came in and looked at these heads. One, two, three. That quickly. "Oh, no, no, Perc! You see, it should look like the seashore, the eye. The water running in and running out." I had spent about 2 weeks, day and night, doing all this modeling and coloring, and he looked at it for 3 minutes! From then on I knew Mr. Laughton and I would be having conflicts.
———Westmore, interviewed for *Hollywood Speaks!* (NY, 1974)

Aside from the broader matter of corrective makeup, there are many little detail tricks a makeup artist can use to make things easier for the cameraman. For instance, there is the familiar problem encountered photographing players with blue eyes.

It has long been a favorite trick of some to focus a baby spotlight fitted with a magenta or even reddish gelatin on the faces of such players, to make the blue eyes photograph darker.

This is not always convenient, but we have found that we can simplify this problem with a little trick of makeup. If any tiny spot of red—so small as to be virtually invisible to the eye—is placed at the inner corner of each eye, we get the same effect as though a magenta-filtered lamp were used, and the eye goes dark.

I hope I may be excused for mentioning what I consider a real achievement in corrective makeup. In *The Life of Emile Zola* [1937] Paul Muni's characterization shows Zola at a number of ages from young manhood to old age.

In the early sequences he plays Zola at a time he weighed approximately Muni's normal weight of 160 pounds; in the latter part of the picture, Zola has aged and put on weight until he weighs approximately 200 pounds.

When these scenes were made Muni's weight was still the same—160 pounds—and no cheek distenders, padded makeup or clothes pads were used, yet he looked a convincing 200 pounds on the screen. This result was achieved simply by an elaboration of the fundamental process of corrective makeup.

——Westmore, in *American Cinematographer*, Jan 38

Haskell W E X L E R
Born in Chicago, 1926. Worked on industrial and educational films before becoming a cinematographer and director.

When I first showed the rushes [*Brazil: A Report on Torture*, 1971] to some friends, I got some interesting comments. Someone said, "That guy doesn't come off too well in the film. What he's saying doesn't seem sincere." Well, she was right. One of the guys just had a manner of speaking and looking that was less convincing. But I *know* he was telling the truth; all his companeros were there, and he couldn't possibly have invented all those fantastic factual things. So here are real people in a real-life situation, speaking directly to the camera, and we evaluate them like actors. Once it's reduced to a medium like film or tape, we automatically make a theatrical judgment. We made them when we were cutting the film. Even though there's very little manipulation in the cutting—it's just interviews interspersed with some demonstrations of the tortures by the people who had been tortured—we still had to say, "Well, is it better to have a woman here and a guy there, or should he say this here or there?" In other words, the degree of manipulation, even through the most honest hands, is still considerable. One of the things that showing the dailies did was convince me that when something is reduced to a *medium*, taken out of reality, it becomes subject to a theatrical evaluation. Nobody gives a shit if it's real anyway, because if you can do it better theatrically you can be more convincing than if you did it actually.

——Wexler, interviewed in *Take One*, July–Aug 71

Pearl W H I T E   (1889–1938)
Born in Greenridge, Missouri.

From the time of my first serial, *The Perils of Pauline* [1914], I have been in training. For a long time I took regular lessons under a competent instructor, hardening my muscles by the use of dumbbells, Indian clubs, pulley machines, and rowing machines. Now I find that fifteen minutes to a half-hour daily keeps me in good trim.

If you have good health, you can keep your temper. If you haven't, you become nervous and go to pieces. The result is that when the director casts for another picture he remembers you all right, but he remembers to leave you out in the cold!

——White, interviewed for *Picture Show*, 4 May 1929

Bernhard W I C K I
Born in St. Pölten, Austria, 1919. After 1945 an actor and theater director in Switzerland, Monaco, Germany. Assistant film director to Helmut Kautner.

The Bridge [1954] was cast with inexperienced youngsters. They were not actors, except for one from an acting school. They were all schoolboys I selected myself. I didn't make them "play theater." I suggested things, explained the situations. You get a more spontaneous performance like that. If I had no success, I tired them, made them run 14 times in the sun, 50 meters there, 50 meters back; and they were at the point where they were crying, and I'd say "Shoot!" I did that film with a lot of unartistic methods; but it was the only way to get the right reaction from these kids.

———Wicki, interviewed for *Films & Filming*, Apr 62

Richard W I D M A R K
Born in Sunrise, Minnesota, 1914. Appeared on radio and stage before entering films.

When I'm reading a script for the first time, I read it for story. As you go along, you see something in your part. Once you start, it's kind of with you all the time. You can be out driving a tractor on the farm, and the part is with you. It demands constant absorption. That aspect of it is pretty much as it is with a play. I learn my part first off, line by line. My wife or my daughter cues me. I learn the whole thing by rote, and then it's out of the way. You don't have to think of the words; they just come. For my recent movie *Judgment at Nuremberg* [1961], it took me 6 weeks just to learn the lines of my part. Rehearsals are for common movement, but you get little time for that. If we had 3 or 4 weeks of rehearsal for movies, it would make a tremendous difference. I've got to be up on a tough scene weeks before I do it for the camera. It's tricky. You have to have the overall idea of what you're going to do firmly entrenched. Then, making one scene match another is tricky, too. When you stop at 6 P.M. Monday, and pick it up again at 4 P.M. Thursday, you need to be absolutely in control of what you're doing if you want it to match. Memory counts a lot, and, fortunately, I have a very good memory.

———Widmark, interviewed for *The Player* (NY, 1962)

I made a new Western with James Stewart called *Two Rode Together* [1961], directed by John Ford.

I don't know what sort of a picture it'll turn out to be, Ford usually gets bored with a picture before the end and takes off. And as he makes a film in such a complicated way that nobody else can put it together, this can create problems.

———Widmark, interviewed for *The Sunday Express*, 28 May 61

Billy W I L D E R
Born in Vienna, 1906. Worked as newspaperman in Vienna and Berlin before starting in movies as a screenwriter. Went to Hollywood in 1934 and collaborated on screenplays with Lubitsch and others before directing his own films.

I try to tell the story as elegantly as I can without any frills or totally unnecessary setups. It makes no sense to me to have bizarre camera angles, because the audience simply becomes aware of the fact that you're using big cranes to get them. One of the greatest directors, John Ford, in the whole of *Stagecoach* had one single panning shot when he took the camera round about 15 degrees. In my films I also like to have the utmost simplicity, though this doesn't simply mean a series of taxicab shots. But for me the most powerful thing man has invented in the cinema is the ability to cut, the ability to make an audience look at what you want them to look at.

—Wilder, interviewed for *The Times*, 19 Aug 69

You remember . . . the scene in *Some Like It Hot* [1959] where Tony Curtis climbs back into the hotel after his night with Sugar and Jack Lemmon tells him he has got engaged to Joe E. Brown—for security! As we rehearsed this it became obvious that the scene would be very funny and provoke a big audience reaction, but we had to allow for this reaction or the audience would miss half the lines. On the other hand, the screen could not just go dead while they laughed, or the scene would lose impetus and fall flat, where obviously the bubble had to be kept in the air. On the morning of shooting we worked out the business with the maracas, so that between lines Jack Lemmon could be absorbed in his tango routine and Tony Curtis would be fighting for his attention while the audience laughed, his frantic attempts to get Jack Lemmon to listen being comic in themselves.

In *One, Two, Three* [1961] I decided to experiment with keeping the tempo up the whole time so that the audience did not have a moment to catch its breath; the whole film is built on speed. Actually, I think it even suffers a little from this, because few audiences have the stamina to pay such close attention so continuously.

I like to make my films as quickly and inexpensively as is compatible with the technical and artistic standards I set myself: I rarely take more than about 60–65 days on the actual shooting and hardly ever look back over what I've done when the film is completed, as I like to get straight on with the next.

—Wilder, interviewed for *The Times*, 8 Feb 62

Know how I got the idea for *The Apartment* [1960]? From seeing *Brief Encounter* [1945] again. Remember how Trevor Howard and Celia Johnson borrowed a friend's flat one afternoon? I wondered about that friend. What sort of a man was it who lent his flat to a friend? That's how the idea for *The Apartment* came. And I wrote it with Jack Lemmon in mind.

—Wilder, interviewed for *The Sunday Express*, 31 July 60

Do you remember the opening shot of *Some Like It Hot*, the close-up of of Lemmon and Curtis wobbling along on high heels? We found the preview audiences howled so much at that, that we went back and added all the footage we'd shot from every angle. You don't notice it, but they're walking past the same railroad car 6 times.

—Wilder, interviewed for *The Toronto Star*, 2 Jan 73

. . . I made *Five Graves to Cairo* [1943] . . . with Erich von Stroheim as Rommel. He was fascinating, . . . He didn't resemble Rommel at all, but that didn't matter either: he gave the audience the proper sense of illusion, a correct impression of the character. Of course, he influenced me greatly as a director: I always think of my style as a curious cross between Lubitsch and Stroheim. . . . [Stroheim] was full of marvelous ideas. His makeup, for instance: it was black on the face and white on his head above the line of the cap—you see, he pointed out that Rommel was always in the sun, and when he took his cap off there would be no colour in the skin underneath.

He insisted on having two cameras slung around his neck. They had to be German; he even insisted on having film inside, saying, "The audience will sense if the films aren't inside; they'll feel they are merely props." Of course, he later contributed ideas to *Sunset Boulevard* [1950] as well: the idea that the butler he plays writes all the fan mail for the lost star Norma Desmond, for instance.

On *Double Indemnity* [1944], adapted from the novel by James M. Cain, I worked with Raymond Chandler. I sat in a room with him and sorted it out; we did the whole thing in 10 or 12 weeks.

We used as many locations for the film as possible. . . . I'd go in and kind of dirty up the sets a little bit and make them look worn. I'd take the white out of everything. . . . John F. Seitz, the cameraman . . . helped me a great deal. I wanted that look that Californian houses get, with the sun streaming through the shutters and showing the dust. You couldn't photograph that, so Seitz made some shreddings for me and they photographed like motes in sunbeams. I like that kind of realism . . . everything in Hollywood always looks like the late Jayne Mansfield's bedroom, and it's ridiculous.

The whole film was deliberately underplayed, done very quietly; if you have something that's full of violence and drama you can afford to take it easy; it's only if you have nothing that you have to "blow it up," to make the sparks fly. I hate arty tricks; suddenly you're shooting a man crossing a street and you take him from the ninth story of a building, and you begin to think in the stalls, "It must be an FBI man looking down from up there," and instead it's just an arty cameraman. Why? Why shoot a scene from a bird's-eye view, or a bug's?

———Wilder, interviewed in *The Celluloid Muse* (Chicago, 1969)

Q. Do you tend to have a star in mind when you're writing a script?

In *The Apartment* you wanted Lemmon, and I suppose you adapted your dialogue to his personality.

Diamond: I'd say that most of the time we have known pretty early on in the script who was going to be in the picture, which of course makes it much more comfortable for the writer.

Wilder: In *Some Like It Hot*, we were way into the script when we found out that Marilyn Monroe was available and wanted to do the picture. I think, as a rule, it's bad to tell the actors, "I'm doing something for you and only you can play it." They don't like that. You just say, "I know that you can do it. You can interpret it because you can play anything." They love to hear that. . . .

Q. You made 2 films with Monroe. What was your experience working with her?

Wilder: My God, I think there have been more books on Marilyn Monroe than on World War II, and there's a great similarity. It was not easy. It was hell. But it was well worth it once you got it on the screen. I've forgotten the trouble I had, and the times I thought, "This picture will never be finished." It's all forgotten once the picture is done.

Q. Do you assume a kind of role with an actor?

Wilder: It's every kind of role. It depends what the actor or actress will respond to. I can become a masochist. I can become the Marquis de Sade. I can become a midwife. I can become Otto Preminger. I can do all sorts of things. It depends on what will work on actors. They're all very different.

Q. How do you decide what method to use?

Wilder: To begin with, I stay away as far as possible. It never gets too friendly because it's just not good: Other actors sense there's a little clique. I remember that I was once making a picture with Marlene Dietrich and Jean Arthur, *A Foreign Affair* [1948]. I had known Marlene from Germany before I ever came to this country, when I was a newspaperman in Berlin, and we were very friendly. In the middle of shooting, one midnight, the doorbell rang, and there was Jean Arthur, absolutely frenzied, with eyes bulging, and in back of her was her husband, Frank Ross. I said, "What is it, Jean?" She said, "What did you do with my close-up?" I said, "What close-up?" She said, "The close-up where I look so beautiful." I said, "What do you mean, what did I do with it?" She said, "You burned it. Marlene told you to burn that close-up. She does not want me to look good." This is typical. It's a little insane asylum, and they are all inmates.

Q. How did the script of *Sunset Boulevard* come about?

Wilder: I was working with Mr. Brackett then, and he had an idea of doing a picture with a Hollywood background. I think originally we wanted Pola Negri or Mary Pickford. Once we got hold of a character of the silent-picture glamour star who had had it, a kind of female John Gilbert, whose career is finished with the advent of talkies but she still has the oil wells pumping and the house on Sunset Boulevard, then we started rolling. The characters of the writer and the director came after.

Soon we had Gloria Swanson and Erich von Stroheim, and we had a whole slew of the old stars, H. B. Warner and Buster Keaton. The part of the writer, Joe Gillis, who becomes the gigolo there, was written for Montgomery Clift. But about 2 weeks before we started shooting, he sent his agent in, who said, "Mr. Montgomery Clift, the great New York actor, will not do the picture, because what would his fans think if he had an affair with a woman twice his age?" You would expect that from a Hollywood actor but not a serious actor. We were then confronted with what to do. It was too late to shelve the picture. So we took William Holden, who was playing second lieutenants in comedies at that time. It had also been difficult to find stars to play in *Double Indemnity*—especially to find a leading man who would play a murderer. We went all the way down, actor after actor, until I finally wound up with Fred MacMurray, who told me, "For Christ's sake, you're making the mistake of your life. I'm a saxophone player. I can't do it."

Q. Were you concerned in *Sunset Boulevard* about having a dead narrator?

Wilder: Yes, but that was the only way out. I shot a whole prologue, a whole reel—that and another reel of the ending to *Double Indemnity* have never been shown. The prologue was very well shot and quite effective. A corpse is brought into the morgue downtown—and I shot it there, too—and it's the corpse of Holden. There are about 6 other corpses there under sheets. Through a trick we see through the sheets to the faces, and they are telling each other the events leading to their deaths. Then Holden starts telling his story.

We previewed the picture, with the original first reel, in Evanston, Illinois, right where Northwestern University is. The picture started. The corpse is brought in on a slab, a name tape is put on the big toe of the corpse, and once the tag went on the toe, the audience broke into the biggest laugh I ever heard in my life. I said, "Oh, my God," and the picture just went straight down. It was a disaster. So that whole sequence went out, but we kept the notion of a man telling of the events which led to his demise.

In *Double Indemnity* I had a final scene with the character in the gas chamber. There are pellets dropping and the bucket and the fumes, and outside is Eddie Robinson watching. They are two great friends, and there is something going on between them, an exchange or whatever. It was very good but just unnecessary. The picture is over when he tells him, "You can't even make the elevator," and he tries and collapses. In the distance you hear the siren of the police, and you know what's going to happen. That was the end of it. I added a postscript which was totally unnecessary.

——Wilder & Diamond, interviewed for *Dialogue on Film*,
in *American Film*, July–Aug 76

Richard W I L L I A M S
Born in Toronto, Canada, 1933. Entered the film industry in 1955 as producer of The Little Island.

[*The Little Island*] is about three little men with fixed ideas . . . so fixed that they are unable to communicate with one another. I call them Truth, Beauty, and Goodness. But it is not about truth, beauty, and goodness—I wouldn't know about them. It's about the way people's eyes are closed. The intellectual critics read things into it that just aren't there. And there's no moral at the end despite the nuclear explosion.

I'm not trying to say that if we all understood one another, we'd all be happy. I'm really having a go at intellectuals.

——Williams, interviewed for *The Evening News*, 19 March 59

Michael W I N N E R
Born in London, 1935.

Q. You have a reputation for working with a low budget on a tight schedule.

A. Well, you see my films are not made on a tight schedule. There is this myth that I am this super-fast director and it's totally untrue. First of all my films are rather expensive. You may read that *Death Wish* [1974] was cheaply made, but that wasn't at all the case. There are just things I do which result in savings in time, and consequently in money. There is enormous waste in most films in terms of work done not showing up on the screen. People often shoot up to an hour more film than they will use in the final cut. What's the point of shooting film you're going to throw away? My films are 97, 98 minutes long, and that is all I shoot. It's not my schedules that are tight, it's my scripts. Second, I will not permit the egomaniacs on some film crews, the lighting and sound men, to spend 2 hours lighting a shot that can be lit as well in 5 minutes. Modern lightweight lighting equipment allows you to shoot 40 setups a day, instead of 6, with no loss of quality. I will not sacrifice that. Another factor in speed of production is my shooting exclusively on location. I always do, never, ever in a studio. Life is lived in real places, and I shoot in real places.

———Winner, interviewed for *Millimeter*, Feb 75

Shelley W I N T E R S [Shirley Schrift]
Born in St. Louis, Montana, 1922. Worked in vaudeville and on the dramatic stage. Made her screen debut in 1944.

The reason for all the wisecracks was that I was determined to get myself some good films. It's not merely talent that brings them your way in Hollywood (or Hollywood as it was then), but being noticed and talked about. So I discussed it with my press agent, and quite cold-bloodedly we invented this personality—a dumb blonde with a body and a set of sharp sayings.
———Winters, interviewed for *The Sunday Times*, 2 May 71

This girl who plays Lolita—Sue Lyon—is gorgeous; a sort of young Bardot. I could murder her. Dammit, she makes me look like Marjorie Main.

It's a tremendous part for her. Every young girl in Hollywood wanted the role. There was this young actress Tuesday Weld, who's very big with the kids now. She begged the director, Stanley Kubrick, to give her the role.

But he said, "No. You're too old." Too old! Imagine! She's 16. Sue Lyon is 14.

Q. Are you supposed to look glamorous in the picture?

A. Stanley Kubrick wants me to, but I'm fighting it. The author, Vladimir Nabokov, said I was ideal for the role, and I think I should play it looking a bit dowdy. It's easier, you know, when you don't look so good.
———Winters, interviewed for *The Sunday Express*, 27 Nov 60

Q. . . . You don't memorize the lines, you first have to understand what the character is about?

A. Yes. The first person I got this from was George Stevens. He didn't mention it this way, but the first time when we started on *A Place in the Sun* [1951], I said, "Now, what do I do in this scene?" And he said, "I don't know. Let's find out." And he said, "If you were such-and-such, would you do this?" Then I did a scene—you remember the abortion scene in the picture, when I go and ask the doctor? He sprang that on me one morning. . . . I did the scene and I was crying, and I thought I was great, and he sat and thought for a while and then he said, "Now, Shelley, let me ask you something about this girl. What is she here for?" And I said, "She's desperate to get the doctor to help her." And so he said, "What she wants in this scene is for the doctor to help her." And I said, "Yes." And he said, "If she does what you just did, would he help her?" And I said, "No, she would scare him." But I was angry at him, because you know, I thought it was so great if I started crying away like crazy. And so he said, "Then the problem in the scene is for her not to cry." And I said, "All right." "Now let's do it again. And you get this doctor to help you." I started the scene, and I wanted to cry, and I had to wait— I don't know whether you remember it, but there were long waits while I got myself under control, and I just sat there and looked at him. Well, it was 90 times more effective than the other. . . . His favorite trick is to rehearse you with the lines and then take the lines away and say, "Now, do the scene— just looking at each other." And in some ways, it's more powerful because you communicate thoughts.

Stevens's sets are like death, they're so quiet. And the crews know it. They move scenery quietly. He knows the actors have to stay quiet, and sometimes he jars you out of the mood purposely because he knows it's getting too long, like he will turn up the air conditioning till you freeze, when it's a scene that you have to be cold in. In the dead of summer in August, he'll put the heating system on if he wants you to be hot. And sometimes he has a thing that's just wonderful—I wish there was a way to use it in the theater. You know, he's from silent pictures and he has a kind of thing—it's a gadget that's next to his chair, and he knows what music works on you, and he pushes the button and he finds the kind of music you respond to; and in preparation for a scene, when he says, "Roll 'em," before you start acting, he will play that music, sometimes he'll play it during the scene.

———Winters, interviewed for *Actors Talk about Acting* (New York 1961)

Robert W I S E
Born 1914, in Winchester, Indiana. Entered the movie business in 1933 in the cutting department of RKO. In 1939 he became a film editor and in 1943 a director.

. . . When [Orson Welles] did *The Magnificent Ambersons*, he was also doing a "Lady Esther" radio program every week. Then the war started and the government offered him the opportunity to do a film in South America as part of their Good Neighbor Policy. Well, Orson got this bright idea: since he owed RKO one more picture, he decided if he went to South America he could wipe the slate clean. So he put *Journey into Fear* into the works while he was still shooting *Ambersons*.

Orson was directing *Ambersons* in the daytime, working all night on *Journey into Fear*, and taping "Lady Esther" radio shows on weekends for the coming week. He was all over the place—and everything suffered because of it. . . .

We had sneak previews of the film in Los Angeles and it was terribly painful—audiences laughed at it and walked out in droves. They were some of the worst evenings I've ever spent in my life! But RKO had a film that had cost close to a million and a half, and they at least wanted a picture audiences would sit through.

So we did the best we could with Orson's material, although we did have to do some serious cutting and bridging to make the thing work. There are probably 30–35 minutes of the original cut out; and we shot several bridge scenes and a new ending which Freddie Fleck, the unit manager, directed.

In terms of a work of art, I grant you Orson's original film was better. But we were faced with the realities of what the studio was demanding. The old bit of art vs. commercialism.

————Wise, interviewed for *Filmmakers Newsletter*, Apr 76

Well, [being a former editor] doesn't make me camera-cut or be overly eco-nomical, let's say, with film. That's, I think, a misconception held very often— that when one has been an editor and then becomes a director that you tend to shoot less film, because you know exactly what you need and how it will go together and all that. I find it just the reverse. As an editor I knew the value of having a lot of film to work with, having that extra angle, that close-up or whatever, that piece of film that would help me out of a spot and make the scene play better. And I was never happier than when I had a director, at the time I was editing, who would give me plenty of film to work with. So I found myself as an ex-editor probably shooting more than the average director who hasn't my background because I can't bear not to have that extra piece of film. And I know that 3 or 4 months later when I'm working on that sequence, if I don't have it, there's no way of getting it. So, that's one way that the editing has influenced my shooting. I suppose, too, in laying out and preparing and planning actual shooting one, maybe, can visualize a little more fully how it's going to come out on film in the cut sequence. So I think that I preplan and prepare to a great degree, physically, how I'm going to shoot the film that one might who didn't have an editing background. I think the biggest influence I ever had was in the use of film and the need to have plenty of it. When I was starting in the editing department with T. K. Wood, he made one statement that always stuck with me even in terms of the work we were doing there, cutting sound effects where you had to order up a lot of film. He always impressed upon me the fact that film was the cheapest single thing that went into a movie and never to be stingy with it.

————Wise, interviewed for *Directors at Work* (NY, 1970)

Q. *West Side Story* [1961] had two direction credits, you and Jerome Robbins. How did you split your duties?

A. . . . I was asked if I wanted to produce and direct it, and I said, "I'd love it." Robbins, who by contract . . . had the right to do the film choreogra-phy, chose not to . . . he didn't want to come out to the West Coast just to do the choreography. He wanted to be more deeply involved in the whole production. I said, "Why don't they let him take over the film and direct it?" But United Artists thought there was no way they could do that. It was going to be a big, expensive, complex picture to do, and they were not willing to let a man inexperienced in film direct it. . . .

Finally, we came to a setup where he would come on the film as the co-director, and he would be involved in all the aspects of the film. . . . But when it came to shooting, he would have the responsibility and deciding voice on the music and dance numbers, and I would have the say on all the "book" aspects of the script. . . . Now, Jerry didn't stay on all the way through; he was on over 50 percent of the shooting. We had some rough moments, not too many, but we managed to work them out, though there were a few times when we rather got at each other. But finally we were getting very far behind schedule, and United Artists was very worried. They decided that the tandem arrangement was slowing us down to a great degree and insisted that I take over the whole show, which I did.

———Wise, interviewed for *American Film*, Nov 75

Frederick W I S E M A N
Born 1930, graduated from Yale Law School; practiced law in Paris and Boston before producing Shirley Clarke's The Cool World *in 1964.*

I like the final film to represent my experience of making the film and not my prior stereotype. I didn't start off *Law and Order* [1969] with, say, "I want to build a bridge between the community and the police." In fact I probably started off with the view, "What a great chance to get the cops. I've been given permission to run around with the cops for however long I want and I'm really going to show what bastards they are." But the experience was very different than that. I have as little information as the general public. I don't have any special knowledge about police or hospitals or anything; but I have an idea, a theory and the theory may be a cliché. What I try and do is set down my initial thinking, my initial point of view about the subject, which I generally do with about a 3- or 4-page outline. This I don't mind because the people I'm asking permission from to make the film want a statement of it, for you still have to deal in words! This may have no relationship to the final film because, particularly in documentary, you don't know what you are going to find out there; all you can do is give your illustrative examples. So what I do is set out a theory and give illustrations of the kind of material I expect to find, but in no way commit myself to finding out; for God knows—you don't know what's going to happen in advance; you don't know the principal is going to stand up and read a letter from a soldier in Vietnam [in *High School*, 1968] or that a cop is going to try and strangle a prostitute. . . . The process reaches its ultimate kind of intensity, where it gets very intense, in the course of the editing. The editing generally takes me anywhere from 4 to 6 months; but the last 3 months are really, you know, 7 days a week, 12 to 15 hours a day—mainly because I like to work that way and because you get very involved in the material. You're really thinking your way through the material and you're beginning to see connections and relationships and development of themes that you only kind of half-sensed before.

———Wiseman, interviewed for *Film Quarterly*, Fall 70

Natalie W O O D [Gurdin]
Born in San Francisco, 1938.

For the first time I had a director, Nicholas Ray in *Rebel Without a Cause* [1955], who actually encouraged me to have ideas and opinions. I kept hearing about the Method, and just about everybody on the set was carrying a copy of Chekhov's book *To an Actor,* and using phrases like "sense memory," and "emotion memory."

I started dropping in at the Actors Studio, and found it was basically the way I'd been working all along. "Emotion memory" is recalling something sad when you have a sad scene to do, and very early on I used to get myself in the right mood by thinking of a pet dog that died. Nobody told me how to do it. It just came naturally.

In *Splendor in the Grass* [1961] I had to portray fear. I'm terrified of heights, and Elia Kazan had me standing on a ledge, safely roped, with two men holding my hands. Just before the take, he whispered something to one of the men, and as the camera turned he let go of my hand. It was just a trick, but it didn't work. I was so angry I forgot to be afraid.

Learning lines is no problem. But what I try to do is learn the entire scene *without* lines. I try to absorb the narrative outline, so that I'll know what the character would do, how she might behave in another scene or situation. In most films I've tried to create a character, but in *Bob and Carol [and Ted and Alice,* 1969] I've used more of myself. It's one of the things I've enjoyed doing most. For one thing we shot it in sequence, and for another thing we shot it pretty quickly. Ten weeks from start to finish.

———Wood, interviewed for *The Sunday Times,* 28 Dec 69

Joanne WOODWARD
Born in Thomasville, Georgia, 1930. Studied at the Neighborhood Playhouse Dramatic School.

When I was very young, I wanted to be a movie star. When I was older I wanted to be an actress. Now I find acting in films an irritating process. It's become a medium of price, hurry, rush, "let's finish this scene today," almost everything except "what are we doing?"

There was a kind of delight in the days when I first started out. But pretty soon, it began to wear me out, all my other drives. [My discontent with acting] has been growing for the last 4 or 5 years, with almost everything I've done since *Rachel, Rachel* [1968]. We made that just around the time the squeeze began. I dislike rushing in to do my little bit, then rushing into my elegant camper, then rushing back to do my little bit again. It's become a drag. I could just as well do my needlepoint at home.

———Woodward, interviewed for *Show,* Feb 73

William WYLER
Born 1902, in Mulhouse, France, but was saved from its business life by a visit from his mother's cousin, Carl Laemmle. Wyler worked in the New York office of Universal before moving to their Hollywood lot. His first films in 1925 were 2-reel Westerns, and he headed second units for Universal's spectacles (he directed the Paris locations for The Phantom of the Opera, *1925).*

Making those routine Westerns taught me the fundamental thing about films— they have *to move.* The picture had to open with action—a girl on a runaway horse, on a runaway stagecoach, or a chase. Then the hero comes along and rescues her, and a little love story develops. Then a plot turn, involving heavies, and sheriff and posse. That was it—love story, big chase, big action, happy ending. `٭

——Wyler, interviewed for *Films in Review*, Oct 71

[My version of *Three Godfathers: Hell's Heroes*, 1929] was all sound, the first all-talking outdoor picture Universal made. We were in the Mojave Desert and in Panamint Valley, just off Death Valley, in July and August of 1930. The cameraman was in a glass booth. It was 120 degrees outside. In the glass booth it was 140. Sometimes after a shot, we would find that the cameraman had passed out. We had a crew pushing this thing, with the microphone hidden in a cactus here and in the sand over there.

When I come on the set, I've studied the scene, and I've got a vague idea of how I want to play it. But I haven't mapped it out exactly, as some directors do. Before I can make up my mind definitely, I've got to see the actors doing it. Also, I want to see what the actors have to contribute, so I don't tell them very much. If an actor asks me, I say, "You show me. You know the scene. Go ahead, you show me." And it happens very often that the actor will have a different idea or an even better idea than I have. When we've got it worked out, then comes the technical part of working out the camera movement, the camerawork, and so on. Then we start shooting. That's when they say I start becoming a sadist, shooting again and again.

Sometimes I'm not very articulate with the actor. If you point out some-thing, it may become too prominent in his thinking, and the scene will suffer. I figure that by putting an actor on his own and letting him use all the re-sourcefulness he has, he won't depend on me. I can't do it for him, no matter what. He's got to do it. He's got to feel it.

I think a director is bound to make small contributions to a screenplay. I'm not a writing director, but that doesn't mean I don't make changes. An example is in *The Best Years*. We had Dana Andrews walking around the airfield seeing all these obsolete airplanes which never saw action, and all the script said was, "He walks around thinking of how the war has done him in." But it's because I did *Memphis Belle* [1944] and rode in a bombardier's compartment on a few missions that I got the idea that he would climb up into his old place and have a dream and lose himself in the dream, or rather in hallucination. It was all invented on the spot because the airfield, those obsolete planes, were conducive to the basic idea of the film, of the man feeling lost.

——Wyler, interviewed for *American Film*, Apr 76

During the shooting [of *The Best Years of Our Lives*, 1946] which began April 15 and ended August 9, 1946, I worked very closely with Daniel Mandell, one of the really fine film editors. Danny has put most of my pictures together, and knows as much about the subject as anybody you could name. Our com-pany met at 8:30 every morning to see the film we'd shot the day before. Danny sat next to me, and I would pick the takes to be used, and briefly dis-cuss the way I intended the scene to be cut. Then, during the course of the day, Danny would come on the set and we would talk over specific problems. Occasionally, every few weeks, I would devote an evening to running the assembled film with Danny, and making suggestions to him. . . . The day after we finished the long 4-month shooting schedule, Danny had a first rough cut ready to show. It ran just a few minutes under 3 hours, and very few changes had to be made in it.

———Wyler, in *The Screen Writer*, Feb 47

Barbra is the only reason I directed this film [*Funny Girl*, 1968]. I could not just think of Fanny Brice and ignore Barbra Streisand. She gave me what I wanted and more. She was very satisfying, very professional and absolutely tireless. I could work this girl round the clock with no complaint. Bette Davis had the same sort of eagerness and desire to get the best and never be satisfied with herself, or anyone else for that matter.

———Wyler, interviewed for *The Sunday Times Magazine*, 12 Jan 69

[With deep focus] I can have action and reaction in the same shot, without having to cut back and forth from individual shots of the characters. This makes for smooth continuity, an almost effortless flow of the scene, much more interesting composition in each shot and lets the spectator look from one to the other character at his own will, do his own thing.

———Wyler in *Documentary; Film News*, Vol. 7, No. 6

Just before [Gregg Toland] died he had worked out a new lens with which he had made spectacular shots. He carried in his wallet a strip of film taken with this lens, of which he was very proud. It was a shot of a face 3 inches from the lens, filling one-third of the left side of the frame. Three feet from the lens, in the center foreground, was another face, and then, over 100 yards away was the rear wall of the studio, showing telephone wires, and architectural details. *Everything* was in focus, from 3 inches to infinity.

———Wyler, letter to *Sequence* 8, Summer 49

Jane W Y M A N [Sarah Jane Fulks]
Born in St. Joseph, Missouri, in 1914.

After the first preview [of *Johnny Belinda*, 1948, Jack Warner] hated it so much he stuck it in cans and nobody knew what happened to it. Everyone was fired at the end of the picture and Jean Negulesco, the director, wasn't even allowed to do his own editing. He has never to this day set foot in the Warner Brothers studio again. One day somebody was rummaging around in a lot of dusty cans of film in the New York office and found some reels of the picture and ran them, and it finally got shown. You know the rest. I made Jack Warner take out an ad and apologize to everyone connected with the film, from the grips to the water boy, and he named every person by name.

———Wyman, interviewed for *The New York Times*, 6 Oct 68

Y

Michael YORK

Born in Fulmer, England, 1942. Prior to film work, he worked with the Oxford University Dramatic Society, the National Youth Theatre, the Dundee Repertory, the National Theatre.

I've been very lucky, working solidly for the past few years. But I suppose *Cabaret* [1972] was the biggest break. I was in Puerto Rico when they were casting it and I heard they were looking for a new Michael York. I thought this was a bit off because it seemed to me that the old one still had a little mileage left in him, so I came back to London and saw the right people and got the part. Oddly enough, I never felt while we were working on it that *Cabaret* would make any vital difference to my career. It was made for $4m, including $1m for the screen rights, which isn't much for a big musical.

   I thought it would simply be another rather good film. It shows how wrong you can be. You see, I thought *Justine* [1969] would provide the breakthrough for me, and it's turned out to be a disaster that did nobody any good at all.

——York, interviewed for *The Times*, 8 Apr 72

Susannah YORK

Born in London, 1942. Entered TV in 1959, films in 1960.

I was shattered at the end of [*Freud,* 1962]. It took me more than a year to recover my nerve, and I'm not sure if I've really done so yet.

   Freud was an incredible experience, though. And it did more to make me understand myself—as a person and as an actress—than anything I have ever done.

   At times I really hated it. After violent arguments with John Huston, I would go to my dressing room in floods of tears.

York, interviewed for *Evening Standard*, 24 Aug 63

[In *The Killing of Sister George,* 1969] I was mentally stripped by the camera. It explores your face, your body, and, yes, searches your soul.

   It terrifies me. The thought that my own feelings, my embarrassment, might show. It was difficult, a very difficult scene. I hated doing it.

As an actress you are doing something to order. Love, lovemaking, is an intensely spontaneous and private thing. Filming, it is difficult not to get self-conscious. Just as if you are snapped unawares at a Sunday picnic.
———York, interviewed for *The Sun,* London, 10 June 69

Terence Y O U N G
Born in Shanghai, 1915. Began as a screenwriter before turning to directing in 1949.

I never rehearse a film in its entirety. This is a theatrical tradition: the essence of cinema is that it captures something *at the precise moment it is occurring.* If it is overrehearsed it loses its immediacy. Quite often I even shoot such rehearsals as I do have—and if they don't work, it doesn't matter. In the same way I keep the number of takes down as low as possible. An actress such as Audrey Hepburn . . . will give a great performance the first 2 or 3 takes, but after half a dozen she becomes tired, and what she was able to contribute at first has gone. In addition a player may tend in later takes to react *before* he hears (for the sixth or seventh time) the line which should cause the reaction.
———Young, interviewed for *The Making of Feature Films* (London, 1971)

Z

Darryl F. Z A N U C K
Born in Wahoo, Nebraska, 1902. In various trades before decision to become screenwriter.

From the very beginning [of *The Longest Day*, 1962] I had 2 units shooting film simultaneously, and at times there were 4. It made it very difficult for me, but everything had been worked out in advance, in great detail, and I used a helicopter to drop in on my directors and supervise the work being done.

Only about one-third of *The Longest Day* was shot in the studio. When we did move indoors, I took over the Studio Boulogne—France's largest—for 3 months. We built 47 separate sets there. Here, too, I had 2 units working simultaneously on different stages. At the studio we reproduced everything from the interior of a glider and of a landing craft at sea (the motions were simulated by having the craft built on a platform which sank and rose with hydraulic pressure) to the Normandy countryside and the interior of a German bunker under bombardment. One scene called for Irina Demich to fight a German soldier in the water. It was freezing out, so we couldn't shoot in the country. I had a stream built on the stage and the water was preheated to keep her and everyone else from catching pneumonia.

—Zanuck, in *Films & Filming*, Nov 62

Krzyzstof Z A N U S S I

At first I thought of *The Structure of Crystal* as a half-hour film for television, yet while I was working on the script I found out that I would have to cut everything that interested me, so I rewrote it as a full-length feature.

Q. How would you describe the main theme of the film, its psychological, moral and social content?

While I was working on it, I feared—as I do now—that I had intellectualized the subject too much. This can be dangerous, a thing Munk always used to tell us; keep your ear to the ground, don't generalize, don't put in "general problems." It's a paradox, as he well knew. He himself saw his rationalism as a danger. . . . I didn't want to "state the problem" with complete intellectual discipline, and then solve it like a mathematical equation; I didn't want to put it exclusively on the level of a social, psychological, or moral problem. This does not mean that I wanted to obscure the picture, shut out all thought and produce a work of little meaning, a trend which I note at times in Resnais. I defended myself from the dangers of facile generalization and too many confused thoughts by using as a criterion my own experiences of life and fellow men. . . .

———Zanussi, interviewed at the Pesaro Film Festival, 1970

Franco Z E F F I R E L L I
Born in Florence, 1923.

[Kate and Petruchio] should have great physical life. Everything is of the flesh, of the blood. They are very attached to physical things—sex, eating, sleeping, hating.

Their instincts are shrewd, decisive—black, white, yes, no, I love you, I hate you. Like cats. When they want to eat, they eat. When they want to make love, they make love.

What I shall do is tell the story [of *The Taming of the Shrew*, 1967] as if I were telling it to an audience of children. Simply. With lots of color, action, atmosphere. And I would like adults to enjoy it as if it were a Christmas pantomime.

———Zeffirelli, interviewed for *The Daily Mail*, 7 Feb 66

I think I have a method, which is very flexible, of catching the actors and letting them go free. It is a combination of the two. You must be as tough as rubber and as soft as steel. You play it by ear and see what they receive best. There are some things they do better if they are not taught. You just feed their imagination and they do the rest.

Q. Do you tell theater actors as much as you do these?

Yes. Cinema is different because you do it bit by bit and you sketch it for them. In the theater I usually demonstrate very much. I am not too good at explaining in words. I don't think it's useful to discuss with actors, who are very simple creatures. They work on simple, basic images. They should be given an image which is clear and not confused. If you are going to discuss motivations, identifications, and why and why not, you're lost.

———Zeffirelli, interviewed for *The Guardian*, 2 March 68

Fred Z I N N E M A N N
Born in Vienna, 1907. Educated in Vienna and Paris. Camera assistant in Berlin and Paris. Began work in the U.S. in 1930, first as an extra then as a screenwriter and director of shorts.

Flaherty taught me more than anyone else. Number one was to stick to your guns. I learned the importance of expressing what you want to say, to make a film the way you see it. . . . I also learned from him not to try to make pictures about subjects *you don't* know. . . .

If you backlight an object, it stands out more sharply in contrast to its surroundings. Similarly, if you use a person who is not right for the part physically, he sometimes brings an extra dimension to the role. You have to imagine how an actor will relate to the other actors in a film. That is as important as the choice of individual actors. Then you must create an atmosphere in which they can function, *give them* as much assurance as you possibly can.

———Zinnemann, interviewed for *Show*, Aug 64

It might be of some interest to know that we rehearsed the entire film *From Here to Eternity* [1953] in detail with props and so on before shooting started. We found that it adds to spontaneity and saves time. The picture was shot in 41 days—and we split it by taking 2 of the leading actors each day and doing their whole story. (Clift and Donna Reed, Burt Lancaster and Deborah Kerr, the Sinatra sequences.) And it gave each of them a sense of continuity.

———Zinnemann, reported in *Sight & Sound*, Autumn 55

One of the best German cameramen that I ever worked with was Eugene Schüfftan. . . . He was responsible for developing some of the trick photographic effects that were widely used at UFA. . . . One trick process involved placing a semitransparent mirror at a 45° angle in front of the camera lens. This reflected the image of a scale model which was out of camera range and made that image blend with the live action that was being photographed in front of the camera. For example, a peasant might be ploughing a field, with a moving windmill in the background. The turning windmill was supplied by the reflection of a scale model.

Floyd Crosby photographed [*High Noon*, 1952] and had the courage to give it the style we had agreed upon. Floyd and I thought that *High Noon* should look like a newsreel would have looked if they had had newsreels in those days, and we studied Matthew Brady's photographs of the Civil War as an aid. Up to that time there was almost a religious ritual about the way that Westerns were made. There was always a lovely gray sky with pretty clouds in the background. Instead Crosby used no filters and gave the sky a white, cloudless, burnt-out look. He used flat lighting and that gave the film a grainy quality. From the first day the front office complained about the poor photography. Most cameramen might have struck their colors, but Floyd went ahead anyway. Subliminally the photography created the effect we wanted; it made the film look more real.

While Franz Waxman was scoring the picture [*The Nun's Story*, 1959] I discovered that he had a deep dislike for the Catholic church and this was coming across in his music. The theme he originally wrote for the convent scenes would have been more appropriate for scenes set in a dungeon. For the final scene, when Sister Luke [Audrey Hepburn] leaves the convent and returns to the world, he wrote an exultant theme to end the film, and I removed it from the sound track so that the film ended in silence. He was very upset about this and at the postmortem after the first preview of the picture he said so to Jack Warner. When Warner asked me about it, I answered his question with another: "What kind of music do you want at the end of a film?

If the music expresses gloom, it will imply that it is too bad that Sister Luke left the convent. If it is joyful, people will think that Warner Brothers is encouraging nuns to leave the convent." And so the film ends in silence, the way I wanted it to.

——Zinnemann, interviewed for *Focus on Film,* Spring 73

The kind of approach you have to filmmaking depends on your background. I was an assistant cameraman—who never became a fully fledged cameraman, incidentally—so I have a cameraman's approach. Someone like David Lean started in the cutting room, so he would rely more on editing. Editing is essential, of course. It is in the cutting room you get the rhythm of a film—the flow. I will spend about 6 weeks editing [*Behold a Pale Horse,* 1963].

It is useful to remember how many different ways you can approach the making of a film. Hitchcock shoots a cut film. He edits in the camera. You can't do anything with his film after it has been shot other than just stick the bits together. Stevens works in terms of camerawork. I like to study other people's work. Particularly Stevens, Lean, Billy Wilder, William Wyler—we have a kind of mutual admiration society. We watch each other's work and get to know the others' methods, their approach, how they think. . . .

——Zinnemann, interviewed for *The Guardian,* 24 Aug 63

ZOUZOU [Danielle Ciarlet]
Born in Algeria.

What I liked about working with Rohmer [on *Chloe in the Afternoon,* 1972] is that I did not feel for one minute that I was wasting my time. Every day we were shooting something that was used. Most directors take 10 shots of everything to cover themselves. Rohmer doesn't do that at all. He takes one shot and that's okay. He knows exactly what he wants, from where he wants to see it, so you don't waste a minute. What was good, too, with Rohmer is that we work with a small crew so everybody's really involved in the movie. Nobody's doing only his own job; everybody's helping the other person. The man at the sound can help the man from the electricity if he's got a problem. The lighting man can go get me a Coke if I'm thirsty. I can get something for Nestor [Almendros] when he is filming because he'd like to have a drink, you know. And that was great! It was like a family for 2 months. We got used to seeing each other every day, having lunch, having fun, even during the work was such fun because Rohmer is a very funny man. Fantastic! He's absolutely hilarious. If I look at him I know that the first thing he says is going to make me fall on the floor laughing. He's so funny. Nobody believes that. His films are very serious, and he is a serious person. But at the same time he has the greatest humor—his sense of humor is absolutely different from the rest of the world. . . . He knows exactly what he wants from the actor. Actually, he never directs you or tells you to do something or explain anything. I don't know how he manages it, but you just do what he wants. There's no way to escape. Ah, you can do it sometimes but he enjoys it so much that you realize he meant for you to escape, to do whatever you had in your mind. . . .

But what I admire about Rohmer is that he doesn't care what other people do. He has his own mind, his own way of thinking. He's an entirely different person from anyone I've ever met. He doesn't care about the business, he doesn't know what's going on anywhere, hasn't seen a film for years because he doesn't want to start thinking about—this man has been doing this and that man has been doing that—why am I doing what I do? He just wants to be on his own little trip, he doesn't care about anybody else, he's got his own things to say and he does not want to be involved in movies that might be more rewarding financially. He could make more money, have a big success but he's not interested. That's not his problem. His problem was doing his 6 moral tales, it's finished now, he's done it. He's in good shape.

——Zouzou, interviewed for *Show*, Feb 73

Vilmos ZSIGMOND
Born in Hungary, 1930. Trained at Budapest Film School.

... We wanted to have [*McCabe and Mrs. Miller,* 1971] look like old photographs, old color photographs. We thought if they had a camera in those days and if they had an old type of color film, that's the way it would have looked. That was one approach; the other approach was the weather. We wanted to shoot this whole story against a very humid, cold, muddy background. To create that feeling, we wanted to muddy up the film a little. That means we flashed the film quite heavily and pushed it.

All we wanted to do on *Deliverance* [1972] was to desaturate the beginning of the picture, which played in a small Appalachian village. We started to shoot in April. Everything was very, very colorful; it was springtime and we had colors, the colors of wild flowers, greens and yellows. *Deliverance* needed something more dramatic, something less colorful. That's why we decided to print black and white over in all those scenes which would need it. The beginning of the picture—the beginning 2 reels and the last 2 reels—were printed that way. The middle section, which plays on the river, we didn't have to worry about, because all we had was water and green foliage. We loved the green. The green, dramatically, was right. ... What we wanted to do was ... to shoot everything in overcast. ... On a sunny day, the river reflected the blue sky and the white clouds. It looked very cheerful, very beautiful. You couldn't use it for the film because it had the mood of Kodak snapshots. ... We shot only the beginning part of the journey on sunny days.

——Zsigmond, interviewed at the American Film Institute, Oct 74

Adolph ZUKOR (1873–1976)
Born in Ricse, Hungary, orphaned in childhood; emigrated to U.S. at 16.

If we knew in advance when we made any picture how it was going to be taken by the public, we'd have to hire a hall to hold the money. You make a picture you believe in. That doesn't mean the public will agree with us. I devoted my time and energy to selecting the material we were making. The story was always most important. At any stage in life, you cannot always do what you think the public wants, but if you study the trends of success in literature . . . A picture is a publication, the same as a book. If a book sells a million copies, there must be a reason for it.

If you try to superimpose your own taste and feel the public has to like something because you like it, you will fail. I was fortunate. Failures were very few and far between, and successes were numerous. I always tried to make pictures that appealed to the young people. I always selected subjects the young people would be fascinated by. That's why we had more hits than the others. Because you know the public taste changes in time just like styles in clothes.

———Zukor, interviewed for *The New York Times,* 4 Feb 73

Index

A Bout de Souffle (*Breathless*) (1959), 28, 170–71, 274
A Nous la Liberté (1930), 75–76
A Tout Prendre (1963), 229–30
Accatone (1961), 34, 346
Accident (1967), 23, 279–280
Act of Violence (1948), 17
Actors, acting: casting, 53, 131–32; child actors, 113; improvisation, 63–65, 77–78, 111, 148, 471; non-actors, 46, 47, 99–100, 146–47, 223; rehearsals, 60, 63–65, 77–78, 96–97, 111, 115, 148, 330, 518; relations with cameramen, 105; relations with directors, 11, 34, 51, 63, 73, 75; tests, 182–83. *See also* individual listings
Actors Studio, 171, 235, 329, 514
Actress, The (1953), 96, 353
Adam's Rib (1949), 95
Adler, Luther, 4
Admiral Nakhimov (1946) 174–75
Adventurer, The (1917), 70–71
Adventures of Tom Sawyer, The (1939), 214–15
Adversary, The (1971), 378
Affaire est dans le sac, L' (1932), 369
Affaires Publiques, Les (1934), 47
African Queen, The (1951), 196
After Many Years (1908), 12–13
Age d'Or, L' (1930), 54
Agee, James, 3
Aimée, Anouk, 267, 468
Airmail (1932), 190
Airport 1975 (1974), 193
Alamo, The (1960), 459
Alatriste, Gustavo, 471
Albert, Eddie, 4
Albin, Charles, 15
Alcoriza, Luis, 55
Aldrich, Robert, 3–4, 444
Alejandro, Julio, 55
Alékan, Henri, 81
Alexander the Great (1956), 406–7
Alexander Nevsky (1938), 126
Alexeieff, Alexandre, 4–5
Alice Doesn't Live Here Anymore (1974), 421–22

Alice's Restaurant (1969), 351
All Quiet on the Western Front (1930), 21, 93, 312
All That Money Can Buy (1941), 199-200
All This and Heaven Too (1940), 103
Allan, Geoff, 27
Allégret, Yves, 88, 356, 434
Allen, Gene, 26
Allen, Woody, 5
Allgeier, Sepp, 6
Almendros, Nestor, 522
Alouette et la Mésange, L' (1922), 9
Altman, Robert, 6, 71
Alton, John, 50, 298
Alvarez, Santiago, 7
America Revisited (1971), 338
American in Paris, An (1931), 443
American Graffiti (1973), 132–33, 285–86
American Madness (1932), 60
American Tragedy, An (unrealized), 424
American Tragedy, An (1931), 443
Amiche, Le (1955), 10
Amour a vingt ans, L' (1962), 338
Anastasia (1956), 32
Anderson, G. M., 464–65
Anderson, Lindsay, 7–8, 246, 304, 307
Anderson, Michael, 379–80
Andrews, Dana, 515
Anger, Kenneth, 8
Angry Silence, The (1959), 188
Animal Crackers (1930), 300
Animal Kingdom (1932), 283
Animators and animation: *see* Alexeieff & Parker, Avery, Borowczyk, Disney, Hubley, Lambart, Lye, McLaren, Reiniger, Starewicz, Williams
Anna Boleyn (1920), 284
Anna Christie (1930), 100, 261
Anstey, Edgar, 9
Anthony Adverse (1937), 162
Antoine, André, 9
Antonioni, Michelangelo, 9–11, 172, 184, 225, 321, 334, 339, 484–85
Apache (1954), 3
Apartment, The (1960), 506
Applause (1929), 294, 491

Apprenticeship of Duddy Kravitz, The (1974), 245
Apfel, Oscar, 105
Arbuckle, Roscoe "Fatty," 83, 236
Arcand, Denys, 12
Arms & the Man (unrealized), 178
Armstead, Mark, 79
Arnold, Victor, 283
Arrangement, The (1969), 113–14
Arsenal (1929), 114
Artaud, Antonin, 245
Arvidson, Linda (Mrs. D. W. Griffith), 12–13
Arthur, Jean, 190, 508
Aryan, The (1916), 186
Arzner, Dorothy, 13–14, 99
As You Desire Me (1932), 114
As You Like It (1936), 336
Asher, Jack, 137
Asphalt Jungle, The (1950), 192
Ashes & Diamonds (1958), 487
Asquith, Anthony, 14, 213, 337
Astaire, Fred, 14–15, 237, 490
Astor, Mary, 15–17
Astruc, Alexandre, 18
Atalante, L' (1934), 232
Atlantis (1932), 310–11, 343
Attack (1956), 4
Attenborough, Richard, 18–19, 188
Aubrey, James, 123
Auden, Wystan Hugh, 67, 495
Audran, Stéphane, 19
August, Joseph, 314, 315
Auric, Georges, 82
Aumont, Jean-Pierre, 471
Autant-Lara, Claude, 19–20, 101
Austernprinzessin, Die (1919), 283–84
Avery, Tex, 20
Avventura, L' (1960), 10, 321, 484–85
Axelrod, George, 21
Ayres, Lew, 21
Aznavour, Charles, 318

Babochkin, Boris, 22
Baby Doll (1956), 160, 235
Bacall, Lauren, 191
Bad Boys (1960), 182–83
Bad Company (1972), 29
Bad Day at Black Rock (1954), 43
Bad Luck (1960), 363
Bad Sleep Well, The (1960), 251–52
Bakaleinikoff, Constantin, 497
Baker, Carroll, 160
Baker, Stanley, 22–23
Balcon, Michael, 319
Ball, Lucille, 23–24
Ballad of Cable Hogue, The (1970), 491
Ballad of the Thirteen Hills Reservoir (1958), 74
Ballet Mécanique (1924), 264
Baltic Deputy (1937), 73
Bambi (1942), 215
Bancroft, Anne, 350
Baranovskaya, Vera, 174, 372
Barbier, George, 94
Bargain, The (1914), 186
Barker, Reginald, 186

Barrault, Jean-Louis, 24
Barry, John, 249
Barry, Philip, 95, 196
Barrymore, John, 15, 24, 94, 97
Barrymore, Lionel, 231
Barthelmess, Richard, 169, 438
Barsacq, Léon, 24–25
Bas Fonds, Les (1936), 385–86
Bass, Saul, 25
Bassori, Timité, 26
Bates, Alan, 134
Battisti, Carlo, 107–8
Battle of Algiers, The (1966), 367
Battle of Colloden (1964), 492–93
Battleship Potemkin (1925), 123–25, 187
Bauer, Yevgeni, 49, 325
Baxter, Warner, 33
Beaton, Cecil, 26–27
Beatles, The, 269
Beatty, Warren, 350, 407
Beau Brummel (1924), 15
Beau Serge, Le (1958), 67, 104
de Beauregard, Georges, 171
Becker, Jacques, 27–28, 433, 470
Becket (1964), 169–70
Beckwith, Frank, 175
Becky Sharp (1935), 296
Bedlam (1946), 397
Beery, Wallace, 48, 51, 425
Beggars of Life (1928), 48
Begone Dull Care (1949), 253
Behind the Mask (1958), 380
Behold a Pale Horse (1963), 522
Belasco, David, 105
Belle de Jour (1966), 344
Belle et la Bête, La (1945), 81–82
Bellochio, Marco, 28
Bells Have Gone to Rome, The (1958), 225
Belmondo, Jean-Paul, 28, 104, 170
Ben-Hur (1925), 122, 331, 456–57
Ben-Hur (1959), 206, 410
Benchley, Nathaniel, 288
Bendersky, Samuel, 311
Benedek, Laslo, 28–29
Bennett, Charles, 319
Bennett, Compton, 239
Bennett, Spencer, 313
Benton, Robert, 29
Berendt, Rachel, 81
Bergkatze, Die (1921), 284
Bergman, Ingmar, 30–32, 335, 452, 458–59, 473
Bergman, Ingrid, 32, 92
Bergner, Elisabeth, 98
Berkeley, Busby, 33
Berlin (1927), 154, 414
Berlin (1945), 375
Bernhardt, Curtis, 33–34
Bertolucci, Bernardo, 34–35, 416
Best Foot Forward (1942), 111
Best Years of Our Lives, The (1946), 461, 515–16
Bible, The (1966), 218
Bicycle Thief, The (1948), 270
Big Parade, The (1924), 456, 479, 481
Big Sleep, The (1935), 3

Big Trail, The (1931), 496
Bigger Than Life (1956), 9
Bill of Divorcement, A (1932), 94, 195
Billion Dollar Brain, The (1967), 412–13
Billy Budd (1962), 473–74
Billy Liar (1963), 417
Bini, Alfredo, 346
Birds, The (1963), 203, 206
Birth of a Nation, The (1915), 36, 168, 177, 488
Bisset, Jacqueline, 471
Bitzer, Billy, 35–36, 357, 452
Black Cat, The (1941), 87
Black Knight, The (1954), 42
Black Narcissus (1947), 61, 450
Blackboard Jungle (1955), 50
Blackburn, Maurice, 306
Blackmail (1929), 202, 320, 328
Blackton, James Stuart, 37–38, 472
Blair, Linda, 156
Blanke, Henry, 134
Blassetti, Alessandro, 166
Blind Date (1960), 22
Blind Husbands (1919), 99
Blithe Spirit (1947), 184
Blitzstein, Marc, 38, 477
Blondell, Joan, 39, 58
Blood and Sand (1941), 296
Blue, Monte, 52–53, 310
Blue Angel, The (1930), 109–10, 161
Boardman, Eleanor, 92
Bob and Carol and Ted and Alice (1969), 514
Body and Soul (1947), 214, 345, 407–8
Boetticher, Budd, 39
Bofors Gun, The (1968), 491
Bogaert, Lucienne, 63
Bogarde, Dirk, 39–40
Bogart, Humphrey, 17, 28, 102, 171, 278, 347
Bogdanovich, Peter, 29, 40–41
Boles, John, 82
Boheme, La (1926), 479, 482
Boleslawski, Richard, 41, 425
Bolt, Robert, 41–42, 145, 262, 421
Bondman, The (1915), 441–42
Bonnie and Clyde (1967), 29, 350–51
Boom (1968), 281–82, 437
Boom Town (1940), 43
Boomerang (1947), 233
Boorman, John, 42, 299–300, 485–86
Booth, Margaret, 42–43
Borgnine, Ernest, 43–44
Borinage (1933), 223
Borowczyk, Walerian, 44
Borzage, Frank, 400
Boston Strangler, The (1968), 8, 139
Boucher, Le (1969), 68
Boulle, Pierre, 145
Box, John, 44–45
Boy With Green Hair, The (1948), 278
Boyd, Stephen, 57, 201
Boyer, Charles, 425
Boyle, Robert, 228
Brabin, Charles, 283
Brackett, Charles, 45, 508
Bradley, David, 200

Brady, Matthew, 521
Brakhage, Stan, 45–46
Brando, Marlon, 34–35, 46, 78, 264–65, 288–89, 292, 300–1, 419, 440, 467
Brasseur, Claude, 66
Brault, Michel, 46, 229, 297
Braunberger, Pierre, 385–86
Brazil: A Report on Torture (1971), 504
Brecht, Bertolt, 8, 207, 278
Bressler, Jerry, 348
Bresson, Robert, 47, 63, 170, 293
Bride Wore Red, The (1937), 13
Bridge, The (1954), 505
Bridge on the River Kwai, The (1957), 145, 191–92
Brig, The (1964), 308
Bright Shawl, The (1923), 397
Brief Encounter (1945), 506
Bring Your Smile Along (1955), 123
Bringing Up Baby (1938), 29
Britten, Benjamin, 47, 67
Brook, Peter, 47–48, 224, 322
Brooks, Louise, 48–49
Brooks, Richard, 49
Brothers Karamazov, The (1958), 50
Brothers and Sisters of the Toda Family (1941), 341
Brown, Clarence, 50–52
Brown, Joe E., 506
Brown, Karl, 52–53
Browning, Tod, 303
Brownlow, Kevin, 53
Brunel, Adrian, 319
Brunius, Jacques, 53–54
Buchan, Alistair, 248
Bullfighter and the Lady, The (1951), 39
Buñuel, Luis, 19, 54–56, 322, 324, 344, 433, 471
Burks, Robert, 206
Burstyn, Ellen, 56, 155, 422
Burton, Richard, 56, 169–70, 218, 281
Bus Stop (1956), 274–75
But Not for Me (1959), 345
Butch Cassidy and the Sundance Kid (1969), 182
Butler, William, 148

Cabanne, Christy, 152, 282
Cabaret (1972), 315, 517
Cabecas Cortadas (1970), 398
Cabinet of Dr. Caligari, The (1919), 255
Cacoyannis, Michael, 58
Cagney, James, 39, 58, 500
Caine, Michael, 59
Calcutta (1969), 294, 403
California Split (1974), 6
Cameramen, cinematography: Arriflex camera, 102, 154, 181, 292, 294; camera movement, 6, 10, 93, 120, 197–98, 214, 255, 327; color processes, uses, 18, 40, 50, 68, 96, 137, 143, 172, 205, 214, 217, 289–90, 296, 300, 316; color experiments, 11, 216, 323, 523; concealed cameras, 154, 323, 480; depth of field, 53–54, 214, 462–64, 516; lighting, 34, 162–63; multiple cameras, 132–33, 169,

Cameramen (*cont.*)
331, 338–39; screen ratios, 335; wide screen, 275; Technicolor, 91, 216, 266, 482. *See also* individual listings
Camille (1937), 94, 97
Candidate, The (1972), 379
Canary Island Bananas (1935), 261
Cantor, Eddie, 33
Canutt, Yakima, 59–60, 200
Capellani, Albert, 158
Capra, Frank, 60–61, 190, 487
Captain Blood (1935), 492
Cardiff, Jack, 61–62
Carefree (1938), 15
Caretaker, The (1963), 111, 359–60
Carey, Harry, 143, 496
Carey, Macdonald, 298
Carle, Gilles, 62
Carmen (1915), 129
Carmen (1918), 284
Carnal Knowledge (1971), 332–33
Carné, Marcel, 9
Caron, Leslie, 188
Carrière, Jean-Claude, 55
Carrosse d'Or, La (1952), 388
Carson, Kit, 303
Casablanca (1942), 242
Casarès, Marie, 63
Casque d'Or (1952), 27–28, 433
Cassavetes, John, 63–65
Cassell, Jean-Pierre, 66, 68, 104
Cat People, The (1942), 398
Catch-22 (1969), 195
Cavalcanti, Alberto, 66–67, 380, 495
Cayrol, Jean, 392
Cenere (1916), 119
Chabrol, Claude, 19, 66–68, 104, 470
Chairman, The (1969), 457
Champion (1949), 113
Chang Chun-hsiang, 68–69
Chapayev (1934), 22
Chaplin, Charles, 46, 69–71, 82, 83, 172, 272, 310, 319, 361, 394, 427, 436, 447, 450, 454, 464–65
Chaplin, Geraldine, 71
Chaplin, Sydney, 447
Chappaqua (1966), 403
Charell, Erik, 196
Charge of the Light Brigade, The (1936), 122
Charge of the Light Brigade, The (1968), 167
Charlie Bubbles (1967), 136, 315
Charly (1968), 329, 396–97
Chase, Borden, 71–72
Chase, Charley, 394
Chase, The (1966), 351
Chasse au Lion a l'Arc, La (1958–65), 409
Chateau en Enfer (1969), 104
Chayefsky, Paddy, 43–44, 72
Chekhov, Mikhail, 514
Cherkasov, Nikolai, 73
Chevalier, Maurice, 73, 211–12, 283
Childhood of Gorky, The (1938–40), 112–13
Children's Hour, The (1962), 291

Chienne, La (1931), 385
Chimes at Midnight (*Falstaff*) (1966), 166–67, 498–99
Chinatown (1974), 466
Chinoise, La (1967), 262
Chin Shan, 74
Chloe in the Afternoon (1972), 400–1, 522–23
Chretien, Henri, 19
Christmas Tree, The (1969), 209
Chronique d'un été (1961), 46
Christie, Julie, 74
Chukhrai, Grigori, 74–75
Cimarron (1931), 122
Cincinnati Kid, The (1965), 228, 258–59
Citizen Kane (1941), 88, 90, 198–99, 208, 213, 320–21, 460–64, 497–99
City, The (1939), 477
Clair, René, 10, 19, 25, 66, 73, 75–76, 88
Claire, Ina, 283
Clark, James, 187–89
Clarke, Mae, 500
Clarke, Shirley, 77–78, 513
Clayton, Jack, 134, 240, 324
Clément, Réne, 35, 85, 323
Cléo from 5 to 7 (1961), 478
Cleopatra (1963), 56–57, 206
Clift, Montgomery, 78, 240, 383–84, 508
Clifton, Elmer, 53
Clockwork Orange, A (1971), 246, 248–49, 304
Close, Ivy, 328
Clothier, William H., 78–79, 501
Cobb, Lee J., 80
Cocteau, Jean, 80–82
Cohen, Emmanuel, 502
Cohn, Harry, 61, 190
Colbert, Claudette, 61
Colour Box (1935), 289
Colman, Ronald, 82–83, 413
Comedy, comedians: *see* W. Allen, Ball, C. Chaplin, Conklin, W. Fields, Horton, Keaton, Lemmon, Lester, J. Lewis, Lloyd, G. Marx, Medvedkin, Perelman, Roach, W. Rogers, Sellers, Sennett, Tashlin, Tati
Comingore, Dorothy, 461
Companeez, Jacques, 28
Compartiment Tueurs (*The Sleeping Car Murders*) (1965), 88–89
Compulsion (1958), 138
Concert of Mr. & Mrs. Kabal, The (1962), 44
Conformist, The (1969), 416
Conklin, Chester, 83
Connery, Sean, 83
Conway, Jack, 425
Construire un Feu (1927–30), 20
Convict's Sacrifice, A (1909), 490
Coogan, Jackie, 70
Cool Hand Luke (1967), 358
Cool World, The (1963), 513
Cooper, Merian C., 425
Copland, Aaron, 83–84, 369, 477
Coppola, Francis Ford, 84–85, 333, 467
Corman, Roger, 40, 84–86, 333, 371
Cortese, Valentina, 471

Cortez, Stanley, 87–88
Costa-Gavras, 88–89, 93
Cotten, Joseph, 90
Courtenay, Tom, 417
Cousins, Les (1958), 19, 104
Coutard, Raoul, 91–92, 350
Coward, Noël, 18, 175, 184–85
Craig, Gordon, 246
Crain, Jeanne, 234
Crash Donovan (1936), 329
Crack in the Mirror (1960), 138
Crawford, Joan, 13, 92, 490
Cries and Whispers (1972), 32
Criminal, The (1960), 280
Crisis (1946), 30–31
Crisp, Donald, 93
Cromwell, John, 72, 424
Cronaca di un amore (1950), 10–11
Crosby, Floyd, 521
Crowd, The (1928), 480
Cruze, James, 102
Cry for Help, A (1959), 444
Cukor, George, 26, 87, 92–97, 161–62,
    172, 257, 264, 426
Cummington Story, The (1946), 175
Curtis, Tony, 139, 506
Curtiz, Michael, 231, 242
Cybulski, Zbigniew, 487
Czinner, Paul, 98

Dames du Bois de Boulogne, Les (1945),
    47, 63
Damned, The (1969), 459, 484
Dance at Eagle Pass, The (1911 ?), 464
Dance, dancers, choreographers: *see*
    Astaire, Berkeley, Kelly, Nureyev
Dancigers, Oscar, 54–55
Dandridge, Dorothy, 429
Dane, Clemence, 184
Danger on the Air (1938), 87
Daniell, Henry, 97
Daniels, Bebe, 99
Daniels, William, 99, 101, 161
Dankworth, John, 279
D'Antoni, Phil, 154
Darbon, Emile, 81
Dark at the Top of the Stairs, The (1960),
    257
Dark Passage (1947), 102
Darrieux, Danielle, 101
Dassin, Jules, 101–2, 354, 356
Daves, Delmer, 102
David and Lisa (1962), 355
David Copperfield (1935), 97–98
David Harum (1915), 120
David Holzman's Diary (1967), 303
Davis, Bette, 34, 102–3, 130, 193, 460, 516
Davis, John, 178
Day, Josette, 82
Day, The (1961), 134
Day for Night (1973), 208, 471
Day of the Locust, The (1975), 419
Day of Waters (1971), 246
Day of Wrath (1942), 115, 436
Days of Glory (1944), 347
Days of Wine and Roses (1962), 383
De Antonio, Emile, 81

Dead Birds, 160
Dead of Night (1946), 380
Dean, James, 318, 376
Death of a Salesman (1951), 29
Death Wish (1974), 509–10
Death Takes a Holiday (1933), 265–66
DeBroca, Philippe, 103–4
Decaë, Henri, 104–5, 350
Decameron (1971), 347
December 7th (1942), 346
Deep End (1970), 436
Deliverance (1972), 486, 523
Delon, Alain, 309, 434
Dementia 13 (1962), 84–85
Demich, Irina, 519
De Mille, Cecil B., 99, 105, 129, 169, 174,
    189, 258–59, 265, 368–69
De Mille, William, 105–6, 129
Démons de L'Aube, Les (1945), 434
Demy, Jacques, 106, 478
De Packh, Maurice, 497
De Palma, Brian, 303
De Putti, Lya, 118
Dernier atout (1942), 27
De Santis, Giuseppe, 9
De Seta, Vittorio, 106
De Sica, Vittorio, 107–8, 276
Design, art direction, settings, costumes:
    see Barsacq, Bass, Beaton, Box, Fegté,
    Herlth, Horner; costumes, *see* Head, 19,
    202
Design for Living (1933), 194
Deslaw, Eugène, 232
Deutsch, Adolph, 108–9
Devil and Daniel Webster, The (1941),
    199–200
Devils, The (1971), 393, 412
Devil's Disciple, The (1958), 254
Devine, Andy, 60
Diaboliques, Les (1955), 80, 433
Dial M for Murder (1954), 205
Diamond, I. A. L., 109, 507–9
Dickens, Charles, 13
Dickinson, Angie, 134
Dietrich, Marlene, 109–10, 161, 275, 425,
    508
Digue, La (1911), 158
Dikii, Alexei, 174–75
Directors, mise-en-scene: relation with
    producers, 4, 22–23, 34. *See also* in-
    dividual listings
Directors Guild, 333
Dirty Harry (1971), 432
Discreet Charm of the Bourgeoisie, The
    (1972), 19
Disney, Walt, 20, 110, 215, 275
Distant Thunder (1972), 378
Di Venanzo, Gianni, 239, 321
Dr. Broadway (1942), 298
Dr. Bull (1933), 143
Dr. Strangelove (1965), 189, 193, 247–
    48
Dr. Zhivago (1965), 41–42
Doctor's Dilemma, The (1954), 14
Dodsworth (1936), 340
Dolce Vita, La (1960), 301
Donat, Robert, 492

Donen, Stanley, 111, 136
Donner, Clive, 111–12, 359
Don Q (1925), 15
Don Quixote (1974), 334
Donskoy, Mark, 112–13, 427
Double Indemnity (1949), 409–10, 507
Double Life, A (1947), 95
Douglas, Kirk, 113–14, 151
Douglas, Melvyn, 114
Dovzhenko, Alexander, 114–15, 234
Dozier, William, 243, 339
Dracula, 263
Dreigroschenoper, Die (1931), 58
Dreyer, Carl-Theodor, 47, 67, 115–17,
    215, 436
Drifters (1929), 176
Drums Along the Mohawk (1939), 143
Drunken Angel (1948), 250
Dudow, Slatan, 207
Duel in the Sun (1946), 481
Dumbo (1941), 215
Dullea, Keir, 165
Dunning, Jack, 213
Dupont, Ewald-André, 80, 117–18
Durante, Jimmy, 277
Duras, Marguerite, 118–19
Du Rififi chez les Hommes (1955), 101,
    356
Duse, Eleanora, 119
Dutchman (1966), 187
Dutta, Dulal, 377
Dwan, Allan, 119–21
Dymling, Carl-Anders, 30

Eason, B. Reeves, 122
East of Eden (1955), 235
Eastman Company, 52, 144, 316
Easter Parade (1948), 237, 490
Eastwood, Clint, 122–23
Easy Rider (1969), 141, 209–10
Ekberg, Anita, 193
Ecoledes Facteurs, L' (1947), 454
Ecstasy (1933), 253
Edge of Doom (1950), 174
Editors, cutting, montage: *see* Arzner,
    Booth, V. Fields, Goldman, Parrish,
    Shub; *also* pp. 99, 120, 173, 263, 270–
    71, 288, 437–38, 464–65, 512
Edwards, Blake, 123
Edwards, Billy and Antoinette, 266–67
Effi Briest (1973), 130
8½ (1963), 132, 501
Ehrlich, Max, 422
Eisenstein, Sergei, 46, 73, 123–27, 165,
    234, 246, 319, 424
Eisler, Hanns, 127–28
Ekman, Hasse, 31
El Dorado (1966), 191
Ellis, Melville, 129
End of St. Petersburg, The (1927), 372
Epstein, Jean, 54
Epstein, Julius and Philip, 242
Eternal City, The (1914), 152
Eva (1962), 22–23, 281, 321–22
Evans, Edith, 128
Every Day Except Christmas (1957), 7
Exodus (1960), 330

Exorcist, The (1973), 56, 155–56, 401
Extra Girl, The (1923), 210

Faces (1968), 64
Fahrenheit 451 (1966), 471
Fail-Safe (1964), 288
Fairbanks, Douglas, 119–20, 265
Fairbanks, Douglas Jr., 21, 339
Faits Divers (1923), 19
Falconetti, 115, 215
Falk, Peter, 65
Fall of the House of Usher, The (1928),
    494
Fall of the House of Usher (1960), 371
Fall of the Romanov Dynasty (1927), 430
Fallen Idol, The (1948), 19
Falstaff (Chimes at Midnight) (1965),
    498–99
Fanck, Arnold, 6
Fantasia (1940), 215
Fantastic Voyage (1966), 360
Far from the Madding Crowd (1967), 74,
    400, 419
Farewell to Arms, A (1957), 216
Farmer Takes a Wife, The (1935), 139
Farnum, Dustin, 105
Farnum, William, 442
Farrar, Geraldine, 129
Farrell, Eileen, 129–30, 199
Farrow, Mia, 282, 370
Fashions for Women (1927), 13
Fassbinder, Rainer Werner, 130
Fat City (1972), 180–81, 236
Father Gets in the Game (1908), 13
Father Goose (1964), 175
Faust (1926), 404
Fear and Desire (1953), 247
Fegté, Ernst, 130–31
Feiffer, Jules, 333
Fejos, Paul, 385
Feldzug in Polen (1939), 6
Felitta, Frank, 422
Fellini, Federico, 131–32, 301
Fellows, Robert, 501
Femme au Couteau, La (1969), 26
Femme de Boulanger, La (1938), 375
Femme Douce, Une (1969), 416
Femme est une Femme, Une (1961), 91,
    171–72
Ferrer, José, 323
Fêtes Galant, Les (1965), 66
Feuillade, Louis, 75, 158, 391
Feyder, Jacques, 367–68, 403, 434
Fiddler on the Roof (1971), 464
Fields, Verna, 132–33
Fields, W. C., 76, 97–98, 133, 502
Fifteen Strings of Cash (1956), 453
Figueroa, Gabriel, 54, 324
Fight to the Last (1938), 270
Fighting Chance, The (1920), 328
Finance, 8, 26, 107, 134
Finch, Peter, 57, 133–35, 167
Finney, Albert, 135–37
Firemen's Ball, The (1968), 147
Firma Heiratet, Die (1914), 283
Fischer, Gunnar, 31
Fistful of Dollars, A (1964), 122–23

Fists in the Pocket (1966), 28
Five Easy Pieces (1970), 334
Five Graves to Cairo (1943), 506–7
Flaherty, Robert, 137–38, 173–74, 176–77, 476, 494, 520
Flame of New Orleans, The (1941), 76
Flaubert, Gustave, "A Simple Heart," 107
Fleck, Fred, 512
Fleischer, Max, 138, 381, 453
Fleming, Victor, 16–17, 139, 194, 268
Flesh and the Devil (1927), 260–61
Flight of the Phoenix, The (1965), 444
Floating Weeds (1959), 341
Flon, Suzanne, 323
Flynn, Errol, 201, 492
Folsey, George, 295
Fonda, Henry, 139–41, 256, 432
Fonda, Jane, 141, 361
Fonda, Peter, 141
Fontaine, Joan, 96, 205, 243–44
Foolish Wives (1921), 99–100
Forbes, Bryan, 142, 188
Force of Evil (1948), 366
Ford, Francis, 142
Ford, John, 8, 39, 40, 59–60, 78–79, 140–41, 142–44, 190, 234, 268–69, 313–14, 324, 345, 425, 444, 500, 505–6
Foreign Affair, A (1948), 508
Foreman, Carl, 144–45
Forman, Milos, 109, 146–48, 194–95
Fort Apache (1948), 78
Forrest, Dave, 108–9
Forty-First, The (1956), 74–75
42nd Street (1933), 33
Four Devils (1928), 327
Four Horsemen of the Apocalypse (1921), 221
Four Horsemen of the Apocalypse (1962), 459
Four Hundred Blows, The (1959), 104, 468–69
Four Hundred Million (1939), 127–28
Fox, William, 148–49, 441
Frail Women (1931), 179
France, Charles, 184
Francis, Kay, 130
Franju, Georges, 149–50, 318
Frank, Gerald, 8
Frankenheimer, John, 21, 150–52, 257
Franklin, Sidney, 152
Frederick, Pauline, 152–53
French Connection, The (1971), 154–55
Frenchman's Creek (1944), 130–31, 266
Frenzy (1972), 206–7, 296
Freud, Sigmund, 283
Freud (1962), 217, 436, 517
Freudlose Gasse, Die (1925), 439
Freund, Karl, 117–18, 153–54, 197–98, 255, 414
Friedkin, William, 56, 154–56
Fröhlich, Carl, 343
Fröhlich, Gustav, 255
Front Page, The (1931), 312
From Here to Eternity (1953), 240, 521
Fry, Christopher, 200
Fugitive, The (1947), 141, 324
Fugitive Kind, The (1960), 292

Fuller, Samuel, 156–57
Funny Girl (1968), 446, 516
Funny Thing Happened on the Way to the Forum, A (1966), 399
Fury (1936), 256–57, 297–98

Gabin, Jean, 24
Gable, Clark, 16–17, 43, 61, 93, 268, 277, 345
Gaily, Gaily (1969), 228
Gance, Abel, 158–59
Gandolfi, Alfredo, 105
Garbo, Greta, 21, 41, 51, 92, 94, 99–101, 114, 159, 161, 260–61, 275, 295–96, 302, 339, 439–40
Garden of Allah, The (1936), 425
Garden of the Finzi-Continis, The (1971), 108, 416
Gardner, Ava, 435
Gardner, Cyril, 93
Garfein, Jack, 159
Garfunkel, Art, 333
Gargan, William, 160–61
Garland, Judy, 237, 302, 315, 490
Garmes, Lee, 161–62, 442, 481
Garner, Peggy Ann, 233
Gaslight (1944), 257
Gasnier, Louis, 313
Gaudio, Gaetano, 162–63
Gauntier, Gene, 163
Gazzara, Ben, 65
General Died at Dawn, The (1936), 314
General Line, The (1926–29), 459–60
Gentleman, Wally, 163–65
Gentleman's Agreement (1948), 234
Georgy Girl (1966), 379
Gerasimov, Sergei, 165–66
Germi, Pietro, 166
Gertrud (1964), 115, 117, 436
Get Out and Get Under (1920), 273
Giannini, Giancarlo, 166
Giant (1956), 160
Gibbons, Cedric, 480
Gibson, William, 350
Gielgud, John, 166–67, 246
Gigi (1958), 26
Gilbert, John, 260–61, 479, 482
Gillespie, Arnold, 480
Gilliatt, Penelope, 167–68, 224
Girl from Trieste, The (see *Bride Wore Red, The*)
Gish, Lillian, 43, 168–69, 438, 479, 482
Glass Wall, The (1953), 205–6
Glazer, Benjamin, 48
Glennon, Bert, 169, 442
Glenville, Peter, 169–70
Gliese, Rochus, 404
Go-Between, The (1971), 265, 282
Godard, Jean-Luc, 28, 91, 170–72, 256, 262
Goddard, Paulette, 172
Goddess, The (1957), 72
Godfather, The (1972–74), 85, 344, 410–11, 467
Goetz, William, 500
Gold, Jack, 491
Gold Diggers of 1933 (1933), 33

Gold Rush, The (1925), 319, 450
Goldman, John, 173–4
Goldwyn, Samuel, 13, 33, 105, 153, 174, 216, 231, 368, 446, 460
Golem, The (1920), 497
Golovnya, Anatoli, 174–75
Gone With the Wind (1939), 152, 161, 194, 217, 264, 426
Goodbye Charlie (1964), 56
Good Earth, The (1937), 325
Goosson, Stephen, 460
Gordon, Ruth, 95
Gospel According to St. Matthew, The (1964), 346
Gosta Berlings Saga (1924), 159, 439
Goulding, Edmund, 451
Graduate, The (1967), 332
Grande Illusion, La (1937), 386
Grand Prix (1966), 152
Grant, Cary, 175, 190, 206, 247, 336
Grapes of Wrath, The (1940), 7, 140, 461
Grau, Gil, 497
Grayson, Helen, 175
Great Dictator, The (1940), 447, 465
Great Expectations (1946), 178
Great Gatsby, The (1974), 379
Greatest Story Ever Told, The (1965), 452
Greed (1923), 99–100, 386, 446
Greene, Graham, 176
Greene, Milton, 275
Greenstreet, Sidney, 278, 431
Greetings (1969), 303
Grido, Il (1957), 10
Grierson, John, 9, 67, 176–77, 495
Griffith, D. W., 12–13, 36, 42–43, 52–53, 88, 119, 152, 165, 177–78, 186, 250, 276–77, 282, 299, 300, 356–57, 427, 451, 456, 488–89, 490
Griffith, Edward, 283
Grumpy (1930), 93
Gruson, Dave, 366
Guerre est Finie, La (1966), 392
Guess Who's Coming to Dinner (1967), 247
Guinness, Alec, 178, 191–92, 329
Gunga Din (1939), 443
Guns of Navarone, The (1961), 459
Guffey, Burney, 182, 350
Gupta, Banshi Chandra, 377
Gypsy Moths, The (1969), 151

Hackman, Gene, 155
Hagen, Jean, 192
Hall, Conrad, 180
Hall, Peter, 182
Hall, Spec, 53
Hallelujah! (1929), 480, 483
Haller, Daniel, 86
Halliwell, Miles, 53
Hammarskjold, Dag, 206
Hani, Susumu, 182–83
Hansen, Einar, 440
Harakiri (1963), 241
Harareet, Haya, 201
Hard Day's Night, A (1964), 269
Hardwicke, Cedric, 183

Hardy, Oliver, 183, 303
Harris, Richard, 183–84
Harrison, Rex, 57, 96, 184–85
Harryhausen, Ray, 185
Hart, William S., 186–87
Harvey, Anthony, 187–89, 437
Hashimoto, 251
Hathaway, Henry, 393
Hawks, Howard, 29, 79, 189–91, 425
Hayakawa, Sessue, 191–92
Hayden, Sterling, 192–93
Hayward, Leland, 268–69
Hayworth, Rita, 110
He Ran All the Way (1951), 214
Head, Edith, 193
Head, Murray, 135
Hearn, Lafcadio, 241
Hearst, William Randolph, 497–98
Hearts Adrift (1914), 357
Hecht, Ben, 190, 193–94, 228, 425
Hecht, Harold, 4
Heiress, The (1949), 83–84, 211, 369
Hellinger, Mark, 435
Hello Dolly! (1969), 237
Hellman, Jerome, 419
Hellman, Monte, 333
Henabery, Joseph, 53
Henry, Buck, 29, 194–95
Henry V (1946), 337
Hepburn, Audrey, 185, 195, 518
Hepburn, Katharine, 95, 195–97, 231–32, 247, 287
Hercules Unchained (1959), 270
Herlth, Robert, 153, 197–98
Hernadi, Gyula, 225
Herrmann, Bernard, 198–200, 213
Heston, Charlton, 200–2, 348
Hi, Nellie (1933), 130
Hiawatha (1914), 314
Higgins, Michael, 274
High Noon (1952), 144–45, 191, 459, 521
Higgins, John, 465–66
High School (1968), 513
Highway Dragnet (1954), 85–86
Hilburn, Percy, 331
Hilde Warren und der Tod (1917), 90
Hill, George Roy, 182, 379
Hill, Jack, 85
Hill, The (1965), 323
Hiller, Arthur, 244
Hiroshima Mon Amour (1959), 118–19, 170
His New Job (1915), 464–65
Hitchcock, Alfred, 25, 67–68, 96, 167, 193, 202–7, 212, 319–20, 347, 353, 475, 522
Hoa Binh (1970), 91–92
Hoellering, George, 207
Hoffman, Dustin, 207–8, 332, 418
Hoffmann, Carl, 208, 404
Hoge, Ralph, 208
Holden, William, 123, 209, 508–9
Holiday (1930), 16
Honegger, Artur, 38
Hopper, Dennis, 141, 209–19
Horn, Camilla, 94
Hornbeck, William, 210
Horner, Harry, 210–11, 361

Horse's Mouth, The (1959), 178
Horton, Edward Everett, 211–12
Hotchkiss, 385
Hotel des Invalides (1951), 150
Houseman, John, 134, 212–13, 243, 316
Howard, Leslie, 213–14
Howard, Sidney, 161–62, 194
Howard, Tom, 449
Howe, James Wong, 214–15
How He Lied to Her Husband (1931), 178
How to Steal a Million (1966), 195
Huang Shao-Fen, 453
Hubley, John, 215
Hud (1963), 394
Hughes, Howard, 213, 339
Hugo, Valentine, 215
Humain, Trop Humaine (1973), 294
Human Condition, The (1958–61), 241
Hunchback of Notre Dame, The (1939), 503
Hurry Sundown (1967), 59
Husbands (1970), 65
Hustler, The (1961), 330, 407
Huston, John, 17, 46, 181, 192–93, 196, 215–18, 235–36, 323–24, 423, 434–36, 488, 517
Huston, Walter, 215
Huyck, William and Gloria, 285–86

I Am a Camera (1955), 220
I Am a Fugitive From a Chain Gang (1932), 325
I Came to Give You Freedom (unrealized), 431
I Shot Jesse James (1949), 156
Ichikawa, Kon, 219
Idiot, The (1951), 251
If I Had a Million (1932), 133
Ikiru (1952), 251
Imai, Tadashi, 219–20
In Cold Blood (1967), 49
In Spring (1929), 233
In the Cool of the Day (1963), 134
In Which We Serve (1942), 18
India (1958), 405
Ince, Thomas, 161, 186, 191, 331
Indiscretions of an American Wife (1954), 324
Informer, The (1935), 3, 331, 496
Inge, William, 220–21
Ingraham, Lloyd, 282, 464
Ingram, Rex, 221, 446
Innocents, The (1962), 240
International House (1933), 133
Interrupted Messages, The (1900), 35–36
Intimate Lighting (1966), 347
Intolerance (1916), 52–53, 152, 277
L'Invitata (1970), 106
Ioseliani, Otar, 222
Iron Duke, The (1935), 90
Is Paris Burning? (1966), 85
Isherwood, Christopher, 220
Isle of the Dead (1945), 397–98
Isn't Life Wonderful? (1924), 250
It Happened Here (1963), 53
It Happened One Night (1934), 61

Ivan Grozny (*Ivan the Terrible*) (1945–46), 73
Ivens, Joris, 222–23
Iwerks, Ub, 110

J'Accuse (1919), 159
Jackson, Glenda, 167, 224, 411
Jaglom, Henry, 209
Jaguar (1958–67), 409
Jannings, Emil, 90, 117–18, 153–54, 197
Jansco, Miklos, 225–26
Jason and the Argonauts (1963), 185
Jaubert, Maurice, 226
Jaworsky, Henry, 226–27
Jazz Singer, The (1927), 211
Jefferson, Joseph, 37
Jennings, Humphrey, 8
Jeremiah Johnson (1972), 379
Jeux de l'Amour, Les (1959), 103
Jewison, Norman, 227–28, 244, 260
Johnny Belinda (1948), 516
Johnny Got His Gun (1971), 471–72
Johnson, Lyndon, 457
Johnson, Martin, 251
Johnstone, Julanne, 265
Jones, Chuck, 20
Jones, Jennifer, 481
Jones, Quincy, 228–29, 287
Jones, F. Richard, 210
Jour de fête (1947), 455
Journal de femme de chambre, Le (1964), 55
Journey Into Fear (1943), 511
Joyce, Patricia, 235
Joyless Street (See *Die Freudlose Gasse*)
Jubilo (1919), 400
Judge Hardy and Son (1939), 302
Judgment at Nuremberg (1960), 78, 254, 429, 505
Jules et Jim (1961), 322, 469–70
Julius Caesar (1949), 200
Julius Caesar (1953), 212, 410
Justin, George, 72
Justine (1969), 40, 517
Jutra, Claude, 46, 229–30

Kael, Pauline, 213
Kafka, Franz, 334
Kanin, Garson, 95, 161, 231–32
Kapital, Das (unrealized), 125
Karina, Anna, 171
Karloff, Boris, 398
Kaufman, Boris, 232, 235, 287
Kaufman, George, 300
Kaufman, Mikhail, 232–33
Kautner, Helmut, 504
Kazan, Chris, 235
Kazan, Elia, 113, 220–21, 233–35, 240, 264, 347, 383–84, 393, 440–41, 514
Keach, Stacy, 181, 235–36
Keaton, Buster, 24, 76, 236–37, 394
Keeler, Ruby, 33
Keitel, Harvey, 421
Kelly, Gene, 111, 237–38, 490
Kendall, Kay, 238–39
Kende, Janos, 239
Kennedy, John Fitzgerald, 396
Kerr, Deborah, 239–40

Key, The (1958), 145
Keystone, 69, 83, 169, 272, 427, 428
Khmelyov, Nikolai, 22
Khokhlova, Alexandra, 249
Kid, The (1921), 70, 272
Kid from Spain, The (1932), 33
Kiley, Richard, 156–57
Killers, The (1946), 434–35
Killing, The (1956), 171
Killing of Sister George, The (1969), 517
Kimbrough, Hunter, 126
Kind of Loving, A (1961), 417
King, Allan, 266
King and Country (1964), 281
King Kong (1933), 496
King of Alcatraz (1938), 368
King of Marvin Gardens (1972), 334
King Solomon's Mines (1950), 239, 449
Kino-Pravda, 233, 479
Kirkwood, James, 490
Kiss, The (1929), 21
Kleine Napoleon, Der (1923), 109
Kline, Richard, 228
Knack, The (1965), 269
Knave of Hearts (1954), 323
Knife in the Water (1961), 363–64
Knott, Lydia, 450
Knox, Frank, 301
Kobayashi, Masaki, 241
Kobayashi, Takeji, 240–42
Koch, Carl, 382
Koch, Howard, 213, 242–44
Koenig, William, 500
Korda, Alexander, 244, 259, 344
Kortner, Fritz, 49
Kotcheff, Ted, 244–45
Kozintsev, Grigori, 165, 245–46
Kozlovsky, Sergei, 174
Kracauer, Siegfried, 130
Kräly, Hans, 247
Kramer, Stanley, 247, 434
Krampf, Gunther, 207
Krasna, Norman, 300
Krasner, Milton, 275
Krauss, Werner, 384–85
Kriukov, Lyosha, 124
Kubrick, Stanley, 113, 164–65, 187–89, 193, 247–49, 304, 510
Kuhle Wampe (1931), 207
Kuleshov, Lev, 249–50, 371
Kuntze, Reimar, 414
Kurosawa, Akira, 250–52
Kwaidan (1964), 241
Kyo, Machiko, 251

L-Shaped Room, The (1963), 188–89
Labiche, 172
Labrecque, Jean-Claude, 229
Lacombe Lucien (1974), 294
Ladd, Alan, 142
Lady from Shanghai (1949), 201
Lady in the Lake (1946), 203
Lady Killers, The (1955), 254
Lady of Shalott, The (1912), 328
Lady L (1965), 473
Lady Windermere's Fan (1925), 285
Lagerfeld, Karl, 19

Laemmle, Carl, 162, 456, 514
Laemmle, Carl, Jr., 21
Lamarr, Hedy, 253
Lambart, Evelyn, 253
Lambert, Gavin, 376
Lancaster, Burt, 3–4, 151, 254
Land, The (1939–42), 476
Landau, Ely, 288
Lang, André, 9
Lang, Fritz, 67–68, 140, 171, 255–57, 278, 297–98
Langdon, Harry, 394–95, 428
Langner, Philip, 287
Lansbury, Angela, 257
Lantz, Walter, 20
LaRoque, Rod, 257–58
Lasky, Jesse, 105, 129, 174, 328
Lassally, Walter, 258, 350
Last Days of Dolwyn, The (1948), 56
Last Laugh, The (1924), 153–54, 197
Last Detail, The (1973), 466
Last of the Mohicans, The (1920), 50–51
Last Picture Show, The (1971), 40
Last Tango in Paris (1972), 34–35, 419
Last Year at Marienbad (1962), 390–91, 396
Late Extra (1935), 300
Lathrop, Philip, 258–59
Laughton, Charles, 88, 93, 97, 160–61, 184, 192, 259, 317, 503
Laurel, Stan, 183, 260, 303, 399
Law, John Philip, 260
Law and Order (1969), 513
Lawford, Peter, 237
Lawman (1970), 80
Lawrence of Arabia (1962), 42, 263, 429
Lawson, John Howard, 261
Lawton, Charles, 102
Leacock, Richard, 77, 261–62
Lean, David, 42, 74, 145, 184, 192, 262–63, 522
Léaud, Jean-Pierre, 104, 468–69
LeBaron, William, 502
LeCarré, John, 189
Leda (1959), 104
Lee, Christopher, 263–64
Left-Handed Gun, The (1958), 349, 351
Leger, Fernand, 264
Legg, Stuart, 67
Legrand, Michel, 478
Lehman, Ernest, 204
Lehrman, "Pathé," 428
Leigh, Vivien, 184, 264–65
Leighton, Margaret, 265
Leisen, Mitchell, 130–31, 265–66
Leiterman, Richard, 266–67
Lelouch, Claude, 267, 468
Lemmon, Jack, 122–23, 267–68, 383, 506–507
Lenin in October (1937), 402
Lenny (1974), 207
Leo, Jack, 149
Leone, Sergio, 122
Leopard, The (1963), 254
Lerner, Irving, 477
Leroy, Mervyn, 268–69
Lester, Richard, 187, 269

Let's Do It Again (1975), 362
Letter from an Unknown Woman (1948), 243–44, 339
Levine, Joseph, 270
Lewin, Albert, 270–71
Lewis, David, 130
Lewis, Jerry, 271–72, 453
Lewis, Robert, 272
Lewis, Roger, 287
Lewton, Val, 272, 397–98
Lichtig, Renée, 389
Liebe der Jeanne Ney, Die (1927), 343
Liebelei (1932), 243, 339
Life and Times of Judge Roy Bean, The (1972), 216
Life of an American Fireman, The (1903), 367
Life of Emile Zola, The (1937), 162–63, 325–26, 503
Life in Death (1914), 325
Life of O-Haru (1952), 318
Life of Villa, The (1912), 489
Lighton, Louis D., 233
Lilith (1964), 407
Limelight (1952), 447
Linder, Max, 13
Lion in Winter, The (1968), 437
Little Caesar (1930), 129, 268, 397
Little Foxes, The (1941), 460
Little Island, The (1955), 509
Litvak, Anatole, 80, 103, 353
Lizards, The (1963), 501
Lloyd, Frank, 93
Lloyd, Harold, 99, 272–74, 394–95
Lockwood, Margaret, 184
Loden, Barbara, 274
Lodger, The (1926), 202–3, 319
Lods, Jean, 232
Logan, Joshua, 274–75
Lola (1960), 106
Lolita (1962), 187–89, 510
Lollobrigida, Gina, 276
London, Jack, 20
Loneliness of the Long Distance Runner, The (1963), 258, 393
Long Day's Journey Into Night, A (1962), 286–87
Long Goodbye, The (1973), 6
Long Hot Summer, The (1958), 393
Long Voyage Home, The (1940), 461
Longest Day, The (1962), 519
Look Back in Anger (1959), 136
Loos, Anita, 276–77
Lord of the Flies, The (1962), 48
Loren, Sophia, 277–78, 473
Lorentz, Pare, 476–77
Lorre, Peter, 278, 431–32
Losey, Joseph, 4, 22–23, 278–82, 265, 321–22, 484
Lourié, Eugene, 388
Louisiana Story (1948), 138, 261–62, 476
Love (1928), 260
Love, Bessie, 186–87, 282
Love Among the Ruins (1974), 196
Love Story (1970), 316
Lovely Way to Die, A (1968), 113
Loves of a Blonde (1965), 148

Low, Colin, 164
Loy, Myrna, 282–83
Lubitsch, Ernst, 51, 93–94, 194, 211–12, 244, 247, 283–85, 298, 310, 314, 376, 505
Lucas, George, 132–33, 285–86
Lucille Love (1914), 142
Lugosi, Bela, 144, 286
Lumet, Sidney, 140, 229, 186–89, 292, 323, 339
Lumière, Louis, 289
Lumière (1976), 322
Lunardi, Toni, 337
Lure of the Circus (1918), 365
Lust for Life (1956), 113–14, 316
Lyarsky, Alyosha, 112
Lye, Len, 289–90, 305
Lyon, Sue, 187, 218, 510

M (1931), 4, 255, 278, 280
M (1950), 4, 280
Mabel's Strange Predicament (1914), 83
Macadam (1946), 434
Macbeth (1971), 251
MacDonald, Jeanette, 211–12
MacDonald, J. Farrell, 273
MacGowran, Jack, 156
Machaty, Gustav, 253
MacKendrick, Alexander, 254
MacKenzie, Donald, 313
Mackintosh Man, The (1973), 216
MacMurray, Fred, 508–9
MacPherson, Jeannie, 129
Madame Du Barry (1919), 284
Madame Bovary (1949), 316
Madame Nicotine (1906), 402
Madden, Owney, 374
Maddow, Ben, 132, 291–92
Maddox, Lester, 338
Mademoiselle Docteur (1937), 420
Madigan (1968), 432
Madison, Larry, 175
Maedchen in Uniform (1931), 416
Magic Mountain, The (unrealized), 339
Magnani, Anna, 292, 388
Magnificent Ambersons, The (1942), 87–88, 498, 511
Maidstone (1969), 292–93
Mailer, Norman, 266–67, 292–93
Majewsky, Virginia, 200
Major Dundee (1965), 348
Makavejev, Dusan, 293
Make-up, *see* Westmore, Perc; *also see* pp. 15, 17, 91, 128
Malden, Karl, 123
Malle, Louis, 293–94, 403
Malraux, André, 3, 427
Maltese Falcon, The (1941), 17, 216, 278
Mamoulian, Rouben, 283, 294–96, 447, 491
Man and a Woman, A (1966), 267
Man for All Seasons, A (1966), 42, 45, 421
Man I Killed, The (*Broken Lullaby*) (1932), 93
Man of Aran (1933–4), 173–74, 494
Man Ray, 264, 369

Man to Remember, A (1938), 231
Man Who Knew Too Much (1934), 319
Man With a Movie Camera (1929), 233
Manchurian Candidate, The (1962), 21, 151, 257
Mancini, Henry, 296
Mandabi (*Money Order*) (1968), 427
Mandell, Daniel, 515–16
Mankiewicz, Francis, 297
Mankiewicz, Herman, 213, 297, 499
Mankiewicz, Joseph, 57, 59, 109, 257, 297–98
Mann, Anthony, 298–99
Mann, Daniel, 374
Mann, Delbert, 43–44, 257
Mao Tse-tung, 457
Marais, Jean, 82
Marat/Sade (1966), 224, 411
Marceau, Marcel, 245
March, Fredric, 13, 82, 93, 151, 265, 299, 447
Marchand, Colette, 323
Maria Rosa (1915), 129
Marius (1931), 344
Marley, Peverell, 169
Marmstedt, Lorens, 31
Marnie (1964), 200
Marquand, Christian, 18
Marriage Circle, The (1924), 285, 310
Marriage Playground, The (1929), 299
Married Couple, A (1969), 266
Marsh, Mae, 168, 186, 299
Marton, Andrew, 239
Marty (1955), 43–44, 72
Marvin, Lee, 42, 299–300
Marx Brothers, 300, 352
Marx, Julius "Groucho," 300, 351–52
Marx, Samuel, 71–72, 300
Mask of Dimitrios, The (1944), 329
Mask of Fu Manchu, The (1932), 283
Mason, James, 97, 187, 300–1, 339
Massingham, Richard, 305
Mastroianni, Marcello, 276, 301, 321
Maté, Rudolph, 76, 116
Mature, Victor, 56
May, Elaine, 332
May, Phil, 27
Mayer, Carl, 153–54
Mayer, Louis B., 13, 43, 61, 92, 152, 237, 297–98, 301–2, 425, 446, 455, 465–66
Maynard, Ken, 302
Mayo, Archie, 502
McBride, Jim, 302–3
McCabe and Mrs. Miller (1971), 523
McCarey, Leo, 303
McCord, Ted, 235, 350
McDowell, Malcolm, 304
McGuire, Charles, 72
McLaren, Norman, 305–7
McMurtry, Larry, 40
Mean Streets (1973), 421
Medvedkin, Alexander, 307
Medwin, Michael, 307–8
Meeker, Ralph, 160
Meerson, Lazare, 75
Meet Me in St. Louis (1944), 315
Mekas, Jonas, 308

Méliès, Georges, 36, 82, 246, 305, 308–9
Melville, Jean-Pierre, 309
Memphis Belle (1944), 515
Men Are Not Gods (1936), 184
Men of Tomorrow (1932), 416
Men Without Women (1929), 331
Mendes, Lothar, 299
Menjou, Adolphe, 310
Menzies, William Cameron, 298–99
Merrill, Gary, 132
Merry Widow, The (1925), 99, 352, 447
Merry Widow, The (1934), 211–12
Metropolis (1926), 255
Metropolitan Symphony (1929), 318
Metty, Russell, 88, 258
Metzner, Ernö, 310–11
Messiah, The (1975), 406
Meyerhold, Vsevolod, 123, 311–12
Meyers, Sidney, 132
Mickey (1917), 210
Mickey One (1964), 350
Midnight Cowboy (1969), 418, 485–86
Midsummer Night's Dream, A (1968), 182
Mifune, Toshiro, 250
Milestone, Lewis, 21, 312, 314, 426
Miller, Arthur C., 234–35
Miller, J. P., 383
Miller, Jason, 155
Miller, Lee, 81
Millhauser, Bertram, 313
Million, Le (1931), 75
Million Dollar Legs (1932), 133
Milner, Victor, 314
Minamata (1971), 183
Minnelli, Liza, 315
Minnelli, Vincent, 56, 238, 315–16, 459, 490
Minsky, Howard, 316
Mintz, Charles, 20
Miracle in the Rain (unrealized), 108
Miracle Worker, The (1962), 350
Misfits, The (1961), 488
Mistons, Les (1957), 468
Mr. Roberts (1955), 140, 268–69
Mrs. Miniver (1942), 301
Mitchell, Margaret, 194
Mitchum, Robert, 191, 316–17, 501
Mitra, Subrata, 317, 377
Mix, Tom, 317–18
Miyagawa, Kazuo, 341
Mizoguchi, Kenji, 318, 414
Moby Dick (1956), 217–18, 324
Mocky, Jean-Pierre, 318
Modern Times (1936), 172
Modesty Blaise (1966), 484–85
Modiano, Patrick, 294
Mogambo (1953), 40
Mohr, Hal, 318–19
Mollo, Andrew, 53
Molnar, Ferenc, 13
Molly Maguires, The (1968), 394
Monkey Business (1931), 352
Monroe, Marilyn, 62, 274–75, 507–8
Monsieur Hulot's Holiday (1951), 454–55
Monsieur Verdoux (1947), 272
Montagu, Ivor, 319–20
Montague, William P., 320

Montgomery, Robert, 61, 203
Moon and Sixpence, The (1942), 271
Moore, Owen, 357
Moorehead, Agnes, 320–21
Moreau, Jeanne, 321–22, 338
Morgan (1966), 380–81
Morgan, Don, 362
Mori, Masayuki, 251
Morley, Robert, 196
Morocco (1930), 110, 161
Morra, Mario, 367
Morris, Oswald, 218, 322–24
Mort d'un Bucheron, La (1973), 62
Mort en ce Jardin, La (1958), 433
Moscow Art Theatre, 41, 294, 340
Moss, Jack, 87
Mother (1926), 174, 372
Mother and the Law, The (1916), 177
Moulin Rouge (1953), 217–18, 322–23
Moussinac, Léon, 125
Moussy, Marcel, 468
Movie Crazy (1932), 273
Mozhukhin, Ivan, 249, 324–25
Mulligan, Robert, 354, 370
Muni, Paul, 17, 130, 162–63, 325–26, 503–504
Munk, Andrzej, 326–27, 363, 519
Munro, Grant, 306
Muriel (1963), 391–92
Murnau, F. W., 153, 197, 327, 404, 447–48
Murphy, Dudley, 264
Murphy, Richard, 234
Murray, Don, 275
Murray, Mae, 352
Music, composers: *see* Blitzstein, Britten, Copland, Eisler, Herrmann, Jaubert, Jones, Mancini, Previn, Rozsa, Steiner, Tiomkin, Webb; *also* pp. 82, 106, 126–27, 477
Mussolini, Benito, 483
Mutiny on the Bounty (1935), 93
My Fair Lady (1964), 26–27, 96, 185
My Little Chickadee (1940), 502

Nabokov, Vladimir, 510
Nagel, Conrad, 328
Nijinsky, Vaslav, 412
Naked City (1948), 356
Nalpas, Louis, 158
Nana (1926), 384
Nanami (1968), 183
Nanook of the North (1922), 137–38, 174
Napoléon (1927), 159
Napoleon Crossing the Alps (1904), 162
Narcissus (1975?), 307
Nashville (1975), 6, 71
Nasser, Gamal Abdul, 429
National Film Board of Canada, 12, 297, 305–6
Native Land (1940–41), 38
Nazi Agent (1942), 101
Neame, Elwin, 328
Neame, Ronald, 185, 328–29
Nouveaux Messieurs, Les (1928), 367–68
Negulesco, Jean, 329, 516
Neighbours (1952), 305

Nel Nome del Padre (*In the Name of the Father*) (1971), 28
Nelson, Ralph, 329
Never on Sunday (1960), 356
Never Steal Anything Small (1960), 58
New Babylon, The (1929), 165–66
New Earth (1934), 232
New York, New York (1977), 422
Newman, David, 29
Newman, Paul, 182, 193, 216, 329–31, 358, 383–84
Nibelungen, Die. Part I: *Siegfried*, 255
Niblo, Fred, 331
Nicholas, Dudley, 29, 331
Nichols, Mike, 195, 332–33, 423
Nicholson, Jack, 209–10
Niemansland (1930), 127
Night After Night (1932), 374–75
Night Mail (1936), 67, 495
Night of the Hunter, The (1955), 88, 317
Night of the Iguana (1964), 218
Night on Bald Mountain, A (1933–34), 4–5
Night Train to Munich (1940), 184
Nine Men (1943), 496
Ninotchka (1939), 114
Nju (1924), 98
No Regrets for Our Youth (1946), 220, 250
Nobody Waved Goodbye (1966), 340
Noda, Kogo, 414
Nolan, Lloyd, 368–69
None But the Lonely Heart (1944), 336
Normand, Mabel, 69, 83, 210, 428
North by Northwest (1959), 204–5
North Sea (1938), 67, 495
Northwest Passage (1940), 482
Notte, La (1961), 321–22
Now (1966), 7
Now About These Women (1964), 31
Nun's Story, The (1958), 134, 521–22
Nureyev, Rudolf, 334–35
Nykvist, Sven, 31–32, 335

O'Connor, Carroll, 42
October (1927), 125
Odets, Clifford, 314, 336, 376–77
Oguni, 251
Oh What a Lovely War (1969), 18–19
Oil and Water (1913), 451
Olcott, Sidney, 163
Old and New (1929), 126
Old Man and the Sea (1958), 448
Oliver! (1968), 45, 381
Olivier, Laurence, 62, 78, 170, 196, 246, 254, 264–65, 336–37
Olmi, Ermanno, 337
Olvidados, Los (1950), 54
Olympia (1936–38), 6, 226–27
On Dangerous Ground (1951), 200
On est au coton (1970), 12
On the Midnight Stage (1915), 186
On the Town (1949), 111, 238
On the Waterfront (1954), 232, 234–35, 420, 440–41
Once There Was a Singing Blackbird (1970), 222

One A.M. (1969), 262
One Flew Over the Cuckoo's Nest (1975), 148
One Hour with You (1932), 43
One Million Years B.C. (1940), 185
One, Two, Three (1961), 506
On a Wonderful Sunday (1947), 250
O'Neal, Ryan, 29, 123
O'Neill, Eugene, 261, 287, 350
Only Angels Have Wings (1939), 190
Ophüls, Marcel, 337–38
Ophüls, Max, 101, 243, 338–39
Ordet (1943), 115, 117
Ordinary Fascism (1965), 402
Ornitz, Arthur, 72, 339–40
Orphans of the Storm (1921), 43
Ossessione (1942), 483–84
O'Toole, Peter, 169–70, 263, 340
Otterson, Jack, 76
Ouspenskaya, Maria, 340
Over the Fence (1917), 273
Owen, Don, 341
Oxbow Incident, The (1943), 500–1
Ozu, Yasujiro, 341–42, 414–15

Pabst, G. W., 49, 310–11, 343, 420, 439
Pacino, Al, 343–44, 467
Page, Genevieve, 344
Pagnol, Marcel, 344, 375
Painted Veil, The (1934), 41
Paisa (1946), 131, 405
Palance, Jack, 344–45
Paley, William, 426
Palmer, Lilli, 345
Pandora's Box (1928), 49
Panic in the Streets (1950), 234
Panzer, Paul, 313
Papendrou, George, 89
Papousek, Jaroslav, 146
Paradine Case, The (1947), 426
Paradise for Buster, 455
Paris la Belle (1961), 369
Parrish, Robert, 345–46
Parker, Claire, 4–5
Partie du Campagne, Une (1936), 53–54, 385–86
Partner (1968), 35
Pas de Deux (1967), 305–6
Pasolini, Pier Paolo, 34, 346–47
Passenger, The (1961), 326–27
Passer, Ivan, 146, 347
Passion, A (1969), 31–32
Passion de Jeanne d'Arc, La (1928), 115, 117, 215, 436
Pasternak, Boris, 41
Pasternak, Joseph, 28
Pathé News, 314
Pather Panchali (1949–55), 317, 377–78
Paths of Glory (1958), 113
Patton (1969), 423–24
Pavese, Cesare, 10
Pawnbroker, The (1965), 287–88
Payment on Demand (1951), 34
Peau de banane (1963), 347–48
Peck, Gregory, 347–48, 457
Peckinpah, Sam, 348–49, 392–93, 491
Pederson, Can, 164

Penn, Arthur, 349–51
Pennebaker, Donn Alan, 77
Perelman, S. J., 300, 351–52
Peries, Lester, 352
Perils of Pauline, The (1914), 313, 504
Perinal, Georges, 80–81
Perkins, Anthony, 141, 353–54
Perlman, Milton, 72
Perrault, Pierre, 46
Perry, Eleanor, 354
Perry, Frank, 354–55
Persona (1967), 30–31, 473
Peter and Pavla (1964), 146
Petit Soldat, Le (1960), 170, 172
Phantom India (1969), 294
Phantom of the Opera (1925), 514
Phantom of the Opera (1962), 137
Philadelphia Story, The (1940), 94–95
Philipe, Gérard, 323, 356
Picasso, Pablo, 44
Picker, David, 356
Pickford, Jack, 356
Pickford, Mary, 162, 299, 356–58
Pickup on South Street (1953), 156
Picture of Dorian Gray, The (1945), 271, 311
Pierrot le Fou (1965), 172
Pierson, Frank, 358
Pink Panther, The (1963), 424
Pinky (1949), 234
Pinocchio (1939), 215
Pinter, Harold, 23, 111–12, 265, 279, 359
Pirosmani (1971), 246
Pitts, Zasu, 394
Place de la République (1972), 293–94
Place in the Sun, A (1951), 510
Play It Again, Sam (1972), 5
Playtime (1967), 454–55
Pleasence, Donald, 112, 359–60
Plymouth Adventure (1952), 410, 467
Poe, James, 361–62
Poem About a Sea (1957), 114–15
Point Blank (1968), 42, 299–300
Pointe Courte, La (1954), 390
Poitier, Sidney, 362–63, 429
Polanski, Roman, 363–64
Pollack, Sydney, 364–65
Polo, Malvina, 100
Polonsky, Abraham, 366–67
Pomeroy, Roy, 257, 491
Pommer, Erich, 153, 184, 197, 255
Ponedel, Dotty, 315
Pontecorvo, Gillo, 367
Pool Sharks (1915), 133
Poor Little Rich Girl (1917), 358
Porgy and Bess (1959), 368, 429
Porter, Edwin S., 312, 367
Porter, Eric, 53
Portrait of Jason (1967), 77
Pour la suite du monde (1963), 46
Powell, Dick, 33
Powell, William, 82
Power, Tyrone, 201
Power and the Land (1940), 223
Préjean, Albert, 367–68
Preminger, Otto, 330, 368
Preston, Robert, 368–69

Prévert, Jacques, 369, 385
Prévert, Pierre, 369
Previn, Andre, 369–70
Prevost, Marie, 310
Prevot, Amédée, 25
Price, Vincent, 370–71
Pride and the Passion, The (1957), 247
Prince and the Showgirl, The (1957), 62
Prisoner, The (1955), 169
Private Life of Henry VIII, The (1933), 244, 259
Procès de Jeanne d'Arc, Le (1962), 47
Proferes, Nick, 235
Professionals, The (1966), 49
Project of Engineer Prite, The (1917), 249
Prometheus-Film, 207
Prokofiev, Sergei, 126–27
Protazanov, Yakov, 75
Prowler, The (1951), 280–81
Psycho (1960), 25, 200, 206, 353
P.T. 109 (1963), 396
Public Enemy (1931), 59, 500
Pudovkin, Vsevolod, 174–75, 223, 371–73
Pumpkin Eater, The (1963), 134
Punishment Park (1971), 492–93
Puppe, Die (1919), 284
Pushover (1954), 171
Puzo, Mario, 85
Pygmalion (1938), 14, 38, 213
Pyriev, Ivan, 75

Que la Bête Meure (1969), 68
Que Viva Mexico! (unrealized), 126
Queen Christina (1933), 295–96
Queen Kelly (1928), 451
Queen of Spades (1949), 128
Quelle Joie de Vivre (1961), 104
Quiet Man, The (1952), 70, 143
Quine, Richard, 171
Quinn, Anthony, 170
Quo Vadis? (1924), 90
Quo Vadis? (1951), 449

Rachel, Rachel (1968), 330–31, 514
Rackin, Martin, 374
Rafelson, Bob, 56
Raft, George, 374–75
Rage (1972), 423
Raimu, 344, 375
Rainbow Dance (1936), 289–90
Rainer, Luise, 13
Rains, Claude, 278
Raizman (or Reisman), Yuli, 375
Raksin, David, 366
Ralston, Vera, 39
Rank, J. Arthur, 178
Ransohoff, Martin, 228
Raphaelson, Samson, 375–76
Rashomon (1950), 251
Ray, Nicholas, 233, 376–77, 513–14
Ray, Satyajit, 317, 377–78
Ravaged Earth (See *Fight to the Last*)
Raven, The (1963), 333
Razin, Stepan, 431
Rear Window (1954), 203, 205

Rebecca (1940), 205, 212
Rebel Without a Cause (1957), 376, 513–15
Rebound (1932), 283
Recuperanti, I (1970), 337
Red Beard (1965), 252
Red Desert (1964), 11, 184
Red Dust (1932), 16–17
Red Eagle, Ron, 345
Red Guelder Rose, The (1975), 430
Red Psalm (1972), 239
Red River (1948), 78
Redford, Robert, 379
Redgrave, Lynn, 379
Redgrave, Michael, 379–80
Redgrave, Vanessa, 301, 380–81
Reed, Carol, 142, 145, 176, 184, 381
Reed, Oliver, 411
Reed, Rex, 156
Reflections in a Golden Eye (1967), 216, 323–24
Reign of Terror (1949), 298–99
Reinhardt, Max, 283, 386
Reinhardt, Wolfgang, 339
Reimann, Walter, 255
Reiniger, Lotte, 381–82
Reisch, Walter, 184
Reisz, Karel, 135, 380–82, 491
Reluctant Debutante, The (1958), 238
Remick, Lee, 383–84
Rennahan, Ray, 61, 481
Renoir, Claude, 18, 317, 388
Renoir, Jean, 24, 27, 53–54, 66, 172, 317, 384–90
Renoir, Marguerite, 386
Repulsion (1965), 364
Resnais, Alain, 118–19, 239, 390–92, 477–78, 520
Revengers, The (172), 44, 374
Reville, Alma, 319
Reynolds, Burt, 355
Richardson, John, 392–93
Richardson, Ralph, 276, 286–87
Richardson, Tony, 167, 228, 324, 380, 393
Riefenstahl, Leni, 226–27, 477
Rien que les heures (1926), 66–67
Ring of Fear (1954), 501
Rink, The (1916), 70
Rio Bravo (1959), 191
Rio Lobo (1970), 79
Rio Rita (1929), 99
Ritt, Martin, 189, 393–94
River, The (1936), 476–77
River, The (1950), 317, 377, 388
Rivkin, Allen, 71–72, 216
Roach, Hal, 272–73, 303, 319, 394–95, 443
Road to Glory, The (1926), 189
Road to Mandalay (1926), 297
Road to Yesterday, The (1925), 189–90
Roads of Destiny (1921), 152
Robards, Jason, 286–87
Robbe-Grillet, Alain, 390–91, 396
Robbins, Jerome, 512–13
Robe, The (1953), 56, 316
Roberts, Meade, 134
Roberts, Rachel, 183

Robertson, Cliff, 396–97
Robeson, Paul, 38
Robin Hood (1922), 120–21
Robinson, Edward G., 397, 508–9
Robson, Mark, 397–98
Rocha, Glauber, 246, 398–99
Rock, Joe, 399
Rock, "Pop," 37
Roeg, Nicholas, 112, 399–400
Rogers, Ginger, 33
Rogers, Will, 143, 400, 496
Rohmer, Eric, 400–1, 522–23
Röhrig, Walter, 153, 155, 197
Roizman, Owen, 401
Roma, Eraldo da, 11
Roman Holiday (1953), 195
Roman Scandals (1933), 33
Rome, Open City (1945), 131, 404–5
Romeo and Juliet (1936), 43, 94, 297–98
Romm, Mikhail, 74–75, 402–3
Rooks, Conrad, 403
Rooney, Mickey, 302
Roosevelt, Eleanor, 196
Rope (1948), 204
Rosay, Françoise, 413, 434
Rose Scarlette (1940), 107
Rose, William, 228
Rosemary's Baby (1968), 364
Rosenberg, Frank, 432
Rosher, Charles, 404, 447
Ross, Frank, 508
Ross, Katherine, 182, 332
Rossellini, Roberto, 9, 131, 404–6
Rossen, Robert, 330, 406–8
Rosson, Harold, 16, 120, 481
Rotha, Paul, 408
Rouch, Jean, 46, 389, 408–9
Roue, La (1922), 159
Round-Up, The (1965), 225
Royal Family of Broadway, The (1930), 93
Royle, Edwin Milton, 105
Rozsa, Miklos, 316, 409–10
Ruban, Al, 64
Rubin, Al, 71–72
Ruddy, Albert, 410–11
Rules of the Game, The (1939), 386–87
Rupture, La (1970), 68
Russell, Ken, 224, 411–13
Russell, Rosalind, 413
Russians Are Coming, the Russians Are Coming, The (1966), 228, 260
Russia, Country of Depression (1910), 312–13
Ruttenberg, Joseph, 316
Ruttmann, Walter, 413–14
Ryskind, Morrie, 300
Ryu, Chishu, 414–15

Saboteur (1942), 212
Sadoul, Georges, 54
St. Denis, Ruth, 48
St. Martin's Lane (1938), 184
St. Valentine's Day Massacre (1967), 86
Safety Last (1923), 273–74
Sagan, Leontine, 416
Salt, Waldo, 418–19, 485

Saltzman, Harry, 412
Samourai, Le (1967), 105
San Francisco (1936), 277
Sanchez, Jaime, 288
Sanda, Dominique, 416
Sanders, George, 424
Sang des Bêtes, Le (1949), 149–50
Sang d'un Poete, Le (1930), 80–82
Sanjuro (1962), 252
Sára, Sándor, 239
Saturday Night and Sunday Morning (1960), 135–36
Savage Eye, The (1960), 132
Saville, Victor, 184
Saving of Bill Blewett, The (1936), 495
Savage Is Loose, The (1974), 422–23
Sautet, Claude, 338
Scarface (1932), 171, 190–91, 325, 425
Scenes from a Marriage (1974), 335
Scenes from Under Childhood (1970), 45
Scharfenberg, Robert, 207
Schary, Dore, 278–79, 449
Schatten (1922), 319
Schatz, Der (1923), 343
Schell, Maria, 18, 416–17
Schlesinger, John, 9, 74, 167, 189, 224, 417–19, 485
Schmitz, John, 449
Schneider, Bert, 41, 209
Schneider, Maria, 419
Schoenberg, Arnold, 127
Scheoenderfer, Erich, 283
Schüfftan, Eugene, 419–20, 521
Schulberg, B. P., 93, 420
Schulberg, Budd, 420
Sciuscia (*Shoeshine*) (1946), 107
Scofield, Paul, 246, 421
Scorsese, Martin, 421
Scott, George C., 422–24
Screen Actors' Guild, 328
Sea of Grass, The (1947), 196
Seagull, The (1968), 301
Seahawk, The (1940), 242
Search, The (1948), 78
Searchers, The (1956), 144
Seberg, Jean, 170
Secret Agent (1936), 167
Secret Ceremony (1968), 282
See No Evil (*Blind Panic*) (1971), 370
Segal, Erich, 316
Seitz, George, 313
Sellers, Peter, 424
Selznick, David, 87, 97, 151–52, 194, 212, 216–17, 264, 424–26, 481
Sembène, Ousmane, 426–27
Semprun, Jorge, 392
Sennett, Mack, 13, 69, 83, 133, 210, 427–28
Sense of Loss (1973), 338
Senso (1954), 484
Serpico (1973), 339–40
Servant, The (1963), 280, 437
Seven Days in May (1964), 151
Seventh Seal, The (1956), 30–31
Seymour, Clarine, 168
Seyrig, Delphine, 19
Shadow of a Doubt (1943), 204, 475–76

Shadows (1960), 63–64, 77
Shakespeare, William, 166, 182, 213, 312; *see also As You Like It* (1936), 336; Hamlet, 167; *Henry V* (1946), 337; *Julius Caesar* (1953), 200, 212, 410; *King Lear*, 80, 466–67; *Macbeth* (1971), 251; *Romeo and Juliet* (1936), 297; *The Taming of the Shrew* (1967), 520; *The Tempest* (unrealized), 245–46
Shamroy, Leon, 368, 429
Shane (1953), 345
Shanghai Express (1932), 442
Sharif, Omar, 429
Shaw, George Bernard, 14, 178–79, 183
Shaw, Irwin, 140
Shchukin, Boris, 402
Sherlock Jr. (1924), 237
Sherwin, David, 8
Ship of Fools (1965), 434
Shimura, 250
Shootist, The (1976), 432
Shortcut to Hell (1957), 59
Shub, Esther, 429–30
Shukshin, Vasili, 430–31
Shumlin, Herman, 319
Si jolie petite plage, Une (1948), 356
Sidney, Sylvia, 140
Siederman, Maurice, 88
Siegel, Don, 431–32
Siegmann, George, 52–53
Sign of the Cross, The (1932), 259
Signoret, Simone, 78, 432–34
Sigurd, Jacques, 356
Silence, The (1964), 458–59
Silence and Cry (1968), 239
Silence est d'Or, Le (1947), 25, 73
Silliphant, Stirling, 329
Silver, Richard, 180
Simon of the Desert (1965), 471
Sinatra, Frank, 21, 34, 240
Sinbad (1958), 496
Sinclair, John, 133, 247, 276, 410
Sinclair, Upton, 126
Sinners' Holiday (1930), 39, 58
Singin' in the Rain (1952), 238
Sins of Rachel Cade, The (1961), 134
Siodmak, Robert, 434–35
Sirk, Douglas, 435–36
Sisk, Robert, 231
Skerritt, Tom, 123
Skolimowski, Jerzy, 436
Sleeping Prince, The (1957), 62
Slocombe, Douglas, 436–37
Smiles of a Summer Night (1955), 30
Smith, Albert, 37, 472
Smith, Fred Y., 437–38
Smith, James, 36
Smith, Lee, 438
Smith, Maggie, 19
Smith, Oliver, 368
Smith, Rose, 36
Snow, Michael, 438
Snow White and the Seven Dwarfs (1937), 215
So This Is New York (1948), 247
Soderberg, Hjalmar, 117

Sodom and Gomorrah (1962), 270
Socrates (1970), 405
Soldati, Mario, 276
Some Like It Hot (1959), 109, 506
Something Wild (1961), 160
Son of Dracula (1943), 434
Song of Ceylon (1943), 495
Song of Life (1930), 127
Song of Russia (1944), 301
Sontag, Susan, 224
Sound, 6, 149, 332; dubbing, 10–11, 278; experiments, 3, 385; transition to sound, 208, 260–61, 480, 483, 491, 515; mixing, 295
South Pacific (1958), 275–76
Sparrows (1926), 447
Sparkuhl, Theodor, 298
Spartacus (1960), 113
Special effects, *see* Gentleman, Harryhausen; *also see* pp. 163–65, 426
Spiegel, Sam, 42, 48, 191, 263, 353, 429
Spione (1927), 256
Spitfire (1934), 196
Spellbound (1945), 205
Splendor in the Grass (1961), 220–21, 274, 514
Sorrow and the Pity, The (1970), 338
Spy Who Came in from the Cold, The (1965), 188
Squaw Man, The (1913), 105
Stagecoach (1939), 59–60, 506
Stahltier, Das (1936), 227
Stair, Bill, 299
Stamp, Terence, 473–74
Stander, Lionel, 361
Standing, Guy, 265
Stanwyck, Barbara, 60, 455
Star Is Born, A (1937), 97
Star Is Born, A (1954), 97
Starewicz, Wladyslaw, 440
Stark, Ray, 181
State of Siege (1973), 89
Steamboat Willie (1928), 110
Steiger, Rod, 288, 440–41
Steiner, Max, 441–42, 496
Steinbeck, John, 140, 235
Sten, Anna, 13
Sterling, Ford, 83, 428
Sternberg, Josef, 109–10, 161, 442–43, 481
Stewart, Donald Ogden, 95
Stewart, James, 79, 143, 203, 444
Stevens, George, 443–44, 452, 510–11
Stevens, Inger, 432
Stieglitz, Alfred, 487
Stiller, Mauritz, 439–40
Stockwell, Dean, 138, 286
Stoney, George, 444–45
Storm in a Teacup (1937), 184
Story of Louis Pasteur, The (1935), 325–26
Stolz der Firma, Der (1914), 283
Stowaway (1936), 314
Stradling, Harry, 96, 174, 445
Strange Love of Martha Ivers, The (1946), 113
Strasberg, Paula, 62

Straub, Jean Marie, 130
Straw Dogs (1971), 349, 392–93
Street of Forgotten Men, The (1925), 48
Street Scene (1931), 480
Streetcar Named Desire, A (1951), 233, 264, 445
Streisand, Barbra, 29, 237, 445–46, 516
Strick, Joseph, 132
Strike (1925), 123, 165
Stroheim, Erich, 99–100, 159, 178, 214, 386, 446–47, 451, 506–7
Strong Man, The (1926), 311–12
Stross, Raymond, 84–85
Structure of Crystal, The, 519–20
Struggle, The (1931), 277
Struss, Karl, 404, 447–48
Sturges, John, 448
Sturges, Preston, 298, 339
Sugata Sanshiro (1943), 250
Sullivan, C. Gardner, 186
Sullivan's Travels (1942), 298
Sun Shines Bright, The (1953), 40
Sunday, Bloody Sunday (1971), 135, 167–68, 224, 418
Sunrise (1927), 404, 447
Sunset Boulevard (1950), 45, 193, 209, 507
Surtees, Robert, 239, 448–50
Suspicion (1941), 96
Sutch, Herbert, 52
Sutherland, Edward, 450
Svilova, Elizaveta, 479
Swanson, Gloria, 93, 450–51
Sweet, Blanche, 451
Sweet Smell of Success, The (1957), 254
Swimmer, The (1968), 355
Sydow, Max Von, 155, 452
Sylbert, Richard, 361
Symphonie Fantastique, La (1942), 24

Tagebuch einer Verlorenen (1929), 6
Taking Off (1971), 109, 147, 194–95
Tale of Renard, The (1930), 440
Talent Competition (1963), 146
Tales of Terror (1962), 371
Tall Story (1960), 141
Taming of the Shrew (1967), 520
Tao Chin, 453
Tarkington, Booth, 498
Tartuffe (1925), 154, 197
Tashlin, Frank, 453
Taste of Honey, A (1961), 258
Tati, Jacques, 453–55
Taxi Driver (1976), 422
Taylor, Elizabeth, 57, 110, 281–82
Taylor, John, 494
Taylor, Laurette, 78, 299
Taylor, Robert, 94, 301, 449, 455–56
Tearing Down the Spanish Flag (1898), 37
Tell Them Willie Boy Is Here (1969), 366–67
Temple, Shirley, 314
Temps d'une Chasse, Le (1972), 297
Ten Commandments, The (1923), 169, 257–58
Terminus (1960), 9

Terra Trema, La (1947), 484
Terror, The (1928), 211
Terror, The (1963), 333
Testament du Dr. Cordelier, Le (1961), 368–69
Testimone (1945), 166
Tête contre les murs, La (1958), 171, 318
Texas Ranger, The (1935), 480
Texas Steer, The (1927), 400
Thalberg, Irving, 43, 92, 94, 260–61, 270–71, 300, 446, 456–57
That Man from Rio (1964), 104
They All Come Out (1939), 466
They Had to See Paris (1929), 400
They Live by Night (1949), 213
They Knew What They Wanted (1940), 160–61
They Shoot Horses, Don't They? (1969), 361–62, 365
Thief of Bagdad (1924), 265
Third Man, The (1950), 176, 381
Thirty-Nine Steps, The (1935), 212
This Gun for Hire (1942), 59
This Land Is Mine (1943), 332
This Man's Navy (1945), 71–72
This Sporting Life (1963), 184
Thompson, J. Lee, 457–58
Thompson, Stewart, 404
Thomson, Virgil, 458
Three Days of the Condor (1975), 401
Three Godfathers (Hell's Heroes) (1929), 515
3:10 to Yuma (1951), 102
Three Strangers (1946), 109
Throne of Blood (1957), 251
Thulin, Ingrid, 458–59
Tide of Empire (1929), 121
Tierney, Gene, 467
T'ien Han, 74
Time to Love and a Time to Die, A (1958), 436
Tiomkin, Dimitri, 412, 459
Tirez sur le pianiste (1960), 469
Tisse, Edward, 459–60
To Have and Have Not (1947), 191
To Kill a Mockingbird (1962), 348
To Paris, With Love (1954), 178
Toland, Greg, 9, 174, 208, 345, 460–64, 499, 516
Tolstoy, Leo, 140, 246
Tom Jones (1963), 135–36, 228, 258, 491
Tomb of Ligeia, The (1964), 466
Toni (1935), 386
Too Much, Too Soon (1958), 492
Top Hat (1935), 15
Topol, 464
Torch Song (1954), 490
Torn, Rip, 209
Torn Curtain (1966), 205
Tortoise and the Hare, The (1934), 20
Totheroh, Roland, 447, 464–65
Touch of Evil (1957), 110, 499
Tourneur, Jacques, 465–66
Tourneur, Maurice, 50–51, 358
Toute la Memoire du Monde (1956), 391
Tover, Leo, 34
Towne, Robert, 466–67

Tracy, Spencer, 43, 196, 231–32, 247, 277, 299, 448, 467
Track of the Cat (1954), 78–79, 501
Train, The (1964), 151–52
Train sans yeux, Le (1926), 66
TransAtlantic (1931), 214
Trauberg, Leonid, 165, 245
Treasure of the Sierra Madre, The (1948), 235
Tree Grows in Brooklyn, A (1945), 233
Trespasser, The (1929), 451, 461
Trintignant, Jean-Louis, 267, 467–68
Trivas, Victor, 127
Trojan Women, The (1971), 58
Trouble in Paradise (1932), 376
True Heart Susie (1919), 168
True Nature of Bernadette, The (1972), 62–63
Truffaut, Francois, 74, 92, 104, 208, 468–71
Trumbo, Dalton, 231, 471–72
Tsuchimoto, 183
Tulipe Noire, La (1963), 105
Tunes of Glory (1960), 178
Turksib (1929), 261
Turner, Florence, 472
Tva Manniskor (1945), 116
Twelve Angry Men (1957), 140, 286–87
20,000 Leagues Under the Sea (1954), 275
Two Bagatelles (1952), 305
Two-Faced Woman (1941), 114
Two Men and a Wardrobe (1959), 363
Two Mules for Sister Sara (1970), 374
Two Rode Together (1961), 444, 505
2001: A Space Odyssey (1969), 164–65, 248
Two Women (1961), 278
Typhoon (1914), 191

Uccelacci e Uccelini (1966), 347
Uegusa, 250–51
Ullmann, Liv, 32, 473
Umberto D. (1952), 107–8
Under Two Flags (1936), 413
Underworld (1927), 193, 442
Union Pacific (1939), 368–69
Universe (1959), 164
Unfried, Emil, 207
Uptight (1968), 101–2
Ure, Mary, 136–37
Ustinov, Peter, 473–74

Valentine, Joseph, 204, 475–76
Valley Town (1940), 477
Vampyr (1932), 115–16
Van Devere, Trish, 423
Van Dongen, Helen, 476
Van Dyke, Willard, 476–77
Van Dyke, Woodward S., 52
Van Gogh, Vincent, 316
Varda, Agnes, 477–78
Variety (1925), 117–18, 480
Vasiliev, Georgi, 22
Vasiliev, Sergei, 22
Veiller, Anthony, 218, 435
Verdict, The (1946), 431

Verneuil, Henri, 88
Vertigo (1958), 205
Vertov, Dziga, 232, 478–79
Vidor, Florence, 310
Vidor, King, 140, 479–83, 456
Vie, Une (1958), 18
Vigo, Jean, 226, 232
Villa, Pancho, 489
Violin Maker of Cremona, The (1909), 357
Viridiana (1961), 55, 433
Visconti, Luchino, 9, 39–40, 254, 483–84
Visitors, The (1971), 235
Vitti, Monica, 484–85
Viva Villa! (1934), 425
Viva Zapata (1952), 234
Vivre Sa Vie (1962), 171
Voight, Jon, 418, 485–86
Von Sternberg (*see* Sternberg)
Von Stroheim (*see* Stroheim)
Vorkapich, Slavko, 180

Wada, Nato, 219
Wagner, Fritz Arno, 310
Wagner, Richard, 55
Wagonmaster (1950), 40
Wajda, Andrzej, 487
Walker, Joseph, 413, 487
Walking Down Broadway (1933), 214
Wallach, Eli, 488
Wallis, Hal, 169, 325, 397
Walsh, Raoul, 488–89
Walters, Charles, 489–90
Walthall, Henry B., 490
Wanda (1970), 235, 274
Wanger, Walter, 491
War and Peace (1956), 140, 483
War Game, The (1965), 493
War Wagon, The (1967), 113
Ward, Warwick, 118
Warm, Hermann, 255
Warner, David, 381, 491
Warner, H. B., 491–92
Warner, Jack, 269, 325, 491–92, 503, 516, 521
Warren, Jack, 205
Watch on the Rhine (1943), 319
Waters, Ethel, 234
Watkins, Peter, 492–93
Watson, James Sibley, 494
Watt, Harry, 67
Waxman, Franz, 521–22
Way Down East (1920), 168–69, 438, 494–96
Way We Were, The (1973), 379
Wayne, David, 4
Wayne, John, 79, 113, 144, 191, 197, 432, 435–36, 496, 501
Webb, Roy, 497
Wedding March (1926–28), 319, 438–39
Wee Willie Winkie (1937), 314
Weekend (1968), 262
Wegener, Paul, 497
Welles, Orson, 40–41, 87–88, 90, 110, 138–39, 166–67, 198–99, 201, 208, 251, 320, 353–54, 381, 393, 460–63, 497–99, 511–12

Wellman, William, 48, 72, 78–79, 97, 499–501
Wertmüller, Lina, 166, 501
West, Mae, 193, 374–75, 502
West Side Story (1961), 512–13
Westfront 1918 (1930), 310
Westmore, Bud, 503
Westmore, George, 502
Westmore, Perc, 15–16, 502–4
Westmore, Wally, 259
Wexler, Haskell, 148, 504
What a Widow (1930), 121
What's New, Pussycat? (1965), 5
What's Up, Doc? (1972), 29
Whiskey Galore (1948), 254
Whistle Down the Wind (1961), 142
White, Pearl, 504
White Sheik, The (1952), 131
Whitney, John Hay, 425
Who's Afraid of Virginia Woolf (1966), 332
Whoopee (1930), 33
Wicki, Bernard, 504–5
Widmark, Richard, 143, 156–57
Widow Coudert, The (1971), 434
Wilbur, Crane, 313
Wild Angels, The (1966), 86
Wild Bunch, The (1969), 209, 348–49
Wild, Harry, 88
Wild Party, The (1929), 13
Wild River (1960), 274, 383–84
Wild Rovers (1971), 123
Wild Strawberries (1957), 452
Wilde, Hagar, 29
Wilder, Billy, 45, 109, 267–68, 291, 505–9
Wilder, Thornton, 108
Williams, Ben Ames, 400
Williams, Dick, 101
Williams, Richard, 509
Williams, Tennessee, 218
Willingham, Calder, 351
Wilson, Michael, 145
Wimbush, Mary, 19
Wings (1927), 499–500
Winner, Michael, 509–10
Winstanley (1975), 53
Winters, Shelley, 88, 510–11
Wise, Robert, 87–88, 511–13
Wiseman, Frederick, 513
Wizard of Oz, The (1939), 268
Woman of Paris, A (1923), 310, 450
Woman Under the Influence, A (1974), 65
Woman's Face, A (1941), 92
Women in Love (1970), 411
Wood, Harry, 313
Wood, Natalie, 376, 513–14

Wood, T. K., 512
Woods, Edward, 59
Woodward, Joanne, 514
Workers Leaving the Lumière Factory (1894), 289
World Changes, The (1933), 17
Wortman, Huck, 37, 52
Wrangler, Chris, 266
Wright, Basil, 67, 495
WR: Mysteries of the Organism (1971), 293
Wuthering Heights (1939), 54–55, 336, 461
Wyckoff, Alvin, 169, 214
Wyler, William, 84, 103, 195, 200–1, 215, 291, 336–37, 353, 369, 410, 460–61, 446, 514–16
Wyman, Jane, 516

Yamamoto, Kajiro, 250
Yank at Oxford, A (1938), 456
Yanne, Jean, 68
Yates, Herbert J., 39
Year of the Pig, The (1969), 103
Yegorov, Vladimir, 312
York, Michael, 517
York, Susanna, 421, 517–18
Young Lions, The (1958), 78
Young, Freddie, 263
Young Mr. Lincoln (1939), 140–41
Young One, The (1957), 160
Young Racers, The (1962), 84
Young, Terence, 518
You Only Live Once (1937), 140, 256
You're a Big Boy Now (1966), 85
Yutkevich, Sergei, 74–75, 245

Z (1968), 88–89
Zanuck, Darryl, 33, 234, 296, 500–1, 519
Zanussi, Krzyzstof, 519–20
Zavattini, Cesare, 107
Zecca, Ferdinand, 25, 158
Zeffirelli, Franco, 520
Zeiss Company, 54
Zero de Conduite (1933), 8, 226
Ziegfeld, Florenz, 133
Zielke, Willy, 227
Zinnemann, Fred, 17, 45, 134, 145, 240, 429, 448, 520–22
Zola, Emile, 165, 274
Zoo in Budapest (1933), 3
Zouzou, 522–23
Zsigmond, Vilmos, 486, 523
Zukor, Adolph, 152, 357–58, 523–24
Zweig, Stefan, 243